THE MUSEUM OF EAST ASIAN ART

JADES *from* CHINA

Angus Forsyth • Brian McElney

Published by The Museum of East Asian Art

ISBN 1 897734 04 2

English text by Angus Forsyth (AHF) and Brian McElney (BSM), Honorary Curator
Chinese translation: Art text, Ming Wilson, Jack Lee
Designed and produced by PPA Design Limited
Designers: Michelle Shek, Leung Yiu Wing, Tracy Hoy
Photography by Arthur Kan
Colour Separations by Fung's Graphic Arts Co., Ltd.
Printed and bound in Hong Kong by Hong Kong Prime Printing Co., Ltd.

THE MUSEUM OF EAST ASIAN ART

JADES *from* CHINA

Angus Forsyth • Brian McElney

11 JUNE 1994
12 Bennett Street
Bath BA1 2QL England

THE MUSEUM OF EAST ASIAN ART

Contents

1 ACKNOWLEDGEMENTS

BRIAN McELNEY ACKNOWLEDGEMENTS

I began collecting East Asian Art in 1958 and developed an interest in Chinese jade in the late 60s. Over the years I have visited collectors and museums all over the world. Many people too numerous to mention have been unstinting in sharing their views and knowledge on jade with me during this time. My thanks in particular are due to James Watt, who I took as my mentor in the field, John Ayers, Terese Tse Bartholomew, Roger Bluett, Emma Bunker, Anthony Carter, Doris Dohrenwend, Robert Ellsworth, Angus Forsyth, the late Ip Yee and all the other members of the Min Chiu Society of Hong Kong, at whose meetings many happy hours have been spent discussing jade, Roger Keverne, Peter Lam, Brian Morgan, Hugh Moss, Jessica Rawson, Jenny So and Mason Wang. My thanks are also due to the support of the Museum staff over the last year. I hope I will be forgiven if I have forgotten to mention anyone.

ANGUS FORSYTH ACKNOWLEDGEMENTS

In the course of a 20 year involvement with the study of Chinese Jade, I have visited collectors, scholars, museums and curators in North America, China and Europe and culture excavation sites in various parts of China. Many people have been very kind in sharing their views and knowledge over this period and I hope that I leave out none in the following very summarised list of principal people who have helped me, answered my enquiries or assisted me in the right directions. My thanks accordingly to Marty Amt, Terese Tse Bartholomew, Bennet Bronson, Emma Bunker, Anthony Carter, Elizabeth Childs-Johnson, Carol Chiu, Betty Lo and Kenneth Chu, Chung Wah Pui, Doris Dohrenwend, Robert H. Ellsworth, Nora Fok, Robert Frey, Sidney and S L Fung, Guo Da Shun, Hsio Yen Shih, Sir Joseph Hotung, Louisa F Huber, John Jamieson, Dominic Jellinek, Roger Keverne, Elizabeth Knight, Simon Kwan, Brian McElney, Malcolm McPherson, Brian Morgan, Mou Yong-gang, Jack Lee, Jessica Rawson, Jack Sewell, Jenny So, Sun Shou Dao, Robert Tang, Suzanne Valenstein, Mayke Wagner, Professor Wang Cheng Li, Wang Ming Da, Jean and Mason Wang, Professor Yang Hu and Yang Mei Li. From the late 1970's to the late 1980's I met regularly in Hong Kong with Malcolm Barnett, Doris Shum and Thomas and Judy Yen to discuss later post-archaic jades.

My thanks are also due to the strenuous effort of my secretary, Patty Chan, the typing energy of Irene and Susanna Wong and, lastly, for many kinds of tolerances and support, my wife Bebe.

2   Introduction

Chinese jade has an immense appeal for many people and is a splendid theme for a public exhibition; but as all students will recognise, as a subject of study it has its difficulties. Because of its great antiquity and the reverence in which it was held from the earliest days, not to mention the unworldly character and beauty of the material itself, jades came to enjoy a uniquely favoured place in the hierarchy of Chinese arts. This state of affairs continued down virtually to modern times, and it is therefore somewhat odd that understanding of its historical development has been relatively poor and even now, remains quite patchy and incomplete. Although Chinese literature with its rich vein of references to things made of jade underlines the fact of its social prestige and importance, it seems that the official records and histories are not informative; there have down the centuries been many collectors of exalted and serious intent, especially of ancient jades, but their zeal seems to have resulted in too little effective scholarship and publication. It is only in the present century that art-historical methods and Western-style archaeology have begun to establish a more credible and durable framework for viewing the material. This however, one is happy to say, is both rich and abundant.

During the long years of relative isolation from the mainland some Western students of jade, in their attempts to bring greater order to the jades in their care, thus found space to perform a useful role; and while building on traditional Chinese connoisseurship, with its undeniable sensibility towards this form of art, were able to bring to bear an analytical scepticism and rigour that were salutary. Among these, the work of S. Howard Hansford in England and the German scholar Alfred Salmony in America can be said to dominate

the mid-century. Hansford did much to clarify the technical basis and procedures of jade carving and its sources, while the latter brought a fresh systematisation to the known jades of the archaic period. Subsequently, Salmony began also to explore the dark area of the long centuries between Han and Ming, and in this was followed by a number of perceptive collectors and scholars, notably King Gustaf Adolf of Sweden, Bo Gyllensvard and Desmond Gure, whose work led to a rare exhibition in Stockholm in 1963, when the reborn Ostasiatiska Museum was opened. An important event also was the publication of a study of jades in the Avery Brundage collection in San Francisco by Yvon d'Argence. These efforts were focused on finding more cogent evidence for identifying specific jades from the more obscure dynasties, studying closely their technical features and drawing support from related material in other arts.

By the 1960s such research was already beginning to receive modest but vital support from the new archaeological movement in China itself, and it was partly this development that motivated the exhibition mounted in London by the Oriental Ceramic Society at The Victoria & Albert Museum in 1975. In bringing together a substantial body of material from widely scattered sources its authors, Jessica Rawson and the present writer, sought to compare and contrast representative examples of many types and all periods from the archaic onwards, while reconsidering the way in which they were classified and dated.

A very significant factor broadening interest in the study of jade by this time was the expansion of collecting in Hong Kong, where direct or sympathetic contact with mainland China offered special opportunities for acquisitions and the fruitful exchange of ideas.

Various exhibitions took place there in the 1970s, culminating in the major event organised in 1983 by the Min Chiu Society and Hong Kong Museum of Art. The catalogue by Dr Ip Yee, with considered contributions also from Professor Cheng Te-k'un and Brian McElney, is a worthy indication of the state of knowledge then achieved. A leading figure in these years was James Watt, the active curator of the Art Gallery of the Chinese University in the 1970s and now senior curator of oriental art at the Metropolitan Museum of Art in New York. It was recognition of his knowledge and abilities that enabled the Asia Society in New York to assemble in 1980 their important exhibition 'Chinese Jades from Han to Ch'ing'.

Common conclusions were now emerging about some of the more difficult problems of identification and classification, and a growing, if cautious confidence prevailed. Brian McElney and Angus Forsyth both became deeply involved in jade studies in the course of lengthy residence in Hong Kong through this exciting period, and it would be hard to imagine a more stimulating preparation for the task they have embarked on here.

Meanwhile, the flow of archaeological and art-historical information from China has continued to swell, and with the greatly-enhanced standard of illustrated book production the world at large has become better able to appreciate the nature and significance of the new discoveries. Of recent years these have been nothing less than sensational in both scale and importance; indeed it may be claimed that the revelation they bring of highly advanced prehistoric, neolithic cultures now identified at sites right across China constitutes one of the most significant archaeological events ever seen in Asia.

The early date of these societies ranging back variously to 5500 BC, as modern scientific methods have established, and in particular the existence of numerous jades showing a striking originality and advanced workmanship, overturns at a stroke many previous assumptions about early Chinese culture. In consequence, it is not too much to say that in some respects the very foundations of Chinese art history have now to be reviewed and rebuilt. As regards the craft of jade, it is beyond doubt that a whole range of familiar forms, technical methods and skills are of far greater antiquity than formerly supposed. And not without justice, scholars are now speaking of an 'Age of Jade' that preceded and in many ways heralded and inspired the coming Bronze Age.

Each year now brings fresh revelations, and the detailed study of this neolithic material has become a prime preoccupation. All those seriously interested in jade will be eager to see the range of rare early pieces on exhibition in Bath, most of which will never before have been seen in the West; and they will be profoundly grateful to Mr Forsyth for the massive and painstaking task of elucidation he has undertaken which occupies a substantial part of the catalogue. It is the first work on this scale in which the matter has been plainly put to an English-speaking public.

By comparison what he has to say about the jades of the Shang, Zhou and Han - exciting as these have long been to us - is bound to seem relatively prosaic, although here too his text contains many revealing insights. Jades of the post-archaic centuries have also not been illuminated to such brilliant effect by the archaeologists, understandably perhaps, in times when burial customs and beliefs no longer imposed a need to deposit jade in tombs. Other methods of research must therefore be brought into play. In the essays which preface each successive section Mr McElney firmly sites the material in the known context of its time, while concentrating also on those pieces and aspects about which we are fortunate enough to possess telling evidence - whether of a technical, stylistic or otherwise rewarding kind. The information he has assembled helps greatly to bring still obscure and difficult areas of the subject into a clearer perspective; indeed the project of the exhibition and catalogue as a whole could hardly be more thoughtfully conceived or well timed.

The new Museum of East Asian Art in Bath will soon have been in existence for a year and this anniversary reminds us of the extent to which its existence is owing to the far-sighted generosity and application of one man; its Honorary Curator, Brian McElney. This first special exhibition devoted to Chinese jade promises to equal in achievement all the expectations aroused by that first opening, and I shall not be alone in congratulating him in this realisation of what has surely been a deeply-held ambition.

John Ayers
January 1994

WHERE JADE IS FOUND IN THE WORLD TODAY

Nephrite Sources
Hualin, Taiwan
Sha Che (Yarkand)
Hetian (Khotan)
Lo Pu, Xinjiang
Chi Mo, Xinjiang
Sui Lai, Xinjiang
Lake Baikal, Siberia
Kyongju, Korea
Turnagain, B.C. Canada
Kobuk River, Alaska
Landar, Wyoming, U.S.A.
Mendocino, Mariposa and Monterey, California, U.S.A.
Amazon River, Brazil
North of South Island, New Zealand
Jordanow, Poland
Graubunden, Switzerland
Ligurian Alps, Italy
S.E. Shuriawi, Zimbabwe

Jadeite Sources
Myitkina, Burma
Niigata, Japan
Sulawesi, Indonesia
Motagua River, Guatamala
San Beneto County, California, U.S.A.

Other miscellaneous jade-type sources
Serpentine, I Li
(Tianmu, Ning Chen near Lake Tai)
Nan Yang, Henan (Metagalbro a form of jadeite, Hornblend and others)
Xin Shan jade, Xiu Yen, Liaoning Bowenite
Lan Tian, Shansi (Serpentinized Diopside)
Chiu Chuan jade, Gansu (Serpentine)

3 PREFACE

The Museum of East Asian Art opened its doors in April 1993 and the occasion was marked by the publication of two substantial volumes describing and illustrating in colour a large part of the collection formed by the founder of the Museum, Mr Brian McElney, and gifted to the Museum. The treasures commemorated in the Inaugural exhibition of the Museum, together with further objects from the Museum's permanent collection and other loans arranged by Mr McElney have been on exhibition during the first year of the Museum's existence, thus firmly laying the foundation of the high regard internationally which the Museum has won for itself.

The present catalogue has been in the course of preparation since shortly after the opening of the Museum and is the joint work of Brian McElney and Angus Forsyth. All the exhibits are taken from the jades presently kept at the Museum. Approximately 50% come from the jades gifted to the Museum by Brian McElney and the balance are on long term loan from the Peony Collection and the Rannerdale Collection. The Peony Collection has been in course of formation by a single collector over a long period with the intention of representing a full chronological representation of the esteem in which the Chinese people have held jade since the Neolithic Era. It is his hope that those viewing this exhibition, and studying this catalogue in later years, will be able to derive their own several benefits from the mostly unpublished selection. The collector wishes to remain anonymous.

The intention to put together an exhibition devoted to jade was foreshadowed in the Inaugural catalogue. Now that intention has come to fruition and visitors will be able to see an outstanding display covering a full range of jade carvings from China from neolithic times up to the early 19th century. Such a comprehensive display of Chinese jades has never been shown before in the United Kingdom. However, in the long term the main importance of the exhibition will undoubtedly lie in the catalogue which with its scholarly essays by Brian McElney and Angus Forsyth will make it an essential part of any library on Chinese Jades.

A number of people have made notable contributions to this work, apart from the two authors, and our thanks must be expressed to John Ayers for his Introduction, to the photographer Mr Arthur Kan, for his excellent work, to Cathay Pacific Airways Ltd who sponsored the photographer's visit to England, to Susan Dewar who reviewed the English text and organised in Beijing the translation of the joint essays, to Andrew Twine who prepared the maps and sketches, to the designers and producers of PPA Design Limited and to Ming Wilson who was responsible for the Chinese translation of Brian McElney's essays and Jack Lee who was responsible for the translations of Angus Forsyth's essays in Hong Kong.

Roger Bluett
Chairman, The Museum of East Asian Art

4 AUTHORS' NOTE

The dating of jade objects within their proper time frames is particularly difficult as the material is so hard that little change in the surface of the jade occurs over centuries. At the present time there is no scientific method, such as carbon-14, or thermoluminescence which help to date organic materials and ceramics respectively to within a few centuries, to assist in their dating. The lack of published archaeological finds and detailed historical records meant that in the past there were few points of reference for the dating of later jades. There have, however, been several important caches of jade published in the last decade or so, notably those of Lady Fu Hao (c.1400 BC) and the king of Nanyue (122 BC), published in the last decade or so which have thrown light on the jades worked from the Shang to the Han dynasties. For this reason the dating of jades from these periods is now better understood. The relative lack of excavated later jades, however, has generally necessitated the dating of jades after the Han dynasty by analogy with objects in other materials. This may well be misleading as it seems to the authors that jade, as the more valuable material, rather than following the styles of objects in other media, probably served as the prototypes for such objects.

Several exhibitions have been held in the past twenty years in which jades of the later periods, i.e. from the Han to the Qing, were presented as such. The three most important of these exhibitions were The Oriental Ceramic Society's Jade Exhibition, London 1975; the Asia Society's Exhibition Chinese Jade from Han to Ching, New York 1980; and the Min Chiu Society's Chinese Jade Carving Exhibition, Hong Kong 1983: All of these have considerably enhanced knowledge of later jades, and we believe have provided a firmer basis for their dating, although even now dating should be made within fairly wide limits.

Numerous excavations in the past decade have brought to light several neolithic cultures, such as Songze, Hongshan and Liangzhu, which were previously unknown or unrecognised. Indeed, several decades ago it was doubted whether jade was even being worked in neolithic times. This opinion has been totally reversed by these recent excavations the full significance of which is still far from clear. Recent writers have suggested a Jade Age, lasting from at least 4000-2000 BC, prior to the Chinese Bronze Age which extended from c.2000-500BC.

With some notable exceptions, it is now possible to recognise most neolithic jades and to assign them to a particular culture. Excavation reports have all assigned dates to the cultures in question, mostly by virtue of carbon-14 dating of the organic material from the same culture levels. However, jade was so precious that whether inherited, excavated or a chance find, it was zealously preserved and jades could have been buried centuries after they were actually worked. There are some jades in the tomb of Fu Hao, for instance, that are considered to be neolithic and may therefore date to a thousand years and more before her burial. The noted expert James Watt, who gave a lecture in Hong Kong on the jades recovered from the tomb in Guangzhou of the king of Nanyue, gave cogent reasons for dating many of the jade objects from this tomb to the period from the 5th to the 3rd century BC, somewhat before the Han dynasty when they were buried. It is important for our purposes to acknowledge the validity and significance of the view that the Fu Hao tomb, and burials from other periods with similarly rich jade contents impossible to associate with one particular product, culture or period, are the last resting places of a jade collector whose eclectic acquisitions may give valuable pointers to the connoisseurship of the period of their burial. These finds may also be the repository of tribute composed of random surface finds of all periods and presented to the ruler either by law or by custom.

The authors of this volume believe that Chinese jades dating from the very earliest times to almost the end of the Qing dynasty are represented in this Exhibition. While it would be a mistake to assign the jades to too narrow a time scale, it would also be inappropriate not to give any lead at all to dating. The aim of the art historian is modest. While not proclaiming certainty, he or she should give an informed opinion on what is probable or improbable, and return an open verdict when the balance of evidence is in question. Unlike the verdict of a jury, however, such conclusions are constantly subject to appeal, and the art historian must therefore clearly distinguish between the evidence and what is deduced from it. This then enables others to correct inferences in the light of new evidence and a deeper understanding. If no conclusions based on available evidence are offered readers are left with false beliefs and woolly notions; and the importance of new evidence is easily missed. For example, some time ago James Watt assigned certain open-work plaques to the Yuan and Ming dynasties, indicating that such plaques did not appear before the Yuan (82 Nos. 175 -182). However an open-work white jade plaque similar to some of those discussed by Watt has recently been excavated from a mid-Liao dynasty tomb (11th century). The significance of the Liao discovery would not have been noticed if James Watt had not previously dated similar plaques to the Yuan

and Ming. It appears in fact from most recent excavations that such open-work plaques were in use at least as early as the Liao dynasty and that their use continued until the end of the Ming dynasty with only minor changes of style.

The art historian must also openly acknowledge his or her own sympathies, for those who pretend to be free of bias unconsciously surrender to the superficial assumptions of the day and can therefore frequently be misleading and often dull.

It must also be realised that once a style had been introduced, the carving of jades in that style probably continued for centuries, and while the style may have gone out of fashion for a considerable time, it could always be reintroduced. This was very much the case in the taste for archaistic forms which developed into a passion for some time from the late 11th century when jades in earlier styles were produced for the scholar/mandarins and other collectors of the day. These deliberately archaistic pieces continued to be made for centuries, and represent one of the most difficult groups to understand and date. In this Exhibition a small group of such pieces has been assembled into a separate category, which follows the Ming dynasty section of this catalogue.

In addition to the archaistic pieces, there has been, particularly in the last hundred years, a substantial industry deliberately producing faked archaic jades to deceive collectors and others. Following every book published on jade (within the last ten or so years such publications have multiplied) modern Chinese jade workers have actually copied the published pieces. Jade animals, for which there is a ready market, have been recent favourites. The feel of such fakes is generally wrong, and the polish seems forced, but many such pieces are sufficiently convincing to take in the inexperienced buyer. The jade-carvers of the past, who worked with pebble jades were restricted in their subject matter by the nature and shape of the pebble itself. While the subject might be repeated, the exact replication of an older jade piece is unlikely to have occurred. The carving of vessels, which could normally only take place in times of relative abundance of the raw material, would not have been so restricted and the carving of vessels of the same shape would in consequence be entirely likely.

We have divided the material in the Exhibition into sections according to the traditional periodization of Chinese history with a special category for archaistic pieces and a lengthy section for the neolithic pieces. An exception has been made in regard to the period from the commencement of the Sui to the end of the Song dynasty. This has been divided into two periods 581-950 and 951-1279 for the reasons given in the introduction "The Fluctuating Jewel" and in the introductory essays to the sections in question. It must also be remembered that stylistic changes did not necessarily correspond with dynastic changes. The neolithic section has also been sub-divided into the main jade cultures presently identified.

Because of the uncertainties of dating jades the textual commentaries may date a piece to a period covered in more than one section. In these instances the jade in question is generally included among the pieces at the beginning of the later section. For example, a jade assigned to the Song to Ming period will be found among jades at the beginning of the Ming section. Since the periods within each section sometimes cover more than three centuries, if in the authors' opinion a narrower time band is indicated, for jades dated after the Han in some cases an indication of the century or centuries to which they consider the jade most likely to date has also been given. For instance, a jade dated Song to Ming may well be followed by the words "(probably 13th to 15th century)". Such dating for periods prior to the Han dynasty is not possible at the present time.

Various references to the bibliography have been included in the essays and commentaries on the objects by means of underlined numerals. These numbers refer to the number of the publication in the bibliography and in most instances also an underlined page plate or exhibit number to which attention is being drawn.

Angus Forsyth
Brian McElney

作者緒言

中國玉器體質堅硬，經歷多個世紀亦絲毫不改其面貌，再加上科學鑒定方法，如碳十四或熱光測試，對玉器不適用，故斷代特別困難。幸好過去十年中，有數宗重要墓葬出土，如殷墟婦好墓（約公元前1400年）及南越王墓（公元前122年），使一般人對商代至漢代玉器有較深認識。唯漢代之後的玉器出土不多，斷代也只能參考同時期他類古物如瓷器、銅器、金銀器等，這一方法未必準確。玉器是非常珍貴的材料，不一定模仿瓷器或銅器，相反地玉器極可能是他類古物模仿的對象。

過去二十年中，有數次重要玉器展覽，如1975年東方陶瓷學會在倫敦的展覽、1980年亞洲學會在紐約的展覽、及1983年敏求精舍在香港的展覽等。這些展覽為以後對玉器的研究和斷代奠定良好基礎。

此外，鮮為人認識的新石器時代文化如松澤、紅山及良渚文化遙有遺址發現，改變了以前認為玉器在新石器時代未有生產的觀念。近年有學者提議在公元前4000至2000年間，有"玉器時代"的存在。"玉器時代"比"青銅器時代"（公元2000至500年）為早。

除少數特殊例子外，一般新石器時代玉器均有其特徵。考古家利用碳十四測試墓葬中其他有機物體，從而斷定玉器所屬文化。必須注意的是，玉器陪葬品的年代可能比出處墓葬的年代要早幾百年，如殷虛婦好墓中部份玉器，是新石器時代產品。著名學者屈志仁在香港一研討會中曾指出，南越王墓中很多玉器早於漢代，屬公元前五世紀至三世紀之物。此現象或反映墓主對該類玉器的喜愛、或間接顯示當時的進貢風俗。玉器研究者在斷代方面應慎重考慮各項可能性。

是次展覽包括最早期至清代玉器。斷代方面，本書作者認為將一件展品的年代範圍定得太窄固然不好，但完全不提供斷代資料亦非善策。藝術史家的責任不是作出權威性的理論，而是分析各項可能性後，再提出一己之見，然而他必須分清事實與推理，亦必須接納他人合理的意見。藝術史家若只筆錄事實，讀者會有模稜兩可的感覺。若他的理論不留商討餘地，考古上的新發現則難獲廣泛注意。例如：多年前，屈志仁曾指出一類透雕玉牌（82圖175-182）的年代不會早於元朝，而此類玉牌最近卻出現於一遼墓中（十一世紀）。若屈氏不曾提出他的理論，玉牌出於遼墓之重要性便會被忽視。

藝術史家亦當承認他有個人的愛惡。自以為全無偏見的作者缺乏立場，亦易流於膚淺及枯燥無味。

玉雕的風格常經歷數百年不變。再者，某種風格在消失了一段時期後又會重現，如宋代之仿古風尚。此類仿古玉自宋開始盛行，為斷代帶來不少困難，是次展覽中一組玉器即屬此類。

除仿古玉器外，近百年中還有偽玉器出現。玉器圖錄的出版使現代玉工很容易按圖仿製。動物玉雕特別受歡迎，故偽品亦多。一般來說，偽玉器的質感不佳，拋光牽強，但間中亦能蒙騙經驗少的收藏家。古代玉工雕製玉器，題材常受璞玉的形狀所限。同一題材雖會多次採用，但兩件形狀完全相同、題材一模一樣的玉雕，出現的可能性不大。相反來說，玉製器皿如杯、碗之類，只會在玉材來源豐富的情況下生產，玉工不受玉材形狀的牽制，故而兩件形狀完全相同的玉器皿出現也就不足為奇了。

是次展覽根據編年作出分類，另特闢一"仿古"類，每類展品說明之前均有導言。新石器時代再劃分不同文化。隋至宋代則分作兩階段——公元581至951及951至1279年，詳情請參閱〈隨時勢遷動的瑰寶〉一文。應注意的是，改朝換代不一定同時引致風格的改變。

若某展品的年代跨越兩朝之間（如宋至明代），則該展品劃歸後一代（即明代）。有時兩朝相距數百年，項目說明將加註公元年數（如十三至十五世紀）。唯此方法不適用於漢代之前的古玉。

本書引用書目，用劃線代表，黑色數字指該書頁數或插圖號數。

5 CHRONOLOGICAL TABLE 年表

NEOLITHIC PERIOD circa 5500 - 1700 BC		
1.	NORTH CHINA NEOLITHIC CULTURES	
	(North and North West China - Liaoning Province and Inner Mongolia)	
	Xinglongwa 興隆洼	c. 5500 - 5040 BC
	Zhaobaogou 趙寶溝	c. 4800 - 4000 BC
	Chahai 查海	c. 4700 - 3000 BC
	Hongshan 紅山	c. 3500 - 2200 BC
2.	YELLOW RIVER NEOLITHIC CULTURES (circa 4800 - circa 1700 BC)	
a.	Shaanxi Province (the central plain) /Middle/Lower Middle Yellow River	
	Yangshao 仰韶	c. 4800 - 3070 BC
	Banpo type 半坡類型	c. 4800 - 4200 BC
	Miaodigou type 廟底溝類型	c. 3900 - 3500 BC
	Qinwangzhai type 秦王寨類型	c. 3400 - 3000 BC
	Henan Longshan 河南龍山	c. 2300 - 1700 BC
b.	Lower Yellow River/Shandong Province/North Jiangsu Province - Huai River Basin	
	Dawenkou 大汶口	c. 4500 - 2300 BC
	Huating 花廳	c. 3800 - 3000 BC
	Shandong Longshan 山東龍山	c. 2300 - 1700 BC
3.	YANGZI RIVER NEOLITHIC CULTURES (circa 5000 - circa 2000 BC)	
a.	Middle Yangzi River-Sichuan, Hubei	
	Daixi 大溪	c. 4000 - 3300 BC
	Shijiahe 石家河	c. 2500 - 2000 BC
	(Qinglongquan III)	
b.	Lower Yangzi River Basin - Lake Tai and East Central China (Ning Shao Plain)	
	Hemudu 河姆渡	c. 5000 - 4800 BC
	Majiabin 馬家濱	c. 5000 - 3900 BC
	Songze 崧澤	c. 3800 - 2900 BC
	Qingliangang	c. 3500 BC
	Liangzhu 良渚	c. 3400 - 2250 BC
4.	SOUTHERN NEOLITHIC JADE INFLUENCED CULTURES (circa 3000 - 2000 BC)	
	South Coastal Provinces Guangdong Province	
	Shixia 石峽	c. 3000 - 2000 BC
XIA DYNASTY 夏		c. 2100 - 1600 BC
ERLITOU PERIOD 二里頭		c. 1900 - 1600 BC
SHANG DYNASTY 商		c. 1600 - 1100 BC
	Erligang Phase	c. 1600 - 1400 BC
	Anyang Phase	c. 1400 - 1100 BC
ZHOU DYNASTY 周		c. 1100 - 221 BC
	Western Zhou Period 西周	c. 1100 - 771 BC
	Eastern Zhou Period 東周	c. 770 - 221 BC
	Spring and Autumn Period 春秋時期	770 - 475 BC
	Warring States Period 戰國時期	475 - 221 BC

QIN DYNASTY 秦		221 - 206 BC
HAN DYNASTY 漢		206 - 220 BC
	Western Han 西漢	206 BC - 8 AD
	Xin (Wang Mang) 新（王莽）	9 - 25
	Eastern Han 東漢	25 - 220
SIX DYNASTIES 六朝		220 - 589
	Three Kingdoms period 三國	220 - 280
	Wu 吳	220 - 280
	Shu 蜀	221 - 263
	Wei 魏	220 - 265
	Western and Eastern Jin 西晉東晉	265 - 420
PERIOD OF NORTHERN AND SOUTHERN DYNASTIES 南北朝時代 386-589		
	North 北朝	
	Northern Wei 北魏	386 - 534
	Eastern Wei 東魏	534 - 550
	Western Wei 西魏	535 - 557
	Northern Qi 北齊	550 - 577
	Northern Zhou 北周	557 - 581
	South 南朝	
	(Liu) Song （劉）宋	420 - 479
	Southern Qi 南齊	479 - 502
	Liang 梁	502 - 557
	Chen 陳	557 - 589
SUI DYNASTY 隋		581 - 618
TANG DYNASTY 唐		618 - 907
	High Tang 盛唐	684 - 756
	Late Tang 晚唐	757 - 907
FIVE DYNASTIES 五代		907 - 960
SONG DYNASTY 宋		960 - 1279
	Northern Song 北宋	960 - 1127
	Southern Song 南宋	1127 - 1279
LIAO DYNASTY (Qidan) 遼		907 - 1125
JIN DYNASTY (Jurchen) 金		1115 - 1234
YUAN DYNASTY (Mongol) 元		1279 - 1368
MING DYNASTY 明		1368 - 1644
QING DYNASTY 清		1644 - 1911

6 GLOSSARY OF ARCHAIC JADES

The names of archaic jade shapes are often confusing with commentators calling different shapes by different names. It seems sensible to agree on a uniform terminology for practical purposes. The origin of the names in use are based mostly on the Han dynasty versions of three books purportedly written over 2000 years ago: Zhouli, Yili and Liji.

The six Ritual Jades - *bi, cong, gui, zhang, huang,* and *hu* described in these books were supposed to be used for paying homage to the Sky, the Earth and the Four Directions. Each jade form was supposed to be of a specific colour. The prescribed colour for the *huang* was black but *huang* excavated so far do not bear out this colour association.

In the commentaries to the Zhouli, Han scholars allocated the six Ritual Jades definite positions in relation to the body. Again excavations have produced no proof of this supposed relationship. Ip Yee suggested a simpler and more uniform set of terminology for practical use in his Chinese Jade Carving (37 at pages 22 and 23) and we intend adopting similar terminology in this catalogue.

TABLE OF SIMPLIFIED TERMINOLOGY

1 *Bi-disc*

This includes *bi* 璧, *huan* 環, and *yuan* 瑗. *Bi-discs* of all three types, first appeared in neolithic times. Their names before the Western Zhou dynasty (c.1100-771BC) are not known.

According to Xia Nai, the classification of *bi-disc* into three types: *bi* 璧, *huan* 環 and *yuan* 瑗, is a Han invention and as the hole can be of any size, never to any specification, it is best to call them all *bi-discs*. The diagrams at the end of this glossary show the traditional classification of *bi-discs* into *bi, huan* and *yuan.*

If a more detailed description is required then they may be called *bi-disc* with big hole, *bi-disc* with medium size hole and *bi-disc* with small hole.

2 *Cong* 琮, *jue* 玦 and *huang* 璜.

All three of these traditional shapes first appeared in neolithic times. The name *cong,* a circular cylinder enclosed by a square or rectangular box , for which no equivalent in English is available, is retained in this catalogue. All *jue* 玦 are referred to as slit discs and all *huang* 璜 are referred to as arched pendants. *Huang* 璜 can be a segment or any fraction of a *bi-disc;* and in later examples, the ends were often modified but the general shape of the piece remained. A simplified English description of arched pendant seems appropriate.

3 Pendants

These would include *heng* 珩, *xibi* 系璧, *xie* 觿, *wengzhong* 翁仲, *le* 瓅 *pei* 珮 and *gangmao* 剛卯. All jades used as pendants should be called pendants and their archaic names discarded.

The term *'heng'* will not be used as it denotes the top piece in a set of pendants. The correct position of any piece of jade in a set is uncertain. The reconstruction of the positioning of buried jades found in different positions of the body is based merely on speculation. Moreover, the arrangement of the pieces may differ from set to set.

'Xibi' will be called 'small *bi-disc'*. The reason for the change is the same as for *'heng'* described above as its function and position is not definite.

'Xie' will be described by its shape and becomes 'pointed pendant'.

'Wengzhong' will be named 'bearded human figure or bearded old man'. It is

unconvincing to call this bearded old man 'wengzhong' meaning the giant warrior.

'Le' is tubular and may be used as a pendant or to form part of a string of beads. It will simply be called 'tubular pendant or tubular bead'.

'Pei' is an expression covering various hanging or suspended shapes not covered by any other specific term.

'Gangmao' is a square tubular pendant with inscriptions on it to ward off evil and may be called 'tubular charm'.

Animals and birds were often made with a perforation to be worn as pendants. If perforated a dragon with perforation or perforations will be described as a 'dragon pendant'.

4 Inlays and Inserts

Jades with perforations or attachments on the back or at the ends were meant for inlays or inserts. For instance, if it is a bear, then we have called it 'bear insert' or 'bear inlay'.

5 Ornaments

Some jades have no perforations or attachments and were meant to be ornaments. Similarly for instance, if it is a dragon, then we will describe it as 'dragon or dragon ornament'.

6 Beads

Beads, including *zhu*, a type of round bead.

7 Bracelets

Jade bracelets (*zhuo* 鐲) have been worked from neolithic times on.

8 Gui-tablet 圭

This name should be confined to the tablet with a pointed end as defined in the Han dictionary Shuowen Jiezi and as shown in the 'Diagram of Six Jades' on a Han tombstone. This type has been found in the Han tombs at Mancheng. More research has to be done on the subject. There are more than ten different types of *gui*-tablets mentioned in Zhouli but the six identified by Wu Dacheng in 81 have all turned out to be weapons or tools of the early Shang period except one with dragon design of spirals which belonged to the Eastern Han period.

9 Zhang 璋

Gui-tablets and *zhangs*, a flat sword form with slender hilt projection, though known since neolithic times, were not popular until the Warring States period and the definition given in the Shuowen Jiezi that a *zhang* is half a *gui* is so far the most convincing.

10 Sword and Scabbard Fittings

Different commentators have used different names for different pieces involved. The following names will be adopted.

a. Pommel (for sword or macehead, called by some *shou* 首)

b. Sword guard or sword hilt (called by some *ge* 格)

c. Sword buckle or sword slide (called by some *zhi* 璏 or *wei* 璏)

d. Chape (*bi* 珌)

11 Axe (*fu* 斧) a flat wide bladed axe head with cutting edge formed by grinding both surfaces.

12 Adze (*chan* 鏟) with cutting edge formed by grinding one surface.

13 Flat Axe (*yue* 鉞) A wide bladed axe with large central perforation and symetrical side notches, generally finely finished. For ceremonial or ritual use only.

14 Chisel or Narrow Axe (*chi* 鑿 and *beng* 錛) a thick chisel form with a flat underside formed by sharply bevelling down one end of the topside.

15 Axe with notches and teeth (*qi* 戚).

16 Blade
This expression covers *dao* 刀 which is a square ended knife and *chan* 鏟, a square shaped blade with evenly thin mid section, and blades of all types.

17 *Bi-disc* with notches and teeth on perimeter (*qibi* 戚璧 or *xuanji* 璇璣).

    Xuanji 璇璣 is included here because it is no more than a *bi-disc* with notches and teeth. The number of notches and teeth is not fixed and its function remains unknown, although various theories have been put forward.

18 *Zan 'Ji'* 笄 for hair or headgears to be replaced by *'zan'* (hairpin or hatpin).

19 Ear plug or Earring
This will replace *'zhen'* 瑱. It has a perforation, and was probably used as an earring. This is sometimes confused with an ear plug which has no perforation. Both types have been found near the ears. Ear plugs with no perforations have been found in the Han graves at Mancheng.

20 Thumb ring or Archers' ring
This expression will replace *'xie'* 韘. Some people called it *'jue'* '決' and called its leather lining *'xie'* 韘. The many purely ornamental ones, which bear little relationship to the traditional archer's ring, *xie* 觿 are pendants and are described as 'pointed pendants', as is mentioned above.

21 Mouth Charm
This expression covers *han* 唅 a flat disc or tear drop shape with central perforation and cicadas of all types found in the mouth of some buried skeletons.

22 Many other names including the following should be retained because of traditional or common usage:
a. Chime
b. Comb *shu* 梳
c. Dagger or halberd blade with tang extension and no projection *ge* 戈
d. Spearhead *mao* 矛
e Belt or garment hook *daigou* 帶鈎
f. Tubular bead *guan* 琯
g. Awl-shaped pendant *chui* 錐
h. *xi* 觿 a pin form, perceived by some as a knot picker.
i. *Bingxingshu* 柄形梳, a handle form object with tenon extension for insertion.

    It is hoped that readers will find the above table useful. It is incomplete and no doubt will require revision as a result of fresh discoveries over the years to some. Diagrams of some of the shapes involved with their traditional Chinese name are set out on the following pages.

1. *Bi-disc* with small hole 璧

2. Short form *cong* 琮

7. *Zhuo* 鐲

1. *Bi-disc* with medium size hole (*huan* 環)

2. Slit-disc (*jue* 玦)

8. *Gui* 圭

2. *Huang* 璜

9. *Zhang* 璋

1. *Bi-disc* with big hole (*yuan*) 瑗

3. *Pei* 珮

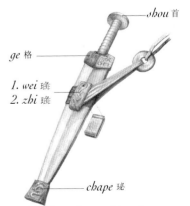

shou 首

ge 格

1. *wei* 璏
2. *zhi* 璏

chape 珌

10. Sword + scabbard jade fittings

2. Long form *cong* 琮

6. *Zhu* 珠

11. Axe *(fu* 斧 *)*

16. *Dao* 刀

22f. *Guan* 琯

12. Adze *(ben* 錛*)*

17. *Bi-disc* with knotches
and teeth on perimeter
(*qibi* 戚璣 *or xuanji* 璇璣*)*

22h. *Xi* 觿

12. Adze *(chan* 鏟 *)*

21. *Han* 唅

22g. *Chui* 錐 - first type

13. Flat Axe *(yue* 鉞*)*

22. *Ge* 戈

22g. *Chui* 錐 - second type

古玉釋名

古玉的名稱，因不同的作者採用不同的稱謂而顯得亂。玉器名稱的來源，出自漢代編纂的〈周禮〉、〈儀禮〉和〈禮記〉。為實際起見，實有統一各稱謂的必要。

礼器中的"六器"，即璧、琮、圭、璋、璜及琥，是用來祭禮天、地及四方之用的。六器應有規定的顏色，如璜應是黑色，但黑璜至今尚未見有出土。

在〈周禮〉註釋中，漢代學者認為六器應放在人體的一定位置，但墓葬出土玉器否定此說。葉義在其〈中國玉雕〉(37頁22-23)一書中作了簡化的統一正名工作。本書除略作更改外，將採用該書的名稱及分類。

一)璧
璧類包括璧、環、瑗。此三項形制在新石器時代已出現，唯西周前此類玉器尚未有定名。

據夏鼐教授研究所得，將璧分為璧、環、瑗三類的制度始自漢代。但因璧孔大小並無特殊規定，所以它們應統稱為璧。本文後之插圖顯示傳統璧、環、瑗的分類方法。若需更仔細分類，可稱為大孔璧、中孔璧或小孔璧。

二)琮、玦、璜
此三項形制最早出現於新石器時代。琮及玦名稱保留，璜可以是璧的某部份，有時首尾兩端被修改，故改稱璜形珮。

三)珮
珮類包括珩、系璧、觿、翁仲、瑚、剛卯。所有作佩飾用的玉器應稱為珮，它們在古代的不同名稱一律廢棄。珩一名亦不用，因其只是代表一串玉珮中最上端的一件，唯珮串中每件玉珮的位置均未有規定，屍首上陪葬玉器的正確擺放位置只是一種臆測，再者珮串中玉器的排列方法往往有差異。

系璧應稱作小璧。如珩一樣，其用途及正途及正確位置不定。

觿應稱作尖珮，因其形狀呈尖形。

翁仲應稱為玉人或有鬚人像，"翁仲"一詞原指武士像。

瑚作圓管狀，可作為玉珮，或玉串的一部份，故可稱管珮或管珠。

剛卯是方形管狀珮，上刻文字以辟邪，可稱作辟邪管珮。

珮泛指一切佩飾。動物或雀鳥形的玉塊常附穿孔作為佩戴之用，若玉塊雕作龍形，上有穿孔，可稱為龍形珮。

四)鑲嵌器
玉雕背面或末端附有穿孔或附件，作為鑲嵌之用，可稱作鑲嵌飾物。如玉塊雕成熊形，可稱作熊形嵌飾。

五)飾物
一些玉雕並無穿孔或附件，是作飾物之用。如其雕作龍形，可名為玉龍或龍形飾。

六)珠
包括圓形、方形、柱狀及管狀小件飾物。

七)鐲
玉鐲在新石器時代已有製造。

八)圭
"圭"一名應限於末端呈尖削形的長玉片，如漢代〈說文解字〉中所載及滿城漢墓碑板〈六玉圖〉所示。此等圖像有待學者作更深入研究。〈周禮〉中記述了十種以上的圭。吳大澂所考定的六種圭(81圖)，五種是商代的武器或工具，另一種飾以渦卷紋的則屬東漢時期。

九)璋
戰國時代以前，圭與璋尚未流行。〈說文解字〉釋璋是縱剖圭之一半，此說較為合理。

十)劍飾
劍飾的名稱並不劃一，本文採用下列數種：
甲、劍首(或儀仗首)，前稱琫或璏
乙、劍格，前稱璲或珌
丙、劍鞘上帶扣，或稱璲或璏
丁、劍鞘末玉飾，或稱珌

十一)斧
從雙面磨成刃部的玉器。

十二)錛
從單面磨成刃部的玉器。

十三)扁平斧，或稱鉞。

十四)狹長斧，或稱錛。

十五)齒牙斧，或稱戚。

十六)刀
包括刀、鏟及各類刃。

十七)齒牙璧，或稱戚璧、璿璣
璿璣歸此類，因其只是具有齒及糟的璧。齒糟沒有一定數目，其用途亦未有定論。

十八）簪

笄為簪（髮簪、冠簪）所代替。

十九）耳塞、耳環

瑱改稱耳塞或耳環。因其有穿孔，所以多是用作耳環。此物常與耳塞相混淆，因兩者均在屍首耳部附近發現。無孔的耳塞曾在滿城漢墓出土。

二十）扳指

韘改稱扳指。也有將扳指稱作"決"，將墊襯之熟皮稱作"韘"的。形狀如觿，但純粹作裝飾用的稱為尖珮。

二十一）唅

唅包括琀及其它放在死人口中的陪葬玉。

二十二）下列傳統名稱，因沿用已久，故仍予以保留：

甲、磬

乙、梳

丙、戈

丁、矛

戊、帶鈎

己、琯

庚、錐

辛、觿

壬、柄形梳

　　　以上的分類或未得周全，但希望對讀者有所幫助。考古上的新發現將對玉器的正名有更進一步的確定。前頁（第20－21頁）插圖為玉器的傳統名稱及形制。

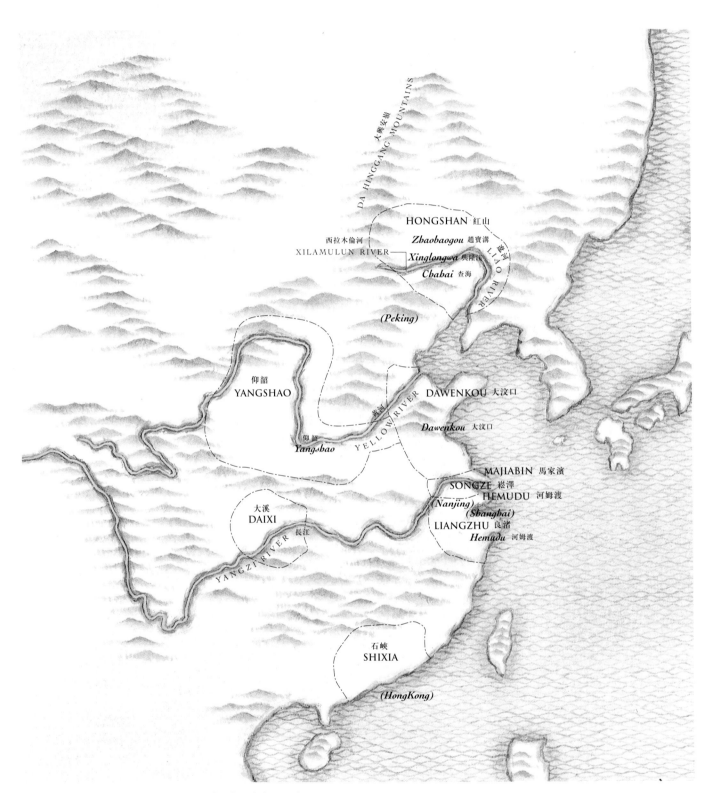

HONGSHAN 红山
Zhaobaogou 趙寶溝
西拉木倫河
XILAMULUN RIVER — *Xinglongwa* 興隆窪
Chahai 查海
DA HINGGANG MOUNTAINS 大興安嶺
LIAO RIVER 遼河

(Peking)

仰韶
YANGSHAO
仰韶
Yangshao

YELLOW RIVER 黃河

DAWENKOU 大汶口
Dawenkou 大汶口

MAJIABIN 馬家濱
SONGZE 崧澤
HEMUDU 河姆渡
(Nanjing) (Shanghai)
LIANGZHU 良渚
Hemudu 河姆渡

大溪
DAIXI
長江
YANGZI RIVER

石峽
SHIXIA

(HongKong)

Mainstream jade using cultures in the early and mid Neolithic Period

大興安嶺
DA HINGGANG MOUNTAINS

西拉木倫河
XILAMULUN RIVER

遼河
LIAO RIVER

黃河
YELLOW RIVER

SHANDONG LONGSHAAN
山東龍山

河南龍山
HENAN LONGSHAN

ERLITOU 二里頭

LIANGZHU 良渚

石家河
Shijiahe

良渚
Liangzhu

長江

SHIJIAHE
石家河

YANGZI RIVER

石峽
Shixia

石峽
SHIXIA

Mainstream jade using cultures in the late Neolithic Period

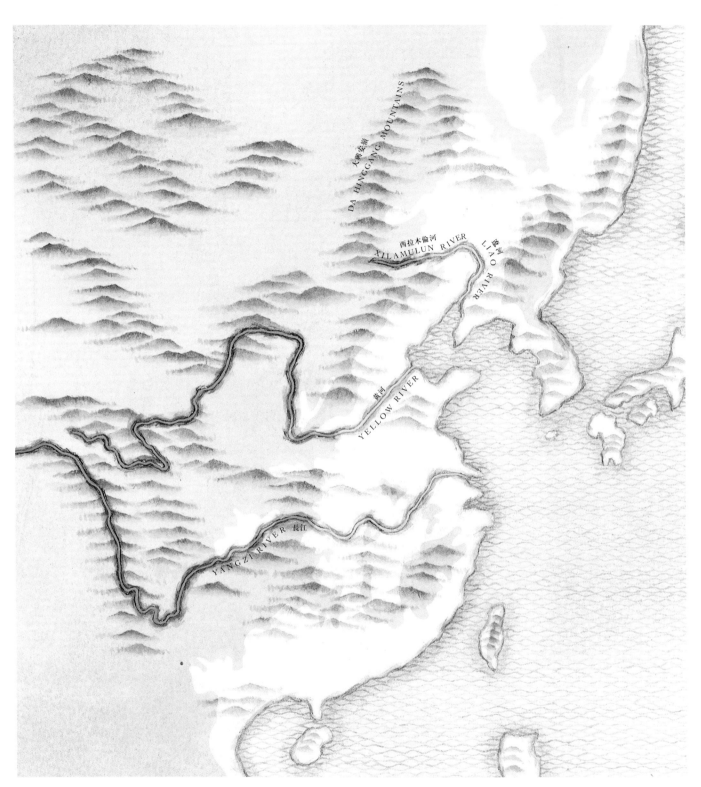

大興安嶺
DA HINGGANG MOUNTAINS

西拉木倫河
XILAMULUN RIVER

遼河
LIAO RIVER

黃河
YELLOW RIVER

YANGZI RIVER 長江

Map with lighter shade showing the extent of the elevation up to 600m which formed the cradle for growth of the principal jade using Neolithic cultures.

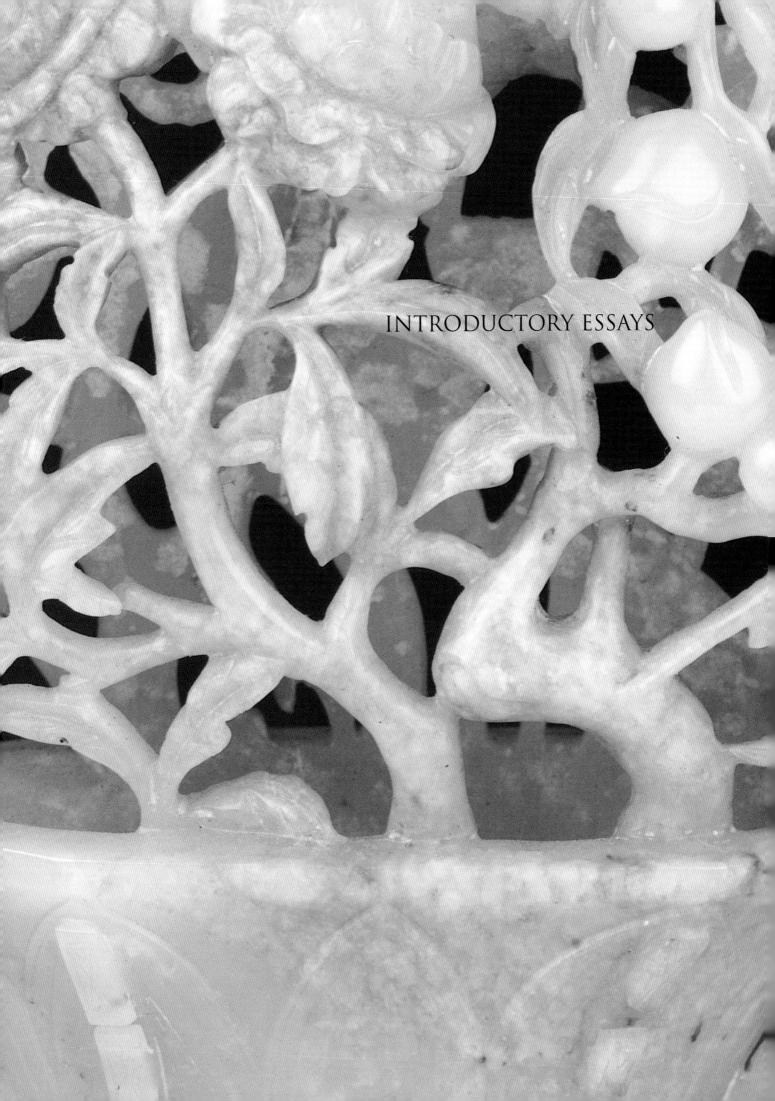

INTRODUCTORY ESSAYS

8 Jade, the Raw Material

Jade is the name currently applied in English to a gemstone group that includes the pyroxene called jadeite composed of sodium, aluminium and silicate ($NaAl\,Si_2O_6$), and the amphibole stone composed of calcium, magnesium and silicate $\{Ca_2(Mg.Fe)_5Si_8O_{22}(OH)_2\}$ known as nephrite. These gemstones of almost entirely different composition are both called jade.(ZBFJ p.24)

Both of these materials are relatively uncommon. A list of the places where nephrite and jadeite are known to occur at the present time is appended to the Introduction. Most of these places would however have been irrelevant as sources of supply for Chinese jade carvers of the past.

The two principal stones in the nephrite group are Toushanshi 透閃石 or tremolite, and Yangqishi 陽起石 or actinolite.

Testing of many Hongshan jades has identified them as a silicate of magnesium, popularly called bowenite. This is of a similar physical structure to nephrite but slightly softer.

Today large deposits of a dark-green fibrous serpentine stone with a hardness range of 4.5 to 5.5 are worked in Xiuyan county in Liaoning province. This stone has been shown to be a magnesium silicate but it differs from those found near sites of neolithic jade workings elsewhere in China. Tremolite and actinolite from the same site have been analysed and found to be of a totally different structure from Khotan nephrite.

The generally accepted view has been that the Chinese did not know jadeite, referred to as *feicui* (kingfisher) in the 18th and 19th centuries, until the 18th century. This date is likely to be far too conservative as earlier historical records mention *feicui* in a 6th century AD context. In a work by Ouyang Xiu of the Northern Song dynasty there is also reference to a vessel as being of *feicui*. It seems probable that the *feicui* mentioned in both instances refers to jadeite (ZBFJ p.40). There are also small pieces of jadeite in the tomb of the Ming emperor Wanli (d.1620). It seems certain, however, that supplies of jadeite (coming in the main from the Kachin hills of North Burma) did not enter China in any appreciable quantities until the 18th century, and therefore in this exhibition we are primarily concerned with the other jade material, nephrite, with only a single jadeite example (Exhibit 354) included for comparison. Jadeite, probably from the source in Japan at Niigata, seems to have been used by the Japanese and Koreans exclusively for the production of magatama, comma-shaped beads or charms found in Japanese and Korean burials of the first half of the first millenium AD. Apart from this one use, the Japanese conspicuously failed to acquire a reverence for jade despite their many influential cultural imports from China. While the Chinese were certainly aware for centuries that Japan had a native source of green jade, since this is mentioned in the histories of both the Eastern Han dynasty, and the Wei Kingdom, there is no record of the Chinese ever having imported or received more than token jade tribute from Japan.

The Chinese character yu 玉, appears at least from the beginnings of Chinese writing in the Shang period, to have referred to any hard beautiful stone, and the use of the character yu 玉 was not confined to nephrite and jadeite until well into the first millenium AD. In this exhibition, therefore, several agates have been properly included as well as cornelian, pudding-stone and certain types of serpentine all of which would have been considered to be jade at the time of their production.

The sustained legitimacy of this perception

in modern China is well demonstrated by the description of a famous winged figurine of the Shang period excavated from a river bank at Xingan, Jiangxi Province in 1989. This figure was published in 21, No. 66 as being made of "jade" when it has been unanimously agreed by those who have handled it that the piece is not nephrite but a soft form of soapstone.

In recent years Professor Guang Wen of China's Institute of Geology has used a scanning electron microscope and a high resolution transmission electron microscope as well as other scientific instrumentation to examine the microstructures and compositions of jades from various archaeological sites. His research has shown that there are two main types of nephrite found in China; nephrite in magnesium marble and nephrite in serpentinised ultrabasic. The quality and colour of the Chinese nephrite concerned is determined by the microstructure and content of ferrous oxide in the tremolite/actinolite ratios. This research is important since it seems to establish that the source of Liangzhu culture jade was probably the southern part of Jiangsu, near Lake Tai Hu, where nephrite of more or less identical composition has been found. His research is continuing with investigation of jades from the Hongshan and Songze cultures and other sites. Professor Guang's initial results co-authored with Jing Zhichun were published in 85. From his research to date, it appears likely that most of the raw nephrite jade material used in neolithic times came from sources within China. 7BFJ p.38-41

The specific gravities of both nephrite and jadeite are within 2.8-3.6 and on Moh's incremental scale of hardness, which ranges from 1 to10, nephrite is about 6.5, jadeite between 6.75 and 7 and agate about 7, whereas a modern steel knife would be 6, and a diamond 10. It is,

therefore, technically incorrect to speak of jade being "carved" although it seems unnecessarily pedantic at this juncture to abandon the use of the word so hallowed by long usage. Jade has in truth to be worked by sawing, drilling or grinding down with the use of abrasives. There is, however, an interesting distinction in Chinese terminology which classifies jadeite as "hard jade" and nephrite as "soft jade".

In their purest form both jadeite and nephrite are the colour of white lychee flesh. Although both occur in various colours jadeite has a wider range of hues and can achieve greater intensity of tone than nephrite. Both jades occur in white, yellow, green, blue and brown but only jadeite is found in pink or mauve or the brilliant kingfisher green associated with jade jewellery. Nephrite occurs mostly in various tones of green and exhibits a wider range of variations in this colour than jadeite. Jadeite jewellery is typically emerald green and the best imperial examples of this colour when placed in a cup of water reflect the light so perfectly that the water appears to take on a pale greenish tinge. If the jade jewellery in question produces this effect it is probably as rare as emeralds. Only nephrite occurs as a true black jade, although a very dark green jadeite can appear black in some lights.

The Chinese have held jade in the highest esteem for at least seven thousand years. It has been postulated by recent writers (particularly Wu Hung in 89) that prior to the Chinese Bronze Age c. 2000 to 500 BC, China enjoyed a Jade Age from about 4000 to 2000 BC. Until a decade or so ago the very supposition of jade working in neolithic times was generally questioned. However, the fact that jades were worked in many parts of China during this period, regardless of environment or economic circumstances, is no longer in doubt and has been amply confirmed by numerous finds over the last decade. Evidence for the perceived Jade Age is now unarguable and there is no reason why this term should not enter general currency as an acknowledgement of the seminal role of this remarkable material in the formation of Chinese culture. The adulation of jade by the Chinese was shared by other peoples such as the neolithic inhabitants of temperate Europe, the Maoris of New Zealand and the inhabitants of early Mexico and Honduras, but only the Chinese have carried its symbolic use to such levels of sophistication 9, pp 35.

The material has a unique combination of obduracy, adamantine strength and beauty. In neolithic times the necessary expenditure of months of labour in the jade carving process would only have increased respect for the material. Such respect can be gauged from the large concentrations of jade found in the richest burials of the late Liangzhu culture from the middle of the third millenium BC. These must surely indicate the existence of a specialist body of administrators and a large number of workers exclusively devoted to the production of jade artifacts. In other words, respect for jade was extended from an appreciation of its beauty and immutability to its investiture into the social order of the state. In consequence, respect for jade and for the state became synonymous, and the attribution to jade of powers and virtues above those of mankind made very understandable its use in religious and court audiences, as a mark of noble or royal rank, and as correct luxury wear for kings - all of these demonstrated and enhanced the qualities society had identified in jade, namely the true virtue, purpose and value of its own structure. In the mid fifth century BC, Confucian precepts were developed that endowed jade with title and rank for the ordering of society,

thus establishing a force which, like the Confucian order itself, entered the heart and soul of Chinese culture for the 2,400 years before the overthrow of the Qing dynasty in 1911.

Something of the sheer depth of the penetrating reality of this legacy can be seen in the use in even "modern" China today, as a newly introduced simplification by the post 1949 Communist Government, of the colloquial written Chinese character "国" "guo" for country or motherland. This simplified character replaced a previous, more complicated one, with the same meaning. Combined with "中" or "zhong" meaning "middle" the new character creates "中国" "zhong guo" for "middle country/motherland" which is the traditional Chinese language term for China - a concept of fundamental living significance for the Chinese as a people. In fact, this new character "国" for "guo" is nothing more than the age old Chinese character "玉" "yu" for "jade" set within the comforting protection of enclosing walls. The adoption of the traditional character for "jade" for this purpose will thus be clearly seen to have signified - even since 1949 - an acknowledgment in a manner uniquely Chinese and heedless of politics of a domestic patriotic allegiance of the highest value - the absolute recognition of the true power of jade.

The five basic human virtues attributed to jade by Confucian teaching were kindness or endearment, found in the benefit that accrued to the people as a result of moderation; integrity, from the confidence that the inside is the same as the outside; wisdom, from the emission of a deep, reverberating sound when the jade is struck; courage, identified with the unbendable nature of the matted nephrite fabric; and finally purity, found in the honest, unstained and natural openness of jade. Any true subscriber to civilised virtue would seek to emulate these five qualities and what better way to do so than to wear and thus be near to one or more pieces of jade.

In the Shang dynasty, jade was considered a form of wealth and it is worthy of note in this regard that the Chinese official responsible for the treasure of the imperial court in all dynasties had the title "Chief of the Jade Storehouse" 3BFJ pp 23. The shapes found from that time include discs, segments and forms taken from nature.

From at least the Shang dynasty on, jade was used extensively for pendant ornaments. As a result assemblages of jade in the form of pectorals, or strings of pendants gradually became popular. Such pectorals were a personal item worn both in life and after death. In burials dating from as early as 800 BC jades of appropriate shapes were arranged on the body to emphasise the features of the face. Different assemblages seem to have been worn by different sexes. Two sets were probably worn on the chest, splitting at the lower part of the body. The practice of wearing such pectorals became particularly common in the Eastern Zhou dynasty, and the wearing of both pectorals and pendants continued well into the Han period. For example, no less than eleven different sets of pectoral assemblages were found in the tomb of the posthumously named Emperor Wen, Zhao Mo, the second king of Nanyue who died in 122 BC (47).

Jade was also valued for its musical qualities. Stone chimes have been known for centuries and there is even a large neolithic hanging jade, that must have served as a gong. This is borne out by the use of jade for tuning pipes, evident from Exhibit 143, and from the later ban on its use for this purpose, mentioned in the commentary to that Exhibit.

According to Confucius (522-479 BC), the equivalent of the nouveau riche gentlemen of his day 'go around clanking their jades'. A true gentleman was apparently expected to move at a leisurely, elegant pace so as to prevent his jade pectorals from clashing together and creating a discordant sound. His graceful, unhurried movements were however expected to produce a pleasing tinkling sound from the pendants.

The pivotal status accorded to jade in society provided rich inspiration for figures of speech. There are, not surprisingly, dozens of examples. The expression "玉碎" or "yu sui", literally "shattered jade" in fact means that it is better to die with glory than live in dishonour. "玉函" or "yu han" besides being "Honorable Sir" can also be interpreted as an admonition to use jade to store letters, meaning that items of the greatest value deserve to be preserved in the finest environment. The phrase "玉石俱焚" or "yu shi ju fen" means "Jade and stone burned together", a reference to the indiscriminate destruction of both good and bad and "亭亭玉立" or "ting ting yu li" connotes a fair, slim elegant woman.

From at least the Han dynasty on the sources of the nephrite jade worked in China were the rivers flowing from the Kunlun mountains in the regions of Khotan and Yarkand. These rivers are called the Black Jade River, the Green Jade River and the White Jade River in the Turkic language spoken by the Uighur natives of the area. The other significant source of nephrite from the 18th century onwards was the Vostochny Sayan mountain range west of the southern end of Lake Baikal. The nephrite jades from this source, commonly called Siberian jades, are deep spinach green with grey or black flecks. There is no evidence that Siberian jade entered China before the 18th century.

Early historical records describe the methods and procedures for gathering jade. The New History of the Five Dynasties - Si yi fu lu records of Khotan "In the east there is the white jade river, in the west the green jade river, also in the west the black jade river, and the three rivers are so named after the colours of their jade. Every autumn when the water is low, the king draws the first jade from the rivers, and only after that may the people draw out jade". 7BFJ pp 29

The vast majority of the nephrite worked in China up to the early 17th century came from pebble jade. However there is a reference to mountain jade in the literature of the Warring States period, and a distinction was drawn from at least the late Ming dynasty between mountain and pebble jade. It is also mentioned elsewhere that Jade was mined in the mountains from the late Ming onwards, but mountain jade was apparently considered much inferior to pebble jade, and generally fetched less than a third of the price. Nephrite pebbles or boulders were recovered from river-beds in the Khotan and Yarkand regions when the rivers were at their lowest in the spring and early autumn. Wood block illustrations show women of the area searching among the alluvial deposits washed down by the rivers. Tradition has it that they entered the water naked since jade was associated with the female principle yin and was thought to be attracted to the women who would locate the nephrite pebbles with their feet.

Nephrite produces a tactile sensation not shared by many stones which is aptly described as a greasy feel.

There is another version, however, of the way in which these nephrite pebbles were collected. In 'Chinese Central Asia' published in 1893 Henry Lansdell records: (pp 136-138)

"Not far west of the river Yarkand was a hamlet called Seh-Shambeh, or Tuesday bazaar, with a serai, where on a subsequent journey, we slept. Now we passed on, and at a quarter past three, at eight miles from the city, came to the Yarkand river (known as Zarafshan), with tamarisk jungle on both banks. Dr. Henderson noticed also, where he crossed, several good-sized trees of Ailanthus glandulosa.

The Yarkand river rises within a few miles of the Karakoram Pass, and is fed by streams descending from the glaciers of Baltistan and Kunjut, so that during the melting of the snows the stream near Yarkand is almost a mile wide, filling its entire channel." So at least says Sir T.D. Forsyth (author of the Forsyth report on the 1873 mission to Yarkand for the Indian government which also visited Khotan, and no relation to the present author); whereas Henderson gives the stream, "now at its highest," from 70 to 180 yards in width, by which possibly he means the principal channel; whilst by another traveller, in August, the stream is said to be 500 yards wide with a rapid current, with eight boats for crossing. The boats measure 40 feet long by nine broad, and two and a half deep, each taking ten horses and their loads.

In September we found the volume of water scanty, and sprawling over its stony bed in many channels, the deepest of which we crossed in a ferry; but in winter, according to Forsyth, most of the rivers of Chinese Turkestan may be crossed dry-shod, stepping from one stone to another. All these rivers contain fish, and are said to be a source of food to the inhabitants. More important, however, than its fish has been, in days gone by, the yield of the Yarkand river in gold and precious stones.

Tchuen-yuen, at the close of the last century, gives some interesting particulars on this subject. "They have a river," he says, "which contains precious stones, the larger as big as a dish or a bushel, the smaller the size of the fist or a walnut, some of them weighing up to 200 or 300 lbs. They are found of various colours; some white as snow, others blue as a kingfisher, yellow like wasp, black like ink, or of a shade of carmine reminding one of cinnabar, all of premier quality. One kind is streaked with bright veins, like mutton fat; another is blue and transparent, like the vegetable called pouo-seu. The same river rolls down also nuggets of gold, which are difficult to find, because the precious morsels are lost in a mass of common stones that cumber the bed.

A military mandarin superintends the search, causing 20 or 30 experienced Mussulmans to plunge into the river up to their shoulders, feeling the stones with their naked feet, and keeping on the move. If they come across a precious stone, they perceive it by a touch of the foot, and stoop to pick it up. A soldier placed on the bank then strikes a gong, the workmen come out of the river, the mandarin passes along a little vermillion, and the find is marked, generally with the character "che" (a stone). Tchuen-yuen adds that about 75 miles from Yarkand lies Mount Mirt'ai, which, he says, "is full of precious stones. To get the purest, which sometimes weigh 10,000 lbs, it is necessary to climb to peaks almost inaccessible. This is done by the help of yaks. The Mussulmans take up machinery by means of which they hammer the cliffs, and allow stones and tools to fall together, to be collected afterwards. Every year Yarkand furnishes in spring and autumn from 7,000 to 8,000 and sometimes 10,000 lbs of precious stones. All are sent to Peking, and private trade in them is strictly forbidden, though among the Mussulmans it is impossible to prevent it entirely."

It seems that the clay deposits on the riverbeds were also sometimes turned and searched over to find the nephrite pebbles deposited there many millenia ago. The pebble jades found in the riverbeds are examples of the survival of the fittest. In their course down the river from the mother lodes in the mountains much of the inferior material surrounding the nephrite core would have been worn off.

Soon after assuming power in 1949, the Communist government of China took control of the sourcing of pebble jade through collecting centres in Kashgar, Yarkand and Khotan. They sent half yearly teams paying very low prices for pebbles gathered by the Uighurs who continued the tradition of combing the great jade rivers after the snow melted in late spring. Collection of raw material in this way continues today with the crop being taken to state workshops in Yangzhou and Suzhou in eastern China to be worked for the handicraft market. A very small workshop in Khotan also works a token amount of nephrite but the "jade" workshops for tourists in Kashgar and Urumqi now apply their electrically mechanised skills to lesser stones.

Angus Forsyth
Brian McElney
January 1994

玉 器 原 料

Jade是英文對一組寶石的通稱。這一組寶石包括成份為鈉、鋁和硅酸鹽的稱作硬玉的輝石(NaAl Si$_2$O$_6$)以及成份為鈣、鎂和硅酸鹽的稱作軟玉的閃石{Ca$_2$(MgFe)$_5$Si$_8$O$_{22}$(OH)$_2$}。這樣兩族成份完全不同的寶石都被叫做Jade (7BFJ第24頁)。

兩族礦物均不多見。附表(見第9頁)列出了當今硬玉和軟玉的已知產地。但作為原料來源,這些地點和中國古代玉匠之間不會有任何關係。

軟玉族中的主要兩種玉石是透閃石(Toushanshi)也叫tremolite,和陽起石(Yangqishi)也叫actinolite。

對紅山文化玉器的檢測證明,其成份是一種硅酸鎂,俗稱鮑文玉(Bowenite)。這種玉石的物質結構近於軟玉,但稍軟。

今天遼寧省岫陽縣大片開採一種摩氏硬度在4.5至5.5度之間的墨綠色纖維蛇紋玉石。這種玉石的成份已經證實是一種硅酸鎂,然而又不同於在中國境內其它地區新石器時代採玉場附近發現的玉石。分析了該地出產的透閃石和陽起石後,發現它們與和闐軟玉(閃石玉)不同。

人們通常認為中國人遲至十八世紀才知道硬玉(輝石玉),這種玉在十八和十九世紀被稱為翡翠。這一年代估計過於保守,因為此前史書論及六世紀時,已經提到了翡翠。北宋歐陽修也曾提及一只翡翠罌。兩處"翡翠"當指硬玉(7BFJ第40頁)。萬曆皇帝(歿於1620年)墓中也發現了輝石小玉件。但無論怎樣說,(產自北緬甸喀傾山脈的)硬玉較為大量地輸入中國當始於十八世紀。所以,本展覽除收進一件硬玉器以供比較外,主要展出另一種玉料即軟玉製成的器物 (Exhibit 354)。

可能出產於日本新潟縣的硬玉,似乎僅僅被日本人和朝鮮人用來製造magatama,一種在公元一至五世紀日、朝墓葬中常見的弧形珠飾。玉石在日本的用途僅限於此。日本人雖然從中國引進了大量影響深遠的文化產品,卻獨獨沒有學得對玉石的一份景仰之情。很久以來,中國人雖然完全知道日本有自己的綠玉礦源,東漢及三國曹魏史籍中均有有關記載,但是沒有任何史料可以證明,中國除象徵性貢品以外,從日本進口和獲得過玉石。

至少自中文初始的商代起,"玉"字象是泛指一切堅質美石,只是在進入公元十世紀以後才專指軟玉和硬玉。故本展覽亦收入數件瑪瑙、紅玉髓、雨花石及幾種蛇紋石器物,這些在當時都會被視為玉器。

直到今天,在中國這仍是正統觀念。對1989年江西新干縣河岸出土的著名商代羽人的描述,清楚地說明了這一點:儘管所有觸摸過這件物品的人

一致認為是軟質滑石不是軟玉,第66號〔報告中〕仍稱其為"玉"。

近年來,中國地質科學院聞廣教授運用掃描電子顯微鏡和高分辨透射電子顯微鏡以及其它科學儀器,對來自不同考古現場的玉石的微觀結構和成份進行了測試。他的研究表明,中國有主要兩類軟玉:一是鎂質大理岩之軟玉,一是蛇紋化超基性岩中之軟玉。

中國軟玉的品質和顏色取決於其微結構和透閃石與陽起石比率中的氧化鐵含量。這一研究成果之所以重要,在於它似乎確認了良諸文化玉器的原材料來自江蘇南部鄰近太湖一帶,這一地區業已發現成份類似的軟玉。聞廣教授正在繼續研究紅山、崧澤及其它文化的玉器。他的初步成果於1985年與景知成(Jing,Zhi-cheng)聯名發表。從他目前的研究來看,中國新石器時代所用軟玉材可能大都出自本土。(7BFJ,38-41頁)。

軟玉和硬玉的比重在2.8至3.6之間,在分為十度的摩氏硬度遞增表上,前者約為6.5度,後者介乎6.75和7度之間,瑪瑙為7度,而現代鋼刀和鑽石則分別為6度和10度。如此看來,"雕"玉從技術上來說是不準確的,然若為此摒棄這樣一個沿用已久倍受尊崇的詞匯則不免過於冬烘氣了。實際上,玉石的加工只能依靠鋸,鑽以及以磨料旋磨等種手段。但中文術語中又有把輝石稱作硬玉、閃石稱作軟玉這樣一種有意思的區分。

質地最純的硬玉和軟玉呈荔枝肉色。雖然兩者均有多種顏色,但硬玉色相更豐富、色調更濃烈。兩者均可呈白、黃、綠、藍、棕等色,但只有硬玉方具有粉紅、紫紅及常見於玉質首飾的翠鳥般明麗的綠色。軟玉多呈不同色調的綠色,綠色中的變化較硬玉為多。首飾用玉為典型的祖母綠色,其中極品置於杯水中反光極佳,清水似為瑩瑩綠色暈染。只有軟玉具有純黑色,極綠的輝石在某些光線裡也可呈黑色。

中國人珍視玉石至少有七千年之久。近來有人(尤其是巫鴻在1989年)撰文提出:公元前2000至500年的青銅器時代以前,約在公元前4至2000年,中國歷史上曾出現過一個玉器時代。十年前僅僅是推測新石器時代有玉石加工都遭到普遍的懷疑。然而,這一時期裡中國眾多地區,無論其自然環境和經濟條件如何都有玉器加工,這已成為毫無疑問的事實,並為近十年來眾多考古發現充分地證實。玉器時代一說的證據既已不容懷疑,就沒有理由不廣泛採用"玉器時代"這一名詞,以肯定這一特殊物質在中華文化

形成中的開創性作用。新石器時代歐洲溫暖地區的
居民、新西蘭毛利人、古墨西哥土著同中國人一樣崇拜
玉器，但唯有中國人把玉的象徵作用發展到了如此精妙
的程度 (9，35頁)。

　　玉石質堅色美，新石器時代加工起來又不得
不耗費數月辛勤勞動，這使人對它愈加珍重。公元前
3000年，良渚文化最豪華的墓葬中聚集了大量玉器，
從此可以窺見古人對玉的珍重。

　　如此大量玉器的匯集只能説明當時已出現了
專門管理玉器的官員和眾多生產玉器的工人。也就是
説，對玉的態度已經從視其為可供玩賞的美麗堅硬之
物，發展成為尊其為等級地位的象徵。結果，尊崇玉器
就等於尊崇國家。玉既被賦予超人的力量和美德，它
在祭祀朝享的場合作為顯赫身世的象徵和帝王得體
的佩飾出現在世人面前也就無足為奇了，因為這一切
無一不是在展示和渲染社會在玉石中看到的品質，
而這又正是社會結構自身的道德、追求和價值觀。

　　公元前五世紀中葉，儒家觀念得以發展，為了
維護社會秩序，賦予玉區分等級和身份的意義，從而
形成了一種力量，這種力量正像儒家秩序本身一樣，進
入了中國文化的精髓之中，長達二千四百年，直至
1911年清王朝的覆滅。

　　中共自1949年立國以後，全國推行以簡體字為
官方字體標準。在"国"這簡體字中，我們可窺看
這些遺產深厚的意思。"国"這個字代替了寫法較複雜的
"國"字，但是意思則一樣。如果與"中"字組合起來，
就成為傳統上所指"中國"一辭。實際上，這個簡體"国"
字的造型是以四面圍壁，中心藏玉而成的。玉字
在這裡的使用，是有它一定的重要性的，它告訴了
我們玉器不管是在中共立國以前或以後，都是絕對
權力的象徵。

　　儒家教育賦予玉以五德：潤澤以溫，仁之方也；
鰓理自外，可以知中，義之方也；其聲舒揚，專以
遠聞，智之方也；不撓不折，勇之方也；銳廉而不忮，
絜之方也。君子比德於玉，故玉不去身。

　　商朝時，玉被視為一種形式的財富，在這方面
值得注意的是，中國歷代管理皇家珍寶的官員稱為
"玉局總管"(3BFJ,頁23)。已發現的那個時候的玉器，
包括璧、片飾和天然形態的玉等別。

　　至少從商代以來，玉就廣泛地用作佩飾。結果，
以胸飾或串飾等樣式的成組玉珮廣為流行。這樣的
胸飾是一種個人隨身之物，生前死後均可佩戴，在早至
公元前800年的墓葬中，就發現在遺體面部五官的
位置上排列與五官形狀相當的玉件。看來，不同性別

者所佩帶的成組玉珮有所不同。也許是在胸部佩戴兩
套，其下部又分成數串。東周時期，佩帶這種胸飾
尤為流行，佩帶胸飾和串飾的習俗一直延續到漢代。
例如：死於公元前122年的南越王趙眜的墓中就有
不同的胸飾、成組玉珮十一套之多 (47)。

　　玉也以其在音樂方面的價值而受到重視。許多
世紀以來，石磬已為人們所知。展品中甚至有一件
新石器時代的大懸玉，它一定是一種打擊樂器，玉笛的
使用也證明玉這方面的價值。展品143以及展品説明中，
更進一步説明了玉是製作樂器的理想材料。

　　孔子 (公元前522-479年) 曾批評當時的新貴"玉珮
叮噹亂響"。君子應步履從容，以避免相互碰撞，發
出不和諧之聲。而他的高雅從容的步履就能使玉珮
產生悅耳的音律。

　　玉在人們的社會生活中具有重要地位，以玉
喻事的例子比比皆是，無足為奇。"玉碎"從文字
上講，是玉被打碎了，而實際上表示捨生取義；"玉函"
的含義則是珍貴之物該小心保護；"玉石俱焚"原意
是玉和石一起燒掉，卻轉指不分好壞，皆予摧毀；
"亭亭玉立"則比喻窈窕淑女。

　　至少從漢代以來，玉料主要來自新疆和闐與
葉爾羌一帶崑崙山脈的河流。這些河流在當地維吾爾
族人的語言裡是烏玉河、綠玉河和白玉河的意思。
從十八世紀起，軟玉的另一重要來源是貝加爾湖南端
的Vostochny Sayan山麓，這裡的玉俗稱西伯利亞玉，
為深綠色帶灰或黑斑，這種玉在十八世紀以前未見
輸入中國。

　　〈新五代史•四夷附錄〉記載，該三條河因其
產玉三種顏色而得名，每年秋季河水下退之後，國王率
先撈取第一塊玉，其後百姓相繼效法。

　　十七世紀之前，中國的玉料絕大多數是籽玉
(Pebble Jade)。但戰國時期文獻提及山產礦玉，至遲在
明朝末年已對礦玉與籽玉加以區分。其它文獻也記載
從明末起人們入山採玉，但礦玉明顯地被認為比籽玉
低劣，通常價格不及後者的三分之一。籽玉撈自和闐及
葉爾羌一帶河床，每年春天和初秋是撈玉的好季節。
有木刻版畫描繪當地婦女在河流沖積物中來回淘玉的
情形。傳説她們是赤身沒水的，原因是玉和女陰氣
相召，玉受到女子的吸引，女人們就能用腳打探到玉的
位置了。

　　軟玉質感細膩，撫之如脂，為其它美石所不及。

　　但是，關於籽玉的採集方式另有一種説法。
1893年亨利•蘭斯德出版的〈中國的中亞〉一書
(第136-138頁)這樣描述：

"在一段旅程之後，我們先在一個離葉爾羌河西側不太遠，當地人們稱之為「星期二市場」(Seh Shambeh) 的小村莊休息。現在我們繼續前進，三點一刻，在離城市8英里處，我們來到葉爾羌河，河兩岸是檉柳叢。韓德森博士在過河時還發現幾棵形狀優美的臭椿樹。

葉爾羌河在離喀拉崑崙(Karakoram)山口幾哩內開始上升，河由數條山川匯集而成，每當冰雪消融之際，靠近葉爾羌的那條川流寬達幾乎一哩，擠滿整個河谷。至少T.D.福西特(Forsyth)是這樣說的；而韓德森卻說，這條川流"現在水位最高時"，是70至180碼寬，也許他這樣說是指主流；而同時，另一位旅行者卻說，在八月，川流最急時水面有500碼寬，需8條船才可跨狀。船長40呎，寬9呎，深2呎半，每條船載10匹馬和馬駱的物品。

九月時，我們發現大水已退，河床上只留下淺淺的數道清流，最深處我們是乘坐小船渡過的。但是，在冬天，據福西特說，大多數河流可踏著石塊乾足而過。所有的河流都產魚，據說是當地居民的一種食物。但比魚更重要的是，葉爾羌河所產的黃金與寶石。

上世紀末，就這個話題，一個名叫椿園(Tchuen-yuen)的人說到的一些事就特別有趣。他說："他們那兒有一條河，河中有許多寶石，大者如盤，小者如拳，有重達200至300磅者，顏色或白如雪，或藍如翠鳥，或黃如蜂，或黑如墨，或赤如硃砂，質地均很優美。有的脈理鮮明如羊脂，有的潔而透明

呈藍色。該河也出金砂，但常被河床中的雜石所掩蓋，難以發現。

下河撈玉，由一武官監察，二、三十個熟練的回人(穆斯林)沒水至肩，赤足探石而行，遇到有玉石就彎腰拾起，此時岸上士兵敲一聲鑼，撈玉者上岸，監察官用硃筆在玉石上作一記號，通常是一個「石」字。椿園又說，離葉爾羌大約70哩處是密爾岱山，山中寶石蘊藏豐富，最純者有時重達一萬磅，要想採得這樣的寶石，必須攀至幾乎無法到達的頂峰。回人騎著犛牛，帶着鎚鑿工具登山，得玉後任由它滾落山下，再行運取。每年春秋可從葉爾羌獲取七、八千，有時甚至一萬磅寶石。所有寶石都運至北京，雖嚴禁私人買賣，然而卻難以完全禁止在回人之間私下賣買"。

看來有時乾涸的河床也被翻遍，以尋找千百年前沉積在下面的籽玉。在河中發現的籽玉是適者生存的例子。在它們從山中原產地沖來河床的途中，包着玉心的劣質石皮就會被磨損掉。

1949年，中共政府獲得權力之後不久，控制了玉石的原料，在喀什、葉爾羌和和闐成立了採集站。他們一年兩次派遣收集隊，以低價向維吾爾人收購。維吾爾人不改他們的傳統，仍在冰雪消融之後的陽春梳理大玉河。這種採集玉料的方法延至今天。而玉材運到中國東部的揚州、蘇州等地的國營加工廠加工，供應工藝市場。在和闐也有一小型工廠進行少量的象徵性玉材加工；喀什和烏魯木齊為派激者服務的"玉"工場現在已運用電動科技進行小件玉石的加工。(AHF/BSM)

9 THE FLUCTUATING JEWEL
THE SUPPLY OF JADE RAW MATERIAL TO CHINA THROUGH THE AGES

The sources of nephrite of the quality preferred by Chinese jade workers and consumers were the regions around the oases and cities of Khotan and its neighbour Yarkand, far to the west of Chinese controlled territory. The raw material therefore had to be transported over a vast disance, over mountains and around the margins of the Taklamakan desert to the jade working centres in China. It has been estimated that it would take a radius of 3,600 kilometres from these regions to encompass all the areas within China where jade was worked even in neolithic times. 9 pp35

One remarkable aspect of the use of Khotan nephrite in China probably orginating in the late Shang period, is that the raw material, far more valuable and meaningful than gold to the Chinese, was found outside the Great Wall and China proper, and yet there was never any real drive to seize control of the source of this vital material.

For most of China's history, these western regions and the trade routes connecting them to China, were occupied by nomadic tribes frequently hostile to China and considered semi-barbarian by the Chinese. Furthermore, the very nomadic nature of their existence frequently led them into violent conflict with their neighbours. The trade in jade was therefore subject to lengthy interruptions as a result of disturbances along the routes leading from the Khotan and Yarkand regions through the Jade Gate or Yumen at the far western end of the Great Wall.

Studies of pre-Han dynasty historical records have so far found virtually no mention of the availability of raw jade material. However, later tradition supported by archaeological evidence suggests that jade from these regions was being transported to China prior to 1000 BC. Inscriptions on Shang oracle bones record obtaining jades and levying jades and a jade halberd in the tomb of Lady Fu Hao (c.1400 BC) bears an inscription stating that it was a tribute to the king of Shang from Lu, a country acknowledging allegiance to the Shang kingdom, but whose location is unknown.

Since the beginning of the Han dynasty there have only been a limited number of periods in which the trade routes to China from the Khotan and Yarkand regions were open without interruption. The first period was during the Han dynasty itself. The nomadic Xiongnu controlled these trade routes at the commencement of the Han dynasty. Although the Han never subjugated the Xiongnu, during the expedition to Ferghana (101 BC) they came to dominate this Central Asian region and a two-way tribute system (i.e. two-way trade which would have included jade) between the Chinese and the Xiongnu was initiated. It was not, however, until the surrender of the Xiongnu chiefs, Jihchu in 60 BC and Hanyei in 52 BC, that Han dominance over western Central Asia became firmly established, and Chinese garrisons and an administrative officer called the Protector General of the Western Frontier were sent by the Han court to control the area. This led to a plentiful supply of jade becoming available in China during the remainder of the Western Han dynasty 96.

However, Han dominance of the western frontier regions was short-lived and came to an end during the civil war (known as the Wang Mang Interregnum) at the end of the Western Han. It was not until the Xiongnu split into two polities, the Northern and Southern Xiongnu, in 48 AD that dominance was reestablished with the Southern Xiongnu surrendering to the Han and becoming one of the minority tribes within Han territory. The Northern Xiongnu subsequently withdrew to the northwest but continued to challenge the Eastern Han dynasty for dominance of the western regions. It appears however, that from approximately 73 AD until the collapse of the Eastern Han in 220 AD, the trades routes to the Khotan and Yarkand regions remained open. For much of the Han dynasty, jade was therefore in relatively plentiful supply. 96 and 51 pp 112-4

The collapse of the Eastern Han dynasty caused a further prolonged interruption of the trade routes to the west and seems to have resulted in relatively little jade entering China during the Wei, Jin, Northern and Southern dynasties and the Six Dynasties period. These were very unsettled times during which Chinese rulers concentrated all their efforts on maintaining their realms and, more significantly, on the new religion of Buddhism.

The reunification of China under the Sui and Tang dynasties, encouraged trade with the rest of Asia and must have enabled a plentiful supply of raw jade from the Khotan and Yarkand regions to enter the Chinese market. The availablity of jade seems to be confirmed by facts recorded about Yang Guifei (mid 8th century). This famous Imperial concubine, known as the Jade beauty, is reputed to have slept on a jade bed, worn only jade ornaments and surrounded herself with objects only of jade. At that time an edict was issued forbidding the use of inferior jades for funerary purposes which would have had no significance if jade were not readily available. The number of foreigners residing in China during the Sui and Tang dynasties was enormous and their influence on Chinese art is well attested by artefacts of all kinds. The fact that foreigners identified gold and silver as the height of luxury seized hold of the Tang court and nobility, with the result that increasingly from the 8th to the 10th century more gold and silver

was produced than at any other time in Chinese history and, for a while, the supreme position of jade was perhaps eclipsed. That the jades today safely dated to the Sui and Tang dynasties are few in number seems partly explained by the ban mentioned above and by the popularity of gold and silver at that time. It nevertheless seems likely that some jades now given a later date should be reassigned to these periods.

With the spread of Islam in Central Asia the Turkic tribes of the Khotan and Yarkand regions were converted to that faith in the 8th century. Religious persecutions in China in 845 and the following decade or so seem to have resulted in the virtual suspension of the entry of raw jade into China. Historical records attest the effect this disruption of the supply of raw material had on the price of jade. Such disruption appears to have lasted until 950. There are jades in the exhibition of a rather distinctive dull brownish-grey colour, sometimes with reddish veins, that appear to date to the late Tang dynasty on the basis of their style or decoration, which could arguably be assigned to the period from 845 to 950, since it is hard to imagine such dull, poor quality material being used at a time when better quality jade was in plentiful supply, as seems to have been the case before 845, and certainly was after 950.

At a seminar on jade in Detroit in February 1981, James Watt stated that Song historical records mention that (i) in 951 the price of the best quality lychee-flesh white jade fell to about one-third of its former value because of oversupply. This glut was apparently caused by the elimination of middle men from the trade routes at that time; (ii) Oversupply apparently continued until about 1028, when trade was completely disrupted by disturbances caused by the Xi Xia in China's north western border regions through which the trade routes ran. (iii) It appears from these historical records that little jade entered China between 1028 and 1077 when it is recorded that the trade routes reopened; (iv) Once they reopened, it seems that there was a considerable problem in getting jade of the preferred lychee-flesh white, and the jade that first entered China is described as having extensive brown flecks. Raw jade was available during the remainder of the Song dynasty although there were still problems with quality.

During the Yuan dynasty China was united with the western regions and Yuan histories record that the court had direct control over jade production. They sent jade craftsmen to Khotan and other areas to acquire jade, and issued orders to local officials to transport it to the capital. It is recorded that in 1273 the jade craftsman Xiu Cai was sent to Khotan with orders to obtain green, yellow, black and white jade, but he was not required to go the following year. In addition to the jade gathering organized by the Yuan court, the material was also collected by the common people. It seems that jade of a yellowish tone or the colour of roast chestnuts was popular at this time, and from historical records it appears that a substantial quantity of jade entered China during the Yuan dynasty. It is therefore surprising that so few jades are currently dated to the Yuan dynasty, and it is probable that future scholarship will assign to this period some of the jades presently labelled Song or Ming.

Jade pieces of any size dated prior to the late Ming have always been rare. The enormous mottled greyish-green jade basin, believed to be the famous piece mentioned by Marco Polo c.1291 and now in Beihai Park in Beijing, decorated with dragons, sea-horses, fish and fabulous animals amid swirling waves, was famous even in the Yuan dynasty on account of its size. It was lost for centuries after the fall of the Yuan dynasty but rediscovered in the late 18th century in a Buddhist monastery where it was being used for pickling vegetables!

At the end of the Yuan and beginning of the Ming dynasty, serious disturbances occurred in the Khotan region, with the local inhabitants and their king having to hide in the valleys and mountains. As a result jade gathering was severely disrupted until the early 15th century when the king of Khotan reestablished his authority over the region and it flourished once more. The king's authority was, however, shortlived. It is recorded that in 1453 a Mongol embassy took 5900 jins (2950 kgs) of jade to Beijing as a diplomatic gift but it was refused and sold on the open market. Between 1473 and about 1530 almost constant warfare between China and the rulers of Turfan disrupted the trade routes. However, around 1550 Turfan itself was conquered by the Khans of Kashgar, but power in the region seems thereafter to have devolved on Khoja families, who were heavily involved in the caravan trade and the trade in jade. The Khoja father of a prominent courtier to the Indian emperor Akbar who settled in Kashgar is said to have been granted a concession on a jade bearing river in the mid 16th century and on his orders jade was conveyed to China. From this time on until about 1600, when political fragmentation in Central Asia virtually halted the jade supply, jade appears to have been plentiful in China. Only two 'tribute missions' from Central Asia reached Beijing between 1600 and 1630 resulting in a shortage of jade that continued into the early Qing dynasty. 6BFJ pp 34-35

The gathering of jades seems to have taken place in spring and autumn when the water levels in the rivers were at their lowest.

It is recorded that in order to increase the productivity of the jade stone industry the mining of mountain jade was started at Ye'erqiang on the western border of the region. The exact date of this is not known but it seems to have been not long before the Jesuit missionary Benedict Goes's visit in the 11th month of 1603. Mountain jade is mentioned rather disparagingly by Zheng Yingwen writing in 1595 so that mining must have started before this date. Goes saw for himself the jade gathering and in his detailed and reliable records wrote "There are two kinds of jade, the first being very shiny and coming from the Tian River, not far from the State Capital, and the gatherers go into the river to gather it, just as one gathers pearls... The second kind is not of the finest quality and is mined out of the mountain where large pieces are cut into slices. These measure 2 ells in width. Then they are ground smaller, making it easier to transport them. The mountains lie far from the city, in remote areas, the stone is hard, and for this reason the practice of jade gathering is not an easy one. The local people say: 'one makes a fire and burns the jadestone, the stone cracks and the jade is easily retrieved'. The right to gather jade is sold by the King to merchants at a very high price. During the validity of the right no one is permitted to look for jade without the permission of the merchants. The craftsmen look for workers and all form teams to go mining, taking with them enough food for one year, because during this time it is not easy to get back to the Capital". 7BFJ pp30-31

During the Qing dynasty, there were numerous political changes and alterations in the regulations concerning the gathering of jade. Broadly speaking the Qing can be divided into four distinct periods; (a) prior to 1761, when the common people gathered jade but supplied comparatively little to the court. A palace memorial of 31 January 1742 indicates that fine jades in the palaces were limited at that time, but another memorial of 7 April 1747, instructing the High Inspector to hire extra jade carvers outside the palace, indicates an increase in supply; (b) from 1761-1821, when both officials and the common people both collected jade; (c) 1821-1862, when the common people again gathered jade, free of any governmental restrictions, and (d) after 1862 when supplies were disrupted and private workshops took over most of the working of jades. During this dynasty the Chinese provincial governor enjoyed the privileges previously exercised by the king of Khotan.

From 1759 onwards, Chinese control of the Khotan area led to many Moghul jades from the royal workshops in Delhi entering China. These were particularly popular with the Qianlong emperor (r.1736-95) who inscribed poems on some of the pieces. The palace records of the time have many references to such items of which Exhibit 348 is considered to be one. Their popularity with the court led to many jades in the Moghul style being produced in China from 1760-1820, some of which are difficult to distinguish from the earlier pieces produced in India for the Indian Moghul court. The Moghul pieces, however, seem to have a much softer polish than their Chinese imitations and are frequently of exemplary thinness.

In 1787, the Qing government decided to end the spring gathering of jade and to retain only the autumn gathering since there was a massive oversupply of jade at the imperial court. In 1799, the government abolished the regulations and ceased operations at most collecting areas. They continued to draw jade only from the Yulongkashe river, where the jade was of the finest quality, for fifteen days every autumn, and from Ye'erqiang. By 1812 the amount of jade at the imperial court was so vast it was impossible to count, and the annual jade take was decreased from over 4,000 jin (2000 kgs) to 2,000 jin. In 1821 the official gathering of jade ceased altogether and was not revived for the remainder of the Qing dynasty. There was major rebellion in Chinese Turkestan between 1862 and 1877 and as a result the jade trade was halted from 1867-77. This disruption led to the Chinese sourcing more of their raw material from Siberia and Burma. Jade was apparently quite scarce and expensive in China in the second half of the 19th century, and it seems that the palace had difficulty purchasing good quality jade at this time. Reports indicate that the enormous stocks held in 1821 had been largely exhausted by this time. However, private workshops appear to have prospered and although imperial patronage ceased on the fall of the dynasty in 1911, export trade stimulated the production of jades by private workshops in the late 19th and early 20th century. 7BFJ pp31-34 and 77, pp 30-41. In the 20th century, Chinese jade-workers have also obtained some of their raw nephrite from non-traditional sources such as Wyoming in the USA.

Angus Forsyth
Brian McElney
January 1994

身 價 難 卜 的 珍 寶 —— 關 於 歷 代 玉 料 的 供 應

歷來，中國琢玉匠人和玉器享有者所鐘愛的玉材是
軟玉。這種玉產於遠在中國西部地區被稱之為沙漠緣洲
的和闐(今和田縣)及其鄰近的葉爾羌周圍。因此，要
把玉運抵中國內地各個玉業中心，需要長途跋踄、翻山
越嶺、繞過克拉馬干大沙漠。據估計，由原產地至
中國內地那些從新石器時代就已經有了琢玉工藝的玉業
中心區，總有三千六百公里之遙(第35頁，9)。

值得注意的是，中國人採用和闐軟玉可能起始於
商晚期，雖然當時的中國人把玉價看得比黃金更貴重、
更有意義，而且在長城內外和中國腹地到處發現了
玉材，但是，中國人卻從來未曾認真地去控制這些珍貴
的礦物資源產地。

在中國歷史上，有相當長的一個時期，西域
以及連結中國和西域的貿易通道，常常由一些敵視
中國人又被中國人視為蠻族的游牧部落佔據。此外，
他們那種游動性的生活方式常常導致與其鄰邦
發生激烈的衝突。結果，玉石貿易不斷受到騷擾，
這條由和闐、葉爾羌穿過長城西部終端玉門關的玉石
商道也時常因之中斷。

查閱漢代以前的歷史文獻資料，很難找到有關
玉材的記載。但是，考古發現支持了一種較晚出的
傳統說法，即：西域的玉料早在公元前1000年以前，即
已傳入中國內地。商代甲骨文刻辭上就記載有採玉、
徵玉的內容。殷虛婦好墓(公元前1400年)中出土的
一片玉戈上寫明該玉器是盧方進貢給商王的。盧方乃是
一個忠於商王朝的方國，不過，她的確切位置至今
尚無人知曉。

自漢朝初年，由和闐和葉爾羌至中原的商貿通道
暢通無阻的時候不多。那時，匈奴游牧民族控制着
這些商貿通道。儘管漢朝從未征服過匈奴。但到公元前
101年通使大宛(費爾干納)的時候，漢王朝就把勢力
逐漸擴展到了中亞的這一區域。中國人與匈奴人之間
形成了一種相互往來的渠道，即：包括玉料在內的
雙邊貿易。以後，雖然公元前60年匈奴首領日逐和公元
前52年呼韓邪先後向漢朝稱臣，但還不能說當時漢朝
已牢牢地建立起了對中亞西部的統治。因此，漢王室着
意派遣了"西域都護大將軍"，由他率部鎮守這一地區。
此後，西漢時期，玉料得以源源不斷進入中原。

然而，漢王室對西域的統治是短命的，由於
內戰興起(歷史上有名的王莽篡位)，西漢瓦解，對
西域的統治遂之終止。慶幸的是，這時匈奴內部分裂
成了北匈奴、南匈奴兩支，形成了南、北匈奴的局面。
公元48年，南匈奴降漢並成了其版圖內眾多少數
民族中之一，漢朝才得以重新恢復對西域這片土地的

統治。隨後，北匈奴遁退西北，但間有挑撥騷擾。
所以，總的看來，大約自公元73年始至公元220年
東漢末世，通往和闐和葉爾羌的商道是敞開的。
漢代大部份時間中，玉料的供應還是相對充足的
(第112-114頁96和51)。

東漢王朝的覆滅招致較長一段時間與西域貿易
通道的中斷，因而在魏、晉、南北朝時期，進入中原地
帶的玉料相對說來好像是不多的。此時正值多事之秋，
中國各方統治者正竭盡全力地維持各自的既得地盤，
或者說，更專注於新興的佛教上。

隋、唐時代中國的統一對沉寂多年的亞州地區
貿易是一大刺激，促使大批的玉料從和闐和葉爾羌地區
源源不斷地進入中原市場。關於用玉的情況，從一段
有關楊貴妃的史書記載中可以得到說明。八世紀中葉，
這位著名玉顏皇妃的臥床、佩飾和其它隨身之物
均為玉質的。當時頒佈過一項法令稱：劣質玉器不得
用於殯葬。由此可見，如果當時玉料來之不易，那麼此
條禁令則就無甚意義了。隋唐時期，到中國來的外國人
很多，從種類繁多的工藝品上都能看到他們對中國藝術
的影響。這些外國人把金銀製品作為豪華高貴的禮品
來討好唐朝王室貴族。結果，從八世紀至十世紀的
二百年間，中國金銀器的產量與日俱增，遠遠超過歷史
上的任何朝代。一時間，玉器就從原來那種光采至尊的
崇高地位上衰弱下來而暗然失色了。今日所見，確屬
隋唐的玉器數量不多。部份原因似乎與上面提到的
禁令有關，主要的恐怕當時金銀器的普遍流行亦是重要
因素之一。不過，一些被訂為時代較晚的玉器或許有
可能會重新確認為屬於隋唐時代。

隨着伊斯蘭教在中亞的傳播，八世紀，和闐和
葉爾羌教地區的突厥族轉而信奉伊斯蘭教。公元845年及
其後十年間，中國所發生的宗教逼害，致使玉料長期
不能進入中國市場。據史書記載，由於玉料供應中斷，
當時玉料價格猛漲。此種混亂狀況直至公元950年才告
結束。本屆展覽會中，有一些玉器色澤晦暗呈灰褐色，
有的還間雜淡紅條紋，從其風格或雕錦的基調來看，當
屬唐代晚期無疑。之所以鑒定在公元845年至950年之
間，是因為如果像公元845年之前，或950年之後那樣
優質玉料供應充足的話，就不會使用如此晦暗的
劣質玉料了。

1981年2月在底特律召開的玉器專題研討會上，
屈志仁指出：宋史文獻記載(1) 公元951年，由於
供大於需，最優質的荔枝肉色白玉價格比先前下降了
三分之二，其原因在於官府當時剷除了貿易通道上的
中間商人；(2) 供大於求的狀況大概一直延續到

公元1028年，因為此時西夏正在貿易通道所經過的中國西北地區鬧事，因而貿易中斷；(3) 從歷史文獻上看，公元1028-1077年間，只有少量玉料流入中原。1077年時貿易通道重新開放；(4)一旦道路開通，就產生了一個很大的問題，最先輸入到中原的一批白玉據說帶有褐色斑紋而非純白荔枝肉色。嗣後，宋代末期，玉料雖然來源無缺，但卻始終存在一個質量問題。

在元朝，中國與整個西域是一個整體。元史記載：王室直接掌管玉石生產，他們派遣玉石匠人前去和闐及其它地區採玉，敕令地方官員把玉料送至京都。史料上曾提到公元1273年，有一位叫"秀才"的琢玉匠人奉旨到和闐徵收綠、黃、黑、白玉。不過，他在次年便棄職而亡了。在元代，除宮廷有組織的採集玉料外，民間私人也有採集。當時，淡黃色的或粟色的玉石似乎最受歡迎。據記載，元朝玉料來源頗豐，但令人奇怪的是目前確認為元代的玉器卻很少，可能在不遠的將來，學者們會把一些現時認為宋代或明代的玉器改訂為元代。

明代晚期以前的玉器，不論大件、小件均極為罕見。現存於北京北海公園內的灰綠色瀆山大玉海，據說就是馬可波羅在1291年的著述中提到的那件刻有翻江倒海的蛟龍、海馬、游魚及許多神獸的著名玉甕。元朝滅亡後，此甕曾失蹤數百年而不知去向。直至十八世紀末，才在一佛寺中發現該物一直被寺內僧侶當作醃菜缸使用。

元末明初，和闐地區發生嚴重騷亂，當地人和他們的頭領紛紛藏匿於荒山野嶺之中，採玉因此一度中斷。直至十五世紀初，和闐頭領重新掌握了對該地區的控制，採玉業才又興旺起來。不過，這些頭領的統治是短暫的。史料又記載：公元1453年，一位蒙古使節攜五千九百斤(2950千克)玉作為外交禮物進京朝貢卻被拒之門外，不得已只好開市銷售。公元1473年至1530年間，中原與吐魯蕃戰事頻仍，波及貿易通道。大約在1550年，吐蕃又被喀什喀爾的可汗征服，該地區的統治權落到了與商隊及玉石貿易有着難解之緣的和卓家族手中。和卓族長為喀什喀爾顯貴，於十六世紀中葉，他從住在喀什喀爾的印度國王Akbar那裡獲得了在河流中撈取玉石的特權，受命將玉料運往中國。從那時直至1600年，中亞局勢動蕩，玉料供應中斷為止，中國的玉料一直是充裕的。從1600年至1630年間，中亞進京"朝貢"只有兩次，因而玉料短缺嚴重，此種狀況一直延續至清初(第34-35頁 6BFJ)。

採玉似乎都選擇在春秋季節，因為此時的河水水位最低。

文獻記載：為了提高玉業生產，開始在西域葉爾羌地區入山開採玉礦。此舉起始的準確日期已無人知，大約是在1603年11月耶穌傳教士本尼迪克特 • 戈斯來中國訪問之前不久的事。有關入山採玉的情況在鄭應文(Zheng Yingwen) 1595年的著作裡已有貶意的述及，說明進山開採玉礦肯定是在此之前。戈斯以其親身參加開採玉礦的經歷作了詳細而又真實的記載，他寫道："玉分兩類，第一類質地優良，光潔明亮，出自京城附近的天河 (Tian River)，採玉者入河採玉猶如採集珍珠一般……。第二類質地稍次，取材於崇山峻嶺之中，在當地就把大至90吋寬的玉材破成小塊，目的是為了方便運輸。礦山遠離城市，玉質堅硬，因此，採玉實非易事。當地人說："用火燒烤，把玉礦石燒裂則玉料就容易採出來了"。採玉的權利由當地頭領以極高價賣給商人，沒有商人的許可，任何人都不得擅自採礦。由琢玉匠人來挑選工人。最後，每人帶足一年的口糧便結隊入山開礦了，因為在此期間回城一趟是非常不容易的(第30-31頁 7BFJ)。

清代，政治風雲變幻莫測，大起大落，有關採玉的政規也朝令夕改，但概括地講，清朝的玉料供應可分為四個不同的時期：(1)公元1761年前，由百姓採玉，只將其少量供應王室。公元1742年1月31日的皇宮記錄上記載，宮中庫存的玉料幾近告罄，但在公元1747年4月7日的另外一份記錄上，卻看到有指令高級官員召僱玉工巧匠進宮的記載。這說明宮中庫存玉料已有增加；(2)公元1761年至1821年間採玉是官營民營並舉的；(3) 公元1821-1862年間，再度由民間採玉，官府不予干涉；(4)1862年之後，玉料供應發生混亂，大部份玉器產自個體私人作坊。整個清代，中國的省級主管都在一直行使先前和闐首領曾經行使過的那種特權。

從公元1759年以來，中國對和闐地區的管轄，使得許多出自印度皇家作坊的莫臥兒玉器流入中國。乾隆皇帝(公元1736-1795年) 嗜好在一些玉器上鐫刻詩文詞賦，當時的宮廷記錄中有許多這類記載，本屆350號展品即其中之一。宮廷的這種愛好使得大量仿有莫臥兒風格的玉器風靡走紅，中國的有些仿製品與印度早期為莫臥兒宮廷生產的玉器相比，幾乎達到了以假亂真的地步。當然，實際還是有區別的，莫臥兒玉器比中國的仿製品來說，玉面拋光更為柔美，而器身往往更薄。

公元1787年，清政府鑒於皇宮積存玉料過多，決定由每年春秋兩季採玉改為只限於秋季進行。公元1799年，政府改變了上述規定，又命令許多採玉地區停止採玉，每年秋季只准在流經葉爾羌 (原文如此，今玉龍喀什河流經和闐，而非葉爾羌——譯者註) 的玉龍喀什河採玉十五天，那裡的玉質品位最高。到了公元1812年，宮廷庫存的玉料已多到難以計數的程度，便把年度徵收量由四千多斤減至二千斤。1821年時，完全停止一切官方採玉，直至清朝到了風雨飄搖的晚年也再沒恢復過。公元1862-1877年間，新疆發生了嚴重騷亂，1867年至1877年間的玉石貿易隨之中斷，中國不得已轉從西伯利亞和緬甸得到材源。十九世紀下半葉，中國市場玉料奇缺 ，價格飛漲，連宮廷當時也很難得到優質玉材。有報導說，1821年的大量庫存此時行將消耗殆盡。而這時的私人作坊玉業則呈現出昌盛的勢頭，儘管1911年清王朝的覆滅，再也得不到皇家的惠顧，但在十九世紀末、二十世紀初，出口貿易卻大大促進了中國私人作坊玉業的發展(第30-41頁，77和第31-34頁 7BFJ)。二十世紀，中國的玉匠們已能從傳統的玉料產地之外，獲得他們所需要的軟玉了，美國的懷俄明州即是其中之一。

10 WORKING WITH JADE

As we have already seen the hardness of the jade material was such that it could not really be carved in the usual sense of the word, but had to be worked by a grinding process using suitable abrasives. It seems, however, that from neolithic times on, saws and drills were used in conjunction with grease and abrasives to drill holes in nephrite or saw it into slices. These saws and drills frequently leave clear marks of their use.

In neolithic times, the huge area of what is now China consisted of various disparate tribal areas, some of which appear to have been in contact with each other and some not. For this reason it is perhaps possible to discern regional differences in the jade worked by different cultures in different regions. The basic addition to a stone artefact was a hole made by using one or more methods, namely chipping, scraping, solid drill head boring, or hollow cylinder core boring. Sawing though a boulder of jade - perhaps with abrasive impregnated string or animal sinew produces a flat face. A flat slice of jade can be produced by sawing, perhaps 0.5, 1.0 or more centimetres away from the original cut. Techniques for making holes could then be applied to the slice. Hand sawing with impregnated string or sinew seems often to have given way to a primitive, but effective, swing sawing process which usually left a tell tale bow shaped scar or scars.

A boulder with a flat surface but irregular outline would be sawn through on all four sides to create a rectangle or square from both faces of the stone. At the point where the two cuts are sawn almost through to the middle, the exterior rough, unwanted in the finished product, would be snapped off leaving a rough line or longitudinal keel. This keel could then be ground away to form a squared edge. However, although smoothed off and "tidied

up" it was often not completely finished and the residual, polished keel, enables the acute observer to see how the laboriously sawn off line was achieved.

In certain cultures only the cutting edge of an axe or knife form would be ground to a sharp edge and the remainder left in a more or less rough condition. In others, such as Dawenkou and Longshan, such pride was taken in their work that the entire blade would be ground and finely polished.

The cutting edges of Dawenkou and Longshan jade blades are in the form of a hollow ground lunette. This appears as a crescentic plane arcing gently from one side of the blade to the other. Both faces of the blade have this feature which results in a very thin cutting edge. This hollow ground lunette form does not appear on the edges or faces of blades from the Liangzhu or other blade-forming cultures. Instead, the body of the piece is cambered gently down from the centre point of the surface to meet a similar shaping from the opposite face. The result is a flattened blade edge with a strong, robust body but which lacks the delicacy and thinness of the Longshan form.

One basic process for making a hole was a solid hand held rod with its hemispherical end covered with an abrasive, possibly grease containing dust of a harder material. Applying circular, downward pressure with the round end of the rod against the piece to be worked gradually results in a wearing down of the host surface. A round depression is created and then a round hole with a dome-shaped profile. Although large drill bit heads made of sandstone and scored on the drill face with circular drilling marks have been found in Yangshao and Longshan culture sites, as yet, small drill bit heads have not been identified in excavations. Credible jade workshop remains and relics have been found in the Hongshan culture region.

Cone-shaped or straight sided holes can be formed by drilling either right through a piece from one side only, or from both sides towards the centre. When drilled from one side a cylindrical tube - a bamboo stem springs to mind - would be impregnated with, or dipped into, abrasive paste and then rotated rapidly against the host face. This effects a ring-form entry, leaving an intact solid circular core or plate with a bevel edge. At the end of the process this core is anchored by only a circular remnant or platform of host material from which it can easily be snapped off - perhaps by the pressure of both thumbs or a sharp tap with another stone. The separated core leaves behind a jagged edge, either from the core itself or from the mother material, which is often not ground or polished down. In thicker stone artifacts, the drilling is done from opposing sides or ends of a piece. Here it is much more difficult to ensure that the two holes meet in a single channel. The platform or ridge that is often created at the junction is also frequently not ground or polished out.

Drilled holes in more than one neolithic Chinese culture, but particularly in North China, have a ring scoring or ridging on the interior surface of the hole that has not been removed during the finishing process. (see for example Exhibit 28). They are separate concentric rings and not of the continuous screw-line type. Although they are presumed to be scars from the hole-forming process, it is not at all clear which technique was used.

Dome shaped, straight sided and cone shaped holes are all found in Jades from the Longshan culture. However, in neolithic flat blade type artifacts from northern China all holes

appear to have been drilled from one side only.

In the Liangzhu culture most shallow holes were formed by drilling from the opposing faces with a cylindrical tube as described above. The shoulder keel was frequently not polished out. There are curved scars on some Liangzhu jades that suggest the use of a rotary wheel "drill".

As already mentioned, Dawenkou jades exhibit simple, but extremely painstaking, workmanship indicating an emphasis on art over utility - at least in regards to jade axe blades. Carefully and immaculately finished holes pierce highly glossed blades of a beautifully elegant and balanced thinness.

Both cone and dome-shaped holes are very meticulously finished. The blade edges of both axes and *dao* of the Dawenkou culture are hollow ground lunette in form and many pieces bear along their sides the carefully polished remnant of a sawn keel-form ridge. The cutting edges are either a straight line, or a very gentle offset curve. This important feature distinguishes them from the gently sweeping profile of the curved cutting edge of Liangzhu culture axes.

In Dawenkou culture holes appear to have been formed by two sided bevelling and, to a lesser extent, by impact abrasion with a dome-ended rod or drilling head rotated with a circular movement or in alternate clockwise and anticlockwise directions. One distinctive characteristic of jades from the Dawenkou culture appears to be the offset formation of holes drilled from opposite sides or dome shaped and cone shaped holes.

As time went by there were various developments and improvements in jade working in China. During the Erlitou period there was a substantial increase in the number and type of objects produced, and the complicated, elegant shapes and cut-out decoration of the jades are clear evidences of the very advanced and skilled techniques then in use. In recent years a series of unexplained bronze implements have been excavated at the Erlitou site, such as a jig saw, a drill tube and bit and a rotating polishing wheel. The currently favoured explanation is that they are jade working tools. Two methods of jade working, *gou* (outlining) and *che* (carving away the outline) are found at this early period. The incised curves are unlikely to have been carved by hand and according to modern jade carvers in China, were probably made with a nail-shaped bronze *tozi*, a grinding tool mounted on a wooden bench, with the help of fine sand. (compare KK 1976 No.4, pps 232). Openwork, probably produced with apparatus resembling a modern bow-saw, is known from late Liangzhu pieces (see Exhibit 37), and became common from the mid Shang period onwards. All of these techniques became common in succeeding periods.

It is probable that in the late Western Zhou, harder and stronger tools enabled more elaborate jades to be carved. Openwork carving, which was rare before this period, became relatively common, as demonstrated by a number of such plaques in the exhibition. The smoothly curved edges of the openwork were produced by a skillful carver with a bow-shaped saw, a technique that was fully developed in the Eastern Zhou and particularly in the Warring States period. No doubt some of these advances were the result of the replacement of bronze tools by those of iron. This was increasingly the case from the Spring and Autumn period, when iron was first commonly used for tools in China. However, the use of such iron tools never eliminated the reliance on abrasion for working jade. To reduce the time needed to work the jade, the only possible option after the introduction of iron was to find harder abrasives and to devise more effective methods for applying them.

Chinese jade workers continued to rely on quartz sand for abrasion until the Tang dynasty when it was reinforced by crushed garnet (MOHS 7.5). At this time there was also a substantial improvement in the working environment and in the tools of the trade - including the diamond stylus used for inscribing the jade books so beloved of emperors. One such jade book was excavated from the tomb of the Southern Tang Emperor Li Bian. Diamonds, the hardest of all abrasives, are thought to have reached China from India in about the 3rd century AD, but their use was mainly confined to drilling fine perforations, and in stylae for Tang book inscriptions. They do not seem to have been in general use for the working of jade before the 19th century. Corundum (MOHS 9) a crystallised mineral of the ruby group, came into use during the Song dynasty (960-1279 AD), and enabled a greater complexity of work to be performed on several levels of a piece, as is evident from Exhibits 218 and 245.

Saws, evidently effective enough to cut nephrite into the relatively thin sheets from which archaic jades were made, and bow-drills must have been available from the very beginning of jade working. The introduction of iron and later steel, for tools such as saws, cutting discs, grinders, gouges and drills, undoubtedly enhanced the jade workers' control over their material. Particularly when hollowing vessels, executing decorative designs in high relief and in such tours de force as vessels with pendant rings, sometimes with lids attached by chains, all carved from the same block of nephrite. A key device was the rotary lathe, operated by a foot-pedal that left the hands free. Lathes were introduced to China perhaps as early as the Ming dynasty when the eastern jade working centres of Suzhou, Hangzhou, Nanjing and Yangzhou came to prominence along with the Ming establishment of the capital at Beijing. Lathes were still being used in the jade workshops at Beijing during Hansford's visit in 1938-9. Despite the constant, slow and painful movement of the raw material over thousands of miles from the mountains and rivers in eastern Turkestan to the craftsmen of eastern China a jade working tradition apparently continued in Turkestan itself. In a 1926 account of his four year tenure as British consul at Kashgar, Sir Clarmont Skrine writes of the overthrow and assassination in 1924 of General Ma, the Imperial Commander in Chief of the Kashgaria military region. The septuagenarian Ma, who for many years had headed an exploitative and exceptionally brutal regime extended his interests from oil wells to a jade cutting factory. When the revolutionary mob rampaged through his palace at the tyrant's final denouement, great quantities of raw and half worked jade were found in the remains of this factory, which Skrine described as having been set up with a forcibly restrained and semi-starved work force of jade artisans kidnapped from their home base in Khotan.

Beijing, as the capital, was the site of the Imperial jade workshops which were kept very busy through much of the Ming and Qing dynasties. At the time of the Qianlong Emperor (r.1736-95) there were eight other jade working centres in China, the best of which was Suzhou. There are records of orders being placed by the palace with the jade workers of Suzhou at this time. Suzhou was a major centre for jade production from probably the early

Ming dynasty on, and the jade workers seem to have supplied much of the market outside the Palace. Jade was reasonably plentiful during the Ming and Qing dynasties, and whenever it was available there were plenty of workers ready to exploit it.

The artificial colouring of jade to improve its visual appeal seems to have first occured in the Tang dynasty, but was apparently never all that popular with consumers. This practice was chiefly confined to copies of archaic pieces or those made to deceive collectors. In the late 19th and early 20th centuries there was a substantial industry producing such jades for the antique trade. It must be remembered that at this time steam driven machinery, and later electric power, greatly facilitated the work of the jade carver. Even Hong Kong had factories expert at artificially ageing jade in the early 1950s. The dyeing and ageing of jade involved the use of various chemicals depending on the desired colour. Such colour introduction is generally fairly easy to detect as the colour seems to be confined to the surface of the jade, and does not blend gradually with the colour, as would usually be the case if the colour of the stone had occurred naturally. In the past some jades were described as "calcified", but this term is considered inappropriate since the changes in such jades may result from cremation (commonly practised by the Liangzhu culture) or other exposure to fire or from the conditions or location in the tomb from which the jades were excavated. The preferred description for such jades today is "altered" and this word will be found frequently in the commentaries on the exhibits.

Angus Forsyth
Brian McElney
January 1994

玉 材 的 加 工

如上所述，玉材質地極硬，無法施以通常所說的雕刻，只能用適當的研磨料磨製成器，然而似乎從新石器時期開始，人們就用鋸和鑽並輔以潤滑脂和研磨料，將軟玉開解或鑽孔。這些鋸、鑽上面往往留有清晰的使用痕跡。

在新石器時代，現今中國的廣大地域乃是各種不同的部族分別聚居之地，其中有些地區看來互有接觸，有些則彼此隔絕。因此，在不同地區之間，或可發現不同文化的玉器帶有地區差別。與石器加工相比較，最主要的新添工藝是用一種或幾種方法在玉材上穿孔，如打鑿、挖刮、用桯鑽或管鑽鑽孔，將大塊璞玉開解(大概用蘸以研磨料的細繩或獸筋)，可以鋸出平整的面。再在距原先開口0.5至1厘米以上的部位下鋸，便可獲得扁平的玉片。然後將穿孔技術用在玉片上。用細繩或獸筋蘸滿研磨料而做成的手鋸，看來往往被一種原始的但卻高效的擺鋸所取代，後者一般都會留下特徵明顯的弧形鋸痕。

兩面已經鋸平但輪廓還不規整的玉坯，四側都得兩面對鋸，才能作成長方體或立方體。當兩面對鋸幾達中心綫時，粗糙的邊緣就會崩掉，留下一條粗道或窄長的隆脊。這條隆脊隨後可以磨掉，使側棱變得平整。然而，儘管作過修整，隆脊往往仍未去掉，帶有磨痕的殘脊使細心的觀察者得以窺見這難以鋸掉的隆綫是怎樣形成的。

有些文化只把斧、刀等器的刃部磨成鋒利的刃口，其餘部位則仍較粗糙。但大汶口、龍山等文化卻以通體磨光為其工藝的顯著的特色。

大汶口和龍山文化的玉製刀斧，刃部磨製成新月形狀，這個新月形的平面有一條弧邊從器身的一側到另一側徐徐彎曲。器身的兩面都有這個特點，形成極薄的刃口。但良渚或其它一些製作刀斧的文化，其器刃和器身都沒有這種磨出來的新月形，而是器身兩面都從中心點開始徐徐下彎，形成扁薄的邊緣。如此將器身做得結實厚重，不像龍山製品那樣做工精緻，器形較薄。

穿孔的工序主要是用一根手執的桯鑽進行的，鑽頭呈半圓形，上面蘸滿了研磨料——可能是含有硬度較大的粉末狀材料的潤滑劑。將圓鑽頭抵住玉料作下壓旋轉，便可在坯體表面越磨越深。先是磨出圓窪，繼而磨出剖面呈弧形圓孔。雖然鑽面上留有圓形鑽痕的大形砂岩鑽頭，在仰韶和龍山文化遺址中已有發現，但小型鑽頭迄至今未見出土。在紅山文化地區，發現有可靠的製玉工場遺跡和遺物。

在坯體上作一面透鑽或者從兩面向中心對鑽，都可鑽出圓錐形或直筒形的穿孔。一面透鑽以管鑽為工具(或許是用竹筒)，先蘸上研磨膏或浸入其中，然後在坯體表面快速旋轉。如此鑽出環形的鑽口，形成邊緣傾斜的圓芯或圓片。臨近鑽頭時，鑽芯還連在圓形的殘留體上或坯料的臺面上，不用費大勁就能取下——大概是用兩個拇指下壓或用一塊石頭敲擊，鑽芯取出以後，鑽孔上留有毛碴，連帶着從鑽芯崩下的餘料或者從坯體崩出的切口，這種碴口通常不加修磨或拋光，製作較厚朋玉石器，穿孔須從坯體的兩側或兩端對鑽。這種工藝難度要大得多，必需把兩孔對準，才能匯成一個孔道。往往在匯合部位形成臺階或凸脊，但一般也不磨平或磨光。

新石器時代的中國，尤其是華北，已有若干文化發現有內壁帶環形旋痕或隆脊的鑽孔，穿孔綫跡在末道工序中沒有去掉(例見28號展品)，這些都是彼此分離的同心圓，而不是連續不斷的螺旋紋，雖然推信這是穿孔工序的遺痕。但其所用技術尚不得而知。

圓頂形，直壁形和圓錐形的穿孔均在龍山文化的出土玉器上見有實例。但是在華北新石器時代的扁體型製品上，所有穿孔似乎都是僅從一面透鑽的。

在良渚文化中，綫孔多是用上文所述的那種以管對鑽的方法從兩面鑽成的。孔內的隆脊往往沒有磨光。有些良渚玉器上留有盤曲的旋痕，説明當時已採用旋轉的輪鑽。

如前所述，大汶口文化的玉器，工藝簡單但極費心機，説明製作者着重藝術超過了實用，至少對玉斧的器身是這樣。這些玉斧穿孔精緻，斧身光滑，薄度均勻，透出優雅的美感。

無論是圓錐形還是圓頂形的孔眼，都做得十分細緻。大汶口文化的刀斧，刃部磨成新月形狀，許多標本的側面帶有隆脊形鋸痕經精心磨光的跡象，刃口或平如直綫，或彎曲成流暢的偏心弧綫。這個重要特點與良渚文化斧形器的弧刃上那徐徐彎曲的側面輪廓迥然不同。

在大汶口文化中，穿孔似系從兩面鑽出斜壁圓洞而形成，間或則是用圓頭桯鑽按圓周運動，或者按順時針方向和遞時針方向交替旋轉而沖磨出來的大汶口文化的出土玉器，似有一個特點，即兩面對鑽的或圓頂形，圓錐形的穿孔呈偏心形態。

隨着時間的推移，中國製玉工藝得到多方面的發展和改進。二里頭時期，玉器的數量和種類都大有增加。複雜而精緻的玉器形剖和刻紋顯然證明當時已有非常先進和熟練的技術。近年來，在二里頭遺址已發掘出一系列尚難解的青銅工具，如堅鋸、鑽管、鑽頭

和旋轉磨輪。目前一般都把它們視為製玉工具。這個
早期階段已採用"勾"和"徹"這兩種製玉方法，那些
彎曲的刻紋，不可能是手刻成，按照中國現代玉匠的
看法，很可能是用釘形的青銅砣子刻出來的，這是一種
支在木凳上的磨具，以細砂為磨料 (參看〈參古〉，1976
年4期232頁)。透雕工藝在良渚晚期的製品上已有
發現 (見37號展品)，至商代中期開始盛行；所用工具
大概與現代的弓形鋸相似。所有這些技術都在隨後
時期風行開來。

西周晚期，似已能使用堅硬的工具在較為精緻的
玉器上雕刻紋飾，從前罕見的透雕這時已較普遍，如
展出的不少透雕飾牌所示，技巧嫻熟的雕工用弓形
鋸作出邊緣圓潤彎曲的透雕花紋，至東周時代特別是
戰國時期，這種技法得到充分的發展。有些進步無疑是
鐵工具取代替銅工具的結果。從春秋時期起，這種
狀況日趨明朗，當時中國開始普遍用鐵製造工具。然而
鐵器的使用從未消除製玉工藝對研磨料的依靠。採用
鐵器以後，唯一可能減少製玉工時的途徑是尋找
更硬的研磨料，並設計更有效地使用研磨料的方法。

唐代以前，中國玉匠一直用石尖砂進行研磨；
從唐代起，增添了粉碎的石榴石(摩氏硬度為7.5)。當時
製玉的條件和貿易工具也大有改善，例為能用金剛
計來刻皇帝非常喜愛的玉冊。這種玉冊在發掘南唐皇帝
李昇墓時即出土一件。金剛石在各種研磨料中硬度
最大，據信是約當公元三世紀從印度傳入中國的，但其
用途主要限於鑽細孔，製作用以書刻唐代玉冊之類的
刻針。在十九世紀以前的製玉工藝中似未普遍使用，宋
朝時期(公元960-1279年)，開始用剛玉(摩氏9度)。這是
一種紅寶石類型的結晶礦物，借助於這種磨料，能在
玉璞的幾個層次上施行更為複雜的製作工藝，為218，
223號展品所示。

鋸顯然是將軟玉開解成薄玉片，以製作古璞玉器
的有效工具；弓鑽當在製玉工藝的初始階段即已使用。
鐵製的及後來鋼製的鋸、切割盤、磨具、弧口鑿和鑽
等工具的採用，無疑提高了玉匠駕馭玉料的能力，尤其
便於他們施展諸如掏挖窾器，製作高浮雕紋飾乃至
整玉雕成帶有垂環和以鏈繫蓋的容器等絕技。一項
關鍵性的裝備是腳踫的旋轉車床，它使雙手可以騰出
空來。中國可能早在明代即已傳入車床，當時蘇州、

杭州、南京、揚州等東部製玉中心紛紛崛起，堪與
明都之建於北京相比。1938-1939年，韓思福訪問北京
時，那裡的製玉工場仍使用車床。儘管玉材源源不斷地
從新疆的山區和河谷，千里迢迢緩慢而費力地運銷中國
東部的玉匠，但新疆本地卻顯然長期沿襲着一種
製玉傳統。1926年，英國駐喀什噶爾領事史觀爵士在其
任職四年後的述職報告中，記述了1924當地駐軍統帥
馬將軍被推翻和謀殺的事件。年逾七旬的馬將軍多年
推行肆意剝削，異常殘忍的統治，從經營油井發展
到開辦解玉工廠，起事民眾在這個暴君的末日來臨時節
沖垮其衙署時，發現在這個工廠的遺存中藏有大量
玉材和玉器半成品，史觀寫到，這個工廠是靠強制和閹
玉工背井離鄉而組成的，備受壓逼、忍饑挨餓的勞動
大軍建立起來的。

作為明清兩代都城的北京，是皇家玉器作坊的
所在地，在很長時間內保持着繁榮興旺的景象。乾隆
年間(1736-1795年)，中國還另有八個製玉中心，景況最
好的是蘇州，史料中載有當時宮廷向蘇州玉工頂貨的
情事。大概從明代初期開始，蘇州就是生產玉器的
一大中心，看來那裡的玉匠還供應了宮廷之外的
許多市場。玉材在明清時期無疑出產豐富，哪裡藏有
玉礦，哪裡就有眾多工匠去開採它。

玉器着色以改變其外觀的技法似始於唐代，
但顯然從未受到用戶的普遍歡迎。這種做法主要
限於製造古玩複製品或欺騙收藏家的贗品，十九世紀末
至二十世紀初，曾已頗大規模興起生產這種玉器的
製造業，以供應古玩貿易。不應忘記，當時的
蒸汽機械和後來的電動機械為琢玉工匠提供了很大
方便。本世紀五十年代早期，甚至香港也有生產
偽古玉頗為在行的工廠。玉器的着色和作舊，要根據
要求的色澤來選用不同的化學原料。這種着色手段
一般都不難識破，因為上色僅限於玉器表面，不能與
玉石的本色漸次交融，而石料自然顯現的自然色澤
通常都是渾然一體的。過去對有些玉器的描述
曾有"受沁"一說，其實這是用詞不當，因為這些玉器
的變化可以由焚燒(常見於良渚文化)、烘烤以及出土
玉器的墓葬所處的條件或地點而引起。我們不妨用
"變質"一詞來形容這類玉器，在展品説明中，這個用語
將反覆出現。

JADE CULTURE AND
DYNASTIC ESSAYS

EXHIBITS AND
COMMENTARIES ON
INDIVIDUAL PIECES

11 NEOLITHIC PERIOD TO ERLITOU PERIOD

INCLUSIVE C. 5500-1600BC

A. INTRODUCTION - THE JADE AGE

The study of neolithic jade working in China and its results can be distilled and drawn with a recently based confidence and accuracy from reliable archaeological dating techniques of carbon 14 measurement of carbonised organic remains and thermo-luminescence measurement of pottery excavated with jades and from jade culture levels. Since 1949, and particularly since 1980, a steady and unbroken programme of scientific and controlled archaeological excavation and analysis in China by increasingly experienced and ingenious experts has furnished new, incontrovertible and often startling evidence of what it is now clear was a very long and readily identifiable jade era immediately preceding the introduction of bronze metal and writing. For many years, distinctive culture names have been taken from the village or area of the first identified site of a particular uniquely distinguishable "culture". For example the Liangzhu village in Zhejiang Province has the name which, since first discovered in the 1930's, has been given to the now famous neolithic jade culture of that region. Every so often however a new, usually older or newer "culture" is found in a particular region that necessitates a minuter stratification of previous perceptions. This 'serendipity' is particularly a factor in the currently fast evolving picture of archaeological work in North China where several villages have achieved neolithic name importance in the last ten years through being the place of innovative archaeology though there may eventually turn out to be dozens or hundreds of sites around represented by that named culture which had been so happily but fortuitously named after the village of first discovery. The cultural map in central and southern China is at the moment much clearer

but, in the north, these developments are currently so fluid that the underlying picture of coordinated cultural sequence is not clear. For this reason the term "North China Neolithic" appears in this" catalogue where it is necessary to attribute a piece to an early date without the certainty of established culture specifics to enable a more positive statement. The relevant presently known jade-using neolithic cultures and approximate dates are fully listed for reference in the neolithic section of the Chronological Table on page 15.

In jade studies, the term "Neolithic" (New Stone Age) is the traditional one used for the period of initiation and development of consciously applied abrasion and drill working or processing of uncarveable jade type stones before the introduction of metal. This was an archaeologically identifiable period extending way back - from a securely dated termination point between 2100 BC - 1600 BC, of the north central China Erlitou period which is now normally considered to be the period which first saw bronze production in China on a large scale - to beginnings which, from the latest archaeological finds are no later than 5000 BC.

This neolithic period seems to have begun with the abandonment of a nomadic hunting existence in favour of settled dwelling and agriculture. Settled communities were organised into villages. These village communities carried on farming of crops on land formed of, and annually fertilised by, rich alluvial silt deposits which were carried by numerous river systems down from the, generally, western mountains in many Chinese Provinces. For hundreds of years, the traditional Chinese and international scholarly view of the beginnings of this settled society sited it on the levels of loess washed down since time immemorial to the erratically formed lower flood plains of China's enormous river, Huang He or Yellow River. The turbulent nurturing by this monster of the civilised development of the Han Chinese heartland on the great central plains area of the China landmass has earned it the name of "China's Sorrow".

This somewhat cosy view of cleanly placed indigenous growth and change has however been disturbed by the findings of archaeology in recent years. The currently revealed picture shows settled agriculture and associated civilised structures such as organised dwellings in villages, unique regional pottery and jade working, developing - apparently independently - in the river flood valley and basin of China's other huge river, the Chang Jiang or Yangzi River and also along the course of the Liao River in the North China areas of Inner Mongolia and the present day Liaoning Province.

In August 1993, Professor Lin Yuen of Jilin University delivered a paper making novel suggestions in regard to neolithic cultural exchange in the north east of China and Baikalia (East Central Siberia) to the International Academic Conference of North China Ancient Culture in Chifeng, Inner Mongolia. He drew upon the existence of ceramic shapes common to North China neolithic cultures and the neolithic cultures of Russian Siberia - some with much older links dating back to 8000 BC. He also mentioned similar examples in the later level cultures of the early Bronze Age more to the west in the Minussinsk basin and in the Altai mountains which border the Ningxia Hui Automous Region and Inner and Outer Mongolia. This thread now requires further isolation and

development - an exercise whose need is noted but is beyond the scope of this catalogue.

In neolithic China animals such as dogs, pigs, goats, sheep and cattle were being domesticated and selectively improved in quality of skin and meat. Stone spinning artefacts found are clear evidence of cloth production and there is some evidence possibly indicative of sericulture.

Society's transition from a nomadic to a settled village type culture brought fundamental changes to social practices in respect of such things as burials. The creation of artefacts of a wholly non utilitarian function from precious materials such as a number of jade categories, both representational and imaginary in form, are evidence of religious or shamanistic beliefs and subscription to ceremonial formalities. At the same time graphic artistic expression begins to make a determined demonstration through incised and painted designs on pottery and these, in association with three dimensional sculpture in clay, stone and jade, lay the foundation for continuous future development.

Very significant, but as yet unrationalised pictograms or designs etched into pottery of the Dawenkou culture of Shandong Province have arguable connection to very similar designs which appear incised on a limited number of neolithic jades - unfortunately none from a controlled excavation but, in at least one relatively recent case, definitely from the Liangzhu culture of Jiangsu and Zhejiang Provinces. Other long known examples may be from the Shandong Dawenkou culture. The pottery pictogram inscriptions are however from securely dated archaeological excavation of Dawenkou culture sites in Shandong. These designs, are considered by some scholars as evidence of the earliest development of writing, or of what eventually developed into writing, in China - at least by communication of ideas through symbols. In early 1993 there was a brief published report on one piece of pottery from a site at Dinggong Village Zouping Country, South Western Shandong dating to the Longshan culture of c.2300 - 1700 BC which is reported to be inscribed with eleven characters in five lines. Written Chinese is of course based on a pictogram or ideographic system but according to present understanding true, ordered pictogram writing, was not to appear in China until the early historical period in the Shang dynasty.

In an extremely perceptive and fundamentally interpretative 1990 paper, published as an introduction to the Mu Fei Catalogue (83), Professor Wu Hung, takes the basic, Herculean, steps of drawing together the tangled skeins of the several legendary, literary, funerary and archaeological facts representing the reality of the "Jade Age".

The identification of this phenomenon can be stated as the perception of society at large that jade was more than a pretty stone or jewel. It was invested with elements of the greatest virtue and respect available and was made, apart from the very significant jewellery type use of earrings, almost exclusively into objects of religio-ritualistic application thus confirming the setting aside of jade onto a plane of appreciation and standing separate from any other material then known to East Asian Man.

In the mere fact that the processing of this very intractable material in extremely primitive circumstances must have involved the exclusive work and labour of a specifically dedicated section of the community, we can see a full measure of the way in which a commonly subscribed and regulated social uniformity of

this respect was fixed into the basic order of the state. Professor Wu identifies the four of the "Tribute of Yu" provinces which lie in a region extending from south Liaoning Province down to Zhejiang as conforming to recent archaeological discoveries in positively endorsing legend in identification of the north to central eastern region of present day China as the place of the Eastern or Bird Yi People. If the general assimilation of divers legends and beliefs from this large area in neolithic terms can be said to have been a fact by the generally agreed time of the existence of the still somewhat legendary Xia dynasty of Yu the Great, then it is no surprise that the "Tribute of Yu" should summarise accurately in material terms all that was then known about what may well previously have been divergent and, indeed multi-strata cultural characteristics. What the slow but ordered findings of archaeology, (some of which are so recent that they were not even available to Professor Wu at the time of his writing his excellent work in 1990), reveal is that not only was the period of the Jade Age pushed back to an origin at least 3,000 years before the Xia period, but the area of the beginning of the Jade Age was situated not along any part of the Eastern Yi Arc of the Liaoning/Zhejiang area but was situated somewhat to the north west of this arc in present day Inner Mongolia.

Profoundly important archaeological work is continuing to unfold and push back the origins of the Jade Age. The currently received wisdom of this work forms the basis of the order and organisation of this section of this exhibition and catalogue. Of particular significance here is the recent publication in 1993 of the basic work of Professor Yang Hu, Associate Professor of the Institute of Archaeology, Chinese Academy of Social

Sciences and his team at the Xinglongwa culture village settlement in south eastern Inner Mongolia. His work which has established what is beyond doubt the currently oldest finding of jade in China, is to be associated with the work of archaeologists in Inner Mongolia in levels of the Zhaobaogou culture which is turning up jade artefacts hitherto associated with the archaeological findings during the 1980s on Hongshan culture levels. The importance of this fact lies in that the Zhaogbaogou culture levels have been scientifically dated in China to 4800 to 4000 BC which is substantially before the earliest beginnings now known for the Hongshan Culture, and certainly up to 1,000 and more years before what one might regard as the "high" Hongshan culture period such as that represented by the famous Mother Temple site at Niuheliang, Lingyuan, in southwest Liaoning Province.

Given these astounding findings of fact, and given also the fact that the bulk of Hongshan jade findings from archaeologically excavated sites are extremely worn and smoothed, it is now legitimate to perceive that the Hongshan culture people, far from being themselves innovators in the use and working of jade as an elemental dynamic of the civilised order of the state, were merely the undoubtedly capable but unoriginal inheritors of an even more ancient jade tradition and users of its jade artefact products - already "archaic" by the time of the Hongshan culture period. The true extent of this tradition is not accurately known but waits to be revealed in the coming years of increasingly exciting and rewarding archaeological examination of an area of north China which is huge today and almost untouched in archaeological terms but which at the time of the Jade Age was an enormous world of its own.

B. TABLE OF CHRONOLOGICAL DEVELOPMENT AND BROAD GEOGRAPHICAL DISTRIBUTION

Principal jade using and jade influenced neolithic cultures in China
c. 6000-1700 BC

1. JADE USING NEOLITHIC CULTURES
North and North West China - Liaoning Province and Inner Mongolia - North China neolithic
Xinglongwa 興隆洼 c. 5500-5040 BC
Zhaobaogou 趙寶溝 c. 4800-4000 BC
Chahai 查海 c. 4700-3000 BC
Hongshan 紅山 c. 3500-2200 BC

Shaanxi Province (the central plain)/Middle/ Lower Middle Yellow River
Yangshao 仰韶 c. 4800-3070 BC
Banpo type 半坡類型 c. 4800-4200 BC
Miaodigou type 廟底溝類型 c. 3900-3500 BC
Qinwangzhai type 秦王寨類型 c. 3400-3000 BC
Henan Longshan 河南龍山 c. 2300-1700 BC

Lower Yellow River/Shandong Province/North Jiangsu Province - Huai River Basin
Dawenkou 大汶口 c. 4500-2300 BC
Huating 花廳 c. 3800-3000 BC
Shandong Longshan 山東龍山 c. 2300-1700 BC

Middle Yangzi River-Sichuan, Hubei
Daixi 大溪 c. 4000-3300 BC
Shijiahe 石家河 c. 2500-2000 BC

Lower Yangzi River Basin - Lake Tai and East Central China (Ning Shao Plain)
Hemudu 河姆渡 c. 5000-4800 BC
Majiabin 馬家濱 c. 5000-3900 BC
Songze 崧澤 c. 3800-2900 BC
Liangzhu 良渚 c. 3400-2250 BC

2. JADE INFLUENCED CULTURES
South Coastal Provinces

Guangdong Province -
Shixia 石峽 Late Phase c. 3000-2000 BC

3. ERLITOU PERIOD 二里頭
Henan Province c. 1900 - 1600 BC

C. NEOLITHIC PERIOD
c. 6000-1700 BC
GENERAL

The map on page 26 shows a distinction between the basic flood plain and river valley regions of Central and Eastern China being broadly set in a contour below 600 metres above sea level and the ranges of hills and mountains which penetrate this low lying littoral and extend up to heights at which primitive agriculture was not possible. As mentioned elsewhere, archaeological excavation is establishing beyond doubt that the Yellow River can no longer be regarded by the Chinese as the exclusive source and wellspring of Han Chinese nationhood and there are equally important areas of the country in the development of man's tenure of the Chinese landmass. These areas are widely separated - but principally to be found on a north south axis along the east coastal region extending between Manchuria in the north down to at least Zhejiang province south of Shanghai so far as our present knowledge goes.

Early Man had signal and well merited success of cultural and artistic developments in this Eastern place of plenty in some of the richest and most fertile land in the world at the Yellow River and Yangzi River lower flood plains and estuaries, along the Liao river draining into the Bohai Gulf and along the various rivers in Inner Mongolia forming the upstream tributary system of the Liao River.

The inordinate length of slow but inexorable time that it took for jade to evolve to its status of extreme value not available to the common man, invested it with an aura and pedestal which in turn engendered a foothold and a respect that even gold and silver were not able to dislodge until very recent times. The only uses that could be made of it were to ornament wealthy or politically powerful citizens or to symbolise meaningful ceremonial purposes.

In considering these neolithic artefacts it is helpful- indeed necessary - to have a working idea of the relevant names in Chinese characters and the romanised forms which, together with line drawings of the principal shapes appear in the Glossary.

In general, and despite, or perhaps as a consequence of, very good organisation of and subscription to, social order, neolithic man seems to have responded, as an essential of social development, to an ethereal imperative associated with his spiritual well being. It is part of traditional human organisation to demand satisfying and credible physical tokens of the value of belief and there is little doubt that jade performed this function with admirable adequacy from the very earliest times. The social order early on certainly associated itself with a considerable respect for the dead. It is a significant fact that, apart from an occasional find in or near the site of a dwelling house, neolithic jade artefacts are found rarely in either dwelling houses or in what are clearly important temple complexes of some of the neolithic cultures - though some of which have yielded up amazingly mature and developed human sculptural forms in clay. In contrast profligate numbers of superb jades have been found in tombs - constituting the beginning of what became the standard funerary practice in China to inter the finest jades as funerary objects appropriate in lavishness to the stature of the deceased. In Hongshan burials at any rate, ceramics - that other great constant of human artisan achievement since very earliest times - were not placed inside the coffin with the body of the deceased. This close intimacy of interment was reserved for jade.

Perhaps in consequence, the application of jade to purely utilitarian expression in neolithic times is extremely rare. In essence it is a surprising fact that the one really hard material available to man in a workable form in pre-metal times was not set to applied uses by him when the need must have been acute. This material which was so difficult to work and consequently represented an enormous concentration of the economic fruits of the community, was shut permanently off from the community through burial. Exceptionally, a remarkably elegant and very usable jade spoon of the Liangzhu/Longshan transition type, in form very similar to the standard contemporary modern Chinese porcelain spoon was excavated in 1985 at Lingjiatan in Anhui Province and is so far a unique form from any neolithic site.

As many of neolithic jade pieces are complex and sophisticated forms, it is clear that they were made with extreme care and attention to detail. This was no small or temporary undertaking and would accordingly seem to suggest that the jade working section of the neolithic community drew substantially upon the basic food and shelter resources of the living in return for services performed almost exclusively for the dead. It is reasonable to presume that the fruits of jade workers' labours did not go unrewarded in economic terms. Production was almost entirely non-utilitarian and with a very low output because a piece might take months, or even years, to make. These workers were clearly a most important segment of a community which was very much principally involved in the daily round of agriculture and animal husbandry purely in order to survive, yet retaining a keen and developed acknowledgement and recognition of the supernatural.

The table of chronology and map distribution on pages 15 and 16, and 24 and 25 respectively show that there are periods and areas of general overlap. That said however, a sequential examination of the site findings of the principal neolithic cultures in different areas affords the easiest overview of the developing story which commences in the north east of China and progresses down to the south via the sub 600 metres contour. As mentioned before, there were other neolithic cultures developing simultaneously in other areas of China but somehow not all demonstrated a systematic ability to work with, or interest in applying and using, jade in their daily lives or after death. For our purposes here, only those identified local cultures which worked and used jade have been taken as part of the overall picture.

Much work remains to be done in examining the communication channels of cross fertilisation and blending of artistic ideas between the different jade cultures. This seems not to have been common despite well established exceptions such as the stone forms of the typical Liangzhu culture *cong* which have been excavated from the contemporary site at Shixia in northern Guangdong Province adjacent to Hong Kong. There are also discernible similarities between the late phase Liangzhu culture and the Shandong Longshan culture towards the close of the third millennium BC.

The disparate and unconnected base of neolithic jade cultures can however be shown to have matured into a reasonably homogenous adolescence by the beginning of the second millennium BC. The geographically mobile and politically strong later peoples of Xia and Shang were quick to draw from this foundation and absorbed such jade cultures into their own syncretic development of artistic form. In that light, these independent generic similarities of neolithic regionalism can and must with increasing clarity be seen and studied as the foundation of the unified concept we call Chinese Art.

D. REGIONAL DEVELOPMENT

1. NORTH AND NORTHWEST CHINA- LIAONING PROVINCE/INNER MONGOLIA - NORTH CHINA NEOLITHIC

(i) XINGLONGWA 興隆洼 – 5500 - 5040 BC
(ii) ZHAOBAOGOU 趙寶溝 - 4800 - 4400 BC
(iii) CHAHAI 查海– 4700 - 3000 BC
(iv) HONGSHAN 紅山 – 4700 - 3000 BC

It is now reasonably well established that the neolithic jade working cultures of north China occupied a large area bordered by, and including, in the east, present day Liaoning Province up to the Korean border, in the South, Jinzhou city of Liaoning Province on the Bo Hai Gulf and North Hebei Province and in the west the east central section of Inner Mongolia. There is as yet no clearly defined idea of the northern boundary which may therefore extend into present day independent Mongolia in the northwest and into the present day Jilin and Heilongjiang Provinces of China, respectively to the north and north east. It may even go beyond into

Siberia where the second millennium BC jade working culture of Cape Burkhan, Olkhon Island, in the Irkutsk region of south Lake Baikal is to be found. This culture used a fine quality white nephrite material to make *bi-discs* and closed rings most likely to have been the inheritor of an older tradition, and was excavated by Professor Alexei Okladnikov of the Soviet Academy of Sciences before and after the Second World War. Henry Michael in his 1958 paper "The neolithic Age in Eastern Siberia" (52) describes the green and white nephrite from the Kitoi River valley worked by Baikal region people in neolithic times and the travelling export and trade propensities of the obviously popular green colour nephrite to far western excavated destinations such as the Minussinsk Basin, the Yenisei Valley and even the Ural Mountain area which had its own, grey-green, nephrite. Yang Meili of the Palace Museum, Taipei, Taiwan has published important observations on the seminal role that the ring shaped jade discs of neolithic north China were to play through interface with those of later cultures further south in the Shandong peninsula.

The northern boundary of the north China neolithic area is taken today for practical purposes as being the Xilamulun River in Inner Mongolia which flows broadly from West to East becoming a tributary of the Liao River.

North of the Xilamulun River begins an eastern pocket extremity of the Mongolian Desert formed in a hook of the Da Hinggang mountains. This desert first became a desert sometime between 1000 and 3000 BC. Geological examination shows us that the present desert was previously pasture land with some afforested parts.

There have been reports in the past of Hongshan culture pottery finds in this desert area. They clearly establish the possibility, if not certainty, that the Hongshan culture, and possibly also its sister cultures in the area, occupied - and antedated - the desertification of what was an agriculturally settled area and, presumably, extended their influence, if not their settlements, right up into the Da Hinggang mountains and north up to the border of the province with the Russian Federation Far Eastern Region of Siberia. There is a present need to make scientific examination of this position.

What is now reasonably clear is that the late neolithic stone ploughshares manufacturing tradition is not found all over China and is in fact restricted to North Hebei, Liaoning, Jilin (possibly) and Inner Mongolia thus establishing a familiarity of the peoples in these regions in very earliest times with the working of stone for strictly utilitarian purposes and with the rich harvest available to represent the success of such working. There could perhaps be no more natural and comprehending an appreciation of a hard and obdurate beautiful stone than by those who had mastered the use of softer stones for everyday life sustaining purposes.

From our present knowledge however, the north Chinese neolithic cultural area seems to have a cross roads or central focus upon the Chifeng area which is now an administrative district of some considerable size in north eastern Inner Mongolia extending about 200 miles north to south and about the same distance east to west. The northern border of the Chifeng district is the Xilamulun River and the Da Hinggang mountains and the southern border can be taken almost as far as the present day city of Chengde, the magnificent former Jehol summer hunting park and playground of the Qing Manchurian Emperors. Between the eighth and eleventh centuries AD. Chifeng district was the heartland of the Qidan Liao peoples who developed a position of immense power in north west China until destroyed by the Tungusic Jurchen peoples from the Bohai area in 1125 AD.

In this Chifeng area have been found the remains of at least four identifiably distinct neolithic cultures which have been named (in chronological order) as Xinglongwa (5500 BC to 5040 BC), Zhaobaogou (4800 BC to 4400 BC) Hongshan (c. 3500 - 2200 BC) and the Xiajiadian Lower Culture (2000 BC to 1600 BC). There is also what might now be regarded as a sub-branch of the Zhaobaogou culture which is the Chahai culture of a similar antiquity sited at the city of Fuxin in the east of present Liaoning Province and adjacent to the south east area of the Chifeng District.

Archaeological evidence has now clearly established that the Xinglongwa culture worked jade as evidenced by the simple *chueh* form slit disc earrings and two *beng* form axe/chisels found in a grave at the excavation site. These are currently the earliest datable worked jades discovered in China.

There is further clear evidence that the Zhaobaogou culture was a jade working culture. Evidence of this is provided by the finding in dated Zhaobaogou levels in the Ningcheng area of a jade cicada or insect with prominent eyes in very fine and even quality yellow jade material, some *chueh* slit discs in the same material ranging from thin and flat to fat and raised and some elongated cylinder beads which exhibit pronounced internal scoring or ridging of a type not previously identified from such an early positive date. Zhaobaogou dating is now ascribed to the level of a very rich excavation in 1980 and 1981 at Naxitai Village,

Balin Right Banner, Inner Mongolia which was fully reported in KK No.6 of 1987. This was a site of settled houses with a pottery kiln which yielded curious and so far unique kneeling human figures in stone and about one hundred mostly yellow green jades of the cicada, spread wing bird, fish, hook-like finial, pig dragon, hoof-shape tube and openwork cloud pendant - some of which have been excavated, generally in a very worn and scratched state from undoubted Hongshan sites such as Niuheliang but which it now seems date from a substantially earlier period. (See commentary on Exhibit 1.)

It is now, at the time of publication of this catalogue, reasonably clear from these archaeological discoveries, and from the discovery of a number of surface or occasional finds that more than one settled culture of distinct characteristics occupied the north China neolithic area over a period of time extending between at least as far back as 5500 BC (Xinglongwa) to as late as 1600 BC (Xiajiadian Lower) and that the Xinglongwa, Zhaobaogou and Hongshan cultures have all been clearly demonstrated to be proficient in the working of jade with the last two mentioned possibly showing particular skills. From these it can be deduced that, given that detailed studies of these cultures on sites in North China is very recent, it is only a matter of time before clear and cogent evidence of the sculptural achievement of these cultures in the field of three dimensional jade working such as the human figure will be revealed. There are in fact already chance finds of human figure sculptures in jade from this area but, due to lack of secure archaeological provenance, they have not to date been included in any published material either in China or abroad. Because of the current impossibility of predicating a secure

origin for these forms which are certainly spread over the three principal cultures mentioned above, they are treated here in a general way. As explained above, the expression "North China neolithic" is used in places where there is no more sensible current option. One cautionary note should however always be kept in mind. This is that, although the neolithic period antedated, and terminated with the beginning of the Bronze Age in China, metal working as such was known to at least one jade working neolithic culture. We are indebted to Mrs. Emma Bunker for her kind confirmation of the excavation at the Niuheliang site of a pair of simple earrings made of copper and each supporting a nephritic stone bead.

Jade working culture sites have been found on riparian lower ground and on low hill tops. Between 1983 and 1985 a substantial temple site was excavated by the Mangniu River, Niuheliang, Liaoning Province. What has been tentatively identified as the core central building of the temple, was a sophisticated earth walled structure with plaster facing now entirely collapsed in rubble which includes often giant fragments of human torsos and limbs and pig dragon forms all in rather low fired red clay which seem to be the remains of what were clearly devotional images of a well developed organised religion. This building is set on a hillside several hundred feet above an arrangement of square and circular altars, not yet fully understood but which are in the midst of a number of shallow and deep tombs which were also excavated. The deep tombs alone contained jades of Hongshan type among the burial objects and to date, no jade of the period has been found in a Hongshan house or temple. Some tombs had more than one occupant arguably indicating human sacrifice.

There are additional burials, also containing Hongshan type jade artefacts. These are in what appears to be a deliberate plan of tomb satellite arrangement on low hill tops at roughly equal distances away from the principal altar platform. Some of these jades are much better finished and formed than others, some are very sketchily and superficially formed and yet others are very worn and scratched. This, in a very hard raw material, appears to indicate interment with both high quality jade objects that were extremely old when buried and with lower quality jades made hastily for burial purposes only.

Sites have been found on riparian lower ground and on low hill tops.

With the exception of Xinglongwa which was an urban site of many houses, we do not have a clear archaeological view of the houses of these culture. However one cultural distinction of interest at the Xinglongwa site was the discovery of burials inside domestic houses and not some distance away. Not only that - entire pigs were interred together with the remains of deceased human beings which is a feature unique to Xinglongwa.

The principal archaeological finds of Hongshan type culture have been of their temples and tombs - the former showing evidence of stone wall foundation and plastered wall superstructure of quite an advanced character. We know from these that the Hongshan people raised pigs and dogs and held particularly the pig in a revered status which would be quite alien to many subsequent peoples although not it seems to the previous Xinglongwa culture. In the excavated Hongshan temples there is evidence of coloured plaster walls and formed floors. In what appears to have been the temple nave many fragments of smashed terracotta female figures - sometimes naked and standing and sometimes clothed and seated - are suggestive of a matrilinear society. Some of these figures are two thirds life size and demonstrate remarkable advanced plastic clay sculpture in the north of China at the time. So far as we now know, this was an artistic sensitivity that on our present knowledge does not seem to appear in other parts of China for another one or two thousand years. This temple area is not however large and is so crowded with these smashed remains that current ideas perceive the structure to have been some kind of inner sanctum store house where the effigies were stored - being carried outside for ceremonial purposes and returned to storage after use.

A singular form of jade artefact possibly unique to the Hongshan culture - and possibly of a much earlier origin but certainly no later - is an open work flat pendant of rectangular or square profile whose retained surfaces are scooped out as broad and smoothed grooves. This form is mostly found well finished and carved on both sides but some are carved more roughly and formed on one side only. The type is ascribed by some observers to a cloud inspiration, but by others to a reptile design origin. In tombs excavated so far, these pendants have been found near the head and also on the chest of the corpse. There have been suggestions that they form a feature in some sort of headdress in wood or other material now perished. Some are very large - as much as 22 cm in diameter.

Small axe forms have been found with three of the four sides rounded. The fourth side forms the blade and there is a highly ground polish on both faces. These axes seem to be made for offering in some propitiatory way connected with burial and, possibly the after life and do not seem intended for every day use.

Beads of tubular, waisted and elliptical shape are strung as jewellery. They are pierced with a channel passing through drilled from each end to meet in the middle.

Another commonly encountered jade form is a hollow tapered tube or scoop taking the shape of an open ended shovel or hopper with a tapered outline and an oblique or diagonal mouth opening at the broader end. See Exhibit 27. The cross section is oval and the walls of the piece are thin. Sometimes there is a hole at each side near the base and sometimes not. No wholly acceptable explanation of the purpose of this form has been offered. It has been found upon the chest of the corpse and sometimes placed crosswise beneath the head like a pillow. This pillow positioning has developed the suggestion that it was some kind of hair piece or ornament. However, many, though not all of these pieces are of a very substantial size. A fist can be inserted into the broad open end. This would form a very unwieldy and heavy fitting for use in connection with the hair of the head. Nonetheless, given the exclusive funerary nature of Hongshan jades, it is possible that a hair piece or ornament of unusably splendid proportions were made purely for interment. The actual utility of the object or the convenience of the user is immaterial after death.

There are two types of flattened rod or finial forms made of jade. The first, less common, type is formed of concentrically ring encircled segments and terminating in a figure of eight or butterfly shaped finial. The end of the rod opposite the butterfly terminal is unfinished and appears ready for insertion into an orifice or matrix such as a wooden base or implement.

In one Niuheliang burial a single, thinly cut, butterfly form jade plaque was found on the pelvic area of the skeleton.

The second type, represented by Exhibit 18, is a curious flat hook-ended object of unknown purpose with, along its length a median broad groove of the same scooped out type as on the openwork cloud scroll pendants. This object again terminates at its lower end with an unfinished insertion haft or tang usually with a hole pierced, presumably for some fastening function. An associated form seems to be Exhibit 17 in this catalogue which is an elegant elongated birdhead type.

Because Hongshan jades have not yet been found in domestic sites but only in burials, it is not possible to ascribe with any certainty an everyday utilitarian purpose to the jade objects found. That said, it is difficult to justify a funerary explanation for one excavated Hongshan type jade object. This is a form of knuckleduster formed with three separate large holes like hoops standing side by side on a flat and narrow base capable of admitting fingers and the piece could be held in a clenched fist. At each end of the piece is a flop-eared and lively pig-head terminal which demonstrates again the regard for this economically, and perhaps also religiously, important animal. The flat narrow base is pierced with four equidistant ox-nose looped holes. This would seem to argue against the weapon form use and more in favour of an attachment purpose or function such as the handle of a lid or vessel. In August 1993, the author was kindly shown at the Niuheliang site a so far unpublished piece of similar structure but smaller, with three holes instead of four, and with much simplified human head profiles at each end instead of the pig-head form. See Exhibit 21 for an animal and directly associated form fully described under its own exhibit entry. This piece has the so far unique features of two holes and a serrated tooth-form base.

Undoubtedly the most dramatic and arresting creations however are the zoomorphic forms. The "Zhulong" or "pig-dragon" is a remarkable jade artefact encountered in the Hongshan culture and which appears perhaps to have been developed at that time. Evolutionary changes to the form appeared until as late as the Shang dynasty Anyang phase in about 1300 BC. The name used is a modern name which takes account of the pig like origins argued for the appearance of the head of the piece with flat ended snout, exaggerated double nostril, big round eyes and big flat pinnas to the ears. The pig-dragon ranges in size from perhaps four centimetres high to fifteen centimetres high. Exhibit 23 is a plaque of the face mask of a pig - a rare example of the animal itself featuring as itself in jade of the period and not as a component element in some composite mythical animal.

Pig remains in Hongshan human tombs are of particular significance in relation to jade. The pig seems to have been quite fully domesticated at this time and to have been an extremely important animal. Dragons have been revered in China since very early days, certainly since neolithic times. Professor Jao Tsungyi (40) and other scholars have made out good arguments for the Zhulong of the Hongshan culture to be the origin of the dragon in China. See Exhibits 24 and 25. As a mythical beast, the dragon has always writhed fittingly in the Chinese cosmos to portend and nurture imperial fortune and bountiful harvest. Perhaps the Zhulong was used for harvest related worship or sacrificial practice being associated with the pig as an important food animal, presumably no less tasty in Hongshan

times than today. As mentioned above a large broken earthenware version of this Zhulong creature has been found at the image repository at the Niuheliang site. This suggests a non funerary, deified function for at least the clay form of the pig-dragon. In one tomb, a pair of large jade pig-dragons were found laid back to back on the chest of the corpse, deliberately facing outwards towards each side.

Whether strictly relative to the Hongshan culture only or also as regards the north China neolithic jades generally, there appear to be two forms of basic body types of the Zhulong. One is a smooth curl shape and the other has the same basic curl but broken down by a larval type body segmentation e.g. Exhibit 25.

There is as yet no very satisfactory knowledge of scientifically controlled excavation of another kind of dragon form now commonly associated with the Hongshan culture but in fact quite likely dating from as far back as the Zhaobaogou culture. This is in the form of an open circle of round or oval cross-section with a median opening or break at one side of the circle. See Exhibit 7. The upper section of the circle above the median opening is formed as the head of the dragon-like creature with pig-like nostrils and head retaining the smooth form of the circle body but more snake-like and elegant and depicting brow, eyes and cross hatching work panels on each cheek and on the forehead. A long crest or mane of continuous fin type with a sharp outer edge extends back from the head to curl out at a point one-third round the circle-form body. This mane or crest has been compared with the mane of the wild boar. Coupled with the flat double nostril, this serves as arguable evidence of the association of the pig with the dragon's origin. The most famous of these is a huge piece discovered from a surface chance find at Sanxingtala, Ongniud Banner, Inner Mongolia in 1971 - which was not attributed by common accord to the Hongshan culture until the 1980's - but there are others including a very fine, pure yellow jade specimen of seven inch diameter seen by the author in 1993 in Chifeng as a find by a farmer and as yet unpublished.

There is no very reliable indication of the originating dynamic which engendered the popularity of zoomorphic jade carving but it may have had a ritualistic base associated principally with bird worship but also extending to the tortoise, the cicada and what is possibly the carp and also the alligator. One classic type is the spread wing bird. Some have round eyes set each side of a round head possibly representing the pigeon or dove. See Exhibit 14. Other bird forms of the same basic spread wing structure have distinct ears raising up from the back of the head in a most probably deliberate owl-like semblance. See Exhibits 15 and 16. Although basically similar in their sculptural structure of a flattish medallion form, the two types convey a rather different feeling - largely through the ears present on one and their absence on the other. Both types are generally drilled on the back with ox-nose looped holes indicating some sort of utilitarian suspension or attachment. See Exhibits 11 to 17 inclusive.

The turtle, or tortoise is found, some with neck extended and some with neck drawn in. See Exhibit 26. One dramatic representation is a pair of palm-sized almost solid tortoise shells in a beautiful and flawless, but distinctly worn, yellow jade material found one in each hand of a skeleton in one of the Niuheliang burials. There are also simple fish plate forms. Another significant, perhaps, secular animal form are fat tubular bodied cicadas. See Exhibit 10. These are relatively numerous and perhaps they are symbolic of the regard that the Chinese people have always had for the cicada. The life cycle of this insect involves a larval stage which burrows into the soil to a great depth for two or three years of torpor to emerge alive and ready to split and reveal the pristine adult insect. There can be no more readily available or eloquent testament to the legendary phenomenon of rebirth. See Exhibits 9 and 10.

Lastly it is proper to mention north Chinese neolithic jade representations of the human figure.

The dated Hongshan site at Dongshanzui, Kazuo County, Liaoning Province has yielded what appear to be small votive figures of fat form females in clay. These are strikingly similar in feeling to those unearthed in south European, Mediterranean and Near Eastern early sites such as Austria, Malta, the Cycladic Islands of the Aegean Sea and Catal Huyuk and Hacilar in Turkey. It is difficult to argue for a physical connection between the different areas of the world producing such works at rather similar times in history but perhaps this may be seen as evidence that the development of man and his artistic sensitivities around the globe advanced at something like a uniform pace.

At the present time, no human figure representation in jade has been excavated scientifically from a Hongshan or earlier site. That both human figure sculptures modelled from clay and carved from stone had reached a high degree of artistic achievement by north Chinese neolithic times has however been definitively established respectively by both the miniature clay female figures found at Hongshan sites as mentioned above, by fragments of much larger human figures found at the Niuheliang Temple site of the Hongshan period and by the two very important stone figures excavated under controlled conditions from the Zhaobaogou site at Naxitai Village, Balin Right Banner in 1980 and 1981.

It has been orally confirmed that at least one human figure in jade has been found accidentally in the Chi Feng area by a professional archaeologist in circumstances indicating a Hongshan period date but no comparative sculptural study of either this piece, or of others in public collections in China, seems ever to have been carried out. What cannot be wished away however is a limited series of human figures in jade which have appeared on the market and of which Exhibits 2 and 3 are interesting examples. In their similar and classic posture of erect bearing, broad shoulders, similar hole formation and seated position with hands on knees, and Exhibit 2 with bull horn headdress, they show a volumetric uniformity with certain figures of jade in western collections which have been commented upon by the writer in the article in 15. Those however also exhibit horn or tine like extensions rising vertically from the top of the head. This feature is also exhibited by at least one published piece in the Palace Museum collection in Beijing. Exhibit 3 demonstrates the same basic posture but shows a much softer and more rounded sculptural treatment of body line and form. Apart from the hands on knee posture having some affinity with one of the stone figures from Naxitai, there is no direct resemblance between these jade figures and the clay and stone figures from controlled excavation sites. Therefore, the available avenue of action in considering these jade figures is to consider the style and manner of their making as representing in all respects neolithic jade working technique and to place them on the threshold of what must certainly

follow as major archaeologically controlled discoveries in the future.

The north Chinese neolithic jade material mentioned above is of a fine quality ranging from a black through semi-translucent dark green and on through a translucent lemon yellow-green to a semi-translucent white. It seems, on the basis of currently available archaeological evidence, that the finer, yellow quality material is older in workmanship as it is found in relatively small quantities in dateable Hongshan culture site excavations and, when found in them, is usually very smoothed and worn as if in use for hundreds of years prior to burial. There are actual finds of fine yellow material at dated Zhaobaogou level finds. From this it may be possible to deduce that the bulk of fine yellow material artefacts antedate the Hongshan culture period. An opaque bean curd white is also found which may be the product of funerary burning practices. The material was worked into a full range of sculptural forms ranging from a flat plate through a three dimensional medallion flat form such as the bird-form already mentioned. Also found as an integral extension of the Hongshan repertoire is a full three dimensional sculptured form represented by the pig-dragons, the cicadas and the full ring dragon-forms and the humanoid creatures mentioned above.

One very distinctive formation of hole making in the Hongshan culture is the ox-nose or looped hole. (15) This typically has twin tear drop shaped orifices leading diagonally into each other with reducing depth bore. This formation is not found in other neolithic jade cultures. On the internal wall faces of deeper holes are often found a form of helical or circular scoring of what appears in some cases almost as a screw line but is in fact not a connected whorl but a series of adjacent concentric incised circles.

The workmanship of Hongshan jade is simple but fine. The edges of pieces are often polished into sharpness. There is also a type which is rough almost to the point of being unfinished - a quality that in fact conveys an additional sense of strength. Very strong and meticulous forms can also be carefully finished throughout and ridge lines are simply executed. Broad grooves are carefully formed. There is a marked general absence of patterning or incised work upon the body of a piece except for the one important exception represented by the diamond cross-hatching patches on the cheeks and forehead of the Niuheliang and other circle dragons and by the very rare fish bone striations of incised designs on the mane of Exhibit 8. Animal form heads of Hongshan pieces have many piglike characteristics and we have seen the funerary importance bestowed upon that animal. Whether or not their currently pronounced dating is wholly accurate, there is legitimacy in argument for north China neolithic jades as forming the artistically original stylistic rootstock or sculptural prototype matrix onto which later jade style development was grafted.

2. MIDDLE YELLOW RIVER VALLEY NEOLITHIC CULTURE/SHAANXI PROVINCE

(i) BANPO 半坡 4800 - 4200 BC

SITE AREA
Xian, the longtime dynastic capital of China in the Western Zhou period and a dozen other periods, bright star of the Eastern Silk Road firmament in the Tang dynasty and now the provincial capital of Shaanxi Province, also holds the Banpo Site.

Banpo is a sub-division of the Yangshao culture which extends alongside the banks of the Yellow River, with a central point at Xian.

Banpo houses were dwellings formed through digging round pits into the ground about three feet deep and twelve or more feet across. The side of the hole formed the protective and solid side wall of the house which was then roofed with a conical shaped thatch structure.

The Banpo culture produced very few jade artefacts. They take the form of chisel and axe as weapons or tools.

A type of golf tee shaped hairpin together with earrings formed as a *jue* or slit disc appear to summarise the extent of personal ornament. Pendants in the form of a *huang* or flat form arch have also been found but there is as yet no indication of ritual or ceremonial or zoomorphic forms of jade artefact.

The difficulty of working the material is clearly evident - in total distinction from the apparent effortlessness with which the Hongshan and Liangzhu people worked stones of the same hardness with no more sophisticated tools. The Banpo workmanship on jade is generally of a rough and sturdy quality and design.

Holes formed by the Banpo People were essentially single cone drillings formed by intrusion into the matrix from one side or face.

(ii) MIAODIGOU 廟底溝 - 3900 - 3500 BC
The Miaodigou People occupied the same general area as the Banpo people. Their jade artefacts were distributed in haphazard form and axe, adze and knife forms are found for tools and weapons type. Personal ornament was satisfied by a stiletto type of hairpin, finger rings, slit disc earrings, *huang* arched pendants and a form of heart-shaped pendant. As with the Banpo culture, there is no evidence of jade performing a ritual or ceremonial function in

this culture and zoomorphic forms have not yet been found. In workmanship and design the pieces found are rough and plain with scant attention to fine detail. Dimensional planes are in the form of blocks and oblong body forms such as chisels.

(iii) QINWANGZHAI 秦王寨
c.3400 - 3000 BC

The Qinwangzhai culture occupied the same basic area as the other two Yangshao cultures mentioned above. Jade artefacts took the form of axe, adze and knife as tools and weapons while personal ornament were found such as stiletto type hairpin, finger rings, slit disc earrings and heart shaped pendants. As in the Miaodigou culture, finds of jade artefacts from Qinwangzhai are not plentiful and fruitful study awaits substantially richer finds in future.

3. LOWER YELLOW RIVER VALLEY/SHANDONG PROVINCE/NORTHERN JIANGSU PROVINCE - HUAI RIVER BASIN

(i) DAWENKOU 大汶口 c. 4500 - 2300 BC

The village of Dawenkou is situated on the Dawen River near Taian in Shandong Province through which flows the lowest reach of the Yellow River.

Surviving clay models of houses found in archaeological excavation help to date the finds and to show that dwellings in Dawenkou stood squarely on the surface of the earth with no need for construction of an internal pit.

Dawenkou artefacts have been found in scattered sites but generally in the lower ground below the 600 metre contour.

The forms of jades found range from tool shapes of axe adze and chisel through weapons of the *dao* squared-end knife blade. It seems clear however that the excavated forms of axe and adze

are all with squared profile and that the rounded blade edge profile is foreign to Dawenkou culture.

In the personal ornament category are finger rings, heart shaped pendant, a long awl shaped pendant or hairpin and bracelets or bangles for the wrists. These bangles are of a surprising delicacy of form and in that regard very different from the much more massive type found in the Liangzhu culture.

Also found in this category are slit ring earrings and *huang* arched pendant. One unexplained form is a type of "V" grooved bridge-shaped fitting of a longitudinal shape and with the flat base pierced with a small number of equidistant holes, perhaps for attachment.

No clearly identified ritual or ceremonial jades have been found in regard to the Dawenkou culture. Although not known to have evident connection with ritual or ceremonial, it is appropriate to mention here a well known group of three jade *bi* and one high sided bracelet ring in the Freer collection in Washington, United States of America. These show minute and faint but often well drawn incised designs which feature spread-wing flying shapes and profiles of elegant standing birds of the song bird type some of which are reasonably clearly of the wagtail type and some of the thrush or misselidae family. Some observers have associated them with the swallow but the profile of the swallow has an entirely different silhouette.

They are incised in conjunction with a crescent moon and with a globe form with "stringball" incisions which is usually taken to represent the sun. Unfortunately, none of these pieces comes from a controlled excavation and no controlled excavation of any neolithic site in China has yet turned up a similar piece. Without absolutely satisfactory present reasoning, these pieces are sometimes ascribed to the Liangzhu culture but as mentioned below, the incised symbolism and its very reticent rendering, are not yet archaeologically recorded at all as Liangzhu characteristics.

However, though they are not identical, these designs can arguably be gathered into a physically homogeneous group which owes little to pure design or decoration for its own sake. They can be dated by direct relation with incised designs appearing upon several large earthenware ritual vessels of the Dawenkou culture level excavated from datable sites in Shandong Province in the years between 1970 and 1980. A number of scholars have tried to analyse these incised symbols and, though a long way from a full explanation, sufficient illustration of orthographic possibilities has been given to stimulate continued thought in this general direction.

The workmanship of Dawenkou jades is simple but extremely painstaking. See Exhibit 46. There is strong evidence of a perfectionist emphasis of art over the craft and utility of earlier jade forms- particularly of axe blades. Very refined thin blades were made and smoothed to a high degree of gloss and with carefully and immaculately finished holes. Exhibit 47 is a good example.

All holes are very meticulously finished. Both axe and *dao* knife edge forms have hollow ground lunette blade ends as mentioned in the "Working with Jade" section of this catalogue to which the reader is now referred for a brief summary of technical evaluation. Many pieces bear along their sides the carefully polished but retained remnant of a keel-form sawing platform. Reference should also be made to Exhibit 47 of lunette blade grinding and overall careful finishing attributable to this culture.

The material for Dawenkou jades is normally a translucent grass green and the texture is nephritic. Further colours are opaque green black and opaque creamy-brown. Translucent white, opaque pea-green and opaque moss-green are also found.

Save for some possible exceptions mentioned below, the dimensional planes of Dawenkou jades are generally flat with very little all round sculptural form.

Holes drilled by the jade workers of the Dawenkou culture are essentially double bevel drilled together from opposing faces.

In a series of three tombs excavated in 1985 at Lingjiatan Village, Hanshan County, Anhui Province dated to middle Dawenkou culture about 2500 BC several very significant jades without easily ascertained parallels were found. Apart from fairly standard forms of *huang*, *Zhuo* bracelet, axe and *bi* there were three flat form slender human figures with lobe earrings and striped flat hat and with both hands held together on the chest with open fingers pointing upwards. They were 9.6 cm. high and 2.2 cm. wide. There was also an astrological form of flat square plate with perimeter bore holes and incised on one side with circle and ray designs which cannot yet be explained. This plate was found sandwiched between two pieces of jade which are formed respectively as the top and bottom parts of a tortoise shell - an arrangement which will itself need considerable further study. The clearly astrological abstraction of the incised designs on the square plate and the human figure representations have no currently known parallels in neolithic Chinese jade. The importance of the tortoise shell in the later Shang oracle bone divination should be borne in mind.

In northern Jiangsu Province is Huating village which is the site of the designated Huating culture that rises from traceable beginnings in the Dawenkou culture period and extends into a group of burials dated to 3000 BC. They contained a wealth of jade artefacts with marked similarity to those of the mainstream Liangzhu culture at the Lake Tai region and Yuhang mentioned below. This argues for some cultural or perhaps political connection or intercourse between the two areas in those times with an accent on pig burial also a shared feature.

(ii) SHANDONG LONGSHAN 山東龍山 c. 2300 - c.1900 BC

Today, the Yellow River debouches into the Bohai Gulf to the north of the beginning of the Shandong peninsula. In times past the Yellow River has exited directly into the Yellow Sea to the south of the Shandong peninsula. This enormous divergence of movement of a huge river over hundreds of years is dramatic evidence of its very turbulent history and its impact upon the north central basin of China through which it has always rampaged in its lower reaches. One positive consequence of this very erratic historical progress has been the deposit over vast areas of north central China, and the Shandong peninsula, of very deep layers of salts and silt from the mountainous upper reaches of the Yellow River in Tibet and Qinghai. In consequence, the Shandong peninsula is richly fertile and has been occupied by man for thousands of years. The evidence of archaeological excavation over the last 20 years clearly demonstrates the development in this area in the late neolithic times of a very sophisticated jade working culture which has come to be known as Shandong Longshan. The sophistication in its jade working is principally to be found in excellent formation of the raised line, in the formation of uniquely characteristic hook form projections out from edge lines and in very

strong, highly intellectualised and rather starkly formal, abstraction of geometric openwork in flat-form jade pieces. No previous neolithic jade working culture developed these characteristics and they seem to have been invented by the Longshan cultures, perhaps in Shaanxi higher up in the lower middle reaches of the Yellow River but perhaps in Shandong. Jade working was brought by them up to the highest possible refinement. So significantly progressive are these developments that it is becoming possible to see in them the natural precursor of an even greater quality of raised line work which seems now to be the principal jade working achievement of the Erlitou period.

In 21, plate 60 is illustrated a form of hairpin excavated in 1989 at Linqu, Shandong Province. This is a white jade open work flat plaque form of terminal which is inserted into one end of a long differentially turned spindle or handle. The openwork of this form repays very careful examination both because of its general organisation and also because of the hook-form projections at each side and on the top.

Very similar hook-form projections are also to be found at the side of the Shijiahe culture jade plaque and human head mask referred to in the Shijiahe section below. There is a remarkably fine example of this type in the British Museum in London which is illustrated in 41, plate XXX1 and we are fortunate in having examples in this Exhibition, being Exhibits Nos. 64 and 65 which demonstrate very similar side edge hook projections while the third, No. 63, shows two vertical projections which can be argued as having a uniform link with the projections on 64 and 65 and on the Linqu hairpin finial. It is interesting to note that the faces of the Exhibits 64 and 65 have a twin bevelled or ridged effect slanting down to each side edge from a central vertical axis. Now we must turn to examine also the hook-form projections extending from the back of the yellow condor, Exhibit 60, and the related but more restrained ones on the perimeter of the *bi-disc* with notches and teeth, Exhibit 61. While the condor's back extensions do in fact constitute a very perceptive representation of the loose, flapping feathers found on the shoulder of the condor/vulture in nature, they also fulfil the additional function of also replicating the hook-form projections at the edges of the Linqu hairpin plaque and of the various monster masks. In passing it may be noted that the Linqu hairpin terminal exhibits two small turquoise roundels inserted at symmetrical interstices near the lower exterior corners of the piece and the eye of the yellow condor, Exhibit 60, is also formed of a small turquoise roundel. Other instances of small turquoise roundels occur in the Shang/Yin period and it seems plausible that the use of turquoise in this way dates from the Shandong Longshan period as a development away from the use of large pieces of turquoise such as the spread wing bird of turquoise from the Hongshan culture period found at Dongshanzui, Liaoning Province.

The internal squared, geometric and angular structure of the openwork of the Linqu hairpin terminal demonstrates an organisational openwork formula found in a number of pieces in public collections both in and out of China. There is a decided abstraction of a sophisticated type which has no clear parallel in contemporary art of the Longshan Period and whose true interpretation continues to be the subject of much careful thought and concentration. The Linqu terminal however may be seen to present something less

of a problem when compared with the abstracted human or devil mask form of the incised line type appearing on the reverse of Exhibit 65. As noted in the caption for Exhibit 65, the same abstracted devil mask design with its uniquely curved bordered eyes also appears as an incised form around the central hole of a *fu* axe blade in the Winthrop Collection, 46, no.192. The Winthrop piece has been well and accurately compared by many writers to the same form appearing sometimes in raised-line work and sometimes in incised line work across the breadth of flat adze form blades of the Longshan culture type. Other geometrical openwork jade pieces in the various public collections mentioned above clearly originate in the same thought processes and period, but are wholly abstract designs of an astonishing ingenuity and for which an adequately interpretative rationale has not yet been developed.

Despite its unique jade achievements the Shandong Longshan culture does share a number of affinities with the Dawenkou culture of the same geographical area. As mentioned above, there are also affiliated Longshan cultures in Henan and on the middle Yangzi River at Shijiahe.

The distribution of Longshan culture sites in Shandong is essentially upon small hill ranges and the isolation of this culture from those of adjacent areas of China will be readily apparent by the dynamic but delicate originality of the design features of raised-line and incised line work.

Here we find tools in jade such as axes and adze and small sharp scraper blades. Most likely following the existing Dawenkou culture also in the Shandong peninsula, the weapon form of jade blade is represented by the *dao* squared end knife blade with margin of several single cone holes drilled equidistantly along the spine of the piece away from the cutting edge of the blade. See Exhibit 67. A very refined and elegant group of this type from the remains of a shallow burial of the Henan Longshan culture at Shih-Mao, Shen Mu County, north Shaanxi Province near the border with Inner Mongolia is now in the new Shaanxi History Museum and identified from pottery types. Again and not surprisingly the axe and *dao* knife blade edge both continue to exhibit the fine hollow ground lunette form which originated with Dawenkou culture and is not found after the end of the Longshan period or in any other jade working. This Shih-Mao site also produced a celebrated form of human head which is formed as a flat round plaque with a crude and massive eye incised on each side and a short and squared nose extending from one edge.

During this culture we see the first appearance of the *bi-disc* with notches and teeth (Exhibit 61). The *Zhang* also appears for the first time with a shape and broad concave bladed structure which, together with the finely made branching projections each side of the hilt are wholly impractical for applied practical use (Exhibit 68). Both types can properly be considered to have ritual or ceremonial purposes and functions whose exact identity and meaning are still a fertile ground for unsubstantiated academic theorizing. Further, although there is no current excavated evidence, it seems reasonable to attribute the everted central flange ring, Exhibit 54, to a Shandong Longshan origin.

There are two other principal design products of the Longshan jade worker. One is the demonic or monster mask already touched upon and the other is a group inspired by bird interpretation. Taking the bird form first, there is a subdivision into three essentially distinct sculptural representations and it is most likely that two of these subforms were developed for and used in a ritual or religious purpose rather than following the guidance of secular precepts whereas something of an informality in the overall concept of the third type permits a greater ambivalence and hypothetical scope.

The first probably ritualistic bird design type is a relief representation of a crested eagle. This is depicted in the softest and most reticent of raised-line carving in a rearing or upward soaring movement with beak and head extended and swept back wings held out and down as though being pushed back by pressure of passing air streams. This form appears as a faint but firm raised-line relief decoration across the breadth of heavy chisel-like flat blades. Sometimes the eagle rises through feathery fronds and sometimes he is placed above a narrow belt of richly ornamented faint raised-line work of curling and fluidly arranged mask form motifs. The same aerodynamic form also occurs together with a long haired human head in profile and has also been found as a raised-line work component on an openwork plaque straddling and clutching in its giant talons a formation of human heads with striated hats, beards and earrings. The feather-form - with an open type of "eye" in an elliptical curve shape but somehow related in feeling to the "eyes" in a peacock's tail feathers, are a definite Longshan innovation and it is possible to see their influence carrying on into the Erlitou period in such work as the softly branching headdress in Exhibit 72.

The same faint raised-line work is evident in a dark green chisel of the same type found in Liangchengzhen which depicts at the end of both faces a very stylised mythical monster mask.

The soaring eagle form is a very magical

one of a typical design unique to Longshan. There is a well published ring or bracelet form in the Musee Cernuschi in Paris where the rearing eagle rises in the same soft raised-line work out of an openwork flange extending from around the perimeter of the ring.

However one feature found on pieces which bear a similar perimeter flange in openwork and thus possibly assignable at first sight to the Longshan culture and period, is a vigorous form of "stringball" raised line design of curling spirals and triangles. The incised work on the forward edge of the hat of the demonic mask piece in the British Museum, 41, plate XXXI is an excellent example and the bas reliefs in the corner angle uprights of the *cong*-shaped bead, Exhibit 71, may be another example. On these, the nature and spacing of the openwork holes coupled with the sense of simultaneous freedom and discipline in the incised work are extremely close to that of some trapezoidal pendants of Liangzhu culture mentioned below, and are very much in the Liangzhu culture idiom. They seem very arguably a link between Shandong Longshan and Liangzhu in the same currently enigmatic way as the bird incised *bi* of Dawenkou culture type referred to above.

The second bird design type is a three dimensional one of a short pen barrel rod surmounted at one end by an alert perching eagle with wings sometimes having raised-line pinion feathers folded behind its back, with an exaggerated but simply rendered hooked bill and sometimes with sharply defined spanner head talons. This form is a sculptural one and also unique to Longshan.

The third bird design type is an openwork plaque form which has an overall profile of a curving trapezoid within much the same perimeter outline as the Linqu hairpin terminal

while the bird, infested with perimeter hook form projections of the type mentioned above, follows a graceful and consistent contoured movement through the base ground of varied openwork movement and forms. There is an excellent example excavated, at a site in Hunan Province in 1991 which also combines incised work for certain of the bird-form contouring. This piece has been published in 1993 as 22 plate 46 where it is dated firmly in the Longshan culture period and attributed accordingly.

The second principal Longshan innovation above referred to is the devil or monster mask. This is based on a human model with distinct bare cheeks, lenticular eyes, distinct bridged nose and firmly profiled chin. This is a clear distinction from the *taotie* mask of the immediately preceding Liangzhu culture period which has been convincingly shown to have had close links with the Dawenkou culture of the Shandong peninsula. Whereas the *taotie* mask has been argued as originally built around the total ferocity of the tiger but clearly represents a supernatural import of some kind, the Longshan devil mask adopts the kinder familiarity of the human face but with distinctly tigerish fangs in a combination with what may well have been the equivalent of designer earrings hanging down with elegance each side.

The workmanship of Longshan jade is very meticulous achieving a fine soft gloss finish and a mellow warmth of smoothed lines and raised areas with the exception however of the openwork edges and borders which, perhaps as a contrast, generally feature a bleak and somewhat distant formalism.

The thin blades produced by the Longshan culture are very refined and some pieces demonstrate a form of "stringball" incised design motifs which are of great interest because of their very close affinity with the same style in the Liangzhu culture.

The materials used by the Longshan jade workers are nephritic and range from opaque olive grey through opaque lentil-brown to translucent white, golden brown and lime green. The dimensional plane of Longshan jades is flat - either blade or plaque. Three dimensional sculpted forms have not to date been found in Longshan culture jade, except for the small folded-wing eagle totems mentioned above and with the possible further exception of certain human mask plaques or fittings from unrecorded sources whose accurate placing into the Longshan culture remains a matter of stylistic conjecture.

4. UPPER AND MIDDLE YANGZI RIVER - SICHUAN/HUBEI

(i) DAIXI 大溪 c. 4000 - c.3300 BC

The Daixi Site is at Wushan, Sichuan in west central China. This province is now the most populous and one of the most mountainous provinces in the country.

Axes, adzes as tools and weapon forms such as the square ended *dao* knife are found in neolithic jade. Also found are personal ornaments of the *jue* slit disc ear rings and the *huang* flat bar pendant with 45 degree ends with biconical holes. There is no real evidence of more sophisticated forms such as ritual or ceremonial jade except for a single find in 1959 which is an oval plaque of 6 cm height, 3.6 cm. width and 1 cm. thickness considered by some to rank as jade and others as jade stone. It has a human face carved in relief on both the front and the back faces. The faces are different but each has a straight nose, open eyes and a mouth form like an "O" shape in a somewhat surprised gape. The raised perimeter rim is polished and so are certain parts of the relief carving such as the cheeks. This piece was taken from a tomb and clearly therefore a funerary object with a hole for stringing for suspension. The tomb was that of a child which renders even more difficult the assessment of a logical explanation of the interment of this particular piece although it may demonstrate that ceremonial of a lavish level was accorded to even some children of the Daixi culture.

The workmanship of Daixi culture jade is careful but not distinguished. The material is nephritic ranging from light translucent green to semi-translucent white. The dimensional planes are of a flat plaque form and holes are biconical drilled from each side or face.

(ii) SHIJIAHE 石家河 2500 - 2000 BC (formerly QINGLONGQUAN III)

This culture has a base situation in Hubei Province along the middle reaches of the Yangzi River commencing just below the Gezhouba Dam at the western extremity of the Five Gorges. Quite large ships are capable of sailing up the Yangzi River to dock at the port of Shashi which is only a short distance from the walled city of Jingzhou, capital of the Chu State from 580 to 220 BC. Jingzhou is one of the three cities left in modern China with its original city walls intact and in good order dating structurally at least from the Ming dynasty. Between Jingzhou and the Hanjiang River which flows as a tributary into the Yangzi River at Wuhan, the provincial capital of Hubei, very significant jade working finds were made at Liuhe in the early 1980's and were given attribution as the Qinglongquan III culture. These pieces were published in 94, plates 12, 13 and 14. In 1988 a further group of clearly related jade carvings was found at Shihezhen at Tianmen County, Hubei Province and these pieces have been attributed to the Shijiahe culture. They were all found in large size funeral pottery urns - one at Shihezhen had more than fifty jades in it. One major importance of these urns is the possibility to date them in a time and culture context.

Both Qinglongquan III and Shijiahe culture jade working finds are remarkable for their sculptural quality and for their scientifically datable origin in the late neolithic era. The workmanship is strong and clear and the sculpture qualities are mature and plastic. One Liuhe piece is a human head which is broken at the neck from a larger body of material. This piece represents one distinct type-form of human head and is of a basic cylindrical shape with a hat formed as an inverted crescent or banana shape. It has well modelled brows, raised-line border eyes set at a slight slant, a modelled inverted garlic-head nose and a raised-line oval form open mouth showing a rolled tongue. Each side of the head features a large modelled ear with a circular drum earring either suspended from, or pierced through, the lobe. Another Liuhe piece is a flat plate-form of tiger head with very particular form of curl twist modelled ears, broad forehead, grooved horizontal brows bisecting the face above a long vertical nose in the side angles of which are the incised eye roundels. This piece, clearly now attributable to the late neolithic period, has strong affinity with the *taotie* mask decorative feature in a traceable progression from the Liangzhu culture period origin of the motive, down through into the Shang and Zhou dynasties.

However, what is perhaps the most significant Liuhe piece is in the basic mask silhouette but formed as a flat surface plaque with minor openwork. The form is arranged symmetrically about a central axis and has hook edge projections at each side of the same type as those encountered in the Shandong Longshan jades mentioned above and which for this reason are normally ascribed to the Shandong area. There is a particular similarity between this piece from Liuhe and a similar piece in the Fuller collection in the Seattle Art Museum 83 No.3 and which is dated and ascribed to the Longshan culture. Another interestingly similar piece is in the Sackler Collection in the Freer Gallery in Washington D.C.

It may only be fancy but there is one possible graphic interpretation of the shape of the piece, based on the Fuller example, which is put forward in the drawing below as representing an eagle about to alight or seize its prey after a swoop from on high, but this is purely hypothetical:-

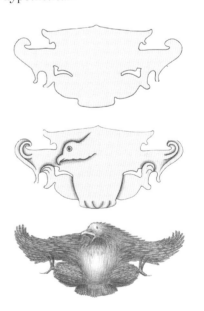

The last major Shijiahe jade carving finds from the Shihezhen excavation in 1988 were firstly of a very strongly but simply formed eagle type bird represented with open wings as if in flight. Dr. Jenny So, Associate Curator of Ancient Chinese Art at the Freer Gallery of Art and the Arthur M. Sackler Gallery in Washington has very kindly shared with us her notes made when handling this piece in the Jingzhou Museum. It is a tiny but brilliantly organised piece with a 4 cm flying wingspan with feathers formed in low raised-line work of classic Longshan type, a strongly hooked, raptorial beak and a most elegant, gull-wing front elevation profile. The features and detail of execution indicate sculptural talent for observation of the highest order.

The other major Liuhe find was the second distinct type form of humanoid head or mask. This is the same form of monster or devil mask of a semi-plaque form with the modelled nose, roundel earrings and side edge hook form projections of exactly the same structural type as those of Longshan culture shown by certain published pieces 11 and also by the demonic mask in Exhibit 64. No adequate explanation for the transmigration of the hook edge projection plaque and of the hook edge projection demon mask between the Shandong Peninsula and the middle reaches of the Yangzi River in Hubei Province has yet been rationalised. Providing further food for thought is the presence among the sandy river bank tomb finds in 1989 at Dayangzhou, Xin'gan County, Jiangxi Province of another demonic mask plaque of the same kind of raised-line, inverted garlic-nose, roundel earring, fanged mouth and side head hook edge projections. By reference to the dateable period of associated bronze forms found with it, this Xin'gan piece has been dated to the late Shang/Yin period of 13th century BC. On the basis of similar structural organisation of this piece to those pieces ascribed to the Shandong Longshan and

Shijiahe cultures, there remain question marks of association and continuity whose pursuit has now become a major preoccupation of the neolithic jade student and scholar. There is, additionally, a famous demon mask plaque of dark green material excavated from an early western Zhou tomb from Fengxi. This also exhibits the specific Shandong Longshan/Shijiahe demon mask characteristics identified in relation to the Xin'gan demon mask plaque mentioned above.

It has been suggested that the finding of such pieces from sites securely dateable from periods between 2500 BC and 1000 BC may indicate the continuity of tradition and development over that period. From the basic structural similarity between these pieces however, even allowing for a certain decadence of developmental detail and evolving floridity in the design, it is very hard to conceive of the jade worker continuing to produce pieces honouring the same canonical formulae without either any discernible development of the tradition or without there being any single representation - or even design influence - of the type in bronze - a much easier material to work and deal with and which, given the obvious importance of this design, is very surprisingly not a medium to which it was introduced. In these circumstances therefore the present writer believes that the Dayangzhou piece and the Fengxi piece together with others of that ilk, whether extant or awaiting excavation, will be dated back to a period commencing in approximately 2500 BC and ending somewhere in the Erlitou period which itself merged into the Erligang phase in about 1600 BC.

Further finds at the Liuhe site were ring form pendants and flat form squared cicada plaques with simple sculptured bodies and broad grooved details which are pierced with head and tail axial holes, probably for suspension. These are not yet possible to associate with published similar finds from the Shandong Longshan area but further interesting types from the Shihezhen site are a ring shape form of pig-dragon which does have similarity to the degenerate early Shang form of pig-dragon found in the Fu Hao tomb of the early Anyang phase of the Shang and which clearly derives from the much earlier form of pig-dragon which we have seen in the Hongshan culture.

Generally speaking, Shijiahe jades are of a calcified or burnt opaque white material and also a semi translucent grey-green. This material is similar to that of jades of the Huating culture.

5. LOWER YANGZI RIVER BASIN - LAKE TAI AND EAST CENTRAL CHINA (NINGSHAO PLAIN)

(i) HEMUDU 河姆渡 c.5000 - c.4800 BC
Hemudu is a small town at Yuyao in Zhejiang Province to the east of Hangzhou. The excavation site there which commenced yielding its rich finds in excavations in 1973, is now the subject of a substantial new museum opened in 1993.

In 1973, the Hemudu site was considered to be one of immense importance for jade studies because the jade artefacts found there in excavation were the earliest examples of jade working then known from China. Since the accurate dating of the Xinglongwa and Zhaobaogou cultures in north China, the Hemudu culture has been toppled from its pedestal of antiquity.

There remains however one dynamic legacy fom the Hemudu culture which has not been in any way diminished by subsequent finds from other parts of China and this is a marvellously facile and spirited drawing of birds and animals. The most famous bird drawings are the incised bird pictures which feature hooked beaks, clutch-ready talons and goggle eyes incised on large slices of bone and the big shouldered bristling bulk of a pig with narrow hindquarters incised on the side of a high sided black pottery vessel.

It is worthy of comment that, despite a clear ability for fresh and creative drawings, no tradition of drawing seems either to have developed further in the Hemudu culture, or to have been applied to the dominant then available material of value, jade. Most Hemudu jade artefacts are in the category of personal ornament such as hairpins, beads, tubes, *jue* slit disc earrings and *huang* arched pendants. The material of the jade used is similar to that found in other parts of neolithic Jiangsu Province which ranges between translucent lemon yellow to light greenish white.

The normal planes of jade working are the flat form taken by discs and beads. Holes are biconically drilled inward from each side of a piece. The workmanship is strong, not always well finished and jade surfaces are plain without embellishment.

(ii) MAJIABIN 馬家濱 [4000 BC]
c.5000 - c.3900 BC
Thermoluminescence ceramic testing and carbon dating of other artefacts have identified this culture which is based around lake Tai in Jiangsu Province. The main sculptural forms in this culture are bone incised carvings and shaped earthenware.

The dating of pottery of the culture has however enabled reasonably accurate attribution to the Majiabin culture of some interesting jade finds at Xiaoxian Qinzhai Village, Anhui Province in 1986. In that year, the archaeologists excavated a small pond which had always been named as the Jade Stone Pond. A number of jade, turquoise and pottery artefacts were found. It was these pottery artefacts which helped to identify the dating of the pieces and their type which indicated the Majiabin culture origin.

However, the jade forms are of the basic Liangzhu culture type. There is one very significant exception to this which is a flat type of handle, see Exhibit 49. The whole of one side of this jade handle type is a sharpened blade edge which is crossed at its central point by three diagonal broad form grooves. In the centre of the handle is a large rectangular elongated opening, well capable of admitting the fingers of the holding hand in tight grip formation. A small number of these pieces are known including Exhibit 49, but the form has no equivalent in the Liangzhu culture jades found to date which perhaps constitutes an acceptable argument for placing the date of the Xiaoxian finds into a suggested late Majiabin to Liangzhu transition for about 3,500 BC. The best known of these "handle blade" artefacts is from the Jade Stone Pond and was exhibited in Beijing in 1992 (21 No. 59). The catalogue entry for this piece in 21, describes it as being "in grotesque shape" and having "no parallel among the ancient jades so far unearthed". The Jade Stone Pond piece however lacks the diagonal grooving across the blade seen in Exhibit 49.

A very rare weapon form possibly related to the "handle blade" is a sort of short bladed cutlass with an enclosed curled knuckle grip aperture which was excavated at the Qing Liangang culture site at Dadunzi, Jiangsu Province in 1976.

(iii) SONGZE 崧澤 c. 3800 - c.2900 BC

The Songze site at Qingpu in Jiangsu Province near Shanghai has yeilded dated finds over the 3800 to 2900 BC period. This culture seems to have been is in fact the introducer of the innovation of the *bi-disc* which appears now for the first time in Chinese jade working.

There is also an interesting beginning of the occasional role played by jade in burial procedures and which seem to relate to, and be influenced by the life cycle of the cicada. The adult cicada lays an egg. The egg hatches into a grub which sits on a green leaf. At the maturity of this stage, the grub splits its skin and reveals a brown chrysalis. The chrysalis burrows into the ground to remain there over the turn of the seasons through the winter into the next year when it will burrow up into the sunlight to split and reveal the perfect insect completing the cycle. In the Han period, the jade cicada was placed under the tongue of the corpse. In the times of the Songze culture, it seems to have been popular to place in the mouth the *han* or pierced plectrum plate which is found for the first time in the Songze culture and may well be the neolithic equivalent to the Han dynasty jade cicada.

During the Songze culture, the *jue* slit disc is a standard tomb feature, *Zhuo* bracelets on the wrists of the corpse are not uncommon and tubular bead making was highly proficient. At this time the development of the *jue* slit disc can be traced from the fully round bead profile, cleaving it in from the exterior circumference to the interior by a double saw cut in parallel. This will form a full opening to the round bead. This *jue* slit disc has been found at the ear position of both male and female skeletons.

Perhaps the highest technical achievement of the Songze culture is the making of the *huang* pendant. These are very well formed and balanced and are burnished to a high gloss. See Exhibit 30.

Several varieties of the type are found ranging from a half horse shoe deep hoop with biconically perforated ends to a much thicker, flat and much more open form of hoop with one straight edge and a median indentation flanked by two small biconically drilled holes. The workmanship of Songze jade is very refined to a soft gloss finish. The material is usually a brittle semi-opaque white but a simpler crystalline form and the translucent yellow pink colour are also found and worked.

(iv) LIANGZHU 良渚 c.3400 - c.2250 BC

From the currently available archaeological evidence, the 1,300 year period of development of the Liangzhu culture jade working tradition was the ideas laboratory and principal development powerhouse in China throughout that period.

The culture area consists of the lower reaches of the Yangzi River, and comprises essentially flat and richly silted agricultural land shot through with an extensive and ancient canal communication system and also embracing several huge lakes.

The area covers the environs of Lake Tai in Jiangsu Province, and extends in influence at least north to some extent into Anhui Province and west to the Nanjing area on the Yangzi River.

The eastern border is the sea at Shanghai with its important suburban Liangzhu settlement of Fuquanshan. The southern extension currently identified includes Hangzhou, the Zhejiang Province capital in whose vicinity are the major sites including, firstly in modern times the eponymous village of Liangzhu, and also the nearby magnificent royal or priestly cemetery at Fanshan with

associated cemetery at Yaoshan, both at Yuhang town 25 kilometers to the north west of Hangzhou.

The short winters of this region are very cold but followed by an early spring which leads in a summer of great heat and 24 hour high humidity. The conditions are excellent for agriculture without undue effort and it is therefore not surprising that the inhabitants of this region in the neolithic period were clearly wealthy and developed from this base of riches ethereal contemplations of philosophy, the supernatural, religion and graphic art which are all so evident in their amazingly sophisticated artefacts in jade.

The uniform structure of excavated Liangzhu tombs finds them situated at a fairly shallow level sunk into the flat tops of low rise but laterally extensive burial hillocks or mounds. In the course of time, the small or low hill structure of each site has frequently been given a local place name which includes the word "Shan" meaning hill.

Sometimes each tomb contains a few objects and sometimes there are hundreds in the tomb. The Liangzhu people also made very distinctive ceramics which are beyond the scope of this catalogue and the interested reader is strongly urged to study the shapes and surface patterns of these which were very well represented in the 1992 Hong Kong exhibition catalogue of the Shanghai Fuquan Shan Liangzhu finds in 70.

Many of the tombs discovered in the last 15 years have been undisturbed since the time of original burial. They demonstrate a careful arrangement of burial objects which punctilious excavation has been able to identify in a particular order and style. To some extent the identity and detail of burial objects varies from place to place in the Liangzhu region but there do seem to be certain basic rules about tomb organisation and arrangement which indicate with reasonable certainty a prescribed formula of intention presumably the product of strong centrally imposed religious or ritual precept. In certain positions in certain tombs there are traces of red relict stain or powder whose exact identity is not clear but may in fact also be the remains of lacquer. In many tombs, but not all, there is evidence of burning. This evidence indicates that sometimes the entire tomb and its contents were subjected to general conflagration. In other tombs it is clear that only certain of the buried artefacts were burnt.

Clearly the body of the deceased was the central focus of grave goods arrangement. The general practice is to place certain artefacts above the head. *Bi-discs* have been found liberally arranged over the chest and stomach interspersed with the long form *cong*. A very interesting artefact also found in the stomach area in certain burials is a form of belt hook or buckle which was presumably the fastening mechanism for some type of garment or belt long since perished. The particular interest of this artefact perhaps lies in the fact that it was not to appear again as an item of fastening apparel until, again made of jade, during the Warring States period of the late Eastern Zhou dynasty.

In certain select graves, the three typical jade pieces associated with the *Yu* axe have been found. These three pieces were in each case clearly arranged upon a wooden handle which has long perished. They consist of an upper end jade finial, the blade itself set at a point about one quarter down the handle from the upper finial, and, lastly, a bottom end haft terminal or finial made of jade which is found in or near the left hand. The arrangement suggests that the corpse was buried with the axe and handle held in the slope position extending from the hand at waist level to lie up and upon the shoulder.

Around the foot area of the corpse were frequently arranged *bi-discs*, axes of stone and pottery vessels. *Yu* axes made of stone are quite commonly found around the foot area but never in the shoulder slope position. This may indicate a ritual need for burial of the axe blade shape under regulations which found it acceptable for the stone form to be used at the feet and the jade form to be used for the shoulder slope position and, sometimes, upon the chest.

In some burials jade artefacts have been found inside earthenware containers beside the body. In most circumstances where jade is found, it constitutes by far the bulk of the grave goods.

One interesting factor which is also very apparent in Liangzhu tomb excavated jades is the fact that many pieces found are clearly broken pieces of other things which have, in the Liangzhu times predating the burial, been recut or fashioned into new, smaller, artefacts.

Jade forming, as it does, such a rich and extravagant tomb asset, it is also interesting to note that by no means every Liangzhu burial contains jades and its presence, in greater or lesser quantity, or its absence, in a tomb seems clearly to indicate in some way the relative status of the occupant in the society of his day.

A brief examination of the various kind of jade artefact found in Liangzhu tombs shows the basic group types to be firstly, weapons or tools such as the *yu* axe, secondly, ritual objects such as the *bi-disc* and the *cong*, thirdly, ornamental pieces such as pendants whether for ritual or personal use, and fourthly, a subgroup of ornamental pieces which are clearly associated only with ritual.

Both the *yu* axe as a tool form, and the battle axe as a weapon form have been found. The former has a rounded blade and the latter has an elongated blade with sides incurving on the blade edge to the butt. See Exhibit 34. Although the former type is slightly thicker than the latter, both of these types are thin flat blades normally having a single double bevel hole drilled together from each side in a median position near the butt. The edge of the butt is often not well finished and squared off as in Dawenkou and Longshan culture *yu* axe blade. This failure fully to finish such a piece marks a refreshing, perhaps human, lapse in the midst of such general technical excellence. The distinction between the pillowed camber to the blade edge from a thick central axis in the Liangzhu culture axe blade in contrast to the much thinner and finer plaque type form of the Dawenkou and Longshan culture axe blade edges in a lunated shape has been drawn above in this catalogue. As mentioned above, the current surmise is that the blade itself was inserted into a wooden handle and then lashed around with cord. One blade has been excavated with traces of a reddish line representing the remnant of a diagonally lashed rouge impregnated cord passing through the central double bevel hole and across the surface of the blade for connection to the haft.

Small personal ornament forms are common and represented by round ball and cylinder shape beads, minature *cong* beads with large eyed animal mask form, *jue* slit disc earrings, quan tube form beads and round *zhu* beads. Cylindrical pendants, very small, delicately made, hole pierced button forms and thick ring bangles are also found.

The most singular and innovative pendant shape can be likened to something between a seaman's net or sailmaker's awl and an Egyptian obelisk. One extremity ends in a fairly blunt point and the other in an extension of reduced diameter which often, but not always is delicately pierced with a biconical bore hole analogous with the rear end thread hole of an awl. These pieces can be four faced with a square cross section (Exhibit 40) or round with a circular cross section and either type can be plain along its shank or with one or more registers of god or animal masks. These have been basically excavated in bunches of between three to nine pieces in varying lengths and found on the upper area of the skull which may have meant a symbolic feather representation on a head dress of the kind worn by the god like being depicted on the lunette pendants and on the trapezoid pendants mentioned below. These pieces vary in length between three and twenty centimeters. There is also a variant form in which the reduced diameter extension is not pierced but fits into a very carefully made jade cylindrical cap tube and there is no helpful guidance yet on the reason for this.

Two kinds of broad form flat ornament have been found.

The first of these takes the form of a trapezoid whose shorter side or edge is formed as a flange or tenon which is usually pierced with three holes. See Exhibits 35 to 37 inclusive.

The second of this type is a half moon form which has a gentle cambered blunted blade edge around the perimeter of the hemisphere. The straight centre side sometimes has a small middle indentation like a very slight part hole remnant and sometimes does not have this feature.

The trapezoid type with the tenon seems clearly to have been made for insertion into some form of slit hole or orifice. In the context of in situ excavation, it appears from long wood fibre traces and red, possibly lacquer stain, remnants that the trapezoid tenon formed the crowning feature of a wooden tablet which was painted with red lacquer or red stain and which has now long decomposed away. Sometimes very small lenticular pieces of jade are found in the area of the reddened earth suggesting that the lacquered wooden board was studded with small jade seeds. The trapezoid is normally solid and flat and often plain with no incised work. Alternatively, some examples have a relief or incised design of monster mask and, exceptionally such as with Exhibit 37, the trapezoid is cut through with intricate openwork designs which are themselves incised with monster or animal mask forms and human god-type images with long and extended arms weaving through the design. One nearly related type is very much in a pig appearance with a blunt snout and large oval shaped saucer eyes and a distinctly domed skull profile. Exhibit 38 is a good example and it is to be noted that this type also has the tenon extension indicating that it was perhaps also somehow set into a wooden plaque or totem.

The lunette form of ornament can be either plain as on the left side of Exhibit 31, or carved in relief with a big eyed face. In some tombs a set of four of these pieces with very fine working has been found at the top of the skull placed at equal distances apart around the circumference of the head. On the plain rear face of each piece are drilled sew hole channels which indicate arrangement and use on a headdress or head. As briefly mentioned above, one further very distinctive artefact among Liangzhu jades is a jade belt hook associated with a textile context. So far, these have not been found in stone and it may therefore be that there was no

alternative, lesser, form of this object in any kind of use and its appearance in Liangzhu times can be associated only with the most lavish ritual or luxury.

Just as the north China neolithic cultures developed what appear to be unique ritual forms such as the cloud-scroll plaque type, so the Liangzhu culture developed its own unique ritual forms. By far the most important and inventive of these is the *cong*.

The *cong* normally takes the form of a cylinder which is enclosed, in short forms by a square sided box, and in long forms by a rectangular box, in each case of square section conforming to the diameter of the cylinder enclosed by the box.

This form definitely appears to have its birth in the Liangzhu period and culture. It also appears to have died essentially as a living tradition with the Liangzhu culture because the Liangzhu form *cong*, subject to some discussion of this question in this catalogue and in some other writings, does not survive the end of the Liangzhu period. For the next 2,000 years however, the basic form of the *cong*, but plain faced and without the Liangzhu type of ornamentation, remains as a very significant ritual shape in Chinese jade. This significance climaxes to the point that the late Zhou dynasty writings in books such as the Zhouli, ascribed to the *cong* and the *bi* certain ritual perceptions and colour coded functions which appear now to us to be rather the inherited product of long evolutionary deviation away from pristine understandings and practices, than an accurate and informed inheritance of truth.

Except for the stone example of the Shixia culture mentioned below, the *cong* is only made from jade. No matter what the period, no other stone, and no metal in later periods, was ever used. There is a single, perhaps rather scholarly exception to this rule which is the production of the *cong* form in the Song Dynasty period in monochrome glazed ceramic and there are well known examples in Guan, Ge and Longquan Celadons of the Song dynasty but these seem clearly to have been made with an eye to respect for the shapes of history, rather than for any utilitarian purpose or in acknowledgement of any ritual precept.

Excavated burials show that the *cong* was always buried with males. It has been found in the tombs of males of all ages. Some of the tombs show evidence of human sacrifice. It is true that on balance most *cong* are found in larger tombs with an associated preponderance of ritual jade contents.

A single heavy circular bracelet form dating from approximately 3000 BC has been found at Zhanglingshan, Wuxian, Jiangsu Province. Around the circumference of this bracelet is a series of four raised level angle masks of an animal character. They are equally placed around the external perimeter of the bracelet and each is separated by a blank, unworked, area.

The very simple, rather crude, but strong structural organisation of the animal mask, with a distinctive inverted ogival shape, follows very closely the shape of the mask with goggle eyes on the *cong* bead Exhibit 71 in this catalogue. It is currently rather difficult to rationalise but the current view of the Wuxian animal mask bracelet is that it may represent the prototype for the *cong* form because, on carbon dating basis, this piece is one of the oldest *cong* forms yet discovered.

If this is true, it may be correct to regard the Wuxian piece as an ornamented bracelet - but commencing a transition to a higher, much more sophisticated innovation for exclusively religious or ritual purposes which became the *cong*.

Following this line of thought, the separated animal masks begin to form corners which cause the mask to be arranged as a bisected angle feature traversing across the squared corner of the surrounding box element of the *cong*. The space between each mask, on what in some *cong* remains the body of the circle, is a blank area centrally placed between the inner borders of the corner angle feature. This space becomes a very precisely made vertical channel or groove up and down the midway vertical axis of each side of the box.

Having set the basic directional evolution of a cylinder enclosed by a squared edge box of either square or rectangular shape, there was a further evolution which divided clearly between the rectangular form box on the one hand, and the square form box on the other hand, each of which continued to enclose a cylinder. In the rectangular box form each vertical squared corner face is a drawn out rectangle in shape and the cylinder did not always project out from each end of the piece and can be regarded in some cases as being reduced to a broad central perforation through the length of the piece leaving only a relatively thin walled cylinder passing through the rectangular squared corner box.

All evidence indicates that the central perforation of all types of *cong* was made from each end of the cylinder resulting in a central join. In the shorter, square form cong, this is usually polished out. In the longer, rectangular form *cong*, this is not polished out and the central join is clearly obvious in all cases.

The short square type of *cong* is wider than it is high. Each vertical squared corner face is approximately square in shape. This type is normally divided into two horizontal registers or layers of the corner angle feature. The corner angle feature assumes the form of an animal mask traversing the actual corner to lie across with eyes represented on each flat side. It is frequently the case that the mask on the upper register corners will feature a pair of round small incised eyes while the lower register mask will feature a pair of much larger, oval or saucer shaped eyes. See Exhibit 39.

The tall, rectangular box type of *cong*, has a greater height than width. This is never formed with the oval, saucer shape of eye but usually either without eyes at all or with the small round incised type of eye appearing either on every divided register or layer of the piece or, sometimes, on alternate layers or registers only. This squared rectangular form type has been found in considerable numbers arranged along the length of the body in some tombs.

Both of these types developed gradually during the Liangzhu period and were clearly a highly important element of ritual or religion in regard to burial. What is clear however is that the most skilled and elaborate work and detail was applied to the short form cong leaving the long form *cong* as a form whose basic message and meaning are in its shape and dimension and not in its applied decorative elements.

Some of the squared rectangular face type are very large extending up to 30 or more centimetres in length. In this type, one end is wider than the other. It was long considered that the narrower end was the upper end but due consideration of the animal faces across the corner angles, with the assistance of the different forms from recent excavations of both long and short types, has now clearly established that proper visual arrangement of the animal faces on each register or layer of the long form *cong*, requires that the broad end must be uppermost.

Of all the Liangzhu jade types, the *cong* and the openwork trapezoid plaque, reflect the most ingenious design and excellence of jade working achievement. This may acknowledge the fact of the importance of the function of these pieces because both types show the incised representation of a humanoid figure with a head formed as an inverted trapezoid shape topped with a feather or sun-ray headdress and with double concentric circle goggle eyes. In the openwork trapezoid plaque, the humanoid is flanked by what may be wolf or, possibly, alligator heads with long, extended snouts and the same double circle concentric goggle eyes but, this time, each side having a small "nick" representing the canthus. The Lower Yangzi River alligator, rare today, is an indigenous denizen of the Liangzhu area. See Exhibits 36 and 37.

On one particular famous short form *cong* found at Fanshan there is a representation of the small-eyed humanoid surmounting and enfolding with extended arms the oval eyed head, much bigger than itself, of a creature whose feet with curving talons are drawn in together beneath its mouth. Some writers have seen this representation of the small incised form of the eye in the humanoid creature taking a superior position over the much larger oval eye form as being the depiction of god in a position of absolute domination over the animal world represented by the mythical beast with oval eyes - a semblance discerned also in the placing of the small eyed cross-corner angle mask in the upper register of the two register *cong* over the oval, concave eyed, mask across the corner angle of the lower register. Much further thought and research is necessary to move on with identifying exactly what animals are depicted in these works but, bearing in mind the rare pig form of trapezoid plaque in

Exhibit 38 with the oval saucer eyes, coupled with the obvious importance of the pig in the lives of the Liangzhu people, it may well be the pig which is represented by the beast face on the lower register of the two level *cong*.

As mentioned in the Songze section the *bi-disc* was developed in the Songze culture but it saw its major development as a ritual jade during the Liangzhu culture. The Liangzhu jade workers produced very large jade *bi-discs* which were entirely plain and undecorated. See Exhibit 32. These very large *bi-discs* appear to be unique to Liangzhu among all neolithic cultures. As mentioned above in the section in Dawenkou culture, there are Liangzhu type *bi-discs* which are incised with the Dawenkou bird emblem and with the other famous Dawenkou symbols for the sun and moon. Although there has not yet been an actual archaeologically excavated Liangzhu *bi-disc* with bird or symbol incising, there are long gathered pieces in the Shanghai Museum and more recently gathered pieces in Hangzhou which are undoubtedly made by the Liangzhu culture and feature these designs. Conversely, no jade *bi-disc* has been excavated in Shandong, the Dawenkou culture area, with these incised designs which are standard of incised design work upon Dawenkou earthenware.

The majority of Liangzhu *bi-discs* are found around the feet of the deceased but there are burials in which they are placed both beneath and on top of the torso.

Another singular design form of jade artefact unique to the Liangzhu culture is a form of trident with the oval, saucer eyed animal mask design in light relief. These trident pieces are normally found on the upper part of the skull. The central prong of the trident is backed with a vertical hollow tubular projection which might have been intended for the insertion of feathers as part of a headdress.

For reasons which are not yet clear, very simple and strong representations of other members of the animal kingdom appear in Liangzhu jades. These range from a very typical and unique form of aerodynamic spread-wing flying bird with pointed beak held directly to the fore and with the flat head featuring goggle eyes in low relief. This kind of bird has been found with an elaborate stringball form of design which has also been used on the square form two register *cong*. It has been suggested by one scholar that this design may be taken to represent feathers when used on birds and to represent fur or hair when used on animal forms.

In the Fanshan burials were found a very small number of fish, flat turtle with head extended forward and feet to each side, a flat cicada and one almost three dimensional piece of a very simplified perching bird, again of the thrush form type.

By means which are still something of a mystery, the workmanship of Liangzhu jades is extremely accomplished. Every surface of every piece is absolutely finished on all angles and with an overall high gloss. The resulting surface can be compared with bean curd or *dou fu* in the east and with junket in the west.

Parallel line work structured in contiguous bands of four or five together are individually no more than one millimeter across and executed with a technical perfection which is a challenge even today. There is as yet no well rationalised study of the manufacturing technique used to such remarkable affect by the Liangzhu jade workers.

A further very important aspect of the designs incised onto Liangzhu jades is that they, together with designs incised upon ceramic forms, represent the only contemporary drawing which has come down to us from those times. A full consideration of the subject is beyond the scope of this catalogue but there seems little doubt that the fanged fury of the composite stringball incising animal mask on Exhibit 36 in this catalogue is a leading candidate for the origin of the *taotie* mask of Shang and Zhou art. From the ogival centre of Exhibit 36 it is possible to imagine the drawing down of a vertical line and the banding of the piece about this vertical axis to create an angled animal mask which would lie across the corner angle of the lower register of the square form two register *cong*. The large round-form eyes of the *taotie* mask in Exhibit 36 are already in place to justify and support this interpretation.

As mentioned elsewhere, Liangzhu burial jades have no trace or evidence of use or wear. There are no chips, no scratches, no bruises and the perfect bean-curd gloss shines smoothly throughout. All the indications of this are that these pieces were made for the most delicate and punctilious ritual use for persons of the highest importance while they were alive, and then buried with that person after death. As mentioned in the section, Working with Jade, in this catalogue, Liangzhu pieces often exhibit swing saw cutting marks or scars of a curved shape.

The largest Liangzhu jade artefacts are the long rectangular form *cong* and the large *bi-discs*. From these huge pieces, there is a range of sizes down to the minute almond shaped chips which seem to have been embedded in the wooden plaque-form totems topped by the trapezoid plaques. The normal dimensional profile of Liangzhu jades, apart from the container form of the *cong*, is flat and low. The holes in Liangzhu jades are normally biconical drilled together from opposing faces. On the walls of deeper holes, such as the boring through the length of the *cong*, there is some trace of ridging on the walls of the holes.

One sculptural note is very strange as regards Liangzhu jade working. Despite proficient work in three dimensional jade production as early as the Zhaobaogou and Hongshan Cultures in north China at a much earlier time, there is, apart from the single small bird found at the Fanshan excavation, no excavated three dimensional Liangzhu jade sculpture. This fact is remarkable given the ease with which the Liangzhu jade workers were able to deal in technically minute ways with a flat surface of jade. Somehow, and for reasons not clear, they do not seem to have been able, or perhaps willing, to rise up to the production of working around different levels and circumference of a piece to create a free standing sculpted product.

6. SOUTH COASTAL PROVINCES - GUANGDONG SHIXIA 石峡 c. 3000 - 2000 BC

The name site for the Shixia culture has been reported as being approximately 30,000 square meters in area in a hilly region in the northern part of Guangdong Province inland from Hong Kong. There is no doubt that settled agriculture of a kind as advanced as any in contemporary neolithic China was well established at Shixia.

Given the great breadth and drama associated with the findings in archaeological excavations of neolithic sites in China over recent years, the Shixia culture could perhaps be described as routine but this routine is shattered by a very significant matter which was the use of the *cong*. Both types of the traditional Liangzhu form of *cong*, the rectangular face form and the square face form, have been found in Shixia burials. Each type also respectively replicates the Liangzhu corner angle small eyed human face and saucer-eyed animal face Liangzhu models although the saucer form of eye is incised only in the specimens known so far and not rendered in bas relief like the majority of Liangzhu examples. One very significant difference however from the Liangzhu *cong* is that the Shixia *cong* are made of a light grey silicaceous stone. There has been no excavated jade *cong* from the Shixia culture. As a side note however it is very interesting to consider the important find in about 1983 of neolithic jade artefacts not currently thought to be the products of the Liangzhu culture - in a sandy site on the beach above the high watermark at Tinkeng town, Hei Feng County on the coast of Guangdong. Artefacts on this site included *cong* and these were made of fine light green jade material.

Returning to the Shixia *cong*, there is one further important distinction from the Liangzhu *cong*. As has been well demonstrated, all Liangzhu *cong* in excavated circumstances are in pristine condition without damage as if either looked after with great care during life and carefully placed in the burial, or as if made specifically for burial and carefully placed in the grave. There are some exceptions but Shixia Stone *cong* are extremely worn and smoothed at the corners. All sharpness of definition on squared corners is smoothed down on certain pieces. The effect is not simply one of showing a certain, limited, amount of use but rather indicates the subjection of the piece to a substantially stressful function which has left great wear, scratches and scars.

There must be a significant explanation for this distinction but the answer must abide further research and contemplation. There is

however also a fine polish on the surface of some pieces of Shixia *cong* in the same manner as in the Liangzhu jade *cong* and there is a little doubt that, despite the very small numbers of *cong* found in Shixia tombs in comparison to the numbers found in the tombs of Liangzhu, their use was a funerary or religious one and the general date period from approximately 2500 BC coincides with the late Liangzhu period. To date however there is no evidence of actual communication between the lower Yangzi River basin of the Liangzhu area and the areas of northern Guangdong. For one thing, there are many ranges of difficult mountains between the two areas. The Guangdong coastal finding of Liangzhu quality jade *cong* however may perhaps indicate a sea route linking central and southern China and greater evidence of this would enable entirely new perspectives of neolithic communication lines across the Chinese landmass.

E. ERLITOU PERIOD JADES
c. 1900 - 1600 BC

We have now seen a slow evolution of quality in both the conceptualisation and execution of neolithic jade working over the period of 3,000 years commencing, on current knowledge, with the Xinglongwa culture. The raising of jade to a secure pinnacle in the social order of man was already well entrenched during the Zhaobaogou culture and the Hongshan culture. Very strong, simple shapes and three dimensional forms with little surface work of the Hongshan culture developed into the minutely drawn detail of, incised working on predominantly flat surfaces of the Liangzhu culture with its lavish artistic licence. This itself in turn somehow tailed away except where retained in rudimentary form in the Dawenkou and Longshan cultures which themselves developed the hook-form edge projection work and style and broad strap-form openwork plaques while the mainstream reverted to the extremely elegant simplicity of the *dao* and the *Zhang*. We have seen the Liangzhu culture engender the astonishingly rapid rise and development of the god and beast engraved *cong* form and we have also seen its equally dramatic subsidence from mandatory ritual pre- eminence. We have seen jade was a popular material of personal adornment form as ear-rings, necklaces, belt hooks, beads and bracelets. By the beginning of the third millenium BC, the Jade Age had established itself, as had jade itself, as a non-luxurious demonstration of perfect quality, essence and balance in the eyes of society generally from top to bottom.

Now, however, neolithic man was on the threshold of a revolution which was to change forever the developed order of society and this was the beginning of the Bronze Age in China over the gradual period commencing perhaps as early as c.2200 - 1600 BC. The beginnings of bronze casting in China wrought huge and permanent changes, principally through the application of bronze to military production because the state that mastered the production of bronze weapons would briskly and decisively vanquish any opposing state in war. There was clearly a need for all states to take up and exploit the new medium of bronze production as quickly as possible and without any delay. Accordingly, by the true end of any remnant of the neolithic period in about 1600 BC, bronze was already an extensively applied medium for production of vessels of various kinds and of weapons of war.

The development of bronze weapon technology particularly was rapid because of the war tested efficiency of the new medium and tremendous economic state resources were set aside and specifically dedicated to bronze production. This seems to have been at all times with the common consent and understanding of the various peoples of the individual bronze producing states - most likely because of the obviously inevitable alternative of decimation without the new material.

In terms of the organisation of society, the traditional Chinese perception of these times invests them with the emergence of the first fully co-ordinated Han Chinese dynastic structure popularly known for at least 2,500 years as the Xia dynasty. In fact, the origin of a dynasty called Xia is wreathed in many shadows and myths and there are many scholars who doubt that such a dynasty existed at all.

What is possible to trace from this period is a distinct leap forward through the rapid adoption of bronze for production of the technical equipment available to the jade worker for easier working of more technically sophisticated jade forms and designs. The principal base site for the period discovered to date is at Erlitou Yanshi Xian in Henan Province which is about 100 kilometres west of Zhengzhou towards Loyang. This being the definitive principal Erlitou culture site, has given its name to the culture. Based upon excavated finds from Yanshi, further sites of the Erlitou period have been identified at what is now Zhengzhou, the provincial capital of Henan Province which is situated on a bend of the Yellow River south of Shaanxi and Shandong Provinces.

The Erlitou period is currently thought to extend from approximately 1900 to c.1700 BC. Erlitou jades can clearly be shown as an evolution from styles and forms of the

Liangzhu and Shandong Longshan cultures. For the first time also in the history of the slow development of jade carving in China, the artefacts of the Erlitou period demonstrate the broad future course of development by the simple fact of aggregation into a single stream of the diverse and widespread neolithic cultural forerunners.

Although it seems that the social position of jade was not at all disturbed by the advent of bronze as a new material of luxurious and expensive creation, there was clearly now an alternative, much more easily produced medium of three dimensional expression. It is very significant that the two materials rapidly developed a symbiotic relationship such that innovative designs in bronze began to be suggested in jade while the continued development of certain innovations in jade gave birth to new bronze designs. Perhaps through greater ease of incised line forming with new rotary tools of bronze, established jade forms such as the *dao* and *ge* blades began to be decorated on the surface with incised line striations. See Exhibit 75. Openwork cutout projections sprouted from the sides of axe blades, from the hilt of the Zhang in some very elaborate forms and, in a more reticent way, from the angled twin ends of the *dao* blade and from the hilt of the jade *ge*.

Across the breadth of the squared blade edge of axe and adze forms however the lunette shaped hollow ground form of the Dawenkou/Longshan culture has gone and the edge has taken on a gradual cambered form.

Erlitou excavations have yielded up magnificent, elegant and sometimes very large blades of the types mentioned above. These buried jades represent the essence of achieved maturity of the neolithic jade worker's craft and art. They also demonstrate in themselves a continuing subscription by the immediate heirs of the Longshan people to the supreme importance of jade for funerary ritual. This point can accordingly be identified as the terminus of the already ancient and quietly inexorable development of jade through egg, larva, crysalis or pupa to final maturity.

A classic Erlitou handle in columnar form excavated at the Yanshi site has a sectioned structure of separate bands or registers of different decoration. The two principal registers show, in the direct Liangzhu tradition, a cross corner angle structure of a human face whose relief details are characterised by fairly low, but very strong and positive actual raised lines. This time however, the corner wrap around face has a long garlic-head nose wrapped around the very corner of the piece and eyes which have diamond-shaped canthus extensions at each side instead of the oval or saucer forms of Liangzhu. Furthermore, their drawn physiognomical characteristics are executed in raised-line detail which more closely follows a Shandong Longshan precept in place of the Liangzhu incised concave bas relief. These features, particularly the vivid and strong linear assemblage of the structure of the face upon a uniformly reduced level surface with its inverted "banana mouth" draws heavily and effectively upon, and is well accentuated by, the plainness of the open bud form of two of the alternating handle sections while the human face registers can almost be said to represent the evolved inheritance from the Liangzhu tradition of cross-corner face albeit now already degenerate and of little value for the study of later periods in jade art historical terms.

Intermediate registers on the same Yanshi handle take the appearance of exterior cladding in a structure of broad leaf-forms each with an everted spiked tip on the upper end. This form, adopting exclusively the broad leaf type of register, developed into a standard in the Shang dynasty and, in a much simplified and flat-form survived into the Western Zhou dynasty. Two very interesting examples from a Western Zhou excavation at Baoji, Shaanxi Province are published in 22, pls 51 and 52 and show what at that time was the actual use of the shape in practice. Of particular interest is their abuttal up against an extension section of small inlaid turquoise and jade pieces but there is no evidence that this arrangement had a neolithic or Erlitou precursor. However the Yanshi piece from Erlitou period is the only one known to exhibit the human face registers and also to combine them with the leaf form.

Of particular interest for comparison with the execution of facial structure and details of this Erlitou handle is firstly Exhibit no. 70 in this catalogue. This is a small but extremely powerful bead in the direct *cong* tradition carved in uniform low relief with a long, lugubrious human face across each squared-corner angle and whose nose treatment and strong relief eyes are very close in feeling to the faces on the Yanshi handle - particularly reflecting the angled canthus extending and drawing out the opposite corners of the eyes.

Exhibit 74 is another piece whose raised-line formation of eyes with extended angle canthus and asymmetrical organisation around a basic triangular plaque-shape shows much similarity with Exhibit 70 and yet in fact occupies a wholly more complex, beautiful and much rarer overall production quality and impact.

Firstly, the back of the neck in Exhibit 74 is worked with a diagonal groove arrangement almost as if to represent thickly stranded or braided hair, perhaps hanging down from inside the elaborate headdress worn by the figure.

Secondly, the structure of the headdress is an elaborate complex of detail expressed by way of minutely organised very finely executed true raised-line design work with a hook meander structure. The creation of this formation involves reduction and lowering of the entire surface of the piece all around the very refined and delicate remnant which is intended as, and is in fact constituted by, the raised-line feature standing proud from the reduced area. On the back of the cheek on each side of the head there is a finely formed, enclosed hook. The nose is large, extending from between modelled cheek bones and the generous, yet not exaggerated mouth and the lips resemble very closely the structure of the mouths of the corner-angle elongated faces on Exhibit 70 referred to above. Although perhaps beginning to adopt an angularity of style that is discernibly more disciplined than the smoothly curving hook and curl motifs both in field and round the perimeter of dateably earlier pieces such as the Shandong Longshan and Shijiahe demonic masks, it is distinctly possible to relate the features of Exhibit 70 to development from the latter - in fact to categorise them as the high point of the style. While it is therefore possible to consider the beginning of the Bronze Age as a sustainable theoretical backdrop to the contemporary Erlitou jade artefacts, it is necessary to indicate the maintained evolution of already existing jade forms and decorative motifs which, together, with ceramics in hollow vessel context were the only available exemplary foundation for the origin of the bronze casters' art.

It seems reasonably clear that there is quite a good case to be made out for, firstly, establishment of bronze rotary tools which were used for the Yanshi handle. Apart from the wondrously fine incised line detail work of the Liangzhu culture, there was no previous neolithic jade using culture of any consequence which brought the line as such, whether raised or incised, to such a high point. Later in the Shang period, jade carvers produced very typical block or chunky form figures decorated only with the celebrated "false raised" lines. Exhibit 85 is an example in the larval form of an insect. It can accordingly be seen that the simple and lazy degeneracy of the false raised line in jade carving securely dateable to the Shang dynasty's Anyang phase, argues well for the much earlier actual origination of the raised line as a feature of the Late Longshan to early Erlitou periods. If so, and if the examples here are representative, it would represent a virtuoso achievement which degenerated over several centuries into the Anyang phase in the 14th and 13th centuries BC.

The very strange, but true fact that the most magnificent and elegant blades - which could easily be made of the newly proficient bronze material only and which have been excavated at Erlitou - are made of jade, indicates something of the continuing tenacity of the importance of jade in terms of funerary ritual. The simplicity, grace and strength of these jades are not the production of an innovative infancy but clearly the natural progression of a civilising imperative with already very old and distinguished roots which we have examined above. In their total sophistication, they contrast very clearly and very interestingly, with the still crude and primitive contemporary artefacts in bronze whose progression to later magnificence had obviously only just begun.

So far archaeologically secure excavation of the Erlitou period has not revealed the *cong* form which is very remarkable given the paramount importance accorded to it in the Liangzhu culture and its continued use, though on a diminished and entirely less lavish, restrained, basis, in the Shang and Zhou dynasties.

Erlitou jade workmanship is characterised by very large blade forms worked with fine incised diamond hatched lines (see Exhibit 75) and long striations and if the above raised-line hypothesis is accurate, with some of the finest raised line work of any jade period. The material ranges from opaque moss-green to semi- translucent off white and it is presumed that local sources supplied it. The dimensional planes so far ascertained are flat forms with occasional squared rod types such as the handle discussed above. Erlitou holes are of the simple cone shaped type drilled from one side.

Angus Forsyth
January 1994

興隆洼文化至二里頭時期

A. 簡介 —— 玉器時代

現今，中國新石器時代玉器的研究，在利用了碳十四斷代法和熱釋光測試後，已可取得可信的結果。自中國解放後，尤其是在1980年間，在一群本土有經驗的專家領導下，就展開了持續的考古發掘和分析，對於一直被認為可能出現先於青銅器時代的玉器時代，提供了令人振奮的證據。多年以來，考古文化都是以其所發掘之遺址而命名，如浙江省的良渚村自1930年代起，就成為該區著名的新石器時代玉器文化。新遺址不斷的發現，無疑是會對過往文化分層的觀念有所改變，此情況在中國北方發展快速的考古工作中是很常見的。一些村落在過往十年因成為新石器時代文化的要址而命名，但其實在它們周圍，還有很多遺址是因發掘得較遲而跟隨其命名的。現時中國中原和南部的文化地圖已逐漸清晰，但是北方的則變化較大，尚未取到一個一致的系統。基於此原因，在本書出現的「中國北方新石器時代」這個詞，是指那些未能準確界定其所屬文化的遺物。新石器時代時間表裡(見第15-16頁)，已列出現今介定為新石器時代玉器文化的大約年期，以作參詳。

在古玉研究中，新石器時代傳統上是指在鐵器出現之前，採用磨蝕和鑽孔方法來處理不能切割的玉石之時期，此時期在考古上至遲可追溯到公元前1900年至1600年間之二里頭時期，而從最近的發掘，更可推斷到於公元前5000年。新石器時代開始的時候，人們似乎已放棄了游牧打獵，轉而定居下來，過著農耕的生活。由於定居聚集，村落亦因而誕生，此時的居民利用中國西面山脈河流沖積下來肥沃的泥土耕種。幾百年以來，中國人或是國際學者皆認為，漢人最初是在黃河流域定居，他們飽受河水泛濫的威脅，故黃河有"中國的憂患"之稱號。

最近考古學上的發現，對這種說法有所修訂。從現今所得的資料，我們可見在其它大型河流如長江流域或遼寧省與內蒙之間的遼河，都發現了人類聚居耕作、製作陶器和玉器的證據。

1993年8月，吉林大學的林雲教授在赤峰舉行的中國北方古代文化國際學術研究會上，發表了一篇想法新穎的文章。在此文裡，他提到中國東北部與貝加爾湖地區(西伯利亞中部與東部)在新石器時代文化上的交流。林教授指出了兩地新石器時代陶瓷在形制上的相似，至少可追溯到公元前8000年。此外，他亦進一步指出，米努辛斯克盆地和阿爾泰山在早期青銅器的次層文化上的相似。

在中國新石器時代裡，狗、豬、山羊、綿羊和牛都是被飼養的動物，而石造紡織器的發掘就是當時製衣的一個最佳證據。此外，我們亦發現到一些關於絲綢文化的証據。從游牧文化過渡到定居文化，葬禮的儀式也有所改變。這時器皿的製造未必純為實際使用，它們在設計上與表達上，反映了對宗教或薩滿教信仰和宗教禮儀的認可。同時，陶器上也開始出現了刻線和油彩的圖案設計，與以泥、石和玉作的立體雕塑，為未來的藝術發展邁開了第一步。

山東省大汶口文化陶器上那些重要的象形刻符和設計與部份新石器時代玉器的設計相似，但是很可惜它們並非來自科學的發掘，就算最近發現可能屬於浙江良渚文化的一件，也是在此情況下找到的。而其它已出土多年的器物，也可能是來自山東大汶口文化。然而，那些陶器上的象形刻符則肯定是從大汶口文化遺址考古發掘所得。一些學者認為，這些設計是中國早期文字上的發展，或者說至少是一種符號上的溝通。在1993年初的一份簡報裡，報導了山東省西南面之鄒平縣郊丁公村出土的一件屬公元2500年至2000年之陶器，器物上刻有十一個字母，分別以五行排列。中國的書寫是以象形刻符或表意系統為基礎，但據現今所知，有系統的象形刻符書寫，至少是在商代始出現。

巫鴻教授在1990年〈木扉〉的論文裡，把盤根錯節的傳說、文學、葬禮與考古資料聯繫起來，冀證明玉器時代的存在。此現象正好說明了玉器在古代社會觀念中並不單只是一種外貌美麗的珠寶，人們其實已懂得從另一層面去欣賞它，尤其把它與宗教祭祀拉上關係起來。

在原始時代的環境底下，玉器的製造需要涉及到大量的工序和社會上某一部份勞動力，這情況在當時的國家已是很普遍。巫教授在最近的考古發掘中，指出了〈禹貢〉中提到的四個州，即今遼寧省南部以至浙江地區為夷族所在地，他以為中國北部至東部是神話中所謂的鳥夷。如果這些不同的新石器時代傳說是屬實的話，那麼〈禹貢〉就證明了過往多層文化之特色。從緩慢的考古發現中(有些發現甚至是在巫教授1990年的論文後始出現)，顯示到玉器時代至少可追溯到夏代的3000年以前，但玉器時代的開端並不是在遼寧／浙江地區，而是在今天西北方的內蒙一帶。

考古上重要的發展繼續把玉器時代的始源推得更早，其中以1993年出版，有關中國社會科學院考古研究所楊虎教授與其隊伍在內蒙東南興隆洼文化村之發掘報告較為重要。此報告所論到的古玉，無可否認是當今中國所發掘到年代最久遠的玉器，它們與內蒙趙寶溝文化層的玉器有關，而趙寶溝文化層玉器，則是迄今與1980年代在紅山文化層的發現有關。趙寶溝文化層可鑑定為約公元前4800年至4000年，即是在紅山文化開始之前，比紅山文化的"高峰期"如著名的凌源牛河梁女神廟還要早約一千年之多。

由這些教人振奮的發現，與紅山文化那些殘破的玉器，我們可正式肯定紅山文化人並不是最早利用玉器作為統治國家制度的手段，他們只是承繼了一個更早期的遠古傳統。這傳統究竟維持了多久，並沒有明確的答案，惟有希望在未來中國北方的考古發掘中可得到線索。

B. 時間發展及地理分佈圖
中國主要使用玉器和受玉器影響之新石器時代文
約公元前6000年至公元前1700年
1. 使用玉器之新石器時代文化
中國北方和西北方 — 遼寧省和內蒙 — 中國北方
新石器時代
興隆洼　公元前5500年 — 5040年
趙寶溝　公元前4800年 — 4000年
查海　公元前4700年 — 3000年
紅山　公元前3500年 — 2200年
陝西省(中原)／黃河中游／中下游
仰韶　公元前4800年 — 3070年
半坡類型　公元前4800年 — 4200年
廟底溝類型　公元前3900年 — 3500年
秦王寨類型　公元前3400年 — 3000年
河南龍山　公元前2300年 — 1700年
黃河下游／山東省／江蘇北
大汶口　公元前4500年 — 2300年
花廳　公元前3800年 — 3000年
山東龍山　公元前2300年 — 1700年
長江中游 — 四川、湖北
大溪　公元前4000年 — 3300年
石家河　公元前2500年 — 2000年
長江下游盆地 — 太湖和中國中部東面(寧紹平原)
河姆渡　公元前5000年 — 4800年
馬家濱　公元前5000年 — 3900年
崧澤　公元前3800年 — 2900年
良渚　公元前3400年 — 2250年
2. 受玉器影響之文化
南部沿岸省份
廣東省
石峽　公元前3000年 — 2000年後期

3. 二里頭時期
河南省　約公元前1900年 — 1600年

C. 新石器時期
約公元前6000年 — 公元前1700年
簡介
頁26的地圖顯示了中國中原和東部主要氾濫平原和河谷地區的分別，它們是以低於600米和連綿山嶺劃分的，其中伸展至沿海地區的山嶺在600米以上是無法作原始耕種的。正如其它文章所言，黃河流域不再是中華民族的唯一搖籃，中國其它地方也是漢人文化的重要泉源。這些地區廣泛分佈，但主要是東面沿岸地區，從我們掌握的資料而言，就是由東北伸展至浙江上海一帶。早期居於遼河東面一帶的人民，他們在文化與藝術上都有很好的發展。玉器要發展成為具有高度價值是需要漫長的時間，唯一能令它攀升到更高的地位，就是將之作為尊貴的飾物，或是賦予它政治或宗教的意義。為了讓大家對這些新石器時代的器物有更透徹的了解，在此書中將會有它們的漢語拼音。此外，我們還會以簡單的線條，繪製各種器物的造型，以便解釋。

普遍而言，新石器時代的人對精神上的安寧似有一種莫名其妙的渴求。人類社會傳統上喜歡証明在信仰上的價值，而玉器在很早期便擔當了此角色。在早期的社會，人們已表現出對死人的尊敬。重要的一點是，除卻一些偶然的例子外，新石器時代玉器極少在居所或是重要的廟宇內發現。相反，在墓穴內則常發現大量高質素的玉器，這正好促成了中國人在禮葬上以適當的玉器去裝飾死者的身軀之習俗。在紅山文化的墓葬中，瓷器並不是和死者一起放在棺木內的，反而玉器則是和死者並放的。

在新石器時代，以玉器作為工具用途是很少見的。玉器是堅硬的材料，在鐵器未出現之前，它不被作為製工具之材料，確是一個奇怪的現象。玉器是一種很難處理的材料，它們是社會富裕之象徵，但卻因偏偏與墓葬有關連，是以長期被埋在地底下，而與社會隔絕。1985年在安徽省凌家灘出土的玉匙，在新石器時代的出土玉器中可說是獨一無二。此匙外貌突出，屬於良渚／龍山過渡類型，與中國當代標準之瓷匙形制相近，具有實際用途之價值。

新石器時代玉器的形制，有很多都是很複雜和精密的，相信它們的製造是要經過很小心的處理的。由於玉匠是要為死去的人服務來換取利益，我們有理由相信他們所付出的努力，是可在經濟上取得回報的。此時玉器的製造雖非為實際使用，每一件作品都需要成年累月的時間去完成，故此它們的製作速度是很緩慢的。這些玉匠肯定是社會勞動力重要的一部份，他們平時要以農耕飼畜來維持生活，但對神秘的超自然界事物也有認識。

頁15及16、24及25新石器時代的年表和地區分佈圖，顯示出某些年代與地區是有重複的。若順序觀察新石器時代不同地區主要的遺址，大約可見到是由中國東北發展至南部低於600米之地區。正如以往所述，中國其它地方在此時也有新石器時代文化之發展，但他們未必全部能在日常生活或墓葬中有系統地運用玉器。故為方便起見，此地圖只包括那些採用玉器的文化。

要考查不同玉器文化的相互作用，以及它們在藝術思想上溝通的渠道，相信還有很多工作要做。雖然這種情況並不普遍，但在廣東省北面的石峽遺址，則發現了一塊在形制上與良渚文化玉琮相同的石頭。此外，約公元前3000年前的後期良渚文化與山東龍山文化亦有相像之處。

在公元前2000年初，新石器時代之玉器文化基礎已變得成熟。後期夏人與商人擁有地理上和政治上之優勢，他們吸收了這些玉器文化之特色，從而發展調和成為自己的藝術形式。由此可見，新石器時代地域特色上的相似，應作為研究中國藝術統一之觀念的基礎。

D. 地區發展

1. 中國北方新石器時代 — 遼寧省/內蒙

(i) 興隆洼　公元前5500年 — 5040年

(ii) 趙寶溝　公元前4800年 — 4400年

(iii) 查海　公元前4700年 — 3000年

(iv) 紅山　公元前4700年 — 3000年

中國北方新石器時代玉器文化包括了東面遼寧省至朝鮮邊界，南面遼寧省錦州市和河北省北部，西面內蒙的東部和中部地帶。至於北面的劃界，至今依然未清晰，它有可能伸展至西北的蒙古和東北方的吉林和黑龍江省，甚至越過西伯利亞，到達伊爾庫茨克地區。在二次大戰之前後，蘇聯科學院的奧克拉德利科夫教授在此區的奧爾洪島上之布爾漢，就發現到公元前2000年的玉器文化。此文化繼承過往傳統，採優質白軟玉製玉璧的玉環。在1985年，亨利 • 米高在其論文 < 西伯利亞東部之新石器時代 > (參考書目52) 中描述了在新石器時代貝加爾區人所製的基托河谷綠色和白色軟玉，以及當時流行的綠色軟玉銷售到西方之情況。這些軟玉是運到本身出土灰綠色軟玉之地，如米努辛斯克盆地、葉利塞河平原和烏拉爾地區。據台灣國立故宮博物館的楊美莉女士對中國北方新石器時代觀察所得，當時的環形玉璧與遼東半島後期文化是互有聯繫的。

為方便研究起見，我們以內蒙西拉木倫河為中國新石器時代北面之邊界。西拉木倫河北面為蒙古沙漠，約於公元前1000年至3000年形成。地質上的考察顯示了現時之沙漠前身本為牧草原和一些人造林。過往，曾有在此沙漠地區發現紅山文化陶器之報告，這正好說明了紅山文化和其同型文化曾在這個昔日有農業定居之地出現過，它們的影響遠至大興安嶺以至西伯利亞遠東地區之邊界。故現今有需要為此作出科學上的考証。

新石器時代後期製造石鏟的傳統，並不是在中國所有地方可見，它只是局限在河北北部、遼寧、(可能在) 吉林和內蒙，這些地區同時以石鏟作為農業器具，令耕種有良好的收成，所以相信沒有一種石器會像它般受廣泛採用。

從我們現今所知，中國北方新石器時代文化區似乎是集中在赤峰一帶。赤峰現今為內蒙之行政區，其北面邊界為西拉木倫河和大興安嶺，南面邊界則伸展到承德市，即昔日滿清皇帝游獵之地。在八世紀至十一世紀之間，赤峰是契丹人的心臟地帶，他們在中國北方擁有強大勢力，直至1125年始被通古斯語族人殲滅。

在赤峰地區，至少已發掘到四個可辨認的新石器時代文化的遺存，它們 (若以時間順序排列) 包括了興隆洼 (公元前5500年至5040年)、趙寶溝 (公元前4800年至4400年)、紅山 (公元前4700年至3000年) 與夏家店下層文化 (公元前2000年至1600年)。此外，還有被認為是趙寶溝文化分支的查海文化，其遺址在遼寧省赤峰東南方之阜新市。

從考古上的證據清楚可見，在墓穴中發掘到的興隆洼文化玉玦和兩件玉鏟，是中國最早期的玉器製品。此外，我們還有更多證據證明趙寶溝文化有玉器之製造。如在寧鎮地區所得的趙寶溝玉蟬或昆蟲，其凸出的眼睛是以優質黃玉所製。有些以同樣材料製的玉玦，它們有扁身的、浮雕的和長筒形串飾的，內設刻線和凸線，在早期是尚未被確定的。

在1980與1981年，內蒙古巴林右旗那斯台遺址豐富的發掘，已認定為是趙寶溝時期，詳情載於1987年6月的〈考古〉內。此遺址為一居所，內裡的陶窰出產了一獨特之蹲身石像，以及百多件大部份是黃綠色的玉器，如蟬、鳥、魚、勾形頂飾、豬龍、蹄形管與鏤空雲狀掛飾，有一部份在發掘的時候，已經是磨損得很嚴重。毫無疑問，它們應屬於紅山文化，譬如牛河梁遺址，其可追溯之時期比以往所定的更早。
（見展品1標題）

從現今考古發現可見，多過一種文化曾在中國北方新石器時代地區出現，它們出現時期約是由公元前5500年（興隆洼）至公元前1600年（夏家店下層），其中興隆洼文化、趙寶溝文化、紅山文化顯示出純熟的製玉技巧，尤以後者擁有特殊的技術。由此可推斷，要揭示中國北方古文化在立體玉雕如玉人的成就，只不過是時間上的問題。實際上，在此地區曾出現過玉人雕塑，但由於不能肯定它在考古上的發展與由來，所以它並未在國內或國外發表過。上面所述的形制可能涉及到三種不同的文化，至今仍未能確定它們所屬的年期，故我們在此只作簡單的處理。

在上面已解釋過，"中國北方新石器時代"這詞只宜在意見分歧不大的情況下使用。有一點值得注意的是，雖然新石器時代是在青銅器時代之前出現，但我們知道至少有一個新石器時代文化除懂得製玉外，還曉得鐵器之製造。在此我們要感謝艾瑪•賓加女士鑒定一對在牛河梁遺址出土的銅耳環，此物外形簡樸，每隻均附有軟玉珠。

玉器文化的遺址在湖濱低地和低山嶺上均可見。

在1983年和1985年間，遼寧省牛河梁牛河發掘了大量廟宇的遺址。其中一幢結構精巧的土牆被推斷為廟宇的核心部份，牆上的灰泥外層已經剝落，當中的發現包括了以紅泥製的人體與屬於腿部之碎片、豬龍，似是以前宗教上被膜拜的塑像之遺跡。此建築物是建在山腰上，與山下的祭壇相距百多呎，位置是在多個被發掘到的淺穴和深穴之間。在深穴內之葬品中發現了紅山文化玉器，但是在紅山時期的居所和廟宇內則找不到該時的玉器。在一些墓穴裡，發現了多過一具屍體，這也許揭示了當時以活人殉葬的情況。在另外的一些墓葬裡，也有紅山文化類型玉器的發現，這些墓葬屬於附屬墓穴設計，位處小山之尖，每個與祭壇的距離相若。當中的玉器參差，有精工雕琢的，也有技術粗糙的、兼且已殘缺剝落。在這些墓葬中，不論是那些高質素的古玉，或是倉卒完工的粗糙玉器都是作為陪葬之用的器物。

在牧草場低地和小山之尖都可見墓穴遺址。

除了現在已知的興隆洼是一個有大量居所的城市遺址外，我們對其它文化的居所遺址的概念還是很模糊的。其中最令人感興趣的是在興隆洼文化中，有些墓穴是藏在居所內或不遠處。興隆洼文化墓葬的其中一特色，就是把豬隻和死者一起合葬。

紅山文化中最主要的考古發現是廟宇和墓葬，其中前者更顯示了建造石牆灰泥外層的先進技術。在這些考古發現中，我們發現了紅山人的豬浮雕和狗浮雕，豬在他們的社會是很受尊崇的。此情況除了在興隆洼文化出現之外，恐怕很難在其它文化中找到。在發掘到的紅山廟宇中，顯示了當時的建築已有塗色的灰泥牆和堅固的地板。

在廟宇的中殿又發現了已破碎的赤陶女像，她們有赤裸的也有穿衣的；有站立的也有坐臥的，不期然令人聯想起母系社會的情況。這些人像有部份是等身的三分二，她們展示了當時中國北方先進的泥雕塑技巧。據我們所知，這種藝術觸角從未在中國其它地方的文化像這般可維持一千或二千年。這些廟宇的範圍不算大，但內裡則藏滿殘破的遺存，故一般認為此處是密室之類的建設，應是用來擺放在禮儀中使用的塑像，每當儀式完畢後，塑像便會儲放在此密室內。

在紅山文化玉器中獨一無二的，可能是一種扁方形鏤空玉珮。物器的表面是挖成闊滑的紋坑，大部份此形制的物器都是精工完成的，底面有刻紋，但有些只是單面有刻紋，而且手工也較粗糙。

一些觀察家認為這些紋飾的靈感是來自雲，但是有些則認為是從爬行類動物設計而來。從以往發掘的墓穴可見，這些玉珮都是放在屍體頭部附近，或是放在其胸口上。曾經有推論指出這種玉珮是頭飾的一部份，而頭飾是以木或其他材料製成，現只因時日久遠而腐爛，當中有的體形巨大，直徑達22厘米。

另外也有小斧的發現。斧身呈三圓邊，第四邊為刃，底面都是經嚴格打磨的。此物器似是用於墓葬，給墓主人在死後使用的，它們並不像日常生活的用具。

管狀、腰狀和橢圓形的串飾是穿繫起來使用的，這些串飾前後鑽孔，貫通中間以便串連起來。

而常見的玉器如斜口錐形管（見展品27）橫切面呈橢圓狀，其底部有時或有穿孔，用途並不明確，被發現的時候是放在屍體的胸前，或是交叉擺放在腦後，當作頭枕之用。此種擺放方法暗示了它可能是頭飾的一種。但是大部份此類型玉器的體積都是很大的，其闊口甚至可容下一拳頭，故若作為頭飾佩戴是很不便的。然而，基於紅山玉器與墓葬的密切關係，有可能此玉器是純作陪葬用的，它的實際功用，對死者來說已經是毫不重要了。

此外有兩種扁身冠頂玉飾。第一種較少見，複環中心呈"8"字形，玉飾的尾部粗略完成，似可插嵌入有孔的木器內。

在牛河梁的墓葬中，發現了在死者骸骨的骨盆部份放有一薄身蝶形玉片。

第二種如展品18，是呈扁身勾尾狀的，其用途並不清楚。物器上亦刻有頗闊之坑槽，與鏤空的卷雲紋和玉珮上的大致一樣，此物器尾部為柄，手工粗疏，柄上穿孔以作穿掛用。與此物器同類的有展品17之長形鳥首器。

由於紅山文化玉器的出土處多為墓穴，而從未在居所遺址出現過，故此我們並不肯定目前找到的紅山玉器在日常生活上的用途。如果單以一件出土的紅山玉器去判斷它和祭祀的關係，是未免過於輕率。

玉三聯璧外型呈指節銅套狀，器身扁窄的底部有三個圈狀孔並列，可供手指插入以緊握。在物器每面的末端有一豬首，呈擺耳生動之態，正好説明了豬在當時社會上之價值，或牠在宗教上之意義，見展品21。其扁窄的底部有四個等距鑽孔，形似牛之鼻孔，觀其外型似是蓋或手柄多於似是武器。在1993年8月，筆者有幸在牛河梁遺址見過一件尚未發表，但是外型一樣的物器。這物器體形較少，有三個穿孔，兩末端各有人首之橫切面。假設展品21是換上了人首，那就會與上述的很相近。

動物紋無疑是一種引人注意的紋飾。在紅山文化中，"豬龍"是其中一種突出的玉器，它在當時可能已有發展。而直至公元前1300年的殷商安陽時期，"豬龍"在外形上始作出轉變。其實"豬龍"這名字是我們現代人後來加上去的，意指其扁平下額、巨大鼻孔、大眼兼扁闊耳廓之貌皆由豬的相貌而來。"豬龍"的高度為4毫米至15毫米。展品23是塊豬臉，在眾多展品中實屬少見，因動物紋在玉器中通常只充當作裝飾的一部份而已。

就玉器而論，紅山人墓穴中豬隻的骸跡是很重要的。在紅山文化時期，豬是極之重要的牲畜，牠們全都似是由人類飼養的。至於龍在早至中國新石器時代已經受人類的崇敬。而饒宗頤教授與其他學者都指出，紅山文化中的"豬龍"其實是中國龍的祖型。見展品24和25。在中華民族裡，龍是神秘的動物，牠往往被視作為帝王之命脈和人民豐收之象徵。故此，豬龍在當時可能是作為收割時的一種祭祀，而豬則為當時重要的佳餚。在上面已提過，在牛河梁遺址放置塑像的墓室中，就發現了一陶製的大豬龍。由此可以推斷，至少泥塑的豬龍並非作為葬禮和崇拜之用。在墓室中找到的一對豬龍，它們是背對著背的放在死者之胸前，豬龍的面部是向外張望的。

不管是就紅山文化或是中國北方新石器時代

玉器而論，豬龍的形制可分兩種。一為綣狀，另一則雖同屬綣狀，但身上卻如幼蟲般節狀，如展品25。

至於在科學控制下發掘到的另一種龍，我們到現在尚未有滿意的結論。它雖被普遍接納為紅山文化類型，但實際上它應還可追溯到更早期的趙寶溝文化。此器物的橫切面呈橢圓形，器身上設開口，見展品7。開口圓形的上部為龍首，鼻如豬之鼻孔，其環形身軀又似蛇，眼部刻劃精緻，雙煩與前額皆刻有斷面紋。自龍首以下，有三分一之身軀帶有鰭狀齒邊之羽冠，這些羽冠與野豬的相比，再加上其扁形豬鼻孔，成為了豬與龍祖型之關係最佳之證據。其中最著名的一件是在1971年於內蒙敖漢旗三星他拉發現的，直至1980年代它始被肯定為屬紅山文化。此外，筆者在1993年於赤峰亦見過一件很精緻的純黃玉例子，直徑若有7吋。此物為一農民所發現，至今尚未發表。

而動物紋玉雕之所以流行，至今未有可信的解釋。它可能與宗教儀式如鳥以至龜、蟬、鯉魚和鱷魚的崇拜有關。其中最傳統的相信是對鳥的崇拜。這些鳥一般呈展翅狀，鳥首每邊均有圈眼，可能是白鴿之形象，見展品14。其它屬展翅鳥型的動物紋，在頭部後面都有凸起的耳，外貌與貓頭鷹相近，見展品15與16。雖然這兩種鳥在雕塑結構和扁平的形狀上相似，但它們有耳和無耳之區別卻表達了不同的感覺。兩種鳥的背部都有牛鼻狀鑽孔，顯示它們是作垂掛或接駁之用，見展品11至17。

在發掘到的龜形玉器中，它們有的是伸脖，有的則是相反。其中在牛河梁墓址出土的一對玉龜，體形如手掌般大小，是以黃玉製成的。這對玉龜雖然已很殘舊，但是龜甲卻毫無瑕庇，被發現的時候還緊握在骸骨的左右手中。另外，在墓中還發現了簡單的玉魚飾和玉蟬，此玉蟬呈闊身管狀，可能是重要的神聖動物，見展品10。玉蟬出土的數量較多，它這種形態可能就是中國人心目中蟬的象徵。蟬在牠的幼蟲時期是鑽進地洞內，然後蟄伏兩至三年，始後才脫殼變成蟲，這種循環生態是重生現象的表現，見展品9和10。

最後，我們應說到中國北方新石器時代中的玉人。

在遼寧喀左縣東山嘴遺址中出土了小型泥塑女像，似是作為奉獻之用。此類型泥像與在南歐、地中海和早期遺址，如奧地利、馬爾他、愛琴海的基克拉迪群島、土耳其之卡塔許于克和哈吉拉爾所出土的相近。雖然這類泥像是在相若的時間製造，但它們分別處於的地域，故若要在歷史上把這些不同地域作出聯繫，似乎是有點困難。但是，我們卻可將這現象作為人類在藝術觸角上同步速的証據。

現今，在紅山或是早期的遺址，尚未發掘到玉製之人像。然而，在上述之小型紅山泥塑女像，牛河梁廟遺址出土的紅山時期人像殘塊，以及在1980和1981年，於巴林右旗那斯台村趙寶溝遺址出土的兩具石像，分別顯示了中國北方新石器時期人像雕塑已達到了很高的藝術水平。

曾經有口頭確証實有一名專業考古學家，在赤峰地區意外地發現了至少一件屬紅山時期的玉人。但在大陸至今尚未見有對此玉人或其它玉人在雕塑上之研究和比較。然而，在玉器市場上亦出現了一批有限量的玉人，如展品2和3。它們垂直的體態、闊肩、穿孔以及手置膝上的坐姿，加上展品2的牛角頭飾，與筆者曾評述過的幾件西方所藏之玉人在體積上很是相似(見參考書目15)。那些玉像的頭頂也有凸出的角或齒狀物，而北京故宮博物館就至少發表過一件類似的藏品。展品3的姿態基本上一樣，但在體形線條處理上更為圓滑流暢。除了手置膝上之坐姿與那斯台出土的石像相似外，這批玉人與上述的泥塑女像或石像都沒有直接關係。故此，要了解此批玉人唯一的途徑，就是研究它們的風格與製作方法，進而了解新石器時代製玉各方面之技術。以此作起點，相信對研究未來在考古上同樣的發現有幫助。

上面所述的中國新石器時代玉材包括了墨玉、半透暗綠色、透明青黃色以至半透白色玉。從現有考古証據看，紅山文化遺址出產的黃玉數量最少，故它應是最早被採用之材料。而且發掘到的黃玉大都已經殘舊和磨損，看起來似是在陪葬前已被沿用了幾百年。

在趙寶溝文化層，亦有黃玉的出土。由此推斷，這批黃玉應是在紅山文化時期之前出現。而另外找到的一件扁身白玉，與上述的鳥形相仿，可能是在葬禮中作為焚燒用的物品。此外發掘到的雕塑尚有豬龍、蟬、龍環和上述的類人動物，它們是紅山文化器物的主要範圍。

在紅山文化中，最特出的鑽孔是牛鼻孔。此種鑽孔狀如兩水滴，孔口尖端相向，其口徑愈斜入愈收窄，在新石器時代的玉器是從未見過的。而在一些鑽孔較深之內側，常有螺旋形或圓形之切線，但細看其實是一組重複的陰刻圓線。

紅山玉器之工藝雖然簡單，但是卻很精細，玉器邊緣位置更是打磨鋒利。此外，有些的製作則較粗糙，看似是另一種粗豪之表現；也有些精細的造型是精工雕琢而成，它們表現出簡單的脊線和闊溝槽。大部份玉器身上都沒有紋飾和線刻，其中只有牛河梁出土的龍環前額與煩上和其它龍環上有斷面線紋，而

展品8羽冠上也有魚骨紋線刻。

紅山動物形玉器的頭部多有豬之特色，這可見豬在當時的葬禮是扮現了很重要的角色。

2. 黃河流域中游之新石器時代文化／陝西省

(i) 半坡時期　公元前4800 — 公元前4200年
遺址地區
從西周時代開始，西安長時期以來已成為中國的首都，它在唐朝時是絲綢之路的起點，現今則是陝西省的省市，也是半坡遺址的所在地。

仰韶文化從黃河流域沿岸伸展，以西安為中心點，而半坡算是仰韶文化的分支處。

半坡時期的房屋是以土坑建成，通常深3呎，闊約12呎。坑身為牆，上蓋以茅草造之圓錐形屋頂。

半坡文化出產很少玉器，通常只有齒或斧等武器和工具。此時的首飾，以貌似高爾夫球座的髮簪和玉玦為表表者。雖然在半坡文化中也有玉璜掛飾的發現，但卻沒有發掘到與宗教禮儀有關之玉器。

這時玉器在雕琢技術上缺乏像良渚文化和紅山文化的先進工具，故其玉器之質素與圖紋設計亦較粗糙和樸實。玉器上的鑽孔，多在器身的一面以單錐鑽成的。

(ii) 廟底溝　公元前3900年 — 公元前3500年
廟底溝居民所屬之地區，與半坡居民的相近。

廟底溝玉器種類夾雜，武器的包括有斧、錛和刀，首飾則有短尖的髮簪、指環、玉玦、玉璜掛飾和一種心形掛飾。正如半坡玉器一樣，廟底溝玉器並沒有顯示出在宗教禮儀上之用途，且當中也沒有動物紋之發現。至於其雕琢技巧亦頗簡單粗糙，對於精細之設計並不講究。至於玉器形狀多為盒形和長橢圓形的齒。

(iii) 秦王寨　公元前3400年 — 公元前3000年
秦王寨文化所處的地區基本上與上述的兩個仰韶文化相近。此文化玉製的武器和工具有斧、錛和刀，而首飾則有尖幼的髮簪、指環、玉玦和心形掛飾。正如廟底溝一樣，秦王寨所出土的玉器並不多，故若要對此文化的玉器作詳盡的研究，唯有寄望在未來更豐富的發掘。

3. 黃河流域下流／山東省／江蘇省北部　—淮河盆地

(i) 大汶口公元前4500年 — 公元前2300年
大汶口的村落是座落於山東省近泰安黃河流域下游之大汶河上。

在考古發掘中僅存的大汶口房屋泥模,有助於對大汶口文化遺存之研究。此時期之房屋是直接建在泥土上的,它們並沒有挖內坑作結構上的支撐。

大汶口物器出土之遺址分散,不過大部份都是在600米以下之低地發現的。其中玉器的工具,包括了斧、錛和鑿,武器則有方尾刀。從發掘到的斧和錛清楚可見,它們的輪廓全是方形,大汶口文化中並沒有圓形輪廓之玉器。至於首飾,包括了指環、心形掛飾、長尖形掛飾或髮簪和腕鐲,這些腕鐲的外形出奇的纖細,與良渚文化中粗大的形制比較相差甚遠。

此類型的玉器尚有玉玦和玉璜掛飾,當中有種玉璜具"V"形坑槽,紋飾呈縱向拱狀,扁平的底部有數個等距之穿孔,可能是作穿掛之用。

大汶口文化中並未有發掘到與宗教禮儀有關的玉器。雖然如此,現藏美國華盛頓弗利爾博物館的兩件玉璧和一件高身玉環卻是值得一提的。此組玉器以陰線刻有展翅鳥和豎鳥,精工細緻。有些觀察家認為這些鳥是燕子,但燕子的輪廓與這些鳥的外型不符。

在這些玉器上除有鳥形外,還刻有一輪彎月,以及可能是象徵太陽的「絨毯狀」紋飾。但不幸的是,這些玉器是在沒有科學控制的情況下進行發掘的,而在有科學控制的中國新石器時代遺址,卻從未有同類的玉器出土過。這批玉器一向都被視作屬於良渚文化的,但原因卻令人費解。在下面我們將會提到,這批玉器無論在符號刻劃和處理上,都不是屬於良渚文化的特色。

這批玉器的圖案設計雖非相同,但它們依然可歸納為同一類。在1970和1980年之間,於山東省出土的數件大型陶製禮器,器身上之刻線圖案與以上玉器的相仿,故這批玉器應是屬於此時期之物。曾經有多位學者嘗試研究和分析這些刻符,他們的解釋雖未詳盡,但若循此方向下去,必定會找到更充分的解釋。

大汶口文化玉器之技藝雖然簡單,但又卻是異常精細的,見展品46。早期的玉器,尤以斧為例,在手工和用途上已達到專業的水準。這些玉斧器身幼薄,光澤明亮,而且穿孔均精工所製,全無瑕疵,展品47正是一好例子。

大汶口玉器上的所有穿孔都是精工鑽製的,斧和刀皆有在此書中〈玉器之製造〉部份提過的減地弧形尾,現正好為各讀者作一簡單的覆述。大部份斧和刀都是精心打磨,器身上留有凸出棱脊。展品47弧形刃的磨光和整體精工完成之特色,亦是此文化值得參考之地方。

大汶口玉器多為青綠透明軟玉,其它則包括不透明墨綠和粉褐色,另外亦有透明白色、不透明青色

苔蘚綠。玉器多呈扁狀,甚少立體雕塑,鑽孔則採底面斜角透鑽法。

1985年,安徽省含山縣凌家灘村發掘了三個墓穴,它們均屬於約公元前2500年的大汶口中期文化,當中有幾件雖沒表面相似,但卻是同等重要的玉器。除了標準形制的玉璜、玉鐲、玉斧和玉璧外,還有三件扁身人像。這些人像穿耳戴冠,雙手按胸而手指朝天,高9.6厘米,闊2.2厘米。另外又有方形扁身玉牌,牌上有穿孔,一面刻有圓圈和輻射狀圖案,未明是代表甚麼意思。此玉牌被發現的時候是夾在一玉龜甲和龜板之間,這種設計之意思尚有待研究。

在中國新石器時代玉器中,並未出現過以上玉牌般之抽象刻線和人像。但值得留意的是在商代的甲骨文中,龜甲和龜殼是很重要的。

江蘇省北部的花廳村是被認為花廳文化的遺址,它應是由大汶口文化時期開始,而當中的一組墓葬更可追溯至公元前3000年。這組墓葬的玉器與下面提到太湖地區及餘杭出土的玉器是有明顯的相似。此表明這兩地在當時可能有文化或政治上的交流,且兩地也有以豬殉葬之特色。

(ii) 山東龍山　公元前2800年—公元前1900年

過去黃河是直接流出山東半島南部的黃海,但現今它是流出山東以北的渤海。這幾百年以來,黃河下游的改道對中國北部的盆地影響深遠,它目睹了期間動盪的歷史演變。然而,黃河亦為這地區帶來積極的影響,它由上游地區如青海和西藏運來的沖積物,就全數的沉澱在山東半島和中北部一帶,使該地肥沃起來,令人民能在此定居數千年。

據過往廿多年考古發掘的証據展示,此區的玉器文化,即今天的山東龍山文化,在新石器時代已有高度的發展。這時玉器的特色,如凸線、棱上之勾形浮雕、扁身玉器鮮明的幾何抽象鏤雕,皆顯示出龍山文化玉已達成熟的階段。

新石器時代的玉器文化從未有過以上之特色,它未必是由龍山文化所發明,可能是在陝西黃河中下游一帶,或是山東龍山文化,無疑把製玉技術推進了一個完美的境界。

二里頭時期的凸線技巧一向被視為當時重要的特色,但觀乎龍山文化在凸線技巧上精湛的表現,實在有理由令我們相信它是二里頭時期之先驅。

參考書目21圖版60是一件髮簪,白玉質,扁狀鏤空,尾部可插入長柄,1989年於山東省臨朐出土。此玉器的鏤空和結構都是出自精工,其中

頂部兩面的勾形浮雕更是經過小心處理。

在以下石家河部份，我們可見到這文化的玉飾和人面紋同樣有上述般之勾形浮雕。在倫敦的英國藝術館藏有一件同樣之作，見圖版41。我們有幸此次展覽可見到展品64和65也有類似的勾形浮雕，而展品63則有兩道垂直浮雕，與展品64和65相連之關係。展品64和65的面部皆有棱脊，由正中垂直傾斜伸展至兩邊。

現在讓我們研究一下展品60和61，前者為一黃色兀鷹，背部有勾形浮雕，後者則為玉壁，其邊緣外圍的勾形浮雕則較隱約。黃色兀鷹背上的浮雕，表現了當時的人對兀鷹羽毛之概念，但這亦重複了臨胸髮簪和多個獸紋勾形浮雕。細看臨胸髮簪，可發現其尾部鑲有兩粒細小的綠松石，對稱的分佈於底部之兩角。展品66玉鷹的眼部，亦是以細小的綠松石所組成。

在商代安陽時期，也有使用綠松石的例子，故有理由相信綠松石之使用是始自山東龍山時期，與紅山文化時期，如遼寧東山嘴出土的展翅鳥上之綠松石並不相同。

在國內或國外公開收藏的幾件臨胸髮簪，其尾部方形、幾何或尖角的鏤空，顯示了這是有系統的鏤空方法。另一件精製的抽象型髮簪，與當時龍山文化時期之藝術沒有明顯的關連，其真正的含意還有待了解研究。展品65底部有以陰線刻有抽象化的人面紋或鬼面紋，若與臨胸髮簪相比，可發現它存有更多的問題。在展品65的標題中，提到了在溫福藏品中的玉斧上近穿孔位置，也有相同的抽象面紋及以陰線刻成的瞳孔，見參考書目46No.192。過去有很多作者以溫福藏之玉斧與龍山文化類型的扁身錛上之陰刻作比較。在以上提過公開收藏的幾何鏤空玉器，它們均源自同一時期和構思方法，對於這些抽象化設計，至今尚未找到合理解釋。

雖然山東龍山文化的玉器發展成就獨特，但它與同一地區的大汶口文化仍存有共同關係。如上面所述，河南和長江中游的石家河，也有與龍山文化有關之文化。

山東龍山文化遺址分佈於小山上，與鄰近地區的文化分隔，此點可從它玉器上獨特的凸線略窺一二。

在此我們可找到玉斧、錛和鋒利的小型玉刮。正如山東的大汶口文化一樣，龍山文化也有方尾刀之出產，刀脊上有等距的錐孔，見展品67。在新建成的陝西歷史博物館，現存有一組從陝西省北部神木縣石峁淺穴出土的葬品，它們的形制已確定與陶器的相同。斧與刀皆有出自龍山文化之減地弧形狀，此種設計無論在龍山文化完結後，或在其它玉器文化中是從來

沒有出現過的。石峁遺址亦出現過一種扁圓狀之人首，兩面皆刻有雙眼和短方鼻。

在龍山文化中，我們首次見到有戚壁，見展品61。玉璋亦是第一次在龍山文化中出現，刃部多為闊凹形，加上柄部兩邊的分叉浮雕，顯示出此玉器是不適合實際上的使用，見展品68。以上的形制應有宗教禮儀上的功用和意義，它們真正的用途和含意，是學術研究上一個很好的課題。此外，現今雖未有證據顯示像展品54這種凸緣玉環是源自山東龍山，但我們將之納入為龍山文化，亦算是合理的做法。

龍山文化也有另兩種主要的圖案。其一為先前提過的怪獸面紋，其二則是鳥形圖案。鳥紋可分三類，當中有兩類是作宗教上之用，至於第三類則比較不拘形式，故它容納了不同的設想。

第一類鳥形圖案為冠狀鷹之浮雕，可能與宗教禮儀有關。此鳥形圖案以凸線刻成，呈振翅飛行狀，鳥首與嘴部伸長，在齒上之浮雕可見。有時則刻在面紋繞曲凸線上的地方。

在一件鏤空玉飾上，也有類似飛行狀的圖案。此圖案中的飛鳥以爪擒著一長髮人頭。人頭是以凸線所刻，呈側面狀，頭上蓋冠，面有鬚髯，耳則穿孔。而鳥羽上有橢圓形"眼狀"之圖案，貌似孔雀羽之眼狀花紋。這些圖紋設計肯定是由龍山文化所發明的，其影響直至二里頭時期之叉形髮飾仍然可見，見展品72。

在兩城鎮出土的一件同類型暗綠齒，也有相同的凸線，它兩面的背部都刻有很神秘的變形怪獸紋。

在龍山文化中，作展翅高飛狀之鳥形圖案是很獨特的。巴黎塞納斯基博物館藏的一只玉環，亦刻有此種圖案。玉環上的圖案是以凸線所刻，環身有鏤空凸緣。

在一些有繞曲漩渦形凸線的玉器上，它們也有類似的凸緣，而且往往因此被誤作為龍山文化的產品。英國藝術館的一件藏品，參考書目41圖版XXX1刻有怪獸面紋，在獸冠上也有這種刻線。另外展品71琮形玉飾之淺浮雕，也是此種線刻的好例子。

這些玉器的鏤雕在分佈處理上同時表現了自由和有規律之持色，這與以下將提到的良渚文化梯形玉珮相近，是具有良渚文化之特色。山東龍山文化可能像上述大汶口玉璧之鳥紋一樣，與良渚文化是有很微妙的關係。

第二類鳥形圖案是立體的，蓋短杆，一端蓋有鷹鳥，雙翼藏背，帶誇張之勾形，或有尖銳勾爪，此種雕塑造型在龍山文化是獨一無二的。

第三類鳥形圖案是鏤雕玉飾，整體呈曲狀平行四邊形，與臨胸髮簪尾部相似，也有上述那種勾形浮雕。

在1991年，湖南省一遺址發掘到的一件玉鳥，它融合了數種鳥形刻線之特點。此玉鳥曾在1993年發表過，已被確定為龍山文化之產物。詳見參考書目22，圖版46。

龍山文化第二種主要的創新，就是其怪獸面紋。這種紋飾以人面作依據，頭額高聳、凸眼拱鼻、面頰輪廓突出。此紋飾很明顯與良渚文化時期的饕餮紋不同，後者反而與山東大汶口文化較近似。饕餮紋一向是被認為依據老虎兇猛之外型而造，用以代表神界裡某種意思。龍山怪獸面紋採用人類較和善之面孔，但又飾以虎的尖牙，且兩耳亦有穿孔。

龍山文化玉器工藝精細，除鏤雕是較為形式主義外，其它玉器都是以凸線刻劃，器身光澤明亮。

龍山文化中的薄身刃雕工精細，有些刻有"絨毬狀"之圖案，與良渚文化有密切的關係。至於玉匠所採皆是軟玉，由不透橄欖灰、不透扁豆褐色、以至透明白色、金褐與石灰綠都有。在龍山玉器中，不論玉刃和玉飾皆為扁身。除了以上提過的小型摺翼鳥圖騰外，龍山文化立體玉雕的所屬時期至今尚未能明確斷定。

在一些沒正確記錄的資料中，它們把人面紋玉飾歸納為龍山文化的遺存，但這純粹是風格上的推想罷。

4. 長江上游與中游—四川/湖北

(i) 大溪　公元前4000年 — 公元前3000年

大溪遺址位於中國四川西部之巫山。四川省是現今中國人口最稠密和山嶺最多之地。

新石器時代玉器常見的武器和工具有玉刀，首飾則有玉玦和雙錐孔玉璜。至於精製的宗教禮儀玉器，則至今尚未有發現。1959年，曾經出土過一精製的橢圓玉飾，高6厘米，闊3.6厘米，厚1厘米，有的人認為它是玉，有的則說是玉石。此玉飾底面皆刻有人面浮雕，兩面的人面都不同，但二者都有直鼻，作睜眼張口驚惶之狀。玉器凸出的邊緣和面頰等浮雕部份均是精心打磨的，另器身上亦有穿孔作繫掛之用。這件玉器是在墓穴發掘所得，故相信它是葬品之一。由於此墓為小孩所有，若我們邏輯地去研究解釋這些葬品，相信會倍覺困難，因為這些葬品可能反映了大汶口文化奢華墓葬的一面。

大汶口文化玉器之手工雕精確，但並不算特出。所用玉材多為軟玉，由薄透綠至半透白都有。至於在造形上則多扁身，底面有雙錐鑽孔。

(ii) 石家河　公元前2500年 — 公元前2000年
（以前為青龍泉三期）

石家河文化以長江中游湖北省為據地，大型船隻可逆流而上，停泊在距蜀都荊州不遠之沙市。荊州是現今中國三個僅存城牆的城市之一，城牆至遲已在明朝建好。在八十年代，荊州和漢江之間的六合，已發掘到屬青龍泉三期之玉器。見參考書目圖版12,13和14。在1988年，河北省天門縣石河鎮出土了一組相關的玉雕，它們已被列作為石家河文化之玉器。

這些玉器被發現的時候，是藏於一大陶甕中。其中在石河鎮發現的一陶甕更盛多過五十多件玉器。這批陶甕重要之處，是在於它們可幫助推斷內裡玉器所屬的文化和時期。青龍泉三期與石家河文化出土的玉器均以雕塑質素馳名，其玉雕造詣和可塑性都極高。根據科學的推斷，二者皆屬於新石器時代後期。

六合遺址出土的一件玉器為已折斷的人首，呈柱體形，有彎月狀冠，眼睛以刻線勾劃，蒜鼻，嘴部呈橢圓之長口露舌狀，人首兩邊有大耳，耳垂穿耳飾。另一件六合玉器為扁身虎道玉塊，雙耳綣曲，具層次感，前額寬，雙眉的水平坑槽把面部一分為二，雙眼以刻線勾劃。此玉器現已當為新石器時代之作品，與源自良渚文化的饕餮紋及商周時的有很密切之關係。

然而，六合玉器中最重要的可能是一件鏤空玉飾。此玉飾具基本面紋之輪廓，亦有紅山玉器的勾形浮雕，故普遍認為它是山東地區的出品。西雅圖美術博物館富拿藏品中亦有一件與上述相通之玉飾，參考書目83No.3，而前者已被定為龍山文化之產品。另外，華盛頓弗利爾博物館錫拿藏品，亦有一件與上述類似的玉飾。

現嘗試對此玉飾作一圖解。下圖描繪了飛鳥準備從高處降落或擒拿獵物之情況，但此解釋純粹是一假設而矣。

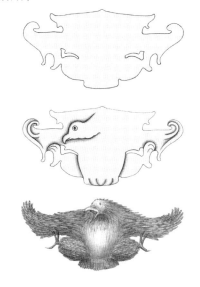

1988年，最後一件出土的石家河玉雕，是在
石河鎮發最後發掘到的玉鳥。此玉鳥為兀鷹，呈展翅
高飛狀。於此我們很高興可以享到華盛頓弗利爾博物館
蘇芳淑博士，在荊州處理這玉鳥時所得的資料。此玉鳥
體型細小，展翅闊距有4厘米，羽毛為龍山類型的
淺凸線，嘴呈勾形，外觀典雅。這些特色顯示了石家河
玉匠觀察準確和在雕塑上之才華。

　　第二類人首或人面紋亦是六合重要之出土玉器，
它與一些已發表的龍山文化玉器和展品64相似，
俱為怪獸面紋玉飾。至於為何山東半島的勾形浮雕會在
湖北長江中游出現，成為勾形浮雕怪獸，則未有
合理的解釋。1989年，在江西省新干大洋洲河岸墓穴
出土了另一件怪獸面紋玉飾，具凸線雕刻、蒜鼻穿耳、
尖牙及勾形浮雕等特點，為研究此種造型的玉飾
提供了另一線索。就青銅器而言，此種玉器應是在
公元前十三世紀的商代安陽時期出現。雖然上述
之玉飾在結溝上與山東龍山和石家河文化的相似，
但究竟它們之間的關係是怎樣，仍是學者們研究新石器
時代玉器的主要問題。

　　除此之外，在灃西的早期西周墓也發掘到一件
暗綠色怪獸紋玉飾，它顯示了上述山東龍山／石家河
怪獸面紋之特色。

　　這些玉器是在公元前2000年至公元前1000年
出現的，有人認為這是繼承和發展該時期之傳統。
從這些玉器基本相同的結構看，很難令人相信當時的
玉匠是一成不變的沿用古舊的製玉方法，而不對傳統作
出改革。這些玉器的紋飾在當時是很重要的，它照理
應在當時的青銅器上出現，但當時的青銅器紋飾，
似沒有受這些玉器的紋飾和圖案所影響。

　　基於這個原因，作者相信大洋洲和灃西及
其他同類的玉器應可追溯到更早的時期，即約由公元
前2500年開始，至公元前1600年二里頭和二里岡
之交接時期。

　　六合遺址出土的玉器尚有玉環和玉蟬。玉蟬
呈扁方形，雕琢簡單，有闊坑槽，頭尾皆有穿孔作繫掛
之用。這些玉蟬尚未可與已發表之山東龍山玉蟬並論。
其他有趣的發現還有石家河出土之環形豬龍，它與
商代婦好墓出土的簡化豬龍相似，應是取材自更早時期
紅山文化的豬龍。

　　一般而言，石家河玉器屬鈣化或燒過之不透明
白玉，與及半透灰綠色玉，這與花廳文化的玉材相似。

5. 長江流域下游盆地—太湖和中國中部東面

(i) 河姆渡　公元前5000年 — 公元前4800年

河姆渡為浙江省杭州東面的餘姚市之一個小鎮。
這裡的遺址在一九七三年始有豐厚的發掘，至1983年
又有大型博物館之落成。

　　在1973年，河姆渡是被認為玉器研究重地
之一，因當時所在這兒所發現的玉器，是所知最早的
中國玉器。雖然自中國北方興隆洼與趙寶溝文化
的年期被確定後，河姆渡文化已失去了它在考古上重要
的位置，但這並未掩蓋它的光采。河姆渡文化獨有
熟練生動的鳥形圖案是很重要的，其中最著名的是骨器
上之勾嘴、爪和凸眼刻線，以及刻在黑陶上的闊肩
幼腿豬形圖案。

　　有點值得討論的是，縱使河姆渡文化以善於繪製
見稱，但這種傳統卻沒有繼續發展下去，或者說沒有在
玉器中表現出來。河姆渡文化玉器以首飾為多，如髮
簪、玉珠、玉筒、玉玦和玉璜，採用透明檸黃色以至淡
青白色玉，與江蘇省新石器時代地區所用的相同。

(ii) 馬家濱　公元前5000年 — 公元前3900年

從熱釋光與碳十四斷代法對馬家濱玉器之測試，
顯示了馬家濱文化是以江蘇太湖地區為據地。此文化的
雕塑以骨刻和陶器為主。馬家濱文化陶器之測定年期，
對於準確判斷1986年安徽省蕭縣金寨村出土
的玉器有很大幫助。當年考古學家發掘的一小池，
是現今所謂的玉石塘。此處出土了相當數量的玉器、
綠松石和陶器，而這些陶器正好幫助推斷馬家濱
文化的時期與源流。

　　然而，馬家濱玉器卻是以良渚玉器的類型為
基礎，其中例外的是一件扁形柄，見展品49。此玉柄
一面為鋒刃，中間有三斜闊溝口。玉柄中部為一修長方
形開口，可套手入內緊握。

　　除展品49外，還有一小部份此類玉器是良渚
文化中沒有的。故此，蕭縣遺存有可能是屬於公元前
3500年，馬家濱後期至良渚過渡期。其中最著名的"握孔
玉刀"是在玉石池找到的，曾於1992年，在北京展出過
(參考書目21)。該展覽目錄把它描述為"造型奇特"和
"為出古玉中所僅見"。但是玉石塘出土的那件玉刀，
缺少了展品49刃身上之斜坑。

　　1976年，江蘇省青蓮崗文化大墩子遺址出土的
一種短刃刀，是一種較少見有拱形手握的武器，它可能
與"握孔玉刀"有關。

(iii) 崧澤　公元前3800年 — 公元前2900年

在江蘇省青浦近上海之崧澤遺址，出土了公元前3800年
至公元前2900年之物器。此文化也許是玉璧之改革者。

　　此外，玉器在禮葬中亦擔當了一個很有趣的角

色，這似是與蟬的生態有關並受其影響。蟬在產卵後，
卵就化成幼蟲而寄居在葉上成蛹，然後躲在地底至
冬天過後，始爬出洞外脫殼成蟲。漢代的時候，玉蟬
通常是放在屍體的口內。在崧澤文化的時候，似乎
流行把玉琀放在口內，這正好相等新石器時代對
玉蟬的處理方法。

在崧澤文化中，玉玦是標準的墓葬品，而玉鐲
也是極普遍的。至於筒型玉飾的製造已是十分熟練。這
時的玉玦是由圓身玉飾所發展而來，以平行雙鋸法由法
面貫通至內心。這些玉玦通常是在骸骨的耳部發現的。

崧澤文化的玉璜飾，在技術上可能已達很高
的成就。這些器物的外型優美，對稱均勻，且都是打磨
得盡露光澤的，見展品30。

此種玉飾款式頗多，如半馬蹄形玉飾，其尾部
是有雙錐鑽孔的，而扁闊蹄形玉飾，則是一邊直身
及有以雙錐鑽成的凹口。

崧澤玉器技術精細，器身表面光滑，多用半透明
呈晶狀白玉，以至透明黃粉紅色玉。

(iv) 良渚 公元前3400年 — 公元前2250年

從現有的考古資料看，良渚文化的玉器製造傳統在
長達一千三百年中，既是中國玉器製作的試驗所，又是
主要發展的動力來源。良渚文化地區，包括了長江
下游一帶，這地區是一塊廣闊而肥沃的農業平原，整個
地區內的運河縱橫交錯，當中並有多個大湖。

良渚文化地區圍繞著整個江蘇太湖地區，
影響範圍西起南京，東至上海，北及安徽，南達杭州。
這範圍內比較重要的古跡，有上海附近之福泉山、
杭州西北廿五里餘杭鎮的良渚村、反山和姚山的
帝王貴族陵墓。

這兒的寒冬很短，夏天又熱又濕，氣候極適
宜農業耕作，無怪此地區新石器時代居民生活是十分富
庶的。良渚文化就是在此基礎上，發展了豐富多姿
的哲學、神話、宗教以及圖案藝術，而它們都是集中
反映在那些鬼斧神功的玉器上。

從已發掘的良渚文化墓葬看，它們都是有
統一的結構。這些墓穴被埋入平頂淺丘後，時間久
遠，當地人便稱之為山。

在葬墓棺木中發現的葬品，由數件至百件不等。
良渚文化的陶瓷同樣是很出色，不過它並不屬於
此次展覽的範圍，對此方面有興趣的讀者，可參閱
1992年在香港舉辦的上海福泉山良渚文化玉器
展覽之目錄，參考書目70。

近十五年來，發現的棺木，大部份是在下葬後

沒被破壞的。而當中發現的葬品，更顯出一種刻意安排
的獨特風格。雖然各地發現的葬品有輕微的差別，
但棺木的置放和葬品的排列都表現濃烈的宗教意識。在
一部份棺木中殘存了一些紅色粉末，可能是紅漆
的痕跡。而很多棺木都有被燒過的痕跡，此暗示了可能
有很多棺木已在大火中徹底毀滅了。在另一些墓地中，
則只有部份工藝葬品被燒毀。

棺中的葬品的排列是以屍體為中心的，一般
的做法是在頭上放些工藝品，在胸前放玉璧，而長型玉
琮則置於腹部。另一種擺放在腹部的玉器是帶勾，
相信是作緊扣皮帶和衣服用的。這種玉飾最吸引之
處，是它直到東周戰國時代始再次出現。

在某些墓中發現到有三件與鉞有關之典型玉器，
它們應是排放在已腐化了的木柄上的。此三個部份，包
括了頂尖的玉冠飾，以下為刃部，在左手旁則為底部
的柄。從這擺設的方式看，它應是放在屍體身旁，
由腰間伸展至肩膊。

在屍體足部的左右，通常是放置了玉璧、石斧
和陶瓷。石鉞通常是放在足部附近，但從不會放在肩膊
位置，這種嚴格的區別可能是喪禮的基本規則。

而有部份玉器則是擺放在屍身旁的陶器內。
假如葬品中是發現有玉器的話，那麼極有可能這些葬品
大部份都是玉器。

另一點有趣的是，在很多良渚墓中找到的玉器，
它們都是由一些器皿的碎片改製而成的，那些較大的碎
片會被改造為較小的玉器。

玉器是價值連城的葬品，當然不是每一個良渚
居民可以此作陪葬。故墓內玉器數量的多寡，實際上
反映了墓主人在社會上之地位。

良渚墓中發掘的玉器可分為以下幾大類：
一為武器或工具，如鉞、二為宗教器物，如璧或琮、
三為製飾品，如項飾、四為與祭祀有關之製飾物。

在良渚文化中，有鉞和戰斧之發現。前者的
刀鋒是圓的，後者則是長的，兩邊向斧角彎曲，見展
品34。雖然前著較後者厚，但兩種斧的刀鋒是很薄的，
一般在斧角都鑽有斜孔。斧角不像大汶口及龍山
文化的一般成直角，也未經細意打磨。

這種在製作上的失誤可能是人為的，但在
良渚文化中卓越之技巧中，這卻顯得格外新穎。至於
良渚文化玉斧變曲形刃邊，與大汶口和龍山文化
玉斧半月形刃邊之區別，我們在此書中已討論過。
正如上面所言，現時一般的推測都以為刃身是插入
木柄，然後再用繩繫緊的。而以往亦曾經發掘到
有綑綁痕跡之斧刃，刃上有紅線痕，暗示了是以染紅的

繩緊綁此物，但因繩褪色而留痕。繩索應是穿過
中間的雙斜孔，繞過身以緊繫柄部的。

　　小型的首飾十分普遍，包括：球形玉珠、柱狀
玉飾、玉琮、玉玦、管形玉飾和圓珠。另外又發現了柱
狀玉珮，體形細小，但卻精工雕製。其他的如玉鐲
亦是常見之玉器。而最特出的玉珮造型，可與漁網或
是埃及方尖塔相比。其中一玉珮末端生硬，另一則
縮短了伸出部份之直徑，且常有雙錐孔，猶如
錐子尾上之針孔。這些玉器有四面，其橫切面呈
正方形（展品40），或是造型與橫切面皆為圖形，兩種
物器的柄都可以是素面，或是刻有一種至多種
神面／獸面紋。

　　這些玉器被發現的時候，基本上是以三件
至九件為一批的，長度不同，是放在屍體頭顱以上的
地方，此可能代表了半月形玉珮上或以下將提到
的梯形玉珮上神人所戴的頭飾。這些玉飾長3至20厘米。
此外，玉珮伸出部份未必有穿孔，它們可能是
套入柱狀玉蓋中，但用意則不詳。

　　在良渚文化玉器中，又發現了兩種扁闊狀的飾物。

　　第一種呈梯形狀，短邊為榫，通常鑽有三個
穿孔，見展品35至37。

　　第二種為半圓形，器身一邊呈彎曲狀，另一邊平
直，在平直邊部有時中有小型凹口。

　　梯形玉飾之榫部明顯是用來套進孔內的。此玉飾
在出土的時候，身上是有木質纖維和紅漆的痕跡，
故有可能榫部是紅色木片的冠狀部份，而木片則因
時日久遠腐化了。在紅土範圍很多時也發現到細小凸狀
的玉片，此正好顯示紅漆木塊可能是有用玉片作點綴
的。梯形玉飾一向都是堅挺扁身的，多為素面，不設
任何刻紋，但有些則有浮雕或怪獸紋。展品37是
眾多中之例外，其梯形上有鏤雕之怪獸或動物紋和
長臂神人的圖案。

　　另一種近似的是豬形圖案。豬有鈍鼻、橢圓大
眼，頭顱外形呈圓蓋狀，展品38即一好例子。這類物器
有榫部，暗示了它們可插入木飾和圖騰中。

　　半月狀首飾有像展品31左邊般之素面，或是
雕有大眼面孔之浮雕。在一些墓穴中，就找到
一套四件的此類物品，它們均是精工雕琢，等距的
繞著屍體頭部分佈。

　　在每件的素面上都鑽有孔道，暗示了作為
頭飾和在頭上掛戴之用。如上面簡述，良渚文化玉器之
另一特色是與衣飾有關的帶勾。至今我們尚未見有
石製之帶勾出土過，表明它能是甚少應用的物器，它之
所以在良渚時期出現，可能是與當時奢華的禮儀有關。

　　正如北方新石器時代獨有綣雲形玉飾之發展，
良渚文化也有自己獨有的宗教儀仗玉器，其中
最重要的是玉琮。

　　玉琮通常為柱體，內圓外方。短身玉琮有方形
節，而長身玉琮則有長形節，外方之長度每以內圓之直
徑為標準。

　　這種造型的玉琮在良渚文化才有，良渚文化結束
後，玉琮亦沒再出現過，此問題在此書或其它書中
也有提過。良渚時期二千以後的基本玉琮造形多
為素面，缺少良渚時期之裝飾，但仍是重要的宗廟儀仗
玉器。這重要性到周代末期至極點，如〈周禮〉把琮
和璧作為宗教禮儀上的一種觀念和色彩標記之用，但現
今，這些觀念只是歷史發展遺留下來的產物，已經
偏離了對玉器本身真正的理解。除了以下將提到的
石峽文化石器外，各時期的琮都是以玉製成，從未有
琮是以石或鐵製成的。

　　從宋代哥窯、鈞窯和龍泉窯雖可見有以琮為形的
單色釉瓷，但它們似為非為宗教儀仗所造，反而可能是因
傾愛它的外型而製。

　　從發掘到的葬墓可見，玉琮通常是男性同葬的，
而且在不同年紀男性的墓也有發現過，有些墓甚至有活
俑的痕跡。但有一點不容否定的，就是在有玉琮的
墓穴裡，通常是以宗教儀仗之玉器佔多數。

　　在江蘇省武進張陵山發掘了一件厚身圓鐲，
估計應屬於約公元前3000年。鐲身外有一組四個的凸起
動物面紋，定距分佈，以空白素面作分界。

　　那些簡單但結構嚴密的動物紋，加上突出之
內外拱狀，與展品71之玉琮上的凸眼圓紋很相似。現時
很難對武進動物紋玉鐲作出推論，但流行的說明皆
認為它是玉琮的祖型。而碳十四斷代法也顯示它是至
今發現最早期的玉琮之一。如果上面所言屬實，
那武進玉鐲是由最初的首飾，演變成作宗教禮儀用
的玉琮了。

　　玉琮上的動物紋分佈在外方的四角，而外方
的曲尺角位正好成為獸面的中軸，把它們一分為二。
每組紋飾之間的空位，是屬於內圓的部份，它們是沒有
任何雕刻的。此空白的地方在外方形成一清晰的
垂直坑道。

　　除了以上玉琮在高矮上的區別外，此外還有
另一方法去分辨二者。在玉琮的外方部份，有凸起呈長
方形之節，內圓部份未必一定比外方部份高。中間
有圓形鑽孔，玉琮整體的外型，就像是一通心的圓柱體
穿入一方角四邊柱體一樣。

　　根據所有的証據顯示，玉琮中心圓孔是以對

鑽做成的。在短身玉琮的圓孔內，這些對鑽痕已被打磨得光滑，但在長身玉琮中，這些痕跡依然清晰可見。短身玉琮高橫闊比直高多，每邊外方也呈正方節，橫向分切為二，每節上刻一獸眼，因方角為面紋之中軸，故每節代表了動物的側面。上節之面紋多刻細圓眼，下節則多刻橢圓大眼，見展品39。

長身玉琮直高比橫闊多，從沒橢圓眼的刻線，通常是沒眼或刻細圓眼，只每節或隔節出現。這些玉琮有若干數量的發現，在一些墓中它們通常是放在死者的身旁。

這兩種玉琮都是在良渚時期逐漸發掘起來的，它們在墓葬中是極之重要的宗教儀仗物品。然而，短身玉琮在雕琢那些細緻圖案上，較長身玉琮為佳。故後者之基本意義往往只在其造型，而非其紋飾成份上。

有些長方節很大，長達30厘米或以上。長期以來，較窄的一端都被為頂部，但是從四角的動物面紋以及最近出土不同形制的短身或長身琮看，較闊的一端始為頂部。

在眾多良渚玉器當中，玉琮和鏤空梯形珮反映了玉器製造中最精巧和傑出的設計，這可歸功於物器本身的重要性，兩者皆以線刻有類人圖案，狀如倒梯，頂上插有光線狀之插羽，重圈為凸眼。在鏤空梯形玉珮類人兩側的是狼或鱷，長嘴並以重圈為眼，每邊有細小凹痕為毗。良渚地區是長江下游鱷現之原居地，但是今天牠們已極罕見了，見展品36和37。

反山出土的一件著名短身玉琮上有類人圖案，細眼、腳有綣爪，雙手抱一物於頂上，此物體積比自己的要大，為橢圓首。一些作者曾在一種圖案中，見過類人的細眼所處之位置比野獸的橢圓眼高，似是意味著神支配了動物的世界。這與玉琮上節為細眼，面紋及下節為橢圓凸眼之處理相同。要確實理解玉琮上所繪的是甚麼動物，還有待繼續研究。但要注意的是展品38梯形玉豬飾是極其罕見的。豬在良渚人的生活中是很重要的，玉琮下節的野獸可能是代表了豬。

在崧澤部份曾提過玉璧雖是自這文化發展而來，但直至良渚文化時，它始發展為主要的宗教儀仗玉器。

良渚玉匠所製之玉璧體積巨大，全是素面和沒有修飾的，見展品32。在新石器時代中，大型的良渚玉璧可說是獨一無二。正如在大汶口部份提過，有些良渚玉璧是刻有大汶口鳥、太陽和月亮圖案的。雖然迄今，尚未在真正發掘中找到有大汶口圖案之良渚玉璧，但在上海博物館收藏多年的玉璧，以及最近從杭州收集的玉璧，卻顯示了這些圖案無疑是出自良渚文化的。相反，雖然這些是典型大汶口陶器

的圖案，但在山東大汶口文化地區，卻從沒出土過這種玉璧。

良渚玉璧多在屍腳部附近發現，但在有些墓中它們是置於屍體身上和底下。

良渚文化另一種獨有之玉器為三叉形器，以淺浮雕刻橢圓眼的動物紋。這些玉器一般都是死者頭頂以上的地方發現，在三叉形中間凸出部份內，又有垂直凹口，可能是供嵌插羽毛，作頭飾之用的。

良渚玉器出現了很多動物的形像，但原因未明。這些動物有鳥形，由作展翅飛行狀至扁首凸眼的淺浮雕都有。在短身玉琮上，亦曾見過這種鳥形和繩球狀之圖案。有一學者就曾指出過這些圖案可能是代表了鳥羽或獸皮毛。

在反山的墓葬中又找到少量的玉魚、扁身玉龜、扁身玉蟬和一近乎立體的栖息鳥。良渚玉器的技巧極之精湛，每件物器每一角落都是精心打磨，拋光精緻，其光滑的表層幾可與豆腐和乾酪相比。

良渚玉器上以四至五條帶狀組成的線刻，每條相距不過1毫米，絲毫不差，對今天的絲刻技術可說一種挑戰。至於良渚玉匠何以能掌握這種鬼斧神功的技巧，則至今未有合理的解釋。

另一種同時在陶瓷上出現的重要圖飾，就是展品36的動物紋，它代表了今天唯一可見的良渚玉器上之繪畫。此動物紋有尖牙，貌相既兇且怒，有繩球狀之刻線。雖然我們不打算在此討論這動物紋的內容，但它極有可能是商周時代饕餮的始源。

假設由展品36中部的尖頂畫一垂直線為中軸，然後將之摺成曲尺形，那麼這獸面紋就與玉琮下節的獸紋相似。而展品36中饕餮紋的大圈眼足以支持以上的推斷。

良渚墓葬的玉器並沒有使用過和穿戴過之痕跡，它們身上沒刮痕或磨損之跡象，器身充滿光澤，暗示了這些玉器是純為禮儀或具有權力的人而製的，這些有權位的人生前使用此物，在死後也以此作陪葬。在〈玉器之製造〉部份提過，良渚玉器時常顯示了搖動式鋸之鋸痕或是曲狀的損痕。

良渚玉器中最大件者為長方玉琮和大玉璧。在這些巨型物器以下，還有一系列不同大小的玉器，小至如杏形玉片也有。這種玉片是鑲在木圖騰上，然後頂部是裝有梯形玉珮的。

良渚玉器之造型除柱筒狀的玉琮外，其它皆是扁身短形，器身上的穿孔均是在底面以雙錐鑽成的，在長玉琮這些有較深的圓孔內，就常有棱脊之痕跡。

良渚玉器在雕塑方面有一點是很奇怪的。在比
良渚文化更早的趙寶溝與紅山文化裡，我們發現了
立體玉雕。但是在良渚文化中，除了是反山出土的
玉鳥外，就從未有發掘過任何立體玉雕。良渚玉匠
既能以精鍊的技巧處理扁身玉器，而良渚文化中又沒
有立體玉雕的製造，實在是很奇怪的情況。這或可
歸咎到一些不明的原因，又或者良渚玉匠不願和
不懂把玉雕提升到立體雕塑之層次未定。

6.　南部沿岸省份

廣東

石峽　公元前3000年 — 公元前2000年

石峽文化遺址佔地約三萬平方米，位於廣東省北部山區。

在新石器時代，石峽也像其他地區一樣有
先進的農業耕作和定居。

中國近年來，在新石器時代遺址出土的大批
文物和有關資料，令到石峽文化看起上來相形見拙，
使人覺得此文化是很普通。但其實不然，石峽文化中
琮的使用正好粉碎了此種想法。

在石峽墓葬中，有良渚傳統的長琮和短琮之
發現。這兩種琮都刻有良渚琮上的細眼和橢圓眼獸面
紋，而在現今所知的例子中，後者只是陰刻，而非像良
渚玉器般之浮雕。

石峽琮與良渚玉琮最大之分別，在於前者是以淺
灰硅石所製，在石峽文化中並未有用玉製的琮之發現。

在1983年，廣東省沿岸的海豐天埗鎮一沙地遺
址，出土了一批曾被列為龍山文化的物器，當中包括了
一件淺綠色玉琮。

石峽琮與良渚玉琮還有另一重要的分別。前面
已提過良渚玉琮在出土的時候，是沒有絲毫損毀的，
它在未入土前應已接受小心處理，而在墓中擺放時
亦是格外謹慎，它們可能是專為禮葬而製的。

除卻一些少數例子外，石峽石琮的角位部份
的磨損是極嚴重的，有多件琮甚至由原來的鋒利的銳角
磨損至平滑的鈍角了。這情況不單顯示出石琮在
使用上的頻繁，更可能暗示它是在撞擊的情況下使用，
以至留下許多刮花磨損的痕跡。

石峽琮與良渚玉琮之分別定有重要的原因，但若
要找出此原因，相信還要作再深入的研究和思考。

有一些石峽琮與良渚玉琮相似，大家的表面都是
打磨得很精緻的。雖然在石峽墓中發現的琮比在良渚
發現的少，但二者俱作宗教儀仗之用，據推斷是屬於公
元前2500年之物，即剛好是良渚文化的後期。

或許是因為良渚地區與廣東北部地區受高山之
分隔，現今未有証據顯示到兩地曾有真正的交流。
而在廣東沿岸出土有良渚特色的琮，暗示了中國中部
和南部可能在水路上有聯繫，如果能在這方面
找到更多線索的話，相信會改觀現時對新石器時代文化
演變之看法。

E.　二里頭時期玉器　公元前1900年—公元前1600年

據現時所知，中國新石器時代是以興隆洼文化為開始
的，而我們也剛看過在這三千年裡，新石器時代
玉器在概念上和實踐上的轉變。

早在趙寶溝文化和紅山文化中，玉器已顯示出
它是統治社會的象徵。紅山文化的玉器形制簡單，立體
雕塑缺少表面的修飾，而直到良渚文化，則多扁狀玉
器，且工於花巧的圖案設計。除了大汶口文化和龍山文
化獨有的勾形浮雕及闊帶狀鏤空玉飾，玉刀和玉璋
簡單優美之風格仍是玉器造型的主流。我們知道玉是
做耳環、帶勾、珠和鐲等首飾常用之材料，在公元前
3000年開始，玉器已建立自己的時代，它向社會
各階層展示了在雕刻上完美的技巧，打破了只是奢華
象徵的框框。

由公元前2200年至公元前1700年之間始，
新石器時代的居民已醞釀要改革社會的制度，這亦是
青銅器時代誕生的時候。

青銅器之鑄造為中國帶來巨大和長遠的轉變。
在當時一些可鑄造青銅的國家，青銅是用來製造武器，
因為只有這樣才可保証在戰爭中稱霸。故此，每個國家
都有急切需要去發展青銅器的鑄造。在公元前1700年，
即新石器時代的末期，青銅已被廣泛利用為多種器皿
和武器之材料。

青銅武器製作技術之所以發展迅速，最主要
是切合戰爭上的需要，在此情況下，社會上大部份的
資源亦落入青銅器鑄造上，這點對當時的國家來說似是
無可避免的。

從社會的組織而言，中國傳統觀念中的夏代
就是在此時候出現。夏代的出現實際上牽涉了很多神
話，故很多學者都否定它的存在。

在此時期，青銅迅速成為鑄造玉器工具之材料，
而這亦促使了玉匠在工藝技巧上有更大的進展。
此時期主要的遺址有河南省距鄭州西面一百公里的偃師
二里頭，故名。鄭州為河南省省市，位處黃河之上，
山東和山西之南。若以偃師之出土為依據，那麼在鄭州
亦有二里頭時期的遺址。

一般都認為二里頭時期是由公元前1900年開始，

直至商初，即約公元前1700年完結。而二里頭玉器可視為從良渚和山東龍山玉器的風格演變過來的。

中國新石器時代玉器的風格多樣化，而二里頭玉器就把這些風格融為一體，為日後長期的發展奠下良好根基。

青銅器之盛行雖然未必可完全打倒玉器在社會上的地位，但有點可以肯定的是，青銅在立體鑄造上，確是提供了較大的自由度。青銅器上的紋飾，成為玉器仿效之對象，而玉器上的圖飾設計，也是青銅器圖案設計之借鏡，兩者能產生相輔相成的作用是很重要的。

由於使用青銅工具可便於線條的刻劃，所以，玉刀和玉戈上開始有多層線刻，見展品75。至於在斧刃、璋柄、刀尾和戈柄則可見到鏤雕。

此時已沒有大汶口／龍山文化的半月狀斧和小斧，這些器物的刃部都是呈弧形狀的。

在二里頭的發掘中，也有以上提到外型優美的刀，其中有些體型還很大。這些葬玉是新石器時代玉匠工藝成熟一面的表現，它們亦顯示了自龍山文化以後，玉器在宗教儀仗和葬禮中的重要性。若把玉器的發展與昆蟲由卵到蛹再變成蟲之進化作一比擬，那麼玉器在經過漫長之發展後，它最終抵達的成蟲階段，就是成為重要的宗教葬品。

在偃師遺址出土的一柱形玉柄，柄上有數節不同的裝飾，其中主要的兩節是繼承了良渚之傳統，以真陽線刻有曲尺人面紋。此人面上有蒜鼻，毗呈菱形，而非良渚傳統之橢圓形，這似乎較接近山東／龍山文化之觀念，多於追隨良渚文化的淺浮雕刻線。玉器上面紋有呈倒轉香蕉形狀的口部，兩側的手柄上有良渚玉琮面紋之特色，但都已經退化剝落，對於研究後期玉器歷史只剩餘少許價值。

在同一偃師玉柄的中節上，其外包層形似闊葉，上端有外翻銳利的尖，此種造型取闊葉形節之特色，在商代時已發展成為一種標準，而至西周時則變得扁平又簡化了。在參考書目22圖版51和52中，曾發表過陝西省寶雞出土的兩件西周玉柄，它們顯示了在當時應用的形制之特色。其中最特別的是有綠松石和玉片鑲嵌的部份連接，但又沒証據顯示此特色是在新石器時代或二里頭時代開始。

然而，偃師出土的這件二里頭玉器是唯一一件以人面紋和葉狀作組合的。

展品70上的人面紋，可與二里頭玉柄上的作一個比較。前者為一琮形之玉飾，四角以淺浮雕刻一修長面孔，貌相憂鬱。它的鼻、凸眼和毗的處理手法，尤以毗為例，與偃師玉柄的有異曲同工之妙。而實際上在整體質素方面，它是更美觀、複雜和具影響力的。

展品74背面頭部有一道斜坑，狀如一條髮辮，相信是供在頭上穿戴之飾物。其次，此頭飾精細的真陽線與勾環設計，表現了很複雜的技術。真陽線的造法，先要把表面沒雕刻的地方減地，以突出陽線設計之輪廓。在頰部後兩側有一勾，巨鼻，由頰骨至大口與展品70之人面紋相似。縱使這時的風格開始變得生硬，但展品70之特色，其實可以說是與山東龍山和石家河的怪獸紋有關的，而此特色實在是這時風格上的一個高潮。

二里頭玉器的發展是與當時剛起步的青銅器文化並駕齊驅的。故此，有一點值得注意是當時玉器在造型上和設計上之演變，以及陶瓷本身的發展，是開啟青銅鑄造藝術的唯一途徑。

偃師玉柄之紋飾，表現出當時已有青銅旋轉工具之製造。除良渚文化外，新石器時代玉器文化中，並未能製出如二里頭時代般精細的凸線或刻線。其後商代的玉匠多以假陽線作線刻，展品85是一呈幼蟲形之玉器。由此可見，真陽線是龍山後期和二里頭早期之特色，假陽線的運用肯定可追溯到商代安陽時期。如果上述和所採之例子是正確的話，那它們就代表了在公元前十四和十三世紀傑出的藝術成就。

在二里頭時期以青銅製刃是很簡單的事，但當時依然還出產很多優良的玉戈，此暗示了玉器仍保持著在宗教禮儀上的重要性。這些玉器簡潔典雅之特色，並非是單從改革而來的，它們其實早已植根於新石器時代的玉器，然後隨著不斷的進步發展而來的，這與當時原始和粗糙的青銅器比較，確是一有趣現象。

琮在良渚文化中是極其重要的，到西周時代，它雖仍繼續被沿用，但已不如良渚時般的廣泛了。而直至今天，二里頭的考古發掘仍未有琮的發現。

二里頭玉器的技巧，最主要是表現在巨型刀刃上的菱形紋陽刻（見展品75）和長條紋，而如果上面對凸線之假設是正確的話，那麼它亦是二里頭玉器技巧上之特色。這時期的玉材由不透明青苔綠至半透灰白色都有，估計應屬本地出產。至於造型以扁身為多，間中亦有如上玉柄般的方棒狀，而穿孔則為簡單的單面錐孔。

1

HUMAN FIGURE COLUMN WITH FLAT TERMINAL

NORTH CHINA NEOLITHIC PERIOD
POSSIBLY ZHAOBAOGOU CULTURE
 (C. 4800 - 4000 BC)

PE475

HEIGHT : 9.3 CM
DEPTH : 1.5 CM
THICKNESS : 1.0 CM

A light tawny green translucent nephrite anthropomorphic handle or column. The form is of a pillar of elliptical cross section tapering down at the lower end to a blunt chisel-shaped projection. The upper section is formed as a human figure with a huge head beneath a high headdress built up of six concentric superimposed rings. The face is long and blank in expression with the eyes formed by a single drilled lateral perforation, the nose flat and wide, the ears long and the mouth a hard slit above a concave protruding chin. The hands are clasped together in front with four fingers and the strong legs straddle each side of the chisel blade and terminate in large simple feet with incised toes.

The piece may be compared with a very similar, but substantively different, piece in the Winthrop Collection 46, No. 122. The eyes of the Winthrop piece are merely countersunk and not through perforated and it has an apical size reduction in the smallest top headdress coil and a damaged posterior extension to the pile of the headdress coils. Furthermore, the lower ear lobe of the Winthrop piece is clearly depicted in contrast to Exhibit 1. The layered pancake form of headdress should also be compared to a very similar form of hat on a stone figure excavated at Naxitai, Inner Mongolia which it is now possible to attribute to the Zhaobaogou culture. The structure and shaping of the flattened and simplified profile form of face may also be compared with a very similar human profile appearing at each end of a small fingerhole piece excavated at the Hongshan site of Niuheliang and seen there by the writer but not yet published. (AHF)

Compare: (i) 46 No.122 (ii) 69 pl.IX No.2a, and 2b
Collection: The Peony Collection

2

SEATED BULL HORNED HUMANOID

NORTH CHINA NEOLITHIC PERIOD
POSSIBLY ZHAOBAOGOU CULTURE
  (C. 4800 - 4000 BC)

PE512

HEIGHT : 7.2 CM
WIDTH : 3.9 CM
DEPTH : 2.0 CM

A fantastic humanoid figure in opaque grey-green nephrite with some black veining and suffusions. The figure is in an upright seated position with its hands on its knees and its lower legs angled in from the knee to meet together at the feet which are in tiptoe position. The broad shoulders support a strong neck on which sits a head with pointed chin, bull-horn headdress and well formed faun ears. There is a smoothly formed horizontal perforation of biconical origin through the sides of the neck and the details are well smoothed throughout with a number of the holes exhibiting concentric internal ridging or scoring.

For a full discussion of this piece and other arguable peers a long time in western collections, see 15. At the date of the publication of this catalogue, no information about the excavation of any similar piece from a controlled archaeological excavation in China has been published. Accordingly, ascription of this piece to the Zhaobaogou culture is a matter of deduction and surmise. The piece, however, bears many North China Neolithic jade characteristics.

The bull or buffalo horns are a so far unique feature of this piece and arguably represent an acknowledgment of the dominant destructive power of the bull and its horns, whether on domesticated or wild cattle is not known, although cattle bones are not a feature of excavated North China Neolithic burials. (AHF)

Previously published: 15 fig.6.
Compare: 15 figs. 7, 8, 9 and 10
Collection: The Peony Collection

3

SEATED HUMANOID

NORTH CHINA NEOLITHIC PERIOD
POSSIBLY ZHAOBAOGOU CULTURE
 (C.4800 - 4000 BC)

PE612

HEIGHT : 5.1 CM
WIDTH : 2.8 CM
DEPTH : 1.7 CM

A fantastic figure of humanoid shape in nephrite which is partly semi-translucent grey-green in colour and partly in opaque white with blackish-brown veining and flecking. The figure is in an upright seated position with its hands on its knees and its lower legs angled in from the knee to meet together at the feet which are in tiptoe position. The face is in the shape of an inverted triangle featuring softly formed and much smoothed angled lenticular eye plateaus with distinctly formed large ears at each side. A broad curve-walled groove rises from behind the head and passes across the top of the forehead to disappear on both sides at the back of the neck into a wide bore transverse conical perforation which is drilled from both sides and has substantial internal groove scoring or ridging. From the back aspect the strong bulging neck rolls smoothly down to the small of the back and swells out in fat buttocks. The details are well smoothed throughout.

The observations with regard to Exhibit 2 apply equally to this piece. There are, however, important sculptural differences. The principal difference is the marvellous swooping line of the massive neck bulge at the back of the piece and its curve down to the small of the back where it splays out to form the swelling buttocks which are almost half flattened beneath as though through the weight of the sitter. The second principal difference is the broadly formed continuous groove running from the back of the neck, round, across the forehead and back behind into the other rear side neck hole. These features possibly indicate a different,unknown but related, contemporary regional producer culture in North China from that of Exhibit 2. (AHF)

Compare : <u>5, No.15</u>
Collection: The Peony Collection

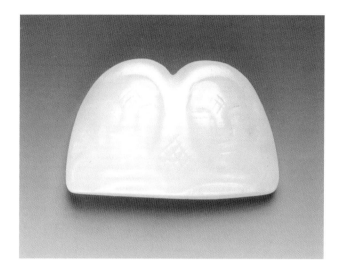

4

TWIN HEAD PLAQUE

NORTH CHINA NEOLITHIC PERIOD
HONGSHAN TYPE
 (C.3500 - 2200 BC)

                              PE603

LENGTH : 2.9 CM
HEIGHT : 1.9 CM
THICKNESS : 0.5 CM

Double oval-shaped plaque in translucent light yellow nephrite. Each rounded top panel is slightly inclined towards the other and carved in well smoothed low relief with a simple human face. On the forehead and between the eyes of each face is a diamond-shaped patch of cross hatching. There is a similar, large diamond-shaped cross-hatch patch between the two heads at cheek level. The flat back is pierced with a horizontal ox-nose or loop-hole for suspension. The details of the piece are well smoothed.

There is no published equivalent of this piece. Equally, there is no published treatment in neolithic jade of a plurality of human figures or faces in a single piece although a very interesting, unpublished, double human figure piece of the same type as Exhibit 3 is known to the writer. Cross-hatch work is known on excavated Hongshan jades and the extreme smoothing of the entire surface is consistent with excavated Hongshan jades. (AHF)

Collection: The Peony Collection

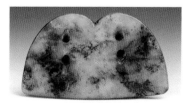

5

DOUBLE FACE PENDANT

NORTH CHINA NEOLITHIC PERIOD
HONGSHAN TYPE
 (C.3500 - 2200 BC)

                    BATEA 588

LENGTH : 5.8 CM
WIDTH : 3.4 CM

Double face pendant of lobed shape decorated with two indistinct human faces resembling large owl-like eyes, the jade of slightly greyish-green colour the reverse with two pairs of small ox-nose perforations for suspension. (BSM)

Compare: Exhibit 4

6

HUMAN MASK

NORTH CHINA NEOLITHIC PERIOD
HONGSHAN TYPE
 (C.3500 - 2200 BC)

BATEA 595

LENGTH : 5.8 CM
WIDTH : 3.1 CM

Blackish-grey and green jade with some brown suffusions depicting a human face, the reverse slightly concave with one large perforation of ox-nose type with extensive alteration in the perforation. (BSM)

7

CIRCLE CRESTED DRAGON

NORTH CHINA NEOLITHIC PERIOD
HONGSHAN TYPE
 (C.3500 - 2200 BC)

PE58

HEIGHT : 4.5 CM
WIDTH : 4.3 CM
THICKNESS : 0.7 CM

Circle bodied dragon of opaque black-green nephrite showing black flecked translucency at the tip of the snout and along the length of the crest. The extended, slightly up tilted snout has a cut- off end featuring twin nostrils. The creature has a long keel-shaped mane or crest with an everted and pointed terminal at mid dorsal point. The body is pierced with a transverse median hole drilled from both sides which forms a symmetrical suspension axis. The eyes are a drawn out tear drop shape set above elongated sunken cheeks.

The classic example of this form was found as a chance surface find at Sanxingtala, Inner Mongolia in 1971 without excavation but in association with nearby burials of Hongshan type. That classic piece which has been published many times is very large measuring 26.4 cm from top to bottom, and exhibits patches of diamond cross-hatch on the cheeks, chin and forehead. The present example is very small without cross hatch work but with a fluid movement and spirit very close to the Sanxingtala example. (AHF)

Compare: 100 No.14
Collection : The Peony Collection

8

BALLOON BODIED BEAST

NORTH CHINA NEOLITHIC
HONGSHAN TYPE
 (c.3500 - 2200 BC)

PE610

HEIGHT : 7 CM
WIDTH : 6.1 CM
DEPTH : 4.7 CM

Beast formed as a head and broad neck rising from a short, bulbous and well stuffed balloon body in semi-translucent yellow-green nephrite with substantial rust coloured blotching on the right hand side. The neck is pierced transversely from side to side with a substantial hole drilled from both sides and with internal concentric ridge scoring. The head has large, oval, bulging eyes which have a blind appearance without pupils, set within a connected series of upper and lower broad grooved, concave band formations constituting the cheeks, forehead and upper nose. Between the laid back calf-like ears is a diamond shaped lozenge area with diamond cross-hatching. Extending down from between the ears and across the back of the neck is a bib or lappet incised with two parallel registers of herring-bone hatching to form a mane and bordered all around by an enclosing broad concave groove. The mouth is closed and surmounted by well rubbed traces of pile-formed nostrils.

The cross-hatch work on the crown of the head is consistent with the cross hatch work on the double head plaque Exhibit 4 and with the cross-hatching on some other published Hongshan Jades. What seems unique here however, are the herringbone striations forming a bib-shaped patch across the back of the broad neck. It is also worth observing the similarity between the broad groove running from the ear base around the bulging eye and back to the ear base with the broad groove from neck hole to neck hole in Exhibit 3. Exhibit 8 is an arguable kindred piece to one that has been in the collection of the Tianjin Museum in China since well before 1949 and is without excavated provenance and which is illustrated in 56 No.17. (AHF)

Compare: 56 , No.17
Collection: The Peony Collection

9

LARVA

NORTH CHINA NEOLITHIC PERIOD
HONGSHAN TYPE
  (C.3500 - 2200 BC)
                            PE640
HEIGHT : 8.6 CM
WIDTH : 4.5 CM
THICKNESS : 1.6 CM

Fat bodied grub or larval stage (presumably of a cicada) in translucent yellow nephrite with a light rust permeation on the curved back. The huge eyes are well and smoothly depicted in low relief on the blunt-ended head of the creature and the curled body is divided into ridged segments which have an externally curved profile.

No equivalent piece with helical whorled segmentation has been published. The huge raised-ring eyes overlapping the corners of the blunt-ended head are another prominent feature without published analogy. The extreme smoothing is consistent with excavated Hongshan jades. (AHF)

Collection: The Peony Collection

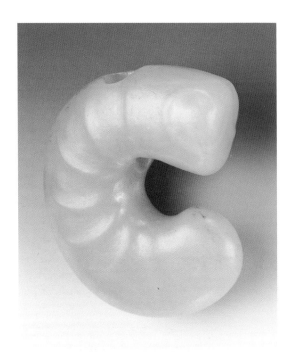

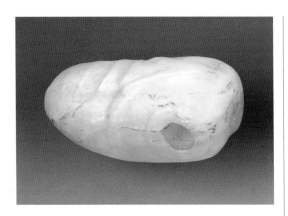

10

INSECT (CICADA)

NORTH CHINA NEOLITHIC PERIOD
HONGSHAN TYPE
  (C. 3500 - 2200 BC)
                            PE614
LENGTH : 5.0 CM
WIDTH : 2.3 CM
HEIGHT : 2.1 CM

A figure of a cicada formed in semi-translucent yellow stone. From the mid forehead a broad raised ridge rolls back to bifurcate behind the head and curve down each side to merge into the body. A transverse internally ridged perforation passes for suspension from the centre of a raised circular platform on each side representing the eyes. At the lower front or mouth area of the head there is an uprising sloped perforation which forms an internal right angled junction with the centre part of the transverse perforation. There is dorsal and abdominal transverse segmentation on the body.

The material of this piece is softer than nephrite. The broad ridged circumference of the hole-form eyes can be compared with the ridged-form eyes of Exhibit 8 but here there is a pupillary central hole feature. Each eye hole exhibits internal scoring or ridging consistent with excavated Hongshan jades. (AHF)

Compare: 100 pl.9
Collection: The Peony Collection

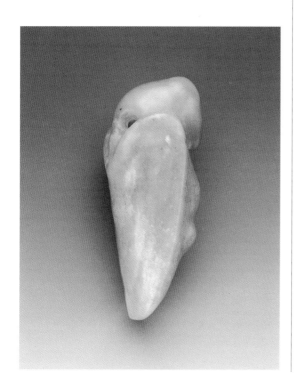

11

PERCHING EAGLE PENDANT

NORTH CHINA NEOLITHIC PERIOD
HONGSHAN TYPE
 (C.3500 - 2200 BC)
                                    PE723
HEIGHT : 5.3 CM
WIDTH : 2.2 CM
DEPTH 2.0 CM

Three dimensional sculpture of a perching eagle in semi-translucent yellow-green nephrite with some light brown suffusions on the beak and belly. The taloned feet are held against the belly and the sweeping wings with smooth long feather grooving are folded together down the back side. The head features a pair of large raised goggle eyes above a prominent beak which is pulled into the breast. At the back of the curved neck is a double loop or ox-nose hole for suspension.

Three dimensional sculptures are rare in North China Neolithic jade birds. The double loop or ox-nose hole at the back of the neck is the typical double drilled suspension hole seen also at the back of the neck of humanoid figures such as Exhibits 2 and 3. The representation of the wing flight feathers by means of down sweeping raised lines is typical. (AHF).

Collection: The Peony Collection

12

PERCHING EAGLE PENDANT

NORTH CHINA NEOLITHIC PERIOD
HONGSHAN TYPE
 (C. 3500 - 2200 BC)
                                    PE694
HEIGHT : 4.9 CM
WIDTH : 3.0 CM
THICKNESS : 1.0 CM

A flattened figure in profile of a perching aquiline bird with half-opened wings depicted with parallel raised lines to represent the wing feathers. The tail is bent forward as if to support the perched body and the curled, gripping talons are held at the front. There is a large, raised plateau form eye on each side of the head and a perforation through the back of the neck for suspension.

The use of parallel raised lines to represent the wing feathers is a typical feature seen also on the open-wing birds of Hongshan type. See Exhibit 14. (AHF).

Collection: The Peony Collection

13

SEATED BIRD PENDANT

NORTH CHINA NEOLITHIC PERIOD
HONGSHAN TYPE
  (c. 3500 - 2200 BC)

                              PE652

LENGTH : 8.0 CM
HEIGHT : 4.5 CM
BREADTH : 2.8 CM

Much simplified three-dimensional seated bird in semi-translucent
yellow-green nephrite with reddish-brown patches. The egg-shaped
body has simple wings folded against the sides and the drawn up legs
are represented by simple grooves beneath. The head is
formed as an oval form extension slightly raised and with a short
stubby beak with lightly incised mouth slit. On each side of the
head is a large oval raised eye of platform structure. The nape of the
neck is pierced by a double aperture connected hole for suspension.
The details of the piece are extremely well smoothed throughout.

There is no published similar example except a resting bird in the
Brundage Collection 1 No.1 which, however, lacks the raised oval
eye and the double connected neck-hole perforation. These features
give additional life to the Peony piece which otherwise has arguable
affinities with the Brundage example. There is as yet no published
example from a controlled archaeological excavation in China.
(AHF)

Compare: (i) 69 pl.II No.3 (ii) 1 pl.1
Collection: The Peony Collection

14

SPREAD-WING BIRD PENDANT

NORTH CHINA NEOLITHIC PERIOD
HONGSHAN TYPE
 (C.3500 - 2200 BC)

PE598

WIDTH : 4.8 CM
HEIGHT : 4.0 CM
THICKNESS : 1.2 CM

A bird in yellow-green translucent nephrite formed as a flattish plaque type structure lying on its back or in gliding flight with spread wings each wing featuring on the underside a straight, relief-raised line from top to bottom, a triangular raised line indication of the bent legs above the feet drawn up against the body and the surface of a fan-shaped tail spreading backwards with faint raised line lateral borders. The eyes are formed in low relief as side by side ridge circles overlapping the top of the head. The back of the bird is carefully and gently contoured down and away from a dorsal axis on each side to the wings and an ox-nose looped hole pierces the back of the neck. The details of the piece are well smoothed throughout.

The basic structure of this piece is a classic excavated Hongshan form and the extreme smoothing is consistent with excavated Hongshan jades. The careful triangle below the feet on the ventral side should be noted and also the suggestion of an undercut chin beneath the beak. The eyes on the crown of the head duplicate the broad ridge eye form of the larva, Exhibit 9. (AHF)

Compare: (i) 74, p.13, Fig.1 (ii) 15, Fig.1
Collection: The Peony Collection

15

SPREAD-WING BIRD PENDANT

NORTH CHINA NEOLITHIC PERIOD
HONGSHAN TYPE
(c.3500 - 2200 BC)

PE563

HEIGHT : 3.4 CM
BREADTH : 3 CM
THICKNESS : 0.3 CM

Bird with open wings in translucent yellow nephrite; the head
features two shaped eyes and is crowned by two erect rounded
auriform extensions on each side of a central peaked extension;
each wing is scored longitudinally with two large and very smoothed
grooves depicting pinion feathers; the extended
fan-shape tail also features four similar smoothed grooves; across the
chest is a feature representing the folded legs.

The erect owl ears each side of the central peak are also found
in a published turquoise example of this type from Dongshanzui in
Liaoning province, which shares the fan-shaped tail and everted ends
of the half spread wings with suggested feather-form grooving and a
single perforation through the right shoulder area. The indications are
that this creature is an owl as distinct both from the more docile,
round capped, pigeon-like form of the majority of Hongshan type flat
bird sculptures, and from the few examples of the more raptorial,
eagle-like form also known. (AHF)

Compare: (i) 74, p.13, Fig.2 (ii) 74 photo Fig.3
Collection: The Peony Collection

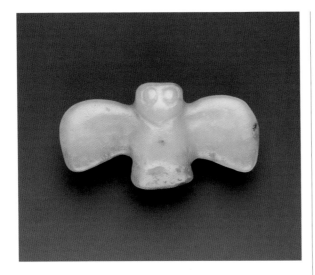

16

SPREAD-WING BIRD PENDANT

NORTH CHINA NEOLITHIC PERIOD
HONGSHAN TYPE
(c.3500 - 2200 BC)

PE655

WIDTH : 4.4 CM
HEIGHT : 2.1 CM
THICK : 0.5 CM

Bird in translucent yellow nephrite with open wings set out from
each side of the elongated convex body on which are
representations of the feet. The beak is pulled into the chest and
surmounted by a pair of huge unblinking eyes. At the back of the
neck is a connected double hole for suspension. The details are
well smoothed throughout.

The subtle thickened ridge forming the line from shoulder to tip
on the inner side of each outspread wing is a finely observed
sculptural fulcrum or reinforcing counterbalance to the relative
weakness of appearance in the lower, thinner wing section.
Although the owl-form "ears" are mere suggestions, the pointed
oval or heart-shaped face with fixed unblinking stare and the
slightly blunted wings both support an owl identification. (AHF)

Collection: The Peony Collection

17

BIRD'S HEAD SHAPED FINIAL

NORTH CHINA NEOLITHIC PERIOD
HONGSHAN TYPE
(c.3500 - 2200 BC)

PE722

LENGTH : 9.7 CM
HEIGHT : 2.9 CM
DEPTH : 0.5 CM

Long plaque-like finial in translucent yellow green nephrite and formed as the big bulge-eyed head of a bird with a curled and striated crest behind the prominent wide eye which is formed in relief on the eye socket bulge. A long pelican-like beak extends in front represented as partly open by a slit-form longitudinal incision formed from both sides of the beak and meeting as a smaller slit hole. The piece is identically formed on both sides.

Extended finial forms are a fairly standard form for North China Neolithic jades. The unusual element about this piece is that it is in the form of a bird's head. A similar, somewhat more elaborate, bird head finial is illustrated in 16 p. 24. (AHF)

Compare: 16 pl.24
Collection: The Peony Collection

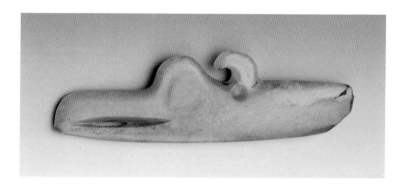

18

HOOKED EXTENSION

NORTH CHINA NEOLITHIC PERIOD
HONGSHAN TYPE
(c.3500 - 2200 BC)

PE713

LENGTH : 10 CM
WIDTH : 3.4 CM
THICKNESS : 0.5 CM

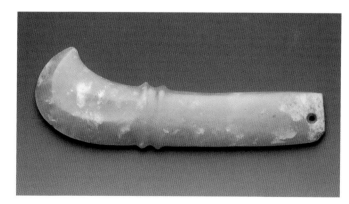

Flattened plaque-form hook or extension finial in translucent light green nephrite. The extended haft or tang has a squared end with a single perforation for attachment. This forms a uniform flattened shank with a double ridged, broad transverse groove formed as a ring all around the entire circumference of the piece. From the upper side of this transverse groove rises a slightly broader and bent over hook form with a broad central groove and a hook terminal mirroring the exterior perimeter of the piece.

This type of finial had a purpose not yet known, although it was clearly intended for insertion into some holding station and attached either by lashing or perhaps by a pin. The hollowing out of the hook terminal is very similar to the curved hollowing out of the flat ribbon or strap-form openwork objects normally described as "cloud-form pendants". (AHF)

Compare: 100 pl.4
Collection: The Peony Collection

19

SERRATED EDGE BAR

NORTH CHINA NEOLITHIC PERIOD
HONGSHAN TYPE
  (C.3500 - 2200 BC)

PE625

LENGTH : 9.5 CM
HEIGHT : 3.0 CM
THICKNESS : 0.6 CM

Flat bar pendant with elliptical section formed as a round-ended oblong with an upper straight edge and a lower edge indented to form five teeth separated by grooved transverse channels cut vertically across the convex face on each side of the piece.

There is currently no well formulated conceptualisation of the use of this piece but the single upper-level two-sided perforation argues strongly for a suspension or pendant application. (AHF)

Collection: The Peony Collection

20

COMB-FORM PENDANT

NORTH CHINA NEOLITHIC PERIOD
HONGSHAN TYPE
  (C.3500 - 2200 BC)

PE596

WIDTH : 9.9 CM
HEIGHT : 4.5 CM
THICKNESS : 0.4 CM

Flat plaque of pendant form in opaque light green nephrite with comb-tooth and curl perimeter excrescences. Each side is identical about a central axis featuring a pair of eyes with pierced pupils and curving brows giving the appearance of a fantastic animated face. In the middle of the "forehead" the piece is pierced with a single hole for suspension.

For a perceptive and analytical treatment of a similar piece in the Sackler Museum in Washington, see 72. There is a cut fragment in the Tianjin Museum 56 p.114. There is as yet no clear fact or surmise which adequately justifies or explains the subtle complexities of marrying curves and crescents in such a format, but the top central perforation argues strongly for a suspended, pendant applied use. (AHF)

Compare: (i) 72 (ii) 56 pl.14
Collection: The Peony Collection

21

KNUCKLE-DUSTER WITH PIG'S-HEAD TERMINALS

NORTH CHINA NEOLITHIC PERIOD
HONGSHAN TYPE
 (c.3500 - 2200 BC)

PE750

WIDTH : 10.2 CM
HEIGHT : 5.0 CM
DEPTH : 1.3 CM

Toothed implement or fitting in semi-opaque dark green nephrite formed as a basic rectangle. At each narrow end is mounted an elongated pig's mask with prominent eyes and flap ears. The lower edge is formed into four prominent teeth of uniform length with squared ends. Through the body of the piece are two large holes which are themselves bordered on their inner sides by a slightly raised line ridge.

There is a famous example of this type of pig's-head ended knuckle-duster, currently ascribed to the Hongshan type which has been published a number of times 100, p. 10. Although the currently known pieces are rare, they all seem to have a flat base which is itself pierced with vertical holes - presumably for attachment. Exhibit 21 is so far unique in its squared tooth-form bottom. The flat base type can be argued as some kind of handle attachment but the exact use of Exhibit 21 is a mystery. (AHF)

Compare: 100 pl.10
Collection: The Peony Collection

22

FLAT OVAL-RIDGED PENDANT

NORTH CHINA NEOLITHIC PERIOD
HONGSHAN TYPE
 (c.3500 - 2200 BC)

PE705

HEIGHT : 6.3 CM
WIDTH : 5.2 CM
DEPTH : 0.3 CM

Flattened ring-form pendant of oval shape in translucent yellow nephrite pierced at the top with a single hole for suspension. At each shoulder of the piece are two angled ridges separated by three smoothed transverse grooves.

This strikingly simple and effective shape of which no other example has been published demonstrates the full range of artistic sensitivity of which the North China Neolithic jade artist was capable. (AHF)

Collection: The Peony Collection

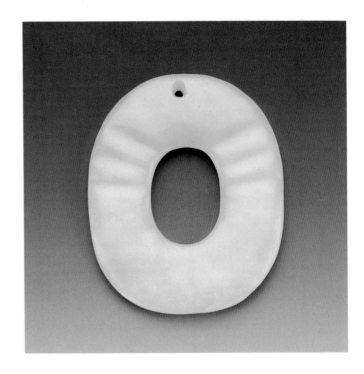

23

GREEN FLAT PIG-MASK PLAQUE

NORTH CHINA NEOLITHIC PERIOD
HONGSHAN TYPE
 (c.3500 - 2200 BC)

PE736

WIDTH : 2.8 CM
HEIGHT : 4.0 CM
DEPTH : 0.5 CM

Flat plaque form pig-mask in translucent green nephrite. The raised ears branch up from slanted, raised plateau-form eyes. The eyes are placed above a broad transverse groove or double ridge which marks the curved beginning of the snout. The end of the snout is pierced with a connected loop hole for suspension.

There is no published piece similar to this Exhibit. Its principal interest lies however in the clear and unambiguous representation of the pig's head or mask in this flat form. (AHF)

Collection: The Peony Collection

24

YELLOWISH JADE PIG-DRAGON PENDANT

NORTH CHINA NEOLITHIC PERIOD
HONGSHAN TYPE
(c.3500 - 2200 BC)

BATEA 454

HEIGHT : 5.2 CM
WIDTH : 3.8 CM
BREADTH : 1.5 CM

Yellowish jade pig-dragon or dragon embryo pendant of
characteristic form, spectacle eyes and ears, the curled dragon
carved almost through and drilled through for suspension from
both sides; the jade with brownish suffusions.

The colour of the stone used here is typical of many of the jades
from this culture type. The shape, which is particularly associated
with this culture type, has been christened by commentators a
pig-dragon though a dragon embryo designation has also been
suggested. (BSM)

Compare: 16 p.62 fig.22

25

PIG-DRAGON

NORTH CHINA NEOLITHIC PERIOD
HONGSHAN TYPE
  (C.3500 - 2200 BC)
                    PE468
HEIGHT : 4.5 CM
BREADTH : 2.5 CM
THICKNESS : 1.8 CM

A pig-dragon with a coiled and segmented larval or silkworm body in translucent yellow nephrite with some chestnut suffusions. The piece is folded round a vertical axis aperture which perforates the stone from side to side. The great head has out-turned and pointed horn or ear-like projections and huge elliptical eyes with large encircled pupils.

No example of a segmented pig-dragon has been excavated or published to date. The writer has seen one single other example in jade, which was altered throughout, and one in turquoise. The pure yellow material with russet suffusions is consistent with a number of pieces of uncertain archaeological provenance that have been in public collections for many years both in China and the West and are currently ascribed to the Hongshan type by most observers. (AHF)

Previously published: 16 pl.13
Compare: (i) 27 pl.54 and 55 (ii) 100 pl.12
Collection: The Peony Collection

26

FLAT TURTLE

NORTH CHINA NEOLITHIC PERIOD
HONGSHAN TYPE
  (C.3500 - 2200 BC)
                    PE455
WIDTH : 2.9 CM
BREADTH : 2.9 CM
THICKNESS : 0.4 CM

A figure of a turtle formed as a flattened plaque in grey-green nephrite with reddish-brown suffusions. The head is slightly drawn in and the two bulging eyes retain the red skin surface. The forelegs are folded back upon themselves and the hind legs are drawn up against the shell while the small tail curves closely to the right. The round shell is perforated between head and tail by two separate holes drilled conically from back to base. Only rudimentary and suggestive outlines only of the shell and legs appear beneath.

The contiguous, adjacent folding of the femur against the tibia and fibula in the hind limbs and of the humerus against radius and ulna in the forelimbs is a distinct characteristic of excavated Hongshan turtle forms 100 pl.11. A piece very similar to this was excavated from the Shang dynasty's Fu Hao tomb at Anyang 36, pl.CXL VII-3 and the indications are that both this piece, and the Fu Hao piece, are considerably older than the Anyang phase of the Shang dynasty.

The analogous anatomical features of the excavated Hongshan turtles make a Hongshan, or North Chinese Neolithic attribution for this piece entirely reasonable. (AHF)

Compare: (i) 35 pl.CXLVII No.3 (ii) 91 pl.68
Collection: The Peony Collection

27

JADE TUBE

NORTH CHINA NEOLITHIC PERIOD
HONGSHAN TYPE
  (C.3500 - 2200 BC)
                        BATEA 590
HEIGHT : 13.9CM
WIDTH : 9.2CM
DIAMETER : 8 CM

Jade tube of oval section with long tail comparable to a nurse's changeable cuff, the jade of yellowish-green colour with extensive fawn coloured alteration. The narrower end drilled through from side to side, possibly for a hairpin.

Several examples of tubes similar to this Exhibit are known and with the pig-dragon (Exhibit 24) are considered the most characteristic shapes of jades of Hongshan type. The shape does not seem to be found among south China neolithic jades. It possibly represents a hair sheath for burial. (BSM)

Compare: (i) 16, p 50, fig. 2 (ii) 99, No. 1

28

JADE SPLIT RING AND
PUDDING-STONE RING

NORTH CHINA NEOLITHIC PERIOD
CHAHAI TYPE
(C.4700 - 3000 BC)

BATEA 593

(I) WIDTH : 3.8CM
   HEIGHT : 3.4CM
   DEPTH : 2.8 CM

BATEA 591

(II) DIAMETER : 4 CM
   WIDTH : 2.8 CM
   HEIGHT : 2 CM

Yellowish-green jade split ring drilled and showing extensive traces of the drilling technique used.

This type of ring has been found at Chahai, an early Hongshan type site.

A thick pudding-stone ring with arched top section and small hole, possibly a very abstract pig-dragon. This is believed to have come from the same source as (I) above. (BSM)

29

GREYISH-WHITE JADE BRACELET

NORTH CHINA NEOLITHIC PERIOD
HONGSHAN TYPE
(c.3500 - 2200 BC)

BATEA 435

LENGTH OVERALL: 10.3 CM
WIDTH OVERALL: 8.4 CM
DIAMETER OF OUTER BAND: VARYING FROM 1.9 CM TO 2.2 CM

Plain white jade oblong, almost rectangular bracelet, the corners all
rounded, the outer edges coming to a blunt point all the way round,
the inner edges of the bracelet smooth, the edges with earth
encrustations and traces of the working process.

The construction of this bracelet, revealing gradual convex
working (from top to bottom and from one side to the other
horizontally) and its almost rectangular shape are both typically
neolithic. The colour of the material suggests a classification as
Hongshan type, as similarly coloured jades have been associated
with this culture type. (BSM)

Compare: 99, No. 12

30

HUANG PENDANT

NEOLITHIC PERIOD, SONGZE CULTURE
 (C.4000 - 2500 BC)

PE427

WIDTH : 9.5 CM
HEIGHT : 6.1 CM

A curved bow-form *huang* pendant in pure and opaque white nephrite material. The middle part is thicker than both ends, each of which is drilled with a small biconical perforation.

This piece is a typical artefact of the Songze culture named for the area round Qingpu in Shanghai municipality on the Lower Yangzi River, China. When found and dated in the 1980s, Songze culture was the oldest known jade working culture in China. Its jade working antiquity has now been exceeded by the more recently discovered Xinglongwa culture of Inner Mongolia and the Chahai culture of Liaoning Province, both in the north of the country. These bow-form pendants can be of a very deep profile like this example or grading down to a much shallower curve, but always retaining the same thinned ends, each with a small biconical perforation drilled very near to the terminal edge. The standard cross section of these *huang* is an elliptical or oval shape. The form is also found in quartz and agate, both hard materials traditionally appreciated as jade. The Songze culture also produced jade slit-discs for ear decoration and as wrist bracelets. (AHF)

Previously published: 16 pl.36
Collection: The Peony Collection

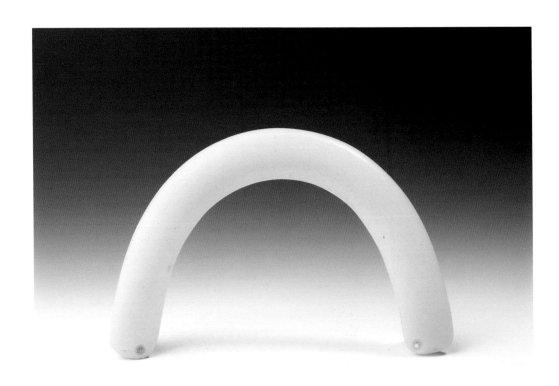

31

HUANG BI-DISC PENDANTS AND BEADS

LIANGZHU CULTURE
  (c.3400 - 2250 BC)

PE259-268

	A	B	C	D	E
			(I) 10.3 CM		VARIOUS
LENGTH :	11.2 CM		(II) 7 CM		1.4 - 3.1 CM
WIDTH :	4.4 CM				
DIAMETER OVERALL:	11.7 CM		3.2 CM		0.9-1.6 CM
HEIGHT :					
DEPTH :	0.5 CM	1.0 CM	(I) 1 CM	1 CM	
			(II) 1 CM		
DIAMETER OF APERTURE:		4.4 CM			

TEN PIECES OF UNDECORATED LIANGZHU NEPHRITE AS FOLLOWS:-

A	B	C	D	E
Huang	*Bi-disc*	Two column pendants	Bored disc	Five cylinder beads

These ten pieces, all except the *huang* and one of the cylinder beads, are of altered material, and are a sufficently homogeneous series to support the view that they come from the same, contemporary source. The *huang*, a semi-spherical form but retaining the merest suggestion of an arc form in the little nick or indentation at the mid point of the long flat edge is of yellowish-green unaltered material with some brownish suffusions. The *bi-disc* retains the double drilled hole with central snap out facility typical of this culture. All the beads are conically drilled from both ends. (AHF).

Collection: The Peony Collection

32

ALTERED JADE *BI-DISC*

NEOLITHIC PERIOD
LIANGZHU CULTURE
 (c.3400 - 2250 BC)
                    BATEA 430
DIAMETER OVERALL: 14.5 CM
DIAMETER OF CENTRAL APERTURE: 6.5 CM

Altered jade *bi-disc* of yellowish-green coloured jade with large
russet sections. (BSM)

Previously published: <u>80, No.4</u>

33

PAIR OF SERPENTINE *BI-DISCS*

NEOLITHIC PERIOD PROBABLY
LIANGZHU CULTURE
 (c.3400 - 2250 BC)
                              BATEA 428
DIAMETER OVERALL : 17.2 CM
DIAMETER OF CENTRAL APERTURE: 2.6 CM

Pair of thick dark green circular *bi-discs* with small holes, the thick
stone slightly convex on one side, the small central holes drilled
from both sides. Both *bi-discs* have two additional small holes drilled
right through, and both have one hole drilled two thirds of the way
through. Both have a distinctly worn section. The stone here is
probably serpentine rather than nephrite.

The existence of the worn sections and the additional holes (some
only going part way through) lead to interesting speculations as to
the original use of these particular *bi-discs*. One suggestion which
seems plausible is that they are parts of a gear mechanism such as
for a potter's wheel with the worn section on both caused by the
hand or foot operating the gear. (BSM)

34

AXE

NEOLITHIC PERIOD
LIANGZHU CULTURE
(c.3400 - 2250 BC)
PE231
LENGTH : 13.6 CM
BREADTH : 10.5 CM
THICKNESS : 0.6 CM

Thin axe formed with elliptical section from translucent dark
grass-green material with uneven patches of alteration. The flat
bi-convex body has straight slightly tapering sides. The butt seems
to have been reground at a time contemporary with manufacture.
The large median hole is drilled from both sides leaving a sharp,
jagged, unpolished snap-out ridge remnant or join around the radial
wall of the hole.

This piece demonstrates Liangzhu type characteristics such as the
slightly tapering sides, the unlevelled butt and the snap-out ridge
remnant in the single hole. The translucent dark green material is
the arguably pristine form of many Liangzhu jade artefacts which
are now altered to opaque, bean curd white (AHF).

Previously published: 16 pl.11
Compare: (i) 46 No.13 (ii) 55 pl.233
Collection: The Peony Collection

35

ALTERED JADE STYLISED BIRD-SHAPED PLAQUE

NEOLITHIC PERIOD
LIANGZHU CULTURE
(C.3400 - 2250 BC)
BATEA 581
LENGTH : 8 CM
WIDTH : 3.4 CM

Altered jade trapezoidal plaque of stylised bird shape with two shallow rectangular indentations in the middle of the top edge. The bottom with slightly narrower section probably for insertion into a slot with two fine perforations at each end. (BSM)

Previously published: 77 no.1
Compare: 98 pl. XXVI.

36

TRAPEZOIDAL PENDANT

NEOLITHIC PERIOD
LIANGZHU CULTURE
(C.3400 - 2250 BC)
PE360
LENGTH : 5.8 CM
HEIGHT : 3.1 CM
THICKNESS : 0.3 CM

Angular pendant plaque in trapezoidal shape and of calcified glossy material of high burnish and ivory-white colour. There is a flange along one side pierced with three small equidistant holes for attachment. Outward flaring sides lead up to the opposite edge which has an ogival indentation in the centre. Each plane face is incised with a symmetrical and complex design formed of a series of connected concentric or vortical circles and structured:

(a) one way up, about an animal face with large round eyes and elongated open mouth showing downward curving fangs, and in each upper corner auriform membranes also representing bisected human heads with sun ray headdress;

(b) the other way up, about a similar animal face with small open mouth, pronounced nostrils and large cheek pouches.

This pendant plaque is the same basic trapezoidal shape as Exhibit 37 but without the openwork. In consequence, the incised surface designs are more complex than those on Exhibit 37 and appear to feature two half-formed beings in attendance at each side of a snarling animal face of great ferocity with lips pulled back over bared fangs. The eye structure represents a third Liangzhu specific type formed as a tight ball of incised concentric circles with radial bar interruptions. There is every stylistic and artistic inspirational reason to associate this central image with the origins of the famous *taotie* form of ferocious animal face. (AHF)

Compare: (i) 55, pl.119
Collection: The Peony Collection

37
TRAPEZOIDAL OPENWORK PENDANT
NEOLITHIC PERIOD, LIANGZHU CULTURE
(C.3400 - 2250 BC)

PE325

WIDTH : 8.7 CM
HEIGHT : 4.0 CM
THICKNESS : 0.4 CM

Angular pendant plaque of trapezoidal shape of altered glossy jade material of high burnish and ivory-white colour. There is a flange along one side pierced with three small, equidistant holes for attachment. The outward flaring sides lead up to the opposite edge which has an elegant and restrained ogival riser in the centre. Each plane face is pierced with a symmetrical openwork design structured about a long armed figure with a sun ray headdress, having arguable feather associations and detailed incised striation devices. A long jawed animal face with similar headdress peers inwards from each upper corner.

The openwork flange pendant in trapezoidal shape is one of the rarest and most accomplished of the Liangzhu jades. It demonstrates the determination of the neolithic artisan who laboured with equipment that we still cannot effectively imagine, presumably for many months, to make this piece but of whom there is no written record to acknowledge his achievement. Two wolves are attacking (or perhaps guarding) the central figure which has a sunburst headdress and long arms reaching through the entwining anatomical coils, perhaps those of the wolves' bodies. It is interesting to note that the eyes of the wolves have an incised, half profile outer border similar in shape to the relief-carved animal eye in the lower register of some examples of the two-register short-form Liangzhu *cong*, Exhibit 39. This eye also exhibits a pupil and a midway side nick to represent the canthus. Note also that these nicked canthus eyes are in stark contrast to the eyes of the central humanoid figure which are simple double circles with no concession to the canthus detail. The symbolism of this assortment is still the subject of much conjecture and discussion. (AHF)

Previously published: 16 pl.41
Compare: 55 pls. 122 and 123
Collection: The Peony Collection

38
PIG-FORM PENDANT
NEOLITHIC PERIOD, LIANGZHU CULTURE
(C.3400 - 2250 BC)

PE363

LENGTH : 6.0 CM
HEIGHT : 3.2 CM
BREADTH : 0.6 CM

Zoomorphic pendant in burnished altered material of ivory-white colour with longitudinal flange pierced with two holes for attachment. The piece is formed asymmetrically and in the round at one end has a saucer-eyed pig-like head and incised massive canine teeth. At the other end is a truncated saucer-eyed beast head with similar teeth. The intervening field is incised with a complex design formed by a series of connected concentric or vortical circles.

It is reasonably clear that this piece is in fact a flanged pendant or perhaps a totem which would possibly have been mounted in some wooden housing, long disintegrated. There has been considerable published commentary on the significance of the pig to neolithic man (40) and pig skulls and bones have been found in Liangzhu type jade-bearing and other tombs showing a high contemporary regard and respect for the pig or wild boar. See also Exhibits 21 and 23 (AHF)

Previously published: 16 pl. 40
Compare: 43 pl.3
Collection: The Peony Collection

39

TWO LAYER *CONG*

NEOLITHIC PERIOD, LIANGZHU CULTURE
 (C.3400 - 2250 BC)

PE345

DIAMETER OVERALL : 8.3 CM
INTERNAL DIAMETER : 6.3 CM
HEIGHT : 6.1 CM

Cong, in ivory-white altered jade with some greyish veins and reddish-brown markings, with a highly burnished finish and in the form of a squat cylinder. The exterior perimeter of the piece is arranged round upper and lower registers of simplified human and animal masks formed as four equidistant "corner-angle" panels. Each upper mask is composed of two horizontal bands of fine *striae* forming eyebrows, a pair of incised, perfect circular eyes, a raised corner angle nose and an incised central circular pupil with midway side nicks to represent the canthus. Each lower mask has two large saucer eyes in concave relief with the same incised inner and outer circular pupil formation as the upper masks and a corner-angle nose. The vertical flat surfaces of both upper and lower corner-angle noses are incised with finger print-like meanders of varying intensity.

There are no known facts capable of challenging the assertion that the *cong* is entirely an invention of the Liangzhu culture. From carbon dating it is thought that a single, one layer *cong* of a low bangle form with four corner mask forms of roughly drawn type is the earliest *cong* form yet discovered and is considered to date from approximately 3600 BC. It was excavated at Zhanglingshan, Wuxian, in Jiangsu Province in the mid 1980's.

From this simple origin of embellishment onto a bracelet form, gradually developed the mature *cong*. Exhibit 39 is a product of the high point of the Liangzhu jade production dating from approximately 2500 BC. Similar pieces were excavated from the Fanshan Hill excavation north west of Hangzhou during the 1980's under the direction of Mou Yongang. No incontestable reason has been advanced for the blenched, opaque whiteness of pieces such as this nor has the precise method of working the extraordinarily fine parallel lines forming the *striae* above and below the corner eye motifs been identified. Although controlled archaeological excavation has revealed that metallic copper was worked by, and known to, North China Neolithic jade cultures of the Hongshan type, there is as yet no similar evidence for the use of copper by the Liangzhu people. Both the much earlier Hongshan type, and Liangzhu culture date from times well before the most optimistic putative dates for the commencement of the Bronze Age now placed at approximately 2100 BC. There is a fearsome, cold reality, at once both metaphysical and yet somehow calculated, about the high precision detail and volumetric organisation of the two register *congs* which sets them far apart from, and above, all other neolithic jades. (AHF)

Previously published: 16 pl.39
Compare: (i) 1 pl.XI (ii) 55 pl.19
Collection: The Peony Collection

40

SQUARED COLUMN WITH POINT

NEOLITHIC PERIOD, LIANGZHU CULTURE
(c.3400 - 2250 BC)

PE297

LENGTH : 6.5 CM
WIDTH : 1.5 CM

Obelisk thick-form pendant in yellow material turning white in small areas
with four plane-faces meeting at the rather abruptly pointed end. The other end
has a square-cut section and a fastening projection with a transverse hole
drilled through from both sides. Towards the pointed end each face of the piece
is carved with separate registers of fine-line incising and, on two sides, with
raised elliptical-eyed animal masks bridging the corner angle between the two
adjacent planes.

The fine lemon-yellow, semi-translucent stone possibly represents the pristine
form of one type of the raw material available for Liangzhu jade workers to
fashion. Across the corner angle formed by the right angled meeting of two
plane surfaces, are arranged two closely packed bundles of parallel lines. These
are arranged around the entire body of the piece and adjacent to, but towards
the narrowed end away from, a large eyed animal mask bridging the corner
angle. Because the greater bulk of excavated and unprovenanced Liangzhu jade
artefacts have been subjected, whether naturally or not, to the whitening
process called alteration, Liangzhu pieces in the pristine material are extremely
rare. A short peg extension from the squared end of the piece is pierced with a
biconical hole sufficient to take a thread for suspension. In contradistinction to
the much more frequently encountered rounded or tapered cylindrical profile, it
is most likely that the obelisk form with a curved, four-faceted blunt pointed
end has a significant meaning. We still await practical or hypothetical
archaeological work to come forward with an adequate interpretation of the
difference. (AHF)

Previously published: 16 pl.37
Compare: 55 pl.135 and pl.148
Collection: The Peony Collection

41

JADE BEAD WITH *TAOTIE* MASKS

NEOLITHIC PERIOD
LIANGZHU CULTURE
(c.3400 - 2250 BC)

BATEA 547

LENGTH : 3 CMS
DIAMETER : 1 CMS

Altered jade tubular bead of ivory-white colour pierced by drillings from both ends with an uneven join, the central portion of the outer surface in-set with a narrow undecorated band, the two end sections each decorated with two *taotie* masks, each showing rectangular mouth and large oval eyes with complicated incised scrollwork in and around the eyes. (BSM)

Compare: (i) A similar bead published in <u>Orientations, April 1988</u> (ii) <u>44, No 13</u> (iii) <u>61, No 27</u>

42

HALF CYLINDER MASK

NEOLITHIC PERIOD, LIANGZHU CULTURE
(c. 3400 - 2250 BC)

PE423

LENGTH : 2.3 CM
HEIGHT : 2.2 CM
THICKNESS : 1.2 CM

Solid semicircular block in translucent yellow-green stone. The curved outer face is carved in relief with a saucer-eyed human mask with splayed nose and wide banana shaped mouth. Two pairs of holes were drilled from the flat top and the other pair from the bottom for some suspension or affixing purpose.

The assymetrical structure of the eyes and the fan shape of the raised relief bridge linking the eyes should be compared with the same structures in the lower register on Exhibit 39. However, there are important distinctions on this half cylinder block. Firstly, the inverted Doric capital form of nose and, secondly the banana shaped raised-level mouth with a single horizontal groove structure. There are a number of solid, half cylinder mask-form pendants of Liangzhu type but these are in fact contemporary polished down corner-angle fragmentations of Liangzhu *cong* forms and not, as with this piece, block pendants or attachment forms in their own right. There is as yet no published archaeological guidance available to identify the precise use for this half cylinder block form of mask pendant. (AHF)

Collection: The Peony Collection

43

TWO RED CORNELIAN
BI-DISCS

NEOLITHIC PERIOD
LIANGZHU CULTURE
   (c.3400 - 2250 BC)
             BATEA 564
DIAMETER : 2.5 CM & 1.9 CM RESPECTIVELY

Two small round flat circular red cornelian
bi-discs, neatly holed from both sides, the stone
with some white patches.

Similar cornelian *bi-discs* have been found in a
Liangzhu cultural context. (BSM)

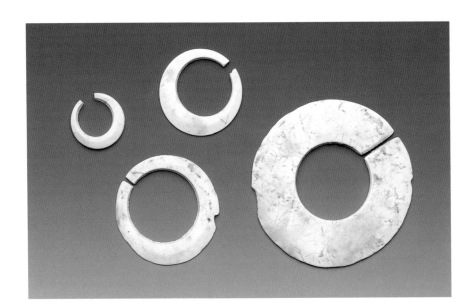

44

FOUR ALTERED ASYMMETRICAL SLIT-DISCS

NEOLITHIC PERIOD
PROBABLY LIANGZHU CULTURE
   (c.3400 - 2250 BC)
             BATEA 437
I) OVERALL DIAMETER 5 CM, DIAMETER OF APERTURE: 2.3 CM
II) OVERALL DIAMETER 3.3 CM, DIAMETER OF APERTURE: 2.2 CM
III) OVERALL DIAMETER 2.6 CM, DIAMETER OF APERTURE: 1.7 CM
IV) OVERALL DIAMETER 1.7 CM, DIAMETER OF APERTURE: 1.1 CM

Set of four altered jade asymmetrical slit-discs each of different size, the smallest two
fitting one within the other, showing them to have been carved from the same piece
of jade, all with band broader on the side opposite the slit, and all flat and uncarved
on one side, the reverse with one plane on the outer rim making the outer edge come
to a point, the inner edge carved from one side leaving the inner edge slightly concave.

This type of slit-disc, probably used as earrings, continued to be made for centuries
in south China with only minor changes of style. The unusual asymmetric form and
the altered nature of the jades, however, both suggest a Neolithic date and a probable
Liangzhu culture provenance. (BSM)

45

HAMMER HEAD

NORTH CHINA NEOLITHIC
(c. 5500 - 2200 BC)
PE452

LENGTH : 10.5 CM
WIDTH : 4 CM
HEIGHT : 3.2 CM

Mallet or hammer head of smooth and well compacted dark green-black schist. Each striking face swells from the side to the centre which is pierced with a large hole that tapers down in width from the bottom to the top.

As with Exhibit 50, this piece, although very hard, is formed of a sedimentary, finely laid and compacted shale-like matrix that nonetheless lends itself well to smoothing. The creation of extremely clear, sharp lines and edges should also be noted. There is no doubt about its utilitarian possibilities although there is no evidence of actual use. (AHF)

Collection: The Peony Collection

46

SQUARED-HEAD BEAD

NEOLITHIC PERIOD, DAWENKOU CULTURE
(c.4500 - 2300 BC)
PE692

HEIGHT : 2.8 CM
WIDTH : 2.3 CM

Cylindrical bead with squared corners on a vertical axis in opaque golden-brown stone. One full side is formed in low relief shallow groove work as a simplified human face with a pair of horizontal diamond-shaped eyes meeting above a vertical, rectangular nose and an open mouth beneath. At each side is a semi-circular groove forming an ear.

There is a flat-form grey-green jade piece with black patches and grooved simple human features in the Tengxian museum in Shandong Province. This piece was excavated from a site at Gangshang village at Tengxian and the use of strong, simple grooving to represent the features of the face and the tapered form of nose is very similar to Exhibit 46 and strongly suggest a Dawenkou culture period attribution and date for Exhibit 46. (AHF)

Compare: 100 pl.17
Collection: The Peony Collection

47

ADZE

NEOLITHIC PERIOD, DAWENKOU CULTURE
  (C. 4500 - 2300 BC)

PE407

LENGTH : 21.5 CM
WIDTH : 10.0 CM
HEIGHT : 0.5 CM

Adze blade in opaque black-flecked grey-green
nephrite with some superficial fracture points.
Each face is smoothed to a high polish and tapers
imperceptibly from the careful semi-lunar
hollow-ground blade edge at one end up and
along to the precisely formed and finished butt at
the other where a transverse scar line on each
face marks the horizontal breakpoint beneath the
flattened central ridge. The butt is pierced with
one small hole drilled from each face to connect
midway through with half the diameter of the
drilling from the other side. One larger hole
nearby is drilled by contusion grinding from both
sides creating a well-formed domed hole on one
side which has a smoothed ridge or join in the
middle of its radial wall.

According to archaeological publications to date,
the lunette-shaped hollow grinding of the blade
edge on the *chan* or adze blade and on axe blades
are exclusive to the Dawenkou culture in the
Shandong peninsula. Because of its occurrence
on this lunette-ground blade edge piece, the
dome shape contusion ground hole can
accordingly also be ascribed to the Dawenkou
culture. (AHF)

Previously published: 16 pl.12
Compare: (i) 100 pl.16 (ii) 46 No.12
Collection: The Peony Collection

48

OBLONG PLAQUE HOLE PENDANTS

NEOLITHIC PERIOD
MAJIABIN CULTURE
  (c. 5000 - 3900 BC)

PE316-PE317

LENGTH : 8.5 CM
BREADTH : 4.0 CM
HEIGHT : 0.4 CM

A pair of large oblong pendants of an almost rectangular shape with rounded corners formed from a greenish nephrite now altered, one a little wider than the other and each pierced with three large equidistant holes on the plane face on the long sides. In between each pair of holes are equidistant pairs of short cuts or nicks.

These two pendants with three-hole piercing are of a so far uniquely large size among published examples of the type which normally has the same form but with two holes or one hole only and are of a much smaller size. The similiar excavated finds to date are drawn from northern Anhui and southern Shandong Provinces in China and have a pale lime-green colour of jade material which, when not altered, is well represented in the published finds from Huating village in Anhui Province. (AHF)

Collection: The Peony Collection

49

HAND IMPLEMENT

NEOLITHIC PERIOD
MAJIABIN CULTURE
  (c.5000 - 3900 BC)
PE405

LENGTH : 12.5 CM
WIDTH : 6.2 CM
HEIGHT : 0.7 CM

Hand-grip or knuckle-duster in translucent pale green nephrite, clouded with incipient alteration and polished overall to a soft gloss. The grip of the piece is formed of a straight back with angled top and bottom bridges traversed by broad gouged channels and joining a frontal blade with two extending spurs top and bottom and a long sharp curving edge between, itself diagonally scored on each side with three broad, gouged channels.

This enigmatic implement can be held like a knuckle-duster and could when wielded as such deliver a vicious wound with its sharp blade edge and projecting spikes. It is, however, a fragile article unlikely to withstand rough use. A very similar piece lacking, however, the angled, broad grooving across the "blade" was excavated at the Huating village site at Xiaoxian in Anhui Province in 1986 and has been published in 21 pl.59 where it is described as a jade knife of the late Neolithic age. It is possible that the form is that of a ceremonial cutter or chopper for preparing ingredients for rite or ritual, rather than having a military or pugilistic significance. On the other hand, the observations made in respect of Exhibit 54 about that piece constituting another rarely found form of the neolithic jade weaponry repertoire may also be relevant in relation to this piece. (AHF)

Previously published: 16 pl.34
Compare: 21 pl.59
Collection: The Peony Collection

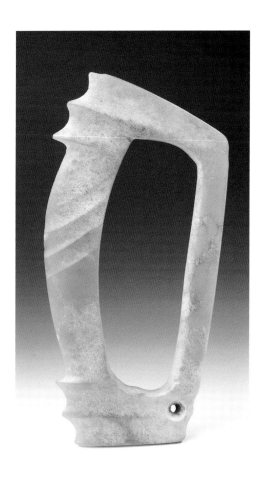

50

Chisel

Neolithic period
Liangzhu culture
(c.3400 - 2250 BC)
PE228
Length : 26.8 cm
Breadth : 3.8 cm
Thick : 1.4 cm

Thick chisel formed of an opaque light green stone. There is a neat conical hole drilled from the side through the median axis near the butt. The thick, massive body tapers sharply towards the blade. The sides have unsmoothed saw keel remnants

The stone is very hard and a form of very finely laid and compacted sedimentary shale type stone not actually nephrite. However, it takes a very precise line definition when worked, as can be seen from the clear strong lines at the sides and butt and on the edges of the very sharply and smoothly drilled hole. There are some nicks on the perfectly contoured curve of the cutting edge of the blade and evidence of superficial scratching indicates a utilitarian application. The principal emphasis of the piece is applied strength coupled with an ancillary aesthetic achievement of elegant simplicity. (AHF)

Collection: The Peony Collection

51

RECTANGULAR FROG PENDANT

NEOLITHIC PERIOD
DAWENKOU CULTURE
  (c. 4500 - 2300 BC)

PE499

LENGTH : 4.5 CM
WIDTH : 3.0 CM
HEIGHT : 1.0 CM

A rectangular plaque form of opaque silvery-grey nephrite pierced with a large dome-form central hole and a smaller one at the rear end. The plaque is carved in low relief on both sides to depict a triangular headed frog with drawn up arms and legs with simply formed digits.

The considerable smoothing of contours and edges in very low relief work are consistent with a North China Neolithic origin. Of particular interest, however, is the dome-shaped hole which is clearly formed by percussion or contusion boring with a hemispherical-ended awl or bit. On the basis of the rarity of the dome shape hole and of the occurrence of such holes in the Dawenkou culture blades of the Shandong peninsula (see Exhibit 47), it is reasonable to attribute this piece to the same cultural origin. (AHF)

Collection: The Peony Collection

52

WHITE TERRAPIN

NEOLITHIC PERIOD
DAWENKOU CULTURE
  (c.4500 - 2300 BC)
PE729
LENGTH : 5.6 CM
WIDTH : 3.3 CM
HEIGHT : 0.8 CM

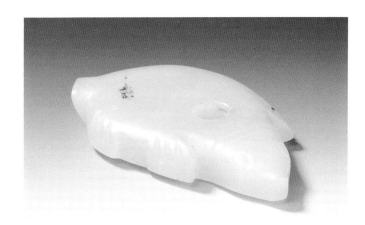

Flat, simplified, white nephrite plaque form of a soft-shelled terrapin with a sharp nosed head with lively eyes turning to the right. Simple fore and hind flippers are held in along each side and a short blunt tail extends behind. Between the shoulders there is a round perforation for suspension which is much wider at the bottom than at the top. The base is completely plain and slightly cambered from side to side.

There is a very similar piece in the Avery Brundage Collection in the Asian Art Museum of San Francisco. The use of white jade is of interest. Such material from neolithic times has been excavated in the Lake Baikal area of southern Siberia. (AHF)

Compare: (i) 1 pl.XXII (ii) 68 pl.XXXIX No.8
Collection: The Peony Collection

53

SCRAPER

NEOLITHIC PERIOD
DAWENKOU CULTURE
  (C.4500 - 2300 BC)
                    PE414
THICK : 0.6 CM
LENGTH : 3.4 CM
BREADTH : 2.5 CM

Small rectangular scraper in translucent honey-brown nephrite
shading to white. The top of the butt is largely altered.
The ground blade bevels sharply away on one side and at a slight
angle transversely across the body of the piece.

Although this piece is small, it takes a very typical form.
The presumed purpose is something akin to the removal of internal
animal fat or the removal of residual flesh when dressing skins
for leather or fur production. It is extremely well adapted for this
purpose with a very sharp cutting edge. (AHF)

Previously published: 16 pl. 33
Collection: The Peony Collection

54
COLLARED DISC

NEOLITHIC PERIOD
LOWER YELLOW RIVER AREA
 (c.4000 - 2500 BC)
                          PE420
DIAMETER: : 9.7 CM
HEIGHT : 1.5 CM

Collared disc in opaque mutton-fat nephrite with soft thrush-breast brown freckles. Around the large central hole on each face rises an encircling wall or flange which is everted outwards towards the perimeter. Each face slopes gently away from the flange to meet at the perimeter forming a surprisingly sharp edge.

There are a few somewhat similar but smaller pieces with a cambered profile encountered in published collections, all with the singular feature of an everted profile to the central flange. All are much later in feeling however, having a sense of softness and rounded edges, and because their overall surfaces have been left in a much less polished or matt state.

A further analogous form is the "ring of Saturn" type *bi*, a concentrically scored flat circle form from the centre of which rises a vertical flange without an everted rim. These non-everted rim flange pieces are a well established Shang dynasty artefact.

Exhibit 54 can be distinguished from both of the above types by the extremely sharp cutting round the edge of both the everted flange and of the exterior perimeter. The coupling of this sharp edge with the undoubted string anchoring capacity of the everted rim flange strongly suggests that this piece was, or was inspired by, some kind of offensive weapon capable of accelerative propulsion by the act of forcefully thrown unravelling of the anchoring string reeled up around the flange. If the reeled string were itself to have its free end tied to a separate stick, even greater force could be available to the operator - rather like the additional momentum achieved for spear throwing in some primitive societies by anchoring the spear in a special throwing stick. (AHF)

Previously published: 16 pl.28
Collection: The Peony Collection

55

CHISEL

NEOLITHIC PERIOD
PROBABLY DAWENKOU CULTURE
 (C.4500 - 2300 BC)

PE432

LENGTH : 8.5 CM
WIDTH : 2.5 CM
THICKNESS : 1.8 CM

Small fat chisel in translucent honey-coloured nephrite shading to brown at the butt. One side is drilled through with a wide-angled, tapered groove with inner wall concentric ring or layered markings.

The proportions of this piece are sturdy enough to enable some forceful use although there is no clear evidence, such as chipping or deep surface scratching to show any applied use. One very interesting, and unexplained feature is the half perforation across one side taking the form of a wide-angled groove whose inner wall is scored with concentric rings. There is a possibility that this groove was once married to another half of the same hole which would indicate some kind of "sister" chisel being formed in parallel with this one and then separated. Each resulting piece would then have a transverse ring, scored groove as the relict of a previous unity. (AHF)

Previously published: 16 pl.26
Collection: The Peony Collection

56

AXE HEAD

NEOLITHIC PERIOD
PROBABLY YELLOW RIVER AREA
 (C.3000 -2000 BC)

PE440

LENGTH : 13.8 CM
WIDTH : 10.0 CM
THICKNESS : 1.2 CM

Round bladed axe formed from an opaque light coffee-coloured stone with a high gloss finish. Each convex face except the butt cambers gently down on all sides to meet the equivalent movement on the reverse. There is a large median hole near the butt that is meticulously drilled from both sides with a central snap-out ridge remnant around the radial wall of the hole.

With its conical hole drilled from both sides, a snap-out ridge remnant unfinished butt end and round-faced cambered blade edge, this piece exhibits substantially the characteristics of a Liangzhu axe, although the Liangzhu axes of this type are normally formed of a plum-grey stone with lighter buff or yellow inclusions. (AHF)

Compare: 66 No.1
Collection: The Peony Collection

57

CONG

NEOLITHIC PERIOD, SHAANXI
HENAN LONGSHAN CULTURE
 (C. 2300-1700 BC)
                              PE370
HEIGHT : 8.6 CM
DIAMETER : 6.5 CM

Cong of light green translucent nephrite with alteration on
two sides. The squared oval aperture formed by a very thin
walled body. On two opposite exterior walls parallel grooves form
a vestigial central channel.

This *cong* has very sharp shoulders, very thin walls and an unusual
"television" screen shaped central aperture. Vestigial channels have
been formed down the vertical axis on each side by the placing of
suggestive bordering grooves running from shoulder to shoulder at
each end. The apparent lack of finish and the clear lime-green stone
indicate that this is a product of a late neolithic but pre-bronze or
other metal-working stage. (AHF)

Collection: The Peony Collection

58

Bi-disc

Neolithic period
Lower Yellow River area
(c.4000 - 2500 BC)
                              PE385
Diameter : 22.0 cm
Thickness : 1.0 cm

Bi-disc in translucent honey-brown nephrite shading to patches of bluish-white, sandy and chocolate-brown in places, and pierced through by a central hole with slightly cambered walls.

A very small, select number of pieces such as this, possibly all cut from the same mother stone and exhibiting a similar colour scheme from moonlight to chocolate have been sporadically published. The surface finish is fine matt and the central hole has smoothed vertical walls with no trace of snap out remnant or other working. (AHF)

Compare: (i) <u>46 pl.11</u> (ii) <u>29 No.49</u> (iii) <u>26 pl.6</u>
Collection: The Peony Collection

59

GREEN AXE HEAD

NEOLITHIC PERIOD
SHANDONG LONGSHAN CULTURE
  (C.2300 - 1700 BC)
                              PE573
WIDTH : 9.5 CM
HEIGHT : 8.8 CM
THICKNESS : 0.5 CM

An axe in translucent moss-green nephrite. The short, broad face is
bounded by two sides which taper out at different lengths to meet
the blade edge thus giving an offset profile to the blade form. The
thickness cambers gently from the butt to the blade edge. The butt
has an oval cross section and one corner is eroded by degradation
of the stone into a soft off-white consistency. The blade is pierced
by a circular perforation drilled in conical form from one side.

A noteworthy feature is the very slight kick out of the silhouette at
each end of the blade edge. The very gradual curve with a
restrained terminal flourish instead of a severe straight line profile
to the side, is a quiet, but eloquent, indication of impeccable
neolithic taste in art form. (AHF)

Compare: 46 No.18
Collection: The Peony Collection

60

CONDOR PLAQUE

NEOLITHIC PERIOD
HENAN LONGSHAN CULTURE
(c. 2300 - 1700 BC)
PE685
HEIGHT : 9.4 CM
WIDTH : 7.2 CM
THICKNESS : 0.5 CM

Plaque in opaque yellow-green nephrite formed as a hunched figure of a vulture or condor. The head, with round turquoise inlaid eye and a predatory beak, stares balefully forward at the top of a long scrawny neck which curves up from pendulous folds of skin. The crown of the head is featured with two tear-shaped bald patches of skin. The talons are held in rounded posture as if gripping a perch, and the back is formed of a series of five projecting serrations representing feathers and extending over in continuation of incised straight lines with inner hook terminals. The broad, squared tail of round-ended feathers juts out at an angle behind the legs.

All available evidence from legend and archaeology indicates the north Chinese neolithic peoples' very real pre-occupation with birds. Having considered various reasons for this it is clear that the unharnessable, majestic power of the huge eagles which inhabit hilly to mountainous regions of the world represents to mere earth bound humans an object of awe and envy. The particular bird represented here does not however appear simply to be an eagle but rather one of the much bigger and more powerful condor or vulture family. The so called European black vulture of our times has a range extending well into China. There is currently no extant member of the condor group of vultures inhabiting north China. The principal surviving relics of this now rare group are the California condor and the Andean Condor of Peru. It is a feature of the condor, and also of most vultures, that the head is bald down through the neck to the breast which is in turn surmounted by a series of loose skin flaps at the base of the neck. There are long, loosely overlaying floppy feathers on the shoulders and back which a slight breeze or perhaps a nervous stiffening of the bird are capable of lifting up and away from the feathered body. These features are all exhibited by this piece, which also has long incised lines with rounded hook ends that appear to have a link with the rounded raised line and hook ends of the Shandong Longshan culture eagle reliefs in jade. This particular aspect of the overlaying free feather activity may be the inspiration for the realistic feather-like extensions rising from the bird's back. These same extensions can also be compared with the irregular perimeter excrescences found on archaeologically excavated jade pieces from the Longshan culture such as various examples of the *bi* form with notches and teeth, such as Exhibit 61, and the famous white jade hair ornament excavated at Linqu, Shandong Province in 1989 and published in 21 pl. 60. Turquoise has been mined in certain parts of China since Neolithic times. (AHF)

Compare: 10 p.72
Collection: The Peony Collection

61

BI-DISC WITH NOTCHES AND TEETH

NEOLITHIC PERIOD,
SHANDONG OR HENAN LONGSHAN CULTURE
  (C. 2300 - 1700 B.C.)

                                BATEA 589

DIAMETER OVERALL: 13.9 CM
DIAMETER OF APERTURE: 7 CM

Yellowish-green jade *bi-disc* with three large notches and twenty
eight teeth on the perimeter. in two groups of 10 and one of eight.
There are traces of encrustation.

The function of the *bi-disc* with notches and teeth is unknown
although various theories have been put forward to suggest an
astrological significance. The number of notches and teeth vary
from example to example. The pale yellow-green colour of the jade
here is typical of many Shandong and Henan Longshan jades.
(BSM)

Previously published: 80, No.31

62

HUMAN HEAD PLAQUE

NEOLITHIC PERIOD
SHANDONG LONGSHAN CULTURE
(C.2300 - 1700 BC)

PE390

BREADTH : 5.6 CM
LENGTH : 5.4 CM
THICKNESS : 1.3 CM

Saddle-shaped convex plaque in translucent light yellow nephrite. The bowed top surface is occupied by a cartouche the central feature of which is a lightly incised human head with full lips and wearing a flat-topped hat with outwardly down curving sides and a high striped neck ruff or collar. The edges of the eyes are formed of raised-line work beneath heavy brows. Each ear is fitted with a round plug from which hangs a curving pendant ornament. To each side of the head is a crescent-shaped panel within a double raised-line border with a raised-line design of curving meanders, and pierced with a small central hole. The plaque thickens from the top to the bottom edge which is centrally penetrated by a vertically bored pit five millimetres deep.

There are a number of known and published, variations upon the theme of a human or humanoid monster mask topped with a sort of junior chef's hat and with long dangling earrings at each side. These are usually seen on silhouette, cut-out, full-face plaque form. For the full representation to be incised with only raised-line work on a full plaque form such as this Exhibit is exceptional. The feathery side-panel designs of raised-line work are typical of Shandong Longshan culture jade designs and the raised-line work forming the borders of the eyes is also typical of the Longshan period. This entire piece of material could be a fragment of a yellow jade bracelet reworked after breakage in Longshan times. Compare the published bracelet in the Freer collection 57 Pl.22. A similar model of full bracelet was excavated from the Fu Hao tomb 91 pl.117 No.1247. The boring of a pit hole in from the bottom edge of the piece presumes some attachment function, a feature shared with a number of published pieces of the same type which are, however, generally of a demonic rather than of a human character. (AHF)

Compare: 69 pl.XII No.3
Collection: The Peony Collection

63

CROWNED HEAD FITTING

NEOLITHIC PERIOD
SHANDONG LONGSHAN CULTURE
 (C.2300 - 1700 BC)
                              PE616
HEIGHT : 4.2 CM
WIDTH : 2.0 CM
DEPTH : 1.0 CM

Human head fitting in semi-translucent light green nephrite.
The back is scored from top to bottom on each side by a broad
double vertical groove. The long, almost sensitive, face featuring
well formed slanting eyes with raised-line border delineation rises
from a high broad neck which has an unfinished, partly drilled
perforation in its flat base. The prominent brow is crowned by
a small slant-sided hat or crown which is drilled down from the
flat top with a short perforation. From each side of the crown rises
a curving or vertical horn-like growth. Each side of the head has
a prominent ear with a circular earring from which is suspended
an out-turning segmented curl form.

There are obvious affinities with Exhibit 62 although the fully
transverse chef's hat has here been replaced by a small, angled pill
box hat. The large earrings and composed facial expression are
shared by both pieces. All surfaces are meticulously worked and
fashioned to the point where there is no visible trace of the original
grinding and scratching that was necessary to reduce the overall
contours of the piece into the present sculptural form. The drilling
of insertion holes at top and bottom, without a direct connection
as a vertical perforation, probably indicates an attachment function
of some kind. (AHF)

Collection: The Peony Collection

64

Demon mask

Neolithic period
Shandong Longshan culture
 (c.2300 - 1700 BC)
                                PE726
Length : 2.9 cm
Height : 2.5 cm
Depth: 1.4 cm

A demonic mask in semi-translucent tawny stone. The back is concave rising to support the convex upper surface which is angled gently to fall away on each side from a central vertical axis. On the front side is a pair of eyes with round pupils each set in a semi-lunar inner and outer canthus. Between the eyes is a prominent sculptured nose which is bordered by raised line and hook formations that branch and curl down the side and around the bottom of the nose to form the nostrils. The nose is set above a horizontal three-bar mouth flanked on each side with an upward sweeping waterspout or rainbow formation, probably representing vestigial fangs. Each ear is represented by a vestigial raised-line formation and has a large round ear-ring pierced through with a central hole. Each side edge has a series of three hook-ended projections. The distinctive chin juts out above a short neck which rises from a convex horizontal groove. The head is crowned by a simple hat, the top of which is formed as a sweeping, laterally hollowed-out corner-angled groove. The piece has a central vertical perforation from top to bottom. The back side is incised with two pairs of crossed triangular grooves .

This piece compares well with the Shijiahe jade demonic mask published in 22 pl.57 although there are many substantive differences of minor detail. Of particular interest in Exhibit 64 is the slender vegetal raised-line formation branching down and around the nose and curling up round the front of the nostrils. This is formed with a lively flourish and a genuine raised line similar in inspiration to the raised-line features around the brow of the agate demonic mask of Exhibit 65. (AHF)

Compare: (i) 46 No.246 (ii) 69 pl XII Nos.5 and 6 (iii) 68 pl.XXXVI No.2
Collection: The Peony Collection

65

AGATE DEMON MASK FITTING

NEOLITHIC PERIOD
SHANDONG LONGSHAN CULTURE
  (C.2300 - 1700 BC)

PE566

WIDTH : 3.9 CM
HEIGHT : 2.8 CM
THICK : 1.3 CM

A demonic mask in translucent tawny agate. On the front side a pair of slanting elliptical eyes in high relief with raised level pupils flanking each side of a high-bridged nose with curled back nostrils. The open lips reveal four upper and four lower teeth clenched together and extending between an inner pair of upright fangs and an outer pair of down-turned fangs. The cheeks are fat and full and bordered by a raised edge that forms a relief hook shape in front of each ear. Each ear has a large round earring pierced through with a central hole. The curved eyebrows on each side are in raised relief with a small median barb extension pointing down. The top of the head is formed as a sweeping V shape with a central perpendicular perforation from top to bottom. The reverse is incised with an intricate design of demonic mask features set equally about a central axis, the upper part of which is drilled out in a semi-cylindrical groove.

There is a well known published piece in the Avery Brundage Collection 1 pl.X which has similar, though less well developed, elliptical plateau form eyes. It also has the very characteristic upward and downward pointing fangs from an open mouth well equipped with strong teeth. Exhibit 65 also exhibits fine raised-line work forming the corners of the cheeks and on the reverse is an extremely important incised geometric mask form which is directly associated with the incised feathery geometric design on a short axe blade in the Winthrop Collection in the Sackler Museum at Harvard University, Massachuetts. The latter is in turn directly related to the incised and raised-line human mask designs on chisel blades in the collections of Sir Joseph Hotung (formerly Richard Bull and Pillsbury Collections) and the former Qianlong imperial collection now in the Palace Museum Taipei. The combination on Exhibit 65 of the incised design on the reverse and the frontal demonic fanged monster with elliptical pedestal eyes establishes an invaluable connection between the two forms and establishes a firm link for both forms to a Shandong Longshan culture context and date. (AHF)

Previously published: 16 pl.29
Compare: (i) 46 No.192 (ii) 1 pl.X
Collection: The Peony Collection

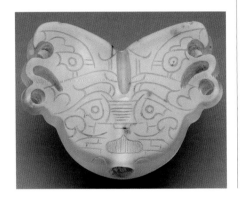

66

RECTANGULAR RITUAL AXE BLADE

NEOLITHIC PERIOD
SHANDONG LONGSHAN CULTURE
  (C.2300 - 1700 BC)

BATEA 538

LENGTH : 21.2 CM
WIDTH : 15.2 CM

Large almost rectangular ritual jade axe blade, the thin slab pierced with two circular holes each drilled from one side only, one from one side, one from the other, placed 2.9 cm from the top edge and 2.5 cm, from the right edge respectively. The colour of the jade is muddy grey-green colour with white inclusions.

The large size of the blade here is typical of the neolithic period and the colour strongly suggests a Shandong Longshan provenance. (BSM)

Previously published: 80, No. 10

67

SQUARE-ENDED CUT BLADE

NEOLITHIC PERIOD
SHANDONG LONGSHAN CULTURE
  (C.2300 - 1700 BC)
                              PE539
LENGTH : 29.7 CM
WIDTH (MAX): 5.9 CM
THICK : 0.5 CM

A *dao* or long square ended knife blade in opaque olive green
nephrite with some light striated banding and internal worm track
meanders. One end is broader than the other. From a straight spine
forming the length of one side each face extends laterally out to the
other side where it has been hollow ground in lunette shape to form
a bevelled, flat surface with curved ends on each side forming the
cutting edge. Two conical holes are drilled along the spine and a
third through the central face nearer to the narrow end.

This artefact achieves a sense of total balance. Without needing to
consider the applied use of such a shape, the senses feel utterly
satisfied by this serene and total statement of man's ability to wrestle
his own perceived beauty out of nature. The extended lunette
hollow grinding of the blade edge is comparable with excavated
counterparts and strongly suggests attribution to the Longshan
culture of the lower Yellow river and Shandong peninsula areas and
a direct inheritance from the earlier Dawenkou culture in the same
area. (AHF)

Compare: 46 No.208
Collection: The Peony Collection

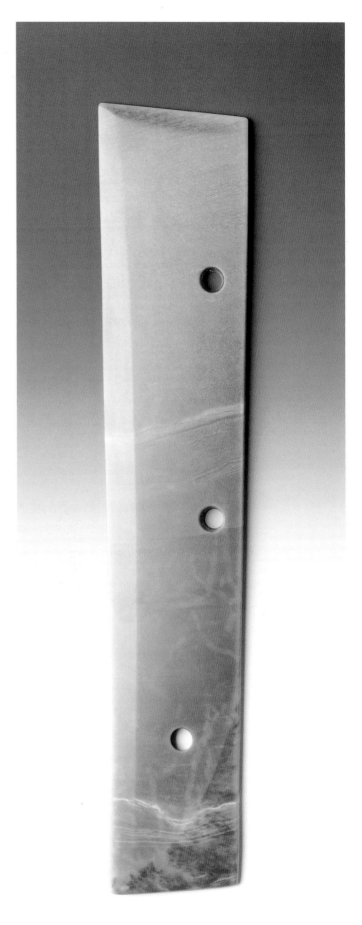

68

DARK GREEN JADE *ZHANG* SCEPTRE

NEOLITHIC PERIOD
SHANDONG LONGSHAN CULTURE
  (C.2300 - 1700 BC)

BATEA 532

LENGTH : 28.8 CM
WIDTH : 5.3 CM
DEPTH : 0.7 CM

Very dark green, almost black, jade *zhang*
sceptre with single conical hole between two
hooked flanges drilled from one side some five
centimetres from the handle end. The handle
shows a rough broken-off finish. The whole
sceptre has gentle lines and a slightly concave
surface.

The colour of the jade, the hooked flanges and
the rough broken-off finish of the handle end of
the sceptre are all indicative of this culture.
(BSM)

Previously published: (i) 77, No. 13. (ii) 80, No. 11

69

TIGER-HEAD BEAD

NEOLITHIC PERIOD
SHIJIAHE CULTURE
 (c.2500 - 2000 BC)
                    PE617
DIAMETER : 3.0 CM
HEIGHT : 3.6 CM

Large drum-form bead drilled through from one side to the other with a broad
perforation. Around the circumference of the cylinder is formed the face of
a wide-eyed tiger with incised pupils, high cheek bones and a simple transverse
groove mouth and a broad nose featuring a central V ridge which extends from
nostrils to the crown of the head. Each ear is formed as a raised plateau concave
groove turning back along the edge of the head from a small pit origin.

A piece of this type has been excavated from what is now designated as a Shijiahe
site near the city of Jingzhou just north of the Yangzi river in Hubei Province.
Three very important jade artefacts were found together at that site, (a) a small
rounded jade finial in the shape of a human head with an inverted *sous-chef's* hat,
round drum earrings and raised line eyes;(b) a silhouette plaque featuring the same
perimeter spikes and curls that typify the classic demonic mask plaques of the
Shandong Longshan culture and (c) a tiger-headed bead of a flatter shape than
Exhibit 69 but similar and with an identical groove eyebrow structure and incised
circular eyes each side of a shaped nose with a central bridge running back and up
through the forehead and between the ears. The lower, exterior cheek pouches and
the twirled-comma scroll-form ears are also features common to both pieces. The
sculptural prominence given to the tiger-head form is unusual in neolithic jade and
here presumably represents the respect paid by at least one culture for the power and
strength of the tiger which, in neolithic times, was an animal widespread throughout
the East Asian land mass. (AHF)

Compare: 68 pl.XXXVI No.6
Collection: The Peony Collection

70

SQUARED FACE BEAD

ERLITOU PERIOD
 (C.1900 - 1600 BC)
                         PE721
HEIGHT : 1.8 CM
DIAGONAL LENGTH : 1.8 CM
WIDTH : 1.4 CM

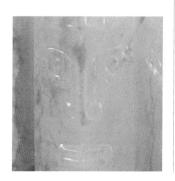

Squared bead of greater height than diameter in translucent off-white nephrite. Each face is equally bisected by a vertical trench. The side faces and corner angle from one vertical trench to the next are each formed as an elongated and realistically modeled face with double raised-line extended canthus eyes, a sculpted long nose and a closed mouth with thick lips, across each corner angle. Above each face is a flat-topped hat of six vertical wavy raised-line contiguous panels the base or brim of which curve up at each side in line with the restraining border trench.

There is no known comparison for this piece, either in the structural arrangement of the subject matter, or graphically in the drawing of the details and the faces. Analogy can however be argued with the Erlitou handle excavated at Yanshi and illustrated in 100 p.49. (AHF)

Compare: (i) 100 pl.49 (ii) 49 No.xxviii
Collection: The Peony Collection

71

CONG-FORM BEAD

ERLITOU PERIOD
(C.1900 - 1600 BC)
PE720
DIAGONAL LENGTH : 3.2 CM
WIDTH : 2.4 CM
HEIGHT : 1.8 CM

Square or *cong*-form bead in translucent off-white nephrite with a large, broad, smoothly finished central vertical hole. Each of the four flat sides is divided by two vertical lines or trenches into three distinct parts consisting of a principal central panel and two side or corner-angle panels. On each of the four reserved central panels between the two vertical trenches is carved a monster mask with a deep gulls-wing feature forming the eyebrows. Below the brows is a pair of circular eyes defined by double incised lines. Below the eyes is an incised open mouth with ogival upper lip, its pointed apex sitting between the base of the eyes. The open mouth sports two long downward-pointing fangs which extend beyond the lower lip to the bottom edge of the piece. The top and bottom of the corner-angle panels are deeply carved with addorsed pairs of double curl or scrolling designs linked to each other by overlapping V shaped formations wrapped around the intervening corner-angle field.

The shape of the mouth replicates that of the incised face on the reverse of the agate demonic mask in Exhibit 65, but the round eyes are similar to those on a mask appearing four times around the circumference of a Liangzhu culture bracelet form, argued by many as the origin of the *cong* and dating to approximately 3,500 BC illustrated at 56 pl.148. (AHF)

Compare: (i) 100 pl.30 (ii) 68 pl.XXXVI No.2 (iii) 55 pl.12
Collection: The Peony Collection

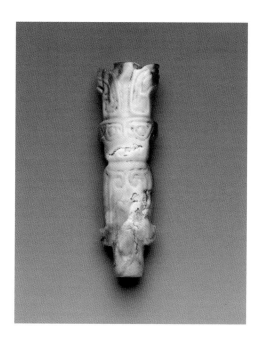

72

HUMAN FIGURE PENDANT

ERLITOU PERIOD
(C.1900 - 1600 BC)

PE681

HEIGHT : 2.6 CM
WIDTH : 0.8 CM
THICK : 0.5 CM

Small elongated pendant in opaque coffee-coloured nephrite, altered on one side to creamy white. There are two identical convex longitudinal faces separated by sides but with a type of machicolated formation. Each longitudinal face is formed as a convex three-dimensional representation of a human figure with arms held to its sides and wearing a raised-line form apron which extends from the waist down towards the feet. The upper arm and arm pit area is defined by vertical raised-line work with prominent everted hook forms at the point of the shoulder. The mouth is formed by a simple raised-line oblate sphere set between and below a pair of large double extended canthus eyes in raised-line work with internal formed pupils and surmounted by a transverse groove. The piece is topped by an elaborate headdress of paired raised-line horn or feather forms curving outwards to each side with further raised-line work extending right around the edge and onto the opposite convex face. On the crown of the headdress is a transverse ridge running from one face to the other that is drilled from each side at a 45° angle to form a short channel for a suspension thread. The rising feather-form headdress of this minute piece has something in common with the feather-form growths springing out from Shandong Longshan culture jade plaques and raised-line representations on flat jade surfaces. Comparison can also be made between the branching hook forms of certain raised-line treatment in the Shandong Longshan culture jade working and the raised-line hook forms in this piece, which also show some characteristics of the Anyang phase of the Shang dynasty and a dating to the transition point from the Erlitou period to the Erligang phase may be appropriate. (AHF)

Collection: The Peony Collection

73

HUMAN HEAD FLAT BEAD

ERLITOU PERIOD
 (C.1900 - 1600 BC)
                            PE719
HEIGHT : 1.8 CM
WIDTH : 1.6 CM
THICKNESS : 0.5 CM

Human head formed as a flattened mask with superimposed hairline above a broad
forehead. The material is opaque chestnut brown and greenish white nephrite with
some alteration. The open eyes are well delineated by fine line work incised onto a
raised lenticular plateau. They stare out from beneath the curved brows which
descend to form the long nose. The lower part of the face features a thick lipped
mouth set between wide, dimpled cheeks.

The piece is pierced at the back with a loop hole for attachment or suspension. The
material is substantially altered in parts but the original stone has a yellow green
colour very similar to Longshan and Erlitou period jades. The small, evenly shaped
eyes and the wide cheeks have no clear sculptural parallel from any culture and the
Erlitou dating, whilst tentative, is a compromise way station which a future
generation of archaeological work will confirm or rebut. There is one interesting, and
seemingly unique feature of the incised line working of the eyes. The line forming the
iris, inner canthus and under profile of the eye is a single one which although
describing several distinct features is continuous and unbroken.(AHF)

Collection: The Peony Collection

74

HUMAN HEAD
EXTENSION OR FITTING

ERLITOU PERIOD
 (C.1900 - 1600 BC)
                        PE728
HEIGHT : 3.3 CM
WIDTH : 2.0 CM
THICKNESS : 0.4 CM

Flattened extension or fitting in translucent golden-chestnut nephrite with a central greenish-white area. The piece is worked identically on each side as a jutting thick lipped male face with a broad nose. Very fine raised-line work delineates the jaw line which curls back at an angle upon the cheek. The same raised-line work is used for the double angle canthus eye with raised central pupil and also for the complex angular, hook-backed headdress from which thick braids of hair fall down the back of the neck. There is a small perforation through the base of the headdress above the forehead.

The fine workmanship on such a small piece indicates the importance of the perfect finishing of the artefact - no matter what the size. The headdress has no currently known exact parallel but there are some jade pieces such as 67 pl.IX No. 3 that appear to have a similar inspiration although the detailed execution is very different. There are immediately superficial parallels to be drawn with some jades from Central America. (AHF)

Collection: The Peony Collection

75

WHITE DAGGER BLADE

ERLITOU PERIOD
  (C.1900 - 1600 BC)
                            PE243

LENGTH : 37 CM
BREADTH : 6.5 CM
THICKNESS : 0.7 CM

Ge dagger or halberd blade, of pure and translucent white nephrite with traces of earth in places, the elegant blade tapering to a sharp tip and curving slightly to one side and with a bevelled surface constituted by a long central ridge and two side ridges extending the entire length through the almost imperceptible shoulders and back to the tang. Each side is bordered by a longitudinal bevelled facet forming the blade edge which terminates in an outward curve at the beginning of the smooth blade tip. The tip is not bevelled but is slightly hollow ground with sides gently cambered to the blade edge. Above the tang, the blade is lightly incised on each side with eight pairs of transverse lines, the third and fourth pairs of which are widely separated by a similarly incised area of double parallel lines forming rhombic cross hatching. The serrated butt of the tang is formed with a series of seven protruding and notched rectangular teeth separated by scalloped interludes which continue identically up the tang on each face as eight flat ribs sequentially bordering seven double walled channels all terminating flush against the first of a series of five adjacent transversely gouged grooves. One large central and one smaller offset perforation are drilled from one side in the centre of the blade above the tang and slightly above the cross hatched area. Both sides are identical in design and concept but with minor differences in execution.

Every aspect of the design and execution is scrupulously conceived, balanced and finished. There are several published examples of Erlitou blades with the same incised diamond cross hatching work. There are also a number of published *ge* with the parallel channel treatment at the end of the tang but the standard number of channels is five. Exhibit 75 is the only one so far published with seven channels. (AHF)

Previously published: 16 pl.49
Compare: (i) 27 pl.20A (ii) 100 pl.47 (iii) 46 No.37 (iv) 46 No.41
Collection: The Peony Collection

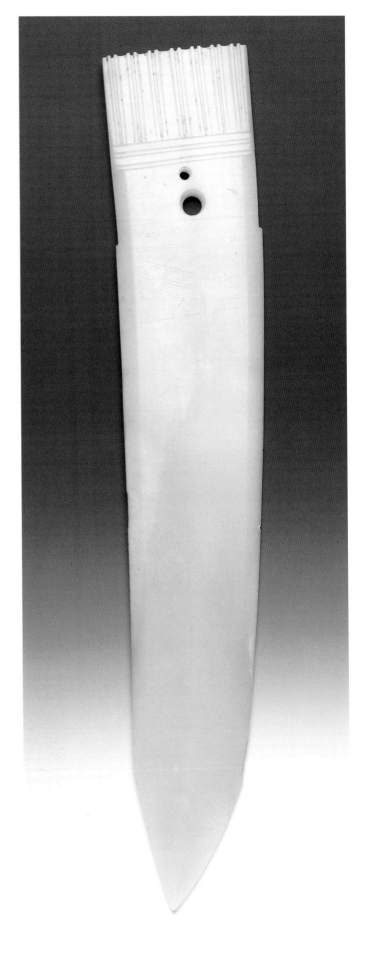

12 SHANG DYNASTY, ERLIGANG AND ANYANG PHASES c.1600-1100BC

A.1 GENERAL INTRODUCTION
SHANG AND ZHOU DYNASTIES
c.1600 - c. 221 BC

This period extends for approximately 1400 years. In terms of western civilisation, this represents an enormous measure of time within whose compass several or many different cultures can rise and fall from and into the ashes of each other. The year 548 AD saw the completion of the architectural glories of St. Sophia's Basilica in Constantinople by direction of the emperor Justinian. It is still intact and visible today in modern Istanbul, and its completion marked the beginning of a 1400 year period which extends to our own 20th century AD whose discernible relationship with the 6th century is nil. In terms of jade, no less a revolutionary development took place over a similarly very long period between c. 1600 and 221 BC and under a slowly developing ethnic Han Chinese milieu and society which survived through gradual honing into the realisation of the truly national Chinese style.

The preceding Erlitou period can be seen as the final phase of disconnected development of regional art styles in China. In, and after, this period a remarkable, but often uncontrollable uniformity of aesthetic preference prevails. The further away from the Central Plain one goes to the west, the less was the uniformity of style. The huge and hideous stalk eyed monster bronze masks of the highly efficient late Erligang phase bronze culture at Sanxingdui, Guanghan, Sichuan Province, are a most eloquent testimony to the dynamic strength of regional creativity maintained in outlying places. Nothing like these nightmarish creations has been found in Central and Eastern China and the contrary way of designing the Sanxingdui bronze sculptures is the more remarkable when seen together

with the jade blades coming from the same burial site - which exhibit all the principal characteristics of the mid Shang or Erligang phase jade artefacts found in the classic and central area of modern Henan Province.

On our present, fully informed, understanding, the first coherently logical known writing in China appeared, for reasons which are not yet clear, in the Shang dynasty's Anyang phase. There were neolithic antecedents of a runic character incised on pottery dateable to the Longshan period and culture (22 plate 4) but limited in number and, as yet, not decipherable. The functional requirement of the Shang's Anyang phase people for the written word was to record the divination of fame or fortune found through oracular pronouncements which were recorded in elaborate pictogram writing on ox scapula and the underside of the tortoise carapace. From this point on, the social history of China becomes accessible for study in contrast to all preceding millennia which were without writing to record any aspect of their society.

Throughout the entire Shang period bronze and jade lived - and flourished - in a revolving kaleidoscopic symbiosis and continued to be applied to, and to be used in connection with, official order and religious ritual with, in the case of bronze, the added and important extension of applied use relative to weapons of war.

In the Erlitou period (c. 1900 - 1600 BC), bronze was in its infancy. Though rapidly developing, it did not achieve any significant fraction of the importance bestowed by the society of the day upon the jade material. By the time of the Anyang phase period however, bronze was being cast into a great variety of sophisticated shapes and forms with a confident mastery of the most fungible metal ingredient combinations and perfect surface non-bubble control of the pouring and moulding methods of manufacture.

Because such a significant sector of the community was involved in the working of bronze, and because this new material assumes a rapidly developing central importance in relation to ritual and burial, it would not have been surprising if bronze were gradually to have replaced jade as a symptom of the momentous changes taking place in society as normal part of the evolution of cultural perceptions allied with, and responsive to, economic facility of production. That this did not happen is an astounding testament to the depth of impact which the jade continuum had by this time made at all levels and in all areas of society in China in consequence of which acceptance of the superior position of jade was clearly a passive, wholly unconscious and unquestioning one which was never in later years to face any serious or genuine challenge. It can be said with truth that the longer the extension of the period of reflecting respect and affection towards jade, the more deep rooted and inalienable its hold on society had become.

In art historical terms, bronze is of enormous value as an easy and infallible mine of information. It takes an easily worked and modest detail of design with an identifiably datable progression, whether through the inscriptions frequently placed on, or in, bronze vessels or by thermoluminescence testing of the ceramic mould core material left within a neck or a handle by the piece mould cast process. As the cultural "close comrade in arms" of the new material bronze, jade was in practice exposed to bronze design development throughout the period and, as we shall see,

the jade worker was influenced by such bronze design development.

Bronze also represented economic deprivation of the society with what must, again, have been the common consent of all. The mining, smelting, moulding, pouring and casting and polishing of bronze was a highly structured activity or series of activities which required substantial, labour intensive, presence, operation and effective control of large numbers of people. In the same way, there is every evidence that the same type of elite work team performance in the production of jade artefacts was not only a continuing reality, but was clearly able to survive without any difficulty through the entire bronze age in China thus constituting even firmer evidence of the great importance attached by the Chinese people to jade stone.

The peoples of the various different cultures in Central and Eastern China during this period were not always at war. They had long periods of settled peace which they utilised to improve their agriculture and to build ever more substantial fortifications to guard their homes and people against the possibility of attack. These fortifications are built with good strong walls and with an attention to personal hygiene. Throughout the period however there was also recurrence of hostility and petty local rivalry and it is appropriate to view the role played by jade as a single, respected and unbreakable thread running, in a constant and reassuring manner, through the entire melee of Chinese historical formation during this period. It is certainly true that, as mentioned above, through times when common sense would argue for the abandonment of jade and the taking up of bronze to the exclusion of jade, no such thing occurred.

B.1 SHANG DYNASTY, (ERLIGANG PHASE) c.1600 - c.1400 BC - CAPITAL AT ZHENGZHOU IN MODERN HENAN PROVINCE

There is still much discussion about the origin of the Shang people. Some have it that they were indigenous to the Shang heartland centred around Anyang in Henan Province. Others hold that the Shang migrated through the Erlitou period from North and Western areas of what is today China albeit outside the traditionally viewed Han Chinese border bastion of the Great Wall which was consolidated into the definitive boundary of Han China proper in the Qin and Han dynasties.

No matter from whence they came, the Shang people were mighty agriculturalists and domesticated the water buffalo and practised irrigated wetland rice cultivation. For what are most likely to have been purely hedonistic reasons, although an associated religious pretext cannot be excluded, the brewing and drinking of wine became an important general activity. Then, as now, wine in North China was made principally from sorghum or gaoliang grain, enormous stretches of which are raised each year in a broad belt extending from Inner Mongolia in the North West, across to Liaoning in the East and down to Jiangsu Province on the Yangzi River. From later inscriptions at the end of the Shang period we know of the great importance of wine and bronze vessels together and there is no reason to discount the possibility that the affinity of man for wine developed much earlier.

The chariot appeared in use as a war machine in the late Erligang/Early Anyang phase. Bronze fittings were made for chariots and better and better quality bronze weapons of war appeared. Offensive military action was not however the exclusive prerogative of any of the settled communities in China in this period and, just as he who had bronze could wage successful campaigns against those who had not, others who had bronze could easily strike back - to the heart of the settled society of the aggressor, if need be. To counter this and to bring reality to the defence of many a civic or national treasure store, massive city perimeter fortifications of rammed earth made an appearance and continued throughout subsequent history to be considered as an essential element of the safety of an urban community.

There is clear evidence of, if not the origin, then of the development and formalisation of ancestor worship - in the sense of obeisance paid to a pluralist family of gods.

Ceramics, bone carving and bronze founding workshops have been excavated in Zhengzhou, Henan Province and all effectively combine to demonstrate the existence of a well run and generally supported society.

Carved bone artefacts made from human bones have been found and there is clear evidence for the introduction of what thereafter remained one of the enduring preferences of the Chinese artists (whether by way of composite participation in an overall design, or whether through more independent highlights) of animal form motifs. This period saw the beginning of the upright pointed cicada panel as a serialised decorative feature around the circumference of a bronze vessel. As we have already seen, the cicada, with its evolutionary life style and its high pitched and ever watchful buzzing sound, had a special place in the mind and belief of the Chinese artist - as much in jade as in bronze and in other forms.

However, the most important development in artistic terms through this period was the making of ritual bronze vessels.

These signified either individual wealth as with a ruler or important local functionary, or signified the product of common effort and belief such as the arrangement of vessels upon an altar.

Through this development grew also the consolidation of the *taotie* mask which was used on spirit related libatory bronze vessels. The *taotie* mask motif is one of the most famous, influential and enduring drawn emblems in China having the horns of an ox, the ears of an elephant, the talons of an eagle, the eye of man and the dragon crest.

It has been argued that the progenitor of this very important design was the Liangzhu incised tiger form mask such as appeared on the trapezoid pendants like that in this exhibition (Exhibit 36). Seen in the Liangzhu period are goggle eyes and the ferocious open mouth with extended fangs ready to be sunk into the side of an identified target or victim. Early in the Erligang phase, the eyes of the *taotie* mask as found on jades are represented by plain hemi-spherical pupillary bulges set centrally into an incised inner and outer canthus which are effectively forced apart and separated by the bulge as pupil. Towards the end of the Erligang phase, this *taotie* mask had thrown up a central diamond shape panel on its forehead which is often picked out with incised line cross-hatching.

Apart from the north China neolithic jades made at a period which is too remote to draw an arguable parallel, we have seen the raised-line in jade carving evolve from its distinct origin as an expression of naturalism in the Hongshan culture period and into the Erlitou period where we have argued that the angled-back hook in raised-line work first appeared. Up to this point, bronze artifacts have been so new a development that their surface decoration had not had time or experience to develop either style or motif. In the middle Shang or Erligang phase however, we find a different story. Here the raised-line on bronze panels or reserves around the circumference or across the sides of a squared piece were formed as thin walls or cloisons, standing proud from the level base or ground surface of the piece and looking almost ready to receive some fluxed or molten material such as finely prepared crystal glass. The cloisons are formed as curlicue lines with branching terminals - usually set symmetrically about a central axis such as with the *taotie* mask. With exactly the same gauge of balance and symmetry the same curlicue cloisons were fashioned out of jade as can be observed on the jade water buffalo, Exhibit 78. Some bronze eyes of the period took the form of a round pupil set between opposed directional canthi, Others, as with the jade water buffalo Exhibit 78, show an elliptical or rectangular eye as a raised pedestal in its own right and without either inner or outer canthus. A third basic point worth making about the overall style of Exhibit 78 is that it shows a plastic and rounded style of basic bodily curves and shaped limbs - something that by the time of the later Anyang phase of the Shang dynasty had became rudimentary to the point of impressionism and distinctly less impressive as examples of the jade worker's art.

What Exhibit 78 also clearly establishes is the reasonably proficient three dimensional sculpture which the Erligang jade workers achieved. There is fluid coupling of positivism and strength in the squared nose end and angled hoofs which is most effectively combined with the rounded haunches and jaw angle curves all within an overall curve ended and rounded exterior silhouette.

As in Erlitou times, bronze manufacture continued to be by piece moulding methods. One unavoidable disadvantage - at least in artistic terms - of the piece moulding technique is that it always leaves a seam where the different piece elements of a bronze vessel are brought together to form a single unit. In terms of the bronze vessel, the seams were soon made to fall into an equidistant vertical arrangement around the external circumference of the vessel. The unavoidable existence of the seams had two principal consequences. The first was that, whether originally by accident or design is not clear, residual bronze metal left as surplus along the line of the seam was seen as giving the potential for development into a flange or low divider between two panels and standing out proud at right angles to the curved wall of the vessel. Almost immediately, these flanges became workable design features with the most popular format being to indent a hook or squared openwork or cut out edge and, as time went by, these flanges developed their own mandatory individualism and style and achieved great originality and elaboration.

The other consequence of the seam divider effect was to place an artificial, but definite, restriction upon the creativity of the design skills of the craftsman whose ingenuity was forced into a measured discipline which might not otherwise have come about. It is astonishing to see the remarkable products wrought by the craftsman in overcoming this limitation. The result is that decoration, although conceived on a continuous register basis around the circumference of a vessel, was constructed as a series of panels with the divider seam or flange forming a central axis about which the two halves of the particular design were arranged. Another motif which in this catalogue we perceive to have originated perhaps in the Erlitou period and which was aggressively developed in the Erligang phase through to the Western Zhou was the angled hook motif. In jade terms it can be seen in raised-line form on Exhibits Nos. 72 and 74 which are here dated to the Erlitou period.

One perceptible disciplinary development in jade carving was the controlled notch edge. The notched or projection extensions on the *zhang* and *dao* hilt guard forms of the Erlitou period, which themselves drew on the exterior projection forms of the Longshan culture, developed a conservatism and reticence in the Erligang phase before disappearing at the time of the Anyang phase of the Shang dynasty. There is no currently understood reason for this notch development and consequently no universally accepted view as to whether the initiative for this device was purely ornamental or whether a utilitarian purpose lay behind these extensions.

From the Erligang phase it is well known that certain jade blades exhibit a patterned remnant of an enfolding textile wrapping. The form of visual remnant ranges from a purely textile weaving close link form to a much simpler basket work or reed matting pattern. At this time it was a common funerary practice to break a jade *ge* blade into two or three pieces and place them in a small pit beneath the back or buttocks of the corpse together with sacrificial bones.

We have mentioned above the burial and funerary sites at Sanxingdui, Guanghan, Sichuan Province which have been dated to the late Erligang or early Anyang phase of the Shang dynasty. We have seen how the quality of the generally bizarre bronze artefacts is extremely high and, while clearly drawing upon the Han heartland in the Central Plain, are so remote in taste and temperament that they must be argued to represent a gifted provincialism. It is possible to see in a somewhat similar light the extraordinary red soapstone figure recovered from the river bank sand burial at Dayangzhou, Xingan country, Jiangxi Province in 1989 (21 pl.66). The bronzes in the burial are generally considered to date from the Anyang phase of the Shang dynasty but this figure with his external notch headdress with free sculpted chain links behind and with extended canthus eyes and small elephant trunk is hard to place in late Shang and may be a collected piece from the Erlitou or Erligang phase - a much more likely explanation.

B.2 Late Shang dynasty, Anyang phase c.1400 - 1100 bc - capital at Yinxu, Anyang (modern day Xiaotun) in modern Henan Province

The confident development of the foundation of urban organisation into cities and towns continued to expand. Urban planning required organised streets, public open spaces within the city ramparts and big and important palace and temple buildings. These last seem generally to have been made of wood and were set upon made up rammed earth platforms.

Big single room tomb structures were established deep in the ground and covered over to the level of the surrounding land following burial. They had wooden walls and rammed earth approach ramps. There is no doubt that, just as in other parts of the world - as with the pyramids of Ancient Egypt - massive engineering projects such as the tombs involved were the dictate of the royal house and the government, so the scale of tomb and public area construction in the Anyang phase of the Shang dynasty in China, is proof of the ability of a strong ruler to levy and organise huge forces of workers.

There is plentiful tomb evidence of human sacrifice and, as seen above, there is no doubt too that bone artefacts were made from human bones. We learn from the oracle bones which became prominent in the Anyang phase as augury, that those consulting the oracle sought assurance of good hunting and those who organised ritual burial ceremonies are recorded on oracle bones as deliberately turning for human sacrifice to foreign "participants" from minority tribes west of the Shang territory.

Agriculture continued to use stone and bone hoes and picks although these were, slowly but surely, giving way to bronze forms which are well known from the large number of excavated moulds for tilling and cutting implements.

However, the sudden explosion onto the social stage of the oracle bone and its futuristic message interpretation service became the dominant desire for all persons in all matters. Even weather forecasts were not excluded. What was important for the effective rule of the King, was to demonstrate that he, although an intermediary between the spirit world and his human subjects on earth, could advise, warn and hold counsel to his subjects very much in the manner performed in recent times by the nomadic Bedouin rulers of Arabia. The spirits with whom the shaman or soothsayer interceded for a supplicant, grew to exercise great influence on those who consulted them - of both high and low estate.

Throughout the period and well into the Western Zhou period, the core of society was bonded by a glue which consisted of a reverberating and alternating predominance of three key components in the basic organisation of social structure. Each of these played upon and affected each other to a greater or lesser degree :-

(i) ZHAOMU - The King and immediate dynastic clan members - both having and exercising mutually exclusive control over their separate perceived leadership requirements.

(ii) ZONGFA - The much wider many tiered group structure of the Royal family common lineage by descent from a single claimed ancestor. This concept allowed a huge membership of self interested persons with subscription to a coherent group motivation and legitimacy.

(iii) FENGJIAN - Branching structure of Provincial new lineages commenced - often by Royal relatives - as breakaway factions creating their own small and distinct urban communities.

These vital principles seem to have engendered gradual individualism of separate regional development and choice and plurality of taste.

Bronze, continuing to evolve in the form of artefacts such as vessels and altar sets, had by this time also developed a very basic dual role in social formality. It was both important for ritual and important for weaponry.

A richer development appears in respect of the piece mould seam on bronze vessels. The formalisation of acknowledging a reality of this excrescence upon every vessel piece is a clear indication of the maturity of the actual development of a need to deal with and exploit to the best account what began as a disadvantage.

The piece mould seam entered a form of baroque extravagance in beginning to be pulled out and extended with crenellations and there is established ground for the view that these flanged crenellations worked a strong influence in jade carving - both on the continuing evolution of the notched edge in jade carving and by the jade workers' acknowledgment of the bronze casting convention that applied surface decoration had to be confined to a restricted space - even in circumstances such as on jade plaque and *huang* forms where no flange existed. The classic, archaeologically excavated example of this genre is the large green nephrite jade *gui* vessel of deep bowl form excavated from the Fu Hao tomb. This vessel has exterior vertical flange extensions well demonstrating the originating mandate of the piece mould seam of the bronze caster's tools but clearly having no practical relevance to jade at all. Very fine detail became possible in bronze casting. The finest cast detail took various raised line design forms. The *Leiwen* or Thundercloud pattern is a typical commonly found example. The exemplars of the times were bronze animal and bird forms with animal groups constituting the basis of ordered, panel relief decoration of bronze vessels with the same feature being observed also on the foot rim of the single actual jade *gui*-vessel already noted and, more plentifully, on the bowl of a similar piece, but this time in white marble, also from the Fu Hao tomb.

Marble, perhaps being an available, and carveable, resource saw a flowering in the Anyang phase of the Shang dynasty as the ideal medium for production of both vessels and also large and small animal and bird sculptures. Monumental examples were excavated by the Academica Sinica at Anyang in the 1930s and some were found in the Fu Hao tomb.

At the back of certain of the really large and massive zoomorphic marble sculptures, there is a hollowed upright groove or channel which appeared to have been designed to admit a new wooden pole or stake support. These large animal and bird forms with their central vertical grooves may well have had a useful application .

It has been held by a number of scholars that the jade or nephrite material available at this time already included supplies from Khotan. This, if true, wholly emphasizes the geographical influence and reach of the Shang State at least - at the end or pinnacle of its achievement.

Specific development during the Shang period can be observed in the neolithic Zhulong or pig-dragon form which, as we have seen originated at least as far back as the North China neolithic or Hongshan era. These have by now developed interesting designs which on the whole can arguably be traced to painted and coiled dragon figures in the cavetto of bowls of the Longshan period and culture.

A crested or maned feature on the Zhulong traces a rising profile from being simply a decorative adjunct to constituting a very pronounced openwork perimeter band of projections and insets while the body itself develops a direct import from the painted pottery of the Longshan period and exhibits decorative triangular and lozenge motifs in false raised line carving. The dragon nose has a short upturned snout and the large ladle bowl shape of ear took a central constriction into a squat bottle or Indian club shape. This ear shape also adopted a common three dimensional form in vessel handles and appliques in bronze. This became popularly known as the bottle-horn dragon form.

In 1976 archaeologists excavated the tomb at Anyang of the Shang Emperor's Consort, Fu Hao. This tomb contained very rich furniture including an enormous range and variety of bronzes but the most significant and important element of the riches buried with Fu Hao were 755 jades. There is no doubt that these pieces were not any later than the death of Fu Hao in the early 14th century BC and they accordingly represent an invaluable measuring stick and primer for many jade dating comparative issues. The burial contained 16 human sacrificial victims whose presence, together with the substantial evidence of bronze wide containers and vessels, well epitomises the at once brutal and hedonistic values of the time.

The burial arrangement of jades in the Fu Hao tomb was to place them both inside the coffin itself and also in the centre of the burial chamber where they were excavated among the lacquer remains of the coffin structure which had been destroyed over centuries of waterlogging. The indications are that the lacquer coffin had a flat top which served as a display platform or simple receiving surface for jade artefacts.

On both bronze and jade a popular decorative device of these times was a straight sided shield form usually arranged in a snake of contiguous end to end forms of separate registers. Another device used in many ways was a diamond or lozenge shape which often had incised or relief cross-hatching work and, as mentioned above, had developed a regular appearance as a motif on the forehead of the Anyang phase *taotie* mask.

Three dimensional sculpture in jade in the form of human figurines and animals continued from the Erligang phase but with significant and explainable changes. They are sculpted as chunky, squat and vigorous forms with feeling and life. The general impression conveyed by these small but monumental works is one of great strength and power - not aesthetic beauty. Their production and style well demonstrates the devotion of much energy and time resource which directed the jade carver to exploit the three dimensional animal forms which were becoming ever more popular in bronze such as the elephant, standing bird and tiger vessel. A basic contrast shown by these animal and bird jade sculptures is great primitivism of execution. The roundness and flow of the Erligang water buffalo (Exhibit 78) has gone and so has the actual raised-line or cloison work style of raised line enclosure. The surface finish of the Anyang phase jade sculptures is rough. Their superficial line designs are executed with the false raised line without any demonstration of the patience and skill inherently necessary for the production of the genuine raised-line which we have noted in the neolithic section of this book and dated as early as the late Longshan period. In marked contrast to the somewhat delicate or the rounded Erligang animal style as mentioned above, the basic form of the Anyang phase animal or bird body is structured on the principle of the squared block with a concession to naturalism through rounded corners and the legs are formed through drilling deep groove channels from one side to the other at right angles across the basic square, (see Exhibit 81. The product is either a two, or a four, peg form which, with a minimum of finishing, constitutes the animal's or bird's legs. There is no structural curvature of the limbs or silhouette. They normally exhibit exterior designs in false raised line execution. One interesting feature of the production of these sculptures at this period is that the inner right angle corners of the legs were not finished by rounding off but, whether through technical inefficiency, or lack of will to proceed, were left squared thus accentuating the overall impression of primitive strength. It is indeed of note that, in this well developed era of the bronze age, there seem to have been

technical limitations upon the capability of the jade worker which certainly formed no inhibition to the creative abilities of the Hongshan and North China neolithic jade workers 2,000 and 3,000 years earlier. However, in the light of what we have seen to have been possible in the Erligang phase, the explanation may perhaps be in the taste of the times - possibly coupled with a laziness or inertia which found satisfaction in the half product rather than the fully finished raised-line effect.

There are very famous human figure subjects (see 91). One striking aspect of these is sometimes the size and, often the very plastic mobility of the features of the small figures. These still retain a roundness of volumetric form that are indeed sculptural work of great memorable intensity. There is one celebrated humanoid figure from the Fu Hao tomb which is a long flat, plaque-form carved on both sides with false raised line work and representing on one side a male figure, and on the other side a female figure.

In addition to the human being, zoomorphic representation included elephants (Exhibit 88), rhinoceros, alligator, tortoise, salamander, bear, tiger, dragon and horse. The designs also created a fat or plaque-form fish with a "chisel" or "screwdriver extension" tail and flat bodies and, sometimes, with round open mouths. Birds and insects are represented by the silkworm, the grasshopper, the dynastically ubiquitous cicada, the cormorant and the owl.

Geometric and quasi-utilitarian forms in Anyang phase jades cover *bi-disc*, plain axes, notched axes, *bi* shaped axes with notches, fat balanced form chisels, *ge* blades which are both notch backed and plain edged, the *cong* form and combs. The representation of the *taotie* mask is very different from even its Erlitou predecessor. It has undergone a radical change of detail. The central, hemispherical box form or feature adopted by the iris of the eye, still stands up on the surface of the eye ball but the piece itself is drilled vertically with a central hole as if an artist wished to endow a pupil onto the somewhat blind and unaggressive form of the earlier type.

Jade *bi-discs* have been found in the foundations of buildings at Anyang. This may well represent an invocation of early blessings upon the fortune of the future structure.

In contemporary association with the three dimensional sculpture forms, flat form jades were plentiful and also took the shape of a number of different animals. Two horses of the small Mongolian type are particularly noteworthy in the Fu Hao tomb. They have well formed but crooked legs which compare well with the more stocky but also crooked legs of the flat plaque-form elephant, Exhibit 88.

There are flat plaque type forms in the *huang* curved shape and formed both as birds with deeply indented perimeter openwork features and also some where the human figure is compressed into the *huang* curved shape and often with long downward curving hair on the head. Both of these types offer considerable opportunity for perimeter openwork although the arrangement into which this work was organised in the Anyang phase has a much more matured and perhaps slick emphasis than the rather more awkward, but freer, feeling which attaches to perimeter openwork in the late neolithic Longshan culture. As already noted, the spatial layout and constrictions seem to observe something of the piece mould flange convention imposed by bronze mould working though without any express need to do so in the case of jade otherwise than as a generally acknowledged design convention.

Another interesting jade form which developed in this period and does not seem to survive it is a form of collared disc where a right angled flange rises on each side of the disc from the immediate inner perimeter around the central hole. The flat surface of the disc is typically scored with concentric rings. (<u>37 plate 31</u>.) Similar pieces has been excavated as far away as Malaya in 1953, (<u>Plate 37, Plate 31</u>) and similar pieces are recorded from Yunnan Province in South West China. At least one good example was recovered in 1989 from the Dayangzhou, Xingan riverside sand burial site in Jiangxi Province.

The Fu Hao tomb has also yielded some jade weapons but they are rough and poor quality shadows of the Dawenkou, Longshan and Erlitou culture periods and would distinctly appear to represent what by the Anyang phase was an art in decline both as regards the overall quality of execution of types such a weapons and also as regards such matters of detail as the false raised line.

There was a continuation of a form of long and slender handle which first appeared in the Erlitou period and whose purpose has not been clearly understood by the modern eye - however two examples from the Western Zhou period were excavated at Baoji, Shaanxi Province in 1992 and are illustrated well in <u>22, plates 51 and 52</u> as already noted above in the Erlitou section. The purpose appears to have been a handle - now, thanks to the Baoji finds, known to be juxtaposed to an inlay area of small pieces of jade and turquoise with, presumably, a fan or other useful service extending beyond but, of course, long since perished.

Jade *ge* were however now made in a simple style and fitted with an extended haft or tang in bronze flat form and in bird head shape.

This extended haft is often inlaid with elaborate designs in turquoise and has also been found made entirely of jade although this is not as common as the bronze, turquoise inlaid extension form. When made entirely in jade, the head of the bird takes the same angled beak form as is found in the three dimensional bird sculptures both in the Fu Hao tomb and in the marble forms now in the Academica Sinica in Taipei, Taiwan. The same beak with angle hook is seen on the cormorant (Exhibit 83) and on the seated bird (Exhibit 89).

As mentioned above in this book, the prolific variety of forms and types of jade in the Fu Hao tomb have given clear evidence of the assemblage of jades of different periods extending as far back as the North China neolithic cultures. Hopefully, there are other, similar, burials of the Anyang phase awaiting excavation and capable of providing further corroboration of the same and other facts.

Angus Forsyth
January 1994

商代（二里岡至殷商安陽時期）

A.1 簡介

公元前1600年 — 221年 —— 首都在今河南省鄭州

此時期維持了大約一千四百多年。從西方文化角度看，在這段期間之內，已經歷了好幾次不同文化的崛起與衰落。公元548年，在查士丁尼大帝的領導下，建築史上著名的聖蘇菲亞大教堂就建成於君士坦丁堡。在今天的伊斯坦堡，我們可見到此教堂仍完整地屹立著，它的落成正好標誌著六世紀至二十世紀，這段相距一千四百多年的歷史的展開。若從古玉方面而言，在中國漢氏族社會的環境底下，在公元前1600年至公元前221年這漫長期間，也經歷了革命性的發展，它已由最初的逐步搪磨發展成為今天真正的中華民族風格。

二里頭階段可以說是中國藝術領域斷續發展的最後一個時期。在此時期或以後，就盛行一種不凡的美學傾向，而這種傾向似是無法阻止的。愈離中原地域向西走，此種風格上的一致性愈是顯得薄弱。在四川省廣漢三星堆發現的二里崗龐型青銅柄眼獸面，可算是邊遠地區在創作領域上精悍一面的助證。在中國中原或以東的地方，從來未有發現過如這般夢魘的創造，與同一墓地出土的玉刃比較，這個三星堆青銅雕塑，更見其設計上之可觀性。這兩件器物顯示了在河南省中部出土的商代中期，或二里崗時期玉器之主要特色。

據我們現今之理解，中國最早有系統的書寫是在殷商時代出現。在新石器時代以前的陶器上（參考書目22圖版4），我們可見它刻有如尼字母，這些陶器應屬於龍山文化，它們的數量有限，而且其文字都是不可闡釋的。殷商人利用書寫字去記錄占卜，這些神諭是以象形文字記錄在牛肩胛骨或龜殼的底部。由此可見，要研究當時中國社會歷史，其實是有入手之處的，這與百萬年前沒有文字記載的社會相比，可謂相去遠矣。

青銅器與玉器在整個商代都盛行，二者相輔相成，經歷了千變萬化的發展，它們先後與官方指令及宗教祭器聯繫起來。在青銅器方面而言，它除作為戰爭之武器外，更被廣泛地採用。

青銅器在二里頭時期（公元前約1900-1600年）只屬於其雛型期。雖然青銅器發展迅速，但它並未如玉器般受到社會的重視。至殷商時代，青銅在精鍊的拋倒技術和完美的氣泡控制下，被鑄造成為多種不同類型的形狀。

由於社會上有部份重要的勞動力是與鑄造青銅有關，也由於此新出現的物料對宗教和祭祀有很大的重要性，所以作為社會經濟和文化意識演變的一種徵兆，我們並不驚訝青銅器能逐漸取代玉器的位置。如果以上的情況不出現，那才會叫人驚歎，因為玉器在當時是影響深遠，社會各階層在被動和無意識的情況下，把玉器作為高級階層的象徵，它們並沒如以後年代的玉器般，在地位上受到嚴正的質疑。故此我們可以說對玉器鍾愛悠長的時期，玉器在這社會的地位愈是根深蒂固和不可剝奪。

從藝術史角度言，青銅器能提供到絕對可靠的資料，故它是具有很大的價值的。譬如發現一個簡單的圖紋在青銅器上或內反覆出現，或以熱發光測試檢定陶器模型內部物料，這都可以為資料收集上取得可觀的進展。玉器乃青銅器在文化上之親密戰友，它此時亦受青銅紋飾發展之影響，這是從玉匠中可見的。

相信大部份人都會同意，青銅器之盛行也同時代表了社會在經濟上之損失。因為青銅器的製造要經過採礦、熔煉、鑄模、倒模、鑄造與打磨，這些都是有高度組織的活動，它們均需要大量的人力來運作和監管，以確保這些工序能有效率地進行。同樣地，玉器的製造也需要這般卓越的勞工，它之所能毫無困難地經歷了青銅時代，加深證明了玉石在中國人心目中的重要性。

在此時期，中國中原和東部的不同文化部落並非時常陷於戰亂之中，他們享有長時期的太平，於是便能有更多空間去改善耕種和建設大型的堡壘，以防禦其它民族的襲擊。這些堡壘均是以優良的城牆所組成，它們的建設亦注意到個人衛生的需要。在這整個時期之中，部落間敵對和內部的紛爭仍有出現。於此，玉器以溫和的姿態擔當了一個受尊敬的角色，穿梭於中國歷史上這個混戰時代。正如上述所言，在經歷長時期之後，人們會以常識辯稱玉器的地位被青銅器所取代，但這種排斥玉器的說法其實是未發生過的。

B.1 商（二里崗時代）

公元前1600年 — 1400年 —— 首都在今河南省鄭州

關於商代人起源的問題，現今依然眾說紛紜。有說他們是殷商人腹地，即今河南省安陽的土著；另有說他們是在二里頭時代從西北方遷徙而來的，此處所指的西北方是漢族邊界以外的地方，即今天長城以外之地。不論商人是從哪裡來，他們是偉大的農種者，他們懂得馴養水牛和耕種稻米。不管是基於純享樂主義，抑或是宗教的理由，釀酒與喝酒對商人來說，是一件極重要的事。今天，中國北方的酒主要是以帝蜀黍和高粱麥釀製的，每年在西北的內蒙古，以至東面的遼寧，南方江蘇長江一帶都有大量出產。從商代後期的刻文看，可見酒與青銅器之間的密切關係，因此我們沒有理由懷疑人類嗜酒是在更早的時候開始。

在二里崗後期或是早期的安陽時代，馬車出現作為戰爭的工具。於是青銅便被用作鑄造馬車裝備的材料，以後質量更佳的青銅武器便出現。在此時期，擁有青銅武器的國家在戰爭上未必一定可佔上風，因為其它擁有同樣武器的國家，也可對侵略者作出反擊。故此，為了保護一國之領土和財產，就有必要建造大規模的城堡，這情況在中國歷史上是從未間斷過的。

我們亦可見到對祖先和不同類型的神的崇拜，以及十進制和日曆的發明。

在河南省鄭州發掘到的陶瓷、骨刻與青銅器鑄造工作坊，它們合力顯示了當時存在了運作良好的社會。

人骨雕刻器物之發現，顯示了中國藝術家日後以動物作為設計的基本圖案的偏好。此時期開始以一系列尖銳直立的蟬為青銅器皿的裝飾花紋，正如我們以往所見，蟬進化的生長特色及其螢螢鳴聲，在中國藝術家的心目中佔有很特別的地位，這正好在玉器和青銅器中表現出來。

然而，此時期藝術上最重要的發展，就是宗教禮儀所採用的青銅器之製造。因為這意味著統治者或官員個人的財富，或是宗廟儀式所採用之器皿。

在這個發展過程中，饕餮紋便已肯定成為了青銅祭酒器特有的紋飾。饕餮紋是眾多紋飾中影響力最深遠的，它是由牛角、象耳、鷹爪、人眼和龍的羽冠所構成。

有人認為饕餮紋的前身，是來自好像今次展品中的良渚文化梯形掛飾上的虎面紋。良渚文化時期的饕餮紋，是凸眼和露出尖牙的，樣貌極其恐怖。在二里崗初期，玉石上的饕餮紋之瞳孔是呈突出半球狀；而在二里崗後期，則在饕餮紋的前額添上菱形設計，以配合陽刻交叉排線。

除了中國北方新石器時代的玉器之外，還有似是表現自然主義的紅山文化時代的凸線玉刻，以及可能是首次在二里頭時代出現的角形倒勾陽刻。由此可見，青銅器在那年代是一種新的發展，它的紋飾設計，基本上，未有足夠時間能發展為一種風格。但是在商代中期或二里崗時期，我們卻發現到另一種發展。此時期青銅器的凸線，從器物的表面上突出，狀似薄薄的隔牆，可放置寶石在內裡。這些陽線猶如花體紋飾，它們在饕餮紋上是以中間對稱分佈的。在展品77的玉水牛中，我們就可看到這種對稱花紋分佈。這時期饕餮的瞳孔是圓形的，分別置於眼角兩端。其他展品像77號

一樣，具有像支柱般的方形眼睛，它們並沒有內眦或外眦之分。此外，值得一提的是展品77號的立體感和曲線體形，這特色在殷商後期可說是一種印象主義，但卻非突出的例子去說明玉匠之藝術。

展品77清楚地顯示了二里頭階段的玉匠，在立體雕塑技巧上，已達到渾圓純熟的境界。如這展品圓形的腿部與傾斜的蹄部，或是方形的鼻尖與曲折的下頷都配合得天衣無縫。

在二里頭時代，青銅器是以范塊鑄造法製成的。這方法其中的一個弱點，就是在把范塊併合為一的過程中，青銅器的表面會產生許多接口。從青銅器皿而言，這些接口就垂直的分佈在器皿外周，它們會產生兩種結果。其一為這些不知是意外或刻意做成的多餘青銅，很大可能發展為器皿上之凸緣和分界。而當其時，它們是被雕凹成勾形或方形鏤空或是塌邊，久而久之，這些凸緣就形成了自己的風格特色。

其次，這些接口限制了工匠在紋飾創作上的自由度。如果一個工匠能夠克服這些接口上的困難，那他的製品必上佳之作。在物器上循環排列的紋飾，本來沒有前後之分，但因為這些接口的出現，反而為紋飾作出了先後之區分。此外，我們在這目錄中亦可看到由二里頭時代發展至二里崗時代，以至西周時代的角形勾紋飾。在展品72和74兩件二里崗玉器中，這紋飾可從那些凸線上看到。

玉器上的凹糟位在玉雕藝術中是有系統地發展的，二里頭時代之玉璋和刀柄上的凹糟或榫子，都是由紅山文化的榫形體制發展而來的，它為二里崗玉器增添了一種穩重感覺，但此特色到殷商時代則消失了。究竟這種凹糟的出現，是純為了裝飾抑或是有功用上的意義，直至現今我們仍未能作出一個合理的解釋。

從部份二里頭時代玉刀裡，我們可見到殘餘的折疊紋。這些紋飾包括了純織布紋和簡單的藍紋或席紋。在這時期的葬禮，人們習慣把戈刃折斷成兩至三節，將之與祭骨一併置於死者的背部或臀部下底。

在上面我們曾經提到四川省廣漢三星堆墓址，是屬於二里崗後期或殷商初期。這些青銅器皿品質極高，它們與中原地帶的比較，在品味和氣質上都相去甚遠，可說具有了天賦的地方特色。在1989年，江蘇省新干郊的大洋洲河床沙葬墓，發掘了一具沙葬紅皂石人像(參考書目21圖版66)。這墓葬裡的青銅器被界定為商代後期之作，但是它的齒狀頭飾和腦後的鏈環雕刻，以及狹長的眦和細小的象牙，叫人難以相信它是商代後期的作品。也許它應是二里頭和二里崗時代所製成的，因這解釋看起來較為合理。

B.2晚商／殷

約公元前1400年 — 公元前1100年 —— 首都在今河南省
安陽殷墟(今日之小屯)

此時期,市鎮的建設繼續擴展,城市設計包括有組織
的街道,在城堡內要有公眾的場地,這些建築都是
以木材建設在堆土上。

巨型的單室墓穴是建在地底深處,當埋葬後,它
們是完全的藏於地下。這些墓穴內建有木牆與堆土的
滑道,正如埃及的金字塔一樣,這般宏偉的工程毫無疑
問是由王室或政府所操縱,所以殷商墓葬正好反映了
當時統治者是要擁有很大的權力,始可調動和組織龐大
的勞動力。從上面所述,我們可見有很多人是在建墓中
犧牲性。因此,骨器也應是由人骨而來的。我們知道
龜甲在殷商時代是用作占卜的,人們希望藉此可帶來狩
獵豐收,又或是以此記錄以蠻夷為祭品的葬禮儀式。

雖然從大量發掘到的鑄模,可知青銅是以作為耕
犁和砍伐的工具見稱,但在農業上人們仍繼續使用石造
和骨製的鋤。然而甲骨在社會上突然被應用,主要是
被為一種可卦告未來,或甚至以此作天氣預測的器具。

作為一個重要和出色的統治者,他除了要顯示
出能貫通天地之間外,最重要的是能做到好像阿拉伯貝
都因人領袖一樣,為人民作出忠告和決策。

薩滿教僧或占卜者替人向神靈請求,令到此神靈
無論在那一階級的心目中產生了很大的影響力。

由此時期至西周時代,社會的核心主要是由三個
基本體系組成,它們彼此間在某程度上是互相影響:—

(i)　昭穆 —— 國君與其代之氏族成員,二者互相
監察對方的權力。

(ii)　宗法 —— 由同一祖先而來,下分不同之宗族。此
概念容納了很大量的成員,他們都服從緊密的整體行動
和嫡系。

(iii)　封建 —— 多為王室的宗支,脫離宗族以建立
自己細小的社會。

青銅器如酒皿和祭祀器皿,在此時期的禮節上已
發展了兩重角色,它既是重要的祭祀禮器,亦是重要的
武器。這時期青銅器上因范塊鑄造法而產生的接口
亦有新的發展,人們已肯定了接口問題的存在,顯示
出是成熟時候去解決這種冶鑄上之缺點。

塊范凸出之接口開始變得舖張誇飾,有証據
肯定它對玉雕是有很大影響的。這些影響包括了玉雕上
凹口邊緣之發展,以及玉匠對青銅鑄造潮流中,紋飾只
可表現在局限的空間之認同,此種紋飾就算在沒凸緣的
玉飾和玉璜亦可見。在考古發掘中這類型的傳統例子

有婦好墓出土之大型綠軟玉簋,此器皿的垂直凸外緣
雖與塊范接口所形成的相同,但對玉器來說卻是
沒實際關係的。此時,青銅之鑄造已開始變得精細,不
同類型之凸線設計,如最普遍的雷紋,都是造得極為
精緻的。而器皿上的圖案設計和雕飾,則以典型的動物
和鳥為本,這些特色在上述玉簋的足緣和婦好墓出土
之白色大理石碗皆可見到。

在殷商時期,大理石是一種製器皿或動物、
鳥雕塑之理想材料。在1903年代,中國社會科學研究院
曾於婦好墓就發掘到這種令人難忘的玉器。

曾經有多位學者認為此時期的玉或軟玉材料,是
包括了由霍堅輸入的,如果此點是對的話,那至少反映
出商代玉器不論在其顛峰或衰落時期影響所及的地方
都是很遠的。

從新石器時代豬龍之造型,可見商代玉器獨特
之發展,此種設計大約可追溯到龍山時期和龍山文化
陶碗上的盤龍像。

豬龍的冠由最初在玉器上的修飾成份,發展為
外周鏤空部份,而其體型則是直接脫自龍山時期
的彩陶,以假身線展示了三角形和菱形紋。龍鼻有上
仰之短頷,耳大而短闊,它們在器皿手柄和青銅器之鑲
飾上是立體的,這亦成為著名的所謂樽角龍造型。

1976年,考古學家們在安陽發掘了婦好墓,
此墓藏有豐富的傢具,其中包括了很多種類的
青銅器以及最重要的七百五十五件玉器。這些玉器
毫無疑問最遲已在婦好去世後出現,即公元前十四世紀
初。它們對於鑑定和比較其他玉器之年代是很有價值
的。婦好墓中包括了十六具活俑,另加上大量的青銅器
皿,正好揭示了當其時帝王殘暴和享樂奢華的一面。

在婦好墓內,玉器分別是擺放在棺木和墓室
內的。在墓室中找到的玉器是與棺狀漆木遺存並置的,
但這些遺存因經歷了幾百世紀的水滲而損毀了。從墓室
的排列情況顯示出木漆棺上應有扁平上蓋,作為擺放
陳列玉器之用的。

此時期最流行的玉器和青銅器紋飾,是分佈
在如縋曲蛇狀玉器上的直身盾形紋。另一種則是菱形
陰刻和斷面線,在上面已提過此紋飾在殷商饕餮紋前額
中已有出現。

緊接二里岡時期發展的立體人和動物玉雕有
重要的轉變,它們有些雕成厚實的、蹲跪的和雄壯的
造型,個個栩栩如生,予人有幹勁和力量的感覺,而非
審美上之美感。這些玉器的製造和風格顯示了玉匠是
需要時間和精力去發掘動物的造型,而在青銅器皿中此
種造型,如象、豎鳥和虎流行起來。這些動物和玉鳥

雕塑最基本的對比，就是在於造型上之質樸風格，二里岡水牛(展品77)渾圓流暢之風格已成過去，而真陽線和凸狀線亦然。殷商玉器的表面是完成得很粗糙，以假陽線為主，玉匠已失去製作新石器時代真陽線之耐性和技術。若與上述二里岡動物渾圓幼細之風格相比，殷商動物和鳥身的基本造型是建立在方盒形上，其圓滑之角位似是容許了自然主義，腿部是在一面以直覺鑽成深坑至另一面而成的，見展品81。製品為兩腿或四腿之動物或鳥，完成得十分之粗疏。在輪廓上或腿部上的曲線是沒有結構的，它們一般以假陽線展示外層的設計。此時期，玉雕製作有一有趣現象，未知是基於技術上的困難，或是玉匠本身不願把動物腿部內側直角部份磨平，動物型玉器的腿部仍保持方狀，予人一種很樸實之印象。在這個青銅器發展優良的年代，玉匠在技術上是受到限制的，而這對於二千或三千年前，新石器時代紅山文化玉匠之創作力則是沒影響的。然而，從二里岡時期可見，這也許是由於時代品味不同，加上玉匠已滿足於非精工的真陽線而停滯不前所致。

參考書目91有十分著名的玉人，其中使人驚訝的是有些細小玉人之體積及其頗高之可塑性。它們仍保留有流暢的體形，實在是令人十分之懷念的雕塑作品。婦好墓中有一著名的類人像，為長扁形玉飾，兩面以假陽線分別刻一男像和一女像。

除人像外，動物紋包括了象(展品88)、犀牛、鱷、龜、蟒、螺、熊、虎、龍和馬。這些設計中也有闊身魚塊，尾部呈齒狀，扁物兼有圓形張口。至於鳥蟲類則有蠶、草蜢、常見的蟬、鸕鶿和鶚。

殷商玉器中幾何和類似用具造型的有玉璧、素面斧、齒斧、璧形齒斧、平衡闊身齒、素刃或齒刃的戈、琮和髮梳。此時饕餮紋與二里頭的不同，其眼珠仍保留了瞳孔的半球形盒狀，但中心的垂直鑽孔，則似是藝術家欲給予以往不兇猛造型的一顆眼珠。

在安陽建築的根基部份有玉璧之發現，它們可說是代表了未來此種玉飾發展之預告。

在當時的立體玉雕中，有很多扁身和動物形玉器。而在婦好墓出土的兩隻小型蒙古型玉馬則是值得一提的，它們造型優美，其曲腿比展品88的扁身象飾之曲腿更優勝。

另外亦有扁身曲狀玉璜飾，它們多為有很深外周鏤空鳥和長髮曲狀人像，為外周鏤空造型提供了很好的機會。在新石器時代龍山文化中，此造型是比較不靈活但卻自由，至商代後期才變得更成熟。正如剛剛提到，在范塊鑄造法的凸緣可發現到空間設計和限制，但對於玉器而言，這是沒有必要的，否則，此已成為了玉器的設計風格。

而另一種只在此時期發展之玉器為翻邊玉璧，璧身兩面近中心孔的內周有直角凸緣，扁平的表面上則刻有典型的複環(見參考書目37圖版31)。類似的玉器於1985年，在遠至馬來亞亦有出土，見圖版31。在中國雲南省也有相似之發現，其中最少在江蘇省新干大洋洲河邊墓址出土的一件現已復合。

婦好墓亦有出產玉製之武器，但製作多粗糙，這些在大汶口文化、龍山文化和二里頭文化影響下產生之玉器，其造型之整體質素和假陽線之運用正代表了商代藝術上的衰落。

這時亦承繼了首次在二里頭時期出現的瘦長形玉柄，雖然至今仍未明其用途，但在1992年，陝西寶雞則出土了兩件屬西周時期之作，見參考書目22圖版51和52。從寶雞出土可見此玉器應為手柄，與鑲嵌的玉片或綠松石並列在譬如是扇或其它已腐化的物品上。

商代玉戈外形簡單，一般是配以銅製扁形或鳥形柄，柄上常鑲有綠松石。它們雖有玉製的，但卻以青銅者漸多。玉製鳥形柄之尖嘴與婦好墓立體玉鳥及台北中央研究院藏大理石鳥相同，在本書中展品89的鸕鶿，也有同樣之尖嘴和勾角。

正如本書前面所述，婦好墓玉器繁多之種類和形制顯示了它集各時代之特色於一身。而現時尚有類似的殷商墓有待發掘，它們應可為此方面或其它方面提供更多的證據。

76

MINIATURE BROWN BLADE

ERLITOU/ERLIGANG PERIOD TRANSITION
  (C.1900 - 1600 BC)

PE528

LENGTH : 5.4 CM
WIDTH : 1.4 CM
THICK : 0.3 CM

A miniature *ge* blade in opaque brown nephrite. The elegant blade tapers and curves gently to a sharp arrow point. It has a double hollow ground surface constituted by a long central ridge and two sides which extend forward from the almost imperceptible shoulders. There is a single hole through the centre of the tang.

A comparison of Exhibit 75 with this piece reveals their common origin, and the smoothing, cambering and finishing of this miniature piece are no less careful or specific. (AHF)

Compare: (i) 46 Nos.60 and 68 (ii) 68 pl.X No.2 and pl.XI No.1 (iii) 66 No.18
Collection: The Peony Collection

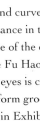

77

GREEN MASK FITTING

ERLITOU/ERLIGANG PERIOD TRANSITION
  (C.1900 - 1400 BC)

PE513

DIAMETER : 3.2 CM
HEIGHT : 3.0 CM
THICKNESS : 1.9 CM

A human face mask fitting in translucent dark green nephrite with some lighter green vertical banding. The eyes are formed as raised roundels above contoured cheeks each side of the inverted mushroom nose and are set within a diagonal frame with pointed outer canthus and downward curving inner canthus. The eyebrows form a slightly angled V bar above the eyes and the mouth is a thick lipped transverse groove raised slightly above the surrounding area of the chin. The ears at each side are formed as a squared and scooped out three-sided rectangle. The piece is pierced from top to bottom by a transversely elongated hole formed by joining four adjacently drilled unsmoothed away channels. The back is pierced at top and bottom with a single conical hole.

This piece is a striking combination of straight lines and curves. The inverted garlic-head form of nose seems first to have made its appearance in the Shandong Longshan culture (see Exhibit 62). The very individual structure of the ears is a feature shared with the ears on a number of the animals found in the Fu Hao tomb at Anyang - such as the elephants. 90 pl.95. The slanted canthus of the eyes is comparable with Shang dynasty Anyang phase bronze decor but the banana form grooved mouth is unusual and can be compared with the curved banana mouth in Exhibit 42 from the Liangzhu culture. There are also elements of this Exhibit which are reflected in the totem poles of the Haida Indians of British Columbia. (AHF)

Compare: 91 pl.95
Collection: The Peony Collection

78

WATER BUFFALO WITH
RAISED-LINE DECORATION

ERLIGANG PERIOD
  (C.1600 - 1400 BC)

                          PE749

LENGTH : 4.2 CM
HEIGHT : 2.8 CM
BREADTH : 2.0 CM

A figure of a relaxing water buffalo in opaque olive green nephrite substantially altered to buff colour. The stocky body has a plastic, rounded profile with curving haunches and curved forelegs which are tucked in a kneeling position beneath the body. The tapered head looks to the front and terminates in a squared muzzle. The eyes are formed in raised plateau relief on top of the head and are set in front of raised-line curving eyebrows. The curving horns are part hollowed out on top, forming chambers separated by cloison-type walls of high raised-line work. The body is covered with curved and hooked designs in fine high raised-line work. The tail hangs behind as a broad V shape with its own raised-line design. The piece is pierced vertically from the centre of the back for suspension.

Three-dimensional jade animals of the Shang dynasty are rare. The Fu Hao tomb (c.1400 BC) yielded by far the greatest known variety and number. There are jade buffaloes in the British Museum, in the Metropolitan Museum in New York, in the Winthrop Collection and formerly in the Meyer Collection. In all these pieces, including those from the Fu Hao tomb, the raised-line work is the degenerate false raised-line, whereas Exhibit 78 clearly exhibits the genuine high raised-line in formal organisation of designs comparable to the raised-line treatment in the reserves on certain bronze vessels of the Zhengzhou period of the early to middle Shang dynasty known as Erligang. This, coupled with a certain liveliness and naturalism derived from the softened and rounded contours of Exhibit 78 strongly suggests an Erligang date. (AHF)

Compare: 46 No.148
Collection: The Peony Collection

79

DARK GREEN JADE BRACELET

SHANG DYNASTY
ERLIGANG PHASE
(c.1600 - 1400 BC)

BATEA 432

OVERALL DIAMETER : 8 CM
DIAMETER OF APERTURE : 5.7 CM.

Jade bracelet of even dark green colour with black flecks, the smooth surface of the bracelet coming gently to the rounded outer edge, the inner edge rounded and smooth.

The colour of the jade is typical of a number of jades from the tomb of Lady Fu Hao (c.1400 BC) which are thought to date to this period. (BSM)

Previously published: 80, No.14

80

DARK GREEN JADE HANDLE

SHANG DYNASTY
ERLIGANG PHASE
(c.1600 - 1400 BC)

BATEA 509

LENGTH : 9.4 CM
WIDTH :2.4 CM
DEPTH : 0.4 CM

Dark green jade handle of thin knife-shaped form with tapering ends and waisted section near the top with one perforation near the base drilled from one side.

A similar handle was found in the tomb of Lady Fu Hao (c.1400 BC). (BSM)

182

Previously published: 77 No. 11.

81

TIGER BIRD

SHANG DYNASTY
EARLY ANYANG PHASE
 (c.1400 BC)
                    PE435
HEIGHT : 7.5 CM
DEPTH : 3.5 CM
WIDTH : 2.9 CM

A feline-headed bird in white stone. The mouth is open and the lips drawn back to reveal two rows of large, straight teeth. The creature stands upright on two square form sturdy legs in front and has a pair of large wings folded closely round to the back of its body. A substantial tail curls under the rear to form a support and terminates in a pair of hooks. There are vestigial remains of incised extended canthus eyes and substantial square form and curved line patterning incised on the wings, back and legs.

A sister piece to this, of a similar small size was excavated from the Fu Hao tomb in Anyang (c.1400 BC). Both follow the characteristic blockiness of late Shang sculpture. The reasons for this are not entirely clear and certainly seem to owe nothing to technical difficulties factors such as those faced by the Neolithic jade workers because, by the Anyang phase, more than adequate knowledge of precision bronze casting was at hand to enable the production of competent and efficient bronze tools. However, the block form of rendering bodies and legs in three dimensions is typical of this period and it is easy to see from pieces such as this the way in which the simplest stone working techniques such as cross grinding were used to form the forelegs, and straight drilling to form the uniform bore hole of the mouth. (AHF)

Previously published: 17 pl.3
Compare: (i) 66 No.50 (ii) 49 No.1 (iii) 91 pl.56
Collection: The Peony Collection

82

JADE TIGER PLAQUE

SHANG DYNASTY
ANYANG PHASE
(C.1400 - 1100 BC)
BATEA 534
LENGTH : 6.3 CM
WIDTH : 3.4 CM

Altered green jade tiger plaque of flat thin form, its paws, ears in
the shape of a recumbent C, and head worked in typical late Shang
style, the reverse similarly carved with extensive traces of cinnabar.
Conical perforation at the mouth. (BSM)

Previously published: (i) 77, No.9 (ii) 80, No.16
Compare: 39 No. 290B

83

FLAT CORMORANT PENDANT

SHANG DYNASTY
EARLY ANYANG PHASE
(C.1400 BC)
PE680
LENGTH : 4.0 CM
HEIGHT : 3.4 CM
THICKNESS : 0.4 CM

A flat-plaque form figure of a cormorant in translucent light golden
nephrite with some white clouding. The bird is in a seated position with
legs drawn up against the humped body. The alert head is held slightly
back at an angle with plateau-form circular eyes. The small forked tail
extends a short way at the rear and the drawn up legs are held into the
body at the lower front with downward curving talons. A ringed hole is
drilled through the base of the chest for suspension and the body is
striated with layered grooves to represent the wing feathers.

Again, the Fu Hao tomb provided one cormorant of this very type but
formed of a thinner slice of jade and lacking some of the partial three
dimensionality of this piece. There is also a very similar piece illustrated
in 29, pl.32. (AHF)

Compare: (i) No.252 (ii) 68 pl.XLVIII No.8 (iii) 28 No.A84 (iv) 1 pl.VII (v) 29 No.32 (vi) 91 pl.70
Collection: The Peony Collection

84

PLAQUE-FORM BIRD

SHANG DYNASTY
ANYANG PHASE
 (C.1400 - 1100 BC)
PE684
LENGTH : 4.0 CM
WIDTH : 3.2 CM
THICKNESS : 0.3 CM

Flattened plaque-form bird with flat base and convex upper profile
in translucent light golden nephrite with some white cloudy
suffusions. The sharp pointed beak extends before a pair of simple
large incised round eyes flanked by the forward outstretched arms
or legs with incised digits. The shoulders and haunches are
depicted by squared inward curling scrolls in low relief and the tail
is formed of a series of paired, striated, incised feather forms
turning out towards each side.

There are a fair number of published pieces structured around this
basic form which consists of a central sharp ended body with a
double-eyed flat head in between short forward extending limbs.
There is also a suggestion – just a suggestion – of a full face human
effigy or mask with a feather form headdress. (AHF)

Compare: (i) 28 No.A85 (ii) 37 No.25 (iii) 1 pl.25 (iv) 1 pl.VII (v) 83 No.14
Collection: The Peony Collection

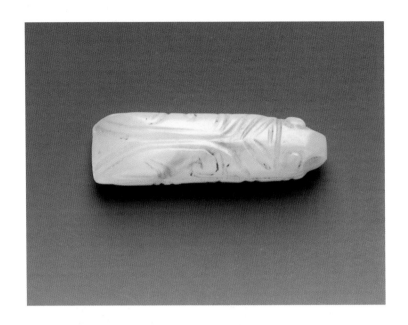

85

INSECT

SHANG DYNASTY
ANYANG PHASE
 (C.1400 - 1100 BC)
                    PE443
LENGTH : 3.2 CM
BREADTH : 0.9 CM
THICK : 0.6 CM

An insect with two pairs of prominent eyes and the proboscis area drilled through from each side for suspension. The thorax and wingcase details are depicted in strong raised-line work formed as hook motifs.

This piece demonstrates a very singular feature that first appeared in the Anyang phase of the Shang dynasty - the false raised-line. In fact the lines are not raised but are the same height as the surrounding surfaces across the single cambered grooves although they give the clever impression of actual raised-lines. The disappearance of the genuine raised-line by, or during the early part of the Anyang phase, is noteworthy. In view of the evolving progression through the Bronze Age from its origin at the end of the third millennium BC of greatly facilitated mechanical assistance for jade working, it is curious that the genuine raised-line of the Shandong Longshan culture that survived strongly into the Erligang period (Exhibit 78) now recedes in deference to this lazy false raised-line substitute. (AHF)

Collection: The Peony Collection

86

CELADON JADE CICADA KNOT-PICKER

SHANG DYNASTY,
ANYANG PHASE
  (C.1400 - 1100 BC)

BATEA 521

LENGTH : 4.2 CM
WIDTH : 1.1 CM
DEPTH : 0.6 CM

Pale celadon jade cicada of long narrow simply carved form, the tail coming to a point, probably a knot-picker. The head pierced for suspension. (BSM)

Previously published: 80 No. 20

87

HUANG SHAPE BIRD PENDANT

SHANG DYNASTY
ANYANG PHASE
  (C.1400 - 1100 BC)

PE469

HEIGHT : 5.3 CM
WIDTH (MAX) 1.1 CM
THICK : 0.3 CM

A *huang* or bow-shaped slice of translucent yellow nephrite formed as the perching figure of a graceful and elegant hawk or eagle with an elongated bifurcated crest and chisel tail. The wings are folded into its sides and the squared head is indicated by transverse incisions between which an incised double concentric circle forms the eye.

The Fu Hao tomb contained a similar bird with a long, extended crest with bifurcated terminals, a squared head with double incised eyes and a strong, simple clawed foot projection. The Fu Hao bird, however, lacks the curve of Exhibit 87 which may have been fashioned along this curved line because it was formed from a broken part of a Shang "ring of Saturn" *bi-disc*. This further demonstrates the respect of the Chinese craftsman for nephrite and his unwillingness to waste even broken fragments. This reluctance to waste jade is a constantly recurring fact throughout the history of jade working. (AHF)

Compare: 91 pl.31
Collection: The Peony Collection

88

ELEPHANT PENDANT

SHANG DYNASTY
ANYANG PHASE
 (C.1400 - 1100 BC)
                     PE674
LENGTH : 2.9 CM
HEIGHT : 1.8 CM
THICKNESS : 0.3 CM

Flat plaque in opaque light honey-brown nephrite formed as a baby elephant with small roughly formed tail and strong bent fore and hind legs. Large ears are situated above lightly incised extended canthus eyes with round central pupils. From the open mouth extends an upward-curving trunk whose tip curls down and in upon itself to form a hole for suspension.

The elephant is a rare form in late Shang dynasty jade plaques. The sculptural structure has moved away from the three-dimensional blockiness more typical of the Shang dynasty's Anyang phase and, indeed the legs are bent almost as if the animal was about to lie down. There are exceptions to the general rule of thickset forms in Shang sculpture such as the pair of horses published in 91 pl.94 and this Exhibit seems a further exception. Today, the elephant in China is confined to Yunnan Province in the extreme south west but, in former times, the elephant ranged widely in southern China and magnificent elephant shape bronze vessels are known from the middle Anyang phase. (AHF)

Compare: 69 pl.XI No.7
Collection: The Peony Collection

89

FLAT BIRD WITH FORKED TAIL

SHANG DYNASTY, ANYANG PHASE TO
EARLY WESTERN ZHOU DYNASTY
  (C.12TH - 9TH CENTURY BC)
                              PE724

LENGTH : 6.0 CM

HEIGHT : 2.0 CM

Elongated thick plaque in translucent off-white nephrite formed as a seated bird with a sharply hooked beak and large round eye with a substantial curved crest lying along its back. The feet are tucked up against the fore part of the body beneath the triple layered wings, which sweep back in relief from a curling form at the shoulder up to the middle of the back with a smooth median corner-angle break. Behind the wings extends a long tail terminating in a short bevelled fishtail fork upon which is an incised escutcheon shape of enclosed double line form with two curled double line panels. Behind the angle of the crouching leg are two separate squared areas of incised hair striation evoking ventral fish fins.

The characteristic hook-end beak, tucked-up leg, the layered relief wings and the fish fork tail are also found in Exhibit 83 which is clearly earlier although these features – and the ventral fish fins – continue through to squarer, cut-out and incised versions of the same bird in the middle Western Zhou period. (AHF)

Compare: (i) 46 Nos.259 and 260 (ii) 68 pl.XLVIII No.2
Collection: The Peony Collection

90

HORNED DRAGON WITH SILKWORM TAIL

LATE SHANG TO EARLY
WESTERN ZHOU DYNASTY
  (C.12TH - 9TH CENTURY BC)
                          BATEA 522

LENGTH : 2.2 CM
HEIGHT : 1.6 CM
WIDTH : 0.7 CM

Yellowish jade horned dragon with a silkworm tail, the shape almost semicircular, the nose pierced for suspension, traces of cinnabar.

The combination of parts from two separate animals seems to have been an innovation of the early Western Zhou. See 84. (BSM)

Previously published: 80, No.27

91

BI-DISC MADE UP OF THREE *HUANG*

SHANG DYNASTY, ANYANG PHASE TO EARLY
WESTERN ZHOU DYNASTY
(C.12TH – 9TH CENTURY BC)

BATEA 529

DIAMETER OVERALL : 12.2 CM
DIAMETER OF APERTURE : 6.7 CM

A set of three thin undecorated jade *huang* pendants of unequal size but making a complete *bi-disc*, each *huang* pendant with a single hole at each end for linking them together, all drilled conically from one side only, the jade all cut from one stone with white cloud-like inclusions in each section, also yellowish-green and brown in places.

Such sets are fairly common and occur in tombs of the Anyang phase or a little later. Some have two holes at one end. (BSM)

Previously published: (i) 77, p. 1 (ii) 80, No.30 Compare: (i) 66, Exhibit 34 (ii) Wenwu 1972/4 p 27 fig 4 (iii) 98, Plate LXIV No 5

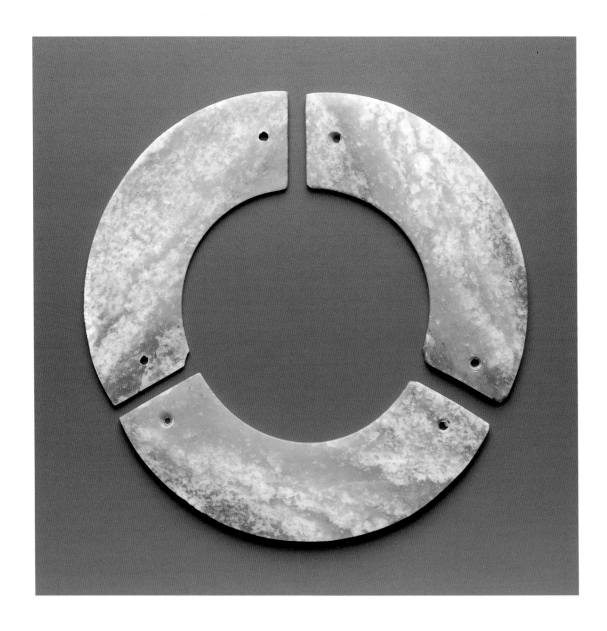

A.1 WESTERN ZHOU c.1100-771 BC
CAPITAL AT XIAN

This period is principally concerned with a geographical area constituted by Southern Shaanxi, Shanxi, Henan, Hebei and Shandong Provinces. However, it had a much wider influence than these direct domains and Western Zhou bronze vessel forms have been excavated as far south as Jiangsu.

Through this period the King of a state continued to exercise central power over the people and in this respect the structure of government continued from the Shang.

What was new to the Western Zhou was the appearance of the concept of linkage of heaven and the direct mandate bestowed from heaven upon the Emperor as intercessor between the people of the state and heaven itself. The emergence of this concept was associated with a closer and more minutely regulated observance of communion between Emperor and people. It is possible in these formalised beginnings to perceive the origins of the massive civil service structure in China which, beginning in the time of Confucius in the early Eastern Zhou period, was to be both the pride of Chinese social organisation and the rigid fetter upon evolutionary beneficial development.

Perhaps concomitant with, or perhaps attributable to, the closer organisation of relationship between the ruler and the ruled, human sacrifice in tombs experienced a massive drop in popularity. Tombs themselves became smaller in scale and, perhaps more significantly, the drinking practices so greatly extolled by the Shang/Yin people were probably banned - and were undoubtedly deprecated. Certainly the drinking ceased with a fair degree of suddenness and there are early Western Zhou bronze inscriptions which condemn the mass drinking habits of the erstwhile Yin as debauched and artificial. In consequence, there being no need for bronze drinking vessels in the type of quantity and variety so beloved of the Yin, bronze vessels were now made to contain food and also to serve as a cache of hidden valuables - many hidden so well that they are only being found today.

Most bronze inscriptions of the period record specific dedications of a commemorative or sacrificial purpose. The verve and flourish of simple naturalism so prevalent under the Yin, gave way to a more modest practicality. This is not in any way to say that greater and greater proficiency of bronze casting did not develop because it did - to the extent that clear and very well written and lengthy records of actual historical events, as well as thoughts and concepts, began appearing on bronzes. These were both of an every day and a dedicatory nature and most of what we know today about the practical social lives of the Western Zhou people are gleaned from bronze inscriptions - a complete contrast to the times of the Shang/Yin people where the information mine was oracle bones - something which had disappeared by the times of the Western Zhou.

The emergence of the family unit as the paramount core of social practice and polity seems to have occurred in contemporaneous juxtaposition with the institution of imperial intercession with heaven. The family unit was structured around the immediately visible, and extant, family members extending in seniority from grandparents, through sons and daughters to grandchildren all dwelling in the same compound. Confucius noted in the sixth century BC the excellent structure of patriarchal society. He was noting the practice which developed in the early Western Zhou onwards and continued to form the central pillar of Chinese private family society from his times up to the present day.

A new simplicity and directness of form in bronze ritual vessels can be traced to the middle Western Zhou period from c.1000 - 900 BC. This period also saw the introduction of bronze musical instruments such as the graduated sets of *zhong* bells suspended on purpose built wooden frames - often 8, 10 or 12 pieces and imposing a considerable weight upon the massive structures built to hang them for playing. One can also see a huge production increase of military implements and weapons dating from this time. It seems to be clear that the central authority was breaking down insofar as it was unable to control and restrain regional and peripheral exploitation of bronze for local and regional personal gain. This beginning of a breakdown of central authority was in fairly short order to introduce the aptly named period of the Warring States.

For reasons which are not clear, the jade worker all but abandoned production of the three dimensional sculpture of dramatic, chunky simplicity so characteristic of the Shang's Anyang phase. He generally confined his productive impulses to flat zoomorphic plaque forms with simple, unlined surfaces. As mentioned above, this type of plaque had begun in the Anyang phase. The Mongolian horse flat plaque-forms in the Fu Hao tomb, and Exhibit 88, are examples. The disappearance of the three dimensional sculpture seems to have been associated with a conceptual simplicity - even austerity - of execution. The entire series of ideas composed into surface decoration is strong and simple and, although often quite complex, there is no concession to rococo floridity or fussiness of detail. On the contrary, the general impression given is of a vitality of manner and lively balance with a soft and even gloss which, as we shall see, was maintained into the Spring and Autumn period and developed into the very high glossy surface finish so popular in the Warring States period.

The flat plaque-form could be a full surface upon which ideas and designs could be engraved or incised or could be individually cut out to profile a particular animal, human figure or bird. There are subtle possibilities of accent and emphasis by which the skilled jade worker can suggest movement and variation in a flat form jade but, this kind of perception and reaction to it being not only possible but normal in the Western Zhou period, it is remarkable that no sustained and major effort to work jade into three dimensional forms was ever made in this period. There are isolated exceptions to this. The small banana form of pendant, Exhibit 100 is a rare example of a three dimensional jade carving of the human figure from the Western Zhou period. The importance of this piece, apart from its uniqueness, lies in its informed and disciplined implementation in jade of certain canons of line and volume interpretation which are even rare in bronze. One signal interesting fact is that this period does not appear to have carved or sculpted marble.

There was also at this time a very important liberating movement in bronze production away from the piece mould seam or flange constraint. The move was a simple one to break out of this by now wholly imaginary limitation in a way that saw the separately arranged registers of tight and formal panels of design break down their borders and spill over into each other. The result was an immediate continuity of design or picture extending right around the neck, shoulder or belly of the bronze vessel. This innovation ushered in an entirely liberated concept of all round freedom of spirit and creativity for the bronze worker - a freedom which the jade worker immediately took up and followed.

From the beginning of this period when surface embellishment of jade was a matter of rather lazy and slipshod incising of false raised lines, there was a gradually higher and increasing profile of sophistication culminating in the great technical virtuosity of the Warring States period. By the 10th to 9th centuries BC, the surface working detail on jades was formed of broadly incised double lines with a fluidity and sureness portraying a remarkable quality of softness wholly unknown to the Shang. The squared form of right angle hook meander, which was first seen in the Longshan Neolithic period raised-line work, is by now reduced and simplified to incised double line detail and worked into a formation of single free standing upright hook with blade form at right angles. See Exhibit 97. From the corner of the blade a single short barb extends to the opposite side. The whole detail is executed in this double incised-line formation with no false or true raised-line work. The hook motif is commonly found as a series in a single band or register on one side of a central line on the surface of the piece.

From the evidence of the Fu Hao tomb jade contents, personal ornament was not a prominent function of jade at that time. In the Western Zhou, personal ornament jades were a definite aspect of jade working. Exhibit 96 of a trapezoid pendant with incised bird design follows a well established form which, sometimes two or three times the size of Exhibit 96, forms a central plaque chest pendant from which strings of beaded jade, coloured or turquoise forms would suspend and, presumably, clank together while the wearer walked about. See 20 Plate 56.

The *taotie* mask whose development we have seen from the Liangzhu period through the Shang dynasty's Anyang phase, degrades and is broken down into much abstracted representative forms that float on an increasingly meaningless sea of diffuse and unconnected motifs resulting in a total loss of the original design stimulus. There is in fact a tendency, together with this looseness of design, for a totality of decoration all over the surface of a piece - almost as if the sight of an undecorated surface was considered a failure properly to bring the work to a finish. One further eccentricity of the early Western Zhou period which carried on into the Spring and Autumn period was a squared, geometric style of incised design deriving perhaps from, among other things, the key fret border pattern which seems to have arisen in Shang.

Flat pendants are executed in a form of "U" shape groove incised false raised line work. Some of these pendants are very large and some are in the *huang* form. Popular incised bevel line motifs are standing crested birds with folded wings, big round eyes, big hooked bills and big talons depicted in an "open spanner head" formation. Dragon forms were also produced at this time with diamond shape eyes whose Anyang phase retrousse nose-form becomes invested both with incised line grooving and also with registers of true raised-line work. Raised-line work was also used to depict on flat *bi-disc* surfaces sometimes simple, and sometimes complex, series of dragon head forms with curled up noses and long curved tongues hanging out in front from the tip of the mouth. (Exhibit 107)

There is a well known series of elongated, rather substantial, oval section handles, *huang* shape pendants and flat rectangular plaque-forms with waisted sides which are all groove incised with the standing crested bird design exhibiting, at the end of strong and confident legs, the "open spanner head" design of open clawed talons.

As touched on above, the beginning of this period had abandoned three dimensional zoomorphic and human form sculptures in favour of incised plaque-form representations whose execution now shows a greater delicacy and lightness than those of late Shang dynasty. These forms also begin to make their appearance in bronze at this time. Later eras of production before the Han dynasty confined the human form representation to the flattened "plaque" form with some important exceptions such as Exhibit 100 with the three dimensional human head mentioned above. The human figure was also shown on the incised line form of flat plaque as associated with dragons and other beasts which are difficult to identify but are possibly the tiger.

There is one exception to the general prohibition on three dimensional pieces and that is the silkworm. These are exclusively three dimensional and range in a wide variety of forms from short and square to elongated and elegant. Examples of the latter can be seen in Exhibit 101 and they can be extremely well formed - which perhaps begs the question as to why it seems that representations of man are not available in such circumstances also.

In summary the following are all found as available forms of jade working art : Handles sometimes carved with standing bird in relief, Bottle-Horn Dragons of the two legged plaque type, the *huang* pendant with incised standing bird relief and the *huang* pendant shape with the human figure or tiger or dragon figures by linear incising or half-trench bevelling. Also

found are slit-discs, "S" shape dragon plaques, masks - both human and *taotie*, small roundels and squares with bird head relief design. Some pieces are very delicate forms of flat tiger, taper bodied flat fish with raised disc form eye and other animals such as stag and doe.

Sometimes the stags, standing with round haunches and forward sloping back, wear huge branched antlers of great spreading splendour. See 22 pls 48, 49 and 50. Other standard forms are silkworms, flat-form and, early in the period also three dimensional form rabbits, drilled bead forms, cormorant, cormorant with fish in claw, cicada, two legged type plaque bottle-horn dragons and certain simple, very residual blades and incised outline human figures with geometrically ordered openwork edges.

As an exciting coda to current Western Zhou jade knowledge, the world awaits published news of the full details of a sensational find in 1990 of many magnificent jades in a horde totalling over 900 pieces in a very important Western Zhouburial of a military general near SanMenXia, Henan Province. 21 pl; 68, 69 and 70. As with the Fu Hao tomb however, preliminary accounts indicate that many of these 900 jades are collected pieces of the Shang and earlier periods - even including one Hongshan culture pig-dragon.

A.2 EASTERN ZHOU (SPRING AND AUTUMN ANNALS)
770-475 BC - CAPITAL AT LOYANG
One of the princely states, the State of Lu, kept annals recording its "Springs and Autumns" from the period of approximately 722 to 475 BC. The dynastic control through the period from 770 to 475 BC is named after these records as the Spring and Autumn period.

As we have seen, the central control of the king weakened through the Western Zhou period. As successive former vassal lords rose to exercise their own control over their own separate small states, the adoption by each of them of the accoutrements of power and civilised society necessarily involved acquisition of jade and bronze artefacts in part of the process which represented a general weakening of the power of the Zhou Emperor. The Zhou Emperor continued his rule at Loyang following the transfer of the state capital from Xian to Loyang. In exercising this rule, he was accorded a nominal allegiance until the third century BC - rather as, two thousand years later, the Emperor of Japan continued nominal rule over his Empire while in fact wholly subservient to the petty despots established throughout the nation by the Shogunate and the associated Daimyo or feudal lord structure. In China it is possible to regard the continuation of the nominal Zhou ruling umbrella as a dynastic fiction giving its name to the exercise of minimal control and protecting without influence the reality of a general sprinkle of small states with their own internal autonomy. State control effectively fell in upon itself and gave birth through its absence to new baby states whose acknowledgment of parental status at the centre continued in name but not otherwise.

The royal land holding system akin to fee simple from the ruler broke down. Private property in assets extended to a private land holding concept with associated powers of willing estates to heirs by testamentary succession. The three generation family unit which was ushered in during the Western Zhou dynasty continued and strengthened its development. The three generations continued to live together in the same compound, to worship their ancestors and generally to continue an emphasis on filial piety.

Each one of the small states arising was obliged to protect its people and govern itself. This created unified self-centred political obedience and an appreciation of territorial integrity and loyalty to state and ruler. Each state was small enough to exercise terrible and minute control over its subjects and legitimacy. Because the creation of a plurality of small states dissipated political power over an increasingly wide area well beyond the boundaries of the original collapsed central authority, the traditional distinction between the central originator of civilisation and the more peripheral outer "Barbarian" states and people became much diminished and, in effect, frequently disappeared.

In about 700 BC there was a reasonably powerful state of Zheng in Henan Province on the Yellow River which had emerged by bringing together smaller local states. The state of Zheng began to contend with the Chu State to its south on the central Yangzi River with its capital at Jingzhou, in the west of modern Hubei Province.

The Chu state was very successful economically and militarily and expanded gradually north through the Spring and Autumn period eventually to defeat Zheng at the end of the seventh century BC.

As the sixth century BC progressed, the Jin State of Southern Shaanxi developed aggressive ability and was in alliance with Chu in more or less loose relations against Zheng.

After the overwhelming of Zheng by Chu, discord developed between Jin and Chu. Each of them called upon the support of smaller states in their respective areas and constant skirmish and feud resulted. The Spring and Autumn period was also notable for reintroducing certain of the brutal customs of the Shang. Human sacrifices were made to celebrate victory in war. There was a reversion to Shang's Anyang phase's preference for burial customs in the development of huge wooden box tombs. Some important ones had a number of chambers even extending in their furnishings to beds. One interesting feature, which may be associated with protection of ancestors, was that it began to be customary to construct these large tombs within the city wall in a place of safety rather than, as previously, in special cemetery areas outside the city walls. The crossbow was introduced in the sixth century and speedily became a very effective weapon of war. The crossbow operated through use of a simple bronze trigger mechanism and came at this time to be made in increasingly large numbers.

There was a scheme to introduce taxes on private land owners and landlords began to make an appearance as private land owners exploited the occupation of their land by others - usually through renting out to farmers for agricultural production. This combination brought about new attitudes to leisure and the social structure of created wealth. These newly available facilities enabled development of handicraft production as a convenience or luxury - to please the touch, to demonstrate social position or status, impress the close circle of the individual and to delight the eye in general alleviation of a hard, fierce and often seemingly insecure existence. The inevitable consequence of a general increase of middle class wealth in combination with ever increasing capacity of mini-state bronze workshops was increased production, leading to increased experimentation. In turn, this led to increased quality of variety. Great advances were made in fine quality line mould casting of complex detail. Part moulding in bronze assisted the composition of more complex composite pieces and greater technical skill developed in alloying the bronze metal components resulting in greater ease of fungible pouring of material to fill out and take the line and form of finer moulded detail. Towards the end of the Spring and Autumn period, lost wax moulding first appeared in China. This enabled even greater detail of design in three dimensional and elaborate trace work moulding in bronze not previously possible and entire new areas of design advance became available for exploitation.

From about 500 BC onwards the use of cast iron for tools and agricultural implements became widespread and the great days of importance for bronze as a means of survival were over leaving only tradition and nostalgia to work their forces upon the further development of bronze - which did indeed continue but in tune only with taste and luxury rather than necessity of life. One interesting element which became a standard feature of tomb furniture was carefully made grave ceramics in great numbers imitating ritual bronze forms. The greater part of these were doubtless attributable to a desire of poorer people to be buried with the trappings of wealth in a cheap and easily obtainable form and they were well able to take advantage of the suddenly available plasticity of well potted clay forms for this purpose.

One interesting manifestation of the ingenuity applied as a direct result of the search for luxury was the creation of decorative patterns constituted by one metal inserted or inlaid into another through technology which is still not clearly understood although being these days the subject of intense study and research. It has been suggested that this practice, frequently associated with gold and silver, was an import into China from the steppe peoples of the Ordos region in contact with places further west. At the time, various Chinese states were having increased contact with the Ordos region people and doing increasing trade with and through them. Gold and silver, or one of these metals or the other alone, were inlaid in assorted patterns into cast or incised shapes or patterns in a bronze body. Bronze was increasingly used for secular works of beauty or art quite separate from any deeper meaning or message. In consequence of this growing demand for luxury, the skills of the bronze founder quickly found a way to satisfy the production of inlaid gold and silver belt buckles and belt or garment hooks made of bronze. From this idea of metal inlay upon metal it was only a short step to conceive of the inlay, or application of jade slices or pieces onto a bronze space and composite artefacts made of bronze, silver, gold and jade either in combination or in separate association were quick to appear and develop.

At the end of the Spring and Autumn period, the state of Jin yielded to the growing strength of the new lower Yangzi River basin states of Wu and Yue. We see the *cong*, almost as a legacy of shadows from former times, described as playing out a role whose nearest written authority is found in the Zhouli. As we have seen in the Neolithic section of this catalogue, the authority of this work, as regards any period but Eastern Zhou is a matter of the gravest doubt. What is very clear is that the dynamic and innovative impetus of the Liangzhu culture which invented the *cong* as a jade form, was, by the time of the Eastern Zhou, very much a part of the long dead and buried past.

One very significant new development in the Spring and Autumn period is the appearance on flat jade pieces of a textured, almost three dimensional, surface carved treatment. This represents a distinct development away from the somewhat detached sterility of the general feeling of most later Western Zhou plaque-form incised jade pieces. The texturing is best seen in the manner of representation of dragons, particularly their heads. At the end of Western Zhou or early Spring and Autumn period, a raised and rounded line form of modelled dragons head became a standard representation and consisted of curved modelled lines forming the outline of the dragon head with prominent eye and an up-curved nose on top and a prominent fang (Exhibit 104) or with an open mouth and a long tongue lolling out of the mouth. (See Exhibit 105.) The raised-line work began to lose its geometric order of arrangement such that individual elements of the dragon design began to assume independent importance without particular relation to the other elements - a phenomenon well described as "dissolving" dragons. Perhaps in corresponding contrast to this undoubtedly degenerate dissolutive tendency, and as a reaction to it, there developed a very much more controlled and tightly organised form of relief feature of the "C" scroll. This frequently took the form of relief carving on a flat surface as arrangement of various bundles with graded contour studding with rounded elegance the entire jade surface and often without any perimeter border. These movements grew away in vigorous compactness of action from the entire dragon head arrangement from which they were spawned. Association with animals was however intricately and intimately retained in this technique through the inclusion of small but deliberately placed panels of rope twist and scales. The overall effect and feeling of this kind of work is one of quiet and soft magnificence. Exhibit 102 is an excellent example of this type.

The period saw production of thin plaques, either trapezoid, rectangular or round, as with Exhibit 106. They were usually carved with "S" scroll incised designs and the method of production seems to have been to carve the essential features of the design over the entire surface of a large sheet or piece. This large sheet or piece would then be cut deliberately from its matrix base and then itself chopped or sawn into smaller pieces of the required size. These plates seem usually to have been made for sewing upon garments as the very small and well drilled perimeter holes would indicate. The evidence of cutting out from a larger, mother, sheet or slice is the interruption round the edges of most of these pieces of the "S" design round the edges where it was clearly cut through. The designs on the thin plate pieces are both squared "C" scrolls with patches of fine hair striation work. There is still some semblance of the dissolving dragon head. The *taotie* mask restored itself, or was restored, to the centre of design and some delicate and sensitive representations resulted of which Exhibit 110 is one refined example.

The *huang* took on this "C" scroll working from its inception in the Spring and Autumn period. However, the style did not lend itself to mass production and production was rather maintained at a steady level, necessary to satisfy the increasing demands of wealth and society.

Connections with the West were strong during this period. There is ample evidence of the movement of ideas in bronze design from the steppes of central Asia and Siberia into China at various points along the long borders outside the Great Wall. The Ordos peoples of the Mongolian and Siberian steppe made and used very characteristic animal bronze fittings and appliques. Such pieces were made in jade. Exhibit 108 of a seated deer with branching antlers, and Exhibit 109 as a flat plaque of a somewhat comic tiger with a sewn up mouth aspect are both examples which seem on stylistic grounds attributable to the late Western Zhou or Spring and Autumn period and have clearly been influenced by the Ordos Barbarians. Ordos animal style jades are very rare. Some 15 pieces are known to have been excavated from one tomb in North China in the early 20th century. These pieces, and others, although rare, are normally flat plaque forms but sometimes have openwork. Some such as illustrated in 82 pls 6 and 7 faithfully portray fighting scenes of animals both real and imaginary and to that extent give a bloody, but presumably accurate, essence of the strength and primeval violence among wild animals - and presumably well understood among human beings - that is very much the central impetus of mainstream Ordos art.

A.3 EASTERN ZHOU (WARRING STATES)
475-221 BC - CAPITAL AT LOYANG, HENAN PROVINCE

This period represents the formation out of the diaspora of ruling families and classes of numerous small city states and kingdoms and leading into the unavoidable backlash of contention between themselves. Wars and skirmishes became so prevalent a characteristic of this period that they have given to it the name by which it is now internationally known and recognised. Huge urban settlements were now the established centres of civilisation and entertainment - some having hundreds of thousands of residents. Considerable resources of man and bronze were devoted to conflict and cavalry forces were by this time fully exploiting the horse for the waging of war.

The burial mound as a deliberately piled up hill of earth over a grave originates in this period. There is no doubt that the Kurgans, or barrows, forming the burial mound tradition of the ancient peoples of the North Central Asian steppes and Central and Eastern Siberia, antedated this period by many hundreds of years and it is reasonable to postulate that, in what we can now regard as metropolitan China this tradition was brought in from the northwest, quite possibly as a result of trading or social contact with the steppe peoples of the Ordos region. It was not lightly taken up in China. The burial mounds quickly became huge features of any tomb of importance and the demonstration of size in depth culminated with the great hillock built over the tomb of the Qin Emperor, Shi Huang Di outside Xian which is still unexcavated. What has so far been excavated of the so called "Terracotta Army" is buried at just one compass point around the periphery of that tomb. The tradition continued in sometimes more, and sometimes less, exaggerated proportions such as the huge mounds in the Tang dynasty and continued to influence the structure of tomb covering in the Ming dynasty.

The opening of this period sees three principal independent countries of strength in the northeast, the northwest and the south of China. Respectively, in the northeast the Qi, in the northwest the Qin and in the south the Chu, states were the most influential individual States.

In the fifth century BC occurred a subdivision of the state of Jin into the new states of Zhao, Wei and Han whose birth as independent political units with different potential pace of development and taste, contributed greatly to the contending variety of appreciation and helped to enrich the overall raw material for synthesis of the design ethic. In about 300 BC the state of Qin began a drive to prominence and assertion of its will over neighbouring regimes - a process which inexorably resulted in the Qin State ultimately emerging victorous and unifying the Han peoples of China into a single state under Qin Shi Huang Di. Communications became a matter of almost mundane excellence with good road systems maintained at public expense. They were built for, and used by, military movement and the needs of trade. The latter spread far and wide creating import and export balances with constant need of redress in one scale or the other. Intensive agriculture generated great farming productivity and wealth and these fundamental developments constituted the rich loam from which fed and sprang leisured class pursuits of creative force and ranging between literary arts and music. The good road system enabled the easy passage of ideas across the national mini boundaries and the satisfaction of a need in one state would soon give rise to a need for the same satisfaction in another. The development of trade furthermore quickly identified the need for a more credible monetary unit than the cowrie shell or its bronze clones. The consequence of this was the introduction of gold as a measure of economic worth - something which did not have a steady subsequent history in China but which did fluctuate quite widely in popularity from one period of several hundred years to the next.

With the added facility of lost wax bronze casting and the consequently enlarged possibilities of complexity in design, the production of three dimensional configurations of man and animals in bronze presented only superficial problems. Bronze exploded out of itself to form, together with gold and silver, or with gold or silver alone, inlaid pieces and very intricate openwork structured around the sinuous writing of snake-like bodies with young dragon heads and apparently undirected, but actually well conceived and planned, movements back and forth and in and out. Very often there were fantastic curls, cloud motifs and interlocking hoop and hook designs. Some of the most elaborately detailed demonstrations of bronze casting virtuosity were interred in the Warring States period tomb of the Marquis of Zeng at Suixian, Hubei Province.

Far from being unaware of, or unconnected with, these developments, jade either led or absorbed them. Although there were pure handicraft limitations upon the carving of, for example, a writhing band of snakes so much more easy to produce in bronze, there was a strong demand for luxury, quality and regionality in jade and this, associated with developed and up to date ideas of animal representation, brought jade artefacts into an almost three dimensional form which could only develop by growing more florid and representational. This necessarily involved a three dimensional profile which accordingly developed in place of the two dimensions thought, until this time, to define the reasonable boundaries of jade expectation in the consumer.

It is possible directly to trace from the "dissolved" remnants of the raised-line dragon curve workings on the sides of small *bi* or slit discs through the deep relief "C" scroll work on the *huang* pendant shape, the beginning of one of the classic field filling decorational design forms. This is the raised curl or "tadpole"

feature. Structurally this consisted of a round ended, tightly curved body and clearly formed fine and wavy tail very much like the tail of the tadpole performing an "S" flip. The tail in fact forms the fish of the parent curl and much resembles the tail of the tadpole, now curled round in a shape curve almost representing the effect of a cracked whiplash.

At about this time the demand for this feature was so great that large jade *bi-discs* would be formed with edges and faces entirely plain except for an orderly arrangement of tadpole tailed "C" scrolls either in ordered lines across the surface from one side to the other or in a more haphazard rendering. Both quality, refined execution of detail and burnished finish were of the highest order and standard. As a variation on the tadpole design, a different organisation of incised hook forms was arranged each featuring a small round terminal centre or boss in relief. The relatively easy to form bronze three dimensional serpent was cleverly interpreted by the jade carver, not as a distinct three dimensional creature separated away from its ground or landscape, but depicted rather as writhing or moving on the background surface, through the background surface or into, and out of, it.

Another popular development was the flat plaque of curling or geometric ribbon-body form of dragon plaque often featuring the phoenix head at the tail end. These are normally pierced half way along their length to enable a balanced suspension hanging, are often made in pairs and sometime are very large - up to 10 centimetres in length and more. (Exhibit 116)

Another design reality enabled by what must have been greatly advanced drilling and sewing techniques with refined bronze tools was the production of very complex and brittle delicacy in openwork. The dragon, the phoenix and the snake interlock in symmetrical moving spirit - after incised shield form or curl edge panels which are decked with fine cross hatching. The "open spanner head" form of bird foot, first seen during the early Western Zhou, continued but with application now, not to the standing crested birds of the Western Zhou, but to tiger and dragon animal forms and as complementary finish to increasingly refined delicacy of detailed outline. By this time it was clear that the dexterity of the jade carver had come full circle. There was very little that he could not do and the evidence is clearly established in the production of very thin slices of jade material faultlessly and without accident, worked into sometimes very complicated openwork designs. (Exhibit 114)

In the Western Zhou period, the incised pattern and designs on the flat forms of *huang* plaque were executed up to the very edge of the flat surface. There was no restraining perimeter border, thick or thin, and no restraint to inhibit the thought processes contemplating the smooth and serene beauty of a jade piece. In the Warring States period this freedom was subjected to a refined discipline. This was brought in by the appearance of perimeter borders with highly polished right angle outer edges and having an internal border bevel inclining sharply down and inwardly away from the edge. This feature is not normally all around the perimeter of a piece but is designed specifically to convey a suggestion of formal containment without the feeling of ordered monotony which would derive from an all around ordered feature of this type. Strategic design breaks were inserted at the personal behest or instinct of the craftsman and the result is an effect which combines a sense of order with a sense of

originality and surprise. The bevelled border also became a natural inner edge and outer perimeter feature of the *bi-disc*.

However, the discipline imposed by this bevelled border did not last. It was effectively broken through by an innovation exclusive to the jade worker which was to move part, but not all, of the decorative elements of a jade design, outside the natural edge or border boundary as a result of which marvellous assymetric balance of consistent design was immediately possible, was thought about and was put into effect. This gave a new sense of freedom to the zoomorphic (and possibly also botanic) elements of a basic design which burst the perimeter chains hitherto imposed by the design border. In implementing the Warring States period intent to develop out of the austerity of the *bi-disc* as a simple flat roundel with a central perforation, the figures of openwork dragons climbed around within the central aperture, dived in and out of the flat surface, writhed around and through vegetal scrolling forms and broke the edge to stand in freedom on the squared surface of the outside in a remarkable and yet contained effect of both discipline and free expression. Perhaps the ultimate excess of luxurious skill was the production of composite carvings from one piece of stone in the form of several linked pieces of limited application but striking effect on a belt.

It is the nature of man to tire easily of available luxury and to spurn its familiarity in seeking new diversion. The inlaying of gold and silver into bronze artefacts and vessels continued on its sumptuous experimental path. The technical quality of fine line gold inlay control and of scaliform gold cloisons enclosing networked areas of polished turquoise and malachite created jewel-like effects not bettered in craftsman-like perfection and intellectual concept anywhere in the world before or since. In purely jade terms, the soft and reticent humour of the Spring and Autumn surface finish was swept aside to be replaced by a brilliant, shining, swaggering surface of mirrored quality of a mettle and worth commensurate with the most insouciant braggadoccio of the Warring States pleasure loving and wealthy society of fops and dandies. This level of quality product is not rare or representative of any particular one of the Warring States. It was a genuine epidemic of excess rampaging throughout the length and breath of Eastern Zhou in China with an intensity as magnificent as it was wanton. The same craving for change and innovation at the highest level of production brought jade to the forefront of the artistic current of the times. Accordingly, jade elements of the highest quality execution were made for incorporation into huge bronze, gold or silver decorative fittings such as belt or garment hooks which commonly feature a series of jade panels or plaques set along the curving shank of the hook (Exhibit 121) and sometimes polished plain and sometimes polished in high relief carving of tadpole coils with bevelled borders or a set of *taotie* masks. In even more ambitious, and presumably expensive examples, the entire garment or belt hook is made of jade, sometimes as a single piece arching unctuously from end to end away from the central underside stud, and sometimes as a composite piece with individual complex elements mounted together end to end and fastened by a common metal core running through a common centrally bored channel. The misfortune sometimes found in the last type is, when the central metal core was made of iron and buried in a part of the country with a wet climate, the iron rusts and expands during its oxidation. The result is to split the exquisite jade housing into fragments whose individual broken glory portrays just a shadow of the original perfection.

Perhaps it was in sympathy with the brilliance of surface gloss, perhaps in response to a sense of actual hardness underlining the pursuit of luxurious pleasure for its own sake but, whatever the originating cause, a significant profile of jade carving in the Warring States period is aligned in an essence of clear cut edges and sharp spikes in a scintillating, light catching exposure of the edges and angles. In consequence, and however difficult to define, there is a palpable sense of harsh and unyielding discomfort in much jade carving of the Warring States period which, however ancillary to the magnificent dexterity of the sculptural achievement of the craftsman, is never obscured by it. In parallel however, a softer feel and sensitivity can also be found that is equally symptomatic of the period. Compare Exhibits 118 and 120.

Specific military applications of jade are a special study. One important function was the finger ring presumed to have been used by archers when pulling back the bow string to be held against the nose or mouth. The notched arrow end was rested upon both the bow string and a groove in, or excrescence from, a jade ring mounted upon the thumb or index finger, as to exactly which currently remains a matter of controversial surmise. Exhibit 122 is an example of a late Warring States archer's ring with a vegetal form arrow support member springing out of one side.

The most popular acknowledgment in the Warring States period of luxurious utility of jade was for sword and scabbard furniture. On the diagram no. 10 on page 20 the four standard pieces of jade sword and scabbard furniture are clearly depicted and the following descriptions set out to summarise the current state of knowledge on them and the variety of available designs :-

(i) The Pommel. (*Shou*) This was fixed by attachment at right angles to the upper end of the sword handle. It was always a circular disc in form and the flat upper face was usually, but not always, worked with decoration. This normally took the form of a central boss of whirling starfish design with intermediate patches of finely worked cross hatching and ringed with an open field usually studded with "tadpole" curls. Alternatively the central boss can be surrounded, or even covered, with open work three dimensioned dragon bodies. Another form lacks the central boss and simply features a four or five petal open flower-like pattern in relief. The sharp vertical sides sometimes incline inwards and, very rarely, are incised with shield and hook designs. See Exhibit 124.

(ii) The Hilt. (*Ge*) This object is pushed down the bronze or iron handle spindle to rest up against the upper termination or tang of the blade. They were used on both bronze and iron blades and in the latter case the normal corrosive processes of rust frequently cause the iron to swell through the centuries and to crack open the jade hilt. The decoration on the hilt is normally a *taotie* face in bright cut relief arranged equally across the span of the piece but it can also be a single or double dragon formula, either free standing or in high or low relief. See Exhibit 125.

(iii) The Scabbard Slide. (*Wei* or *Zhi*) This object is attached to the scabbard and is one of the fittings through which the baldric passes for suspension to the user's belt. There are two basic forms of decoration of the rectangular panel forming the top face of the scabbard slide which are:-

(a) an arrangement of low relief "C" scrolls within longitudinal bevelled borders and bordered at the short end by a *taotie* mask in low relief which always has long striated eyebrows. (Exhibit 126)

(b) a formation in high or low relief of a crawling dragon and sometimes with a second, smaller, dragon across one end of the rectangular panel. (Exhibit 139) In the exuberance already noted both the body of the dragon and vegetal excrescences can be found overspilling the geometric contours of the platform surface even, in one so far unique example, featuring a monkey, playfully seated astride the edge.

Sometimes this object is formed from a reworked chape showing a consistent acknowledgement of the value of the raw material and unwillingness to waste the pieces of an already broken artefact.

(iv) The Chape. (*Bi*) This was the finial at the end of the scabbard and is always of a waisted quadrilateral or trapezoid profile and with a lenticular cross section just like the scabbard. Fastening to the scabbard was by permitting entry of a male extension peg from the scabbard end into a special female shaft bored into the lenticular cross section face for the purpose. By virtue of its lenticular cross section, the chape always had two bi-cambered faces sloping down to an edge that was sometimes finely squared off or sometimes left sharp. These faces were always worked with decorative design in Warring States times and most frequently enclosed by a bevelled perimeter border. See Exhibit 127, though later, in the Han dynasty, they were often left plain. As with the scabbard slide, decoration was of more than one type and the following summary can be made:-

(a) Incised and part hollowed spade block and curl form relief work

(b) Tightly formed curled tadpoles, with or without tails and on a plain field

(c) High or low relief single or double dragons often extending over the geometrical border or edge of the piece. In some of these forms the extreme end of the chape away from the scabbard attachment face, has a stepped form so that the end face is on two levels of which advantage is taken by overlapping three dimensional curled dragon forms. (Exhibit 127)

There were also two additional functional jade pieces used in conjunction with the second. They are not often found but consist of the following:-

(v) Scabbard Fitting. This was a fitting on the scabbard through which the leather or textile strap was threaded or affixed to the scabbard on the reverse side of the scabbard slide. These were generally of plain "D" Section but Exhibit 140, probably of the Han period, is an example decorated with *taotie* design.

(vi) Jade ring toggle intermediate between the scabbard and the belt. These are invariably plain and Exhibit 142 is a Western Han example.

There was also a demand for jade in purely personal ornament such as grooved twisted rope form rings with a flattened contour, "*Pei*" dragon and phoenix form pendants in white jade with subtle arrangements of dragon and phoenix each side and low relief cloud formation work on the thin walled main body. See Exhibit 160 for an excellent, if slightly later, example of this type. Smaller pieces were also made for inlay into lacquer vessels and generally in the form of dragons but sometimes of tortoise and birds.

The skill of the Warring States jade worker was also turned to the production of jade vessels (46, 47 & 48). They have perfectly contoured, hollowed bowls, thin walls and beautifully formed and sculpted feet or footrims. They are both incised and low relief carved with exterior designs, "C" scroll relief billows, or rope twist and scaliform islands. The normal provenance of such artefacts are tombs of royalty or the highest nobility with no real indication of applied use in life. All indications accordingly are that, were the matter ever to have been in doubt, they were made to demonstrate the absolute mastery of man over matter in conquering jade as the hardest of the known materials and bending it to his will thus representing the ultimate panacea to the endless craving for luxurious materiality however insatiable it appeared to be. In so serving such a common place end, the jade carver rose high above himself and we are fortunate that limited numbers of his achievement in this regard have survived down to the present day for our enjoyment and appreciation.

Without doubt, the Warring States period represents an accomplished zenith of man's mastery over the jade medium. In ways still not entirely clear except in what appears to be their practiced ease of production, it was not only possible but almost common place to produce perfect curves, rings, right angle corners, perfectly finished relief carving work and bevels down to the smallest detail. Very thin slices of jade were worked with the greatest plastic artistry which represented a tremendous achievement in contemporary working of material such as bone and iron but which in jade are a stupefying achievement. No better work was performed in this medium between the period of the Warring States and the introduction of carborundum abrasives in the

19th century AD and of the electric drill in the 20th century AD which is universally and exclusively used in modern China for the working of jade.

In this period also small three dimensional human figures were made. Some were finished to a high degree of technical quality and some with a softer message. Some have elaborate hair style and others feature complex openwork headdresses. Exhibit 118 is an example of the latter. The human figure also appears in finely executed flat-form pendant dancers who usually wear long flowing robes and seem normally to have formed the central member of a pectoral formation suspended on the chest from a complex arrangement of *huang* shaped pendants and intervening beads. The three dimensional work was also put into the production of the cicada. Exhibit 120 are excellent examples of the hard and brilliant technical and life-like finish of an insect wing and demonstrating also the lively and alert eyes giving almost the impression of an insect about to trill out its high pitched summer buzzing or leap away into flight.

The three dimensional carving work is of a particular interest in that, after a long hiatus of essentially flat-forms of jade working since the Shang's Anyang phase, jade as representational sculpture was re-emerging in the late Eastern Zhou and, as we now know, having so re-emerged, was never again to be subdued to deprive us of the ensuing dynastic evolution of brilliant sculptural achievement in the jade medium up until the Qing dynasty - many excellent examples of which are illustrated in this catalogue and featured in the exhibition.

The Warring States period also featured allegorical designs in jade. The *bi-disc* was sometimes carved to show zoomorphic designs on the field which are usually dragons but sometimes we find the beasts of the four directions - the Black Tortoise of the North, the Red Phoenix of the South, the White Tiger of the West and the Green Dragon of the East. The *bi-disc* can also be pierced through in open work. It was sometimes buried in quantity around the corpse of the deceased within the inner coffin. Sometimes it is found as an element in a pendant complex on the chest. An additional use - certainly in painting and possibly in actual application - is as the enclosing fastener anchor or buckle for the tension point of a textile sash or ribbon passed through it and around the human body or around a large container such as the burial coffin.

A.4 QIN
221-207 BC - CAPITAL AT XIANYANG SHAANXI PROVINCE

This period represents the final military and political triumph of the Qin State led, at this time, by the great Qin Shi Huang Di. The dynastic period is in fact the period of his reign. He died in 207 BC - an event which marks the establishment of the great Han dynasty which, apart from the Wang Mang Interregnum between 9 and 25 AD, was to endure for four hundred stable years. The reign of Qin Shi Huang Di saw the cataclysmic overturning of traditional belief in various aspects of Chinese social administration through the pushing and forcing together of the various components of the Warring States into the single national ethnic unit which we have since that time regarded as China. Under his reign, the Chinese nation saw the introduction - or rather, the imposition - of uniform writing, uniform system of weights and measures and of bureaucratic civil service administration -

a break with the past so radical and artificially abrupt that it was conducted in the light of funeral pyres of all books of law and philosophy of the individual Warring States, the better to meld them all into a new unified whole. The concept of the Great Wall of China as a continuous defensive rampart to preserve and protect the nation against the wearisome and random incursions of barbarians was largely completed under his reign.

This very short period is a difficult one for general observation of jade development. It will be very interesting to see what by way of jade was buried with the Emperor in his huge tumulus outside Xian - as yet unexcavated. In all probability, Qin jade working is, if not a continuation, then certainly a fluid and unremarkable transition from the harsh brilliance of the Warring States jade working into the more settled sureness and control of the Han period. However, there was one very significant find of jade pieces categorically dateable to the Qin dynasty excavated in 1971 in Xian. See 26 plates 47-58 inclusive. More than 80 jades of grey-green colour were found in this group and all were clearly made for burial purposes being simple renderings of the *bi*, *gui* tablet, *huang* pendant and tally. However perhaps the most interesting pieces were plaque form, flat human figure representations both male and female with very simple facial details incised upon the front side. Exhibit 128 is an example of this type which, although direct and simple in expression, is a clear and strikingly drawn message of the art of the times - times which, thanks to the dateable find at Xian mentioned above, we know to be of the Qin dynasty.

Angus Forsyth
January 1994

西周至東周(戰國)及秦代

A.1 西周

公元前1100年 — 公元前771年 —— 首都在西安

此時期有關的地區，包括了陝西南部、河南、河北和
山東省。然而，其影響並不只在這些地區，在南邊的
江蘇亦發掘到西周青銅器皿。

這時期，國君依然控制中央之權，政府的架構
是繼承商代而來的。

西周時，出現了一種新的觀念，由於國君與人民
間之關係拉近了，國君成為了人民與上天溝通之橋樑。
在這個形式化的開展時期，其實已可預見始自東周孔子
時代鞏固的中國文職制度，它是中國社會強大的表現，
但亦是對有權益發展的一種束縛。

可能是隨着統治者與人民之間的關係拉近了，
西周墓葬中以人殉葬的情況大幅下跌，墓穴的體積
開始縮細。而可能更重要的是，此時已反對和禁止了
殷商人飲酒的習慣，在某程度上它是被突然終止的。
西周初期青銅器上的紋飾，就有斥責昔日集體
飲酒之習慣為虛偽和放蕩，而最後的結果，就是西周時
不再需要殷商人喜愛的酒器，此時所製的青銅器是用
作盛載食物和貯藏寶物的，有些寶物甚至是在今天
始被發現的。

這時青銅器上的刻紋記錄了當時特有的紀念
和祭祀，殷人盛行簡單和具備神韻的自然主義已被質樸
和實際之風格所取代，但從正史上清楚的記載及當時
思想和概念所見，熟練的青銅鑄造並沒有再發展
下去。我們今天對西周人生活的認識是從青銅器上的
刻紋而來的，此與在西周已失傳的以甲骨載事方法是有
很大的差別的。

隨着國君成為了溝通天地之橋樑，當時的
社會又出現了一種以世系為中心的情況。世系結構是以
祖父母為最高位，以下是子女，再下者為孫，大家
都是一同居住的。孔子在公元前六世紀，已道出了父系
社會的好處，他指出的是西周早期發展至今天以男性為
中心的家庭制度。

青銅儀仗器新有簡化和直接的造型，可追溯到
西周中期約公元前1000年至公元前900年。此時期已出現
青銅樂器，如懸掛在木架上的鐘，它們通常是以八片、
十片或十二片組成放在架上敲打的。我們也可見
此時軍事用品和武器有大幅度的增加，中央似已不能控
制地區上和外圍地方為私利而開發青銅之情況，
它的權力在瓦解後便出現了戰國時代。

不知是基於甚麼原因，玉匠此時已停止製作
殷商時期令人印象深刻的立體雕塑，他們基本上專注在
簡單、沒設線的動物形玉飾。正如上述，此種玉飾
在殷商時已出現了，婦好墓出土的扁身蒙古馬
玉飾為一好例子。而立體雕塑之消失似是與簡化和
樸實的製作概念有關，這時器物表面修飾的整體構思
強烈而簡單，雖然有時頗為複雜，但卻並不流於洛
可可式的浮華和過份雕琢。相反，它們予人生動
和諧的印象，其柔和的表層維持到春秋時期後，
在戰國時期更發展成為當時流行的高度光亮表面。

這時扁身玉飾的表面可以是刻滿圖案的，
或是割切成個別動物、人像或鳥的輪廓，技術純熟
的玉匠很少製造顯示移動和變化之扁身造型，
這種概念在西周時期是很普遍，蓋此時是沒有立體
玉雕之製造的。但這情況亦有例外，本書中展品
100香蕉形小玉珮，乃西周時期罕見的立體人雕。
此玉珮除獨一無二外，其重要之處表現在它標準的
線條和體積，這些甚至在青銅器中是很少見的。
另一點有趣的是，這時期沒有大理石刻和雕塑。

此時期，青銅在塊范鑄造法和凸緣限制上有一
重要的解放，塊范上本來分開處理的圖案已可互
相連接在一起，如此紋飾便可連續的伸展到青銅器皿的
頸、肩或腹部。這種改革為青銅工匠帶來創作上和
精神上的自由，而這亦為玉匠所採納和承接的。

在春秋初，玉器表面的裝飾是以較隨便的假陽線
為主，但至戰國時，技術上已變得更精細。公元前十世
紀至九世紀時，玉器表面的紋飾是以闊雙陰刻線組成，
它們流暢柔和的效果是商代玉器所沒有的。在新石器
時代，龍山文化首次出現的方狀綣曲陽線，這時已
被簡化為雙陰刻和立體直立勾狀，直角部份更呈刃狀，
見展品97。在刃狀的角位則有一短倒勾伸展至對面，
整體紋飾都是以這種雙陰刻線製成，當中並沒有
真陽線或假陽線。而在玉器一面的中線部份，常見
一排的勾形紋飾。

由婦好墓之出土可得知當時的玉器並非以
首飾為重。在西周時期，玉器首飾是一項專門的製造。
展品96為一梯形玉珮，與比它大兩倍或三倍之玉珮同樣
是刻有鳥形圖案，是和玉珠、綠松石穿起掛帶在心胸中
央的，佩戴者在走動時會因它們的撞擊而發出噹噹
之聲，見參考書目20圖版56。

自良渚時代到商代，饕餮紋的發展已變得
很抽象，它已失去了本來設計之原創性。而實際上，
有趨勢顯示出像這種鬆散的設計，成為了器身上
所有的紋飾，這彷彿是說器身沒裝飾的地方會是一種
瑕疵。春秋時代依然出現的西周怪現象，是一種
幾何形之刻線設計，它應是取材自商代的回紋。

扁身玉珮上有"U"形之假陽線，有的體型
很大，而有的則呈璜狀。流行的斜切線陰刻，包括了
豎鳥、頭上帶冠、摺翼、有大圓眼、大嘴和巨爪。
此時亦有龍的造型，眼呈菱形，鼻如殷商時的向上仰，
以假陽線或真陽線製成。在玉璧上亦有真陽線刻之
龍形紋飾，它們有的簡單也有的複雜，龍鼻呈向上
捲狀，張口露長曲舌，見展品107。

另外，亦有一系列著名的長形橢圓柄、璜形玉珮
和扁長身收腰玉飾，均是刻有張牙露爪之豎鳥。

上面已提過此時期摒棄了立體動物和人體
雕塑，轉為流行有刻線之玉飾。這些玉飾的刻線比晚商
的更為幼細和輕浮，它們此時亦開始有在青銅器上出
現。除了展品100立體人首外，漢以前的人形圖案只是局
限在扁身玉飾上，這些玉飾上的陰刻人形應是和龍，以
及其它好像是虎的動物一起出現的。

玉蠶是唯一可知的立體雕塑。它們是完全的立
體，備有各種造型，由短方形至長身都有，後者在本書
展品101可見，其造型優美，令人不禁疑問為何在此時
的環境下沒有立體玉人雕塑。

要之，以下是已發現的玉器造型：鳥浮雕玉柄、
兩腿樽角龍玉飾、陰刻鳥浮雕玉璜、以直線陰刻
或半斜坑製成的人像、虎或龍玉璜。另外，又有玉玦、
"S"形龍飾、人面紋及饕餮紋、鳥首浮雕設計等。
有的玉器十分幼細，如扁身虎、尖長扁身凸眼魚和其它
動物像雄鹿或雌鹿。

很多時，這些雄鹿的造型是有圓大的臀部，
雙腳立地，身向前傾，頭上有巨大枝叉狀鹿角。見參考
書目22圖版48、49和50。其餘標準之造型為蠶、扁身
而早期更是立體的兔、鑽孔珠形的鸕鷀、蟬、兩腿樽角
龍飾和一些相當簡單，似是玉碎製的陰刻鏤空人形。

A.2 東周（春秋）
公元前770年 — 公元前481年 —— 首都在洛陽

魯國著〈春秋〉，載公元前772年至公元前481年之事，而
公元前770年至公元前481年這段時間亦以此命名。

我們可見在西周期間，國君之權力已被削弱，
諸候代之而起，各自管理其所屬之小國。這些小國在
武力裝備和其有文化的社會都滲及對玉器和青銅器
之渴求，此也代表了國君被削弱權力的其中一個過程。
周王由長安遷都至洛陽，繼續執政，但直到公元前
三世紀，他只是受到諸候們名義上的效忠，這好比二千
年後之日本皇帝名義上為王，實際卻順服於將軍和
藩王之下。在中國歷史裡，周代各諸侯國皆有內在的統

治體系，中央並未能對它們作出任何保護和影響，
但在名義上卻可繼續統治下去，確實是朝代裡的一個
傳奇。而各小國都各自為政，新誕生之小國雖然名義上
承認中央，但其實已是名存實亡了。

由王室控制的土地制度已粉碎，私人亦開始
可擁有土地作為財產。由周代開始的三代家庭模式繼續
加強發展，三代的成員照舊一起生活，敬拜他們的
祖先和提倡孝道。

每個小國都有義務保護人民和管治法紀，
這就產生了固定中心的政治管轄，以及對完整領土和
忠心奉國之重視，它們是有足夠能力治理本身細小
的國土的。眾多小國的出現正好瓦解了中央之權力，
小國的範圍已超越原來中央的邊界，傳統上認為是文化
之源的中原與偏遠的"蠻夷"的分野現已消失。

在公元前約700年，河南省黃河上有一
強國名鄭，是由兼併多個小國而成的。鄭與長江南面
的楚爭霸，楚都為荊州，在今天湖北省之西面。

在春秋時期，楚國在經濟和軍事上有成功的發
展，勢力逐漸向北擴展，最後於公元前七世紀末敗鄭。

公元前六世紀的時候，山西南部之晉發展迅速，
與楚結好而與鄭為敵。

楚滅鄭後，晉楚交惡，兩國分別向小國拉攏，
兵戈輒生。春秋時期又重現了商代殘暴的風俗，
人們是以活人來祭祀戰爭勝利的。這時又回復了商代
流行的巨型木盒形墓葬，有些重要的墓裡更有多間
墓室，甚至有床的裝備。其中一有趣之特色，就是這些
大型墓葬是築在城內的，比起以往建在城外安全，
這也許是與保護祖先有關。六世紀時已有弩的出現，
它迅速成為了戰爭中有效的武器。弩的使用是要靠簡單
的青銅起動裝置，故它這時開始有大量的出產。

此時開始出現向私地徵稅之計劃，地主租借
土地予農夫作耕種用。這種組合為消閑和創造財富的
社會結構帶來新的看法。新有的設施促成了簡便，或者
是奢華的手工藝品製造，它們表現了社會地位，取悅
封閉在圈中的人，緩和了艱難、兇猛和不穩定之存在。
中產階級在財富上無可避免的增長，以及小國的青銅
工作坊增加生產令青銅製作有更多實習機會，這亦導致
了質素上的改進。青銅局部鑄造法幫助製造更複雜的
造型，從而發展了更先進的鑄造合金技術，方便了灌銅
中造出精細的紋飾。春秋末，中國首次出現失蠟法鑄
造，令青銅器在立體雕塑上可做到以往無法達到的
精細效果，全新圖紋設計之改進就可有待發掘。

由公元前500年開始，鐵鑄之農業工具開始盛行，
而以青銅器作為求存工具的時代亦已過去，剩下來的

只是對傳統的懷緬。青銅器的繼續發展，實際上也只是著重品味的奢華一面，多於照顧生活所需。仿傚青銅器造型製的陶瓷，成為此時墓葬中傢俬的基本特色，它們大部份顯示了貧苦人家欲以貴重物品陪葬之心態，而價值便宜的陶瓷有很高的可塑性，它正好滿足這些人的需要。

在追求奢華底下，亦產生了一種飾紋，它是以一金屬插入或鑲嵌進另一金屬組成的，但現今仍未明此技術是怎樣的，故這已成為一專門研究的題目。曾經有人指出這種與金、銀有關之設計，是經鄂多斯草原地區的人與西面接觸再傳入中國的。春秋時已有多國和鄂多斯地區有貿易上的接觸。各種花紋的金、銀，或是二者與其它金屬是鑲嵌在青銅品器上的，青銅器開始表現的是世俗美，它已遠離深厚的意義了。隨着對奢華的渴求，青銅器在技術上已可做到鑲金和銀的衣帶勾、帶扣飾。從這種金屬鑲嵌在金屬上的概念，可見玉飾鑲嵌在青銅器，或是由青銅、金、銀和玉合製的器具上之出現和發展是不遠的。

春秋末年，晉屈服放長江下遊的吳、越底下。〈周禮〉中指出玉琮扮演了重要的角色，而從本書新石器時代部份可見，此器物的出處對西周人來說是一重大的疑惑。在良渚時期，創新的推動力底下產生的玉琮，於東周時期已是埋藏久遠的事了。

春秋時期的一重要發展為有表面紋飾，幾乎是立體的扁身玉片，這個發展與西周後期大部份的玉飾是有很大分別的，玉器上龍形的圖案，尤以龍首最能表現這些紋飾之特點。西周末或春秋初期，標準的龍首造型是以層次分明的凸圓線製，龍首輪廓以曲狀線勾出，鼻向上彎，張口露舌，見展品105。這些凸線開始失去幾何形的分佈，龍形圓紋每部份都各有重要，此現象可形容為"解體龍"。可能是基於對這種解體趨勢的反應，此時又發展了一種較嚴謹的"C"形卷渦浮雕，通常在器物扁平的表面以浮雕刻成的。而在動物紋飾中保留了此種技巧之餘，也加上了細小扭曲繩狀，它們整體上給人一種寧靜柔和的感覺，展品102為一佳例。

這時期出產了梯形、矩形、圓形和展品106般的薄身玉飾，常刻有"S"卷渦圖案，製法似是先在一大塊玉飾上刻滿這種圖案，然後再按個別需要切割成不同形狀。從這些玉飾上的鑽孔看，它們應是縫在衣物上的，而玉飾的邊緣部份"S"形卷渦清晰的切口，也顯示出它們是由一大塊玉飾細分的。在薄身玉飾上的圖案包括了"C"形卷渦和幼細髮絲之排線，與解體龍首尚有相似之處。至於饕餮紋

仍是保留在圖案之中心位置，其中有些設計像展品110般精美幼細。

春秋時期雖然有玉璜"C"卷渦出現，但卻未有大量製作，它穩定的出產數量已足以應付富裕社會的需要。

此時期與西方有很強之聯繫，有足夠証據顯示中亞細亞和西伯利亞大草原的青銅器設計，是從長城以外數處傳入中國的。蒙古和西伯利亞草原的鄂多斯人製造和使用很有特色的動物形青銅裝備和器具，而在中國，它們是玉製的。展品108為有叉角坐鹿，展品109為扁身玉虎，貌甚滑稽，二者之風格似是西周後期或春秋時期，明顯是受鄂多斯蠻族之影響。玉製的鄂多斯動物形是十分罕見，所知的是在二十世紀初，於中國北方發掘了十五件此種玉器，雖然它們數量極少，但多為扁身，有時甚至鏤空。參考書目82圖版6和7，真確地描繪了動物爭鬥之場面，生動的反映了它們血腥和暴力的一面，也似是反映人性的一面，此乃鄂多斯藝術主流的中心原動力。

A.3 東周（戰國）
公元前418年 — 公元前221年 —— 首都在河南省洛陽

此時期代表了各小國散居的統治階層之間的對抗，戰役頻繁，故名為戰國。大量的城市定居成為了文化和娛樂中心，有些地方更有成千上百的居民。這時大量的人力資源和青銅都用在戰爭和軍事上，馬匹已被調作戰爭之用。

在墳墓上的墓丘亦是源於此時。西伯利亞的史前戰墓墳場，毫無疑問是中亞細亞北部草原和西伯利亞東面古人的習俗，它比東周的出現早幾百年，所以，此習俗可能是透過與西北面的鄂多斯草原人民經商和接觸而傳入中國的。這些丘墓迅速成為了中國墓葬之一大重要特色，在西安郊仍未發掘的秦始皇陵墓上所建的小丘之深度，就正好顯示了此種墓丘的體積，而現今的所謂"兵馬俑"就是在陵墓邊緣附近出土的。這種墓丘的習俗繼後的發展時多時少，有時還很誇張，如唐代的大型墓丘和明代的墳墓結構亦受其影響。

這時期開始有三個獨立強國，它們分別為東北之齊、西北之秦和南面之楚，三者皆有很大的影響力。

公元前五世紀，趙、魏、韓三家分晉，成為獨立之政治體系，各有不同的潛力和風格，對於圖飾設計和綜合物料有很大貢獻。在約公前300年，秦展露了欲統一天下之野心，而在秦始皇瘋狂的窮兵黷武底下，終把漢人統一成為中國。秦始皇令百姓廣築道路，以作

軍事調動和貿易經商之用，其中出入口貿易更擴展至
遠方。大量的農業生產又帶來財富，這些基本發展
為有閑的階級營造了文學和音樂創作的環境。良好的
道路系統令思想容易傳播，邵縣之間因而可互相效法。
貿易上迅速的發展顯示出需要可信賴的貨幣制度來
取代貝幣或青銅複品，最後黃金成為了量度經濟之標
準，但它在中國歷史裡卻沒有穩定的發展，其流行程度
在隨後的幾百年都是起伏不定。

在失蠟法和增進了複雜紋飾製造的機會的出現
後，立體人雕和動物雕塑所面對的只是表面問題。在
一些有龍首和蛇狀綣曲身形的飾物上，出現了以青銅與
金或銀，或是一起組成的鑲嵌飾和細小的鏤雕，它們很
多時候還有綣曲紋、雲紋和交合蹄形和勾形紋飾。在
湖北省隨縣曾侯乙墓，就有技巧精湛的青銅鑄造出土。

在與此發展有關或無關的情況下，玉器領導
或是吸收了此種發展。雖然玉器在純手工技藝上，譬如
說綣曲狀蛇的製造，所受的限制是較青銅器為多。
但是當時對奢華、質素和地方風格卻有很大的需求，
這再加上已發展的動物圖飾，令玉器發展成近立體的
造型。此時立體玉雕已取代平面玉雕之地位，成為
時人心目中定義的玉器。

從玉璜上的"C"形卷渦深浮雕，可追溯細小
玉璧或玉玦上殘餘的"解體"曲狀凸線龍紋，此是綣曲凸
狀或"蝌蚪"狀的特色。在結構上，它包括了圓形、緊密
綣曲之身體和呈"S"跳動狀幼細的尾部。紋飾的尾部
實際上很似蝌蚪，其綣曲狀有如鞭索斷裂了的效果。

此時期對這種特色有很大的需求，大件的玉璧
表面和邊緣可能只是鋪滿了這種"C"形卷渦，
它們有的整齊劃分，有的則是隨意安排。這些玉器
無論在質素上、精細的紋飾和打磨上都是達到很高的
水準。另一種從蝌蚪紋變化而來的，是圓形中心凸起的
勾狀刻紋。玉匠以聰明的手法演繹了在青銅器中較易
製的蛇，他們並不是把玉蛇造成全立體型，而是將之造
成在地上綣曲或蠕動狀，似是在地面鑽出鑽入的。

另一種流行的發展，為扁身綣曲或幾何帶狀之
龍飾，尾部常有鳳首。物件中央通常有鑽孔，可作平衡
的懸掛，以一對為整，有時體形還長達10厘米或以上，
見展品116。

在精銳的青銅工具和先進的鑽孔、切割技術
協助下，又出現了一種十分精細複雜的鏤雕。繼盾形
刻線造型或綣曲邊上的紋節後，龍、鳳和蛇交織成
對稱的推動力。在西周初出現之"旋槳形"鳥爪，此時
仍繼續發展，但它們已不再是鳥爪，而是屬於虎和
龍等動物的，在外形和線條上更為精細。玉匠此時的

技巧已臻完美，那些薄身無瑕疵，甚至有複雜
鏤空的玉飾正好顯示了玉匠們無所不能的鬼斧神技，
展品114。

在西周時期，扁身玉璜上的刻線和圖案擴展
至邊緣部份，它們已沒有外周的範圍，對於構思
和製造光滑美麗是沒有限制的。在戰國時候，這種自由
受到了限制，玉器光滑的外緣凸邊是做成直角，
而內邊則呈向內傾斜，此特色並不是在所有玉飾上
出現，但它卻暗示了在形式上的抑制。玉匠本能或
刻意做成關鍵的間斷紋飾，令玉器加添了整齊和地方
色彩的效果。而斜凸邊也開始成為了玉璧內周和外
周上的特色。

然而，這些斜邊設定的規律並沒有維持下去，
玉匠把玉器部份的紋飾推移到原有的界限以外，
做成了不對稱的設計，令基本的動物紋和植物紋
與外邊上的紋飾融合，產生更自由的感覺。在
戰國時期，在簡單的扁圓玉璧中，鏤空龍是繞著其
中心孔攀爬的，它在扁平的壁面上穿插蟠動，穿過
植物形卷渦，又越過邊緣，同時具備了有規律和隨意的
效果。綜合雕塑可能是最後的一種浮華技巧，它是
從一塊石頭雕成似由多塊組合的，其實際用途有限，
但是卻很特出。

人類的天性容易對已得的奢華感厭倦，而摒棄
舊有的去尋找新的出路。青銅器具和器皿仍有金、銀的
鑲嵌。此時幼金線鑲嵌技術的質素，以及包嵌綠松石
與孔雀石的金邊，可說是在世界上前無古人，後無
來者的。單就玉器而言，春秋時期玉器的表面是柔和
的，到戰國時期已變成耀眼浮華，正相當於其時
富裕社會的紈絝子弟。這種質素的製作，在戰國時並
不罕見，亦沒甚代表性。東周時期戰亂頻密，而在玉器
方面也渴求轉變和改革，這把玉器帶進了當時藝術
潮流的前線。高質素的玉器製品是用來配合大型
的青銅器、金或銀裝飾配件，如帶勾或衣扣的。
在帶勾曲狀的器身上，常有一連串的紋飾，有的為
素面、有的打磨成深浮雕斜邊蝌蚪紋或饕餮紋。
在一些更珍貴的例子中，有的帶勾為全玉製的，它們
有單件拱狀的，中間底部有紐；有時配合個別複雜
的元素，在各中央位置以金屬心線穿連起來。由於
金屬心線是銅製的，故當它葬於天氣潮濕的郊外時，
會因氧化而生銹，結果就是玉飾從中脫下來成殘件，
所見的只是器物原來完美的一部份。

戰國時期，玉雕在輪廓上有清脆的切邊和凸出
的釘狀，邊位和角位反射出明亮的光澤。任何對這些
尖刻的緩和，都即時解去日後製作上的疑慮。最終，

戰國玉匠熟練的技巧雖達到很高的成就，但這仍掩飾
不了玉雕給人艱澀和不快的感覺。

　　　軍事上使用的玉器又可作另一門研究。其中
最重要的一種為箭手使用弓箭時所穿戴的指環，名鰈，
至於箭尾的凹口是否同時插進弓繩和指環的坑上使用，
則仍是現今有所爭論的問題。展品122為戰國後期
的鰈，上有植物形的托位。

　　　戰國時期被公認為最奢華之玉器是玉劍飾。
在頁20圖10清楚地展示了四件標準的玉劍飾，以下的描
述概括了現今對它們之認識和現存紋飾種類：

(i)　首　　它是以直角的裝置在劍柄末，通常為圓璧形，
扁形的上半身多有紋飾，為中央凸起旋轉盤車魚紋，
中間有精細的交叉斷面線和蝌蚪形綣曲環。此外，中央
凸起狀可被立體龍紋圍繞或覆蓋的。而另一種沒中央
凸起狀的，則似四、五片花瓣形的浮雕紋飾，其
垂直邊位有時向內傾，極少的刻有盾形和勾形圖案，
見展品124。

(ii)　格　　在劍刃末端和青銅或鐵柄頂端呈紡綞狀之
物，它用於銅劍和鐵劍，其中後者因鐵銹長期的腐蝕作
用，令到玉格部份爆裂開來。格上紋飾多為饕餮浮雕，
清脆均勻，但也可是單龍或雙龍，有立體、淺浮雕或深
浮雕的，見展品125。

(iii)　璏　　此物是連接在鞘上的，可穿掛在用者衣帶上。
璏面的矩形短管有兩類基本造型：

(a)　在縱向斜凸邊內有淺浮雕"C"卷渦，末部有淺浮雕饕
　　餮紋，眼球呈縱線紋狀。

(b)　匍匐龍淺浮雕或深浮雕，有時矩形短管上有多一條
　　較小的龍，展品139。龍身和植物狀凸出物有時是可
　　蓋過幾何等線，其中有一獨特例子，更是以一隻
　　猴子坐在短管的邊緣部份。

很多時，璏是由玦翻製過來的，這表現了人們認同玉材
之價值，不願浪費任何雖己破碎的玉料，見展品126。

(iv)　珌　　此乃劍鞘上之頂飾，呈梯形，橫切面與鞘
相仿，俱為凸透狀，鞘末的凸出栓部是插入珌內的。
由於它有凸透形的橫切面，珌通常是有兩彎弧邊，末
端或削平成方形或收窄。戰國時的玉珌常有紋飾，有斜
凸狀的外邊，見展品127。在漢代則多為素面，其紋飾
亦有多種，可概括如下：

(a)　刻線和部份鋤形減地，以及綣曲浮雕

(b)　素面上有尾或無尾緊密的蝌蚪綣曲紋

(c)　深或淺的單龍或雙龍浮雕，龍飾跨越幾何凸邊。
　　在這些造型中，有的珌末端是呈梯級狀的，使
　　表面形成不同的高度，有利於製造重疊的立體龍，
　　展品127。

另外，尚有兩種玉飾是配合以上第二類的使用，它們
並非時常可見，但是包括了以下所述：

(v)　鞘上繫緊璲與皮帶或布條的裝備，並非時
常使用，其橫切面呈"D"狀展品140為漢之製品，
上刻有饕餮紋飾。

(iv)　緊扣鞘與皮帶間之玉環，素面，展品142為
西漢之作。

　　　此外，這時亦有對玉製首飾的需求，如扁等線
紐繩坑紋的玉環、白玉製的龍鳳玉珮，兩面有隱約的
龍鳳和雲紋浮雕，展品160為此類型後期的好例子。
而細小的玉飾則是作為鑲嵌在漆木器皿上用的，造型
以龍為主，但間中亦有龜和鳥。

　　　戰國時期的玉匠，也開始製作玉器皿(參考書目
46、47和48)。它們有幼薄等身的空心碗，足緣位置製作
優美，表面常有刻線或淺浮雕、"C"形卷渦浮雕
或紐繩狀紋。這些器皿通常在貴族的陵墓發現，
並沒有顯示實際使用的跡象，它們的製造可能是要
表現出人類能克服玉這種堅硬的材料，可隨心所欲將之
做成任何形狀，而那些奢華的玉雕亦應運而生，如此
玉匠已超越他本身之地位。今天我們有幸從僅存的製
品，仍能欣賞到這些玉匠當日之成就。

　　　無疑，戰國時期代表了人類駕馭玉器之巔峰
時期，玉匠慣於製作完美的線條、環、直角角位、精工
完成之浮雕以至精細的紋飾。就算是十分薄身的玉器，
他們也可靈活塑造，這對於當時的骨雕和牙雕來說，
是一項很重要的成就，但對玉器而言則是很普通的事。
在戰國期間至十九世紀碳化硅磨蝕法的出現，以至
二十世紀尤其在現代中國製玉使用的電鑽發明後，
並未有如上述般傑出的玉器出現過。

　　　這時期也有製造立體人雕，有的精工完成，
有的則較鬆散；有的髮型精巧，也有的表現了複雜的
鏤空髮飾，展品118為後者之例子。在扁身玉珮上亦有
這些人像，他們穿長袍跳舞狀，似是與玉璜和玉珠組成
複雜的胸前掛飾的中央部份。此外也有立體玉蟬的
製作，展品120為一好例子，蟬翼栩栩如生，其生動的
眼睛教人想起它在炎夏的鳴叫和飛動。

　　　自殷商後立體玉雕中斷了，代之而起的是扁身
玉雕，到東周後期它又復現，直至清代仍沒有被
其它形式所取代。而在今次的展覽和本書中亦有很多
清代優良的製品。

　　　在戰國玉器上亦有寓意的紋飾，玉璧常刻有動物
形紋，如玄武、朱雀、白帝和青龍象徵了四個方位。
玉璧亦有鏤空之作，它們有時大量的放在內棺屍體
的身旁，有時則作為掛在胸前的玉珮用。玉璧另一用途

是在繪畫和實際使用上，作為索緊腰帶的環扣，這可
應用在人體的衣服，以至是大型的棺木上。

A.4 秦
公元前221年—207年 ——首都在陝西省咸陽

在秦始皇的統治下，這時期代表了秦在政治上和軍事
上最後的稱霸。秦始皇於公元前207年薨，之後漢代統一
天下，在四百年內，除了公元9年至25年王莽新朝外，
其餘時間均享有太平。秦始皇執政對傳統的觀念作劇烈
的改動，他命令統一文字、設定度量衡、廢封建
而設中央集權政治制度，但又焚書坑儒。而他下令
修築萬里長城則防禦了蠻夷之入侵。

由於秦國祚短，故很難觀察其玉器的發展，
如能見到至今在西安仍未發掘的秦皇墓內的葬玉，將會
是十分之有趣。無論如何，秦代玉器若不是承接戰國
之特色，也應是漢代之前的一個不是十分出眾之
過渡期。然而，在1971年，西安則出土了一批屬秦代的
玉片，見參考書目26圖版47-58。這批玉片包括了八十件
作陪葬用灰／綠色玉，有玉璧、玉圭、玉璜珮飾和
玉符。而最有趣的可能是扁身玉人，它們有男有女，
面部紋飾簡單。展品128為此類之例子，它們的表情雖然
簡單直接，但卻代表了從西安出土，可鑑定為秦代
特色之玉器。

92

CONVEX MONSTER MASK

SHANG DYNASTY, ANYANG PHASE
TO EARLY WESTERN ZHOU DYNASTY
   (C.12TH - 9TH CENTURY BC)
                              PE688
HEIGHT : 5.7 CM
WIDTH : 5.2 CM
DEPTH : 5.2 CM

Monster mask formed as a convex plaque of translucent green nephrite. The top surface of the piece is highly polished. The underside is matt and pierced with a single hole drilled through the forehead from the front. The piece features a pair of outspread false raised-line horns structured as addorsed hooks placed above inverted semi-lunar shaped eyebrows which sit above inverted extended canthus double incised line form eyes with central circular pupils. Below the eyes is an incised V-form nose with rounded sides placed above a canoe-shaped mouth with upturned ends. At each side profile are square hook-form incisions and insert cutouts which form the ears.

There is a similar but thicker, stockier form of this piece with false raised line and raised plateau structure eyes from the Fu Hao tomb see 91 pl.78. Of particular interest is the clear representation of a banana-form mouth as seen on Exhibit 92 with upward curling ends. This feature survives strongly from the Anyang phase of the Shang dynasty right through to the middle or late Western Zhou as indicated by Exhibit 100.
(AHF)

Compare: 91 pl.78
Collection: The Peony Collection

93

TIGER CUT-OUT PLAQUE

EARLY WESTERN ZHOU DYNASTY
(C.11TH - 9TH CENTURY BC)
PE174

LENGTH : 9.3 CM
WIDTH : 4.0 CM
DEPTH : 0.3 CM

A figure of a crouching tiger massively carved from a thin plate of translucent olive-green nephrite. The big head has a squared silhouette and a bottle-shaped horn with club finial. The back is a convex arc between powerfully bunched shoulders and haunches and the tail curls up and over the back. Strong, simple incisions depict the details of limbs and face and fore and hind feet each with four claws. There are some earth and cinnabar incrustations and the forehead and crook of the tail are each drilled through with one large conical hole, and the mouth is drilled through with one small straight hole.

This flat but expressive plaque form with its great economy of detail owes much to the bunching of muscular structure. Each proportion of limb, haunch, back, shoulder or stomach reflects a harmonious and synchronised contribution to a masterful whole. This piece is larger than the usual size of the plaques of animals and birds from this period and clearly demonstrates again the awe with which the people of these times regarded the supple beauties and dangers of the tiger. The bottle-horn in this piece is a vestigial remnant of a bifurcated form of three dimensional bottle or club-shape horn found slightly earlier in the Shang dynasty's Anyang phase. (AHF)

Previously published: 17 p 16
Compare: (i) 46 No.301 (ii) 68 pl.XXXVII No.13 (iii) 37 No.52 (iv) 1 pl.VI No.360 J 916
Collection: The Peony Collection

94

RABBIT CUT-OUT PLAQUE

EARLY WESTERN ZHOU DYNASTY
(C.11TH - 9TH CENTURY BC)
PE660

LENGTH : 3.8 CM
HEIGHT : 2.8 CM
THICKNESS : 0.2 CM

Plaque in translucent grey-green nephrite with the outline of a big-eared, crouching rabbit with a large incised oval eye. Incised features depict the angled elbow and the hind quarters.

The rabbit is a commonly found animal in jade suspension plaques. Exhibit 94 has singularly sharp outline cutting and the rabbit is in a posture of alert readiness. (AHF)

Compare: (i) 46 No.158 (ii) 68 pl XL
Collection: The Peony Collection

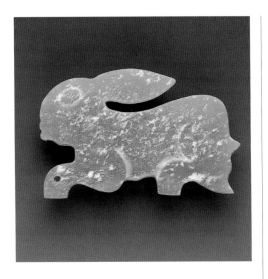

95

FISH PENDANTS

WESTERN ZHOU DYNASTY
(c.1100 - 771 BC)
PE682-PE683

LENGTH : 4.5 CM
HEIGHT : 1.3 CM
THICKNESS : 0.2 CM

Pair of short, fat-bodied fish pendants carved in translucent green nephrite. The dorsal fin and two sets of abdominal fins are finely incised. The lively tails are very sharply carved and formed and the lower jawline is cut as a thickened incurving movement back from the pointed nose. Each is pierced through the mouth area for suspension.

Jade fish, which vary considerably in quality, were hung in bunches, interspersed with beads on necklaces. Paired pieces are uncommon and this pair exhibits exceptionally sharp, clear precision grinding and finishing with very individual details such as the angled tails and curved gills. (AHF)

Previously published: 27 pl.19
Compare: (i) 46 No.278 (ii) 68 pl.XLIV
Collection: The Peony Collection

96

TRAPEZOIDAL BIRD PLAQUE PENDANT

EARLY WESTERN ZHOU DYNASTY
(c.1100 - 771 BC)
PE733

WIDTH (MAX) : 3.8 CM
HEIGHT : 3.8 CM
THICKNESS : 0.2 CM

Trapezoidal breast ornament or plaque pendant in translucent grey-white nephrite with some opaque beige suffusions. The piece is delicately worked on both sides with a figure of a single bird with an alert big-eyed head centrally placed amid a centrifugal swirl of geometric, finely worked low relief wings and tail feathers. At both the top and the bottom is a row of obliquely pierced small holes to take strands of beads or other strung pendant forms.

There is a very similar example published in 67 pl. XXV No.7. The excavated forms of pieces such as this have strings of beads hanging from the holes at the base. This piece, however, also has a row of holes at the top thus indicating that it occupied a median position with pendants above and below. It is interesting to note that one half of the string holes in each row are angled in one direction and the other half in a different direction. (AHF)

Compare: (i) 67 pl.XXV No.7 (ii) 46 No.379 (iii) 68 pl.LXIII No.10
Collection: The Peony Collection

97

SQUARE BIRD'S-HEAD PLAQUE

WESTERN ZHOU DYNASTY
(c.1100 - 771 BC)

PE296

SIDES: 2.2 CM
THICKNESS : 0.2CM

Square plaque or button with rounded corners, in greenish-white translucent nephrite pierced with a central hole and with a formed border. The piece is incised on one side with a double line design of curving hooks and the head of a crested bird with a large curving beak.

The round ended, forward turned crest of this incised form of bird is the typical bird representation of the late Shang/early Western Zhou transition and the form is found incised on pieces ranging from small ones such as this through to relatively large forms of handle where the bird has a long geometrical tail folded up and over and stands on massive thighs which themselves extend into large taloned open claws. (AHF)

Compare: (i) 46 No.335 (ii) 68 pl.LXIII No.6
Collection: The Peony Collection

98

TAOTIE MASK APPLIQUE

WESTERN ZHOU DYNASTY
(c.1100 - 771 BC)

BATEA 1217

LENGTH : 1.8 CM
WIDTH : 1.2 CM
DEPTH : 0.6 CM

Taotie mask applique in pale celadon coloured jade with fake raised line decoration, pierced for affixing and with concave channels on reverse and top. (BSM)

Previously Published: 80, No.28
Collection: The Rannerdale Collection

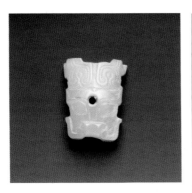

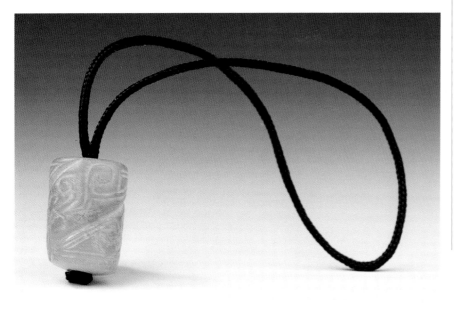

99

JADE BEAD

WESTERN ZHOU DYNASTY
(c.1100 - 771BC)

BATEA 434

LENGTH : 1.5 CM
DIAMETER : 1.2 CM.

A small jade circular bead pierced from both ends, the outer surface with spiralling decoration of monster masks featuring prominent eyes and snouts carved in double line technique.

The decoration on this bead is comparable to bronzes of the Anyang phase. (BSM)

Compare : 37, No. 76.

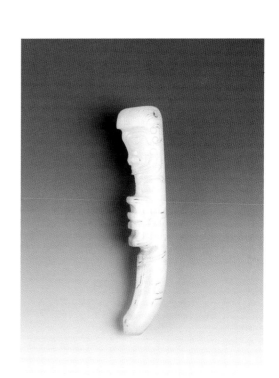

100

HUMAN HEAD TOTEMIC PENDANT

WESTERN ZHOU DYNASTY
(c.1100 - 771 BC)

PE641

LENGTH : 6.0 CM
DEPTH : 1.2 CM
THICKNESS : 0.7 CM

Pendant in off-white greyish semi-translucent nephrite formed as an elongated rod of oval cross section with the last quarter of its length bent at an angle of 15 degrees; one end of the rod is carved as a human head in totemic style capped with a pudding basin style of hair cut with an all round fringe above an elongated face with well formed eyes, nose and nostrils, ears, mouth and narrow chin. The rod extends on one side below the chin through a squared excrescence resembling caterpillar or silkworm feet incised on each side with a simplified *taotie*. On each side of the remainder of the rod are incised line borders within which are regular addorsed double hook motifs.

As with Exhibit 77, parallels can be drawn with the totem pole carving of British Columbia. Certainly as far as Western Zhou China is concerned, the full, round three-dimensional human face is extremely rare and this piece is interesting because it exhibits all the club antenna finial line forms typical of the period arranged around a three-dimensional face. (AHF)

Compare: 69 pl.XIV No.4
Collection: The Peony Collection

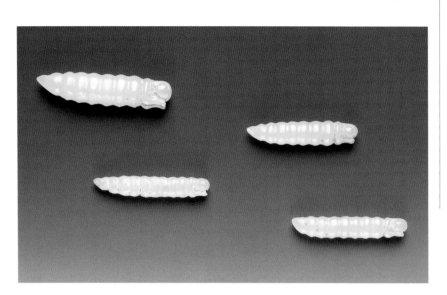

101

SILK-WORMS

WESTERN ZHOU DYNASTY
  (c.1100 - 771 BC)
                              PE562
THE LARGEST
LENGTH : 3.2 CM
HEIGHT : 0.7 CM
WIDTH : 0.5 CM

A group of four silk-worms in translucent white nephrite with fatly segmented bodies and the crooked elbow and fore legs held together with an alert air beneath the large-eyed head.

As with the flat fish form of this period, these silk-worm forms were made for stringing in a bunch as part of a pendant or pectoral ensemble of the type that would have been suspended from a trapezoid plaque similar to Exhibit 96. (AHF)

Compare: (i) 27 p.19 (ii) 46 No.310 (iii) 68 pl.XLI (iv) 37 No.26
Collection: The Peony Collection

102

WHITE *HUANG* PENDANT

SPRING AND AUTUMN PERIOD
  (770 - 475 BC)
                              PE251
LENGTH : 5.6 CM
BREADTH : 2.5 CM
THICKNESS : 0.4 CM

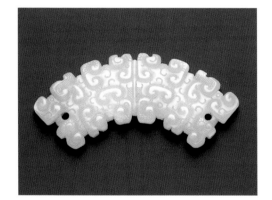

Huang-shaped arc, possibly an applique, in translucent white nephrite, deeply carved and decorated on one side only with an open-mouthed striated horned dragon's head at each end. There is a field or body of C scrolls, curls and incised ring dots extending back from each head towards the centre where it terminates against a carefully formed horizontal median fissure.

This shape was popular as a pivotal element in a complex pectoral made up of a number of strung pieces hanging on the chest. The *huang* normally has a central hole at the top of the arc and either a drilled hole at each end or, as with this piece, a hole at each end forming part of the design. Here the end holes are formed by the open mouths of the terminal dragon's heads and are cleverly designed to avoid slippage of the inserted string . (AHF)

Previously published: 17 pl.28
Compare: (i) 28 B22 (ii) 66 No.105
Collection: The Peony Collection

103
FIGURE IN CHEQUERED SKIRT

SPRING AND AUTUMN PERIOD
 (770 - 475 BC)

PE731

HEIGHT : 3.6 CM
WIDTH : 1.2 CM
DEPTH : 0.8 CM

A figure of a man in translucent greenish-white nephrite somewhat suffused with white clouding. He stands with long sleeves across his stomach and his hands held before him. He wears a full floor-length skirt to his robe. The front of the skirt is picked out with an incised pattern of alternate cross hatched and plain squares. His face is well defined with open eyes, a distinct nose and small pursed mouth. His head has ears and a small topknot.

A group of small plaque-type silhouettes of the human figure with simple incised facial details, a chequered skirt and a horned crescent headdress is published in 100 pl.119. Exhibit 103 has a more three-dimensional treatment but shares many features with those illustrated, including the flared skirt outline and its chequered design with alternating internal cross-hatched with plain squares. (AHF)

Compare: (i) 46 No.413 (ii) 69 pl.XXV No.5
Collection: The Peony Collection

104
WAISTED TUBULAR BEAD WITH STYLISED DRAGONS' HEADS

SPRING AND AUTUMN PERIOD
 (770 - 475 BC)

BATEA 456

LENGTH : 7 CM
DIAMETER : 2 CM - 2.8 CM

Pale celadon jade waisted tubular bead pierced through from both ends and decorated with two bands of two stylised dragons' heads, one on top of the other and facing in different directions all in low double raised-line relief showing eye, upturned snout and fang. There is a border of incised diagonal lines at the wider end and in the narrow band in the middle of the waisted section, separating the decorative bands of dragons' heads.

The decoration of stylised dragons' heads as here was a very popular subject in both jade and bronzes both in the Spring and Autumn and the Warring States periods. In the late Spring and Autumn period and the Warring States period, however, the elements of the design became almost unrecognisable as the period progressed. The fact that the eye, snout and fang can all be distinguished here dates this example fairly early in the Spring and Autumn period. The raised-line relief decoration of the Shandong Longshan and Erligang periods was revived at this time, as on this example, but is quite rare. (BSM)

105

SLIT-DISC

SPRING AND AUTUMN PERIOD
(770 - 475 BC)

PE557

DIAMETER : 3 CM
BREADTH : 0.3 CM

Slit-disc in translucent green nephrite carved on one side with confronting dragons' heads in raised-line work and extending back around the surface in a series of moulded C scrolls also in raised-line work.

The origin of this design goes back to Neolithic times. In the early Western Zhou period the surface work of the dragon's heads and abstract forms are incised but in the Spring and Autumn period the linear elements of the design revert to the genuine raised-line structure of the Longshan culture/Erligang phase and rise out of the surrounding surface. (AHF)

Compare: 27 pl.23 No.1
Collection: The Peony Collection

106

THREE ROUND PLAQUES

SPRING AND AUTUMN PERIOD
(770 - 475 BC)
PE255 PE256 PE257
DIAMETER: : 2.8 CM
THICKNESS : 0.1 CM

Three round plaques of translucent off-white nephrite, carved with composite designs derived from dragons' heads and pierced at equidistant points round the edge as if for sewing thread attachment.

This type of plaque is normally either square or rhombic with slightly oblique slanting sides slanted in the same direction. The round form is unusual. One of the pieces in Exhibit 106 retains a central boss of glass which puts it at the beginning of glass working in China. The dragon's head designs are partially dissolved. (AHF)

Previously published: 17 pl.24
Compare: (i) 46 No.383 (ii) 69 pl.XXI No.5 (iii) 68 pl.LXXXVIII (iv) 28 B25
Collection: The Peony Collection

107

JADE *BI-DISC* WITH DRAGONS' HEADS

LATE SPRING AND AUTUMN PERIOD, EARLY
WARRING STATES
  (6TH - 5TH CENTURY BC)

BATEA 458

DIAMETER OVERALL : 5 CM
DIAMETER OF APERTURE : 3.1 CM
DEPTH : 0.4 CM

Circular jade *bi-disc* of greyish-white colour with deep brown
patches on some of the outer edges, decorated on both sides with a
continuous single band of five partially dissolved dragons' heads in
the style typical of this period.

The more dissolved nature of the dragons' heads here should be
compared with Exhibit 104. Whilst the eye is still to be seen the
fang here has become a tongue. The design is however still
recognisable and must be assigned to this period. As the Warring
States period progressed the elements in the design ceased to be
even recognisable. (BSM)

108

RECUMBENT ANTLERED STAG

SPRING AND AUTUMN PERIOD
ORDOS TYPE
  (770-475 BC)

PE209

LENGTH : 5.0 CM
HEIGHT : 4.1 CM
BREADTH : 2.5 CM

A figure of an antlered stag, of grey-green semi-translucent stone. The body is resting
on the ground. A triangular tail with incised striations and traces of iron encrustation
hangs down to the ground behind. The fore and hind legs are drawn up and folded
beneath the body and the graceful line of the chest follows through the slightly
upturned chin with small incised beard to the well shaped head. Well formed ears
extend out of each side of the head and a pair of six-tined antlers reach back to rest
upon the top of the haunches.

A directly related sculptural form is found in four bronze stags seated equidistantly
around the perimeter of a flat round plate or lid of bronze in the Avery Brundage
collection in San Francisco and attributed to Mongolia and the Warring States
period. The interaction between China and the nomadic tribes of Mongolia and
Siberia between the late Western Zhou and Han periods is a complex area of study in
its own right. Works in jade of the Ordos style from this period are extremely rare.
(AHF)

Collection: The Peony Collection

109
TIGER CUT-OUT

SPRING AND AUTUMN PERIOD
ORDOS TYPE
 (770 - 475 BC)
                              PE236
LENGTH : 10.6 CM
HEIGHT : 4.4 CM
THICK : 0.3 CM

Plaque of opaque off-white nephrite partly calcified and with some black inclusions, formed on both sides as a crouching feline beast with a high gloss. The centre of the looped tail, hip joint, shoulder joint and eye are all formed as a dot surrounded by two sharply incised concentric circles. The small ear lies flat and points forward. The mouth is a single incision with three small transverse incisions to depict the teeth. The long claws are depicted by two curving incisions on each paw and partly enclose a single dot placed behind.

There are very similar pieces in bronze which are unarguably attributed to the Ordos style and dated to this period. A particular feature common to both jade and bronze forms is the target form of concentric circle enclosing a central dot. (AHF)

Collection: The Peony Collection

110

ANGLED *TAOTIE* MASK APPLIQUE

WARRING STATES PERIOD
(475 - 221 BC)

PE249

LENGTH : 4.4 CM
BREADTH : 2.2 CM
HEIGHT : 0.3 CM

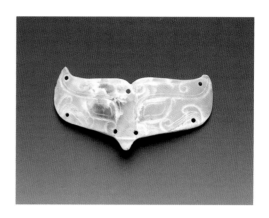

Taotie mask in white nephrite, a band of plum-grey suffusing through the left hand side. The basic silhouette is a double inverted ogival arc enclosing the carved field with a pair of extended eyebrows sweeping away on each side above the angled eyes and long whiskers incised on each cheek. The perimeter is pierced on top with three small holes and on the bottom with four small holes presumably for suspension threads. The overall top surface has a very high gloss and the bottom side is rough hewn with a semi-matt finish. The entire piece is formed as two angled halves meeting at a median ridge.

The material is delicately sliced at an angled pitch with very finely drilled holes (compare Exhibit 106) and demonstrates the mechanical ability of the jade carving in this period. (AHF)

Previously published: 17 pl.25
Collection: The Peony Collection

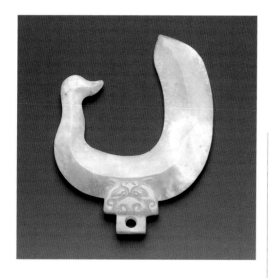

111

MINIATURE HALBERD HEAD

WARRING STATES PERIOD
(475 - 221 BC)

PE462

HEIGHT : 5.3 CM
BREADTH : 4.3 CM

Head of a ceremonial miniature halberd or *ge* in translucent honey-coloured nephrite. The principal vertical blade terminates in a squat point and the conjoined ancillary vertical blade terminates in a simplified bird's head or kris blade finial. Both are gracefully shaped and hollow ground on each side of a single median ridge through their common length on each face. All edges are bevelled and sharpened. The curved centre base of each side is bitten by a *taotie* mask with extended fangs, from the back of which extends a squared flange pierced by a single hole for fastening.

There is a very elegant halberd blade in the Von Oertzen Collection, 28 pl.C1 which is much larger and more elaborately worked on the surface than Exhibit 111 modelled on a well established contemporary bronze form but with the same elegantly mannered overall shape. The main difference between the two is size. The blade of Exhibit 111 is very fine and sharp and is translucent when held against the light. (AHF)

Compare: 28 No.C1
Collection: The Peony Collection

112

'S' DRAGON PLAQUE

WARRING STATES PERIOD
(475 - 221 BC)

PE595

LENGTH : 16 CM
BREADTH : 6.5 CM
THICKNESS : 2.3 CM

Dragon silhouette plaque in translucent light golden-green nephrite
formed identically on both sides as a sinuous but chunky curling
body terminating at one end in a sharp-nosed dragon's head with
an incised oval eye and at the other with a sharp beaked bird or
phoenix-crested head. The field of the body is well worked with a
series of large, broadly incised, low relief C scrolls with a regular
plain border all around. The exterior curvature of the body is
broken at the corners by striated curved protrusions with squared-
end terminals. Internally the plaque is pierced and there are
openwork linear meander holes in two places, cut around the
contours of a club-headed extrusion with a continuous field of C
scrolls in relief. There is one suspension perforation through the
central curve of one body scroll and another near the base of the
dragon neck.

This form, with a squared, almost geometric shape, is typical of the
period and represents the true beginning of the dragon and
phoenix appearing together - a combination which rapidly became
common in Chinese art and remains so to the present day. (AHF)

Compare: 27 pl.29C
Collection: The Peony Collection

113

HIGH-SIDED RING

WARRING STATES PERIOD
(475 - 221 BC)
PE357

LENGTH : 3.9 CM
HEIGHT : 3 CM

High-sided ring of translucent white nephrite carved with a narrow plain border top and bottom. The field between is carved with a series of interlocking spade and triangular-shaped motifs.

The field design represents the final point of the dissolved dragon's head design where the individual dragon features have been wholly absorbed into the C scrolling and spade-shaped design. This piece may have been used as a ring for the hair. (AHF)

Compare: 28 B33
Collection: The Peony Collection

114

WINGED TIGER OR DRAGON OPENWORK PENDANT

WARRING STATES PERIOD
(475 - 221 BC)
PE237

LENGTH : 7.3 CM
HEIGHT : 1.8 CM

Plaque formed from honey-coloured translucent nephrite with an overall high gloss polish on both faces and on the surface round all edges. The piece is fashioned as an elongated dragon or tiger figure with short wings, surface body patterns of incised concentric double curves and a striated median tail band. The head of the beast has an incised bow form eye, prominent scooped ears and open mouth with well marked incisor teeth. The foreleg terminates in a circular clenched claw enclosing a hole and a long tail with internal double bevel to a central groove extends out behind - the design identical on both sides.

The form of a dragon or tiger in this elegant pendant with a clearly delineated wing appears to be unique. The delicacy of the piece makes it hard to contemplate an utilitarian application. The perimeter bevel with deliberate design breaks is a typical feature of the period. (AHF)

Previously published: 17 pl.33
Collection: The Peony Collection

115
RETICULATED *HUANG* DRAGON PENDANT

WARRING STATES PERIOD
  (475 - 221 BC)
                    BATEA 511
LENGTH : *7.9* CM
WIDTH : 2.5 CM.

Jade reticulated *huang* pendant carved through as two dragons their bearded heads turned to face each other, their tails intertwined, the edges of the *huang* pendant indented; the dragons' heads with beards. (BSM)

116
DRAGON AND PHOENIX PLAQUE

WARRING STATES PERIOD
  (475 - 221 BC)
                    PE725
LENGTH : 16.5 CM
THICKNESS : 0.3 CM

S-shaped flat plaque form of dragon and phoenix that appear separately at either end of the same sweeping, curved ribbon body with a raised border, studded with "curled worm" or comma bodies modelled in high relief. The elegant coil-nosed dragon's head with upturned crest is looped back to face the turned back head of the crested phoenix. The piece is worked identically on both sides.

This rounded elegant sweeping S-form of curled dragon and phoenix is typical of the period. Exhibit 112 has incised C scrolls. Exhibit 116 has raised "curled worm" bodies. (AHF)

Compare: (i) 27 pl.45 and 46 (ii) 46 No 433
Collection: The Peony Collection

117

TORTOISE BEAD

WARRING STATES PERIOD
  (475 - 221 BC)

PE552

LENGTH : 1.9 CM
WIDTH : 1.3 CM
HEIGHT : 0.5 CM

A figure of a tortoise in semi-translucent olive-green nephrite. The head with open mouth extends forward and forms the commencement of a perforated horizontal channel emerging by the tail. The upper surface of the shell is formed in deeply moulded C-form motifs depicting two separate dragons' heads. The base is flat.

The body of this piece exhibits the typical C motifs with two clear dragons' heads in an undissolved form. It is probably a bead that formed part of a pectoral complex. (AHF)

Collection: The Peony Collection

118

ROBED STANDING OFFICIAL

WARRING STATES PERIOD
  (475 - 221 BC)

PE523

HEIGHT : 6.6 CM
WIDTH : 2.1 CM
THICKNESS : 0.8 CM

Standing figure of an official carved in the round from semi-translucent green nephrite with some dark brown suffusions and internal fracture lines. The figure wears a wrap-around overgarment that partially encloses a long underrobe with a deeply pleated hem all round. Two pairs of long and short sash ribbons fall down in front and part of an anchoring belt is seen at the back. A two-tiered double collar bib arrangement extends from the neck down over the chest. The arms, folded over the stomach are covered by long sleeves from which emerge the clasped hands with the left thumb extended upwards. The head is crowned with an elaborate openwork headdress and there is a short central braid of hair hanging down behind.

There is a very similar example in the Palace Museum in Beijing, which is a collected piece with no excavated provenance. An important feature of Exhibit 118 is the overlapping arrangement of long pleats hanging at the rear of the robe. (AHF)

Collection: The Peony Collection

119

GARMENT HOOK WITH DUCK'S HEAD FINIAL

WARRING STATES PERIOD
(475 - 221 BC)

BATEA 426

LENGTH : 3.2 CM
WIDTH : 2.2 CM

Small white jade garment hook carved in low relief with a *taotie* mask pierced above and below with three hooks drilled from both sides, the underside carved with linear scrolls from which rises an oval button incised with cross-hatching. A stylised cicada is incised on the underside of the gently curving hook, which terminates in a duck's head. The softly polished translucent white stone has traces of cinnabar.

Garment hooks are thought to have been introduced to the Chinese from the Central Asian/Mongolian steppe in the Spring and Autumn period. They became common in the Warring States and Han periods. This one with its duck's head finial and other decorative elements can be dated with confidence to the Warring States period. (BSM)

Previously published: (i) 77, No. 21 (ii) 80, No 35

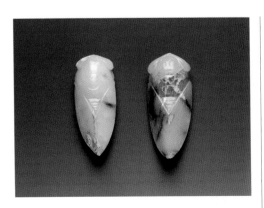

120

TWO FREE STANDING CICADAS

WARRING STATES PERIOD
(475 - 221 BC)

PE272-273

LENGTH : (I) 4.8 CM(II) 4.6 CM
BREADTH : 2.2 CM 2.0 CM
HEIGHT : 1.2 CM 1.1 CM

A pair of cicadas formed of highly polished translucent grey-white nephrite with three- dimensional bodies, the heads with bulging eyes, the veined wings folded back to the body, and the legs curved beneath the segmented stomach, each pierced from end to end by a continuous hole.

The polished gloss on these insects exemplifies the high point of Warring States jade working. (AHF)

Compare: (i) 46 Nos 367-369 (ii) 69 pl. XXII No.4 (iii) 10 p.131
Collection: The Peony Collection

121

TAOTIE MASK PLAQUE

WARRING STATES PERIOD
(475 - 221 BC)
PE607
WIDTH : 4.7 CM
HEIGHT : 3.3 CM

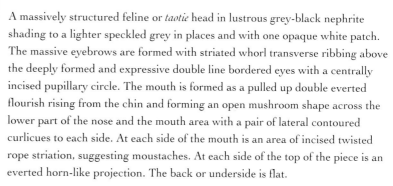

A massively structured feline or *taotie* head in lustrous grey-black nephrite shading to a lighter speckled grey in places and with one opaque white patch. The massive eyebrows are formed with striated whorl transverse ribbing above the deeply formed and expressive double line bordered eyes with a centrally incised pupillary circle. The mouth is formed as a pulled up double everted flourish rising from the chin and forming an open mushroom shape across the lower part of the nose and the mouth area with a pair of lateral contoured curlicues to each side. At each side of the mouth is an area of incised twisted rope striation, suggesting moustaches. At each side of the top of the piece is an everted horn-like projection. The back or underside is flat.

Several examples of this mask type have been published and all form the terminal of a belt hook made up of strongly designed and worked jade components. The double everted flourish forming the mouth is a characteristic design of this period. The expressive contrast between the small and finely drawn eyes and huge eyebrows is another classic combination of this period.(AHF)

Compare: (i) 47 pl.116 (ii) 46 No.472 (iii) 46 No.473
Collection: The Peony Collection

122

ARCHER'S RING

WARRING STATES PERIOD
(475 - 221 BC)
PE242
LENGTH : 5.0 CM
BREADTH : 3.5 CM
HEIGHT : 1.0 CM

Pendant in the form of an archer's thumb ring, formed from partially altered translucent pale green nephrite. There is a large fluent curvilinear hook branching from one side with a bifurcated terminal and auxiliary shoot. The basic form is oval with a large round hole through the upper section and the lower section with a convex surface either side of a longitudinal control ridge. The lower section of the reverse is concave and the whole subtly facetted and ridged at various points throughout.

This form derives from Shang dynasty antecedents (eg. 91 Pl.118 No.973). Pieces of this type are found until the Han period and towards the end of their period of use the exuberant vegetal-looking growth either disappears completely or is reduced to a stub. (AHF)

Compare: 46 No.453
Collection: The Peony Collection

123
MOSS-GREEN AGATE BRACELET

WARRING STATES PERIOD
  (475 - 221 BC)

BATEA 524

DIAMETER OVERALL : 9.78 CM
DIAMETER OF APERTURE : 6.8 CM

Circular agate bracelet with extensive moss-green inclusions and some of red, white and yellowish colour, the overall tone dark green, the stone polished to a high gloss, the outer edge coming to a narrow vertical plane, the inner edge rounded in six flat planes, the main band flat, with some traces of burial.

This type of bracelet was used during this period as part of a pendant or pectoral set. The outer edge of this bracelet is a narrow vertical plane, such as that recorded on similar bracelets found in Warring States burials. It should be compared with similar bracelets from late Warring States to early Western Han burials where the outer edge comes to a point without a separate plane, see Exhibit 131. (BSM)

Previously published: (i) 77, Pl. VI (ii) Hong Kong 1987, Chinese Antiquities from the Brian S McElney Collection, Exhibit 145.
Compare: (i) 44, No. 86 (ii) 66, No. 162

124
SWORD POMMEL

WARRING STATES PERIOD
  (475 - 221 BC)

PE215

BREADTH : 4.5 CM
HEIGHT : 0.8 CM

Sword pommel in greyish-white nephrite, the circular disc with a bevelled perimeter band enclosing a sloping field studded with raised comma spirals arranged in lines. The raised central medallion has an incised-line border enclosing a deeply carved scroll or cloud motif, with secondary incised spirals and patches of incised cross hatching. The plain sides taper to the flat base which is pierced diagonally with three perforations placed equidistantly around a circular groove.

This is the uppermost jade fitting of a warrior's sword. The standard type of pommel's central upper face design is that represented here. It later develops into either a central open stylised flower with as many as five petals although this number is rare. It sometimes also developed into raised three-dimensional prowling dragons in the late Warring states/Western Han period. (47 pl.74 - 76 and 86). (AHF)

Previously published: 17 pl.22
Compare: (i) 27 pl.53A (ii) 46 No.459
Collection: The Peony Collection

125

BLACK JADE WINGED SWORD GUARD

LATE WARRING STATES PERIOD
(4TH TO 3RD CENTURY BC)

BATEA 446

LENGTH : 5.4 CM
WIDTH : 2.0 CM

Jade sword guard of diamond lozenge-shaped cross section and winged (rounded ear) front section, the jade of natural black colour petering off on one side to brown-flecked grey, decorated in relief with angular scrolls and dissolved *kui* dragons.

Similar examples from late Warring States excavations are known. (BSM)

Compare : (i) 67 Pl. LXV 3-4 (ii) 47 No.183

126

SWORD SCABBARD SLIDE

WARRING STATES PERIOD
(475 - 221 BC)

PE221

LENGTH : 9.5 CM
BREADTH : 2.7 CM
HEIGHT : 1.8 CM

Sword scabbard slide in very translucent white nephrite with a slight patch of alteration in one place, formed as a long rectangular plate with projecting, asymmetrically downward-curving ends and backed by a rectangular pendant slot placed off centre. The overall cutting is sharp and there is a very high polish throughout on the top side only. The surface decoration consists of a *taotie* mask with striated eye brows at one end followed by regularly arranged pairs of relief and incised C-shaped volutes interlocking longtitudinally and diagonally within straight raised border lines.

It is important to note the very high gloss finish on the top surface of this piece and the unpolished matt finish below. The material is excellent and pure and was clearly used to satisfy a popular demand for luxury. There is little mechanical strength in the thinness of the piece although it was obviously used on a scabbard. This type of sword slide is also commonly found with a raised crawling dragon, sometimes with a pair of dragons, see Exhibit 139. (AHF)

Previously published: 17 pl.37
Compare: (i) 27 pl.53C (ii) 46 No.569
Collection: The Peony Collection

127
SWORD SCABBARD CHAPE

WARRING STATES PERIOD
  (475 - 221 BC)

PE424

WIDTH : 5.0 CM
HEIGHT : 3.2 CM
THICKNESS : 1.2 CM

Sword scabbard chape in highly polished white nephrite with some brown suffusions. The terminal is asymmetrical with one half stepped higher than the other. On one face writhes a young *kui* dragon with twisted tail in high relief. On the other side is a relief of a beaked phoenix with ribbon body extending over the side edge of the piece, and a *kui* dragon with bifurcated twisted tail, its body entering the main mass of the piece and emerging through the level surface on the end to writhe back against the curving edge of the step.

Some of the most imaginative asymmetrical designs of the late Warring States period are found in these chapes. The emergence from the surface of part of the dragon's body, which also overlaps the terminal at the edge of the piece and one or other of the side faces, is a good example of the available design skills of the times. (AHF)

Compare: (i) 27 pl.53D (ii) 47 pl.206
Collection: The Peony Collection

128
GREEN STANDING FIGURE PLAQUE

QIN DYNASTY
  (221 - 206 BC)

PE447

LENGTH : 9.9 CM
BREATH : 2.3 CM
THICKNESS : 0.6 CM

A spinach-green jade plaque with human features, the stone of flat rectangular shape and with a high gloss finish. The piece is crossed at the centre on both front and back with a single line representing a belt. One end has narrowly formed sloping shoulders and a regularly formed human head incised with simple eyebrows, eyes, nose and mouth.

The fortunate find in Xian, Shaanxi Province, of a tomb securely dateable to the Qin dynasty brought to light a number of these figures. They can accordingly be assigned without any difficulty or controversy to the Qin dynasty - a period so short even if cataclysmic that before the Xian find it was not possible categorically to attribute jades to it. (AHF)

Compare: (i) 26 pl.49 and 50
Collection: The Peony Collection

HAN DYNASTY 206BC-220AD

In the past Chinese commentators considered the Han and Song dynasties to be the pinnacles of the Chinese jade carvers' art. Although today, the premier accolade would probably be awarded to the jades of the preceding Warring States period, there is no doubt that fine jades were produced during the Han dynasty. These are now better understood since a large number of examples from excavations accurately datable to the Han dynasty have been found in the last thirty years. These include the jades found in the tomb of the posthumously named Emperor Wen, Zhao Mo, second King of Nanyue who died in 122 BC, and whose intact tomb was found in the 1980s in Guangzhou.

The introductory essay "The Fluctuating Jewel" discusses the availability of jade during the Han dynasty. From at least the time of the Han Emperor Wudi's expedition to Ferghana in 101 BC, jade was in fairly plentiful supply. Many Han jades are of particularly pleasing colours, including black, yellowish-white, beige with brownish flecks, and greyish-green. At this time, agate was also considered within the *YU* (jade) classification, and two agate pieces dated to the Western Han dynasty are included in this exhibition (Exhibits 130 and 131).

Many of the jade styles that commenced in former periods, such as openwork rings, *huang* pendants, pectorals and belt hooks of all types, continued to be produced during the Han dynasty.

To make discussion of the jades in this essay more manageable they have been divided into six broad distinct categories as follows:

Ritual jades, burial jades, human and animal sculptures, articles for decorative use, sword and scabbard fittings, utensils and articles for domestic use

Almost all the jades that have survived from this period must have been found in tombs, but documentation of jades excavated from Han tombs has in the past been comparatively rare.

RITUAL JADES

These had been comparatively common since neolithic times and were still being produced in the Han dynasty in the traditional *bi-disc*, *huang* and *cong* shapes, although by the Han period the quality of most ritual jades was already in decline. The political and ritual functions of jade had also greatly diminished by this time and *bi-discs* are even found incorporated into the heads of jade burial shrouds 47 No.9, which seems to indicate that they had lost much of, if not all, their former ritual character. The most common ritual jades still in use during the Han dynasty were the *bi-discs*. The rice pattern and nipples that had been worked on such *bi-discs* for several centuries were still present, but by this time they had frequently been reduced to rather perfunctory decoration. On some *bi-discs* the nipple pattern was achieved by wearing away of the background in straight lines, leaving a hexagonal nipple raised above the surface (Exhibit 147). On a number of the more prestigious *bi-discs*, however, there are elaborate outer rings of decoration which are occasionally even reticulated. By the end of the Han dynasty the use of ritual jades appears to have virtually ceased, although *bi-disc* continued to be used. A jade *bi-disc* has even been recorded from a tomb of the 10th century AD, but this piece is probably a survivor from a much earlier period.

BURIAL JADES

As has already been explained, almost all jades that have survived from this period must have come from burials, but this category is confined to the jades that were specifically made for burials. These include the plain, thin plaques of jade sewn together at the corners to form a burial shroud which are well known from major Han dynasty burials, and the jade plugs or covers that were inserted into the body orifices such as the ears, nose and eyes. Most of these plugs and covers are plain and Exhibit 148 is a typical example. In addition to the shroud plaques, plugs and covers two other items are included in this category, namely cicada (*chan*), which were placed on the tongue of the deceased, and jade pigs (*wa*), frequently placed in the hands.

By the Han dynasty, there seems to have been a belief that jade was possessed of some magical property that helped to preserve the body, and this was the reason for the jade burial shrouds. Forty such shrouds, mostly in a fragmentary condition, have been found. During the Western Han, only gold thread was used for sewing the plaques together to form shrouds and at that time virtually all such shrouds were confined to royal tombs. However, in the Eastern Han, gold, silver, gilt-bronze or bronze thread was used, depending upon the rank of the noble being entombed (47, p. 68). The plugging of the orifices was also apparently thought to prevent the soul escaping the body.

Jade pigs and cicadas specifically made for burial are also commonly found in Han tombs. A cicada was placed on the tongue and one pig in each hand of the deceased. While some early Han pigs are comparatively naturalistically rendered, they became progressively more stylised, and the highly stylised jade pigs and cicadas made in the Eastern Han do not appear to have survived the dynasty. First appearing in the mid Western Han, this "Han 8-cut" or Han badao

style was seldom used for objects other than pigs or cicadas which, when carved in this style, are generally called sandao-chan or "3- cut cicada" (Exhibits 151 and 154). A bearded man amulet in highly stylised form of carving is also included (Exhibit 144). The burial of cicada, probably because in its larval stage the cicada lives for a long period underground, started before the Han dynasty. Examples from the Warring States period are included in this exhibition (Exhibit 120).

HUMAN AND ANIMAL SCULPTURES

Whilst representations of humans are common among the pottery figures found in Han tombs, human representations in jade, other than in the form of a bearded man amulet such as Exhibit 144, are very rare. We are therefore, particularly fortunate to have an example in the exhibition. Exhibit 134 probably represents a mourner and is certainly comparable to known Han dynasty bronze and pottery examples in a similar posture. The headdress is also comparable to those of some Western Han figures, and the colour of the jade is very similar to that of a *taotie* mask door handle found in the tomb of Princess DouWan (c. 113 BC). Bearded man amulets, such as Exhibit 144, have been known for centuries, but until one was found in the tomb of the second King of Nanyue (d. 122 BC), no similar amulet from a Han dynasty excavation had been recorded. A Western Han dating has accordingly been assigned to both Exhibits 134 and 144.

Animal sculptures from this period are comparatively numerous with animals from both the natural and imaginary worlds being included in the repertoire. Han jade carvers seem to have paid particular attention to the depiction of wild animals in all their ferocity, and both fighting and roaring animals (Exhibit

146) are known. The animals are generally shown in an energetic posture with a tendency towards naturalism. The claws and feet are emphasised, and even if not depicted in relief are incised (Exhibit 133). The flat bases of the animals are always undecorated, and many of them particularly the *kui* dragons, have their necks and heads retracted and, in some cases coiled, giving the pieces a vitality seldom seen in later depictions (Exhibits 133, 139 and 141).

Animal sculptures in silhouette continued in the Han period, and those sculptured in the round, rare in earlier periods, became comparatively common. Many Han dynasty animals have an elongated neck, with very simple slashes for the ears and eyes. One characteristic feature is the rendering of all the feet in a straight line or in two groups of two. Exhibits 146 and 149 are typical examples. Examples in jade and bronze are well known from dated Han tomb excavations.

The types of animals from the natural world sculptured in jade include bears with exaggerated manes, eagles, horses, lions, tigers and other felines, rhinoceros and buffalo, although buffalo appear never to have been used as a main motif. Mythological animals include dragons, *kui* dragons, depicted with a tiger's head and a sinuous dragon body, very commonly used to decorate sword and scabbard fittings, phoenix, normally depicted as a form of parrot with either a long or short feathery tail, a mythical animal with a long pointed snout, sometimes shown together with a *kui* dragon, and the ubiquitous *taotie*. It is also thought that the custom of presenting a bird-topped walking stick to respected 70 year old males was introduced at this time. Bronze bird finials from this period are well known but so far no jade examples have been published.

Some Han dynasty animal carvings also

bear very fine incised lines to indicate hair. This very distinctive feature can be found on the famous Western Han jade spirit figure riding a horse (99, No.119), and on a number of other jade animals that appear to date from the Han dynasty, or slightly later and on bronze animals of a similar date.

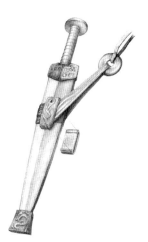

ARTICLES FOR DECORATIVE USE
There are jades for decorative use dated to the Han dynasty including articles for personal use such as garment and belt hooks, pectorals and pendants of all kinds. Other decorative items still in use at this time were *huang* pendants, split rings, discs, figurines, plaques and pointed pendants, many of which would probably have been parts of pectorials. Exhibit 138 is a particularly fine example of a pointed pendant from this period.

Jade pectorals are one of the commonest categories of decorative jades from the Han dynasty and it is noteworthy that no less than eleven sets of pectorals, each containing from four to nine jades were found in the tomb of the second King of Nanyue 47.

Jade belt and garment hooks, and garment rings made of jade, agate, or bronze inlaid with jade from this period exist in considerable numbers. However, garment hooks in similar designs were made from the Song to the Ming dynasty, and it is frequently difficult to differentiate between the Han originals and later copies. Some of the earlier hooks are, however, asymmetrical, a feature not found in the later examples (Exhibit 162).

SWORD AND SCABBARD FITTINGS
Sword and scabbard fittings probably comprise the largest category of Han jades that have survived to the present day. Once used by the nobles of the Han dynasty, these fittings

include a sword pommel, a sword guard, a scabbard chape, a sword slide and a fitting on the reverse side of the scabbard to the sword slide, through both of which a leather or fabric baldric was threaded and hung from a toggle ring placed between the scabbard and the belt. A group of such fittings, probably all datable to the Western Han dynasty or just before, is included in the exhibition. A drawing in the margin illustrates how the various fittings were placed on the sword and scabbard and between the scabbard and belt (Exhibits 124, 125, 133, 139, 140, 141 and 142).

The use of jade for sword and scabbard fittings began in the Warring States period and continued through the Han into the succeeding Six Dynasties period. Many of these fittings, particularly those from the Western Han dynasty, are beautifully carved. No less than fifty-eight of the 244 jades found in the tomb of the second King of Nanyue were sword and scabbard fittings 47, p.58.

The most important of these fittings, and together with the pommel also the commonest, is the sword slide (Exhibit 139) which was bound into the scabbard with the inner surface of its rectangular lower section level with the surface of the scabbard, and its longer tail section facing in the direction of the pommel. The flat bottom surface of the slides hanging section resting in a recess in the surface of the scabbard was seldom polished, or only superficially so. When placed on a level surface both ends of the slide should be elevated from the surface by at least the depth of the lower bar. Genuine slides also frequently show traces of iron or bronze and signs of considerable wear on the lower section. All of these factors point towards the authenticity of the slide. However, sword slides have been extensively copied since Song times, but during this later period their method of use does not seem to have been fully understood.

The *kui* dragon is frequently found on sword and scabbard fittings of all types and several examples are included in the current exhibition (Exhibits 133, 139 and 141). The *kui* dragon was probably the most popular animal in the Han dynasty jade repertoire, and care seems to have been taken to ensure that all the claws or feet of such dragons and those of other animals were shown either in high relief or indicated by incisions (compare Exhibit 133). Such care did not extend to later copies.

UTENSILS AND ARTICLES FOR DOMESTIC USE

The development of the Chinese bureaucracy during the Han dynasty led to a demand for seals, and examples of very fine quality seals, some of them made of jade, were produced at this time. Jade seals are normally square and are frequently topped by an animal such as a tortoise or *kui* dragon (Exhibit 159). Exhibit 159 may, however, date to slightly after the Han dynasty, since a similar piece found in a Han dynasty tomb does not have the extensive ribbon-like excrescenses seen on this exhibit. In addition to seals, rhytons, covered boxes, beakers and cups 99, p.208 are known from the Han dynasty, but such vessels are rare 47.

During the second century BC a great interest in music developed, and jade was used to tune musical instruments. Exhibit 143 is an example of a jade tuning pipe dated to this period. We know from Han historical records that the use of jade for this purpose was banned in 9 AD with bronze tuning pipes being substituted therafter 87.

Brian McElney
January 1994

漢 代

過去，中國學者們均認為漢宋兩代為玉雕之巔峰期，
而近代學者則將這巔峰期提早至戰國時代。
無可否認，漢代玉雕質素極高。近年來漢墓屢有出土，
如完全未經擾亂的南越王趙眜墓，更增加近人對
漢玉的認識。

本書<隨時勢遷動的瑰寶>文中，已提及自公元
前101年張騫出使西域開始，玉材便源源進入中土。
漢玉顏色分黑、黃白、米白帶褐、灰綠等，瑪瑙亦為
美石之一，入"玉"的範圍，展品130及131即為西漢瑪瑙。

漢前已出現之透雕環、璜、尖珮、組玉珮及
帶鈎繼續流行。為方便討論起見，漢玉將分為六大類，
即禮器、殮葬器、肖生器、裝飾品、劍飾及日用器。
傳世漢玉大多來自墓葬，但有確切文獻的出土
漢玉不多。

禮器

禮器如璧、璜、琮等自新石器時代已有製造，到漢代
仍繼續，但其政治作用已明顯地減少，故品質亦大不如
前，璧甚至間或充當殮葬玉衣片之用(47,圖9)。璧的
紋飾大多為穀紋或乳丁紋，部份琢工苟簡，有時只以
縱橫交錯的直線剷去玉的表面，從而特出六角形的
乳丁紋(展品147)。較高質素之璧，外區多雕繁複
或鏤空紋飾。至漢末，玉禮器除璧外幾乎絕跡。十一世
紀墓葬曾出土玉璧，但該器應是較早之物。

殮葬器

殮葬器包括縫製玉衣用之玉片，用以充塞或掩蓋死者
五官之琪、塞、瞑目等，此類大多素面無紋(展品148)。
此外，尚有放在死者舌上之蟬和手中之豚。

漢人認為玉可保屍體不腐，故有玉衣的出現。
過去三十年中出土玉衣四十套之多。西漢玉衣多用縷，
為王室專利，東漢玉衣則分金、銀、銅縷，按死者的
爵位而定。九竅玉，是為使死者魂魄不出竅。

豚和蟬是殮葬器中最常見的。蟬放在死者舌上，
豚則分置左右手中。漢早期玉豚造型逼真，後無論是豚
或蟬都趨於簡化，一般稱為"漢八刀"或"三刀蟬"(展品
151及154)。類似此種雕工的，還有一種有鬚人形佩飾
(展品144)。蟬作為殮葬品，漢代之前已有，想是因為蟬
之幼蟲長時期居於泥土中之故。本展覽之蟬(展品120)為
戰國時之物。

肖生器

漢代陶俑屢有出土，但除上述有鬚人形佩飾外，人形玉
雕極為罕見。展品134玉製哭喪者是稀有之作，與西漢
青銅人像或陶俑頗接近，其顏色則類似滿城中山靖王

劉勝妻竇琯墓出土之玉鋪首。有鬚人形珮傳世品甚多，
唯出自漢墓者則以南越王墓中玉人為首宗。因此，
展品134及144斷為西漢之物。

動物肖生，無論是圓雕或片狀雕，均極普遍，
題材取自自然界或神話傳說。動物多形態兇猛，作
搏鬥或吼叫狀(展品146)。玉工特別強調動物的
四肢，多以浮雕或細線刻劃(展品133)，底部不刻
紋飾。各種動物，尤其是螭龍的頭及頸部向下旋，充
滿動感，為後期作品所不及。值得注意的是，動物
頸部細長，耳及眼部只寥寥數刀，四肢一排並列或
分為兩組(展品146及149)，此類動物除玉製外
亦有青銅製。

取自自然界之動物有熊、鷹、馬、獅、虎、
犀、水牛等，唯水牛甚少作為主要題材。神獸則有龍、
螭(龍身虎首)、鳳、饕餮、和一種長鼻獸(間中與螭一起
出現)。龍及螭多用於劍飾，鳳形如鸚鵡，尾部或長或
短。相傳獻鳩杖首予七十高齡老人之習俗始於
漢代，傳世有銅杖首，但玉杖首未有發現。

漢玉雕另一特徵，是以細微的剔線刻劃動物的
毛髮，如漢昭帝平陵遺址出土之仙人奔馬(99,圖119)。
此特徵在漢或稍後玉器及青銅器均可見到。

裝飾品

裝飾品包括帶鈎、珮及組玉珮。璜、玦、環、人形珮、
尖珮(展品138)等可能是組玉珮的成員。此時，
組玉珮極盛行，南越王墓即出土十一套之多。帶鈎、
衣環亦普遍，多為玉或瑪瑙製，亦有青銅嵌玉者。宋明
多仿漢帶鈎，幾可亂真。漢帶鈎形多不規則和不對稱，
後仿者往往忽略此點(展品162)。

劍飾

劍飾傳世品極多，有劍首、劍格、璲、珌及用以連繫
劍鞘及衣帶之環，各項均可在本展覽中見到。它們的
用途可參考插圖。

玉劍飾始於戰國時期，漢代六朝繼續使用，漢劍飾雕工尤為精美，南越王墓出土二百四十四件玉器，其中五十八件為劍飾(47,頁58)。

劍飾又以璏(展品133)及劍首最為普遍。璏背面有長方銎孔，兩端有鉤向下垂卷，銎孔繫於劍鞘，長鉤向上，銎孔大都不拋光，或只略作打磨。古玉璏大都有磨損痕跡，或附銅鐵殘留，後仿器因未經使用，大多完好無損，亦無金屬殘跡。宋代多仿製玉璏，唯對其用法不甚了解。

螭為劍飾中最常見之紋飾(展品133,139及141)，螭足及爪多以高浮雕或線刻表現(展品133)，雕工之精細為後仿者所不及。

日用器

漢代實行中央政權，公文來往促進璽印的使用。漢印多為方型，有龜及螭鈕。展品159或許稍晚於漢，但類似玉印曾出土漢墓之中。此外，角形杯、蓋盒、杯等均有玉製，但不多見(47)。

漢代音樂發達，玉管時有被用來釐定音律，展品143即為其中之一。據史書記載，玉莽始建國時期，禁用玉管，而以銅管代替(87)。

129

OPENWORK FLAT CIRCULAR DRAGON

WESTERN HAN DYNASTY
(206 BC - 8 AD)

PE715

DIAMETER : 2.9 CM
THICK : 0.5 CM

Openwork ring in opaque green-white nephrite worked into the
contained form of an open-mouthed, long eared and toothed dragon
rolled or curled around itself into a circular posture with hair
striations and muscular curls picked out in finely modeled detail.
Both sides are identical.

There is much graceful movement in the confinement of the curled
up posture of this piece. (AHF)

Compare: 28 No.B 50
Collection: The Peony Collection

130

BLOOD-RED AGATE
DAGGER SCABBARD SLIDE

WESTERN HAN DYNASTY
(206 BC - 8 AD)

BATEA 449

LENGTH : 5 CM.
WIDTH : 2.5 CM
HEIGHT : 2 CM

Blood-red spotted brown and clear agate dagger scabbard slide,
the plain arched top with three undecorated longitudinal bands,
the outer bands concave, the inner band convex, the rectangular
section pendant below the central section of clear but crackled
uncoloured agate.

Agate of this colour seems to have been popular in the Western
Han dynasty and has been found in some burials of this period.
Agate of this colour is thought to have been found in China's
extreme south. (BSM.)

131

BRICK-RED AGATE BRACELET

WESTERN HAN DYNASTY
(206 BC - 8 AD)

BATEA 550

DIAMETER OVERALL: 7 CM

DIAMETER OF APERTURE: 5.1 CM

Agate circular bracelet the outer edge coming to a point in contrast
to Exhibit 123, where the outer edge is itself a narrow plane, the
whole formed by six planes round the inner edge, the colour deep
brick-red and smoky-grey with veins.

Agate rings of this type were part of a pectoral set. The fact that the
outer edge comes to a point dates this piece after Exhibit 123.
(BSM)

Previously published: 77, pl. VII

132

OX-MASK *BI-DISC*

WESTERN HAN DYNASTY
(206 BC - 8 AD) (2ND CENTURY BC)
PE656

DIAMETER : 10.7 CM
THICKNESS : 0.5 CM

Bi-disc of "*huan*" type with a small central hole. A plain narrow bevel forming the outer edge inclines down to a continuous band of rope twist form in high relief which in turn encloses a broad band formed as three equidistant animal faces with sweeping outward-curving horns or brows forming a double S-shape in high relief. Above the forehead of each animal face is a thistle-shaped patch of convex cross hatching and flanked by rudimentary body silhouettes. The interstices between the double curving horn or brow formations are filled with high relief comma curls and stylized floral-spray or snake-body forms incised with spaced pairs of transverse lines. A similar high relief rope twist band divides the animal head band from a broad band of flattened field on which modelled tadpole or curled worm spirals are scattered in linear formation. This band abuts a bevelled inner border that encloses the central aperture.

Similar discs were found in the 1983 excavation of the tomb of the King of Nanyue who died in 122 BC (47 pl.32). The current English translation for this ox-mask form is "bucranium". This writer sees no problem with the word skull. Later in the Han period, the ox-mask feature is incised whereas in the period to which Exhibit 132 is assigned, it was executed in low relief in uniformity with all other details on the surface of the piece. (AHF)

Compare: (i) 47 pl.32 (ii) 27 pl.38A
Collection: The Peony Collection

133

BLACK JADE DAGGER
SCABBARD SLIDE WITH *KUI*
DRAGON IN HIGH RELIEF

WESTERN HAN DYNASTY
(206 BC - 8 AD)
BATEA 505
LENGTH : 5.1 CM
HEIGHT : 2.5 CM
DEPTH : 1.3 CM

Small jade dagger scabbard slide of greyish colour with extensive black inclusions, surmounted by a spirited *kui* dragon its head twisted over the back of its body, its claws, spine and incised tail all accentuated.

The *kui* dragon was a very popular motif during this period, particularly for sword and scabbard furniture. The specific inclusion of all its claws either in relief or by incisions both seen here, though not essential to the overall design, seems typical of the Han dynasty rendering of animals in jade. (BSM)

Previously published: 77, No. 30.

134

JADE MOURNER

WESTERN HAN DYNASTY
(206 BC - 8 AD)
BATEA 436
HEIGHT : 7.7 CM
WIDTH : 6.4 CM
DEPTH : 5.1 CM

Light yellowish-green jade squatting figure of a male mourner, his arms bare to the elbows protruding from pendant sleeves; his hands, one resting on its palm, the other bent back with thumb extended as if grasping, the head with a rectangular flap headdress at the back, the garment with extensive folds.

Compare: This piece is the same colour and type of stone as the famous jade *taotie* mask door handle from a Western Han tomb in Shaanxi, illustrated in 99 Exhibit 172. The posture and headdress of this piece are also similar to some Western Han pottery and bronze figures. (BSM)

Previously published: 51 p.123, fig. 28

135

GOLDEN STONE *BIXIE*

WESTERN HAN DYNASTY
 (206 BC - 8 AD)
                        PE727
LENGTH : 4.4 CM
HEIGHT : 3.6 CM
WIDTH : 2.5 CM

Bixie or fearsome beast in opaque tawny-gold stone with some cream patches. The animal is standing in a position of expectant fury with snarling open mouth showing fangs and teeth. There are tufts of hair behind the cheeks, on the bushy eyebrows, on the top and back of the head, along the short spine, behind the lower legs, elbows and knees and sprouting in layered wing-like formations on the sides. The massive tail springs from the end of the spine and curls downwards bifurcating towards each side. A ribbon-like feature hangs down the front of the chest and bifurcates near the bottom to curl round into rounded terminals. The piece is pierced vertically from the middle back through to the base for suspension. The base is flat.

A very similar structure of sculpture was found in 1975 in the vicinity of the tomb of the Han Emperor Wendi at Xinzhuang village, Zhouling near Xianyang near Xian. There is marked similarity in the round shape of the head, the tufts of hair springing from the neck and the jaw, and the open mouth and the snarling fierceness but Exhibit 135 is a little more wooden and static than the magnificent Xianyang piece. Exhibit 135 can also be considered in association with an inspiration for the somewhat later early celadon pieces of the Western and Eastern Jin tradition, particularly in the structure of its upper tail which is formed in the characteristic shape of an inverted barley grain head. (AHF).

Compare: 100 No.171
Collection: The Peony Collection

136

JADE SLIT- DISC

WESTERN HAN DYNASTY
 (206 BC - 8 AD) OR EARLIER
                    BATEA 420
DIAMETER OVERALL: 5.4 CM
DIAMETER OF CENTRAL APERTURE : 2.1 CM

Thin circular undecorated jade slit-disc, the jade stone of yellowish white colour with deep orange flecking.

Such slit-discs were made for centuries but the lovely colour of the stone used here and the polish both strongly suggest a Western Han date at a time when exceptional quality jade, such as this, was in good supply. (BSM)

137

YELLOWISH JADE TOGGLE

HAN DYNASTY
 (206 BC - 220 AD)

BATEA 597

DIAMETER OVERALL: 4.5 CM
INNER DIAMETER: 3.4 CM
HEIGHT: 2.5 CM

Brown flecked yellow jade toggle with two broad concave bands, the whole undecorated.

The working of the concave bands is similar to that on other jade pieces from this period, and is also comparable to a gilt bronze of the period seen by the writer. (BSM)

138

YELLOW JADE POINTED PENDANT WITH *KUI* DRAGONS

WESTERN HAN DYNASTY
 (206 BC - 8 AD)

BATEA 433

LENGTH : 5.8 CM
WIDTH: 4.1 CM.

Yellow jade pointed pendant of slightly convex pointed shield shape. There is a *kui* dragon astride the hole in the centre of the pendant one leg and the rear of its body partially obscuring the hole and the head of the dragon in the centre of the top of the shield also partially obscures the hole, with one front leg clutching the rim. A baby *kui* dragon is depicted on the rim of one side. The pointed pendant has traces of earth encrustation. The reverse is concave in the centre with incised scrolling patterns.

This type of pendant used to be called an ornamental archer's ring but its resemblance to an archer's ring is very remote. The use of such pointed pendants as a mortuary orifice plug has been suggested. Several pointed pendants of a similar shape, but somewhat simpler design were found in the tomb of the posthumously named Emperor Wen, Zhao Mo, King of Nanyue who died in 122 BC. The position of their discovery suggests that they are individual pendants and not items from a pectoral or orifice plugs. (BSM)

Compare: (i) 47, Nos 66-67, 145 and 155 (ii) 19, No. 79

139

JADE SWORD SCABBARD SLIDE WITH *KUI* DRAGONS IN HIGH RELIEF

WESTERN HAN DYNASTY
(206 BC - 8 AD)

BATEA 440

LENGTH : 7.1 CM
WIDTH : 2.3 CM
HEIGHT : 1.9 CM

Sword scabbard slide of yellowish-white jade with blackish-brown suffusions decorated with a *kui* dragon in high relief on the top, its head and neck typically retracted, and a baby *kui* dragon emerging from the shorter end of the slide. The longer end of the slide is pierced with a hole for hanging decorative appendages.

The additional hole for hanging decorative appendages is unusual, but there is a similarly dated slide in the National Palace Museum in Taipei, which also has this feature. The way the smaller dragon emerges from the end surface of the slide and gazes at the larger dragon is typical of such scabbard slides. (BSM)

Previously published: 51 p.119 fig. 20
Compare: 19, Exhibits 86 and 88.

140

SWORD SCABBARD FITTING WITH *TAOTIE*

WESTERN HAN DYNASTY
(206 BC - 8 AD)

BATEA 444

LENGTH : 5.4 CM
WIDTH : 3 CM
HEIGHT: 1.6 CM

Greenish-white jade sword scabbard fitting of shallow elongated horizontal D-section carved with *taotie* eyes at one end, the small vertical face with a stylised mouth, the top with a narrow raised central band, each side of which has C and S patterns in low relief like a flattened foliated monster body, the rear vertical end with stylised C and S scrolls and split tail. Signs of wear are evident on the bottom bar, the underside of which is unpolished.

Such sword scabbard fittings were normally placed on the underside of the scabbard from sword scabbard slides, such as Exhibit 139. They are usually undecorated, no doubt to avoid snagging on the wearer's clothing. The elaborate decoration here is unusual. The pattern on the top of this piece is, however, very similar to that on the jade pillow found in the tomb of Prince Liu Sheng dated to c.113 BC. (BSM)

Previously published: 51, p. 119, fig. 19

141
SWORD SCABBARD CHAPE
WITH *KUI* DRAGON AND BEAR

WESTERN HAN DYNASTY
 (206 BC - 8 AD)
                                    BATEA 582

LENGTH : 5.4 CM
WIDTH : 4.5 CM
DEPTH : 1.2 CM

A sword chape of slightly tapered rectangular lozenge form, one side carved with a lively long-tailed *kui* dragon rearing up its body addorsed, its head grasping the foot of a small bear-like creature depicted in relief in the corner. The dragon's tail is powerfully twisted and comes to a point. The reverse face of the chape is decorated with interlocking scrolls. The top pierced for affixing to the end of the scabbard.

The bear-like animal shown on this example is occasionally found with *kui* dragons but seems never to be found on its own. (BSM)

Previously published: 51, p.119, fig.19
Compare: 97, No. 162 19, Nos. 93 and 95

142

GREYISH JADE TOGGLE

WESTERN HAN DYNASTY
 (206 BC - 8 AD)
                          BATEA 445
OVERALL DIAMETER: 4.7 CM
DIAMETER CENTRAL APERTURE: 1.4 CM.

Jade toggle of round fat *bi-disc* shape with both the inner and outer edges neatly rounded, the jade of greyish-white colour with extensive brown and black rivering.

This type of toggle was apparently called a *sui* and was used with bindings between the scabbard and the belt. Similar toggles, distinguishable from this type by being thin and lacking the body of this piece, were used to tie a monk's robe.(BSM)

Previously published : 51, p.119, fig. 17

143

CIRCULAR JADE PITCH PIPE (*LÜGUAN*) WITH INSCRIBED DATE 122 BC

WESTERN HAN DYNASTY
(206 BC - 8 AD)

BATEA 530

LENGTH : 5.6 CM
DIAMETER : 1.8 CM

Small white jade pitch pipe with slight light brown suffusions and a faint inscription in clerical script "*Yuanshou yuan nian liu Yue Bing wu shuo ri zao zhonglu*" which translates to: "1st day of lunar month, 6th month cyclical 1st year of reign Yuanshou, this zhonglu made". The date corresponds to 122 BC and is particularly interesting in the inclusion here of the cyclical month date, very seldom used in later periods.

Zhonglu is a note on the Chinese musical scale. The history of the Han dynasty (Han shu) records considerable developments in music during the Western Han dynasty and the use of jade tubes for the tuning of musical instruments at this time. They also record the banning of jade for this purpose in the 1st year of the Wang Mang Interregnum corresponding to 9 AD. The use of jade for pitch pipes as here is dicussed and the subsequent prohibition of its use for this purpose is mentioned in 87, but other than the present example, few, if any, are known. (BSM)

Previously published : 77 No. 31.

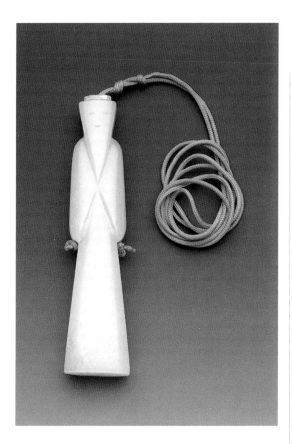

144

BEARDED OLD MAN PENDANT IN (HAN) 8-CUT STYLE

WESTERN HAN DYNASTY
(206 BC - 8 AD)

BATEA 442

HEIGHT : 7.5 CM
WIDTH : 1.8 CM

White jade standing figure of a bearded old man, his hands hidden by the long pendulant sleeves of his robe, the jade with some rust coloured suffusions at the back where the robe's belt.is visible. Pierced for suspension from the top the hole splits in two like an inverted Y and emerges at the bottom of the robe-covered arms, the carving extremely simple in so-called Han 8-cut style.

This type of figure is well known with copies being made as charms for centuries. Such copies however are generally incorrectly pierced through from top to bottom. No example from a recorded excavation had been found, however, before a similar figure to the present example was excavated in the 1980's from the tomb of the posthumously named Emperor Wen, Zhao Mo, King of Nanyue who died in 122 BC. That example is now exhibited at the Guangzhou Museum containing the treasures from his tomb, but was not included in the exhibition of the tomb's jade treasures published in 47. (BSM)

Previously published: 51, p.124, fig. 30
Compare: 37, No. 115

145

LARGE BEARDED OLD MAN

WESTERN HAN DYNASTY
  (206 BC - 8 AD)
                                    PE748
HEIGHT : 14.2 CM
WIDTH : 5.7 CM
DEPTH : 2.3 CM

Huge figure of a "bearded old man" formed in semi-opaque olive-green nephrite with cream parts as a robed long sleeved and bearded figure of a man. There is a broad perforation drilled horizontally from side to side through the neck for suspension.

This piece may be compared with Exhibit 144 with which it has strong similarities and is clearly of the same period. Similar examples exist in wood but jade examples are rare. Comparison may also be made with the famous similar piece in the Avery Brundage collection (1 pl.XX). Exhibit 145 is of unusually large size and the horizontal perforation through the neck is to be distinguished from the normal form of inverted Y-perforation clearly demonstrated in Exhibit 144. (AHF)

Compare: (i) 1 pl.xx (ii) 46 No.550-552
Collection: The Peony Collection

146

BLACK JADE TIGER

WESTERN HAN DYNASTY
 (206 BC - 8 AD)
                BATEA 411
LENGTH : 4.3 CM
HEIGHT : 3.7 CM
WIDTH : 3.8 CM

Tightly curled jade tiger, its raised head turned
sideways with all four paws facing to the front,
its long tail coming up between the legs and
extending over the back, its mouth open in a
roar, the dark stone of smooth blackish colour
with brown veins and markings. The base is flat
and undecorated and the ears are depicted as
simple slashes.

The arrangement of all the paws in a row or
sometimes in two pairs can be seen on a number
of animals both in jade and bronze of this period.
The form is very similar to the famous inlaid
bronze leopards excavated from the tomb of Princess
Douwan (c.113 BC). (BSM)

Previously published: (i) 82, No. 9 (ii) 37, No. 123 (iii) 51, pp 121, fig. 22

147

INCISED PHOENIX *BI-DISC*

WESTERN HAN DYNASTY
(206 BC - 8 AD)

PE618

DIAMETER : 15.0 CM
HEIGHT : 0.3 CM

Bi-disc of semi translucent grey-green nephrite suffused with some blackish-brown and some off-white blotching and veining. Each face is polished to a very high gloss and carved with a narrow plain perimeter border surrounding a broad band of incised scrolling curl-form volutes and spirals. This in turn encloses a narrow band of vortical striations which itself encloses a broad band of raised honey-comb hexagonal raised reserves created by the diagonal cross hatching of widely spaced parallel lines. A small plain band surrounds the central hole. The rim is plain but scored with vestigial circular abrasion marks.

The style can be properly compared with Exhibit 132 but in Exhibit 147 there is a developed laziness that avoids raising the individual curl bodies - in fact, they are reduced to hexagonal flat forms created by cross-rubbed grooves. The outer border of dragons and the interstitial design have been reduced from low relief to incised work. The very flat profile of the design enables the imparting of a very high gloss polish on the piece which is typical for this type in the Han dynasty. (AHF)

Compare: 46 No.537
Collection: The Peony Collection

148

PAIR OF EYE COVERS

WESTERN HAN DYNASTY
 (206 BC - 8 AD)
 PE428

LENGTH : 4.5 CM
HEIGHT : 1.9 CM
THICKNESS : 0.3 CM

A pair of eye covers in translucent greenish nephrite of convex oval shape with pointed ends each pierced with a small hole for sewing thread attachment. The back is flat.

The eye covers form part of a set of seven stoppers inserted into the body orifices of important corpses at burial. It is not uncommon to find the full set - with or without the famous jade suits of the Han period. (AHF)

Compare: (i) 46 No.581 (ii) 68 pl.CIV No.9, 10, 11 (iii) 66 No.153
Collection: The Peony Collection

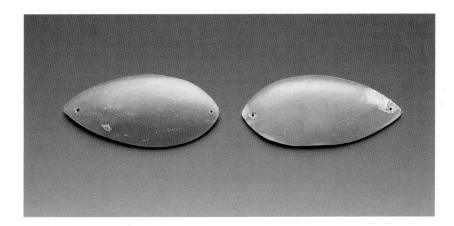

149

BLACK JADE RECUMBENT BEAR INSERT

HAN DYNASTY
 (206 BC - 220 AD)
 BATEA 479

LENGTH : 4.5 CM
HEIGHT : 2.5 CM
DEPTH : 1.6 CM

Black jade recumbent bear with prominent ruff, its feet and paws all aligned together, its eyes and ears made by simple indentations, the base flat undecorated but pierced for mounting. The design and depth of the body suggests that this was an insert for a metal mounting, such as a belt buckle.

The bear was a very popular subject in the Han dynasty and is generally depicted with a prominent ruff as here. The aligning of all the feet or pairs of feet is a convention found on many jade animal carvings of this dynasty, such as Exhibit 146. (BSM)

Previously published: 77 No. 28
Compare: 82, No. 9

150

WHITE DRAGON HEAD BELT HOOK

WESTERN HAN DYNASTY
  (206 BC - 8 AD)

PE404

LENGTH : 3.8 CM
HEIGHT : 1.8 CM
WIDTH : 1.5 CM

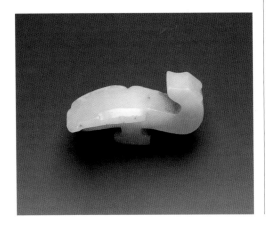

Belt hook in translucent white nephrite discoloured down one side to coffee-brown with black flecks. The piece is entirely sculpted at an angle out of true and stands on a square foot placed midway. A much simplified horned dragon's head forms the terminal hook and the shaft is bordered on the right side with a bevelled edge and a wing-like projection.

By the time of the Han dynasty, the jade belt hook in the form of a single carved piece of jade was very well established and remained so until the Qing dynasty. See Exhibits 313 and 314 for archaistic examples of the Song to Ming period. The interest in Exhibit 150 is the strong cubist slashed structure which falls well into the so-called 8-cut style of three-dimensional sculpture in animals such as the pig, rabbit and cicada which can be seen in Exhibits 151 to 154 inclusive. (AHF)

Collection: The Peony Collection

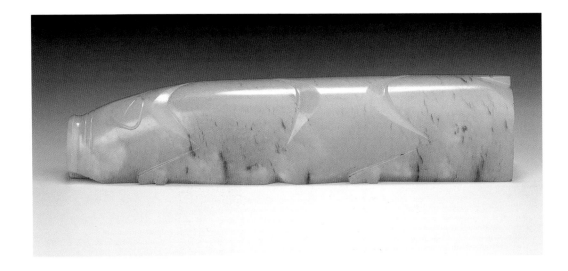

151

STYLISED JADE PIG

HAN DYNASTY
  (206 BC - 220 AD)

BATEA 438

LENGTH : 12.4 CM
HEIGHT : 2.5 CM
WIDTH : 2.4 CM

A jade pig of typical stylised Han 8-cut form, the jade of glassy pale celadon-green colour, the cutting very powerfully done and showing some minor earth inclusions.

There is no perforation and this unusually large example would therefore have been made specifically for burial. Similar examples have been found in the approximate position of the hands. Whilst the 8-cut style started in the Western Han dynasty, most examples date to the Eastern Han dynasty. (BSM)

Previously published: 51, p.115, fig. 6
Compare: (i) 37, No. 120 (ii) 84, No. 18

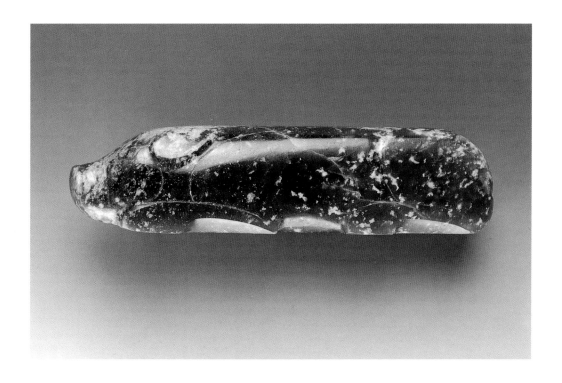

152

GREEN 8-CUT PIG

HAN DYNASTY
 (206 BC - 220 AD)
PE576
LENGTH : 9.6 CM
HEIGHT : 2.2 CM
WIDTH : 2.0 CM

Pig in dark green semi-translucent nephrite altered to grey-green in parts. The highly burnished body is cut with curving bevels, slashes and a series of incised lines variously to indicate flanks, shoulders, limbs and jawline. The ears are separately modeled to lie flat back along the head, the eyes are incised and the small snout ends with two circumferential wrinkles.

This piece is the classic 8-cut form of pig but already less mechanically austere in feeling than Exhibit 151. There is a feeling of roundness and softness not discernible in Exhibit 151. Exhibit 151 may accordingly represent an earlier development than Exhibit 152. As always with this style, the base is completely flat. In Han burials, the corpse was usually laid on its back with the arms down by the sides and a pig such as this placed crosswise below each hand. (AHF)

Compare: 46 No.554
Collection: The Peony Collection

153

WHITE CROUCHING RABBIT

WESTERN HAN DYNASTY
  (206 BC - 8 AD)

PE453

LENGTH : 5.0 CM
BREADTH : 2.6 CM
HEIGHT : 2.6 CM

A compact crouching rabbit in smoothly translucent white nephrite with a perforation drilled transversely through from elbow to elbow. The softly burnished body, limbs and long laid-back ears are delineated by a series of deep cut curves and slashes in the 8-cut style. The eyes and nostrils are simple dots and the base is almost flat.

The rabbit is the only mammal other than the pig and the horse featured in the Han 8-cut style. The horse and rabbit are both rare and very possibly had an auspicious significance. (AHF)

Collection: The Peony Collection

154

STYLISED 3-CUT CICADA

EASTERN HAN DYNASTY
  (25 AD - 220 AD)

BATEA 1216

LENGTH : 3.1 CM
WIDTH : 2.3 CM

Jade cicada in extremely stylised three-cut form made for burial, the whole consisting of four undecorated planes.

Jade cicada were commonly placed on the tongue of the deceased in early burials. The extremely stylistic nature of the cicada here is an example of the Han 3-cut style which can be compared with the 8-cut pigs (such as Exhibits 151 and 152) specially produced for burial particularly in the Eastern Han dynasty. (BSM)

Collection: The Rannerdale Collection
Previously published: 80. No.26

155

STANDING ROBED LADY

EASTERN HAN DYNASTY
(25 - 220 AD)

PE745

HEIGHT : 7.5 CM
DEPTH : 4.6 CM
WIDTH : 2.0 CM

Figure of a standing lady in fractured grey-green jade with black
flecking and one altered patch of black-flecked white to the rear.
The figure leans slightly forward and wears an all over enveloping
robe of quiet elegance. The robe has two vertical folds or grooves
from the elbow to the ground on each side. Her hands are held
together and extended in front of her with the long sleeves folded
over. The hair is arranged around the centre of the head into a
series of eight distinct panels and is pulled up at the centre into a
coiled bun.

There are very similar human figures among Eastern Han ceramic
ladies and there is a pair of similar jade ladies in fine white jade in
the collection of the British Museum (27 pl.65). The British
Museum pieces have a slenderness and elegance absent from
Exhibit 155 which is of a stronger and sturdier build yet it retains a
quietness and determination that seem to strongly evince Eastern
Han dynasty confidence and certainty of power.(AHF)

Compare: (i) 27 pl.65 (ii) 66 No.207
Collection: The Peony Collection

156
STANDING PHOENIX WITH OPENWORK CRESCENT

EASTERN HAN DYNASTY
(25 - 220 AD)

PE718

HEIGHT : 6.5 CM
WIDTH : 1.7 CM

Elegant openwork plaque form of thinly cut honey-brown opaque nephrite formed as a long tailed standing phoenix with a short upward curling wing. A curl-form excrescence matching and balancing the wing moves up from the chest to curl back beneath the chin. The long legs ending in open clawed feet stand on an upper curl of the long tail feathers. Another tail feather forms an adjacent curl and a third extends beyond to complete the overall crescent profile of the piece. There are incised and modeled curls at the angle of the jaw, on the breast and at the top of the legs. Both sides are identical.

This piece is so delicate and fragile that it is difficult to conceive of an independent use. For this reason, it was most probably made to be inserted into some other matrix, perhaps a lacquer vessel. There is an obvious and easy flow of movement that is clearly developing away from the stark 8-cut style. (AHF)

Compare: 69 XXVIII No.2
Collection: The Peony Collection

157
YELLOW JADE FINIAL WITH STYLISED *TAOTIE*

HAN DYNASTY
(206 BC - 220 AD)

BATEA 1232

LENGTH : 5.3 CM
WIDTH : 3.5 CM
DEPTH : 2 CM

Yellow jade finial with brown flecking and deep indentation on the base as if made for mounting as a jade handle onto metal, pierced through horizontally for suspension . The top with stylised *taotie* eyes and face, and convex bands and scrolling decoration on the sides.

The deep indentation on the base is very similar to that found on Han dynasty jade sword pommels, which are however normally circular. The carving of the bands, colour, polish and indentation all combine to suggest a Han dynasty date for this finial. (BSM)

Collection: The Rannerdale Collection

15 SIX DYNASTIES 220-589

During the Six Dynasties period China fragmented into separate kingdoms and there were rapid changes of dynasties, with the north and south generally being governed by different ruling houses. In some instances these kingdoms were dominated by nomadic peoples, who were outsiders without a jade working tradition.

It appears that the supply of raw jade was also severely interrupted at this time and that jade was scarce throughout the period. Few jades can in consequence be assigned to the period, and from published reports of excavated tombs jade finds appear to be rare.

RITUAL JADES

There are several points to note regarding changes that occured at this time. The use of ritual jades had virtually ceased by the end of the Han dynasty, and there have been only occasional finds of jade *bi-discs* in later tombs. A very fine jade *bi-disc* dated to the early Six Dynasties period is included in the exhibition (Exhibit 161). This dating was assigned on the basis of the similarity between the dragons depicted on this piece and gilt-bronze dragons from published tomb finds of this period.

BURIAL JADES

Jade burial suits are not known from tombs later than the Han dynasty, but jade pigs continued to be used for some time. The jade pigs from this period tend to be smaller and somewhat more naturalistic than those of the Eastern Han (Exhibit 170), and stone pigs were increasingly substituted for those of jade. Literary sources, such as Yan shi Jia xun, by the 6th century writer Yan Zhitui criticised the use of jade pigs by his family as an unnecessary extravagance. It certainly appears probable that the use of jade pigs went out of fashion towards the end of the Six Dynasties period since they are not found in published reports of later excavations. The placing of cicadas on the tongue also continued into the Six Dynasties period but this custom also seems to have gradually died out.

HUMAN AND ANIMAL SCULPTURES

Animal sculpture flourished during the Six Dynasties period and there are many fine pieces mostly in stone and marble that still exist today, such as the stone *bixies* in Nanjing. Most of these sculptures are of imaginary animals and are characterised by a great sense of movement and energy with some of the animals striding or slinking forward. Many of the animals have wings or ribbon-like protrusions sprouting from their shoulders, chest or hocks. Although such growths are also found on some Han dynasty animals, their popularity was at its peak during the Six Dynasties period. The fine line incisions indicating hair that first appeared in the Han dynasty, probably continued into this period since this author has seen such incisions on a *bixie* that compared well with some notable Six Dynasties sculptures.

Some of the animal carvings of this period also appear to have acquired human features (Exhibit 158) and occasionally several animal motifs are depicted on the same piece.

Buddhism developed and gained many adherents during this troubled period. The art of early Buddhism is acknowledged for the dramatic and radical role it played in the development of the Chinese sculptor's treatment of the human figure. It was also the handmaiden attending upon the necessary vehicle of picture images for educating the ignorant believer and non believer with illustrations of the stories from the Jataka series depicting scenes from the Buddha's life. One very popular and significant scene is that in the deer park at Sarnath near modern Varanasi, North India, where the Buddha preached his first sermon on turning the wheel of law through the Middle Way of the Four Noble Truths and the Eightfold Path. The concept of a huge park with wide expanses of green landscape, forests and hills inhabited by all manner of natural life such as flowers, trees, birds and animals filling up a vacuum as much abhorrent to the artist as to Nature itself, was the origin of a naturalistic turn taken by the art of China and which was changed by it forever. From this time, as is well represented in the Northern Wei period mural paintings in some of the earliest cave grotto paintings at Dunhuang, the entire subservience of natural things to the grand scale of the Buddha was vividly and effectively depicted. Floral, vegetal, mountain and landscape and common grouping designs appeared - not only for the first time in the applied arts of China (as was indeed the case) but as an innovative response to the need to reflect an integration of the natural world as a whole structure. Tenets and rules for communicative pictorial representation of animal and plant life had to be created and these became the bench mark for future development. There are numerous statues of Buddhist subjects in stone and gilt bronze, and no doubt, jade examples will eventually be discovered. Some figures of dwarfs such as Exhibit 172, are thought to date from this period since they can be compared to pottery figures from Six Dynasties tombs, but human figures in jade from controlled excavations of tombs dated to this period are presently unknown.

ARTICLES FOR DECORATIVE USE

While gilt-bronze plaques and belt hooks are known from this period, no examples in jade have so far been recorded from published excavated tombs. It also appears that the fashion for jade pectorals and pendant sets did not survive the Han dynasty, although individual pendants continued to be worn throughout all later dynasties. Some jade belt hooks appear to have been made at this time, and Exhibit 162, assymetrical in form and combining three different animals, could well be assigned to this period.

SWORD AND SCABBARD FITTINGS

The use of jade sword and scabbard fittings continued into the Six Dynasties period although it appears that at some point the use of the style of sword and scabbard with which such jade fittings were associated was discontinued. Even before this however, there had been an increasing tendency to substitute the cheaper material gilt-bronze for jade in fittings such as the pommel.

UTENSILS AND ARTICLES FOR DOMESTIC USE

Apart from jade seals which continued to be made, it seems that the scarcity of raw jade made the production of other jade articles a rarity. It was in this period that gold began to be seen as the height of luxury, and jade may have been sidelined by metal articles popular with the then dominant nomadic peoples.

Angus Forsyth
Brian McElney
January 1994

六 朝

六朝是分裂及動盪時期，北朝統治者大多為外族人，
對玉器的喜愛遠不及漢人。此時，玉材的供應亦甚稀少
(見<隨時勢遷動的瑰寶>一文)，故斷為六朝之傳世玉器
不多，亦鮮見出土。

禮器
禮器除璧外已絕跡。本展覽有一六朝璧 (展品161)，飾
龍紋，造型與同期鎏金銅器上之龍紋相似。

殯葬器
殯葬玉衣不再出現，但玉豚仍沿用，六朝豚體積較小造
型比東漢豚逼真 (展品170)，此後玉豚陸續被石豚代替。
六世紀時，顏之推在其<顏氏家訓>一書中，批評玉豚為
奢侈之物。六朝末期以玉脈和玉蟬陪葬之習俗已消失。

肖生器
動物雕塑以六朝為鼎盛期，質地多為石或大理石。
石辟邪到今日仍可在南京見到。動物多取自神話，充滿
活力和動感，作向前邁步狀。它們肩上長翅膀，胸前
及後足之毛髮像絲帶。六朝雕刻匠師繼承漢代以
細線刻劃動物毛髮之傳統，動物有時人像化(展品158)，
亦有數種動物共出現於一器上者。

六朝時佛教盛行，佛教藝術對中土藝術的影響至
為深遠。描繪佛祖生平事跡的畫像，由北印度傳入中
國，成為敦煌北魏大型壁畫的靈感泉源。傳世石佛像及
鎏金銅佛像不少，相信將來會有玉佛像發現。侏儒像
(展品172)因類似同期陶俑，被認為是六朝之物，但
六朝墓未見有玉人像出土。

裝飾品
六朝有鎏金銅牌及帶鉤傳世，但未見有玉牌或玉帶鉤
出土。組玉珮在漢後已絕跡，但玉佩飾繼續流行。展品
162想是六朝之物，因其呈不對稱狀，又以三種動物為
紋飾之故。

劍飾
劍飾似乎在六朝沿用了一段時期便中斷，未中斷之前，
玉劍飾已陸續為鎏金劍飾代替。

日用器
此時玉材來源短缺，除玉璽印外，其他日用器甚少玉
製，金器起而代之，其他金屬製品亦開始流行。

158

JADE TORTOISE

EASTERN HAN DYNASTY OR EARLY
SIX DYNASTIES
(25 - 420)

BATEA 455

LENGTH : 6 CM
WIDTH : 4.1 CM
DEPTH : 2.6 CM

Jade tortoise with snake-like head on longish retracted concertinaed neck emerging from its front, the legs bent like human arms at the elbows and held close to the body, the tail swirling to a point, the carapace covered with worn hexagonal patterns divided into four planes by a central ridge and two additional lower ridges, the whole carapace with a stylized key-fret surround, the jade of buff colour with dense light-brown rivering.

The tortoise was a sacred animal in China and an emblem of longevity, strength and endurance and was a popular subject in Chinese art from the Han dynasty on. This example is undoubtedly an early representation of the subject and the human-like arms suggests an Eastern Han or early Six Dynasties date as appropriate. The incorporation of anthropomorphic features into animals was popular during this period. (BSM)

159

SQUARE SEAL WITH *KUI* DRAGON FINIAL

EARLY SIX DYNASTIES
(220 - 420) OR EARLIER

BATEA 450

EACH SIDE: 3.2 CM
HEIGHT : 2.3 CM

A square jade seal of fatty-white coloured jade with blackish-brown suffusions surmounted by a bearded *kui* dragon, its one horned head coiled like a spring on its body, its bifurcated tail curled to a point; some of its haunches with planed ribbon-like protrusions, the sides of the seal plain, the shoulders with one narrow concave sloping facet.

The *kui* dragon was a very popular subject with jade carvers in ancient times, particularly in the Han dynasty. The development of the Chinese bureaucracy at that time led to a demand for objects serving the needs of scholars and mandarins and numerous jade seals have been found in burials from the time of the Western Han dynasty on. The severely retracted screwed down posture of the dragon's head is typical of that found in the Han and early Six Dynasties periods. The planed ribbon-like protrusions on this example, however, can be compared to similar protrusions on sculptures dating from the early Six Dynasties period found in Southern China and an early Six Dynasties date for this piece seems appropriate. Such protrusions however started to decorate animals in the Han dynasty and a Han dating cannot be entirely ruled out. Such ribbon-like protrusions however had their greatest vogue in the Six Dynasties period. (BSM)

Compare: 19, No. 75

160

DRAGON AND PHOENIX POINTED PENDANT

EASTERN HAN DYNASTY TO EARLY SIX DYNASTIES
(25 - 420 AD)

PE214

LENGTH : 7.8 CM
WIDTH : 6.5 CM
THICKNESS : 0.5 CM

Chicken heart pointed pendant in fatty and translucent off-white nephrite. The top and side edges are elaborately ornamented with smoothly carved openwork in ornate designs of curved hooks and curvilinear motifs which contain a horned and winged *kui* dragon with a sinuous curving body and rope-twist tail at one side and a phoenix-headed creature with a curving double tail on the other side. The details of the dragon differ between front and reverse. The body of the pendant is carved in relief with an abstract intaglio of scalloped cloud scrolls among lightly incised feathery lines.

The style of this piece can be traced to the development of the archer's ring from the Shang dynasty through the Warring States period (Exhibit 122). It is associated with the emergence of the dragon and phoenix motif in the Spring and Autumn period. This directly led to the dragon and phoenix being mounted up on each side of an archer's thumb ring in the Warring States period - probably as a typical demonstration of the taste for imaginative luxury of the day. Once introduced in the Warring States period, this form had a long life of uniform production with only slight, but definite, differences of finish and taste. The marriage in Exhibit 160 of refined but reticent workmanship with Han lacquer and bronze surface designs together with an overall gloss of great softness and delicacy, supports an Eastern Han or perhaps slightly later date. Regard should however be had for the cloud scroll and dragon body forms in murals in the importart Qianjingtou tomb at Luoyang published by Li Hou Bo in May 1994 Orientations and dated to 32 BC to 9 AD in late Western Han period. There is a great subtlety in the formation of the opposed double-sided hole plane levels through the body of the piece. (AHF)

Compare: <u>69 pl.XXVII</u>
Collection: The Peony Collection

161

BI-DISC WITH DRAGONS

EASTERN HAN DYNASTY TO EARLY SIX DYNASTIES
(25 - 420 AD)

PE164

BREADTH: 10.2CM
HEIGHT : 0.7 CM

A *bi-disc* of translucent greenish-white nephrite encrusted in parts on both sides with eroded iron residue, the central opening formed of a band sharply bevelled away from the centre; the perimeter rim is bevelled in and away from the elevated outer edge. One side is evenly studded with a grain or silkworm pattern of small tightly coiled roundels of comma shape on a plain surface. The other side is worked in relief of varying depths and angled planes with an old and a young *kui* dragon swirling and writhing on opposite sides of the central opening through a fantastic land or cloud-scape of waves, troughs, vortices and sharp peaks, some of the latter incised - like the dragons' bodies - with tightly ranged sets of small parallel lines forming comb-shaped striations. The sinuous bodies and long curving tails of the beasts appear from and disappear into, the body of the piece. The forepart of the smaller dragon, seen from above, has a long bifurcated club-tipped crest flowing from between two small ears. The forepart of the larger dragon, seen in profile, has an open mouth with a sharp incisor springing down from the upper jaw, and with a plain crest or mane lying along the top contours of the arching neck and partially obscuring a patch of incised diamond hatching situated behind the angle of the much extended lower jaw.

The long snouted form of dragon's head with an open mouth and a single upper incisor is found in relief around the base of some bronze lamps of the period of the Eastern Han and slightly later. The comma or curled worm design is perfectly worked and in excellent order and formation on a level base with an overall softness of finish which can be compared to that on Exhibit 160. Despite the violent representation of swirling clouds and dragons, there is a reticence and restraint which gives a feeling of maturity and which can be seen to reflect an Eastern Han independence in the production of Warring States design ideas, as with Exhibit 160. (AHF)

Collection: The Peony Collection

162

PHOENIX-HEADED
GARMENT HOOK
WITH *KUI* DRAGON
AND PIG IN RELIEF

EARLY SIX DYNASTIES
(220 - 420)
BATEA 467
LENGTH : 5.5 CM
WIDTH : 1.8 CM

Asymmetric phoenix-headed garment hook of whitish-grey jade with several black patches and a plain button on the reverse. The top is carved with three animals in low relief, a stylised phoenix, its head serving as the hook, its body depicted as a long curling streamer tail, a *kui* dragon round the end opposite the hook and a striding pig on the main body of the hook, all in low relief.

The multiplicity of animal motifs on the same object is suggestive of an early Six Dynasties dating and the asymmetric nature of the hook is also an early feature. The depiction of the phoenix by a long streamer tail as here, was common in the Han dynasty as mentioned in the essay on that dynasty. (BSM)

Previously published: 79, No. 54

163

OPEN-MOUTHED BEAR BEAD

EARLY SIX DYNASTIES
(220 - 420)
PE613
HEIGHT : 2.2 CM
DEPTH : 2.0 CM
WIDTH : 1.9 CM

A small bead formed in opaque sandy-gold nephrite as a seated round-eyed bear with erect ears, big frog-like eyes and collapsed breasts sagging onto a vast protruding belly. The snub nose features large simple pit nostrils and the large open mouth a double row of uniform teeth and the tongue resting on the lower palate. The left leg is crooked and pulled across the front of the belly and the spine is formed as a vertical ridge with a concave grooving on each side. The bead is pierced through vertically for suspension.

Jade entered into a phase of three-dimensional sculpture in the late Warring States period. Both human figures and animals appear although sparingly at first. By the late Eastern Han and early Six Dynasties period the jade workers had mastered all aspects of jade three-dimensional sculpture and a new sophistication developed in an intent and ability to portray humour. This piece is an excellent example of a fat, hideous but comic creature of a Walt Disney ingenuity. The slightly twisted open mouth is a feature typical of the Eastern Han or slightly later as are the distended belly and collapsed breasts, the particular significance of which is not yet clearly established, unless simply due to humorous exaggeration. (AHF)

Collection: The Peony Collection

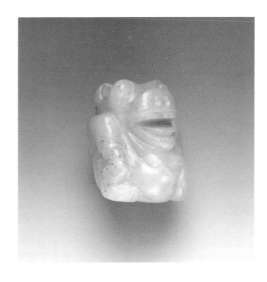

164

STRUTTING DRAGON

EARLY SIX DYNASTIES
(220 - 420)

PE205

LENGTH : 12.3 CM
HEIGHT : 4.7 CM
BREADTH : 0.9 CM

A figure of a sinuous crested feline or dragon-like animal. The creature is composed of a series of elaborate but smooth and muscular curves in a position of forward motion, the right foreleg extended in front, the long slender nearside rear leg held back and the chin held into the chest. The crest is in two parts with a short upper section and a longer lower curling section. There is a short curling projection above the rump and the tail bifurcates into a shorter, forward curling prong between the rear legs and a longer backward curling extension behind. The legs have clearly defined tendons and the feet have strong, elegant curling toes and claws.

Strength combined with elegance is a notable feature of this piece. The classic curled-back lower jaw is a direct inheritance from the Warring States dragon's head design but now somewhat softened. Despite the smoothness of the outline, there is still a tautness and tension in the angle of the right foreleg. The forward movement of this piece is typical of many animal sculptures of this period. (AHF)

Collection: The Peony Collection

165

MYTHICAL BACKWARD-LOOKING BEAST

EARLY SIX DYNASTIES
  (220 - 420)

PE437

LENGTH : 6.4 CM
WIDTH : 3 CM
HEIGHT : 2.8 CM

A mythical beast with small ears and a long single horn in off-white nephrite, in part suffused with brown and the whole right side with an opaque skin of decomposed chalky texture. The open-mouthed head is bent back to look along the spine and the vertebrae are individually modeled and lined on each side with hair striations. The spine ends in a bifurcated tail and the shoulders and haunches are adorned with double flame-like features in relief.

This animal captures tense listening and close attention. The vertebral treatment is very similar to that on the Western and Eastern Jin period celadon *bixie* animal vessels and is coupled with a naturalism which can perhaps be attributed to the incipient rise of Buddhism. (AHF)

Collection: The Peony Collection

166

WHITE SNARLING *BIXIE*
EARLY SIX DYNASTIES
 (220 - 420)

PE651

LENGTH : 7.0 CM
WIDTH : 3.0 CM
HEIGHT : 2.2 CM

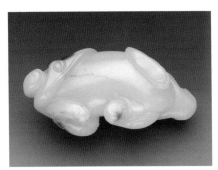

Bixie or mythical beast in translucent white nephrite suffused in places with reddish-brown. The creature is crawling along on its stomach with its head held at a slight tilt to the right and sunk into the shoulders. The well formed collapsed pinnas protect deep ear holes. The spine is formed as a sharp ridge which curves back in an S-shape from the right side to the left in alignment with the crawling posture of the body and limbs. On each side of the spine are short incised hair striations. On each side of the head is a formed jowl with incised hair striations. The mouth is open to reveal a set of clenched upper and lower incisor-like teeth fronting a lateral cavity, behind which the upper lip is curled up and pulled back against the nostrils in wrinkled formation to expose the upper set of teeth. Each foot has a comma incision on the sole and large retracted claws. From the front of each of the fore and hind limbs grows and curls back a pair of wing or flame-like extensions formed in relief and enclosing a small patch of diamond cross-hatching on each shoulder and haunch. The rear part of each of the lower fore and hind limbs is formed with incised hair striations. At the rear a long tail curls between the right hind leg and the body with a hair-striated side branch and terminates with a final curl on the right haunch.

The ridge immediately behind the nose is a very characteristic feature on animal heads of the Eastern Han period and immediately thereafter. It is found in dragons, horses and in *bixie* and in materials ranging from pottery, through jade to both plain and gilt bronze. The tail has the hair striated side branch or adventitious growth which, being asymmetrical, is also a typical design feature of the period. Beneath the pads of the feet is a very characteristic incised circular feature which sometimes shows a distinct bulge or swelling perimeter at the rear side. The small foreshoulder patches of incised cross-hatching are also typical of the period. (AHF)

Compare: 67 pl.XLII No.2
Collection: The Peony Collection

167
SEATED DEER WITH TINED ANTLERS
EARLY SIX DYNASTIES
  (220 - 420)
                    PEAAA
LENGTH : 8.8 CM
HEIGHT : 5.8 CM
THICKNESS : 3.8 CM

A hollowed-out three-dimensional figure of an antlered stag in translucent green nephrite. The piece is formed as a lying animal with cloven-hoofed legs simply indicated at each side and folded up beneath the animal. The head is held at an angle of 45° with the seven-tined antlers held along the length of the back. Large ears are well formed behind the simple and massively structured face with a broad forehead between large sensitive eyes and ending with tear-shaped nostrils and closed mouth. The body sits upon a separate flanged oval base of similar material to form a shallow covered box.

The treatment of the half relief folded legs follows very closely that shown in late Eastern Han and slightly later related ram-form bronze lamps. There is also a similar jade animal dated by James Watt to the Six Dynasties period in 82 pl.30. Laying long, many tined antlers along the back is also well demonstrated by a number of bronze and gilt bronze deer with the same squared shape to the face and whose fat bodies are formed of a single natural cowrie shell, which are securely dated to the the late Eastern Han period. (AHF).

Compare: 82 pl.30.
Collection: The Peony Collection

168
TURQUOISE MYTHICAL BEAST

EARLY SIX DYNASTIES
  (220 - 420)
                    PE619
LENGTH : 4.1 CM
WIDTH : 2.5 CM
HEIGHT : 1.5 CM

Bixie or mythical beast formed in turquoise stone with flecked sandy soil adhesions. The beast is squatting down on its belly. A long bifurcated crest with club terminals and transverse ridging lies back along the top of the spine. From each shoulder twin-flame or ribbon-forms lie back towards each haunch. The broad tail springs from a double comma formation at the base of the spine and curls straight down and back under the rear of the animal.

There are similar squat *bixie* type animals in gilt bronze, one particularly famous one in the Nanjing Museum being inlaid with turquoise spots. (AHF)

Collection: The Peony Collection

169

BIXIE MYTHICAL BEAST

EARLY SIX DYNASTIES
  (220 - 420)

PE649

LENGTH : 9.0 CM
HEIGHT : 3.7 CM
WIDTH : 3.0 CM

Mythical beast or *bixie* in semi-translucent honey-coloured
nephrite. The long body is tensed in an alert crawling posture with
the right hand fore and hind limbs set before their left hand
equivalents. The stalk-eyed dragon-form head has a laterally
flattened skull sprouting a single club-shaped horn with curling
finial which lies atop a bunched hair mane. The head is held at a
45° angle down toward the left side as if the creature is listening
with rapt attention to some important sound. The fore shoulders
are clad with serried scales. From each shoulder and each thigh
there sweeps back on each side a curved, flowing double ribbon or
flame-like structure formed as a smoothed longitudinal, concave
groove with occasional pairs of incised, transverse striations. Across
the strong chest is a curved, broad, smooth grooved collar or chest
plate and the lower spine is transversed with a series of grooves.

As with Exhibit 166, this piece demonstrates the small patches of
incised cross-hatching on the foreshoulders, partially covered by
the flames or wings. The exaggerated strength and power and the
slight swellings in the genital area separated by a longitudinal
groove are typical sculptural habits of the period (89, pl. 30).
The pads of the feet are incised as with Exhibit 166, but this time
with a pear-shaped outline. The tail has been damaged in
antiquity. (AHF)

Collection: The Peony Collection

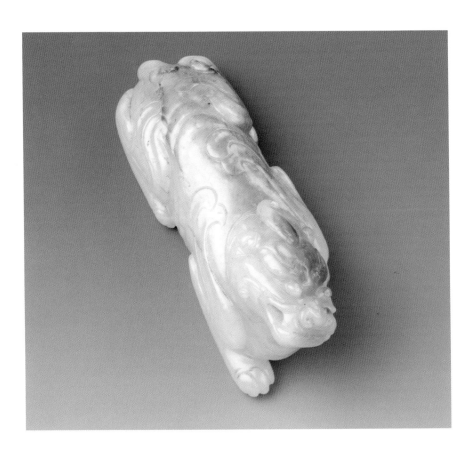

170

JADE SWAY-BACK PIG

SIX DYNASTIES
(220 - 589)
                    BATEA 402
LENGTH : 6 CM
HEIGHT : 2.9 CM
WIDTH : 2.4 CM

Jade sway-back pig of creamy brown colour with smoky black patches rendered realistically in squatting position; its snout slightly upturned, its tail curled to the side of its body. The swayed back pig here may have been designed for use as a brush-rest in a scholar's studio.

Jade pigs were used in burials throughout the Han dynasty and for much of the Six Dynasties from the third century BC on. At the end of the Han dynasty the pigs became more realistic as here, and this trend to realism continued into the Six Dynasties period, though at this time there was a tendency, no doubt because of the scarcity of raw jade material, towards substitution of stone pigs for jade ones. Yan Zhitui (531 to after 590) is recorded as having forbidden his family to use jade pigs and other burial accessories, stressing frugality as a virtue, and from about that time on the burial of jade pigs seems to have gone out of fashion. (BSM)

Previously published: 51, pp 115 Fig 7
Compare: 82, Nos. 15-17

171

JADE DOG-LIKE ANIMAL

SIX DYNASTIES
(220 - 589)
                    BATEA 465
LENGTH : 4.4 CM
HEIGHT : 3.7 CM
WIDTH : 3.3 CM

Jade dog-like animal of rather square shape, its front feet turned in, its claws pronounced, with long flap-like ears twisted to a point, beetling eyebrows and bushy tail finely incised, the pads underneath with extensive details, the jade of celadon green colour with extensive brown patches.

The jade used here is of poor quality which seems to indicate production in a period of shortage of the raw material such as this one. The claws and extremely detailed pads are unusual, and in combination are considered early features. The stance of the animal here is also comparable with gilt bronze animals of the period suggested. (BSM)

Previously published: 77, No. 34

172
BEARDED SQUATTING DWARF

SIX DYNASTIES
(220 - 589)

BATEA 122

HEIGHT : 5.2 CM
WIDTH : 3.1 CM
Depth : 2 cm

A degraded squatting figure of a dwarf with prominent breasts holding a ring and squatting on his exaggerated haunches, the jade very extensively degraded. (BSM)

173
SEATED UPRIGHT LARGE BELLIED *BIXIE*

EARLY SIX DYNASTIES
(220 - 420)

PE741

HEIGHT : 8.2 CM
WIDTH : 3.4 CM
DEPTH: 3.0 CM

A figure of a horned bear or *bixie* in semi-opaque burnt nephrite. The animal is squatting upright on its haunches with a great round stomach extending in front supported by massive hind feet with large claws. The creature holds its right forearm up to touch the right side of its chin. The left forearm is held atop the left side of the stomach. Large breasts hang flatly down above the stomach. The mouth is wide open and features well modelled fangs. There is a double horn hanging down the back of the neck. The shoulders and haunches are the origin of serried-wing or flame-form curving features and the small pointed tail is tucked between the legs.

There is much in common between Exhibit 173 and Exhibits 168 and 169 in relation to the extended wing or flame-type streamers. The fat bellied humour of the piece mirrors well that of the bear bead Exhibit 163. It is also appropriate to compare the long deep-toe structure, almost like a turtle or seal flipper, with the long, deeply furrowed toe structure of a number of well published animal pieces such as the striding *bixie* with a feathered man on its back now in the Sackler Collection in Washington 24 pl 9. (AHF)

Compare: 66 No.177
Collection: The Peony Collection

174

SEATED REARING PHOENIX

EARLY SIX DYNASTIES
  (220 - 420)

PE138

LENGTH : 4.2 CM
HEIGHT : 3.2 CM
BREADTH : 1.6 CM

A figure of a phoenix in fatty translucent greenish-white nephrite. The head is drawn back to touch the tips of wings which are folded across the back and the breast is puffed out, the tail feathers forming a fan and the foremost one curling forward at the tip to rest on the back of the head. There is a lower level extension of the tail feathers to the rear which forms a triangular support. The details of wing and tail feathers are incised and the eyes are simple shallow holes. There is one perforation between back and neck and hole drilled from the underside to the top of the back, emerging at a point at the back of the neck.

This shape is well known as forming an equidistantly spaced triumvirate on the lid of the typical late Warring States and Han period bronze vessels such as the simple low cylindrical *lian*, which often have bear-form feet. It is possible that this piece, whose sensibilities seem more rounded and softer than in late Han times, was one of a set of three on a lian top. The hole drilled from the base to the top of the back may be designed to take some attachment peg because the over-curling tail effectively prevents the through passage of any other kind of useful fastening. (AHF)

Collection: The Peony Collection

175

GREY ARCH-NECKED HORSE

NORTHERN AND SOUTHERN DYNASTIES
  (386 - 581)

PE746

LENGTH : 5.0 CM
HEIGHT : 3.6 CM
WIDTH : 2.0 CM

A seated jade figure of a horse with a short strong neck forming a distinct arch down into strong shoulders and a rope halter lying on its back. The haunches are rounded and undercut to the rear and surmounted by a transversely-pierced vertical ring formed by the looped tail. The legs and hoofs are well formed beneath lifting the body off the ground.

A similarly modelled horse at the famous White Horse temple between Luoyang and Longmen in Henan Province has been famous since the foundation of the temple in the Six Dynasties period. The animal is modelled on one type of the "blood sweating" horses of Ferghana (modern Kyrgyzstan) the centuries-old source of fine horses for the Chinese military. This originated in the Western Han period but tailed off after the end of the Tang dynasty until the Mongols subdued the whole of China with their small fast ponies in the 13th century. (AHF)

Compare: 31 pl.50
Collection: The Peony Collection

16 Sui and Tang dynasties, Five Dynasties, The Birth and Rise of Liao dynasty 581-950

This essay covers the period from the beginning of the Sui dynasty in 581 to 950 at the end of a period when jade ceased to be in short supply. The period starts with the reunification of China following several centuries of fragmentation. The Sui dynasty was followed by the Tang dynasty and both ruled over the whole of what was then China. One of the chief characteristics of these dynasties was the influx of foreigners into China. These foreigners bought with them all kinds of art forms and contemporary designs and shapes taken from Persian and Sassanian metalwork and other Central Asian motifs which were absorbed at this time into the Chinese artistic vocabulary. The whole period was very outward looking with a strong sense of exuberant energy and vitality, sometimes even of an aggressive form. The Tang period in particular was one of considerable luxury until the religious persecutions in the mid 9th century resulted in internal disorder and the dynasty entered a period of gradual decline. Before these persecutions, which reached their height in the decade between 845 and 855 and indirectly resulted in the supply of jade being interrupted, jade must have been in plentiful supply - a late 8th century decree banning the use of inferior jades for burial would have been senseless if jade were scarce at the time. It is worth mentioning that jades are rarely found in Tang burials, and it has been suggested in the introductory essay "The Fluctuating Jewel" that the popularity of jade was sidelined at this time.

The main products in jade during this period appear to have been items for personal use, such as jewellery and cups (Exhibit 180). Sword and scabbard fittings had ceased to be made of jade before the start of this period, and the swords and scabbards, with which jade fittings had been used in the Han dynasty and for a short while thereafter, had given way to a different type of sword and scabbard. Jades specifically made for burials such as pigs, cicadas and shrouds had ceased to be produced before this period, although the occasional *bi-disc* has been found.

The use of jade for belt plaques has been important since at least the Tang dynasty. The earliest known plaques, datable to the Tang dynasty, are solid and square or rectangular in shape. Larger, rectangular plaques called *chawei* equivalent in size to two squares, have their corners rounded at one end (Exhibit 191). These larger *chawei* pieces were meant to hang from a belt and their decoration is therefore to be viewed differently from that on the smaller plaques which were affixed to the belt itself. All these belt plaques are pierced at the back, generally at the corners, for sewing onto the leather or textile of the belt. Several examples are included in the exhibition (Exhibits 189 to 194). All the examples from the Tang and Five Dynasties periods are, (with three exceptions, one that has a buddhist lion motif and one set from the tomb of Wang Jian (d. 918) and Exhibit 194 that both have a three-clawed dragon motif), decorated with seemingly foreign (probably Sassanian) musicians or dancers.

The sumptuary laws of the late Tang dynasty restricted the use of jade belt plaques to the three highest ranks of mandarin and from that time on jade belt plaques were one of the favourite uses to which jade was put. These or similar sumptuary restrictions persisted until the end of the Ming dynasty, although no doubt when imperial control was lax they were frequently ignored, as was the case in medieval Europe. Jade comb tops, such as Exhibits 185 - 187, were another popular item at this time.

Whilst prior to the Tang dynasty the chief subjects for jade carving were animals and birds generally taken from the mythological world but occasionaly also from the natural world, the Tang dynasty for the first time introduced into the artistic repertoire flowers of all types. Initially these were introduced only as secondary decoration but by the end of the dynasty floral decoration had become in some instances the main decoration, and by the time of the Song dynasty it was commonly the main decoration. By now, the Buddhist inspired naturalism of art interpretation had taken a deep hold from its beginnings noted in the essay on the period 220-581, and a distinctive kind of flower and bird representation in the early Tang dynasty became widely used on metal wares, particularly gold and silver, and also on jade - see Exhibits 185, 186 and 187. Associated with this vegetal inspiration was the refined development of such features as the fern-sprout tail of such birds as the phoenix (Exhibits 188 and 198), as the coiled cloud scrolls along the bottom of Exhibit 183, and as the flower and leaf groupings and open lotus leaf curvature on Exhibits 185 and 187.

As we have seen from the essay The Fluctuating Jewel, it is believed that raw jade was in fairly ample supply throughout much of the period under discussion with the exception of the years 845-950 when the trade routes from the jade producing regions appear to have been badly disrupted and little jade entered China.

The Tang court's international outlook led to a fascination with exotic animals and ostriches, brahman bulls (Exhibit 200) and broad-tailed sheep (Exhibit 206) started to be imported at this time. Tang dynasty jade animals are similar in conception to those in the bronze and ceramic media with animals from both the natural and imaginary worlds being depicted. A deer with fan-shaped crest is occasionally seen in both jade and metalwork from this time but is seldom represented in Chinese art after the 10th century. Points to note are the emphasis placed by the jade carvers of the period on the musculature of the animals concerned, and the fact that while Tang jade carvers endeavoured to render animals in a naturalistic way they frequently had to compromise in order to bring their subject within the confines of the pebble. This is demonstrated by Exhibit 178, a jade horse with a knotted tail (such tails are found on both ceramic and jade horses from the Qin to the Yuan dynasty and in paintings up to the Yuan dynasty although not, it seems, thereafter). The horse (Exhibit 178) has one leg curving in around the body in a wholly unnatural manner (christened by the author "the India rubber leg syndrome"). The author believes this to be a typical Tang compromise and a number of other examples, dated to the Tang period are known 37, No.132, 82 No.64. Many animals from this period, both in jade and other media, are depicted in an alert posture, as if about to rise, and the author believes this to be a valuable pointer to a Tang dating.

It is suggested that a number of rather grey jades with reddish suffusions (Exhibits 198 and 199) were probably produced during the period of jade scarcity from about 845 to 950, since the use of such inferior material at a time of plentiful supply would be illogical. The designs on exhibit 198 with its phoenix with fern-sprout tail also accord well with those of the period suggested.

Brian McElney
January 1994

公 元 581至 951年

本文以隋代為起點，以公元951年為終點(951年之歷史
意義見<隨時勢遷動之瑰寶>一文)。隋唐之世，
甚多外國人在中土定居，波斯及薩珊朝金屬器和
中亞藝術對中國藝術，無論在器形或裝飾方面均有一定
的影響，玉器亦不例外。此時的社會活力充沛，唐代
更有趨向奢華的現象，直至九世紀中葉的宗教逼害，
引致內部不穩，自此之後，唐朝便走上沒落之路。
宗教逼害間接影響玉材的供應，但這之前玉材來源
充足，八世紀末，甚至有通諭禁止以劣質玉器陪葬。
一般來說，唐殮葬玉數量不多，金銀器受歡迎，玉器
退居次要地位。

此時，玉器多為裝飾品如佩飾，或日用品如杯碗
(展品180)、劍飾、殮葬玉衣及用以陪葬的玉脈和玉蟬已
停止製造，唯璧仍會間中出現。

最常見的是玉帶板，多是實心，呈正方或長方
形。銙(又稱鉈尾)比帶板大型，長度可能是兩個正方
形，一端的角修圓(展品191)。它們是自腰部向下垂懸
的，故紋飾有別於橫排的帶板。此兩類帶板背部均有穿
孔，便於釘縫於皮革或紡織物之上。

晚唐時，有法令規定三品或以上之官員才准用
玉帶板(展品189及194)，此習俗一直維持到明代。

但法令雖存在，是否嚴格執行則不得而知了。另一流行
飾物為梳背，如展品185至187。

唐之前的玉雕，多為神獸或大自然間的動物，唐
玉工則首創以花卉作題材。花卉先是作輔助紋飾，進而
演變為主要紋飾，到宋代，以花卉為題的玉雕已是
極常見了。

845年之前，輸入中土的玉材數量豐富，但845至
951年期間，貿易通道受到嚴重的干擾，因而進入中土的
玉料幾等於零。

唐朝對異邦之物有濃厚的興趣，進口的動物
包括：駝鳥、印度牛(展品200)、寬尾羊(展品206)等。
動物玉雕與同期之青銅塑和陶塑相似。較為少見的是
一種玉製或金屬製、頭上帶扇狀冠的鹿。此種鹿在
十世紀後不再出現。唐玉工注重刻劃動物的肌肉，造型
亦力求逼真，但常受玉子形狀所限。如展品178之尾部
打結的玉馬，馬的一腿圍繞着馬身，位置極不自然，
是受客觀條件所限的現象。動物多作警醒狀，像是隨時
會一躍而起，這是唐玉雕特徵之一。

本展覽中有數件灰色帶紅斑紋的玉器(如展品198
及199)，被斷為845至951年間產品，因這期間玉材
來源稀少，較次玉石亦被選用之故。

176

JADE IBEX PENDANT

TANG DYNASTY
(618 - 907) OR EARLIER
BATEA 461

LENGTH : 3.9 CM
HEIGHT : 2.8 CM
WIDTH : 1.7 CM

White jade ibex, the front leg, tail and one side with patches of light-brown skin, one front leg bent as if the animal is just about to get up, the horns carved in Han style; pierced through for use as a pendant.

The fashion for stringing jade animal carvings for hanging about the person developed at quite an early time and examples are known from at least the Eastern Han dynasty (see 37, No.120). The posture here, as if just about to rise, was particularly popular among Tang dynasty depictions of animals, but the convention is also found in some Six Dynasties animal sculptures to which period this piece may date. The ibex was an animal found in Chinese art from the Warring States period on. (BSM)

Previously published: 73, No. 35

177

BACTRIAN CAMEL AT REST

TANG DYNASTY
(618-907) OR EARLIER
BATEA 401

LENGTH : 6.9 CM
HEIGHT : 2.9 CM
WIDTH : 1.8 CM

Recumbent Bactrian camel in yellowish-green and brown jade, the camel lying down and its head stretched out. The base is flat and undecorated.

The Bactrian camel was a common motif in Chinese art from the mid Six Dynasties period through the Tang dynasty. A date slightly prior to the Tang has been suggested for this piece in 89 No. 32. (BSM)

Previously published: i) 82, No. 40 (ii) 37, No.129 (iii) 51, pp 122, fig. 27

178

JADE HORSE WITH
KNOTTED TAIL BITING
ITS REAR FOOT

TANG DYNASTY
 (618 - 907)
              BATEA 464

LENGTH : 5.7 CM
HEIGHT : 4 CM
WIDTH : 2.7 CM

Jade horse with brown and black suffusions, the
horse lying on its back biting its rear leg, its tail
knotted. The back shows the animal's powerful
muscles. The horse's front leg is curled round the
body to fit the shape of the pebble.

The treatment of the front leg (curling round the
body in an unnatural way to fit the pebble's
shape, christened by the author 'the india rubber
leg') and the depiction of the animal biting its leg
are both typical of this period. The emphasis on
the muscles is characteristic of the animals in the
naturalistic style and appears on many early
animals from the Tang dynasty on. Horses with
knotted tails are found in the Qin's emperor's
terracotta army and there are numerous
instances of such horses in pottery and in
paintings until the end of the Yuan dynasty but
thereafter this dressing of horses' tails seems to
have gone out of fashion. (BSM)

Previously published: 79, No.55
Compare: 37, No. 132 82, No. 64

179

PEACOCK HEADDRESS FINIAL

TANG DYNASTY
 (618 - 907)
PROBABLY HIGH TANG
 (684 - 756)
                        BATEA 506
HEIGHT : 4 CM
WIDTH : 3 CM
LENGTH : 3.5 CM

Jade peacock headdress finial of slightly yellowish-white colour, its raised and extended fan-tail with incised palmette feather eyes, its head held back and touching the tail, its beak holding a short lingzhi spray, its wings partly raised their tips touching the raised tail, the body with three pierced holes merging into one hole in the undecorated base, probably for affixing to a headdress.

Peacock and phoenix headdresses are occasionally found on the more elaborate pottery court ladies and dancers found in the tombs of the High Tang period. Compare for a pottery example No. 212 illustrated in William Watson's, "Tang and Liao Ceramics." The famous Imperial concubine Yang Guifei (d.755) is recorded as having worn only jade artefacts and such a headdress ornament in jade as here seems a likely accoutrement for the ladies of the court during this period. However, no example in jade other than Exhibit 179, is known. (BSM)

180

SMALL JADE CUP
WITH INCISED BORDER

TANG DYNASTY
 (618 - 907)
PROBABLY HIGH TANG
 (684 - 756)
              BATEA 1250
DIAMETER : 4.3 CM
HEIGHT : 2.7 CM

Small circular jade cup with incised border close to the rim, from which hang four pendant trefoil tendrils of obvious metal inspiration.

Jade cups are known from Tang dynasty excavations and similar examples to this, but in metal, are also known. (BSM)

Collection: The Rannerdale Collection

181
WHITE DANCING FIGURE

TANG DYNASTY
 (618 - 907)

PE581

HEIGHT : 7 CM
WIDTH : 2.3 CM
THICKNESS : 1.3 CM

Figure in translucent white nephrite formed as a soft booted dancer with loose gathered smock garment drawn in at the stomach by a belt from the back of which seven strip-form fittings, all depicted in very low relief, dangle over the buttocks. The strip fittings lie atop a hanging rear train which ends in a swirling fold behind the right foot. The right arm is held crookedly across the chest with the end of a long falling sleeve obscuring the right hand. The left arm, also in a long sleeve is raised behind the soft cap. The left elbow is missing due to old damage. The torso is twisted slightly to the right above the waist and the left leg is raised and folded at the knee across the right thigh in an attitude of motion. The centre of the back is pierced by a large and later cavity that joins a smaller hole pierced through the rear flap of the soft cap. There is a further small perforation above the right instep.

The strip fittings hanging from the belt of this man are typical of the leather strips with small bronze rectangular plates found in excavations from Tang and Liao tombs and widely featured in Tang mural paintings such as those in the tomb of the Princess Yongtai near Xian. The overall soft and loose smock-like garment is typical of the garb of Central Asians in the Tang dynasty. This piece is the only known jade piece featuring this kind of figure as a three-dimensional representation. The usual represention of these dancing foreigner figures in jade are in low relief on the top surface of belt plaques such as those in Exhibits 189 - 193 and three-dimensional ceramic representations are unusual; the type is only seen as a regular feature on impressed stamp cut-outs on Changsha ware glazed ceramic pots of the Tang period (21 pl.30) and on thicker walled bottle forms of the *Xixia* and *Qidan* late Tang and Five Dynasties period in northwest China and in relief panels forming the sides of some silver cups. There is also a very vigorous demonstration of the type, swaddled and spinning on a round mat, engraved on the two panels of a dowel-hinge double stone door found at Yanchi, Ningxia Hui Autonomous Region. (AHF)

Collection: The Peony Collection

182

ROUND OPENWORK DRAGON PLAQUE

TANG DYNASTY
(618 - 907)

BATEA 598

DIAMETER : 4.6 CM
DEPTH : 0.3 CM

An almost circular dragon plaque, the dragon of
the three-clawed variety with long snout, one leg
extended over the tail, its legs and claws forming
the outer edge of the plaque.

This type of dragon with leg crossed over the tail is
typical of the dragons dating from the Tang to late
Song dynasty. Most Tang dragons have three
claws, but this number of claws seldom appears on
dragons after the Yuan dynasty. The style of
carving seems typical of the Tang period. (BSM)

183

FLYING APSARA

TANG DYNASTY
(618 - 907)
PE446

LENGTH : 4.6 CM
MAXIMUM HEIGHT: 3 CM
THICKNESS : 0.7 CM

A figure of an apsara flying from right to left carved front and back in low relief openwork in translucent white nephrite.
The head has well formed facial features and a small stepped crown. The uplifted right hand holds a small plant in a dish.
The figure is bare chested with a close fitting robe or cassock tied across the back with a bow knotted sash. A single
ribbon undulates round the curved body to terminate on each side in a twin ended tassel beside the feet. Below the
stomach is a small openwork register of scrolling vegetation or clouds.

The apsara entered China through the extreme west along the Silk Road as a cultural camp follower journeying with
Buddhism from north India between the 1st and 3rd centuries after Christ. There are directly precedent examples in
Gandharan sculpture seen by the writer in Pakistan and in the Kushana sculpture of Mathura, north India even
possessing the idiosyncratic cross-over feet. Although the first popular imposition of Buddhism as a state creed was by the
Mauryan Empire in northwest India, following the ascent of the Emperor Ashoka to its throne in about 269 BC, the then
dying embers of the Macedonian invasion under Alexander across the Indus in 326 BC did not engender any
iconographic religious art with Grecian influence. The principal reason was that, for its first 500 years, Buddhism was a
religion without human form icons and the first production of the Buddha image, was not to occur until mid First Century
AD under the Kushana King, Kanishka. He supported the growth of learning at Taxila and of Gandhara art which was
firmly based upon Roman imperial art - a familiar influence through well established trading contact at that time. Hence
the Buddha's robes are modelled on the Roman toga. It is accordingly quite likely that as an acolytic supplement or
support for the principal object of religious devotion, the apsara itself was derived from, or from an origin common to, the
angel of early Christian art. The "lobster claw" terminals of the bifurcated ribbons flying around the body are more typical
of those on earlier jade apsaras in China rather than those on the later representations of this figure. The tight - and
curiously somehow asymmetrical - organisation of small rolled cloud scrolls is also indicative of an early date for the type
(compare the more uniform cloud scrolls underlying Exhibits 215 and 223). (AHF)

Compare: 100 pl.227
Collection: The Peony Collection

184

HOLLOW FLAT DRUM

TANG DYNASTY
 (618 - 907)

PE567

DIAMETER : 4.7 CM
THICKNESS : 1.2 CM

Flat drum form in opaque off-white nephrite. Each face has a
central roundel carved in low relief with a somersaulting dragon
with broad shoulders, hair tufts on the elbow, flowing mane and
trifurcated tail. Each roundel is surrounded by a border of key-fret
design. The edge of the thick convex perimeter is incised with a
series of lozenges with double scroll extensions.

The up and over formation of the dragon's body - rather like an
acrobatic act and not to modern eyes in any way befitting the
splendour or magnificent ferocity of the dragon - and the elongated,
spiking tufts of hair at the elbows and on the hindlegs, are typical
features of the late Six Dynasties period and early Tang dynasty. In
gold and in gilt bronze the dragon is found in free standing
formation but these have not yet been encountered in jade.
Compare the rounded back turning profile of the back of the
dragon on Exhibits 182 and 194. The tail of the Tang dragon either
terminates in a scrolling flourish as in Exhibit 184, or tapers away
to a spike as shown in Exhibit 194. The use of the key-fret border is
a frequent Tang dynasty device. (AHF)

Collection: The Peony Collection

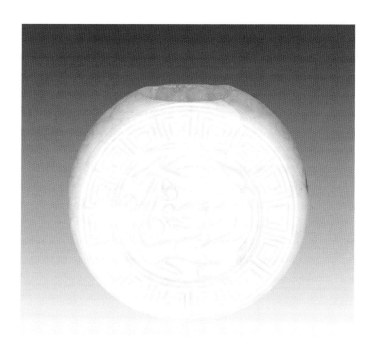

185

PEACOCKS AND FLOWERS COMB TOP

TANG DYNASTY
 (618 - 907)

PE223

LENGTH : 13.2 CM
HEIGHT : 4.0 CM

Comb top, in translucent grey-white nephrite with some traces of incipient alteration. The surface of one side is carved in bas relief with a design of three fully open flower heads arranged over an outspread leaf design extending beneath and out at each end of the flowers. The other side is carved in bas relief with a pair of strutting peacocks, wings raised and tails outspread, the curved outer edge of the piece lined by a raised ridge on each side.

The use of jade in the Tang dynasty seems to have been principally restricted to personal articles, whether for the boudoir or of a sartorial character. Exhibit 185 provides a good example of the naturalism of the decorative motifs that flourished in the Chinese art of the Tang dynasty. This naturalism is also well represented by the grouped open flowers and leaves on one side of Exhibit 185 worked in a strong and almost impressionist manner. Naturalism also guides the equally impressionist, peacocks strutting on the other side - again in very Tang dynasty taste. As is standard in such comb tops, there is a raised exterior border which confines the reduced ground level upon which the design details are arranged in low relief. (AHF)

Compare: 66 No.230
Collection: The Peony Collection

186

DOUBLE PHOENIX COMB TOP

TANG DYNASTY
 (618 - 907)
                                PE627

LENGTH : 9.5 CM
HEIGHT : 3.3 CM

Comb top in translucent white nephrite. Each side is carved in bas relief within a plain perimeter border with a pair of flying long-tailed phoenixes with spread wings, the foremost turning its crested and coxcombed head back to review the approaching progress of the other. The body and tail of the first bird are formed of overlapping foliate feather shapes. The body of the second bird is decked out in fine cross-hatching from which the bushy leaf-form tail extends behind.

There is an element of sophistication in this piece in contrast to Exhibit 185 that might argue for a Five Dynasties date or simply a late Tang date. The long sprouting fern clump streamer tail is a typical feature of late Tang phoenix motifs as is the arrangement of the crest and wattle on the head of the leading bird which recalls Sassanian forms from further west along the Silk Road. (AHF)

Compare: 83 No.31
Collection: The Peony Collection

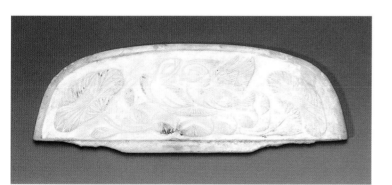

187

DUCKS AND LOTUS COMB TOP

TANG DYNASTY
 (618 - 907)
                                PE637

LENGTH : 8.6 CM
HEIGHT : 3.0 CM

Comb top in translucent white nephrite. Each side is carved in bas relief within a plain perimeter border. On one side is a pair of ducks fluttering their wings amid a huge open lotus flower with a partly curled open lotus leaf spread to each side. On the other side, a pair of ducks fluttering their wings are enfolded by a huge open lotus leaf with simple arrow shaped leaves set to each side.

The rolling swell and dip of the lotus leaves in Exhibit 187 is typical of the Tang period and is well demonstrated on silver work. The inverted triangular form of the simple incised eye, the oval head and the backward sweep line of the neck and breast, which interpret the naturalism in art at this time are typical features. (AHF)

Compare: (i) 66 No.228 (ii) 10 pl.106 (iii) 26 pl.96
Collection: The Peony Collection

188

LEAF-TAILED PHOENIX

TANG DYNASTY
(618 - 907)

PE498

HEIGHT : 3.5 CM
LENGTH : 3.0 CM
THICK: 0.6 CM

A figure of a phoenix in translucent white nephrite suffused with a dark brown crackle. The bird looks straight ahead from under a large rounded plume or crest. The body curves around beneath the short open raised wings to the luxurious tail of unfurling leaf-bud forms which extends round to overhang and touch the crest.

This piece appears to have been made for sewing onto clothing. The short beak, horizontal tear-form eye with a straight upper edge and the long ear, all argue for a mid Tang date. Here, the typical long sprouting "fern clump" form of streamer tail is well developed and the up-swept "shark's fin" open wing is a form that commenced in the Tang period and continued well into the Song (compare Exhibit 215). (AHF)

Collection: The Peony Collection

189

BLACK MUSICIAN BELT PLAQUE

TANG DYNASTY
(618 - 907)

PE542

LENGTH : 5.0 CM
HEIGHT : 5.0 CM
THICKNESS : 0.5 CM

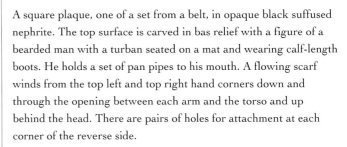

A square plaque, one of a set from a belt, in opaque black suffused nephrite. The top surface is carved in bas relief with a figure of a bearded man with a turban seated on a mat and wearing calf-length boots. He holds a set of pan pipes to his mouth. A flowing scarf winds from the top left and top right hand corners down and through the opening between each arm and the torso and up behind the head. There are pairs of holes for attachment at each corner of the reverse side.

Considering the general paucity of carved jade definitively dateable to the Tang period, there seems to have been a distinct predilection for these small belt decorations exclusively (except for some rare lion examples and the ubiquitous dragon) featuring foreign musicians and dancers from Central Asia. Black nephrite is rare at any time. There are examples of these pieces whose relief carving technique is deep and very positively executed. (Exhibit 189). There are others whose relief work is much slighter and more superficial (see Exhibit 192) but all indications are that the two types are contemporary with each other. (AHF)

Compare: 66 No.221 and 222
Collection: The Peony Collection

190

MOTTLED BLACK SQUARE
BELT PLAQUE WITH
DRUMMER IN RELIEF

TANG DYNASTY
 (618 - 907)

BATEA 482

LENGTH : 3.5 CM
WIDTH : 3.5 CM

Mottled black jade square belt plaque with slightly sloping sides, decorated in low relief with a seated Sassanian drummer with a flowing scarf; the reverse pierced with double holes at each corner for affixing to a belt.

Several similar jade plaques of different sizes are known and similar decoration to that here is found on the frieze of the mausoleum of Wang Jian, ruler of the Former Shu kingdom, who died in 918 AD and whose tomb is at Chengdu. The sumptuary laws of the late Tang restricted the use of such plaques to decorating the belts worn by very senior mandarins. An iron statue of King Wang Jian at Chengdu dated 916 AD, shows him wearing similar plaques decorated with dragons. The plaques are shown on this iron statue affixed to the belt at the back of his robe. (BSM)

Previously published: (i) 77, No. 37 (ii) 37, No. 241
Compare: (i) 66, Nos. 221 and 222 (ii) 82 No. 157

191

CHAWEI END BELT PLAQUE

TANG DYNASTY
 (618 - 907)

PE659

LENGTH : 11.5 CM
WIDTH : 5.0 CM
THICKNESS : 0.8 CM

Flat rectangular plaque with one rounded end being the *chawei*, a single long terminal member of a full set of square plaques for sewing onto a belt. The opaque off-white nephrite piece is carved in full low relief with a large dancing figure of a foreigner with slender torso pivoting on the right leg, the left knee raised and the hands clapping above the head. He is wearing a tight fitting tunic, breeches which are tucked into soft leather boots and a full length apron-like garment falling down from the hips both front and back and lifting and moving with the motion of the dance. The performance is taking place upon a mat. A single ribbon winds from one side of the figure, through his up-raised arms, round the back of his head and forward again through the arms down to the other side. The squared end has a rivetted step on the back with four sets of double holes for attachment.

It is interesting to compare the form of dress worn by this figure with that on Exhibit 181. This belt - or at any rate, this plaque - clearly had extremely heavy daily wear as evidenced by the smoothing of all details. It is, however, together with Exhibit 181 depicting the human figure and Exhibit 194 depicting the dragon, an excellent demonstration of the ability of the Tang jade carver to portray vigorous movement within the restricting limitations of a small area in low relief, which has not been bettered, before or since.

The foreshortening of the raised arms seems to be a deliberate use of perspective to accentuate the drawn out, languorous elegance of the full body movement. (AHF)

Compare: <u>66 Nos.221 and 222</u>
Collection: The Peony Collection

192

FOUR MUSICIAN/DANCER BELT PLAQUES

TANG DYNASTY
(618 - 907)

	PE675 (I) *CHAWEI*	PE676 (II) FLUTE PLAYER	PE677 (III) RATTLE PLAYER	PE678 (IV) *SHENG* PLAYER
LENGTH :	9.9 CM	7.4 CM	7.4 CM	6.8 CM
WIDTH :	3.3 CM	3.4 CM	3.3 CM	3.3 CM
THICKNESS :	0.5 CM	0.5 CM	0.5 CM	0.5 CM

A group of four rectangular belt plaques, one a longer piece or *chawei* with one end with rounded corners and three shorter squared pieces. The upper face of each of the four pieces has an all round perimeter bevelled border enclosing a figure in low relief.

The *chawei* features a dancing curly-headed male figure with long soft leather boots performing on a round carpet. He wears a collarless tunic pulled together into a vertical join at the front of his body and secured by a belt from which falls a full length apron-like garment with incised folds or pleats that swings with the motion of the dance. A single ribbon winds from his left side up and over the head and down again to the right armpit.

The second piece features a standing flute player attired in similar fashion to the dancer with curly hair and a flying sash and standing on a square carpet.

The third and fourth pieces feature figures with long curly hair and swaddled garments tucked into long soft leather boots, seated on square carpets. One is holding a toothed-form rattle above his head in his right hand. The other is playing a *sheng* or multi-pipe wind instrument held to the right of his head. The latter also wears on his head a simple ring diadem the smooth line of which is broken at the front by a pair of incurling terminals.

These pieces come from a set carved in a less deep relief and conveying more of a sense of sketchiness rather than finished work. The piece featuring the *sheng* player is particularly interesting because the diadem which he wears on his head is the earliest definitive appearance of this break front form of hair containing ring in jade, and, it seems, in any other medium. This type of diadem became widespread and popular in Yuan and Ming times. There are representations of simple ring diadems restraining the long hair of foreigners on a number of Tang dynasty artefacts but these are continuous rings and not broken at the front. (AHF)

Compare: 66 Nos.221 and 222
Collection: The Peony Collection

193

ELEVEN MUSICIANS AND
DANCERS BELT PLAQUES

TANG DYNASTY
(618 - 907)

PE752 - PE763

	(i) CHAWEI	(ii) LARGEST SIZE RECTANGLES (FOUR PIECES)	(iii) NEXT SMALLEST RECTANGLE PIECES (TWO PIECES)	(iv) SMALLEST RECTANGLE PIECES (FOUR PIECES)
LENGTH:	5.0 CM	4.5 CM	4.3 CM	3.8 CM
WIDTH:	2.8 CM	3.0 CM	2.8 CM	2.5 CM
THICK:	0.5 CM	0.5 CM	0.5 CM	0.4 CM

A set of eleven rectangular belt plaques in pure sweet-white nephrite and comprising one longer piece or *chawei* one end of which is with rounded corners, four squared end rectangular pieces, two smaller squared end rectangular pieces and four additional, yet smaller, squared end rectangular pieces. The upper or top face of all of the pieces has a continuous perimeter bevel border enclosing a human figure in low relief.

(i) The *chawei* features a dancing curly haired male figure with long soft leather boots performing on a round carpet. He wears a collarless tunic which is pulled together into a vertical join at the front of his body and secured below the belly from which falls a full length apron-like garment with incised folds swinging with the motion of the dance. A single ribbon winds from his left side, up and over his head and down again through the crook of his right arm.

(ii) The four, large rectangular pieces each feature a musician seated on a squared carpet and with encircling ribbons. One pair of these each features a long-haired, bearded flute player. The other two feature curly-haired drummers. One holds a small round drum with perimeter cross stringing to his right side and the other holds an elongated drum, tapered at both ends and cross strung to the centre in two halves, to his left side.

(iii) The two medium sized rectangular pieces each feature a long-haired *sheng* pipe player, one bearded and one clean shaven seated on a square carpet with encircling ribbon.

(iv) The smallest, four rectangular pieces feature respectively two *sheng* pipe players, one pipes of Pan player and one tambourine player, all with long, curling locks and all seated on square carpets and with encircling ribbons.

There are a number of interesting features about this set. The first is that it appears to be one of the largest published sets. There is a set of 16 pieces of this type comprising three different shapes (100 pl.219) and another comprising 15 pieces but depicting seated lions (100 pl.225). There is another set of 9 pieces of this type, but made of agate in the British Museum. (No.66 pl. 222). There is a set of 11 made of jade in the Metropolitan Museum of Art in New York of two different shapes, one of which matches the *chawei* here, and a set of seven jade pieces in the Museum of Fine Arts Boston. Exhibit 193 however, has pieces of four different sizes in the same set, including the *chawei* and this is very singular and unusual. As with nearly all other sets, Exhibit 193 features only musicians and one dancer and all are either seated on, or standing on, a carpet. The theme of a ribbon twirling dancer on a carpet between two lines of musicians on a long rug appears in one lively Tang dynasty mural vignette in cave 320 at Dunhuang although in this celestial example the figures are an idealised Chinese type and not foreigners. Swaddled central Asian dancers are featured on a published pair of dowel-hinged stone doors excavated in Yanchi, Ningxia Hui Autonomous region and on one of a series of white marble relief panels showing central Asian scenes and people published by J.J. Lally in 1992(pl.12). Exhibit 193 is of a very fine sweet-white nephrite and all pieces are pierced on the reverse side with four sets of double holes for threading onto a belt. (AHF)

Compare: 66 Nos.221 and 222
Collection: The Peony Collection

194

WHITE DRAGON BELT PLAQUE

TANG DYNASTY
(618 - 907)

PE633

LENGTH : 7.8 CM
HEIGHT : 6.8 CM
DEPTH : 0.8 CM

Rectangular plaque, one of a set from a belt, in translucent white nephrite. The face is carved in bas relief with the contorted figure of a furiously whirling dragon with its right foot raised and talons extended, spiked tongue flickering forward in the ferocious open mouth, leaf-like proboscis curling upwards and tufts of hair at elbows and pastern. The body is incised with flat, elongated diamond-hatched scales.

The dragon here should be compared with a sister representation of a dragon on a jade belt dating from the Five Dynasties period and published in 21, pl. 84. The flat, bright, cut incised fish-scale design relates to identical depiction of dragons' scales worked on some published white jade saucer dishes and *bi-discs* from Tang period excavations in China. The effective conveyance of such demonic frenzy on a small flat relief surface is a work of genius. An interesting feature of Exhibit 194 is the small double-ribbon bow at the front of the left shoulder which replicates the ribbon bow that sometimes appears at the top of the long leather boots of Central Asian musicians on some jade belt plaques. A further interesting point to note on Exhibit 194 is that there is no bevelled perimeter border and the surface reduction on the entire face commences at the very edge on all sides. (AHF)

Compare: Tianjin Art Museum Collection
Collection: The Peony Collection

195

SPOUTED KUNDIKA

TANG DYNASTY
(618 - 907)
PE456
HEIGHT : 7.5 CM
DIAMETER : 4.5 CM

A squat spouted kundika or lustral pouring vessel in off-white nephrite with eroded surface patches of iron brown. The vessel is formed in two separate parts. The lower part is a flattened, rounded bulb shape representing the cosmic mountain Meru and with a turned peripheral double shoulder ring encircling the whole piece on each side of the short spout. From the summit of the cosmic mountain rises the second part in the form of a turned column of ascendant and separate discs of decreasing size representing a furled umbrella or parasol. The slightly concave base of the lower part is incised with a crossed double vajra or thunderbolt motif.

There are a well established group of elegant and simple bronze kundika and bottle forms which follow the simple basic contours of the body of this piece. The unique aspect of Exhibit 195 is the furled, pagoda pinnacle form of the sacred umbrella which, as can be seen, is a turned, separate piece. The double vajra on the base is a motif known from embossed medallions around the belly of a silver vessel excavated from the Famen Temple near Xian which was interred together with many other precious objects and important relics of the Buddha in 874 AD in the Tang dynasty. The very fine drawing of the double vajra on Exhibit 195 however, closely follows excellent line detail drawing of the same type that is featured in many drawing and painting works recovered from the famous blocked chamber in cave 17 at Dunhang as acquired by the Stein and Pelliot expeditions in the early 20th century. Although appearing to be lathe turned, this piece world have been made by abrasive attrition - possibly with the assistance of a kick operated forward and back movement spindle. (AHF)

Collection: The Peony Collection

196

LION ON LOTUS

TANG DYNASTY
 (618 - 907)
                PE501
HEIGHT : 5.7 CM
WIDTH : 4.0 CM
THICKNESS : 1.5 CM

A lion in translucent off-white nephrite suffused with brown. The beast is seated on scrolling vegetal tendrils above an open lotus flower and his right paw is raised to touch a lotus bud in front of his curving ridged chest. His flanks are incised with vestigial wing or flame formations and his tufted tail arches up and over the rump. The disproportionately massive head has an open mouth with finely formed teeth and is encircled with a curving ruff or mane with incised hair striations.

The openwork lotus flower forming the base of this piece connotes its Buddhist association. The continuous S-flow from the nose to the elbow of the lion is a typical Tang dynasty sculptural mechanism. In detail, the curved ruff or mane extending from the ear round to the front of the chest, and the tightly-scrolled erect tail formation are also typical of the late Tang period. Note the comparatively idle manner of forming the inner bend of the S by simply drilling out a core above the elbow on each side. (AHF)

Collection: The Peony Collection

197

Open lotus boss

Tang dynasty
 (618 - 907)
PE485
Diameter : 5.3 cm
Thickness : 1.5 cm

A boss or button in translucent honey-coloured nephrite with some black crack veining and formed as an open lotus flower with eight sloping petals, each carved with a raised border surrounding one of the eight precious objects of Buddhism. The underside is concave and plain.

This piece seems intended as some kind of base, perhaps the anchor for a figure of the Buddha or Avalokitesvara. It is massively conceived and formed and the concave underside may be compared with the concave underside of Exhibit 195. (AHF)

Collection: The Peony Collection

198

GOURD PENDANT WITH PHOENIXES, FLOWERS AND CLOUDS

LATE TANG, FIVE DYNASTIES OR
EARLY LIAO DYNASTY
(845 - 950)

BATEA 460

HEIGHT : 4.5 CM
WIDTH : 3.2 CM

Greyish red-veined jade of double gourd shape, pierced for
suspension probably as a pendant, decorated on its bottom half
with two phoenixes with stylised feathery tails separated by
trefoil clouds, the top half of the gourd with incised stylised
flower heads.

The colour of the jade is discussed in the introductory essay
The Fluctuating Jewel. The stylised flower-head decoration is
comparable to examples found on parcel-gilt silver of the
period assigned. Similar stylised feathery-tailed phoenixes are
also found in both late Tang and early Liao contexts. (BSM)

Previously published: (i) 37, No 198 (ii) 77, No 36

199

DEER WITH BROAD TAIL

LATE TANG, FIVE DYNASTIES OR
EARLY LIAO DYNASTY
(845 - 950)

BATEA 545

LENGTH : 6.0 CM
HEIGHT : 4.5 CM
WIDTH : 4.3 CM

Jade recumbent deer with two three-pronged horns and broad fat
stubby tail, its front legs bunched up and folded under with knee
protruding, its head massively formed, and thrust back, the jade of
roughly triangular shape and of poor grey-brown colour tinged
with red showing considerable wear.

The posture, with the animal depicted as if about to rise, was
popular during the Tang dynasty. The dating of pieces of this
colour to this period is discussed in the introductory essay The
Fluctuating Jewel. (BSM)

Previously published: 77, No. 38 (as a ram).

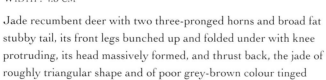

200

YELLOWISH JADE
BRAHMAN BULL

TANG DYNASTY
(618 - 907) OR LATER
BATEA 462
LENGTH : 6.5 CM
WIDTH : 3.5 CM
HEIGHT : 3 CM

Yellowish jade brahman bull with ridged back, its neck, jaws and hocks all with brown-speckled markings; the animal lying down and to one side, its front leg bent as if the animal is about to rise.

The brahman bull was first introduced to China in the Tang dynasty as an exotic animal and became a popular subject in Tang tomb pottery but does not seem to occur in the art of later periods. The posture, as if the animal is about to rise, is a posture common in animals of the Tang period and this piece is believed to date to that period (see Exhibits 176 and 200). (BSM)

Previously published (i) as a longma or dragon horse in <u>37 Exhibit 145</u>, where it is given a late Song to early Ming dating which would be appropriate if it were longma or dragon horse. The identification of the animal as a brahman bull seems the more likely identification, however, since the head and neck appear more brahman bull-like than dragon-like. (ii) as an ox in <u>77 Plate IX</u>.

17 NORTHERN AND SOUTHERN SONG DYNASTIES, THE MATURITY OF LIAO AND JIN DYNASTIES

951-1279

A decade ago in an article entitled "In search of Song Jade" <u>50</u> this author suggested that jades such as a lychee-flesh white broad-tailed sheep (Exhibit 206), a brown-flecked cup (Exhibit 219), certain pieces that followed Longquan and Junyao shapes, (Exhibits 250 and 251) and astragals such as Exhibit 253 and 254 could well be dated to the Song dynasty. For this purpose the Song included the roughly contemporary Liao and Jin dynasties which ruled Manchuria, Inner Mongolia and large parts of northern China for most of this period. It was further suggested that one of the most significant features of Song art was the heightened interest in nature and that motifs from the natural world were the principal subjects of the art of the period. Jade animals were modelled on those occuring in nature rather than in the imagination, and stress was laid on the accuracy of anatomical details.

This article also mentioned that early Chinese commentators on jade credited the Song dynasty (by which they meant the Northern and Southern Song dynasties) with the invention of two characteristic jade techniques; the first was the use of two-colour jade for differing objects in the same piece, for example Exhibit 242, which shows a boy in greyish-white jade holding a greyish-black cat; the second invention was the carving of jade in several levels of relief, as seen on the finial in Exhibit 218. Both of these techniques continued through the Yuan and Ming dynasties.

Although a great many books have been written on jade in the last ten years and several significant excavations, particularly of Liao dynasty jades, have enabled stylistic features to be clarified, these remarks seem largely to have stood the test of time.

The period under discussion in this essay covers also not only the whole of the Northern

and Southern Song dynasties (960-1279) but also the the whole of the Jin dynasty (1115-1234), a small part of the Five Dynasties period (951-960) and most of the Liao dynasty (951-1127).

The date chosen to start the period covered by this essay marks the time when, according to the historical records, a plentiful supply of fine quality jade again entered China after just over a hundred years of scarcity. Jades dating from the earliest years of the Liao dynasty and most of the Five Dynasties period, which are probably indistinguishable from those of the late Tang, are dealt with in the preceding essay.

The introductory essay mentions the glut of lychee-flesh white jade during the period 951-1028, the scarcity of fine quality jade from 1028-77, and the availability of fine and of brown-flecked jade after 1077. Lychee-flesh white jade does not appear to have been available after the mid 15th century, and therefore the colour of jade can be indicative of dating although the use of this criterium alone should be avoided. Earlier this century Chinese antique dealers referred to all naturally black jades as Han jades, but this is certainly not necessarily correct although most naturally black nephrite jades, such as Exhibits 189 and 190, do date to before the Ming dynasty. It has been suggested that black nephrite was collected from the Karakash river ('Karakash' means 'Black Jade' in the local language) from pre-Han times until the Yuan dynasty but not later <u>7BJF p.49</u>.

It appears that although raw jade was in reasonably plentiful supply during the period covered by this essay, it was not subject to commercialisation, which only began in the Yuan dynasty but flourished during the Ming dynasty <u>92</u>. This author takes Yang Boda's remarks in his essay to mean that jade use at this time was confined to the upper echelons of society and did not extend to other social groups. In this sense only his comments may well be correct.

The time has come for an attempt, albeit on a tentative basis given the limited amount of published excavated material, to distinguish between the jades that should be assigned to that part of the Liao and Jin dynasties covered by this essay herein referred to as 'the Northern School', and those that belong to the Northern and Southern Song dynasties herein referred to as 'the Southern School'.

THE NORTHERN AND SOUTHERN SONG DYNASTIES 'THE SOUTHERN SCHOOL'

Early commentators considered Han and Song dynasty jades, i.e., those of the Southern School, the epitome of the jade workers' art, but largely ignored the arts of the sinicized Liao and Jin dynasties, which they considered barbarian dynasties.

The attribution of jades to the Southern School can only be made with some understanding of the background to the periods concerned and the artistry and styles of the preceding period. The artistic products of the Tang dynasty reflected Chinese attitudes and lifestyles at that time characterised by exuberant energy and sometimes even aggression. In the Northern and Southern Song dynasties, which followed a period of economic crisis and military disasters, a different outlook developed that, in due course, was equally reflected in their art.

The Northern Song dynasty court, its courtiers and scholars were connoisseurs who indulged fully in the pleasures of aesthetic appreciation, an appreciation that continued into the Southern Song. The Northern Song emperor Zong Hui (r.1101-25) was an

aesthete, archaeologist, painter and collector and his palace contained many treasures. The imperial collection begun in the mid 11th century had, by the end of his reign, grown to many thousands of objects. The Northern and Southern Song way of life did not have the same international outlook as the Tang. Buddhism had been assimilated into Chinese life for centuries, and in this process had become sinicised. During the Northern Song period, Neo-Confucianism, Chan Buddhism (known in the West by its Japanese name Zen Buddhism) and Daoism were almost unconsciously syncretized, with the result that the principles of solitude and aesthetic contemplation were adopted by the intelligensia and in turn reflected in their art. Purity and simplicity were thus translated from philosophy to the arts, and the mainstream taste of the Southern School was reflected in a monumental simplicity of form and line. However, the change from the vitality of the Tang to the quiet reserve of the Southern School did not occur overnight. Strong and robust animals such as the Tang camel should be compared with another camel from the Southern Tang royal tombs (10th century) in Nanjing which is depicted in a collapsed, comfortable heap 82, p.17.

The author suggests that Southern School animals are normally depicted singly, for example Exhibit 236, rather than in groups. Standing animals in jade are almost unknown in Chinese art before the Ming dynasty, since the carving of such an animal would have been an extravagant waste of the jade pebble. Depictions of animals holding fungus (Exhibit 284), acanthus (Exhibit 294), peaches (Exhibit 324) or other flowers or objects unrelated to their natural lives are far removed from the aesthetics of the Southern School and it is suggested that they should be assigned a later date. In all these cases the flower, object or group conveys an auspicious meaning, which accords well with Ming dynasty interest in good fortune and a Ming date may be appropriate for such pieces.

While animals and flowers from the natural world seem to have been the main subjects of the Southern School, certain motifs from the imaginary world, such as the dragon and phoenix, whose depiction in Chinese art were of very long standing, continued to be occasionally included in its repertoire.

The production of animals and floral motifs in jade continued into the Qing dynasty and the major problem in the absence of published excavated examples is to separate the products of the Southern School from those of later periods. Stylistic changes, including changes in emphasis and decorative conventions, that occured over the long period from 951 to the end of the Qing in 1911, are dealt with in the essays covering the later periods, or in the commentaries on the individual pieces. These help to resolve the dating of many objects, but there still remains a residue of pieces for which no such additional criteria exist and it is these that present the most difficulty. It has been suggested by the author in his essays In Search of Song Jades 50 and Han to Song 51 that the jade animals and flowers truest to nature should be attributed to the Song and this is still considered to be the best pointer to dating. During the period covered by this essay, the emphasis on musculature and the spine (first noticed in respect of Tang animals) continued; considerable attention was also paid to finely incised decorative patterns and to fine line incisions for the tails and beards of animals. Although this naturalistic style continued into

the Ming, jade workers at that time frequently compromised by skimping on details such as the eyes, and had no interest in depicting the sexual organs of animals, which appear to have fascinated some Song jade carvers.

The Northern and Southern schools influenced each other, however, and it would be wrong to assign, for example, all openwork pieces, to the Northern School.

From the late 11th century on there was a revival of antiquarian interest, which is discussed in a separate essay on archaistic pieces following the Ming section of this catalogue.

There can be little doubt that the majority of Southern School jades became treasured heirlooms, which probably accounts for the scarcity of archaeological evidence for such jades.

THE LIAO AND JIN DYNASTIES 'THE NORTHERN SCHOOL'

The Tartar patrons of the Liao and Jin dynasties (the Northern School) demanded luxury items of more exotic taste than those of the Southern School, and were apparently satisfied by a continuation of the Tang traditions. While a quiet reserve pervades the jade productions of the Southern School, this author suggests that although the jades of the Liao and Jin dynasties were undoubtedly influenced by this southern tradition they also frequently incorporate Tang vitality and a continuing foreign influence. In this context it seems likely that the jade workers of the Liao and Jin inherited the Tang dynasty's jade working methods. Tang influence on Liao ceramics has been amply demonstrated. Tang society was much more international and outward-looking than those of the Northern and Southern Song dynasties. The Liao in particular maintained and even appear to have extended Tang contacts with Central Asia and the Near East. This occured to such an extent that the inhabitants of medieval Europe at this time commonly referred to China as Cathay, a word derived from Khitai, the very name used by the Liao for their own people.

The Liao and Jin dynasties continued Tang artistic traditions in taking animals and flowers from the natural and imaginary worlds. Figures such as an apsara (a Buddhist angel, Exhibit 223) and kinnara (human-headed birds, Exhibit 215) are typical subjects in the Liao/Jin tradition. The depiction of a goose or swan being attacked by a small hawk, considered emblematic of spring in the Liao, Jin and Yuan dynasties, was a favourite motif during this period (Exhibit 218) but the hawk seems to be absent in the Ming examples of this subject. One or more deer in an autumnal landscape, symbolising autumn, was another motif common to the Northern School and several plaques illustrating this subject are known 19, No.145. Again, this symbolism does not appear to have carried on into the Ming dynasty. There was also a tendency for Northern School artists to embellish their animals with C scrolls or other decoration to accentuate the legs (Exhibit 207).

Plaques and finials of all kinds, frequently reticulated and sometimes including animals among or on top of flowers, birds amid floral sprays or flowers alone are, I believe, typical of the Northern School. Motifs such as a moth or a butterfly (Exhibit 222) were popular motifs in Liao art and should be dated to this period. Stem cups in shapes also crafted in silver, such as Exhibit 255, and a boy with a lotus (Exhibit 252) can be firmly dated to the Jin or Yuan dynasty. Tribute bearers and foreigners are also frequently depicted in Tang and Liao art and representations in jade are normally dated to these periods (Exhibits 224 and 225).

The use of jade for belt plaques mentioned in the essay on Tang jades continued until the end of the Ming dynasty, although from the mid Liao dynasty onwards the shapes of such plaques changed. Most are rectangular but some are heart-shaped and the large rectangular plaques with corners rounded at one end, such as Exhibit 191, continued in use.

All pre-11th century plaques recorded to date are solid, and several good examples in different shapes and sizes are included in the current exhibition. The excavation from a mid 11th century Liao tomb of a reticulated plaque provides an approximate starting date for this stylistic feature. This plaque bears a long-tailed bird with wings placed as if saluting (compare Exhibit 220) surrounded by a border of concave pearl-shaped roundels. James Watt had previously suggested that such plaques did not antedate the Yuan dynasty, 82 so this find was of major importance in dating such plaques.

One of the commonest finds from the Jin dynasty are jade flowers (probably originally sewn on to mortuary veils as decoration). Similar objects are not found in Northern or Southern Song tombs. Contrary to the author's previous opinion stated in 50, it appears that the earliest jade flowers were plain with six petals, those with five petals apparently being of Yuan date. In the field of ceramics there was a gradual progression from the three to five petal shapes of the 10th/early 11th century to six petal shapes in the late 11th and 12th century. Ceramic bowls of six petal form were fashionable during the Jin dynasty and it is possible that their popularity gave rise to the use of this form in jade during this period (Exhibit 256).

Brian McElney
January 1994

公元 951至 1279年

十年前，筆者曾撰<宋玉探索>一文(50)，文中提出
荔枝肉色的寬尾羊(展品206)，帶褐斑的杯(展品219)，
仿龍泉及鈞窰的玉器皿(展品250及251)，及距骨(展品
253及254)均為宋代之物(「宋代」包括同期之遼及金代)。
筆者又提出宋人對大自然各生物興趣濃厚，神獸甚少
出現，玉工對動物的生態有極準確及詳細的刻劃。

宋玉工又發明了利用玉子的原色雕出雙色玉器，
展品242灰白男童手抱灰黑貓即為上佳例子。另一宋代
發明為多層面浮雕，如展品218嵌飾。這兩項新技術
延用至元及明代。

十年後的今天，玉雕的著述出版了不少考古上
新的發現，特別是遼墓的出土，更增加人們對玉器的
認識，唯筆者的理論大致上經得起時間的考驗。

本文涉及的範圍，除兩宋外亦包括五代後期(951-
960)、遼代後期(951-1127)及金代(1115-1234)。951年是
中土重新獲得大量玉材供應的年份(詳見<隨時勢遷動的
瑰寶>一文)。五代及遼早期玉器類似晚唐產品，在
<公元581至951年>文中已提及。

<隨時勢遷動的瑰寶>文中，亦提及荔枝肉色白玉
斷斷續續的供應，此類白玉在十五世紀中葉後，便不再
出現，因此可作為斷代標準之一，但應避免只憑玉的
顏色斷代。有些骨董商將黑玉一律稱為漢玉，那是
不正確的，黑玉在漢以前，便由烏玉河採集，至元代才
告中止(7BJF,頁49)。

此時期雖然玉材來源充足，但商用玉似乎到元代
才開始蓬勃(92)，玉器仍是上層社會的專利品。本文
另一目的，是將宋玉和遼、金玉分開，前者簡稱為"南
派"，後者簡稱為"北派"。

北宋與南宋(南派)
早期作者多推許漢宋兩代是玉雕的巔峯期，但大都忽略
了遼和金代的玉器，認為它們是蠻夷之作。

要正確地分清南派和北派玉雕，須先明瞭當時的
政治背景。唐代社會充滿活力，其藝術品也是如此。
隨後而來的連串經濟混亂及軍事上的失敗，使北宋王朝
採取了不同的態度。

兩宋的帝王及朝臣一般都沉酣於藝術鑑賞，
宋徽宗本人便集鑑賞家、考古家、畫家及收藏家於
一身。宋室的庋藏由十一世紀中葉開始，至北宋
末年已達數千件。唐人對外來之物興趣濃厚，宋人
則相反。北宋時，儒家思想再度盛行，佛教禪宗
及道教亦提倡獨處、靜思，故宋代藝術無論在造型或
線條上均趨向簡單。但由唐代的動感演變至兩宋
的平淡，不會是突然而來的，像唐早期的駱駝，它

跟南唐王室墓葬出土，軟作一團的駱駝相去
甚遠(82,頁17)。

兩宋的畫家在描繪動物時力求寫實。漢代受
歡迎的作戰鬥狀動物，在宋代不再流行，起而代之的是
臥着的動物(展品232及233)，或舔足(展品237)，或
互相親暱(展品288)，或是水鳥蓮花(展品235)，
均是宋玉的上佳候選者。它們刻劃細緻，追求逼真
不遺餘力。

筆者認為南派動物玉雕，大多數是單獨的
動物(展品236)而非成雙成對。站立的動物在明代之前
絕無僅有，因那會做成大量的浪費。口銜靈芝(展品
284)、或枝葉(展品294)、或桃(展品324)的動物，
跟南派一貫取材於自然界的作風不同，應屬後期之物。
此類玉雕多寓意吉祥，吻合明代傳統和風格。

除取材自自然界的動物及花卉外，神獸如龍鳳
亦間中出現。玉雕動物及花卉，自宋至清千多年中源源
有出產，要對它們作出正確的斷代十分困難。風格及雕
刻手法間中會有幫助，但部份玉器仍令人有模稜兩可的
感覺。筆者曾指出，宋玉製動物花卉造型最自然寫實，
尤注重刻劃動物的肌肉及脊骨，這習慣在唐玉器
已初步形成。此外，宋玉雕多以細線刻劃毛髮、鬍鬚及
尾部。明代玉工繼承此項寫實風格，但很多時草率
了事，對刻劃動物的生殖器毫無興趣。南派與北派玉雕
則互相影響，例如透雕玉器，不一定是北派之物。

十一世紀末仿古風盛，本書有<仿古>專文討論。
南派玉雕多為傳世珍品，出土器甚少。

遼、金(北派)
遼及金代的貴族對奢侈品的需求，跟兩宋大不相同，
他們雖受南派藝術的影響，一般來説他們較接近
唐代的活力充沛及喜好外來之物。遼陶瓷深受唐陶瓷
影響，便是有力証據之一。遼人跟中亞各國往來
密切，比唐代有過之而無不及。中古時，歐洲人稱中國
為"CATHAY"，源自"契丹"一詞。

遼金繼承唐藝術風格，飛天(展品223)及人首鳥
(展品215)是典型題材。最著名的是春水(鶻鷹擒鵝，如
展品218)和秋山(山林群鹿，如19,圖145)玉雕。此類玉雕
明代亦有製造，但已失去原有的象徵意義。北派玉雕多
以C形渦紋強調動物的足部(展品207)。

以動物、花卉為題的透雕牌和嵌飾亦是北派
典型製品。蛾及蝴蝶(展品222)是遼代題材，仿銀製
高足杯(展品255)及童子蓮花(展品252)則是金元之物。
貢人和胡人常見於唐遼藝術，玉製品亦當屬此期
(展品224及225)。

玉帶板自唐至明代歷有沿用。自遼中葉開始，帶板的形狀略有改變。除長方形、角部修圓帶板外（展品191），出現了心形板。

十一世紀中葉以前的玉牌均為實心，本展覽囊括了多件形狀大小不同的代表作。自從有透雕玉牌出土於遼墓（十一世紀中），"透雕玉牌不早於元"一說便被推翻，該遼玉牌刻有一長尾鳥，作振翅欲飛狀，圍以珍珠減地邊紋。

玉花是金代常見之物，相信原是縫於殮葬面罩上作裝飾之用。玉花不見出土於兩宋墓葬。和前說相反（50），最早期玉花為六瓣素面，五瓣玉花是元代產品。陶瓷上的花朵，由十、十一世紀時的三、五瓣，進展為十一、十二世紀的六瓣。玉花是金人的創作，靈感想是來自當時流行的六瓣瓷碗（展品256）。

201
PEACOCK OPENWORK APPLIQUE

LATE TANG TO LIAO DYNASTY
(9TH - 11TH CENTURY)
PE686

HEIGHT : 5.5 CM
WIDTH : 4.4 CM
THICKNESS : 0.6 CM

Openwork plaque of essentially square form in semi-translucent off-white nephrite with white/grey clouding suffusions. The piece is worked on one face only with a gracefully ordered and confined figure of an open-winged crested peacock with a massively luxuriant eyed flowing tail.

This piece may be compared both with the fighting peacocks on Exhibit 185 and also with the line of the neck of the swan or goose in Exhibit 204. There is an arguable transitional median position occupied by Exhibit 201 but, whatever the developmental arguments behind the composition and design, this exhibit shows the remarkable skill of the craftsman in incorporating so much life, sensitivity and luxury of movement into such a small, flat area. (AHF)

Collection: The Peony Collection

202
CELADON JADE LOBED OVAL CUP

LATE TANG TO EARLY LIAO DYNASTY
(PROBABLY 9TH - 11TH CENTURY)
BATEA 507

LENGTH : 8.3 CM
WIDTH : 5.7 CM
HEIGHT : 2.1 CM

Pale celadon jade lobed cup of oval shape divided into three concave sections lengthwise in imitation of a 9th century metallic form, with scalloped rim and high spreading foot.

This form, common in late Tang silver, is also found in ceramics from the late Tang to the Liao period. A jade cup of this basic shape but without lobes has also been found in the foundations of a pagoda built in the late Tang dynasty (9th century). The lobing on the present example, which also appears on the early Liao ceramic examples, renders a dating to the early Liao dynasty probable. (BSM)

Previously published: 51, p.124, fig. 31
Compare: Tang silver example illustrated in The Golden Age of Chinese Art by Hugh Scott, No. 22

203

FLOWER DISH

EARLY LIAO DYNASTY
(907 - 1125)

PE602

LENGTH : 5.4 CM
WIDTH : 3.9
HEIGHT : 1.3 CM

Small lobed petaliform dish in translucent off-white nephrite formed as a hollowed elongated flower head, the opposing two long and two short sides describing the simple double curves of the flower. The vessel stands on a short foot rim which is hollowed out beneath.

Purity and integrity are the principal elements and strengths of this small but remarkable piece. The overall form seems to have developed a Chineseness lacking in the arguably slightly earlier Exhibit 202, which has clear origins in Sassanian metalwork from the far west. (AHF)

Collection: The Peony Collection

204

SEATED SWAN OR GOOSE

LIAO DYNASTY
(907 - 1125)

PE691

LENGTH : 3.0 CM
HEIGHT : 2.5 CM
THICKNESS : 0.7 CM

A flat plaque form of a seated swan or goose in pure translucent white nephrite. The wings are folded up along the sides and the elegant neck sweeps back from the distended breast with a double S-curve. The back is flat but hollowed out and with a rectangular formed hole for attachment. The eye is a single dot.

The excellent composition of simple and graceful curves and relief scooping and grooving represents the pinnacle of the northern Chinese Liao jade sculpture. The sophisticated strengths of this very small piece are conceived on a massive scale. (AHF)

Collection: The Peony Collection

205

U-SHAPE PHOENIX

LIAO OR JIN DYNASTY
  (951 - 1234)
                    PE629
LENGTH : 7.7 CM
WIDTH : 5.5 CM
THICKNESS : 2.2 CM

Phoenix in opaque pure white stone. The entire form sweeps around in a compressed arc from the rounded and finely crested head to the tail finial. The legs are represented on the ventral upright of the arc by vestigial curling incisions. The wings are fully feathered with detailed rendering in high relief. The tail is constituted by a fountain formation of broadly separated U-shaped members. The head, neck and chest are twisted on the vertical axis towards the right hand side.

As with Exhibit 204, the remarkable simplicity of the elongated curves and rounded perimeters combine with the fine white material to evoke a timeless perfection of form. However, in its quietness and directness, the Liao-Jin period and taste are very evident. (AHF)

Compare: 1 pl.XXXI.
Collection: The Peony Collection

206
WHITE JADE BROAD-TAILED SHEEP

NORTHERN SONG DYNASTY
 (960 - 1127)

BATEA 408

LENGTH : 7.5 CM
HEIGHT : 6.0 CM
WIDTH: 2.5 CM

Lychee-flesh white jade bearded, broad-tailed sheep depicted in a seated position, its raised head showing the face divided into distinct planes, its chest protruding and legs folded underneath; the whole executed with a minimum of surface decoration.

The tail of the broad-tailed sheep, a native of Central Asia, became a sought after exotic delicacy in the Tang dynasty and numerous depictions are known from the Tang and Song dynasties. The colour of the jade and the division of the face into distinct planes are both typical of the period assigned. (BSM)

Previously published: i) 77 pl. XXI ii) 37, No. 142 iii) 51, p.121, Fig. 23

207

STANDING MYTHICAL ANIMAL

SONG OR EARLY YUAN DYNASTY
(PROBABLY 11TH - 13TH CENTURY)
BATEA 517

HEIGHT : 4.5 CM
LENGTH : 3.8 CM
WIDTH : 2.5 CM

Pale celadon jade mythical animal with bifurcated horns, ears and a long trifurcated mane, the tail carefully incised, its hocks with double-line flaming accentuations, the head rodent-like and divided into distinct planes slightly turned to the left, the pronounced claws with double-line accentuation.

The detailed incising of the mane and tail and the division of the face into distinct planes and pronounced claws all point to a probable Song dating . The mythical nature of the animal itself and the accentuation of the hocks suggests however that an early Yuan dating is also possible. (BSM)

Previously published: 77, No.53

208

LYCHEE-FLESH WHITE JADE
HAIR CHIGNON AND PIN

THE CHIGNON,
NORTHERN SONG DYNASTY
(960 - 1127)
THE PIN, MING DYNASTY
(1368 - 1644)
BATEA 535

LENGTH : 5.5 CM
HEIGHT : 3.5 CM

Lychee-flesh white jade chignon, the sides pierced for a hairpin and for ventilation, the chignon undecorated but with a flap extending at the rear. A white jade hair pin for affixing a chignon such as this (probably of Ming date) is shown in position.

The wearing of hair chignons, such as the present example, ended with the Manchu requirement making pigtails compulsory (1652). Jade of this most sought after colour was readily available from 951-1028, and this starkly simple example, so in accord with the best of Northern Song taste, probably dates to this period. Hair chignons are known to have been worn by some officials from at least as early as the Tang dynasty. (BSM)

Previously published: 77, pl. XIV
Compare: (i) 82, No. 190 (ii) 37, No. 248

209

GILT-BRONZE MOUNTED JADE BELT FITTINGS

LIAO DYNASTY
 (907 - 1125) OR EARLIER
                                BATEA 451
TANG APPLIQUE:
LENGTH : 4.8 CM
WIDTH : 1.9 CM

TREFOIL APPLIQUES:
LENGTH : 2.8 CM
WIDTH : 1.9 CM.

A set of three gilt bronze mounted white jade lobed appliques for a
textile belt consisting of one narrow plain tang with lobes at both
ends, the back mounted with plain gilt bronze, with a fragment of
textile between gilt bronze and jade, the top of the tang mounted
with a gilt-bronze striding lion holding a fungus spray, the other
two appliques of trefoil flower shape with indented borders each
pierced with an oval hole for suspension (probably of a purse or
tassel), each fitting with three gilt bronze nails for affixing to the
textile of the belt.

Very similarly shaped belt fittings from a royal Liao dynasty tomb
of early 11th century date were seen by the writer in an exhibition
at Hohhot, Inner Mongolia in August 1992, but similar jade fittings
also seem to have been in use in the Tang dynasty and the striding
gilt-bronze lion is also consistent with a Tang or Liao dating.
(BSM)

Previously published: 51, p.117 Fig. 12
Compare: 97, No. 218

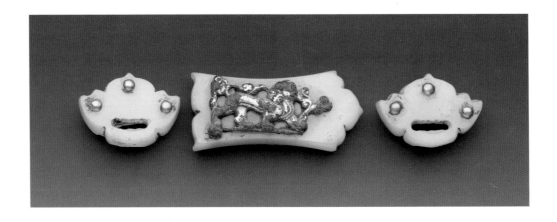

210

WHITE JADE HARE

SONG DYNASTY
 (960 - 1279) OR LATER
                BATEA 496
LENGTH : 5.1 CM
HEIGHT : 3.5 CM
WIDTH : 2 CM

A white jade hare facing directly forward its tail
upcurved, the whole naturalistically carved. (BSM)

Previously published: <u>77 No.43</u>

211

OVAL SEAL WITH
PHOENIX FINIAL

TANG TO NORTHERN
SONG DYNASTY
 (PROBABLY 9TH - 11TH CENTURY)
                BATEA 499
LENGTH : 3 CM
WIDTH : 2.4 CM
HEIGHT : 2.3 CM

Oval seal of yellowish jade with brown suffusions topped by a
phoenix, its bifurcated tail extending over the edge of the seal, the
neck and parrot-like beaked head coiled over the body, the seal
with a concave band round its shoulders.

The screwing down of the head is an early convention and the beak
of the phoenix is comparable with birds depicted on some Yue
celadons of this period. The concave band around the shoulder is
also consistent with an early date. (BSM)

Previously published: <u>77, No 54</u>

212

BELT ANCHOR FOR ACCESSORIES

LIAO DYNASTY
(907 - 1125)

PE599

LENGTH : 7.9 CM
WIDTH : 3.2 CM
HEIGHT : 1.5 CM

Vertical belt fitting for suspension of accessories in semi-translucent partly off-white and partly grey nephrite. The face is worked with a pair of cavorting fish-tailed winged dragons with long manes and pointed noses. Each has spread wings with well delineated pinion and flight feathers. At one end is a flattened slit aperture for suspension purposes and at the other is a carved representation of a rock. The piece is pierced from side to side with a rectangular slit for a belt to pass through.

The fish-tailed, winged dragon, a popular motif in Tang and Song art was taken up with great vigour and enthusiasm by the Liao people or Qidan in the north of China outside the Great Wall. The unusual feature of Exhibit 212 is the deep openwork relief of this subject resulting in a very spirited and dramatic tumbling wariness displayed by the two dragons. (AHF)

Compare: 83 pl.41.
Collection: The Peony Collection

213

FISH-TAILED DRAGON PLAQUE

LIAO DYNASTY
(907 - 1125)

PE586

LENGTH : 4.2 CM
HEIGHT : 2.6 CM

Plaque in translucent off-white nephrite formed as an arching, flying fish-tailed dragon with well formed mane, ears, incised horn, curled retroussé nose, bearded chin and having an open mouth with well formed teeth gripping a large pearl. The goose-form open wings feature two serried rows of pinion feathers. On the left side of the piece is a serrated crest running along the dragon's back which plunges and then continues along the last third of the underside of the curving tail.

The wings, it should be noted, have a clear affinity to the wings on a number of pieces in this section, particularly Exhibits 188, 215 and 218. (AHF)

Collection: The Peony Collection

214

OPENWORK BIRDS AND DRAGONFLY PENDANT

LIAO DYNASTY
(907 - 1125)

PE417

WIDTH : 5.5 CM
HEIGHT : 4.5 CM
THICKNESS : 0.5 CM

A flat openwork plaque in translucent white nephrite with some beige clouding and formed as a pair of confronted birds with open wings. Between their heads is a large dragonfly, the tip of its outspread upper wings touched on each side by the upraised beak of each bird. The long tails of the birds curl below to form bifurcated ends which meet together in the middle.

There may be a rebus meaning associated with this subject, but even without such a double entendre the striking compositional balance of the piece is remarkable. (AHF)

Collection: The Peony Collection

215

THREE FLYING KINNARAS

LIAO DYNASTY
(907 - 1125)

PE478

LENGTH : 4.0 CM
HEIGHT : 3.2 CM
THICKNESS : 0.4 CM

Three figures of flying kinnara with the sprouting fern-clump-form of tails redolent of earlier times (see Exhibits 186 and 188). Shark's fin wings rise together over the back and a curving headdress with two streamers extends behind. The forearms are extended together in front with upturned palms cradling a round fruit or offering.

Jade kinnara are very rare. The small belt of cloud scrolling below is to be noted and also the sprouting-fern new growth form of tail which is more reticent than, but can be well compared with, the more exuberant growth of the tail on Exhibits 186 and 188. (AHF)

Collection: The Peony Collection

216

FLYING STORK ON CLOUD SCROLL

LIAO DYNASTY
(907 - 1125)

PE697

LENGTH : 4.2 CM
WIDTH : 2.2 CM
THICKNESS : 1.1 CM

Extension or fitting in translucent white nephrite formed in openwork as a scrolling base of clouds over which flies an open-winged stork with a hooked neck and legs extended behind.

The style, structure and execution of this piece place it firmly within the same group as Exhibits 204 and 215 with its narrow scrolling cloud base, the beak to wing tip S-curve and the wing shape. The function of this piece is not at all clear but it was most likely an applique or, possibly an extension of a hairpin, perhaps made of gold or silver. (AHF)

Compare: 100 pl.240
Collection: The Peony Collection

217

LONG-TAILED BIRD APPLIQUE

LIAO DYNASTY
(907 - 1125)

PE479

LENGTH : 6.9 CM
HEIGHT : 4.0 CM
THICKNESS : 0.5 CM

An openwork applique in softly translucent white nephrite formed as the curving figure of a long tailed, crested bird in flight with open wings and holding in its beak the stem of a camellia blossom with long stamens. The back is pierced with three pairs of holes for attachment.

Again, wing shape and tail treatment bring this piece into a central position in this uncommon group. There is a very similar piece published in 23 pl.59. (AHF)

Compare: 23 pl.59.
Collection: The Peony Collection

218

Two geese amid lotus with hawk

Liao, Jin, or Yuan dynasty
 (probably 11th - 13th century)
BATEA 512

Length : 4.7 cm
Height : 4.5 cm
Width : 3.2 cm.

White lychee-flesh coloured reticulated jade finial depicting two geese in flight among lotus with a small hawk attacking the head of one goose, the base with two pairs of holes probably for attachment to a hat.

In the Liao, Jin and Yuan dynasties, a hawk attacking a goose or swan was a well known motif in the north of China and Manchuria and was considered emblematic of spring in the arts of these dynasties. The hawk seems to disappear from the Ming versions of this design. The nobles of the northern regions such as the Qidan, Nuzhen and the Mongols used to wear large hats with jade finials which were highly valued at the time. This seems likely to be an example of such a finial. (BSM)

Previously published: 51, p.118, fig. 18
Compare: 92 p.131 fig. 7

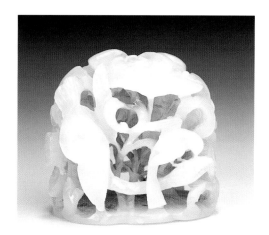

219

Yellowish jade deep cup with brown flecks

Northern Song
 (960 - 1127)
 (probably late 11th century)
BATEA 418

Diameter : 7.2 cm
Depth : 6.5 cm

Deep undecorated circular jade cup of U-shape, the jade of yellowish colour with vertical flecks of reddish-brown tone, the base with no foot rim but with a shallow inset circular central section.

The base is comparable to some ceramics of the 11th century (such as Yaozhou). The flecking of the jade is also like that complained of in the Song historical records immediately after the supply of the jade raw material was resumed in 1077. (See The Fluctuating Jewel). (BSM)

Previously published: (i) 37, No. 201 (ii) 51, p.113, fig. 3 (iii) 77 pl. XIII

220

CHATELAINE WITH COCKATOOS

LIAO OR NORTHERN SONG DYNASTY
(PROBABLY 10TH OR 11TH CENTURY)
BATEA 439

LENGTH : 8.6 CM
HEIGHT : 4.0 CM
WIDTH : 1.8 CM

A jade chatelaine of roughly semicircular shape with two indentations on the upper edge giving a lobed effect, pierced at the upper edge with three holes for hanging probably from a belt, the bottom half of the front with seven short tubes for suspension, the outer surface of the tubes incised with formal back-to-back C scrolls; the upper half of the front with two cockatoos in low relief, their short wings outstretched and almost touching their heads, their long tails intertwined; the reverse with C and S scroll work; the stone of brown-flecked buff colour.

The birds, with their small "as if saluting" wings and the intertwining of their long tails, are both comparable with similar birds on late Tang to early Song Yue celadon boxes of the 10th and 11th centuries. An excavated jade reticulated plaque with a border of pearl roundels with birds with similar "as if saluting" wings has been excavated from a mid 11th century Liao tomb. (BSM)

Previously Published: 51, p.116, fig. 10

221

PEONIES AND GARDEN FENCE OPENWORK PLAQUE

NORTHERN SONG DYNASTY
(960 - 1127)

PE489

WIDTH : 5.2 CM
HEIGHT : 4.5 CM

An openwork plaque of translucent off-white and partly altered nephrite depicting a low fence formed of four upright newel posts with garlic-head finials joined by a single curving rail. Behind the fence stand a pair of peony flowers in bud on each side of a third flower which is fully open.

The representation of a formal garden in works of art other than paintings was a popular diversion in Northern Song times. The same subject is found moulded in the cavetto of Northern Song Ding ware porcelain. Representations in jade seem to be extremely rare. (AHF)

Collection: The Peony Collection

222

OPEN-WINGED BUTTERFLY PLAQUE

NORTHERN SONG DYNASTY
(960 - 1127)

PE488

WIDTH : 6.3 CM
HEIGHT : 5 CM

A butterfly with open wings in lustrous translucent off-white nephrite partly altered; the panels of each wing are formed as openwork scrolling vegetation surrounding a flower. The antennae branch out into carved scrolling openwork of vegetal design.

There is a control and studied discipline discernible in the otherwise riotous complex of movement and style. In fact, the body of the insect is reduced to an almost insignificant proportion of the whole. (AHF)

Collection: The Peony Collection

223

YELLOW FLYING APSARA

NORTHERN SONG DYNASTY
(960 - 1127)

PE747

LENGTH : 6.0 CM
HEIGHT : 3.5 CM
THICK: 0.4 CM

A flat openwork plaque of sweet-yellow nephrite maturely carved front and back as a horizontally flying apsara on a bed or nimbus of tightly curled scrolling clouds. The right hand holds a lotus bud and the left hand gestures with an open palm. A ribbon winds around the back of the head and along the flowing body, the lower half is clothed in an enfolding skirt. The chest is bare.

When compared with Exhibit 183 it can be seen that there is a roundness, supple flow and warmth lacking in the earlier piece. This, added to the lustrous effect of the yellow material, suggests a sense of warmth and humanity. The cutting of the cloud scroll formations is also softer and less sharp to the finger tip than Exhibit 183. The lotus flower and the cloud scroll are both Buddhist sacred symbols. (AHF)

Compare: Senator Hugh Scott Collection
Collection: The Peony Collection

224

CROSS-LEGGED SEATED PERFORMER AND DOG

NORTHERN SONG DYNASTY
(960 - 1127)

PE611

HEIGHT : 5.5 CM
WIDTH : 4.8 CM
DEPTH : 3.8 CM

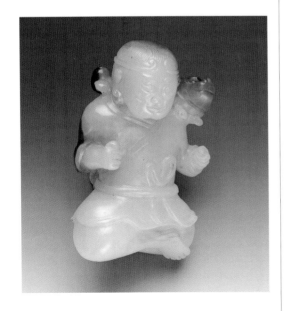

A figure in translucent sweet-yellow nephrite with russet-brown patches. The man is seated with bare legs crossed beneath him and bare feet. He is wearing a wrap-over calf length jerkin tied loosely with a broad rope or thong knotted and looped through itself at the front. Draped across the back of the neck and shoulders is a small dog with a curly mane, deeply sunken eyes, formed nostrils and a broad collar. The figure wears large ring-form earrings and a diadem or band encircling the head and meeting above the forehead as two curls turned back upon themselves. There is a bald patch on top of the head. The eyes slant with a double line canthus and a separate half-moon shaped eyebrow. Each cheek is cleft at the side of the mouth and there is a central vertical cleft at the chin. The arms are held in a half-extended position.

The quality of the yellow jade is very similar to that of Exhibit 223. The practice of foreigners carrying small dogs on their shoulders has been established from ceramic figures. The sculptural details of the dog with a squared jaw and small body with curly mane, collar and sunken ring-bored eyes are closely mirrored by other examples. The barefoot figure in this lively piece is unusual since foreigners are usually depicted wearing long leather boots. The unusual cleft chin is an older feature and the slanting, double line canthus eyes and cheek dimples or clefts are directly related to similar features that are standard on terracotta portrayals of Lokapala guardian figures of the Tang period. The circle ring diadem on the hair is notable for its break front with curled terminals already commented on in respect of Exhibit 192. (AHF)

Collection: The Peony Collection

225

YELLOWISH JADE
KNEELING TRIBUTE BEARER

TANG OR LIAO DYNASTY
  (PROBABLY 9TH - 11TH CENTURY)
                          BATEA 504

HEIGHT : 5 CM
WIDTH : 3 CM
LENGTH : 2 CM

Yellowish jade figure of a foreign tribute bearer
kneeling on one knee the other leg bent, his
hands holding up to one side his tribute, possibly
a lamp, his head and knee with brown suffusions,
his long hair extending down the back and
dividing into three tresses, his head crowned by a
circlet with a break in the centre, the ends of the
break curled like a celtic torc and wearing a
prominent scarf.

Similar figures with similar circlets are known in
several media and are generally given Tang to
Song or Liao dates. Exhibits 192 and 224 are
similar in this regard. (BSM)

Previously published: 77, No 46
Compare:(i) 89, No. 41 (ii) Exhibits 192 and 224

226

CAPPED BOY ON ELEPHANT

SONG OR YUAN DYNASTY
  (960 - 1368)
                          PE8

LENGTH : 4.5 CM
HEIGHT : 4 CM

An elephant carved in translucent honey-coloured jade with the fine-haired tail
sweeping round to the side of the mid hind quarters. The head is turned to the
left and framed by the small ears with the trunk falling to the ground and
passing through the well formed forefeet. On its haunches the animal carries a
boy with a spike or goad in the left hand and a conical hat on his head.

For a long time it was acceptable to attribute such figures with smoothed
conical hats to the Tang period but there is in fact little discernible relationship
between the sculptural structures of the Tang period and the rounded, bland
facial details in this figure. Additionally, the treatment of the elephant seems
much broader in scope than the Tang depictions of the elephant. A later date is
postulated for this piece - Song or even maybe Yuan. (AHF)

Compare: 27 pl.68.
Collection: The Peony Collection

227
ROBED AND HOODED STANDING MAN

NORTHERN SONG DYNASTY
  (960 - 1127)

PE292

HEIGHT : 6.7 CM
WIDTH : 1.2 CM

Figure of a man in grey-green nephrite with upright stance. The hands are covered by coil-ended sleeves and the right arm is held across the stomach. The left arm is held up and over the pointed head-gear and a broad belt gathers in the full length robe which is curved up in front to expose the left toe and foot.

The geometrical compression of this lively piece into an elongated strip is an unusual feature. The conical cap and the long sleeves connote the traditional attributes of the itinerant foreigner of Tang, Song and Yuan times. (AHF)

Collection: The Peony Collection

228
LYING, CURLED IBEX

NORTHERN SONG DYNASTY
  (960 - 1127)

PE135

LENGTH : 7.8 CM
BREADTH: 5.7 CM
HEIGHT : 3.0 CM

A figure of an ibex in grey nephrite partially veined and speckled in black. The left rear leg and the right foreleg are tucked and flattened into relief under the body which is curled round. The head with a sharp angular face turned back to the right side, the chin resting on the right rear shin where a small leaf is carved. The left side of the body is crooked back at the knee and the spine is bevelled smoothly and ridged between head and shoulders and a short stumpy tail behind.

Exactly this form of goat-like ungulate in lowered curling profile turned to bite the right ankle is found in bronze as a weight from as early as the Han dynasty. These Han bronze forms also bear the smooth double grooving between the skull and shoulders. There does however seem to be an elegance in Exhibit 228 that has developed away from the perhaps somewhat stumpy strength of the Han period but attribution of an appropriate date for Exhibit 228 remains very difficult and a conservative preference places it in the Northern Song period in this catalogue. (AHF)

Compare: 37 No.130
Collection: The Peony Collection

229
GREYISH WHITE LOTUS PETAL PALETTE
NORTHERN SONG (960 - 1127) OR EARLIER
BATEA 543
LENGTH : 10.7 CM
WIDTH : 5.2 CM
HEIGHT : 1.5 CM

Greyish-white jade palette in the shape of the petal of the lotus flower, one end coming to a point, the other end slightly open, the jade with black and reddish-brown flecking.

This sophisticated yet simple palette would have been used in a scholar's studio to ensure that the end of the writing brush was facing in the right direction before the scholar started writing or painting and its stark simplicity accords well with Northern Song taste and aesthetics. An almost identical palette, but in rhino horn was among the treasures deposited at the Shoso-in at Nara in Japan by the Empress Jimmo in 762 AD so that a slightly earlier date cannot be entirely ruled out. (BSM)

Previously published : 79, No. 56

230
BLACK AND YELLOW MYTHICAL FELINE
SOUTHERN SONG OR YUAN DYNASTY
(12TH - 14TH CENTURY)
BATEA 527
LENGTH : 5.9 CM
WIDTH : 4 CM
HEIGHT : 3.4 CM

Black grey and yellowish jade half-curled mythical feline with a blunt muzzle looking up, a sinuous ridged spine, its divided, finely incised tail swept up over the body. There are comma-shaped incisions on the base of the paws and incised spirals on the hocks, and the claws are powerfully modelled.

The colours on this animal may have been enhanced by dyeing at the time of its carving. Dyeing of jade from the Tang dynasty on seems to have been practiced. The powerful modelling, emphasis on the spine and fine incised hair all seem indicative of a pre-Ming dating for this piece. Comma-shaped incisions on the base of the paws of animals are common from the Tang dynasty on into the Ming . (BSM)

Previously published: 77, No. 40

231

WHITE JADE *QILIN* PENDANT

SOUTHERN SONG
(1127 - 1279)

BATEA 441

LENGTH : 3.8 CM
HEIGHT : 3.6 CM
WIDTH : 2 CM

A two horned *qilin,* the jade of white lychee-flesh colour with some
brown flecking, seated on its haunches, its nose in the air, its tail
with incised lines curled up by the left rear leg, its long incised
beard all along the jaw ending in two long curling incised side
burns, the neck with incised hair; the base plain, the eyes incised
with two rings. Pierced for suspension.

This treatment of the hair and colour of the jade are both suggestive
of a Southern Song date. (BSM)

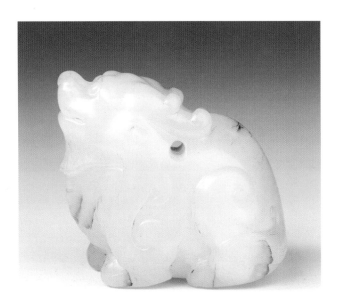

232

RECUMBENT BROWN-FLECKED HORSE

SOUTHERN SONG
(1127 - 1279)

BATEA 552

LENGTH : 7.3 CM
HEIGHT : 3 CM
WIDTH : 2 CM

Jade recumbent horse of brown-flecked white colour, its head
straight forward resting on its two front legs, its tail down and
coming up and over the left leg, the details naturalistically
rendered.

The posture of the horse and its relatively small head can be
compared with horses depicted in Southern Song paintings and
those on the imperial processional way to the tombs of the
Southern Song emperors at Nanjing. (BSM)

Previously published: (i) 77, No. 44 (ii) 51, p. 122, fig. 26
Compare: 59 No. 120

233
RECUMBENT HORSE

SOUTHERN SONG
(1127 - 1279)
BATEA 424
LENGTH : 5 CM
WIDTH : 2 CM
HEIGHT : 1.8 CM

Whitish jade recumbent horse its small head collapsed onto its outstretched front legs, the base flat and undecorated, the mane and tail carefully incised, the whole showing considerable wear.

The flat undecorated base strongly suggests a dating for this piece to the Yuan dynasty or earlier. The very small head and the posture are both typical of horses depicted in extant Southern Song art, to which period this piece has therefore been assigned. (BSM)

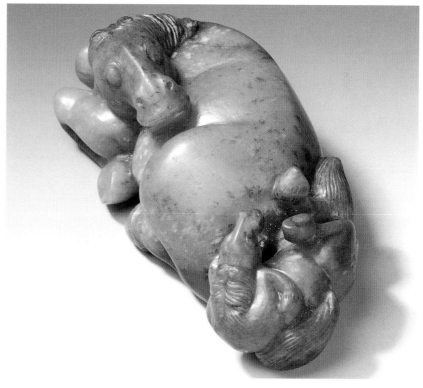

234
TWO RECLINING HORSES

SONG DYNASTY
(960 - 1279)
PE716
LENGTH : 10.5 CM
WIDTH : 4.2 CM
HEIGHT : 3.0 CM

A group of two horses in opaque grey-green nephrite with russet golden suffusions and skin in parts. The larger animal is reclining in a kneeling posture with its front legs folded beneath the head which is turned sharply round to the left with the chin resting on the left side of the stomach. A broad, luxuriant tail curls out behind and partly enfolds the body of the much smaller second horse which lies on its back with its hind legs kicking in the air and its fore legs folded back each side of the alert and quizzical head. The mane of each animal is well defined into large locks of hair falling on each side of a central crease or parting and extending down the neck away from a pair of very small ears. The head of each animal is massively and sensitively modelled with huge wide-open eyes and the smooth line of the forehead descending down to the large oval nostrils set above the generous curling lips of the closed mouth. Each animal has folded legs of exaggerated and mannered elegance with hoof frogs and fetlocks carefully represented.

There is a relaxed but confident aura of innate nobility and uncomplicated peace about these animals. The clear limpidity of the huge innocent eyes communicates sympathetic compassion. This feeling is accentuated by the seemingly random folding and exaggeration of the gangly legs beneath. The piece may be compared with the slightly larger horse of equally sensitive sculpturing in the Sonnenschein Collection (66 pl 203a and 203b). (AHF)

Compare: 66 pl.203a and 203b
Collection: The Peony Collection

235
Goose with lotus flower
Song dynasty
(960 - 1279)

BATEA 417

LENGTH : 4.5 CM
HEIGHT : 1.6 CM
WIDTH : 4.5 CM

Jade goose holding a lotus flower, the jade of yellowish colour with brown flecks, the whole very naturalistically rendered with even the base showing the webbed feet with full details.

The goose was a popular motif in Song art and this very naturalistic carving seems in the best of the Song tradition. Animals holding floral sprays were common from the Tang dynasty on. The brown flecking of the stone also reminds one of the brown flecking complained of when supplies of the raw jade material resumed in 1077 (see The Fluctuating Jewel). (BSM)

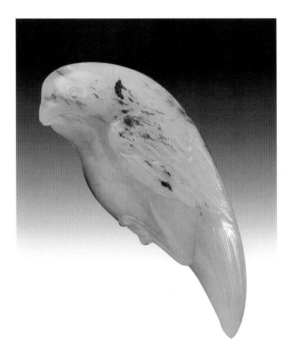

236
Bird of prey
Song dynasty
(960 - 1279)
BATEA 487
LENGTH : 7.3 CM
HEIGHT : 3 CM
WIDTH : 2.5 CM

Jade bird of prey, the jade of pale-celadon green colour with deep reddish suffusions, very naturalistically rendered with detailed eyes, its feet with claws retracted and rendered naturalistically in relief, the underside plain, the top with incised feathers.

The naturalistic carving with its monumental simplicity of form, the detailed eyes and claws all combine to suggest a Song dynasty date for this jade. (BSM)

Previously published: 77, No. 66
Compare: 89, No. 44

237

WHITE JADE LAP DOG

SOUTHERN SONG DYNASTY OR LATER
(1127 - 1279)

BATEA 447

LENGTH : 4.3 CM
WIDTH : 3 CM
HEIGHT : 2.1 CM

White jade lap dog lying curled up, nibbling its rear paw, its tail up over its back, one floppy ear stretched out, its collar with pendant bell and ribbon, the white jade stone with small brown flecks.

This beautifully observed naturalistic rendering of a lap dog seems from the sensitive treatment of the subject most likely to be of Southern Song date but an early Ming dating cannot be entirely ruled out. Animals, such as dogs nibbling their rear foot were popular from the Tang dynasty on. (BSM)

Compare: 82, No.28

238

WHITE BELL COLLARED HOUND

NORTHERN SONG DYNASTY
(960 - 1127)

PE112

LENGTH : 6.4 CM
HEIGHT : 4.3 CM
BREADTH: 2.0 CM

A figure of a recumbent dog in white nephrite with the legs and pads of the feet well rendered beneath. The muscles of the flanks are suggested and the ribs and folds of skin at the shoulders appear distinctly. The tail is short and curls up against the rear of the right flank, the relaxed ears fall down each side of the head. The forepaws are crossed and extended in front and the neck is drawn back with the chest held out, the head looks directly forward. A bell hangs in front from a neck collar.

A famous example of this subject is the hound with a bell collar formerly in the Desmond Gure collection and now in the Sackler Museum in Washington (66 pl 204). The Gure/Sackler piece is, however, more relaxed than Exhibit 238 which shows an alertness and attention more appropriate to a watchdog at work. (AHF)

Compare: 24 pl.25 No.1
Collection: The Peony Collection

239

EAGLE AND BEAR

SOUTHERN SONG DYNASTY
(1127 - 1279)

PE120

LENGTH : 6.8 CM
BREADTH : 2.8 CM
HEIGHT : 2.5 CM

A figure of a recumbent bear in off-white nephrite. The strong shoulders extend forward into paws which meet slightly to the left of the creature and support the chin. An eagle struggles up between the hind legs at the back of the bear, where its long tail is still depicted and the rest of its body emerges with its wings starting to unfold.

The subject matter is a rebus for heroism or courage derived from the sounds of the Chinese words being "Ying" meaning "eagle" and "bravery" and "hong" meaning "strength" and "bear". The dating of Exhibit 239 to the Southern Song period is tentative and rests more upon the quiet strength of the sculptural feeling than any other single factor. (AHF)

Collection: The Peony Collection

240

FEMALE PRAYING MANTIS

SOUTHERN SONG
(1127 - 1279)

BATEA 416

LENGTH : 5.5 CM
HEIGHT : 2.9 CM
WIDTH : 1.5 CM

Female praying mantis naturalistically depicted with prominent sexual organs, the jade of greenish-grey colour with dark brown markings.

The praying mantis was considered a symbol of bravery and was a popular subject of Chinese art in the Song and Yuan periods, but during later periods the motif is seldom seen. The explicit depiction of the sexual organs on animals is considered a feature of the naturalistic animal carvings of the Song dynasty. The colour of the jade here can also be paralleled by some jade vessels in the shapes commonly found in Longquan and Junyao ceramics of the period assigned, such as Exhibit 250. (BSM)

Previously published: (i) 37, No.182 (ii) 51 p. 121 fig 24

241

RECUMBENT MALE BUFFALO

SOUTHERN SONG
(1127 - 1279)

BATEA 423

LENGTH : 6 CM
WIDTH : 4.2 CM
HEIGHT : 2.4 CM

White jade pebble with orange suffusions carved as a recumbent male buffalo, its male sexual organs explicit, its front leg bent in an alert posture, its forehead with small incised button.

As mentioned in the commentary on Exhibit 240 the explicit inclusion of the sexual organs as here seems a feature at this period. (BSM)

Compare: <u>25, No. 270</u>

242

CHUBBY BOY HOLDING A BLACK CAT

SONG DYNASTY
(960 - 1279)

BATEA 502

HEIGHT: 7.3 CM
WIDTH: 4.6 CM
DEPTH: 3.3 CM

Off-white jade group of a standing chubby boy holding a greyish-black cat in his arms, its body and feet dangling down.

The use of stone with two colours by the Chinese jade lapidary has a very long history stretching back to at least the Shang dynasty (see the tortoises and birds in Lady Fu Hao's tomb c.1400 BC). The use of two colours as here to define separate subject matters was particularly popular in the Song dynasty. The depiction of chubby children (certainly depicted in the Song and Yuan dynasties (see Exhibit 252) continued to be popular well into the Ming dynasty. The position in which the cat is held, though an inappropriate way, is typical of how a child holds a cat. This well observed depiction seems to fulfill all the criteria for a Song dating and the writer believes it should be so dated. (BSM)

Previously published: <u>73, pl. XVIII</u>.

243
RECUMBENT PIG

SOUTHERN SONG DYNASTY
   (1127 - 1279)

PE51

LENGTH : 5.9 CM
BREADTH : 3.2 CM
HEIGHT : 3.1 CM

A recumbent pig in pearly-grey opaque nephrite discoloured brown through burial on both front knees, the nose and entire left hindquarters. The material has been carefully and smoothly reduced in every particular and the legs and cloven hoofs are well finished beneath. The creature has a long hairy tail of fine work carved round to rest on the lower right rump.

The re-emergence of the pig, which we have seen as having particular importance in the North China Neolithic period and in the Han dynasty, is most likely without particular significance in this period. The beautiful subtlety of the undulations of the body, suggesting both fatness and grace, should be noted together with the very carefully worked and uncommon form of eye in punctilious relief. (AHF)

Collection: The Peony Collection

244
BIRD AND LILY PLAQUE

JIN DYNASTY
   (1115 - 1234)

PE524

LENGTH : 6.2 CM
BREADTH : 5.2 CM
THICKNESS : 1.0 CM

An oval plaque in translucent white nephrite rising to a small ogival point at the top. The flat-based perimeter rises on each side in a low, flattened arch. From the base rises and extends a convex and complex openwork carving of some depth and perspective depicting a tangle of stems and leaves and a massive open lily flower with long stamens. A small bird, with crested head turned back, perches on a twig at the top right hand corner.

This can be considered a classic Southern Song period, Jin taste, piece of excellent composition and material. There are adequate comparative examples of this type in pure gold openwork. (AHF)

Collection: The Peony Collection

18 YUAN DYNASTY 1279-1368

Little is known about the jades of the Yuan dynasty, although, as mentioned in the essay "The Fluctuating Jewel" jade was in fairly plentiful supply during this period. There also seems to have been a fashion for jade of yellowish or roast chestnut colour at the time.

In 1234, on their way to their conquest of China, the Mongol founders of the Yuan dynasty overran the Jin dynasty and absorbed its art including its jade working traditions, into their own artistic repertoire. The Jin had overthrown the Liao dynasty in 1125 and were themselves heirs to the jade working traditions of the Liao. Following their conquest of China the Yuan dynasty fell heirs in addition to the jade working traditions of the Song dynasty.

The fashion for jade flowers continued from the Jin dynasty through the Yuan dynasty and continued into the Ming. The earliest undecorated Yuan flowers appear to have only five petals or lobes but there was a tendency towards more elaborate forms and a multiplication of the flowers as time went on (Exhibit 256).

A range of pierced plaques, finials and motifs inherited through the Liao and Jin dynasties, such as a hawk attacking a goose or swan, Exhibit 218, continued to be produced at this time.

This period was one of economic prosperity, flourishing foreign trade, social change and cultural enrichment. The Mongol rulers of the Yuan, however, operated an exploitive regime under which the Han and southern Chinese people were slaves by law. After eliminating the civil service examinations, the Mongols themselves monopolised the civil service. As a result, the Chinese intelligentsia were forced to earn a living with their creative skills. This led to considerable achievements in artistic fields such as painting and drama. The monopolisation of the civil service by the Mongols, some of whom were illiterate, led to an increase in the need for seals, a number of which were of jade.

Historical material on Yuan jade carving indicates that during this period there was increased emphasis on craftsmanship and decoration and the beginning of the commercialisation of jade. Yuan craftsmen turned away from the monumental simplicity of atmosphere, form and line so characteristic of the Song period.

Jade was widely used by the Mongol rulers for adornment, even more so than during the Song, Liao and Jin periods. For example, it is recorded that all the emperor's head-dresses, garments and carriages were decorated with jade, and ritual tablets and the imperial seal were made of jade. On the fall of the Yuan dynasty in 1368, the emperor Shundi, left behind many jade items such as a bed and a white jade archway in the Jade Virtue Hall. All his ornaments and accoutrements were made of or decorated with jade. 92 p.106.

The jade wine basin decorated with dragons and fabulous animals amid waves mentioned in the essay 'Raw Material', is recorded as having been commissioned in 1265, before the conquest of China, by the Yuan Mongol ruler of the day.

Imperial restrictions on the use of jade by officials continued during the Yuan, and only first-ranking officials were allowed to wear belts of jade, whether plain, decorated or made of eight pieces; officials of the first to third ranks were allowed vessels of gold or jade and only the first rank were permitted to use jade on their horses. Laymen were forbidden to wear jade or gold on their caps, but jade was used to indicate rank on the hats of nobles. Although a nine dragon design with a front facing dragon is recorded as having been worn by the emperor, the designs of those worn by other ranks of nobles are not known.

Three imperial workshops were established in the capital in 1278, 1279 and 1280. The most important of these during the Yuan dynasty was that located at Dadu. There also appears to have been an important jade centre at Helin which was later moved to Hangzhou.

The fashion for collecting ancient bronzes and jades, which stimulated the craft of jade carving and, in particular, encouraged the manufacture and collection of jade reinterpretations of ancient bronzes, continued from the Southern Song into the Yuan. It is also possible that jades in the shape of Junyao bowls and Longquan celadon vases continued to be produced in the Yuan dynasty, Exhibits 249 - 251.

Apart from belt plaques, few jades have been found in Yuan dynasty tombs. A seal and a covered *zhu*, a reinterpretation of a Shang bronze form, were found in the tomb of Fan Wen hu at Anqing, Anhui province which is dated 1301. On the cover of this *zhu* is a flower with leaves which would certainly not have appeared on the Shang original. Yuan dynasty cups in the shape of flowers with pierced handles in high relief, and cups with ring handles have also been excavated. Jade cups were popular during this period and rhytons, flanged cups, those of petal form and drinking cups with goose head handles, are all known from Yuan excavations 92 pp 130-134. A cup with a lingzhi fungus handle in this exhibition (Exhibit 262) is

considered a good candidate for a Yuan date.

Jade belt hooks and pendant rings for use on belts, frequently depicting a dragon, were popular during this period, as were jade openwork belt plaques although the latter continued to be produced well into the Ming. Other popular motifs were mythological animals, such as flying sea dragons, dragon headed tortoise and animals of all types with wings. Exhibits 258 and 261 are considered typical Yuan examples.

In many Yuan jade sculptures, animals are depicted among clouds or waves, or on vehicles composed of clouds. These decorative conventions certainly originated in the Yuan dynasty and continued through the Ming into the Qing, although examples of animals among clouds or on a vehicle of clouds from this latter period are very rare. There were, however, changes in decorative style over this long period and the somewhat mannered earlier style became freer during the Ming dynasty. Waves with great curling crests similar to those on the David vases dated 1351 appear on the 1265 jade wine basin already mentioned. While the depiction of animals in the Yuan followed Song naturalistic styles, the mythical animals, particularly the dragon that were part of the jade worker's menagerie in the Liao and Jin dynasties also returned to favour. Yuan dynasty animals often have no decoration on the base, but after the Yuan undecorated bases are rare except on modern copies of early pieces.

Brian McElney
January 1994

Included in this section is a group of jades featuring bird-shaped headed figures with human or other zoomorphic characteristics (Exhibits 271 - 276). Some of these figures have human hands holding a mirror and it is possible that they were once associated with Shamanistic practices. Since certain aspects of Taoism were linked to Shamanism, these pieces may represent main stream Chinese taste but it seems more likely that they were produced by one of the cultures practicing Shamanism outside China, such as the Tungusic peoples of northern Manchuria and some groups within Mongolia and Siberia. Most of these jades are pierced hat ornaments and some of the figures have circlets on their heads similar to those found on jade depictions of foreign tribute bearers such as Exhibit 225.

The dating and provenance of this group will remain uncertain (25 and 82, p. 90 - 92) until an example from a scientifically excavated source is found. They are grouped together here for ease of reference, and also because the authors believe that they should be dated no later than the Yuan dynasty. Dates generally assigned to this group range from the Tang to the Yuan, but in all probability, such styles began during the Six Dynasties period when there was extensive foreign influence in China.

Angus Forsyth
Brian McElney
January 1994

元 代

今人對元代玉器認識有限，除<隨時勢遷動的瑰寶>
文中提及元代玉材供應充足外，其他資料顯示
黃玉及栗子色玉最受歡迎。

　　蒙古人繼承了金人的藝術傳統，金人的藝術則受
遼的影響。金代流行的玉花，到元明仍有製造。元代早
期玉花多是素面五瓣，後來逐漸變得繁複（展品256）。透
雕牌及嵌飾如春水、秋山等繼續出現（展品218）。

　　元代經濟蓬勃，對外貿易尤其發達。此時期社會
及文化變遷亦大。蒙古統治者對漢人多採剝削態度，
他們廢除了科舉制度，壟斷了中央政府要職，漢族知識
份子被逼另謀出路，轉向藝術領域如繪畫、戲劇等發
展。部份蒙古官員為文盲，故印章（包括玉印）激增。

　　元玉器注重雕工及裝飾，一反宋代線條簡潔傳
統。商用玉亦於此時開始。

　　蒙古帝王用玉，比宋遼有過之而無不及，除皇帝
的頭飾、衣飾和車飾均玉製外，圭和璽印亦用玉。據稱
元順帝去位時遺有玉榻，玉德堂中有玉拱門，其隨身用
品及裝飾物皆玉製或飾以玉片（92,頁106）。

　　<玉器原料>文中提及的瀆山大玉海，傳說是
元世祖在1265年還未完全統一中國之前下令雕製的。
元朝廷對官員用玉亦有限制，玉腰帶，無論是素面，附
紋飾或由八塊組成，只有一品官員才能佩用，玉馬飾
亦如是。一至三品官才准用金製或玉製器皿，庶民
不准用金玉冠飾，貴族的玉冠飾有等級之分，天子用
九龍紋，其他官階用的紋飾不詳。

　　官辦的玉作坊在1278、1279及1280年，分別在大
都（北京）各處成立，和林似乎亦有玉業工場，後遷往
杭州。大都始終保持其重要製玉中心的地位。

　　元代對古銅古玉的興趣不下於南宋，玉工遂以
古銅器作藍本。此外，亦流行仿當時名窰（如鈞窰）及青
瓷器皿（展品249至251）。

　　除玉帶板外元玉器出土不多，安徽省安慶市
范文虎墓（1301年）曾出玉印及玉觶，觶蓋飾花葉，當
非商器原紋。其他出土元玉器，有帶鏤空柄或活環之花
形杯、闊沿杯、鵝首杯及角形杯等（92,頁130-134），顯示
玉杯在元代極受歡迎。展品262之靈芝柄杯想亦是元器。

　　飾龍紋之帶鈎及帶環相當流行，透雕帶板亦是此
期特色，唯此類透雕延續至明代。翼龍、龍首龜及其他
有翼神獸比比皆是，展品258及261即為典型元代作品。

　　1341年出版之<古玉圖>說及名畫家趙孟頫
（1254-1322）曾購一古玉辟邪作鎮紙之用，證實了在
元代已有用玉雕作鎮紙的習慣，也證實了動物玉雕的
長久歷史。元動物玉雕多作乘雲或乘波濤狀，此傳統
維持至明清，唯表現手法不同。早期雲紋較生硬，
至明代才顯得自然奔放，至清代已日益少見了。
元波濤紋多帶捲浪，此手法在瓷器（如大維德至正
十一年瓶）和玉器（如瀆山大玉海）上均可見到。除取自
自然界之動物外，神獸及各種形式的龍均為普遍題材。
元動物玉雕底部不刻紋飾，元以後此手法不多見，
現代製品則是例外。

245

OVAL OPENWORK PLAQUE

LATE SONG OR YUAN DYNASTY
(12TH - 14TH CENTURY)
PE522

DIAMETER : 7.8 CM
THICKNESS : 6.4 CM

An oval plaque in translucent off-white nephrite formed with an undercut basal perimeter right inside which rises and extends a convex and complex openwork carving of some depth and perspective depicting a long-tailed bird with finely wrought feathers, half opened wings and crested head. It stands amid a series of stems, branches, leaves, buds and open flowers of wild plum or prunus.

Very similar, even if only in low relief and without openwork, examples occur on lacquer vessels and boxes securely dated to the Yuan period. Other renderings of this subject in jade are known but Exhibit 245 displays an unusual delicacy and refinement such as is shown in the curling of the individual leaves. (AHF)

Compare: 100 pl.255
Collection: The Peony Collection

246

THREE IN ONE BELT BUCKLE

JIN OR YUAN DYNASTY
  (12TH - 14TH CENTURY)
                                    PE558
LENGTH : 14 CM
BREADTH: 4.4 CM
HEIGHT : 1.8 CM

Front belt fitting or buckle in translucent white nephrite formed as
two side panels arranged horizontally about an elliptical vertical
panel, the whole integrally connected and created from the same
orange/chestnut skinned white jade pebble. Each side panel has an
external loop projection and is carved in deep openwork with a
goose diving through twisting stems of lotus leaves and flowers.
The central panel is carved with a single half open lotus bud and a
leaf arranged across the upright stalk.

A taste for composite structures of connected but separate pieces
formed from the same stone re-emerged in the 12th or 13th century
after disappearing for 1,600 years after the Spring and Autumn
period. See 37 pl 246 for a slightly more sophisticated and mature
example. Exhibit 246 is in a fine white material displaying the
popular subject of a goose diving through lotus stems, leaves and
flowers but without the often encountered accompaniment of a
perching hawk or kestrel, as seen on Exhibit 218. See 83 pl 40.
(AHF)

Compare: 37 pl.246
Collection: The Peony Collection

247

FANTAIL PHOENIX PLAQUE FITTING

LATE SONG TO YUAN DYNASTY
(12TH - 14TH CENTURY)

PE699

LENGTH : 4.2 CM
WIDTH : 3.5 CM
HEIGHT : 1.8 CM

A convex plaque-form phoenix in translucent off-white nephrite with an elaborate openwork squared fantail extending behind the elegant vertically held S-form neck and head. The head sports a bifurcated crest, one furl of which curls up and forward while the other curls down to strike the centre of the back. The shoulders are incised with cross-hatched feather work. The openwork tail is formed as a fan shape supported at each side by scrolling vegetal forms. At intervals there are hollowed out cups for holding small precious stones.

James Watt comments on an almost identical piece in the Fuller collection in Seattle in 83 pl 38. which he dates to the Song dynasty, but there seems to be no reason why a Yuan date for Exhibit 247 should not be considered appropriate. (AHF)

Compare: 83 pl.38
Collection: The Peony Collection

248

WHITE HOBBY-HORSE RIDER

LATE SONG TO YUAN DYNASTY
(13TH - 14TH CENTURY)

PE588

LENGTH : 6.7 CM
HEIGHT : 6.5 CM
BREADTH: 2.0 CM

A male figure in translucent sweet-white nephrite riding a hobby-horse. He stands with crooked knee astride the hobby-horse with his body twisted to face right. He wears a simple cloth headdress with a short central two-faced ribbon or streamer and his arms are covered with extended narrow sleeve terminals, that on the right side falling behind his back and that on the left side curling around and across the right of the hobby-horse's neck.

The immaculate smoothness of movement extending to the furled cuff at the end of the long left sleeve has a Song period softness but is perhaps belied in this case by the rather typical Mongol form of headdress indicating a Yuan dating. The subject matter of one or more of the 100 boys riding hobby-horses so popular a motif in the Song dynasty and later. The depiction of a bearded adult riding a hobby-horse is unusual. (AHF)

Collection: The Peony Collection

249

Hard stone bowl of Junyao shape

Southern Song or Yuan dynasty (12th - 14th century)

BATEA 1205

Diameter: 14 cm
Depth: 6.5 cm

Undecorated circular hard stone bowl of classic Southern Song/Yuan dynasty Junyao ceramic shape, the hard stone of yellowish fawn colour with well-formed foot rim and gently rising sides. The composition of the stone, which does not appear to be nephrite, has not been analysed. It is however hard stone. (BSM)

Collection: The Rannerdale Collection

250

JADE BOWL OF JUNYAO SHAPE

SOUTHERN SONG OR YUAN DYNASTY
  (13TH - 14TH CENTURY)
                              BATEA 1234
DIAMETER: 8.7 CM
HEIGHT: 4 CM

Undecorated black and grey jade circular shallow bowl of typical Junyao ceramic form.

This broad, shallow, straight-sided form with distinctive foot is typical of Junyao ceramics of the 13th and early 14th centuries. The influence of the forms of Junyao ceramics on other contemporary Chinese arts has been commented on elsewhere and is also true in regard to jade. (BSM)

Previously published: 37, No. 203
Collection: The Rannerdale Collection

251

JADE BOWL OF
JUNYAO SHAPE

SOUTHERN SONG OR
YUAN DYNASTY
 (13TH - 14TH CENTURY)
              BATEA 422
DIAMETER : 9.6 CM
HEIGHT : 3.6 CM

A thinly-walled, circular, undecorated shallow jade bowl
on high slightly splayed foot, the jade of pale straw colour
with extensive brown flecking; the bowl of typical 13th to
early 14th century Junyao shape. (BSM)

Compare: Exhibit No. 250

252

BOY WITH LOTUS LEAF AND FLOWER

SONG OR YUAN DYNASTY
(11TH - 13TH CENTURY)

BATEA 542

HEIGHT : 5.2 CM
WIDTH : 3.3 CM
DEPTH : 2 CM

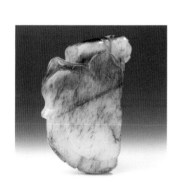

Chubby jade boy holding a lotus flower with thick petals and a lotus leaf over his left shoulder with both hands, his left foot and knee raised, his hair tied in two top-knots, the skin of the pebble at that point black, his waistcoat tied at the waist with tassels at the back, the stone with extensive brown rivering.

A child holding a lotus plant was a popular subject in Chinese art in the Song and Yuan periods. On the festival of *Qixi*, the seventh evening of the seventh lunar month when the constellations of the cowherd and weaving maid met, the streets in China, especially the capitals, would be filled with children dressed in waistcoats and holding a lotus leaf or plant. They were, as the records tell us, imitating the Moheluo cult object of the festival. Reproductions of this object made of clay, ivory, gold and aromatic substances are recorded. There is no doubt that some Moheluo figures were made of jade, as one of the most popular stories of the Song-Yuan period entitled *"Guan yin* of Carved Jade" mentions the owner of a jade stone consulting his artisans as to what to carve the jade into, and during the discussion one of the artisans suggested that the shape of the jade would lend itself well to that of the Moheluo. It was eventually decided to carve it into a *Guan yin*. The Moheluo cult continued well into the Yuan dynasty for it also figured prominently in one of the best known Yuan dramas, named "Zhang Gongmu Zhikan Moheluo". However, the cult seems to have ceased rather abruptly in the Ming period, though the image of a boy holding a lotus remained popular and many authors simply refer to these figures as a boy holding lotus. The detailed modelling and the clever employment of the skin of the pebble to give brown edges to the leaves of the lotus and flower are reminscent of early paintings. This piece seems a good example of a Moheluo figure of the Song or Yuan period. (BSM)

Previously published: <u>77, No. 49</u>
Compare: (i) <u>82, No. 94</u> (ii) <u>19, No. 127</u>

253
SINGLE WHITE JADE ASTRAGAL

LIAO OR JIN DYNASTY
 (10TH - 13TH CENTURY)
                    BATEA 415

LENGTH : 3.2 CM
HEIGHT : 2 CM
WIDTH : 1.6 CM

Single white jade astragal naturalistically carved and pierced for supension.

Astragals, the ankle bones of cloven-hoofed animals such as sheep, have been used extensively in north China from the Liao period on as dice or for the casting of lots. Replicas in jade as here, probably for use as pendants, were popular in the Liao and Jin periods and have been found in a number of tombs of those periods (10 - 13th centuries) in Inner Mongolia, but have not so far been recorded from other areas of China. Jade astragals more conventionalised and not so naturalistic as the present example, were made apparently for the Tibetan market in the 18th and 19th centuries. (BSM)

Previously published: 51, p.123, fig. 29
Compare similar pieces published: (i) 82 Exhibit 161. (ii) WW 1977 p.58 from a Jin tomb

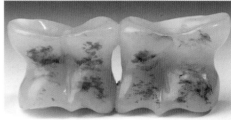

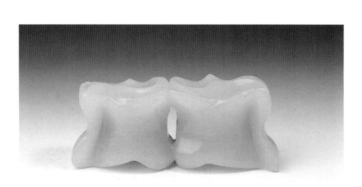

254
JADE DOUBLE ASTRAGAL

LIAO OR JIN DYNASTY
 (10TH - 13TH CENTURY)
                    BATEA 483

LENGTH : 5.8 CM
HEIGHT : 1.7 CM
WIDTH : 1.4 CM

Jade double astragal joined horizontally and naturalistically rendered, the jade of whitish tone, one side retaining part of the orange skin. (BSM)

Compare: (i) 82, No. 161. (ii) Exhibit 253

255

STEM CUP WITH FLARED STEM

JIN OR YUAN DYNASTY
 (12 - 14TH CENTURY)

BATEA 1296

HEIGHT: 12.5 CM
DIAMETER: 7 CM
HEIGHT OF STEM : 5.2 CM

Circular jade deep stem cup with hollow flared stem, the jade of light greyish-green colour, the inside of the U-shaped cup well hollowed out, the rim of the cup and base of the stem with borders of incised classic scroll decoration confined between two incised lines.

A gold cup of identical shape with similar incised classic scroll borders has recently been excavated from a Jin dynasty tomb. Such classic scroll borders are, however, commonly found in the art of both the Jin and Yuan dynasties and it may belong to either dynasty, though this recently excavated piece makes a Jin date more likely. (BSM)

Compare: 20 No. 157
Collection: The Rannerdale Collection

256

SIX JADE FLOWERS

JIN TO EARLY MING DYNASTY
(12TH - 15TH CENTURY)
BATEA 586
LENGTH : 4.7CM - 2.7CM
WIDTH : 3.0CM - 2.2CM

Six flowers in pale whitish celadon jade, one with five petals, two with six petals and three others of varying forms, one of them a multiple of five flowers.

Jade flowers of the types shown here are one of the most common finds from Jin, Yuan and early Ming tombs. The plain Jin examples appear to be six-petalled, and the plain Yuan examples five-petalled. Multiple flowers first appeared during the Yuan dynasty but continued into the Ming dynasty. The single flowers are chiefly confined to the pre-Ming period. Jade flowers are discussed at length by Professor Cheng Tekun in 6. (BSM)

Compare: 82, No. 164-174

257

PHOENIX HAT OR
DRESS ORNAMENT

YUAN DYNASTY
  (1279 - 1368)
                    PE549
LENGTH : 5.4 CM
BREADTH : 4.0 CM
HEIGHT : 2.2 CM

A phoenix in translucent white nephrite, possibly a headdress ornament. The body is formed as a flat plate with a central depression in the fore part, and features the crested head on the topside and a convex chest swelling on the underside. The highly stylised wings are decked with incised feathers on the shoulders and swept back to meet the lyre-form openwork tail feathers extending behind. A small lateral tail feather on each side curls forward to touch each wing. Two connected holes are pierced on the underside, presumably for attachment.

This form of openwork tail and swept-back crest is well established on embroidered textiles of the late Song and Yuan dynasties. (AHF)

Collection: The Peony Collection

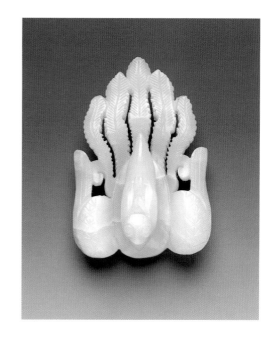

258

MYTHICAL ANIMAL

YUAN DYNASTY
  (1279 - 1368)
                    BATEA 491
LENGTH : 4.4 CM
WIDTH : 3.5 CM
HEIGHT : 3.1 CM

Tubby roast-chestnut-yellow and brown jade mythical animal with triangular head, pointed nose and cornucopia-shaped ears, the feet placed to frame the underside in an almost diamond formation, its hocks accentuated by incisions, the jaw and long tail with some hair incisions.

The roast-chestnut colour is reputed to have been popular in the Yuan dynasty. (BSM)

Previously published: 77, No. 58

259
MYTHICAL ANIMAL WITH BAT

JIN OR YUAN DYNASTY
(12TH - 14TH CENTURY)
BATEA 466

LENGTH : 7.1 CM
WIDTH : 4.8 CM
HEIGHT : 3.8 CM

A mythical animal slinking forward, the right front and left rear legs advancing, its beaked head facing to the right, its tail bifid, its claws prominent. A bat, with wings outstretched rests on the body of the animal. The jade partly of black colour on the base and neck, the spine knobbly and showing off the white body with extensive brown flecking.

The posture of the animal here is reminiscent of some Six Dynasties sculptures of animals but the inclusion of the bat with its good luck connotations is indicative of a later date. The beaked nature of the animals' head is a feature frequently found in animals from the Tang through to the Yuan dynasty and its inclusion here, combined with the natural black colour and other details mentioned, render a dating to the Jin or Yuan dynasty appropriate. (BSM)

260
BACTRIAN CAMEL WITH HANDLER

YUAN DYNASTY
(1279 - 1368)
BATEA 546

LENGTH : 9 CM
HEIGHT : 5.7 CM
WIDTH : 3.4 CM

Jade recumbent Bactrian camel and handler of greyish-celadon colour with extensive brown inclusions. The handler wears a baggy garment and cap with a feather and he may be striving to control the animal.

The dress of the handler is similar to that found on some Yuan tomb figures. The camel was a common subject in Chinese art from the Wei dynasty through to the Yuan, but thereafter its depiction seems comparatively uncommon. The wearing of a feather in the cap is also found on some Yuan dynasty figures. (BSM)

Previously published: 77, pl. No.XV
Compare: (i) 89 No. 276 (ii) 89 No. 32

261
STANDING *QILIN*

YUAN DYNASTY
(1279 - 1368)
BATEA 468
HEIGHT : 7.6 CM
LENGTH : 5.5 CM
DEPTH : 1.5 CM

Jade standing *qilin* its long neck drawn back, its head with bulging eyes, the neck showing extensive muscles and tresses of incised hair, the body covered with scales, its long tail between the legs and curling up to touch the back of its neck, the legs like an eagle's with flame-like projections at the front of each leg, the jade of mainly greyish-celadon colour, the hind quarters mainly brown. (BSM)

Previously published: 79, No. 57

262
CIRCULAR JADE CUP WITH LINGZHI HANDLE

JIN OR YUAN DYNASTY
(12TH - 14TH CENTURY)
BATEA 453
DIAMETER : 7.1 CM
HEIGHT : 3.2 CM

Circular greyish-white jade cup with small low foot and narrow band thickening the rim; the handle formed as a pierced lingzhi fungus head.

The writer has seen a silver cup of identical shape and handle with the complex classic scroll border commonly found on late Jin and Yuan porcelains and bronzes. Lingzhi handles are common on bronzes and porcelain vases of the Yuan period. Jade cups are one of the most common items found in tombs of the Yuan dynasty and a Yuan dating seems probable. (BSM)

263

CUP WITH *KUI* DRAGON HANDLES
YUAN DYNASTY
(1279 - 1368)

PE401

WIDTH : 14.5 CM
HEIGHT : 4.5 CM

A hemispherical cup formed from greyish off-white translucent
nephrite with some brown suffusions. The piece has a well-formed
foot rim, inside the base perimeter of which is an incised Mongolian
inscription. At each side is a free standing *kui* dragon with a single
horn and flowing mane rising to bite the lip of the vessel and using
its short arms on powerful shoulders to grip the rim with large well
finished claws forming the handles. Each animal has a bifurcated
rope twist tail extending round the side. The interior and exterior
are finished to a high gloss overall and the entire exterior is incised
with an elaborate flowing field of dragons among clouds below an
incised rim border of a broad *leiwen* pattern.

James Watt mentions in <u>82 No.139</u>, that there are well known
instances of this simple bowl-form cup with a raised vertical
footrim and opposing long-tailed *kui* dragons forming with their
bodies side handles in Yingqing glazed ceramics of the late Song
to Yuan periods. There is no reason to ascribe this piece to a later
date and the Mongolian inscription inside the base is another
indicator of a Yuan date. The dragon handles display immense
strength, poise and power which contrasts well with the finely
incised dragons and clouds covering the exterior. (AHF)

Compare: <u>82 No.139</u>
Collection: The Peony Collection

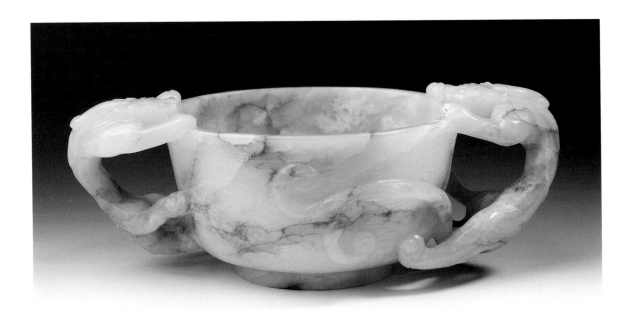

264
KNEELING MONKEY HOLDING PEACH

YUAN TO EARLY MING DYNASTY
(13TH - 15TH CENTURY)
BATEA 523
HEIGHT : 5.7 CM
WIDTH : 2.6 CM

Yellow jade kneeling monkey holding up a peach with both paws, its expressive face looking forward and resting against the peach, its back, stunted tail and left arm and top and left side of its head in a rich brown colour.

A monkey with the peaches of longevity became a common decorative element in Chinese pottery in the 13th and 14th century. The similarity of the iconography to that of Hanuman on bas-relief carvings on Javanese Hindu-Buddhist monuments is striking. The colour of the jade used here is also suggestive of a Yuan date but an early Ming date cannot be ruled out. (BSM).

Previously published: (i) 82, No. 69 (ii) 37, No. 148

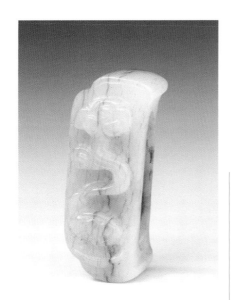

265
FITTING WITH TORTOISE BELCHING CLOUDS

YUAN OR EARLY MING DYNASTY
(14TH - 15TH CENTURY)
BATEA 1215
LENGTH : 3.4 CM
WIDTH : 1.4 CM

Jade belt or dagger fitting of pierced lobed roughly rectangular shape with slight hooks at both ends, decorated on the top with a tortoise belching clouds in high relief, the jade of greyish colour with brown flecks.

The tortoise was a Daoist motif and popular in the period assigned. The clouds depicted here are done in a way reminiscent of some of those on Yuan and early Ming ceramics. (BSM)

Collection: The Rannerdale Collection

266

WINGED STANDING *QILIN* ON BED OF CLOUDS

YUAN TO EARLY MING DYNASTY
(13TH - 15TH CENTURY)
BATEA 495

HEIGHT : 3.6 CM
LENGTH : 3.4 CM
WIDTH : 2.7 CM

One-horned jade *qilin* carved with wings sprouting from its front legs, its bi-forked tail going between the legs and up over the back, the whole standing on a thin layer of stylised clouds.

The depiction of animals standing on clouds was a convention associated with the art of popular Daoism in the Yuan dynasty, for example the sculptures and wall paintings of the Daoist temple Yongle Gong. The convention continued throughout the Ming dynasty but the style of the cloud vehicle here suggests that this is an early depiction. (BSM)

Previously published: 77, No. 57

267

MYTHICAL ANIMAL

YUAN OR EARLY MING DYNASTY
(14TH - 15TH CENTURY)
BATEA 1225

LENGTH : 7.8 CM
HEIGHT : 4.8 CM
DEPTH : 1.8 CM

Pale-celadon jade one-horned mythical animal, its head turned back and touching its knobbly back, its hocks with C scrolls and flaming excrescences, its eyebrows pronounced.

This animal is far removed from the naturalistic style of the Song, and the inclusion of C scrolls at the hocks and flaming excrescences on the legs suggest a Yuan or early Ming dating as appropriate. (BSM)

Collection: The Rannerdale Collection

268

MYTHICAL ANIMAL AND OFFSPRING

YUAN OR EARLY MING DYNASTY
(14TH - 15TH CENTURY)
BATEA 1224

LENGTH : 8.9 CM
HEIGHT : 6.3 CM
WIDTH : 0.5 CM

Greenish-celadon jade carving of one-horned mythical animal and offspring both seated with flaming hocks, C scrolls and bi-forked tail.

This representation was probably a belt plaque. (BSM)

Collection: The Rannerdale Collection

269

SAGE, WATER POT, DEER AND CHILDREN

YUAN TO EARLY MING DYNASTY
  (13TH - 15TH CENTURY)
                              BATEA 516
LENGTH : 19.5 CM
HEIGHT : 6.2 CM
WIDTH : 7.4 CM

A white-flecked celadon jade group for the scholar's studio of a sage seated with his back to a waterpot depicted as a wine jar with a lotus leaf cover, two supine deer and a boy at the back and to the left side of the group, three boys playing on the right side of the sage, two of them holding a fungus spray forming two brush-rests.

The face of the sage can be compared to those of figures in Yuan paintings and the lotus cover for the wine jar waterpot is found on many Yuan ceramic jars. (BSM)

Previously published: Chinese Antiquities from the Brian S. McElney Collection Hong Kong City Hall 1987, Exhibit 149

270

MONSTER HEAD SCROLL WEIGHT

YUAN OR MING DYNASTY
(13TH - 16TH CENTURY)

BATEA 599

WIDTH : 6.2 CM
LENGTH : 5 CM
HEIGHT : 3.1 CM

A naturalistically carved one-horned monster head with curled up
eyebrows, deep set eyes and snub nose, the monster head with only
an upper jaw, the base with some incised decoration. The jade of
yellowish-white colour with dark brown suffusions. Probably a
scroll weight for the scholar's studio. (BSM)

271

BIRD-SHAPED HAT ORNAMENT

TANG TO YUAN DYNASTY
(7TH - 14TH CENTURY)

BATEA 492

WIDTH : 3.7 CM
LENGTH : 3 CM
HEIGHT : 2.5 CM

A bird-shaped hat ornament *(chi)* in dark, predominently black
jade, the head bare with wig-like fringe, the wings and tail spread
out, the front with humanoid breasts and hands, the flat base
perforated for attachment.

This type of hat ornament seems to have been used from the Tang
to the Yuan dynasty with comparatively few changes in style over
this long period. A shamanistic or Daoist origin for the design has
been suggested. (BSM)

Previously published: 77 No. 41
Compare (i) similar bird hat ornament discussed in 25, pl. 4LB, with a late Tang date
suggested. (ii) 82, No.74 where a Tang date is also suggested. (iii) 51, p. 116, fig. 9

272

Large Breasted Bird-Headed Creature

(7th - 14th century)

PE744

Width : 5.0 cm
Height : 2.4 cm

Nephrite pebble of semi-translucent tawny colour with brown suffusions and a reddish patch at the left hand shoulder area. The piece is formed as a large breasted, big bellied, rabbit-legged, bird-headed humanoid type figure. The bird's head rests on the chest between the breasts. Nipples are depicted on the breast and the bottom right hand corner of the stomach has an incised navel. On the back there are bifurcated ribbons in relief carving and a large, piled, concentric rope-form tail.

This piece has been grouped together with the hat ornaments for comparison since it features a bird-like head but there may in fact be no connection. There is very little of purely Chinese design or concept in this piece. It is however clearly nephrite and most likely Khotan nephrite. There is a single heart-shaped motif on each shoulder, which is similar to a well known Sogdian motif from Central Asian excavations such as Pandjikent and Tillya Tepe and which was also carried into China in the Tang dynasty. It also appears in the double vajra design incised on the base of Exhibit 195. The idea is retained through the Song and Qing dynasties as a featured element in the border designs of the Sino-Turkish taste rugs of Khotan. The combination of rabbit feet, a bird's-head and large breasts may indicate a Central Asian influence, or even origin. Associated with these questions is a sketchiness and superficiality of execution which is also somehow un-Chinese. Set against all this however, is the big breasted, big bellied wholly Chinese humorous evocations of the late Eastern Han and immediately subsequent period shown by Exhibits 163 and 173. (AHF)

Collection: The Peony Collection

273

BIRD HAT ORNAMENT

YUAN DYNASTY
(1279 - 1368)

PE673

LENGTH : 5.1 CM
BREADTH: 3.6 CM
HEIGHT : 0.7 CM

Headdress ornament in translucent white nephrite with some russet suffusions on the head modelled in relief with an encircling diadem, which meets above the forehead as two confronted outward scrolling spirals and encloses finely striated hair. The eyebrows are represented as jagged or toothed features above the sunken tear-shaped eyes which have central pupillary pits. A flowing scarf-like ornamentation or ribbon flows in an arc over the pinion feathers at each side of the head. On top of the bird there is a similar double band or streamer formed in relief as two loops of ribbon passing through a centrally placed flat ring. The tail itself is of a closely rounded fan form with parallel feathers with striations in relief. The wings rise from narrow, bare shoulders and extend back to fold along the sides with incised feather details. Each well rounded and smooth arm is encircled at the wrist with an incised bracelet or bangle. Both arms are folded into the sides with the elbows crooked and backward curving cup-form hands with scooped palms and modelled fingers are held beneath the rounded chin which is laterally pierced with a hole for suspension. The underside of the piece is formed as a plain concave roundel pierced at each side with a separate pair of joined holes for attachment. A similar pair of joined holes is pierced transversely across the underside of the tail.

The iconography of this piece closely follows that of a piece in the Freer Gallery in Washington 27 pl 70B. Exhibit 273 shares the braceletted wrists, everted palms, circular diadem broken at the front and ribbon streamers passing through a restraining ring on the tail or rump. Other common features are the flaming eyebrows and the full upturned tear-form eyes.

Professor Chuner Talesami and Dr Larisa Pavlinskaya of the Siberian Department, Peter the Great Museum of Anthroplogy and Ethnography, Russian Academy of Sciences, St Petersburg, on being shown and handling Exhibit 273 confirmed that there is no Siberian shamanistic tradition involving artefacts of this type. (AHF)

Compare: 27 pl.70B
Collection: The Peony Collection

274

BIRD HAT ORNAMENT

YUAN DYNASTY
(1279 - 1368)

PE117

LENGTH : 4.2 CM
HEIGHT : 2.6 CM

Bird, possibly a headdress ornament, of white nephrite, with red and brown on the crown of the head. The piece is of generally circular shape with the short wings folded flat upon the back and the back incised with undivided feathers, the tail feathers falling to the ground behind. The head has a ring diadem compressing long hair which is combed back and falls down around the back and sides. The feet are depicted beneath and the claws are drawn together under the head which is perforated from side to side. There is a connecting loop-form pair of holes in the centre beneath.

This piece follows the basic profile of Exhibit 273 but with less refinement and with a single loop-hole beneath for suspension rather than the base perimeter sets of holes such as those on Exhibit 273. (AHF)

Collection: The Peony Collection

275

SEATED CROSS-LEGGED GARUDA

YUAN DYNASTY
(1279 - 1368)

PE730

HEIGHT : 5.3 CM
WIDTH : 3.6 CM
THICKNESS : 1.8 CM

Figure of garuda of human-form with wings and a bird's beak in opaque-green nephrite with black and reddish-brown suffusions. The figure is seated cross-legged with bare feet folded under the distended belly. The talon-like fingers of the hands are clasped together across the chest and each arm features a plain wrist bangle and a thicker upper arm armlet with a central crosshatched band. The figure wears a necklace and has large ears from which round earrings hang down on each shoulder. The slanted eyes are wide open beneath raised line brows and the nose forms a prominent beak extending down to the chest. The figure wears an elaborate headdress with a frontal band of flame-like formations and from the crown a pair of bands falls down to each side of the back. Long fronds of hair fall down from the back of the headdress and disappear between two small wings folded across the back. The wings do not meet together and are separated by a vertical line of five vertebrae.

There is no published analogy with this remarkable piece in jade and it is difficult to identify clear Chinese parallels in other materials. There is a published gilt-bronze type of hat or belt fitting of a round plate-form garuda with human arms and spread wings but with standing legs and without the distended belly of Exhibit 275. The overall sculptural feeling of the piece is cruder from the back perspective than the somewhat more sophisticated frontal aspect - particularly the pinched and reduced contours of the lower back and buttocks. This may indicate a regional workshop or tradition. The dating of this piece to the Yuan period is consistent with the gilt-bronze piece mentioned above and also with the directly related garuda forms in gilded-wood carving of the early Ming period which show greater sophistication but similar inspiration and which can be seen today in certain temples in Beijing. (AHF)

Collection: The Peony Collection

276

STANDING ROBED BIRD-HEADED FIGURE

YUAN DYNASTY
(1279 - 1368)

PE751

HEIGHT : 4.5 CM
DEPTH : 1.7 CM
WIDTH : 1.7 CM

Robed figure in semi-translucent grey-green nephrite standing with the upper torso angled slightly back from the waist and featuring the hatted and eared head of a bird with a long beak held downwards upon the chest. The arms, formed as long feathered wings emerging from short sleeves are held at an angle in a downward folded position across the front of the body. A short sleeve cuff above the beginning of the wing feathers is finely incised with a crosshatched design. The piece is pierced from the crown of the head vertically down through the flat base for suspension.

As with Exhibit 275 there is no published analogy for this piece. It seems to be unique since no easy guidance can be gleaned from other sculptures in stone, wood, bone, ivory etc. The indications of a bird persona and very possible shamanistic associations argue well for the piece to be placed in this anthropomorphic group for the purposes of this catalogue and there is a distinct similarity with Exhibit 275 in the fine line incised band of cross-hatching on the upper arm armlet in Exhibit 275 and the short sleeved cuff in Exhibit 276. The piece is pierced for suspension and this may also indicate a shamanistic connection. Professor Wang Cheng li of Jilin University has observed to the writer that bird symbolism of the eagle is very much a feature of Tungusic Shamanism of north east China whose priests wear bird emblems on the front shoulder area of their costumes and also on a belt worn around the stomach. Sometimes these bird emblems are made of jade. (AHF)

Collection: The Peony Collection

19 MING DYNASTY 1368-1644

Most Ming dynasty jades have decorations that are part of the general currency of the Ming applied arts. These consist of either naturalistic representations of plants, birds and animals or figurative schemes, which may or may not have particular resonances of allusion 6BFJ p.39. Ming jade carvers appear, however, to have given precedence to the theme of "good fortune" in their designs, frequently to the detriment of the artistic quality of the piece. This should be contrasted with the attitude of Song craftsmen for whom the aesthetic and artistic quality of the jade carving was of paramount importance.

Jade has only occasionally been excavated from Ming tombs. In one study of thirty-four tombs only nine contained jade items and a mere four of these held jade objects other than jewellery or jade decorated belts, usually in the form of simple cups or pointed *gui*-tablets, an archaic shape for which no context other than burial can be found in Ming sources 6BFJ p.45. It is interesting to note that of the 857 jade items confiscated by the State in 1562 from the disgraced Ming politician Yan Song, no less than 284 were cups. In addition to these objects Yan Song owned 202 jade belts of either leather or fabric with jade plaques attached 6BFJ p.37. Jade belt plaques and in particular Liao dynasty reticulated plaques are discussed in the essays covering the periods 581-950 and 951-1279. Reticulated plaques and those of similar shape to excavated Liao example were still being made in the Ming dynasty with few changes in design 82 Nos. 175-183, although both Yuan and Ming plaques, which were either plain or reticulated, lack the concave rendering of the pearl-shaped roundels seen on the Liao example. Diaper background patterns, such as those on Ming lacquers and bronzes, are also frequently found

on plaques of the period. The number of plaques in any individual belt set varied between eight and fourteen, no doubt to accommodate the size of the wearer, and the plaques themselves vary in size. The use of jade belt plaques indirectly as badges of rank was commented on by the Jesuit Matteo Ricci who visited China in the late 16th century, but their use in this context was not continued into the Qing dynasty.

The frequency with which belt plaques are discovered in Ming tombs probably indicates a desire on the part of the deceased's family to ensure the same high rank in death as in life. In addition, if the plaques could not be worn by the next generation because of their lower rank, there would have been no incentive to retain such jades in their possession. For both of these reasons it is probable that jade plaques were specifically chosen for burial. Other jades were probably kept by family members as heirlooms, which could explain why so few pieces have been found in excavated Ming tombs.

Because of the lack of published excavated Ming jades it is difficult to separate those produced early or in the middle of the dynasty from those of a late Ming date. The comparatively large number of jades dated late in the dynasty (1550-1644) are characterised by their extravagant use of the material (not surprising in view of its relative abundance before 1600) the use of rebuses and certain stylised decorative conventions.

Jades produced in the early and middle years of the dynasty appear closer to the naturalistic style of the Song dynasty; they lack stylised decorative conventions and the material is not used extravagantly. There is, however, a tendency towards an emphasis on good fortune. Animals holding a lingzhi or floral spray or with their young were common subjects (Exhibits 283 and 290), and the mid Ming emperor Jiajing's (1522-66) fascination with Daoism led to the popularity of subjects associated with longevity (Exhibit 293).

Many lacquer and wooden screens made in China during the 19th and early 20th centuries have jade inserts. Although most of these inserts are of Qing date, there are also numerous examples in the decorative styles normally associated with the Ming dynasty and they should be so dated. Some of these inserts may originally have been used as belt plaques. It should be pointed out that until the late 1960s, no distinction was made by Chinese collectors between Ming and Qing jades or, indeed, between the jades of any post-Han period - all post-Han dynasty jades, other than those of the 19th and 20th centuries, were indiscriminately labelled "18th century". Nineteenth and 20th century jades were, in contrast, generally so labelled, since they were usually made with diamond abrasives they were distinguished and denigrated and supplied mainly to the tourist trade. The re-use of jades or the re-working of broken pieces of jade has occurred since neolithic times; many examples are known and several are included in this exhibition. The use of Ming pieces, particularly belt plaques, in screens during the Qing dynasty is therefore not surprising and represents a happy inspiration for their public use.

A high proportion of the jades now considered to be Ming are in the form of small figures or animals. According to Ming authors Gao Lian and Wen Zhenheng such objects were used as paperweights. These objects are, however, rarely found in Ming tombs although one tomb dated before 1539 contained a small animal and human figures, and religious figures have also been found 6BFJ p.44. Yan Song, the disgraced Ming politician, had seventeen small jade flowers, birds and figures, one jade lion paperweight, nine horses and other beasts of jade of various sizes and two jade fishes 6BFJ p.45.

There is no Ming evidence for the concept of the "fondling piece" or for the appreciation of the tactile qualities of jade carving at that time. It is therefore possible that the small jade animals normally associated with the Ming dynasty may simply have been paperweights 6BFJ p.46.

The Ming dynasty provides the only jade artist about whose work much is known. Lu Zigang was, it seems, the only jade artist normally to sign his works, and records of the time make it clear that his reputation was such that his work commanded a substantial premium. The textual evidence for Lu's life does not provide a firm date for his activities, but he is mentioned in a poem by Xu Wei who died in 1593, and in a piece by the major writer Wang Shizhen who died in 1590. The 1642 edition of the gazetteer of Taicang prefecture claims him as a native son with the words - "fifty years ago there was of this prefecture a certain Lu Zigang whose skill at carving jade with a knife remains unsurpassed to the present day. Jade hairpins by Lu fetch sixty gold pieces each. His skill was not handed on at his death." A box decorated with narcissus signed by Lu dated 1561 is generally accepted as genuine 37 No.210. A signed hairpin is also recorded 6BFJ p.42, and numerous white jade plaque pendants are inscribed with his signature, but very few, if any, are likely to be by the master. Such plaque pendants, normally of very fine quality white jade, have been referred to in this century as "Zigang" plaques. They were certainly produced from the late

Ming period (mid 16th century) right through the Qing. The earliest such plaque pendants have an auspicious seal inscription on one side and a corresponding rebus on the other 82, p.205. The earliest Zigang plaques generally depict animals and their frames are topped by cloud scrolls. During the Transitional period (1620-1683) such plaques had no frames but by the late 17th century the frames had become complex with many of the decorations being borrowed from wood-block book illustrations of the time. The seal inscriptions on the plaques had by this period ceased to have any connection with the pictorial decoration on the front. The frames were frequently rectangular and surmounted by two facing stylised kui dragons. Such plaques continued to be made after the Kangxi period, but the designs, quality of workmanship and inscriptions of those produced after the Qianlong period are markedly inferior.

During the Ming period, and particularly in the late Ming (1550-1644) there was a great vogue for the use of rebuses in the decorative arts. For example, the combination of a monkey, horse and bee, is a rebus for "may you be immediately elevated to the rank of marquis". Many of these rebuses used in the Ming period remained in use into the 20th century. The Chinese fascination with rebuses stretches back to at least the Song dynasty, but by far their greatest period of popularity was in the Ming dynasty. At this time, jades were considered particularly suitable presentation items for auspicious occasions and what better wedding present than a jade with a hidden meaning such as "may you have sons every year".

Animals riding on a vehicle of clouds or amid clouds or waves, decorative conventions which began in the Yuan dynasty, continued throughout the Ming. In the Ming waves were depicted with multiple whirlpools at their base or with the waves leaping up around an animal. Exhibit 293 is a good example of this Ming treatment. At this time the cloud bases and vehicles also became more regular and stylised.

In addition to a naturalistic style of animal carving certain decorative conventions that were anything but natural continued until the end of the Ming dynasty with some modifications in style. For example, in the later Ming dynasty, birds' wings and beaks were sometimes carved with stylised squared spirals, and other animals had additions such as incised spirals, stars, circles and flaming eyebrows. Simple stars and spirals, although rare, are known from the Song dynasty (Exhibit 241). All of these became common conventions in the Ming dynasty, and Exhibits 304 and 320 are typical examples.

Some of the jades excavated from the tomb of Wanli (d. 1620) are polished to a hard rather glassy finish which is not normally associated with such an early date. Such a high polish is considered much more indicative of a Qing dating. The polish on most Ming pieces, including all those dated prior to 1600, is also generally much softer.

Finally, some comments seem desirable on the colour of jades available or popular in the Ming dynasty. Natural black nephrite and red jade, although highly valued, do not appear to have been available at that time, although jade stained black or red would have been possible. The beautiful lychee-flesh colour so favoured in the Song dynasty was available early in the dynasty since a piece in this colour with a Xuande inscription (1422) is mentioned by James Watt in 82, p.33, but few later pieces in this highly desirable colour are known. A dated jade seal (Exhibit 298) comes close to this colour. The preferred colour depended on the use to which the jade was being put with 'vegetables' (presumably some shade of green) jade being the desired colour for belt plaques. The 16th century Ming commentator, Gou Lian, ranked a shade of yellow (*gou huang*) highest followed by 'mutton fat' white. He was also enthusiastic about deep green jades such as 'spinach' and green jade flecked with black or white 6BFJ p.36.

Brian McElney
January 1994

明 代

明代玉雕，多跟隨明藝術潮流，題材為人物花草、動物飛鳥。明玉工極喜雕製寓意吉祥的玉器，甚至影響玉雕的造型美亦在所不計，這跟宋玉工美觀至上的態度大相逕庭。

明玉器出土不多，有統計稱三十四處明墓中僅有九處出陪葬玉，多為佩飾、帶板、杯及圭，後者除陪葬器外，別無實際用途(6BFJ,頁45)。1562年，嚴嵩失勢被抄家，清單列出玉器八百五十七件，包括：二百八十四件玉杯。清單上另一項為玉帶二百零二條，即革製或絹製，上縫以玉板之衣帶(6BFJ,頁37)。透雕玉牌自遼開始使用，至明代並無重大改變(82,圖175-183)。元明玉牌除光素無紋者，多為透雕，但缺少了遼代的珍珠圍飾。晚明(1550-1644)玉牌多帶錦地紋，跟同期漆器及銅器相呼應。組成一條玉帶，帶板的數量由八塊至十四塊不等，視用者的身材而定，帶板本身的尺寸亦不劃一。十六世紀末，耶穌會士利瑪竇訪華，曾指出玉帶為官階的象徵，唯此習慣在清後便有失。

出土玉器多為帶板，想是死者親屬希望他來生重居高位，再者，如死者子孫官位稍低，玉帶便不能用，也就沒有保留的必要。但此類玉器大都世代相傳，故墓中出土甚少。因此，要分開明早期及晚期的作品不太容易。斷為晚明的玉器較多，其特徵為(甲)用料慷慨，想是與來源豐富有關，(乙)多含隱喻，(丙)裝飾手法簡化。

明早、中期玉器，則較接近宋代的寫實逼真，但多帶吉祥意味。動物口銜靈芝或花枝，子母獸等是常見題材(展品283及290)。明世宗(嘉靖)篤信道教，這時期的作品多與長壽有關(展品293)。

很多十九、二十世紀漆或木屏風嵌有玉片，部份玉片為清器，但部份帶明代風格的當為明器，推想它們原是帶板。六十年代以前，中國收藏家不甚注重分清明玉和清玉，漢代之後的玉器，除十九、二十世紀者外，一律稱"十八世紀"。十九、二十世紀玉器則不受重視，多售與遊客。殘損玉器的改裝及重雕，這習慣始自新石器時代，本展覽有數件展出。以明帶板嵌入清屏風這措施自不足為奇，亦是物盡其用。

大部份明玉雕是人物或動物肖生，高濂和文震亨均指出它們多作鎮紙用。此類玉雕極少出土，1539年墓出土之動物、人像和神像是少數例外之一(6BFJ,頁44)。嚴嵩被抄家時藏有"十七件小型玉花鳥和人像、一玉獅鎮、玉馬九件及其它玉獸玉魚"(6BFJ,頁45)。供把玩之用的玉雕此時尚未出現，動物雕多是鎮紙。

唯一為後世人所知的明代玉工為陸子剛，他亦是唯一在其製品上留款之人。他生時已極享盛名，作品倍

於常價。陸的生平活動年份不詳，詩人徐渭(卒1593年)及作家王世貞(卒1590年)均提到他。1642年<太倉州志>中記載說："五十年前州人有陸子剛者，用刀雕刻，遂擅絕。今所遺玉簪價，一支值六十金。子剛死，技亦不傳"。一署"嘉靖辛酉陸子剛製"，飾折技水仙蓋拿，一般認為是真品(37,圖210)。此外，亦有署子剛款玉簪(6BFJ,頁42)。數量眾多，帶子剛款的白玉牌(俗稱"子剛牌")，雖是質地優美，多是晚明或清代製品。早期子剛牌正面飾風景人物(多含隱喻)，背面刻吉祥句語(82,頁205)，牌頂飾雲紋。明末清初，牌的邊闌紋完全消失。至清代，邊闌紋又重新出現，並日趨繁複，紋飾多取自同期木刻版畫。此時牌背上的字句變得和牌面的風景人物毫無關連，牌頂多飾相對夔龍。乾隆後，此類玉牌無論是圖案或書法均顯著衰退。明代，特別是明晚期，寓意吉祥或語帶相關的題材極度流行，如"馬上封侯"(馬、猴、蜂)之類，中國人對隱喻的興趣在宋代已見跡象，但以晚明為最盛，至二十世紀仍不減。玉器更是吉慶場合最佳禮物，如婚禮中贈以"連生貴子"玉雕，最為適合不過。

乘雲或乘海壽的動物，自元代開始至明代，陸續有雕製。明代的波濤多以重重疊疊的旋渦構成，波濤躍起圍繞動物，如展品293。雲層則有規則而簡化。

站或臥於岩石上的動物為明代玉工首飾，另一別開生面的手法是將動物、飛鳥或其它物件以布包裹起來，如展品302。

<公元951至1279年>文中指出，宋代動物玉雕多力求寫實，但亦有距寫實甚遠之表現方法，此類方法持續至明代，如雀鳥的翼部和咀部飾回紋，動物飾回紋、星紋、圈紋，或眉毛呈火燄狀等等。簡單的星紋和回紋宋時已有，但不常見(展品241)，至明代此類紋飾已極普遍，展品304及320即為典型例子。

明神宗(萬曆，卒1620年)墓中出土某些玉器呈極強玻璃感，此種高度拋光較接近清代作風，明玉器(指1600年之前)的拋光一般來說較柔和。

最後一談明玉的顏色。黑玉和紅玉評價極高，但不可得(染色者例外)。宋時極受歡迎的荔枝肉色白玉，在明初仍可見，如屈志仁提及之帶宣德款玉雕(82,頁33)，但例子不多。展品298玉印跟此顏色最接近。玉的顏色視乎所製之物而定，如帶綠色的"菜玉"被認為適宜製帶板。高濂以甘黃為上品，羊脂白次之，此外，他亦推許深綠及帶黑或白斑的綠玉。(6BFJ,頁36)。

277
RECUMBENT RAM

EARLY MING DYNASTY
  (1368 - 1644)
                    PE123
LENGTH : 7.5 CM
HEIGHT : 6.4 CM
BREADTH : 3.0 CM

A figure of a recumbent ram in greasy yellow-white nephrite. A rope halter around the neck extends over the back. The head is turned directly to face the rear and slightly raised while the lip curls in a sneer. The legs are folded beneath with cloven hoofs. The fetlock hair is depicted in detail while the right hand foreleg is raised with crooked knee.

This is a particularly well observed piece which could justify an earlier dating. (AHF)

Compare: 66 No.259
Collection: The Peony Collection

278
ANGLED PLAQUE

EARLY MING DYNASTY
  (1368 - 1644)
                    PE585
LENGTH : 10.3 CM
HEIGHT : 5.0 CM
DEPTH : 1.0 CM

Plaque or tiara fitting in translucent off-white nephrite formed in an inverted fan-shape rising from each side to a convex apex about the vertical central axis. The piece is formed in openwork with a central open peony flower amid a profusion of leaves and stems set directly above a phoenix or parrot perched upon a rock at the base of the vertical axis.

The busy detail of this tour-de-force of jade carving does not lose the salient details of the open peony flower apex, the wide-spread leaves and the phoenix seated upon the rock. The delicacy of the piece is the more remarkable in the light of the difficulty of forming such complex openwork in an angled convex curve. (AHF)

Collection: The Peony Collection

279

OPENWORK DRAGON PLAQUE

EARLY MING DYNASTY
 (1368 - 1644)

PE657

WIDTH : 6.5 CM
HEIGHT : 5.5 CM
THICKNESS : 0.5 CM

Flat plaque in off-white nephrite, essentially square in shape with rounded corners and with the top and bottom sides slightly longer than the lateral sides. The piece is flat on the back and pierced at each back corner with a double hole for attachment. The front or top of the piece is carved in elaborate openwork featuring a vigorous standing dragon writhing through and among a riot of stems, buds, flowers and curling leaves carved on two levels. Some aspects of the vegetal decor are placed lower than the flattened top level of the dragon body which is finely cross hatched with an incised scale pattern.

As with Exhibit 278, the busyness of well conceived openwork at different levels in jade does not obscure a well thought-out design concept, in this case of a standing dragon twisted back in mid section. However, the overall feeling of this excellent work is that it is a softer and tamer rendering of the dragon in art when compared with Exhibit 194. (AHF)

Collection: The Peony Collection

280

FLOWER-HANDLED CUP

EARLY MING DYNASTY
 (1368 - 1644)

PE559

MAXIMUM DIAMETER : 9 CM (INCLUDING HANDLES)
DIAMETER : 5.9 CM (EXCLUDING HANDLES)
HEIGHT : 3.7 CM (EXCLUDING HANDLES)

Two-handled cup in translucent off-white nephrite with a raised foot rim and opposing bracket handles formed as the stem and leaves of an open chrysanthemum flower on each side. The exterior of the bell-shaped bowl is hollowed out into two registers of oval-shaped depressions all around. The interior is plain.

There are similar shapes in silver of the period and the chrysanthemum flower was a popular contemporary design inspiration in both China and Japan. The exterior double register of oval hollowing is rare and the openwork of the handles mirrors the plaque form openwork of Exhibits 278 and 279. (AHF)

Collection: The Peony Collection

281
DRAGON-HEADED TORTOISE

YUAN TO EARLY MING DYNASTY
  (13TH - 15TH CENTURY)
BATEA 497
LENGTH : 5.5 CM
HEIGHT : 3.5 CM
WIDTH : 2.5 CM

Jade carving of a dragon-headed tortoise, its bearded head with a two-barbed horn and swept-up mane, its snout upturned and its slightly open mouth showing teeth and a free-standing tongue, the raised tail divided into three, the carapace with knobs on the top, its sides smooth with two concave planes, its feet, neck and tail with scales, the jade of yellowish-celadon colour with brown mottling. The tortoise is a sacred animal in China and an emblem of longevity, strength and endeavour. Here, combined with a ragon's head, it is rendered as a divine reature. The dragon-headed tortoise (*tuo-lung*) probably took on this aspect when it appeared in Yuan literature as one of the sons of the dragon (*naga*) king of the sea. (BSM)

Previously published: <u>77, pl.No.X</u>
Compare: <u>82, No. 61</u>

282
TWO CHICKENS WITH FLORAL SPRAYS

EARLY MING DYNASTY
  (1368 - 1644)
  (14TH OR 15TH CENTURY)
BATEA 410
HEIGHT : 4.6 CM
LENGTH : 4.4 CM
WIDTH : 3.1 CM

A pair of chickens, with feathers, eyes, ears and feet all naturalistically rendered. Each chicken holds a floral spray, one a chrysanthemum type flower its petals detailed in a manner similar to those found on jade flowers of the Yuan and early Ming periods.

The naturalistic rendering of the animals has not been skimped and the flower details accords well with the period assigned. (BSM)

Compare for flower: <u>89, No.61</u>

283

CIRCULAR JADE CUP

EARLY MING DYNASTY
(15TH CENTURY)
BATEA 421
DIAMETER : 5.8 CM
HEIGHT : 3.5 CM

Small undecorated circular jade cup of off-white colour and attractive grey-brown rivering flaring gently from a small foot with shallow foot rim.

The shape of both the cup and the footrim are reminiscent of Chenghua Doucai cups. The grey-brown flecking, shape and sophistication of this piece accord well with an attribution to the 15th century. Jade cups are one of the most common categories of jade found in Ming tombs published to date. (BSM)

284

BUDDHIST LION DOG WITH LINGZHI

YUAN TO MING DYNASTY
(13TH - 16TH CENTURY)
BATEA 405

LENGTH : 7 CM
WIDTH : 2.9 CM
HEIGHT : 2.7 CM

Jade buddhist lion dog with lingzhi fungus held in its mouth, its detailed eyes protruding, its striated eyebrows curling like horns, its haunches with C scrolls, its claws accentuated.

Animals with floral sprays were common features on jade animals from the Tang dynasty on. The substitution of the lingzhi, with its good luck connotations, for the floral spray, was popular from the Yuan dynasty on. The accentuated horns and claws as well as the details of the underside suggest a dating within the centuries assigned. (BSM)

Compare for eyebrows on 83, No. 49

285
LOTUS AND FISH

MING DYNASTY
  (1368 - 1644)
  (14TH - 16TH CENTURY)
                    BATEA 559
LENGTH : 6.1 CM
HEIGHT : 4.9 CM
WIDTH : 2.8 CM.

White jade carp-like fish, its fat rounded body enveloped by a leafy lotus frond held in its mouth, the leaves curling back on the fish's spine and resting on another leaf below. The lotus flower rests on the fish's pointed snout. The jade is of pale-celadon colour with slight opaque mottling and brown markings. The underside veins of the leaves, the fin of the fish's tail and the gills all rendered in low relief.

The relief carving of the underside veins of the lotus leaf and fin suggests a date no later than the early 17th century. This motif however goes back to at least the Jin dynasty (see pl.VII Wenwu 1977.4) and was especially popular in the Ming dynasty. The type of fat carp depicted here is a motif commonly found on Chinese blue and white porcelain from the 14th to the 16th centuries, to which period this exhibit is accordingly dated. (BSM)

Previously published: (i) 82. No. 89. (ii) 77, pl. No. XXIV

286
THREE BOYS AND BOWL

MING DYNASTY
  (1368 - 1644)
                    PE156
LENGTH : 6.8 CM
BREADTH : 4.8 CM
HEIGHT : 2.6 CM

A group of three boys playing around a large rimmed bowl, in off-white nephrite discoloured with reddish brown. To the right a single boy kneels on one knee with his hands placed on the bowl rim and facing the other two boys, one of whom stands firm on the ground. This boy holds and supports the third boy at his back who is climbing up to the bowl rim and has his cheek pressed hard against it. All three are dressed in tunics and trousers and have their hair in topknots.

This subject was very popular in small Ming bronzes portraying themes from the hundred boys tradition of the Song period. All surfaces and interstices of this piece are finely finished with a soft and appealing gloss. (AHF)

Compare: (i) 1 pl.XLII (ii) 37 No.204
Collection: The Peony Collection

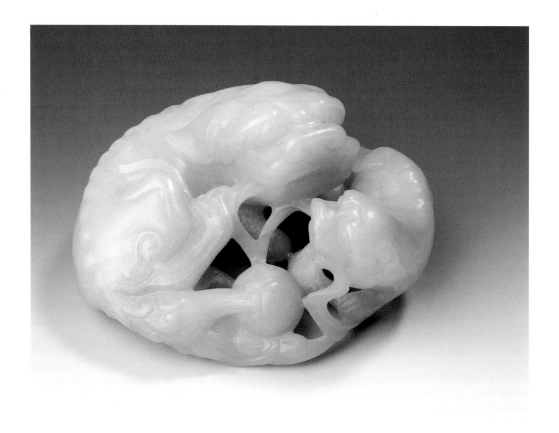

287

LION DOG AND CUB
WITH BROCADE BALL

MING DYNASTY
(1368 - 1644)
(PROBABLY 15TH - 16TH CENTURY)
BATEA 531

LENGTH : 8.1 CM
WIDTH : 6.7 CM
HEIGHT : 3.9 CM

Jade group of lion dog and cub playing with a ribboned
brocade ball, the jade of pale celadon colour with slight
brown skin, the feet with prominent claws, beetling
eyebrows with curls and flames above the eyes. The spine is
prominent and considerable attention has been given to the
details of the hair.

Lion dogs playing with a brocade ball are a well known
subject from at least the Jin dynasty on, with particularly
well-known examples in both lacquer and ceramics dating to
the Ming dynasty. The modelling here compares well with
some 15th century lacquer and ceramic examples. (BSM)

Previously published: 77, No. 63.

288

Two cats at play

Ming dynasty
(1368 - 1644) or earlier
BATEA 494
Length : 4.8 cm
Height : 3 cm
Breadth : 3.5 cm

White jade group of two cats at play, one cat rubbing its head against the neck of the other and pushing the other cat away with one paw, the tails of both free standing one of which curls round one of its back paws, the jade skin of the pebble used to good effect.

Cats and kittens were a very popular subject in the Qing dynasty. However, the beautifully observed details here avoid the coarseness of the Qing representations and this piece has accordingly been placed among the Ming examples. The aesthetic beauty and simplicity involved in this rendering and the naturalistic rendering of cats at play, with the actions depicted so typical of the animals concerned, reminds one of some late Northern Song paintings and could well justify a dating to the Song period. (BSM)

Previously published: (i) 77, No. 86 (ii) 37, No. 154

289

Mythical animal

Yuan to Ming dynasty
(13th - 15th century)
BATEA 493
Length : 5.7 cm
Height : 2.6 cm
Breadth: 2.3 cm

Pale greyish-white jade crouching rodent-like mythical animal, its back showing pronounced vertebrae and its stomach ridged; its hocks with flaming extensions, its tri-forked tail with the bushy central section curling to one side; the ears small and cornucopia-shaped; the claws accentuated by double lines, its rear legs large in proportion. The animal gives a sense of impending movement. (BSM)

Previously published: 77, No. 62.

290
ELEPHANT

MING DYNASTY
(1368 - 1644)
BATEA 481
LENGTH : 6 CM
HEIGHT : 2 CM
BREADTH: 2 CM

Small jade elephant of low form, its legs spindly and deer-like, the stone of greyish colour, the ears showing veining and good details throughout on the body. (BSM)

Previously published: 77, No. 60

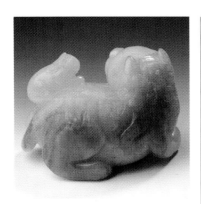

291
FELINE WITH CUB ON ITS BACK

MING DYNASTY
(1368 - 1644)
BATEA 471
LENGTH : 6.5 CM
WIDTH : 4.3 CM
HEIGHT : 4.2 CM

Jade carving of a feline with a cub on its back, its head turned sideways, its back and tail with detailed hair incising, one side white with slightly greyish tinge, the other showing the orange-brown of the jade pebble's skin. The feet have detailed rendering of the pads and claws.

Animals with their young were a popular motif in both the Ming and Qing dynasties. The detailed rendering of the pads and claws as here and the fine incising of the hair, involving considerable work are considered early features and a Ming dating seems certain. (BSM)

Previously published: 37, No. 157

292
MYTHICAL ANIMAL WITH EAGLE

MING DYNASTY
(1368 - 1644)

BATEA 560

LENGTH : 6.5 CM
HEIGHT : 5.2 CM
BREADTH : 2.4 CM

A pale celadon green jade mythical animal in crouching position, its head turned towards an eagle with wings half open perched on its back, its bushy tail and long mane with incised fur markings, the wings and the tail of the bird with similar details, the eyebrows of the mythical animal incised and flame-like, C scrolls and striated hair-tufts decorate its legs.

An eagle on a mythical animal was a popular motif in the Ming dynasty and a rebus for bravery. The flame-like eyebrows were also a convention at that time. (BSM)

Previously published: <u>77, No.61</u>
Compare: Exhibit 239

293

DRAGON-HEADED CARP RISING FROM WAVES

MING DYNASTY
(1368 - 1644)
(PROBABLY 16TH CENTURY)
BATEA 472
LENGTH TIP TO TAIL ROUND
THE OUTSIDE EDGE : 15.8 CM
HEIGHT : 6.3 CM
WIDTH : 3.8 CM

Jade carp rising from waves, its large head already changed into that of a dragon, the jade of greyish colour with extensive brown degradation, the waves with several swirls and breaking onto the carp's prominent back with extensive details.

This depicts a carp ascending the Longmen (dragon gate) falls at the top of which it will turn into a dragon. This was a popular subject in the Ming dynasty being symbolic of the student becoming a mandarin after success in the imperial examinations. The method of depicting the waves here with multiple whirls and waves leaping up around the animal is typical of the treatment of waves on Ming examples from the 16th to early 17th century. (BSM)

Previously published: (i) <u>37, No. 187</u> (ii) <u>77, pl. XXIII</u>
Compare: <u>82, No.61</u>

294

CRANE AND DEER WITH ACANTHUS

MING DYNASTY
 (1368 - 1644),
 (PROBABLY 16TH CENTURY)

BATEA 475

LENGTH : 7.7 CM
WIDTH : 4.3 CM
HEIGHT : 4 CM

Crane and deer lying side by side holding between them an acanthus spray, the jade of greyish-white colour with brown veining, the details realistically carved.

Both these animals are associated with longevity and Daoism and were particularly popular subjects in the mid-16th century. (BSM)

Previously published: (i) 37, No.185 (ii) 77, pl. XIX

295

DOG-LIKE ANIMALS WITH LINGZHI AND ACANTHUS

MING DYNASTY
(1368 - 1644)
(PROBABLY 16TH CENTURY)
BATEA 477

LENGTH : 5.9 CM
WIDTH : 4.2 CM
HEIGHT : 2.5 CM

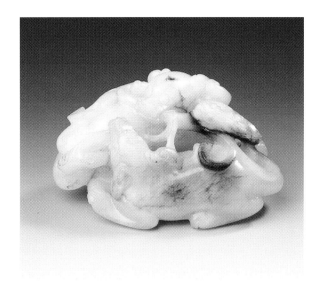

Two dog-like animals carved as a group head to tail, one holding a spray of lingzhi and the other acanthus over their backs; their heads with spiralled ears and pronounced eyebrows, the jade of yellowish-white colour with brown and black (sometimes called "mare's hair") inclusions.

The so-called mare's hair inclusions are considered typical of some Ming dynasty jades. The lingzhi and acanthus are both motifs popular during this period. Dogs and dog-like animals were popular motifs in Chinese art from the Tang dynasty on. (BSM)

Previously published: 77, No. 64

296

TWO LION DOGS WITH LINGZHI

MING DYNASTY
(1368 - 1644)
BATEA 463

LENGTH : 6.3 CM
WIDTH : 4 CM
HEIGHT : 2.8 CM

Jade group of two lion dogs holding a lingzhi spray, the whole (particularly the tails and feet) with naturalistic details, the jade of even pale celadon colour with brown edging. (BSM)

297

HAIRPIN

MING DYNASTY
(1368 - 1644)
PE543
LENGTH : 20.4 CM
WIDTH AT TOP : 2.6 CM

A hairpin in translucent off-white nephrite with a hollowed out openwork elliptical head carved with two open-winged phoenixes disporting among flowers. The fully carved, tapering shaft has a round-nosed *kui* dragon turning back upon itself above a border ring around the circumference. Between the dragon and the lowest ring, the shaft is carved with an intertwined representation of the Three Friends of Winter, pine, prunus and bamboo. Below the lower ring are entwined leaves, flowers, buds and lingzhi fungus.

The openwork of the hollowed upper terminal swelling of this piece can be compared with certain aspects of the openwork on the handles of Exhibit 280 and in Exhibits 278 and 279. The additional distinction between those and Exhibit 297 is the low relief work around the shaft depicting the typical Ming decoration of the Three Friends of Winter. (AHF)

Collection: The Peony Collection

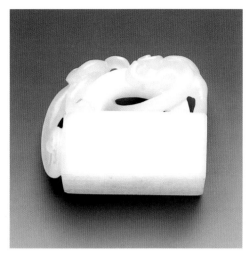

298

INSCRIBED RECTANGULAR
WHITE JADE SEAL WITH ARCHED
HANDLE AND *KUI* DRAGON

MING DYNASTY OR LATER
DATED 1565

BATEA 490

LENGTH : 4.5 CM
HEIGHT : 3.5 CM
WIDTH : 2 CM

Rectangular white jade seal surmounted by an arched loop handle placed lengthwise over and through which a *kui* dragon entwines. The seal base is carved with a poem in seal script, and on one side is an inscription in running script dating the piece to the second month of 1565, and signed "San Qiao", the studio name of Wen Peng (1489-1573). He is recorded as the son of the famous artist Wen Zhenming. Wen Peng was known as an artist and seal carver in his own right.

The quality of the calligraphy and of the jade used for this seal are both very high and the running script used was popular in the Ming dynasty. This seal stands a reasonable chance of being made by or for the artist named, a possibility enhanced by the use of his studio name. Artists such as Wen Peng would have had such a seal carved by the jade worker at the artist's own house and under his personnel supervision working to Wen Peng's own design. Entwining of dragons as part of the decoration on objects for the scholar's studio as here, was popular in the Ming dynasty and examples are known in other media. However although he was known as a seal carver, Wen Peng is not recorded as having carved seals in jade and it may be that this represents an attempt by a Qing carver to create a convincing Ming seal and a Qing date cannot therefore be entirely ruled out. (BSM)

Previously published: <u>77, No. 72</u>

299

CIRCULAR RING WITH TWO BIRDS AND LINGZHI

MING DYNASTY
(1368 - 1644)

BATEA 489

DIAMETER OVERALL : 5.8 CM
DIAMETER OF CENTRAL APERTURE : 3.2 CM
DEPTH : 2.3 CM

Speckled white jade circular ring with two birds separated by lingzhi sprays on the outside and on top of the ring, all in high relief, the jade with black staining on the birds and lingzhi.

The black colour here may be the result of deliberate staining and the motifs probably represent a rebus. (BSM)

Previously published: 77, No. 70

300
SLEEPING BOY AND WHEEL

MING DYNASTY
(1368 - 1644)

PE122

LENGTH : 6.4 CM
HEIGHT : 5.5 CM
BREADTH : 2.4 CM

A figure of a boy in sweet-white nephrite carved from a natural pebble with an axial trend to the left from close to the front. The figure is seated upon the ground with the feet placed each side of a large wheel-shaped disc upon which the hands hidden in long sleeves rest, the head rests upon the hands. The face, with a marked dimple on the right cheek, is turned to the right with the eyes closed and an expression of absolute peace.

This jade carving captures well the bliss of absolute repose. (AHF)

Collection: The Peony Collection

301
JADE TOAD IN LOTUS

MING DYNASTY
(1368 - 1644)

BATEA 485

LENGTH : 7.7 CM
HEIGHT : 3.6 CM
WIDTH : 3.4 CM

Jade pebble of a toad in hiding, peering out from under a small dead lotus leaf and clutching a large lotus leaf wrapped round him. The toad's back has many nodules. The underside of the larger lotus leaf has the veins in relief and the upper side has the veins incised.

The natural depiction of the veins of the lotus leaf both incised and in relief as here is typical of Ming carving. The imaginative use of the skin for the dead leaf and the edge of the lotus leaf wrapping make this an example of the Ming lapidary's art at its best. The toad was associated by the scholars of the Ming dynasty with the much-admired artist-connoisseur Mi Fu, and the depiction of toads in jade from the Song dynasty on is one of the many instances pointing to its close association with Daoism. (BSM)

Previously published: (i) 37, No. 184 (ii) 77, No. XVI

302
PANEL OF DRAGON AMID FLORAL SCROLLS

MING DYNASTY
  (1368 - 1644)
  (PROBABLY 1550 - 1644)
                        BATEA 1229
LENGTH : 10.4 CM
WIDTH : 6 CM
DEPTH : 1.4 CM

Pale celadon jade reticulated straight-sided panel rounded at both ends and decorated with a three-clawed dragon amid floral scrolls. The spirited dragon is depicted with a split feathery tail and its body with patches of scales, both features commonly found in dragons from the late Ming dynasty. The reverse of the dragon's body is neatly hollowed to ensure the jade is of even thickness throughout.

Panels such as this were probably made as inserts into the sides of lanterns where the even thickness of the jade would result in a better, even light. (BSM)

Collection: The Rannerdale Collection

303
FIVE-CLAWED DRAGON IN CLOTH WRAPPING

MING DYNASTY
  (1368 - 1644)
  (PROBABLY 1550 - 1644)
                        BATEA 476
LENGTH : 5.5 CM
HEIGHT : 2.8 CM
WIDTH : 1.7 CM

Jade carving of a five-clawed two-horned dragon with a tightly curled-up figure of eight tail, the tail end feathered, the animal gift-wrapped with a knotted cloth, one leg protruding from the cloth, the jade of greenish-white colour, the head and leg of brown colour.

The feathering of this dragon's tail end is typical of some late Ming dragons. The wrapping up of an animal or inanimate object in cloth has also been discussed by James Watt in 82, page 98, where he considers such wrapping to be a typical Ming mannerism, an interpretation with which this writer agrees. (BSM)

Previously published: 77, No. 77

304

DUCK WITH WATERWEED

MING DYNASTY
(1368 - 1644)
(PROBABLY 1550 - 1644)
BATEA 525

HEIGHT : 4 CM
LENGTH : 5.2 CM
WIDTH : 2.6 CM

Jade figure of a duck carved from a white pebble with russet skin with no details for the feet, the wings incised with a stylised squared spiral, the bird with head turned over its back holding a spray of kidney shaped waterweed in its bill.

The motif of an animal holding a plant in its mouth can be traced back to at least the Tang dynasty. It was however a particularly popular motif in the Ming dynasty. The elaboration of parts of animals by decoration derived originally from ancient bronzes, in this case the stylised squared spirals, is typical of the late Ming period. (BSM)

Previously published: 77 No. 67

305

FINIAL OF MANDARIN DUCK AMID LOTUS

MING DYNASTY
(1368 - 1644)
(PROBABLY 1550 - 1644)
BATEA 470

LENGTH : 4.5 CM
HEIGHT : 3.8 CM
WIDTH : 3.3 CM

White jade reticulated finial with four holes in the base for attachment carved as a mandarin duck sitting on a lotus leaf holding in its mouth a lotus flower spray, with leaf and water weeds all in delicate tracery with slight orange suffusions.

A very similar finial was found in the tomb of the Wanli emperor (1572-1620). The mandarin duck was symbolic of conjugal happiness and a popular subject, particularly in the Ming dynasty. (BSM)

Previously published: 77, No. 73

306

PHOENIX PEBBLE

MING DYNASTY
  (1368 - 1644)
  (PROBABLY 1550 - 1644)
                          PE14
MAXIMUM LENGTH : 11.2 CM
BREADTH : 6.4 CM
HEIGHT : 3.4 CM

A large natural pebble retaining its original shape with the surface reduced all round to create the figure of a massively crested bird in three-dimensional form with a sprig of vegetation held in its bill and the feet drawn up beneath along the stomach. The pearly grey-green stone has a high sheen with ample blotching of natural russet.

This piece is an effective demonstration of the skill and taste of the scholar literati of the late Ming to Qing transitional period. Naturalism in restrained and barely assisted contours display both the ingenuity of structuring a full bird from an almost entirely retained pebble, and the evident respect for, and effective use of the natural colour in the stone. (AHF)

Previously published: 53 pl.80
Collection: The Peony Collection

307

CAT AND BUTTERFLY

MING DYNASTY
(1368 - 1644)
(PROBABLY 1550 - 1644)
PE126
LENGTH : 6.8 CM
HEIGHT : 5.8 CM
BREADTH: 4.6 CM

A figure of a cat in off-white nephrite with black colour on top and beneath. The whole animal, cunningly carved from a single square block of material, tramples plantain type leaves with its big, powerful feet while a sprig of banana leaves is clenched in its jaws. The tail passes forward through the leaves on the left side of the animal and a large, plump butterfly perches between the ears at the back of the triangular-shaped face and head.

There is a positive feel about the determination of this cat to retain its vice-like grip on the leaf stalk in its mouth. The skill of the carver in retaining the almost square shape for the top of the piece and yet conveying the softness traditionally associated with the feline form is remarkable. The cat and the butterfly are a rebus for long life. (AHF)

Previously published: 53 pl.70
Collection: The Peony Collection

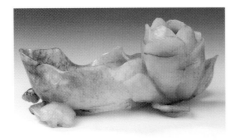

308

LOTUS BRUSHWASHER
WITH FROG AND DUCK

MING DYNASTY
(1368 - 1644)
(PROBABLY 1550 - 1644)
BATEA 448
LENGTH : 12.4 CM
WIDTH : 6.4 CM
HEIGHT : 5.5 CM

Slightly greyish-celadon jade brushwasher with brown suffusions, consisting of a lotus leaf formed as a brushwasher and water container, the sides curled up and one end pinched to form a pouring spout. A lotus bud at the other end is hollowed out to serve as the brush holder, its thick petals with edges turned back, the group held together by stalks on the base, a small duck on one side and a small frog and a snail under the leaf, all forming the rebus "may you have an abundance of sons every year".

Note here the naturalistic carving of the interior and exterior veins of the lotus leaf in incised and relief carving respectively a feature involving considerable work. From early in the Qing dynasty. the interior and exterior veins would have been incised. The inclusion of the rebus in the decoration of this brush washer group is also consistent with a late Ming dynasty dating. (BSM)

309

BOY WITH GOURD BACKED BY PLANTAIN LEAF

MING DYNASTY
(1368 - 1644)
(PROBABLY 1550 - 1644)

BATEA 500

LENGTH : 6.2 CM
HEIGHT : 5.2 CM
BREADTH : 2 CM

Seated boy holding a gourd backed by a large naturalistically carved plantain leaf, the jade of white colour with some black "mare's hair" inclusions, the edges of the leaf turned over in places.

The pebble used here has been carved in late Ming style and in such a way as to enable the piece to stand upright without the support of a display stand, though at first sight this appears likely to be impossible. The author considers this a typical refinement of the late Ming carver. The plantain leaf was a popular motif in the late Ming dynasty. (BSM)

Previously published: 77, No.74
Compare : 82, No. 105

310

"Long Eliza" figure

Late Ming to early Qing dynasty
  (17th century)

BATEA 484

Height : 11.4 cm
Width : 3.3 cm
Breadth : 1.7 cm

Pale celadon jade, "long Eliza" figure carrying what is probably a hand warmer, her clothes with long pendant sleeves elegantly draped and her hair in a bun at the back of her head in late Ming style, her tiny feet possibly bound.

Long Eliza, from the dutch "lange lijsen", is the name given to the elongated female figures that decorate many blue and white porcelains of the 17th century and to which this jade figure bears such a resemblance. (BSM)

Previously published : (i) 77, No. 76

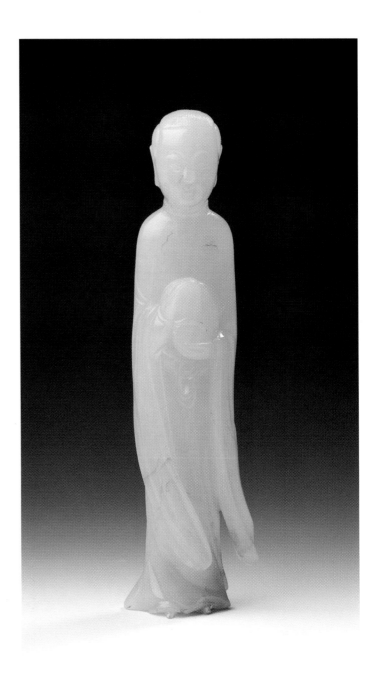

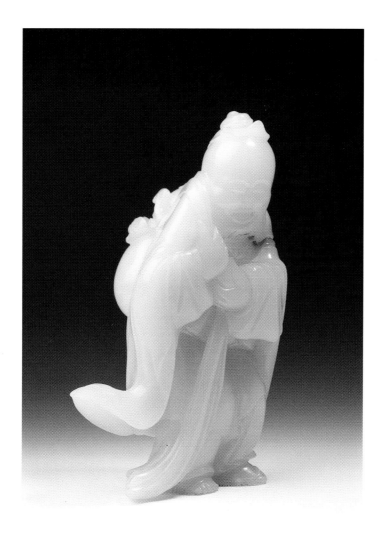

311

DONG FANGSHUO WITH GOURD
AND PEACH SPRAY

LATE MING DYNASTY
 (1368 - 1644)
 (PROBABLY 1550 - 1644)

BATEA 520

HEIGHT : 10.3 CM
WIDTH : 5.8 CM
DEPTH : 4.2 CM

White jade figure of Dong fangshuo, a Daoist immortal, depicted
as a laughing old man with windswept cloak and cloth cap, holding
over his shoulder a gourd tied with a cloth to a peach spray.

The use of a cloth cap as shown here was popular from the mid
16th century on to the end of the Ming dynasty, and paintings and
carvings of the late Ming frequently show scholars and Daoist
immortals wearing such caps. Dong fangshuo stole the peaches of
immortality from the garden of Xi Wangmu, the Queen Mother of
the West, and is frequently depicted with a peach or a peach spray.
(BSM)

Previously published: 82, No. 101

20 ARCHAISTIC GROUP

Interest in the nation's past has been a recurrent feature throughout much of Chinese history. Although this interest waxed and waned over the centuries it was particularly strong in the Song, Yuan and Ming dynasties. This archaising tendency however seems to have started in the Tang dynasty, although contemporary evidence is scarce. In the northern Song period, however, various books illustrating antiques, such as *Kaogu tu* and *Xuanhe bogu tu*, became popular with scholars and mandarins giving added impetus to this archaising tendency. All kinds of bronze and jade objects were created, chiefly in the then perceived styles of the Zhou and Han dynasties. Reinterpretations of bronze shapes and designs from these earlier dynasties were particularly popular. Late Song, Yuan and Ming dynasty workshops, particularly those at Suzhou, are recorded as having produced jade objects copying ancient bronze forms. However, few archaistic pieces have been found in published excavated tombs of these periods, and it has been convincingly argued that the taste for archaic and archaistic jades, at least in the late Ming, was restricted to a minority even among the elite, and perhaps centred on Suzhou itself 6BFJ p.43.

Jade belt hooks and sword slides were favourite subjects with the jade craftsmen who specialised in archaistic pieces. However, they did not seemingly appreciate how the jade sword slides had actually been used in ancient times. They polished the base of the hanging section of the slide, which in ancient times would have been bound into the scabbard and was never highly polished, and they extended both ends of the sword slide to the same level as the bottom of the hanging section. This would have prevented the hanging section of the sword slide fitting neatly into the insert made in the scabbard surface thereby rendering it less effective. Two archaistic belt hooks have been included in this section (Exhibits 314 and 315).

The most desirable archaistic jade pieces seem to have been those following Zhou bronze shapes and decoration.

This group is, however, probably the most difficult of all to assign to its correct time frame. I think the key to doing so is to draw a distinction between pieces that were conscious imitations of genuine archaic material and those creative reconstructions in the style or decoration of earlier periods. The latter seem to have been much finer, although they attracted strong criticism from one early commentator, Shen Kua (1031-95).

The creative reconstructions are beautifully hollowed out and worked, and can be compared to contemporary archaistic bronzes as works of art in their own right. Most of these creative reconstructions should probably be assigned to the Southern Song, Jin or Yuan dynasties. The lack of examples in this style from published Ming tomb excavations suggests that such pieces were rarely produced in the Ming dynasty. One such creative reconstruction, a *hu*-shaped vessel, is reported to have come from the Yuan dynasty tomb of Fan Wenhu who died in 1301, but this writer has been unable to trace any other published example.

Rhytons and vessels with a kui dragon biting the rim to form a handle and decorated with juxtaposed bands of archaistic decoration and complex borders are typical of these reconstructions (Exhibit 316). Loosely linked engraved C and S scrolls and a petal palmette with three incised vertical lines are commonly found on this group of jades (Exhibit 318). This author agrees with the Southern Song or Yuan dating suggested for the group by Desmond Gure 24 p.41.

Late Ming reproductions were

reproductions, not reinterpretations and, by comparison, are very coarse and poorly hollowed. Qing copies, to which the same remarks apply, were outright forgeries designed to deceive the inexperienced collector.

In the late 16th century, when raw jade was readily available, there was intense interest in most aspects of the distant past, and a whole spate of editions of illustrated catalogues of antiquities, which had originated in the late 11th/early 12th centuries, were produced. For example, between 1588 and 1603, there were no less than seven editions of two of the most important catalogues, *Kaogu tu* (preface dated 1092) and *Xuanhe bogu tu*, (purportedly an illustrated catalogue of the bronzes in the imperial palace and thirty-seven private collections) as against only six editions over the preceding 400 odd years. It is said that the original Song printed copy of the early twelfth century *Xuanhe bogu tu* could not be found so a copy of the Song edition with many additions was published in the Zhida period (1308-11) of the Yuan dynasty. It is therefore unlikely that this work was used as a reference for the production of jades in bronze shapes before the 14th century 25 p.43. Only the *Kaogu tu* contains jades, which are confined to a single chapter which does not appear in the earliest editions.

Interest in the forms and decoration of earlier metalwork stimulated by these books did not spread evenly through all the Chinese applied arts. The chief antiquarian interest seems to have been centred on epigraphy with the styles of the bronzes attracting little attention. However, early jades are singularly lacking in inscriptions.

Only twenty-one of the 857 jade items confiscated in 1562 from Yan Song are described by the names of early metalware shapes, and not a single example of the major early ritual jades, such as *bi* and *cong* is included in the detailed inventory. The largest single group of jade objects described were cups, but only thirty-nine out of a total of 284 had decoration such as *kui* dragons, which can be identified as coming from archaic sources.

The 16th century scholar Gao Lian confirms that jades of ancient pattern were being worked at that time, "Nowadays, the ingenious craftsmen of Suzhou imitate Han and Song jade half-rings, belt-hooks and rings using greenish, yellow and mingled colour "onion" jade with an edging of rind (Exhibit 314), or else jade with black streaks. The jades are worked according to patterns falsely confusing the antique style. They all go for high prices. However, men of today cannot manage the double hook style. The forms are rather like the genuine article, but how can the hook grinding imitate the antique. Those who are in the know can recognise the fakes at a glance." 6BFJ p.39-40 Recognition of fakes was not as easy as Gao Lian pretends for even the Qianlong emperor thought a piece identified by the carver's grandson as having been carved by the Suzhou carver Yao Zongren early in the 18th century, to be a Han dynasty original 6BFJ p.41.

The famous jade carver Lu Zigang, who was also from Suzhou, is known to have made and signed jades in the form of archaic metalwork. Lu Zigang's dates are uncertain but he is thought to have worked in the second half of the 16th century. He is reported to have produced water-droppers with animals masks and diaper grounds like ancient bronze *zun* or *lei* or in the shape of hollow *bixie*, and a *zhi* vessel with a hundred nipple design, swing handle and a chain of thirteen links all carved from the same piece of jade 6BFJ p.41-3.

Brian McElney
January 1994

仿古玉

在中國，仿古是常見的現象，尤以宋、元、明三代為甚。仿古風氣始於唐代，唯傳世實物甚少。北宋時，<考古圖>及<宣和博古圖錄>相繼出版，刺激當時的仕人學者仿製戰國和漢代的銅器及玉器。宋元明時，蘇州玉作坊最擅雕製以古青銅器為藍本的玉器，但此類仿古玉甚少出土，故有學者認為仿古玉，特別是晚明仿古玉器，只是少數上層社會人士的愛好(6BFJ,頁43)。

仿古器中又以帶鈎(展品314及315)和璏最多見。當時的玉工似乎不大明瞭璏的用法，因而將長方鋬孔的背部加以琢磨，這跟古璏的製法截然兩樣。再者，他們將璏兩端的鈎加深，深至與鋬孔平行，致使璏本身不能穩固地繫於劍鞘上。

以周代銅器為藍本的玉器最受歡迎，亦最難斷代。重要線索之一，是分清蓄意的模仿品及帶古風的創作。後者一般較為精細，雖然沈括(1031-1095)對它們作出苛刻批評。

帶古風的玉雕大都琢工精美，本身便是上佳藝術品。一般的意見是，帶古風的銅器屬南宋、金或元代，故類似玉器應是同期之物。古風玉雕不見出土於明墓，想是到明代此類玉器不再流行。范文虎(卒1301年)墓曾出玉觶，除此之外不見有其它例子。

角杯及螭龍柄杯即屬古風玉雕中典型之作，多飾以古典花紋(展品316)。C形或S形渦紋，卷葉紋或三度平行直線亦極普遍，如展品318。此器當為南宋或元代之物。

晚明仿古玉則為純粹模仿器，琢工亦粗糙。清代更每下愈況，完全是用以欺騙收藏家的偽品。

十六世紀末葉，玉材來源富足。此時人們對古物興趣大增，十一、十二世紀出版之古物圖錄選被重印。1588至1603年的十五年內，<考古圖>及<宣和博古圖錄>便重印七次之多，而在1588年以前的四百年中，此二書才重印了六次。<宣和博古圖錄>原是北宋宮廷及私人皮藏古器圖錄，據稱原刻本已失。元至六年間(1308-11)重編，又加添了很多項目，但十四世紀前，根據此圖錄中銅器雕製玉器的可能性是不存在的(25,頁43)。<考古圖>收有玉器，但只一章，且不見於早期刊本。

明人對古銅器的興趣又以銘文為首，器形及紋飾次之，唯古玉器鮮見帶銘文。

1562年，嚴嵩被抄家時清單中列出八百五十七件玉器，其中以古銅器為藍本者才二十一件，璧和琮更是完全不見。最大宗是玉杯共達二百八十四件，但只有三十九件帶紋飾，如螭龍。

十六世紀時，高濂對當時的仿古玉業作了如後評語："近日吳中摹擬漢宋螭玦、鈎、環，用蒼黃染色邊皮蔥玉或帶淡墨色玉，如式琢成，偽亂古制，每得高值，孰知今人所不能者，雙鈎之法。形似稍可偽真，鈎碾何法擬古，識者過目自別奚似偽為"(6BFJ,頁39-40)。事實上，要辨別玉器的真偽，並不如高濂所說一般容易。清高宗(乾隆)以為是漢器的玉杯，蘇州匠師姚宗仁指出乃是他祖父所製(6BFJ,頁41)。

另一蘇州碾玉名家陸子剛，擅長雕製古銅器形玉器。陸的生卒年份不詳，據稱活躍於十六世紀下半，曾製獸面錦地水注，"與古尊疊同"。此外，亦有雕玉辟邪，百乳白玉觶等物(6BFJ,頁41-3)。

312

VESSEL WITH *KUI* DRAGON HANDLE

SONG DYNASTY
(960 - 1279)

BATEA 544

LENGTH : 7.8 CM
WIDTH : 4.1 CM
HEIGHT : 3.2 CM

Undecorated pouring vessel of *Yi* form, the jade of pale celadon colour with brown flecking, the foot rim well carved and the rim slightly thickened; the handle formed by a single-horned *kui* dragon with flattened head, its stylised body with two spurs.

The colour of the jade is reminiscent of the brown-flecked jade, about which complaints were made in Song historical records in relation to the jade received immediately after resumption of supply in 1077 (see introduction, The Fluctuating Jewel). The shape is derived from the bronze *yi*-form pouring vessels of the Zhou dynasty. (BSM)

Previously published : 77, No.52
Compare : A similarly shaped and handled piece, but decorated with incised key-fret borders and lychees in low relief, is illustrated as Ming or earlier in 99, No. 280

313

CROUCHING *BIXIE*

MING DYNASTY
(1368 - 1644)

PE739

LENGTH : 7.8 CM
WIDTH : 5.5 CM
HEIGHT : 2.4 CM

A figure of a crouching winged *bixie* in translucent white nephrite with golden-brown suffusions. The strong curled tail is held between the taut narrow profile hind quarters while the back slopes down and forward to meet the powerful neck which is held in an alert position between the action-ready shoulders. The head has a pair of horns extending back along the neck in relief. Round eyes glare below heavy brows and above a small nose and an open mouth with bared fangs. Extending back from the shoulders along the sides is a serried platform arrangement of double layered wing or flame forms in relief.

The piece feigns all the drama and aggression of the *bixie* of the Six Dynasties period but this is somehow mollified by a roundness of contour such as that evident in the big club-finial eyebrows. Although these eyebrows speak of archaism, the fire of the sculptor's imagination is very much alive in the additional curling feature on the left shoulder which is not repeated on the right. (AHF)

Collection: The Peony Collection

314

Garment hook with *kui* dragon

Late Song to mid Ming dynasty
 (13th - 16th century)

BATEA 473

Length : 8.5 cm
Height : 2.1 cm
Width : 2 cm

White jade garment hook with pale brown suffusions, the hook ending in a dragon's head, a *kui* dragon with a contorted body depicted in full relief on the handle with some fine incised-line details; the base with plain circular stud.

Garment hooks were introduced into China from the Central Asian steppe in the middle of the first millenium BC. This hook is in the style of the Western Han dynasty, but the polish and the reserved nature of the carving of the *kui* dragon in relief makes it likely that this hook dates to the late Song to Ming dynasties (13th-16th century), when such hooks in Western Han style were popular. One Ming commentator Gao Lian (16th century) mentions that the Suzhou craftsmen making jade belthooks in Han and Song style used greenish-yellow and mingled colour "onion" jade with an edging of "rind" which fetched high prices. This may be such a piece and the colour here may be that referred to as "onion" jade. (BSM)

Previously published: (i) 77, No. 47 (ii) 37 No. 244

315

Jade garment hook with ram's head finial and rice pattern spirals

Song dynasty
 (960 - 1279)

BATEA 474

Length : 9.2 cm
Width : 2.8 cm
Height : 2 cm

White jade garment hook, the hook formed by a ram's head with twisted horns, detailed eyes, mouth and jowls, the body of the hook covered with raised rice pattern spirals.

The rather beaked nature of the head can be paralleled in Tang and Song animal carvings. This archaistic hook is based on a Han original. (BSM)

Previously published: 77, No. 48

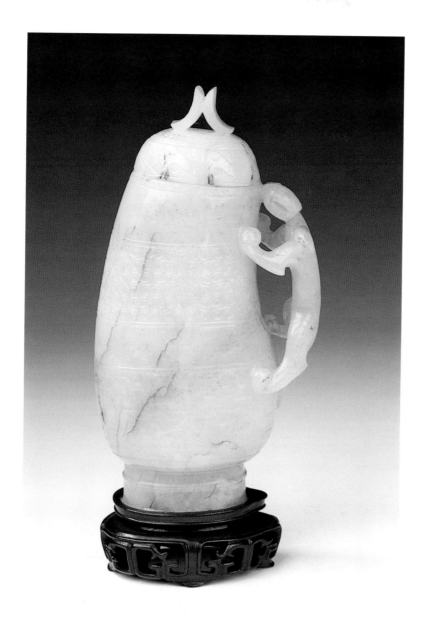

316

COVERED GOURD SHAPED *HU*
WITH *KUI* DRAGON HANDLE

SOUTHERN SONG OR YUAN DYNASTY
(12TH - 14TH CENTURY)
BATEA 583
HEIGHT WITH COVER : 14.4 CM
LENGTH : 7.7 CM
DEPTH : 4.5 CM
LENGTH AT BASE : 4.5 CM
WIDTH AT BASE : 3 CM

Gourd shaped *hu* vessel and cover with archaistic decorations standing on a tall foot with raised ridge. The handle is in the form of a *kui* dragon. The four bands of archaistic motifs on the body, all in low relief, are an initial band of hatching on the rim, set off by an incised line from a plain band; a band of comma patterns in tight formation bounded by double incised lines; another band of incised C scrolls; and a final band of alternating inverted and vertical combinations of dragons' heads, paws, and claws, and varying spiral motifs. The cover is decorated in two bands, one of a rope pattern, the other of waves and scrolls with fine cross-hatching in the troughs, and surmounted by a knob formed by two segments of a circle.

The walls of the vessel are extraordinarily thin and the fine rendering of the geometrised dragon profiles in the lowest band is far superior to their rendering on the late Ming examples of this design. This is a reinterpretation of a gourd shaped *hu* vessel of the 4th - 5th century BC. (BSM)

Previously published: (i) 82, No. 133 (ii) 37, No. 209

317

GU SHAPED BEAKER WITH
FLOWERS AND LEAVES

SOUTHERN SONG TO YUAN DYNASTY
(12TH - 14TH CENTURY)
BATEA 548

HEIGHT : 13.7 CM
WIDTH : 9 CM
DEPTH : 3.7 CM

Pale celadon jade vase of archaistic *gu* hexagonal shape with peonies, peach blossoms, lingzhi and lotus leaves sprouting from the top edge and coming together at an apex, which has three holes for the hollowing instruments, the vase hollowed to provide a thin wall to the whole vessel which is decorated with *taotie* and a blade pattern copying *gu* bronzes in low relief; the whole carved out of one pebble.

This piece is reminiscent of the vases with flowers that are to be seen on Southern Song ceramics. The Southern Song period saw the popularity of flower arranging as a pursuit, and by the 16th century there were several treatises on flower arrangement that survive to this day. *Gu*-shaped bronze vases are mentioned in these works as most suitable for winter displays. The earliest depiction of vases with flowers seems to be in a late Liao tomb (early 12th century). Jade vases with flowers are recorded in the 13th century by the contemporary writer Zhou Mi. (BSM)

Previously published: (i) 82, No. 132 (ii) 37 No. 211

318

EWER WITH *KUI* DRAGON HANDLE

SOUTHERN SONG OR YUAN DYNASTY
(12TH - 14TH CENTURY)

BATEA 425

WIDTH : 9.2 CM
HEIGHT : 7.5 CM
DEPTH : 4.1 CM

A mottled buff-white and brown, well hollowed jade archaistic ewer carved with a central band of linear motifs ending in whorls to form a cruciform pattern, shallowly incised C and S-scrolls and spade-shaped palmettes in low relief in the bottom band with three line incisions in each, the handle formed by a *kui* dragon biting the rim, the base with two archaic characters in relief.

The decoration is derived from Eastern Zhou bronzes, which were popular subjects among the archaistic bronzes of the Southern Song and Yuan dynasties. The spade-shaped palmettes on similar jade pieces are discussed by Desmond Gure in 25, where a Song dynasty date is suggested for this decorative motif. However, the inclusion of characters in relief on the base is known on several Yuan pieces and a Yuan date may be more appropriate. (BSM)

Compare: 66, No. 311

319

BIRD VESSEL IN WARRING STATES BRONZE STYLE

SOUTHERN SONG OR YUAN DYNASTY
  (12TH - 14TH CENTURY)
                            BATEA 452
HEIGHT : 7.6 CM
LENGTH : 7.3 CM
WIDTH : 3.5 CM

Jade vessel designed as a standing bird, its tail curled between its legs, its wings turned up, the body well hollowed out to form a container, its well hollowed head and beak with slits so that it can be used as a water dropper, its feathers incised, the jade of pale celadon colour with several brown inclusions.

The style is reminiscent of 4th - 5th century BC bronzes, but this piece is within the archaistic tradition of the Song and Yuan reinterpretation of bronze forms discussed at the start of this section of the catalogue. (BSM)

Previously published : <u>51, pp 124, fig. 32</u>

21 QING DYNASTY 1644-1911

Qing jade carvers were heirs to the jade carving traditions of all previous dynasties. As mentioned in "The Fluctuating Jewel", from the late 16th century the mining of mountain jade had supplemented the pebbles taken from rivers. Shortly after 1600, however, the supplies of jade to China were again interrupted with comparatively little jade entering China from then until about the mid 18th century. The amount of mined mountain jade entering China before the mid 18th century and available to eastern Chinese workshops was therefore probably very small.

The strong reigns of the Kangxi (r.1662-1722), Yongzheng (r. 1723-35) and Qianlong (r. 1736-95) emperors led to a great increase in prosperity. Jade objects of any real size were a rarity prior to the Qing dynasty, but from the mid 18th century on the enormous increase in the supply of jade led to the production of sizeable pieces. The taste of the times also seems to have been for large objects of all kinds, including those of jade. The use and collection of jade by rich merchant and landlord families, which began at least as early as the Ming continued into the Qing and was stimulated in the second half of the 18th century by the abundant supply of raw material. There were jade vases and enormous mountains of jade decorated with human figures, trees, pavilions, birds and animals. The fashion for such mountains carved from mined or pebble jade, a translation of orthodox landscape painting into sculpture, started in the late Ming period and many such pieces, particularly from the 18th century, exist to this day. They were favoured objects for inclusion in the Qing scholar's studio. Exhibits 330 and 331 are comparatively early examples.

The custom of burying artifacts to accompany the deceased into the after life declined in the early Qing dynasty, and whilst fairly substantial burials exist from the very early years (1644-1680), such burials appear thereafter to have been confined to those of the emperors and their immediate families.

Jade belt plaques, which in earlier times had been indirect badges of rank, ceased to have any relevance during the Qing dynasty since the wearing of badges of rank, sewn onto the back and front of a mandarin's robe, had been made compulsory in 1652. Old jade belt plaques were quite commonly used as screen inlays in the late Qing.

It became mandatory under the Qing dynasty for virtually every subject to have a pigtail, which made the wearing of jade chignons such as Exhibit 208 impossible. Even the style of hairpins that had become common in the late Ming dynasty (Exhibit 297) fell into disuse. A different type of hairpin was used in the Qing dynasty and when made of jade they took the form of nephrite jade in metal mounts. Emerald green jadeite was increasingly substituted for such nephrite in hairpins produced from the late 18th century on.

The quantities of jade available from the mid 18th century onwards meant that such items as bowls could be produced and Exhibit 340 is an excellent example. An examination of the amount of jade available to the imperial palace between 1741 and 1753 is extremely interesting. In 1741 the entire collection of the Qing imperial court comprised only ten complete pieces and sixty-six fragments, whereas in 1753, 101 pieces of uncarved jade with a recorded weight of 2 1/3 tons were selected and orders placed with Suzhou, one of the great jade making centres in China, for 100 bowls and 100 *zhuomu*. Exhibit 340 may well be one of the bowls carved as a result of this order (77 p.42, 12, and 92 p.153).

White jade *zigang* pendants and pendants with relief and openwork carving are known from the late 17th century. Subjects such as Liuhai and toad, buddha's hand, fruit, vegetables and fruit such as pomegranate, and cups with *kui* dragon handles, are typical of the Qing period. Vegetables were seldom, if ever, made the subject of art in the Ming dynasty.

Some of these items are very highly polished like some of the jade found in Wanli's tomb. This high gloss became comparatively common in the Qing period, particularly with the improved polishing materials available from the early 19th century on.

Although the Ming tradition of jade carving continued into the early Qing, several points should be noted in regard to jades from the later period. The lack of three dimensional form in some of Qing animals is obvious, for example Exhibits 329 and 343. Ming dynasty jade carvings all are capable of standing upright, without the assistance of a stand, but this is sometimes not the case with Qing dynasty examples. Exhibits 309 and 329 provide a useful comparison in this regard. Other points to notice are the less laborious methods used for executing the wave bases compare in this regard, Exhibits 293, 327 and 344, which demonstrate the changes in treatment over the period 1550-1750.

From the Yongzheng period onwards, jade craftsman spent more time and effort on fine carving and careful production, which led to technically superior jades being produced during this and the Qianlong period. The second half of the 18th century also saw a revival of interest in yellow jades which seems to have become a favourite colour at this time. Eighteenth century white jades are nearly always opaque or translucent with opaque fibrous veins, quite different from the lychee-flesh white that was popular from the Song to the early Ming dynasties.

During the period after 1755, the Manchu army came to control the northwestern border regions of China and the centres of jade production in Khotan. The Qianlong emperor subsequently received many fine jades from Chinese Turkestan, one of the main types being known as Moghul jades. These were generally of a very fine white colour and quality, very thin and with a beautifully soft polish that is difficult to emulate (Exhibits 348 and 350). The Qianlong emperor so admired these tributes from Turkestan that he ordered poems to be inscribed on them in the beautiful calligraphy of the time. Exhibit 350 appears to be one of these pieces so inscribed. The popularity of Moghul jades led to the Chinese copying their designs and patterns. Although the decorative motifs are not as well polished as those of the Moghul originals and are somewhat coarse by comparison, many are *tours de force*.

Apart from the fine quality jade imported by the Imperial authorities, material of excellent quality was also available in the marketplace, and Suzhou and Yangzhou workshops making jade artifacts chiefly for the private sector flourished throughout the second half of the 18th century. Imperial jades were produced in eight different departments under the control of the imperial court; in Suzhou, Lianghuai, Hangzhou, Jiangling, Huaiguan, Changlu, Jiujiang and Fengyang. Jade was produced for the private sector, in Suzhou, Yangzhou, Hangzhou, Jiangling, Huai'an, Tianjin, Beijing and Guangzhou. Beijing had been a centre for the production of jade since the Yuan dynasty, and Guangzhou also had a long history of jade craftsmanship. Huai'an and Tianjin were new centres and did not last long. The other centres mentioned were all traditionally associated with jade production. It appears that Hanjing, Xi'an and Nangang also produced jade on a relatively small scale, and there were many jade craftsmen who travelled around the country plying their trade (92 p. 155).

The most important centre for jade craftsmanship in the south of China was Suzhou, which was particularly famous at this time for the carving of characters and the staining of jade. Guangzhou was the political, economic and trading centre of the southern region during the Qing dynasty, but its level of craftsmanship never reached that of the Suzhou and the Yangzhou carvers and Guangzhou does not appear to have received any commissions from the Imperial court. However, there does appear to have been some foreign input into the region, and Guangzhou craftsmen were particularly good at combining jade with jewels to make landscapes and jade jewellery.

Spinach green nephrite, from sources close to Lake Baikal, seems to have become quite common in the late 18th century.

The concept of the fondling piece was certainly adopted during the Qing period and continues to this day.

Jade vases and vessels of all types with covers attached by a jade chain, the whole carved from one piece of jade, continued to be produced in ever increasing quantities in the 19th and early 20th centuries. Working jade with diamond drills led to a large increase in the quantities of jades produced at this time, but the care and artistry of the carver went into decline. There was also an increasing tendency to use jadeite (Exhibit 354) rather than nephrite during this period.

Brian McElney
January 1994

清 代

清代玉工繼承了數千年的治玉傳統。<隨時勢遷動的瑰寶>文中,提及十六世紀末開始了入山採玉的活動。唯1600年至十八世紀中葉,玉材供應受阻,吳中一帶玉作坊生產遂受影響。

康熙、雍正、乾隆三代是太平盛世,加上十八世紀中葉以後玉材來源充裕,清代之前罕見之大型玉雕遂大量出現,豪門富戶亦相競收購。除玉花瓶外,最著名的是玉山子,以山產玉或水產玉根據當時的山水畫雕製而成,飾以亭台樓閣、人物鳥獸、花草樹木等等。此風氣在明代已開始,清時成為文人書房中不可缺少之物(展品330及331)。

陪葬品在清代已式微。除早期(1644-1680)墓葬外只有王室及其近親的墓葬才見器物出土。1652年,有法例規定官員袍服前後須縫有補子,故玉帶不再成為間接的官階象徵,甚多明帶板淪為屏風嵌飾。

清律例又規定男子必須剃髮留辮,因而如展品208之髮飾便失去實際作用。清代髮簪亦異於明代,多為金屬製鑲玉,十八世紀晚期,鑲嵌之角閃玉多為翡翠所代。

玉碗則是十八世紀中葉後大量玉材供應下的產品(展品340)。清廷在1741年藏有的玉器玉材,跟1753年所藏大不一樣。1741年庫藏為金器十件、半製成品六十六件。到了1753年,一百零一件玉璞,共重二又三分一噸,被送往蘇州,用以製造碗一百隻及鐲一百隻。展品340恐是其中之一(77,頁42注12,92,頁153)。

白玉子剛牌、浮雕及透雕牌,在十七世紀晚期仍有製造。此外,螭龍柄杯、劉海、瓜果如佛手、石榴、各類蔬菜均是清代典型題材。蔬菜在明藝術品中甚少見。

清玉雕拋光強烈,類似明神宗(萬曆)墓中出土者(見<明代>一文)。強度拋光當是與十九世紀時打磨原料有所改良有關。

清初玉雕仍有明代遺風,但亦有其特徵。清動物玉雕缺立體感,如展品329及343。明玉雕本身能屹立,不必依賴木架支持,清製品則不然,展品309及329是清晰的對比。清玉雕的波濤紋刻工略顯鬆懈,展品293、

327及344,是1550至1750年間兩種不同手法的代表作。

雍正年間,玉工較注重刻工,故此期及之後的乾隆期玉器質素頗高。十八世紀後期,黃玉再度成為寵兒,此時的白玉大多不透明或帶不透明纖維脈理,有異於流行宋明兩代的荔枝肉色白玉。

1755至1759年間,清廷控制了中國西北邊疆一帶,包括和闐的產玉區。自此,土耳其斯坦玉便入貢中土。其中以莫臥兒玉器為最佳、顏色潔白、雕工極薄、拋光柔和,本展覽有三件展出(展品348及350)。清高宗(乾隆)對此等玉器極為喜愛,為此製詩,又命玉工將詩句鐫刻其上,展品350想是其中之一。莫臥兒玉器受歡迎,中國玉工遂有仿製,但器身不如前者薄巧,拋光亦較粗糙,但仍不失為藝術佳品。

十八世紀下半,蘇州及揚州私人玉作坊亦能獲得優質玉材,從而供應王室以外的顧客。由清廷直接控制的製玉工場分設在蘇州、兩淮、杭州、江陵、淮關、長蘆、九江及鳳陽八地,而蘇州、揚州、杭州、江陵、淮安、天津、北京及廣州等地玉作坊則供應其他買家。北京的製玉業始自元代,廣州亦有長久的製玉歷史。除淮安及天津是新起場所外,其他各處均有製玉傳統。此外,漢江、西安及南崗亦有小型治玉工場。所注意的是,大部份玉工的工作範圍不局限於作坊,他們慣於上門到顧客家中雕製各種玉器(92,頁155)。

南部各治玉中心又以蘇州最著名,特別是鐫刻銘文及染色。廣州在清代是政治及經濟重鎮,但製玉技術不及蘇揚,故未獲朝建青睞,但用玉配其他寶石製成的首飾和山水插屏,顯然是受了來自廣州的外國藝術影響。

十八世紀末,流行出自貝加爾湖耽的墨綠色角閃玉。供把玩的玉雕亦變得普遍,這現象維持到今日。

由一塊玉樸雕製而成,帶蓋及活環的花瓶或器皿是鬼斧神工之作,由十八世紀末至二十世紀初陸續生產。鑽石鑽頭的使用促進玉器的產量,但藝術質素卻有下降趨勢。輝石玉(展品354)亦開始接替了角閃玉的地位。

320

BRUSH REST FORMED BY TWO PHOENIXES WITH LINGZHI

LATE MING TO EARLY QING DYNASTY
(17TH CENTURY, PROBABLY 1ST HALF)
BATEA 549

LENGTH : 8 CM
HEIGHT : 4.8 CM
WIDTH : 3 CM

Pale celadon green jade brush rest group of two phoenixes, one smaller than the other, arranged tail to tail, both birds with heads turned inwards, the larger holding a large spray of lingzhi, the wings of both birds decorated with a stylised design.

The designs on the wings are an elaboration of the late Ming dynasty convention of squared spiral carving on bird's wings such as appears on Exhibit 304 and this piece should be dated to the late Ming period or just after. (BSM)

Previously published: 80, No.59

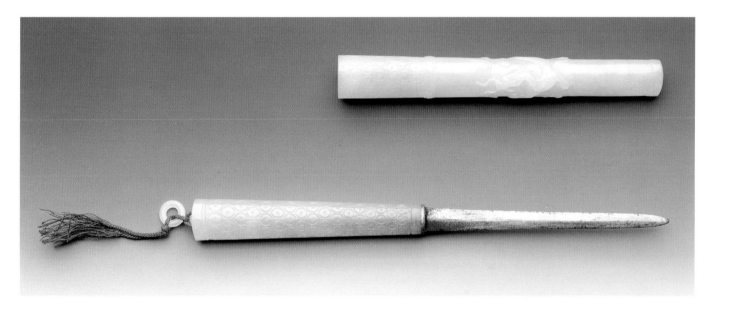

321

JADE MOUNTED EATING DAGGER AND SCABBARD

LATE MING TO EARLY QING DYNASTY
(17TH CENTURY, PROBABLY 1ST HALF)
BATEA 431

LENGTH : 19.7 CM
WIDTH : 1.6 CM

Steel eating dagger with pale celadon jade handle and scabbard, both decorated with an overall pattern of hexagonal diapers; the scabbard with a *kui* dragon in relief and a raised section at the back.

Similar daggers mounted in bamboo have been dated to the 17th century. The hexagonal diaper was a popular late Ming decoration. This dagger was probably made for use by Manchu nobles on their travels on horseback over the vast Mongolian steppe just prior to or just after the establishment of the Qing dynasty. (BSM)

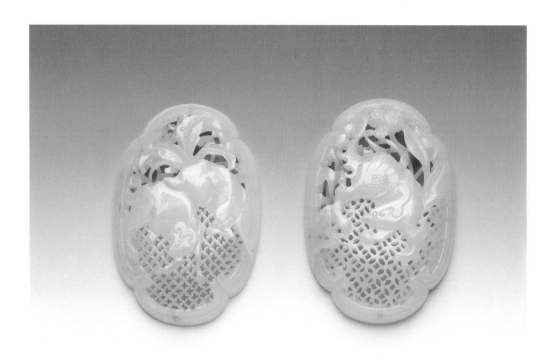

322

RETICULATED JADE OVAL BOX

LATE MING TO EARLY QING DYNASTY
(17TH CENTURY, PROBABLY 1ST HALF)
BATEA 501

LENGTH : 5.8 CM
WIDTH : 4 CM
HEIGHT : 2 CM

Greyish-white jade reticulated perfume box of elongated oval form, the top half carved and pierced through depicting a mythical animal striding on a foreground of cell diaper, with dense scrolling foliage in the background, the bottom half depicting two goats on a similar ground in front of a plantain tree; all within plain, rounded borders, both halves pierced through for stringing together.

This type of mythical animal and plantain tree design are comparable with decoration occuring on many blue and white ceramics dating from the first half of the 17th century but both motifs are seldom depicted thereafter. This type of box was probably used as a pomander. (BSM)

Previously published: <u>77, Plate XXI.</u>

323

Reticulated plaque of Daoist paradise

Late Ming to early Qing dynasty
(17th century, probably 1st half)
BATEA 584

Length : 10 cm
Width : 7 cm

A reticulated roughly rectangular plaque of Xi Wangmu, the Queen Mother of the West, seated under a pine tree with a crane and incense burner by her side. A tortoise belching clouds on which a pagoda floats is on the other side of the pine tree. A fairy riding a cloud vehicle is in the sky above and to one side. The whole scene is set against a backdrop of perforated rocks.

This carving contains many motifs commonly found in Chinese art of the 17th century that are all related to Daoism. Also included are symbols of good fortune, which are typical of Ming dynasty jades. The perforated rocks in the background are also consistent with a 17th century date. Whilst the author believes this piece is 17th century in date, a similar piece in the Beijing Palace Museum collection has been dated to the Song dynasty by Yang Boda. A date earlier than the 17th century is therefore possible, but seems to the writer unlikely. (BSM)

Previously published: 37, No.257

324

Bird with peach spray

Early Qing dynasty
(1644-1911)
(17th century, probably 2nd half)
BATEA 586

Length : 7 cm
Height : 4.5 cm

White jade group of bird with peach spray, one peach protruding; the head sensitively carved, the body showing the russet marking of the original pebble. (BSM)

Previously published: 77, No. 83

325

BUFFALO WITH *QILIN* ON ITS BACK

EARLY QING DYNASTY
 (1644-1911)
 (17TH CENTURY, PROBABLY 2ND HALF)
                           BATEA 518
LENGTH : 7.2 CM
HEIGHT: 2.6 CM
WIDTH : 4.8 CM

A white jade group of a buffalo with a small *qilin* starting to climb up onto its back, the *qilin*'s head turned towards the head of the buffalo which holds the tail of the *qilin* in its mouth.

This combination of animals from the natural and imaginary world suggests a Qing 17th century date. (BSM)

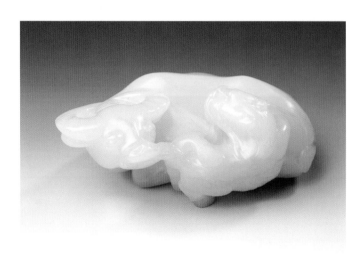

326

BUDDHIST DISCIPLE STANDING ON A LOTUS

QING DYNASTY
 (1644-1911) OR EARLIER
                           BATEA 1227
HEIGHT : 12.2 CM
DEPTH : 3.4 CM
WIDTH : 2.8 CM

Buddhist disciple standing his hands clasped in attitude of prayer on top of a small lotus flower, the jade of pale celadon colour.

Buddhist figures on a lotus have been found in Ming tombs but this standing figure with his hands clasped in prayer in a Christian manner seems more consistent with a Qing date. (BSM)

Collection: The Rannerdale Collection

327
CARPS AMID WAVES

EARLY QING DYNASTY
(17TH CENTURY, PROBABLY 2ND HALF)
BATEA 407

LENGTH : 12 CM
HEIGHT : 6.2 CM
DEPTH : 5 CM

Celadon-green jade group of two carps one large and one small amid swirling waves, the base showing a whirlpool in early Qing style, the larger fish with iron rust markings. The large carp with flat lustrous sides and prominent dorsal fin is followed by a smaller carp across a bed of waves, the waves being both mannered and realistic.

This piece exhibits the first signs of the Qing style of treating wave bases, exemplified in the somewhat later Exhibit 344. The dark celadon-green of the jade stone is typical of some of the jades that are probably dateable to the second half of the 17th century. (BSM)

Previously published: (i) 82 No. 90 (ii) 37 No. 188

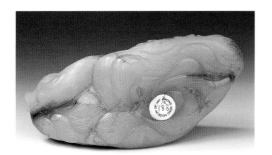

328
TWO PEACHES AND A BAT

EARLY QING DYNASTY
(17TH CENTURY)
                    BATEA 536

LENGTH : 9.5 CM
WIDTH : 7.5 CM
DEPTH : 4.5 CM

Celadon green and brown coloured jade pebble of two peaches with leaves and a bat, the reverse of the leaves showing the veins of the leaf carved naturalistically in relief.

The bat and peaches convey wishes for happiness and longevity and would be a suitable design on a present. The relief carving of the underside of the leaf is an early feature and a 17th century dating is appropriate. (BSM)

Previously published: <u>77, No. 90</u>

329
LION DOG

EARLY QING DYNASTY
PROBABLY KANGXI
(1662-1722)
                    BATEA 433

LENGTH : 10.2 CM
HEIGHT : 6 CM
WIDTH : 4.4 CM

White jade lion dog with a few brown suffusions; its large fat tail with four tightly incised hairy curls where it joins the well-muscled body, all with fine line incisions, the paws with well defined and detailed claws, the back and chest ridged and its rib cage showing, the legs with concave planes, its head tucked in and turned towards the rear.

This piece with its fine treatment of the muscles and hair suggests a Ming dating as appropriate, but the fact that it requires a stand seems to indicate that an early Qing date is more likely, since it is thought that the Ming lapidary would have so worked the pebble that the piece would stand unassisted. (compare Exhibit 308). (BSM)

Previously published: Min Chiu Society 30th Anniversary Exhibition, Hong Kong, November 1990 No. 218

330

PEBBLE OF TETHERED HORSE AND SCHOLAR

EARLY QING DYNASTY
PROBABLY KANGXI
(1662-1722)

BATEA 414

HEIGHT : 8.9 CM

WIDTH : 3.7 CM
LENGTH : 8.7 CM

A pale celadon and russet jade pebble carved with a travelling scholar in a rocky landscape, his horse tethered to a paulownia tree, the reverse decorated with bamboo in relief by a flowing stream under a crag.

The colour of the pebble is typical of the early Qing dynasty and probably of the Kangxi period and the paulownia *Wutong* tree with its Daoist associations was a popular motif at that time but was seldom depicted later. (BSM)

331

PEBBLE OF BODHIDHARMA
CROSSING RIVER

QING DYNASTY
  (1644-1911)
PROBABLY KANGXI
  (1662 - 1722)

BATEA 539

HEIGHT : 11 CM
WIDTH : 8.5 CM
DEPTH: 3.5 CM

Green jade pebble with prominent black markings
down one edge, depicting Bodhidharma crossing a
river on a reed under a cliff; the reverse with pine
trees, the whole deeply carved.

The subject chosen here was particularly popular
in the late 17th century and occurs in several
media. Some of the piece appears to have been
artificially dyed black. The dyeing of jade to
enhance its visual appeal is known to have
occured since at least the Tang dynasty. (BSM)

Previously published: 77, No. 84

332

JADE REBUS OF BAT AND WATER CALTROP

EARLY QING DYNASTY
(1644-1911)
PROBABLY KANGXI
(1662-1722)

BATEA 412

LENGTH : 4 CM
WIDTH : 2.3 CM

Jade pebble of a water caltrop or moustache fruit with a few leaves and stem, on top of which a bat envelopes almost the entire top of the fruit, the jade with light brown suffusions.

The combination of the bat "fu" which has the same sound as the Chinese word for prosperity and water caltrop "ling" which sounds the same as intelligence here form the rebus "fuzhi xinling" meaning "with prosperity comes intelligent use of opportunities". The depiction of fruit (other than the peach and pomegranate) and vegetables as the principal decoration does not seem to occur in Chinese art until the Qing dynasty. The peach and pomegranate both have special connotations connected with longevity and many descendants respectively and are depicted frequently before the Qing dynasty. (BSM)

Previously published: 37, No 286.

333

JADE CAT

EARLY QING DYNASTY
(1644-1911)
PROBABLY KANGXI
(1662-1722)

BATEA 556

LENGTH : 5.6 CM
WIDTH : 3.8 CM
HEIGHT : 2.6 CM

A pale celadon jade cat with patches of orange-brown skin on the top of the head, the ears and the back.

The cat was a very popular subject in Qing jade carving, and this is a good example. The inclusion of so much of the skin and the treatment of the animal itself and the colour of the jade all suggest an early Qing date. (BSM)

Previously published: 77, No. 81

334
BIRD WITH LINGZHI BULB AND PRUNUS

EARLY QING DYNASTY
(1644-1911)
PROBABLY KANGXI
(1662-1722)
BATEA 469
LENGTH : 5.5 CM
WIDTH : 3.3 CM

Oblong jade pebble carved as a long-tailed bird on top of two lingzhi with prunus spray and bulb with berries, the head of the bird and the prunus blossom using the rich orange skin with extensive carving of details.

This type of very detailed carving is in the typical style of the Suzhou school of the period. Very clever use has been made of the skin to depict the plum blossom. The combination probably represents a rebus. (BSM)

Previously published: 37, No. 82

335
GROUP OF GOLDFISH, CLAM AND FROG

EARLY QING DYNASTY
(1644-1911)
(18TH CENTURY, PROBABLY 1ST HALF)
BATEA 1222
WIDTH: 3.6 CM
DIAMETER : 3.5 CM
HEIGHT : 1.5 CM

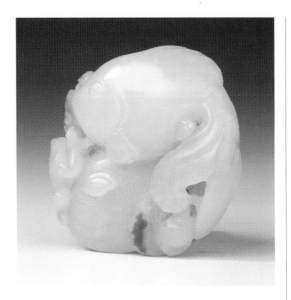

White jade group of goldfish, clam and frog in white jade with orange suffusions and particularly finely incised details.

The very fine incised carving on this particular piece, seldom seen in jade, the author considers typical of the Suzhou carvers' work in the 18th century. Such work was continued into the famous Suzhou agates of the late 18th and 19th centuries. (BSM)

Collection: The Rannerdale Collection

336

GOLDFISH AND SHELLS

QING DYNASTY
  (1644-1911)
  (18TH CENTURY, PROBABLY 1ST HALF)
                              BATEA 457

LENGTH : 5.9 CM
WIDTH : 2.6 CM
HEIGHT : 2.2 CM

White jade group of goldfish and shells carved to retain the orange skin of the pebble with fine incised carving of details.

The author considers the finely incised carving here typical of Suzhou work and the retention of so much of the orange skin of the pebble suggests a date in the first half of the 18th century. The Chinese in the Qing dynasty developed an enormous interest in the goldfish. The breeding of goldfish into ever more exotic forms developed into a craze in the 18th century. (BSM)

337

PHOENIX WITH PEACH SPRAY AND FUNGUS

QING DYNASTY
  (1644-1911)
  (18TH CENTURY, PROBABLY 1ST HALF)
                              BATEA 566

LENGTH : 8.7 CM
WIDTH : 4.8 CM
HEIGHT : 4.7 CM

White jade phoenix retaining the form of the crescent-shaped pebble, one side with extensive traces of the bright russet skin highlighting details of the design. The bird is shown seated, its head turned and holding a fruiting peach bough in its beak, with a clump of fungus at its back. The phoenix's long tail feathers are curled to one side; the other side and the flat base show the white colour of the interior of the pebble.

The use of the skin here is typical of the best 18th century carving. In the second half of the 18th century there seems to have been a tendency to remove the skin on jade of this quality as sullying the pure white of the jade carving. (BSM)

Previously published: 77, Plate. XXV

338

REBUS OF TWO ARROWROOT AND A MAGPIE

QING DYNASTY
(1644-1911)
(18TH CENTURY)

BATEA 478

LENGTH : 6.5 CM
WIDTH : 4.4 CM
DEPTH : 2 CM

A jade group of two arrowroots (*cigu*) with leaves emerging from the top, and a long-tailed bird probably a magpie (*xigue*), the combination a rebus for xibao shuangxi "Happy tidings for parents".

The depiction of vegetables in Chinese decorative art as here seems confined to the Qing dynasty. (BSM)

Previously published: (i) 77, No. 96 (ii) 37, No. 290

339

DEER AND DOG

QING DYNASTY
(1644-1911)
(18TH CENTURY)
BATEA 498

LENGTH : 6 CM
HEIGHT : 4 CM
WIDTH: 2.5 CM

A reclining deer in white mutton fat jade, its head turned to the rear, its legs bunched up. The deer holds a daisy frond in its mouth, and a small dog is climbing onto its back and nuzzling up to its head. (BSM)

Previously published: 77, No. 87

340

GREENISH-WHITE JADE BOWL

QING DYNASTY
(1644-1911)
(18TH CENTURY)

BATEA 540

DIAMETER : 15.3 CM
HEIGHT : 6.2 CM.

Plain, transparent, smoothly polished pale greenish-white circular jade bowl of even colour with outward curving rim; the base with well-formed rectangular footrim.

This piece can only have been made in a period when stone of this almost flawless quality was in abundant supply as much of the original raw material would have been wasted in fashioning such a piece. A Qing dynasty date is therefore very likely. The sensitive modelling and lack of any embellishment imply a respect for the stone itself, and these combined with the lovely polishing suggest an 18th century dating. It could well be one of the bowls ordered by the imperial palace from Suzhou in 1753 mentioned in the introduction to the Qing dynasty section. (BSM)

Previously published: (i) 82, No. 152 (ii) 77, No. 95

341
LOBED SAUCER WITH CATFISH AND FUNGUS

QING DYNASTY
  (1644-1911)
  (MID 18TH CENTURY)
                 BATEA 519
DIAMETER : 13.5 CM
DEPTH : 2.5 CM

White transparent, shallow jade saucer of foliated circular shape, the centre of the interior with two catfish holding a linghzi fungus spray in relief, the inset centre of the base with small fungus spray also in relief.

The base design is one commonly found on enamel pieces dateable to the Yongzheng (1723-1735) and early Qianlong (1735-1795) periods and dating to this period is considered appropriate. (BSM)

Previously published: (i) 77, Plate XXVIII (ii) 37, No. 220

342

YELLOW BUFFALO

QING DYNASTY
(1644-1911)
(18TH CENTURY)
PE80

LENGTH : 4.8 CM
HEIGHT : 2.7 CM
BREADTH : 2.0 CM

A recumbent female water buffalo in flawless yellow nephrite with honey-brown suffusions on the left cheek, shoulder and flank and meticulously worked all over to a fine burnish. The chin rests on the right fore hoof and the left foreleg is drawn under the body at an angle. The head looks straight in front and a corded rope passes from the mouth, between the legs and underneath the animal to emerge and climb up the left side through several coils and terminating upon the back.

This piece depicts the sexual organs in a way redolent of the late Song dynasty. Exhibit 341, however, is clearly of Qing date and is distinguished by its flawless warm fatty-yellow stone so popular in the Qing, the sculptural composition and perfection of finish. (AHF)

Collection: The Peony Collection

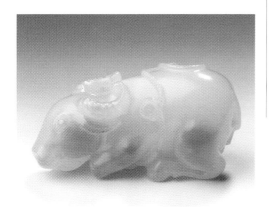

343

MANDARIN DUCKS WITH LOTUS

QING DYNASTY
(1644-1911)
(PROBABLY 18TH CENTURY)
BATEA 561

LENGTH : 7.1 CM
WIDTH : 6.3 CM
HEIGHT : 4.9 CM

Greyish-celadon green jade pebble carved in the shape of two mandarin ducks, each holding a lotus spray, showing in places the orange outer skin of the pebble, the entire group seated on a lotus leaf; the birds' crests and tails and the lotus leaf incised with fine lines.

Mandarin ducks have been symbols of marital fidelity in Chinese art for centuries and two such ducks have been a popular subject since at least the early Ming dynasty. The comparative lack of three-dimensional modelling here, however, suggests a Qing date for this example. (BSM)

344

TWO CATFISH ON BED OF WAVES

QING DYNASTY
(1644-1911)
(18TH CENTURY)
BATEA 488

LENGTH : 8.8 CM
WIDTH : 5.8 CM
DEPTH : 2.9 CM

Mottled white jade of two catfish, each with a sprig of lingzhi entwined together head to tail (Yin-Yang), the base with schematized whirlpool divided into segments in Ming style but further divided by concave bands into groups of incised lines.

Probably a rebus for "every year as you wish". The separation of the incised waves by concave bands is typical of the mid Qing style of executing wave bases found on many Ming and Qing animals. Such concave bands involve much less work than the overall incised lines found on the earlier renderings of such wave bases. (BSM)

Previously published: (i) 82. No.91 (ii) 77, No.80

► 345

SET OF FOUR PEBBLE PAPER WEIGHTS

QING DYNASTY
(1644-1911)
(PROBABLY 18TH CENTURY)
BATEA 528

MAXIMUM DIMENSIONS : 1: 6 CM, 2: 4.5 CM, 3: 7.5 CM, 4: 8 CM.

Set of four natural greenish-white jade pebble paperweights with varying degrees of russet-brown markings, undecorated but for regular *kaishu* inscriptions on one side.

1. (lower left) inscribed with the title of their place of use Chunhe Yuan ("Garden of Peaceful Spring"). 2. (lower right) inscribed with a couplet "The peaches of the Mountain of Immortals (Suishan) are beautiful and everlasting; natural gems of jade have the same longevity"; followed by "recorded by Chunhe" (the name of the garden being transferred to its owner), with seal Chunhe. 3. (upper right) with a poetic description of jade "Unsophisticated [as a virtue] like a pebble from Khotan; embracing the moon, condensing the mist; having the longevity of the pine; with the brilliance of a new year flower," followed by the signature "written by the Master of the Chunhe Yuan" with seal Chunhe. 4. (upper left) also has a poetic description of the stone: "Outstanding jade, naturally produced; collected from the streams of Khotan; treasure of the waters and mountains; essence of ten thousand years of gathered beauty", followed by the seal Bao() Zhai ('Precious [?] Studio' - part of the middle character has been worn away by handling and is no longer legible).

This set of paperweights demonstrates clearly the esteem in which jade was held, quite apart from the workmanship expended upon it. Here seemingly humble pebbles have been simply polished, their natural beauty allowed to speak for itself, and transformed into treasures for the scholar's studio. Although the poems add a level of meaning to them as works of art, it was the simple pebbles that first inspired the poems. In the 19th century pebbles such as these were re-used as snuff bottles and original pebble paperweights such as these are rare.

It has not been possible to trace the ownership or location of the Chunhe Yuan, but we may be fairly certain that it included a place where the scholar/artist/poet could sit, enjoy the peace of the garden and meditate. Here would have been kept the necessary equipment to write or paint, to play music and drink wine or tea while engaging in elegant conversation. Such objects as these would have been associated with that place, and even if used elsewhere would have carried with them the tranquillity of this special garden, as indeed they do to a degree today despite our ignorance of its details. There may well be some connection between this garden and the Hall of Peaceful Spring (Chunhe Tang) which is recorded as having belonged to the Qing dynasty prince You Li.

The same poem and Chunhe seal as on the third (upper right) pebble, are inscribed on the inkstone (Exhibit 346). (BSM)

Previously published: (i) 53. No. 154 (ii) 37, No. 277 (one only)

346

BOULDER INKSTONE

QING DYNASTY
  (1644-1911)
                PE395
LENGTH : 14.5 CM
BREADTH : 12.5 CM
THICKNESS : 5 CM

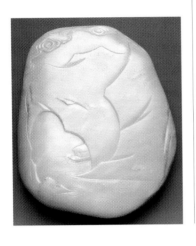

Inkstone formed from a flattened natural pebble of greyish-green translucent nephrite with a soft gloss. On one side two scholars are depicted in relief standing at the foot of a precipice and looking across space over a waterfall pool, formed by the ink grinding surface, to the moon wraithed in cloud and coming out from concealment behind a rock overhang on which is engraved a sixteen character poem. On the other side, clouds cover the summit of massive cliffs towering over a river where a pleasure boat begins to appear at the head of the rapids.

The theme of Red Cliffs with the boatload of scholars riding the rapids was popular in the late Ming and early Qing period. The inscription on the cliff by the moon across the ink grinding surface or pool from the two gesticulating scholars is the same poem and reference to the same Chunhe Yuan as mentioned in Exhibit 345. (AHF)

Collection: The Peony Collection

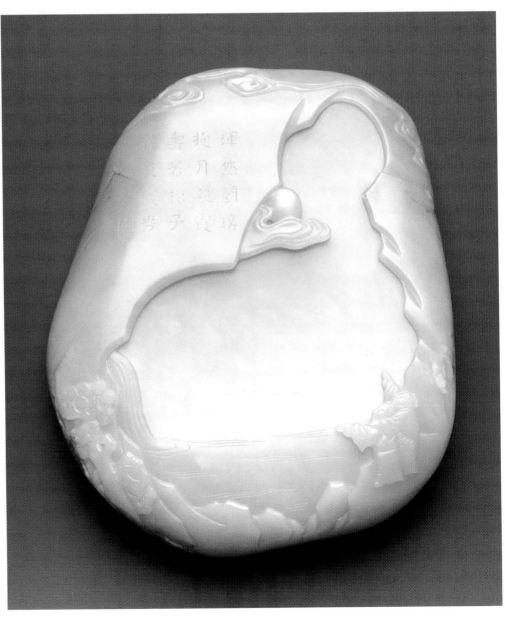

347
PEBBLE WITH PRUNUS AND INSCRIBED COUPLET

QING DYNASTY
(1644-1911)
(QIANLONG PERIOD 1736-95)
BATEA 486

LENGTH : 6.1 CM
WIDTH : 4.6 CM
HEIGHT : 1.9 CM

Greyish-white oval jade pebble with knarled prunus blossom branch with buds and five-petalled flowers carved in low relief. A thirteen character couplet in praise of spring, and two seals reading Ancient and Fragrance, beautifully inscribed in typical Qianlong (1736-95) *kaishu* calligraphy, reads to the following effect:-

"A twig reflects its shadow over the clear water,

Witness to the endless flowers of spring".

The simplicity of the conception and design here is typically 18th century. The calligraphy is typical of the Qianlong period and renders a date within the Qianlong reign almost a certainty. (BSM)

Previously published: <u>77, No. 101</u>

348
FLOWER-SHAPED HANDLED MOGHUL CUP

INDIAN MOGHUL WORK
(17TH OR EARLY 18TH CENTURY)
BATEA 419

LENGTH : 8 CM
WIDTH : 6.4 CM
HEIGHT : 1.7 CM

White translucent jade cup thinly carved in the Moghul style as a lobed oval open flower head standing on a shallow foot formed by the flower head base with petals. A small spray forms the integral handle. The soft polish, form and handle are typical of the best Indian Moghul work.

The Qianlong Emperor admired such work greatly when he first saw it in 1759 and thereafter inscribed poems on many such pieces. Chinese jade carvers from then until well into the 19th century carved many pieces in the Moghul style, but the polish on the Chinese pieces is not so soft, and the carving can be quite coarse. Many Chinese pieces are however difficult to tell from the Indian originals. The extreme thinness, the soft polish, form and the handle all indicate a Hindustan origin for this piece. The more primitive tools and abrasives used by the Moghul jade carvers are thought to have led to the softer polish of their work. (BSM)

Previously published: (i) <u>37, No. 231</u> (ii) <u>77, pl. XXVII</u>

349

CURLING LEAF OR FLOWER PETAL KNOP

MOGHUL, PROBABLY NORTH INDIA
(C.17TH CENTURY)

PE609

WIDTH : 6.3 CM
HEIGHT : 4.4 CM
THICKNESS : 1.5 CM

Knop or handle formed in opaque grey-green nephrite as a long leaf or flower petal shoot with substantial axial supporters rising and turning outwards from a central core or tip which is pierced with a central cavity; the base of the tip drilled horizontally through from the exterior to the base of the central cavity in three places; the out-turned leaves are rendered separately from those below by way of shaped holes drilled right through from side to side. The entire growth rises from a low oval base the exterior perimeter of which is a concave groove. The bottom of the base is flat.

This piece may be well compared with a piece having the same terminal structure but of a slightly more formal and elegant character and illustrated as 49A p.55 No.10, and there described as a representation of a blossoming iris in the Bharat Kala Bhavan, Varanasi in India and ascribed to a North Indian Moghul jade origin and dated to c.1625. Somehow, the feeling and spirit of Exhibit 349 is freer, wetter and more succulent than the Varanasi piece but considerable further thought and study will be necessary before possibly assigning a different provenance and dating to this piece. (AHF)

Compare: 49A p.55 No.10
Collection: The Peony Collection

350

IBEX-HEADED CUP WITH INSCRIPTION

MOGHUL, PROBABLY NORTH INDIA
 (18TH CENTURY)

PE238

LENGTH : 8.5 CM
BREADTH : 6.2 CM
HEIGHT : 2.5 CM

Half gourd-shaped cup with integral handle formed as an ibex head with gold-mounted ruby eyes turning elegantly back on a slender neck enfolded with acanthus leaves. The lobed walls of the vessel are smoothly carved and of great thinness and delicacy. The interior is inscribed with a commemorative tributary elegy of some length. The flower form foot has been damaged and its remnant is encased in a silver ring.

In her excellent work "Hindustan Jade" 1983, Teng Shu-p'ing sets out an exhaustive research into the recorded series of birthday poems and inscriptions of the Qianlong emperor (1736-1795), many of which were inscribed onto the bodies of Hindustan taste jade vessels. Ms. Teng notes that a number of the inscribed poem vessels have been dispersed throughout the world and there seems every reason to believe that Exhibit 350 is one of the missing examples. It bears the text of a poem or song known to be no.51 in the series, the text of which has not yet been identified upon a jade piece. The strength combined with delicacy of Exhibit 350 are typical of the amazing achievement of the Hindustan or Moghul style of jade carving of the 18th century, set off in the case of Exhibit 350 by the small ruby eyes set in gold mounts. The text of the inscription translates as follows "This jade ram's-head petal cup dedicated to the emperor is a famous product of Lutai. It is engraved by an excellent craftsman. It is a cup with a shape quite different to the Han cup and Shang containers. Its body is mainly crafted with exquisite curves while the petals are engraved with leaves and its handle is twisted in the shape of a ram's head. It is crafted with heavenly handiwork, made of the finest material and has a texture such that no one in China can make such a fine cup." (AHF)

Compare: (i) 76; 27 pl.92 (ii) 76; pl.25   (iii) 83 No.99
Collection: The Peony Collection

351

LEAF TRAY WITH WEEVIL HOLES

QING DYNASTY
(1644-1911)
(LATE 18TH - EARLY 19TH CENTURY)
BATEA 429
LENGTH : 15.3 CM
WIDTH : 10 CM

Greyish nephrite jade transparent leaf tray, carved in Moghul style with ring attached and integral to the stem handle, the leaf rendered realistically and showing two weevil holes.

The ring handle integral to the piece can only have been carved in a period when jade was in plentiful supply as in the period indicated. (BSM)

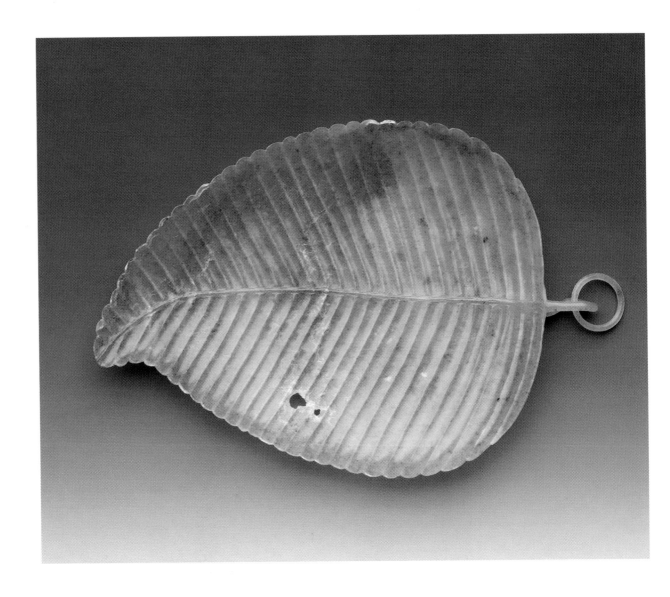

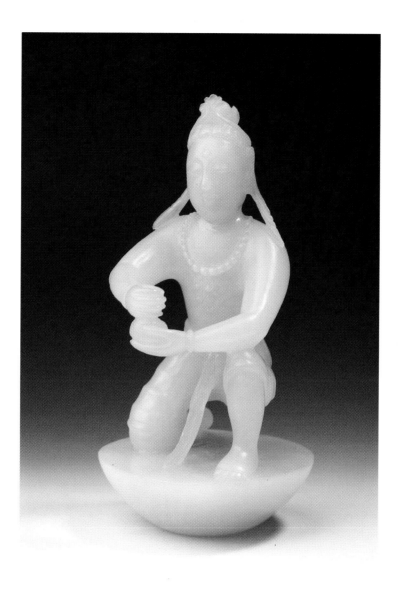

352

Half kneeling buddhist disciple

Qing dynasty
(1644-1911)
(late 18th - early 19th century)
BATEA 1207
Height : 9.5 cm
Width : 4.8 cm

Half-kneeling buddhist disciple, his outstretched hands holding an ointment jar, the tassels from his headdress and belt very thinly carved, the jade of pale celadon colour. The type of jade carving here is reminiscent of some Chinese Moghul work.

This piece with its very fine, thinly carved tassels from the headdress and belt can only have been done in a period when jade was in plentiful supply, and a date late in the 18th or early 19th century seems appropriate. (BSM)

Collection: The Rannerdale Collection

353

JUGGLER WITH FIGURE ON HIS BACK

QING DYNASTY
(1644-1911)
(LATE 18TH - EARLY 19TH CENTURY)
BATEA 596

HEIGHT : 6 CM
WIDTH : 4 CM

White jade male juggler pretending to have a woman on his back.

During the Qing dynasty one of the commonest acts performed by jugglers in villages and towns throughout China was pretending to have what appeared to be another figure on their backs. That figure was a total fake and the denoument of the act was to reveal this. In the meantime both figures appeared to move in unison. The author has seen this act performed very realistically even in the third quarter of the 20th century. (BSM)

354

JADEITE SNUFF BOTTLE WITH SCHOLAR, SERVANT AND ROCK

QING DYNASTY
(1644-1911)
(19TH CENTURY)
BATEA 541

HEIGHT : 6.1 CM
WIDTH : 5 CM
DEPTH : 2 CM

Jadeite snuff bottle of white jade with traces of lavender and emerald green on one side (colours not found in nephrite), decorated on the other side with the orange-brown skin worked to depict a scholar in relief, worshipping by a rock, being fanned by his servant.

This is the only jadeite in the Exhibition and has been included to show two of the additional colours found only in the jadeite material. Jade snuff bottles were not made before the 18th century and most would date to the 19th century. (BSM)

Previously published: 79, No. 60

22 SELECTED BIBLIOGRAPHY

MUSEUM OF EAST ASIAN ART - BATH
1994 JADE EXHIBITION
SELECTED BIBLIOGRAPHY

Abbreviations:

CASS	Chinese Academy of Social Sciences
BFJ	Bulletin of the Friends of Jade
CPAM	Committee for the Preservation of Antiquities and Monuments
BMFEA	Bulletin of the Museum of Far Eastern Antiquities, Stockholm
BOCSHK	Bulletin of the Oriental Ceramic Society of Hong Kong
IA	Institute of Archaelogy, Peoples Republic of China
TOCS	Transactions of the Oriental Ceramic Society
KG	kao gu, archaelogy periodical
WW	wen wu, cultural relics periodical

1. **D'Argence Rene-Yvon Lefebvre**   Chinese Jades in the Avery Brundage Collection Asian Art Museum of San Francisco, 1972

2. **Ayers, John**   A jade menagerie, creatures real and imaginary from the Worrall Collection 1993. Azimuth Editions, London 1993

3. **Burkart-Bauer, M.F.**   Chinesische Jaden aus drei Jahrtausenden, Museum Rietberg, Zurich 1986

4. **Chang K.C.**   An Essay on Cong, Orientations, Hong Kong, June 1989 pp 37-43

5. **Cheng Te Kun**   Some standing Jade Figurines of the Shang-Chou period, Artibus Asiae, vol. XXVIII, 1966 pp 39-52

6. _____   Jade Flowers and Floral Patters in Chinese Decorative Art, Chinese University of Hong Kong, 1969

7. _____   Chinese Jade - a general survey: Urban Council Hong Kong and the Min Chiu Society 1983

8. **Childs-Johnson, Elizabeth**   Dragons, Masks, Axes and Blades from Four Newly-documented Jade-producing Cultures of Ancient China, Orientations April 1988 pp. 30-41

9. **Clarke, Grahame**   Symbols of Excellence, Cambridge University Press 1986

10. **Dohrenwend, Doris**   Chinese Jades in the Royal Ontario Museum, Royal Ontario Museum, Toronto 1971

11. _____   Jade Demonic Images from Early China, Volume X of Ars Orientalis 1975

12. **Fang Dianchun and Liu Baohua**   Excavation of the Jade Tomb finds of the Hongshan Culture at Hutogou, Fuxin County, Liaoning Province, WW 1984: 6 pp 1-6

13. **Chinese Art Series**   Five Thousand Years of, Chinese Jade, Part 1, From Neolithic Age to Early Shang, Taipei 1985

14. **Fong, Wen, ed.**   The Great Bronze Age of China
An Exhibition from the People's Republic of China,
New York: Metropolitan Museum of Art, 1980

15. **Forsyth, Angus**   Five Chinese Jade Figures, a study of the Development of Sculptural Form in Hongshan Neolithic Jade Working, Orientations May 1990 pp. 54-63

16. _____   Neolithic Chinese Jades in "JADE" - Consultant Editor, Roger Keverne; Anness Publishing Ltd. London 1991

17. _____   Post-Neolithic to Han Chinese Jades in "JADE" - Consultant Editor, Roger Keverne; Anness Publishing Ltd. London 1991

18. _____   Jades and Unicorns: Specialist Tour of Jiangsu Province, China 19th-25th April 1984 - BOCSHK No. 6, Hong Kong

19. **Fu Zhong Mo**   Gu Yu Jing Ying (The Art of Jade Carving in Ancient China) Hong Kong 1989

20. **Gems of China's Cultural Relics**   People's Republic of China: Cultural Relics Publishing House, 1990

21. **Gems of China's Cultural Relics**   People's Republic of China: Cultural Relics Publishing House, 1992

22. **Gems of China's Cultural Relics**   People's Republic of China: Cultural Relics Publishing House, 1993

23. **Gugong Museum**   Guyu Jingcui (The Cream of old Jades) Shanghai 1987

24. **Gure, Desmond**   Desmond Gure, Selected Examples from the Jade Exhibition at Stockholm 1963 - A Comparative Study, BMFEA

25. _____   "Some Unusual Early Jades and Their Dating, TOCS: 1960-61

26 **Han Bao Quan**   Jade Wares: China Shaanxi Travel and Tourism Press, 1992

27. **Hansford, S.**   Chinese Carved Jades, Faber & Faber, London, 1968

28. _____   Jade, Essence of Hills and Streams, The Von Oertzen Collection of. Chinese and Indian Jades, Purnell & Sons (S.A.) Pty Limited, Capetown and Johannesburg 1969

29. **Hartman, Joan M.**   Ancient Chinese Jades from the Buffalo Museum of Science, China Institute in America New York 1975

30. **Hongshan Culture**   Excavations at Naxitai, Ba Yin Yeo Banner, Inner Mongolia, KG, 1987:6 pp.507-18

31. **Huang Jun**   Hengzhai Cangjian Guyu Tu Peking 1935

32. **Huang Xuan Pei**   Liangzhu Jades in the Shanghai Museum, Orientations, Hong Kong February 1991, pp.32-36

33. **IA, CASS**   "1976-78 nian Chang'an Fengxi Farjue jianbao" (Excavations at Fengxi in Chang'an 1976-78) KG 1981.1.

34. _____   Mancheng Han mu fajue baogao (Report on the Excavation of the Han Tomb at Mancheng) Beijing, 1978

35. _____   Yinxu Fu Hao mu (Tomb of Fu Hao at Yinxu in Anyang). Beijing, 1980

36. _____   Yinxu yuqi (The Jades from Yin Sites at Anyang). Beijing 1982

37. **Ip, Yee**   Chinese Jade Carving, Urban Council, Hong Kong and the Min Chiu Society 1983

38. **IA, Zhejiang Province**   "Excavation of the Altar Remains of the Liangzhu Culture at Yaoshan in Yuhang". WW 1988.1.

39. **James, Jean M**   Images of Power: Masks of Liangzhu Culture Orientations, Hong Kong, June 1991 pp.46-55.

40. **Jao, Tsungyi**   Some notes on the pig in early Chinese myths and Art. Orientations, Hong Kong December 1988. pp.38 - 41.

41. **Jenyns, Soame**   Chinese Archaic Jades in the British Museum, British Museum London 1951

42. **Kwan, S.Y.**   The Dating and Identification of Jades, B.O.C.S.H.K. No. 9, Hong Kong

43. **Lally & Co, J.J.**   Chinese Works of Art, New York 1988

44. _____   Chinese Archaic Jades and Bronzes from the estate of Professor Max Loehr and others, New York 1993

45. **Li Jiu-fang, ed.**   Chinese Jade Volume 6 - Qing Dynasty, Classified Chinese Art Series, People's Republic of China: Hebei Art Publishing Co., 1991

46. **Loehr, Max & Huber, Louisa F.**   Ancient Chinese Jades from the Grenville L. Winthrop Collection in the Fogg Art Museum, Harvard University, Cambridge, Mass.: Fogg Art Museum, Harvard University 1975

47. **Lam, Peter Y.K. ed.**   Jades From the Tomb of the King of Nanyue, Hong Kong The Chinese University, and Woods Publishing Company, 1991

48. **Lawton, Thomas**   Chinese Art of the Warring States Period; Change and Continuity, 68. BC. Washington, D.C. : Freer Gallery of Art, Smithsonian Institution 1982

49. **Lyons, Elizabeth Smith**   Mr and Mrs Ivan B. Hart Collection of Archaic Chinese Jades, College Museum of Art, Northampton, Massachusetts 1963

49A. **Markel, Stephen**   The World of Jade. Marg Publications, New Delhi 1993

50. **McElney, Brian**   In Search of Song Jades, Chinese Jade carving, Urban council Hong Kong and the Min Chiu Society 1983

51. _____   Han to Song Chinese Jades in "JADE" - Consultant Editor, Roger Keverne; Anness Publishing Ltd. London 1991

52. **Michael, Henry N.**   The Neolithic age in Eastern Siberia. The American Philosophical Society, Philadelphia, USA. 1958

53. **Moss, Hugh and Tsang, Gerard**   Arts from the Scholar's Studio, Hong Kong. The Oriental Ceramic Society of Hong Kong 1986

54. **Morgan, Brian**   Dr. Newton's Zoo, Post Archaic small jade Animal Carvings, Bluett and Sons, London 1981

55. **Mou Yongkang**   Jade from the Liangzhu Culture, Wen Wu Publishers and Woods Publishing Co., Hong Kong 1989

56. _____   ed. Chinese Jade Volume 1-Primitive Societies, Classified Chinese Art Series, People's Republic of China, Hebei Art Publishing Co. 1992

57. **Murray, Julia K.**   Neolithic Chinese Jades in the Freer Gallery of Art, Orientation Hong Kong, November 1983, pp.14-22.

58. **Na Zhiliang**   Chinese Jades: Archaic and Modern from the Minneapolis Institute of Arts, Rutland, Vermont and London: C.E. Tuttle, Co. 1977

59. _____   Zhongguo Guyu Tushi (Commentary on Guyu Tu), Taipei 1990.

60. _____   Dictionary of Chinese Jade, Taipei 1982

61. **National Palace Museum**   Illustrated Catalogue of Ancient Jade Artefacts in the National Palace Museum. Taipei; National Palace Museum, 1992

62. **Pearlstein, Elinor**   Salmony's Catalogue of the Sonnenchein Jades in the light of Recent Finds, Orientations, Hong Kong, June 1993 pp.48-59.

63. **Pelliot, Paul** — Jades Archaiques de Chine appartenant a M C T Loo, Paris and Brussels, Librairie Nationale D'Art et D'Histoire, 1925

64. **Qin Yongsheng and Hu Baoxi** — Highlights of the Huating Neolithic Site, Orientations, Hong Kong, October 1990 pp.54-56

65. **Rawson, Jessica** — Ancient China, Art and Archaeology, British Museum Publications, London 1980

66. **Rawson, Jessica and Ayers, John** — Victoria and Albert Museum: Chinese Jade Throughout the Ages London: Oriental Ceramic Society, 1975

67. **Salmony, Alfred** — Carved Jade of Ancient China, Berkeley, California, 1938

68. _____ — Archaic Chinese Jades from the Edward and Louise B. Sonnenschein Collection Chicago, The Art Institute of Chicago, 1953

69. _____ — Chinese Jades Through the Wei Dynasty, Ronald & Company, New York 1963 pp. 218-193

70. **Exhibition from the Shanghai Museum** — Gems of Liangzhu Culture, Hong Kong Urban Council, 1992

71. **Siggstedt, Mette** — Jan Wirgin ed. The Ernest Erickson Collection in Swedish Museums, 1989, pp. 10-11.

72. **So, Jenny F.** — A Hongshan Jade pendant in the Freer Gallery of Art, Orientations, Hong Kong, May 1993, pp. 87-93.

73. **Strassberg, Richard E.** — Enjoying Jade, Pacific Asia Museum, 1992

74. **Sun Shoudao and Guo Dashun** — "Primitive Culture of the Liao River Valley and the Origin of the Dragon." WW 1984.6.

75. **Sun Shoudao** — A Study of the Jade Dragon of the Hongshan Site, Sanxingtala, WW 1984: 6 pp. 7-11.

76. **Teng Shu-p'ing** — Catalogue of a Special Exhibition of Hindustan Jade in the National Palace Museum, Taipei, 1983

77. **Till, Barry, and Swart, Paula** — Chinese Jade; Stone for the Emperors, Art Gallery of Greater Victoria, 1986

78. _____ — Mountain Retreat in Jade, Arts of Asia, Hong Kong, July/August 1986

79. **Till, Barry** — Arts of the Middle Kingdom, Art Gallery of Greater Victoria, 1986

80 **Till, Barry**   Wonders of Earliest China, Art Gallery of Greater Victoria, 1988

81. **Trousdale, W.**   W. Trousdale, The Long Sword and Scabbard Slide in Asia, Smithsonian Contributions to Anthropology no. 17, Washington, 1975

82. **Watt, James C.Y.**   Chinese Jades from Han to Ch'ing New York. The Asia Society/John Weatherhill Inc., 1980

83. _____   Chinese Jades from the collection of the Seattle Art Museum, Washington: Seattle Art Museum, 1989

84. _____   The Arts of Ancient China, The Metropolitan Museum of Art New York 1990.

85. **Wen, Guang and Jing, Zhichun** Chinese Neolithic Jade: A preliminary Geoarchaeological Study, Geoarchaeology: An International Journal, Vol. 7

86. **White, William Charles**   Tombs of Old Lo-yang, Shanghai; Kelly & Walsh, Ltd. 1934

87. **Wu Dacheng**   Guyu Tukao (Studies and illustration of Ancient Jades) Shanghai 1889

88. **Wu Hung**   Bird Motifs in Eastern Yi Art, Orientations, Hong Kong October 1985 pp. 30-41.

89._____   A Great Beginning: Ancient Chinese Jades and the Origin of Ritual Art, in Chinese Jades from the Mu-Fei Collection, Bluett and Sons London 1990.

90. **Xia Nai**   Jade and Silk of Han China, Lawrence, Kansas; Spencer Museum of Art, University of Kansas, 1983

91. **Xia Nai and others**   The Jades from Yin Xu, Wenwu Press, Beijing 1982

92. **Yang Bo Da**   The Glorious Age of Chinese Jades in "JADE" - Consultant Editor, Roger Keverne, Anness Publishing Ltd, London 1991

93._____   Jade: Emperor Chien Lung's collection in the Palace Museum Peking, Arts of Asia, Hong Kong March/April 1992

94. **Yang Xiaoneng**   Sculpture of Prehistoric China, Tai Dao Publishing Limited, Hong Kong, 1988

95._____   Sculpture of Xia and Shang China, Tai Dao Publishing Limited, Hong Kong, 1988

96. **Xinru Liu** Ancient India and Ancient China, Trade and Religious Exchanges
Oxford University Press 1988

97. **Yao Qinde introduced** Spring and Autumn period Jades from the State of Wu,
by Hsio-Yen Shih Orientations, Hong Kong, 1991, pp.47-52.

98. **Yeung Kin Fong** Jade Carving in Chinese Archaeology, Vol. 1, Chinese University
Press, Hong Kong 1987

99. **Zhang Xuqiu** Jade Artefacts of the Shijiahe Culture; Jiangsu Kaogu,
January 1992

100. **Zhongguo Meishu** Zhongguo Meishu Quanji (Treasures of Chinese Arts and Crafts),
Arts and Crafts Section Vol. 9, "Jade", Wenwu Press, Beijing, 1986